THE PASTORAL EPISTLES

FOR PASTORS

JOHN A. KITCHEN

Kress Christian
PUBLICATIONS

The Pastoral Epistles for Pastors
© 2009 John A. Kitchen

All Rights Reserved
No part of this publication may be reproduced, stored in a retrieval system, or transmitted in any form or by any means—electronic, mechanical, photocopy, recording, or any other—except for brief quotations embodied in critical articles or printed reviews, without prior written permission of the publisher.

Published by:

Kress Christian
PUBLICATIONS

P.O. Box 132228
The Woodlands, TX 77393
www.kresschristianpublications.com

ISBN 978-1-934952-35-1

Text Design: Valerie Moreno
Editorial Consultants: Garry Knussman, Kevin McAteer

Unless otherwise noted, Scripture taken from the *NEW AMERICAN STANDARD BIBLE®,* © Copyright 1960, 1962, 1963, 1968, 1971, 1972, 1973, 1975, 1977, 1995 by The Lockman Foundation. Used by permission. (www.Lockman.org)

The Greek text used is *Novum Testamentum Graece*, Nestle-Aland 27th Edition. Copyright © 1993 Deutsche Bibelgesellschaft, Stuttgart, Germany.

Scripture quotations marked (ASV) are taken from the American Standard Version, 1901. Scripture quotations marked (ESV) are taken from The Holy Bible, English Standard Version™, copyright © 2001 by Crossway Bibles, a division of Good News Publishers. Used by permission. All rights reserved. Scripture quotations marked (JB) are taken from the Jerusalem Bible, Copyright © 1966, 1967, 1968 by Darton, Longman & Todd Ltd. and Doubleday & Company, Inc. Scripture quotations marked (KJV) are taken from the King James Version. Scriptures quotations marked (NEB) are taken from the New English Bible, Copyright © 1961, 1970. The Delegates of the Oxford University Press and The Syndics of the Cambridge University Press. Scripture quotations marked (NIV) are taken from the New International Version®. Copyright © 1973, 1978, 1984 by International Bible Society. Used by permission of Zondervan Publishing House. All rights reserved. Scripture quotations marked (NKJV) are taken from *The New King James Version*. Copyright © 1979, 1980, 1982 by Thomas Nelson, Inc. Used by permission. All rights reserved. Scripture quotations marked (NLT) are taken from the *Holy Bible*, New Living Translation, copyright © 1996. Used by permission of Tyndale House Publishers, Inc., Wheaton, Illinois 60189. All rights reserved. Scripture quotations marked (NRSV) are taken from the New Revised Standard Version. Copyright © 1989 by the Division of Christian Education of the National Council of the Churches of Christ in the United States of America. All rights reserved. Scripture quotations marked (RSV) are taken from the Revised Standard Version of the Bible, Copyright © 1952, 1946, 1971 by the National Council of Churches of Christ in America. Scripture quotations marked (TEV) are taken from the Today's English Version © 1966, 1971, 1976, 1992. American Bible Society.

Dedicated to

John McGarvey

true friend
brother in Christ
co-laborer in ministry

ὁ λόγος τοῦ θεοῦ οὐ δέδεται

—2 Timothy 2:9b

CONTENTS

Abbreviations	9
How to Use this Book	11
Introduction	13
1 Timothy	
Chapter 1	37
Chapter 2	83
Chapter 3	121
Chapter 4	159
Chapter 5	195
Chapter 6	245
2 Timothy	
Chapter 1	299
Chapter 2	339
Chapter 3	389
Chapter 4	425

Titus
- Chapter 1 — 477
- Chapter 2 — 513
- Chapter 3 — 543

Appendix A: A Pastor's Self-Guided Study of the Pastoral Epistles — 577

Appendix B: Training Local Church Leaders from the Pastoral Epistles — 581

Appendix C: A Topical Index to the Ministry Maxims — 587

Appendix D: Preaching/Teaching the Pastoral Epistles — 595

Appendix E: Annotated Bibliography — 615

Abbreviations

Old Testament

Gen.	Genesis	Eccl.	Ecclesiastes
Exod.	Exodus	Song of Sol.	Song of Solomon
Lev.	Leviticus	Isa.	Isaiah
Num.	Numbers	Jer.	Jeremiah
Deut.	Deuteronomy	Lam.	Lamentations
Josh.	Joshua	Ezek.	Ezekiel
Judg.	Judges	Dan.	Daniel
Ruth	Ruth	Hos.	Hosea
1 Sam.	1 Samuel	Joel	Joel
2 Sam.	2 Samuel	Amos	Amos
1 Kings	1 Kings	Obad.	Obadiah
2 Kings	2 Kings	Jonah	Jonah
1 Chron.	1 Chronicles	Mic.	Micah
2 Chron.	2 Chronicles	Nah.	Nahum
Ezra	Ezra	Hab.	Habakkuk
Neh.	Nehemiah	Zeph.	Zephaniah
Esth.	Esther	Hag.	Haggai
Job	Job	Zech.	Zechariah
Psa.	Psalm	Mal.	Malachi
Prov.	Proverbs		

New Testament

Matt.	Matthew	1 Tim.	1 Timothy
Mark	Mark	2 Tim.	2 Timothy
Luke	Luke	Titus	Titus
John	John	Philem.	Philemon
Acts	Acts	Heb.	Hebrews
Rom.	Romans	James	James
1 Cor.	1 Corinthians	1 Peter	1 Peter
2 Cor.	2 Corinthians	2 Peter	2 Peter
Gal.	Galatians	1 John	1 John
Eph.	Ephesians	2 John	2 John
Phil.	Philippians	3 John	3 John
Col.	Colossians	Jude	Jude
1 Thess.	1 Thessalonians	Rev.	Revelation
2 Thess.	2 Thessalonians		

Bible Translations

ASV	American Standard Version
ESV	English Standard Version
JB	Jerusalem Bible
KJV	King James Version
NASB	New American Standard Bible (1977)
NASU	New American Standard Bible: Updated Edition (1995)
NEB	New English Bible
NIV	New International Version
NKJV	New King James Version
NLT	New Living Translation
NRSV	New Revised Standard Version
RSV	Revised Standard Version
TEV	Today's English Version

Miscellaneous

c.	*circa*, about
cf.	*confer*, compare
contra	contrary to
e.g.	*exempli gratia*, for example
etc.	*et cetera*, and the like
ff.	following (verses, pages, etc.)
ibid.	*ibidem*, in the same place
i.e.	*id est*, that is
LXX	Septuagint
n.d.	no date
NT	New Testament
OT	Old Testament
PE	Pastoral Epistles
rpt.	reprint

Footnotes

BAGD	*A Greek-English Lexicon of the New Testament and Other Early Christian Literature*
DNTT	*The New International Dictionary of New Testament Theology*

HOW TO USE THIS BOOK

Allow me to share a word about how you may use this volume for your personal growth and for that of your congregation. *The Pastoral Epistles for Pastors* weaves three distinct features into the fabric of one helpful volume. It will serve your needs in any number of different ways. Three of the most obvious ways it will serve you are as a commentary, a counselor, and a coach.

As a *commentary* you will find that *The Pastoral Epistles for Pastors* provides a wealth of exegetical information regarding the text of the Pastoral Epistles. This will aid you in personally understanding God's Word, in preaching and teaching these texts, and in explaining the meaning of these Scriptures to the people whom you shepherd.

As a *counselor* you will find generously dispersed throughout the text what I call Ministry Maxims. These are pithy, pointedly stated principles of ministry which arise from or are suggested by the verse where they are found. Each is stated in such a way as to distill the wisdom of the given Scripture into a pointed—and sometimes provocative—statement of principle which applies in ministry contexts of all cultures and at all times. Do you wonder if that is possible? Have a debate with one of the Ministry Maxims? Then they have served their purpose! They are stated in thought-provoking ways in order to stimulate thought and rouse you to interaction with the truth. While the commentary speaks facts into your mind, the Ministry Maxims are designed to speak truth into your heart.

As a *coach* this companion never allows you to leave a section of Scripture without stopping to ponder how its truth applies to your life and ministry. It provides bridges of application from the truths found in the text of Scripture to the work of ministry in your local church. Through the Digging Deeper questions dispersed generously throughout the text, the reader is stimulated to think of how the truths of the PE apply to the reader's life and local church ministry. If the commentary is designed to speak facts into your mind and the Ministry Maxims are designed to speak truth into your heart, then these Digging Deeper questions are intended to put skill into your hands as you serve the Lord by serving His people. Additionally, the appendices provide practical ideas on how you can use the PE in personal ministry growth, training local church leaders, and preaching the PE.

Finally, may I suggest that *The Pastoral Epistles for Pastors* is suitable for diving, wading, and dipping. That is to say, you may want to dive in and immerse yourself in the fullness of its content (see appendices A and B for ideas). Or you may want to wade into a particular section of one of these PE by studying the commentary at that point in the text. Or you may simply want to dip into its contents by perusing the Ministry Maxim call out boxes, and only then stopping to examine the exegetical work behind those statements which peak your interest. In my mind, the deeper you dive the better, but there is benefit in all these approaches.

INTRODUCTION

The letters of 1 and 2 Timothy and Titus stand alone among Paul's letters as having been written to individual coworkers, rather than to churches.[1] We have come to know these letters as the Pastoral Epistles (PE). They were not, however, given this title until 1726 when Paul Anton so dubbed them in a series of lectures which were later published after his death.[2] Many have made the point that neither Timothy nor Titus were pastors in the exact sense in which we understand that role today. They functioned more as apostolic representatives who spoke with Paul's authority concerning matters of doctrine and practice within the churches to which they were assigned. Despite these nuances, the title has stuck because these letters were written to men who in a unique way shepherded and had spiritual oversight of the churches in Ephesus and Crete. Pastoral leaders through the generations have found in these letters special insight and guidance. All of the epistles—indeed all of Scripture (2 Tim. 3:16-17)—offer guidance to pastors, but these three stand in a unique position to address the issues that confront pastors in their ministries. Thus the title Pastoral Epistles is apt.[3] Beyond the fact that these three letters are written to individuals in such a distinct role of spiritual leadership, the content, style, and historical situations into which they speak are so similar as to have bound them together in a unique sub-set of the Pauline epistles. Of course this is not to say that the PE speak only to the pastor. Here is truth for all the members of Christ's church, laymen and pastors alike.

---

[1] Sometimes Philemon is added to this list, but upon closer examination that letter was actually addressed to multiple individuals (Philem. 1-2). Philemon seems to have been the *primary* recipient of that letter (as evidenced in the use of singular forms nearly twenty times in the letter). Others, however, were also intended, including "the church in your house" (v.2). Thus Towner can say of the PE, "... they are the only Pauline letters addressed to individual coworkers rather than to churches" (NICNT, 1).

[2] Barclay, 2; Knight, 3.

[3] contra, Towner, *The Letters to Timothy and Titus*, 88.

This introduction is prepared with the pastor in mind. This is in distinction from an introduction prepared for the academic community. Certainly the two cannot and should not be divorced entirely. The goal here is to be well informed regarding the scholarly discussions, but not to become pedantically mired in technical debate. This introduction aims to provide the pastor with what he needs in order to approach rightly the text of the PE and to glean from the text of these epistles all God intends for his life and ministry. To this end I will from time to time direct the reader to other sources which will expand upon the issues at hand.

Authorship: Who Wrote the Pastoral Epistles?

In many people's minds this has become the great question regarding the PE. One need look no further than the introductions of most commentaries. The great bulk of space is often dedicated to this very issue.

The letters of 1 and 2 Timothy and Titus all claim to have been written by the Apostle Paul. The voice of the early church is squarely behind Pauline authorship. In fact the Pauline authorship of the PE was not in doubt until the nineteenth century when Friedrich Schleiermacher became the first of what has become a long line of detractors. Some suggest a second-century writer used the Apostle's name in order to add a greater weight of authority to his compositions. Others propose that a later disciple of Paul used genuine fragments of his writings to piece together these three letters. A.T. Hanson is among those who doubt the authenticity of these letters. He claims disdainfully, ". . . if Paul wrote the Pastorals he must have been afflicted with approaching senility."[4] In sweeping fashion he casts aside the PE saying, "The Pastorals have no authentically Pauline elements in them at all. They are wholly pseudonymous, and were composed by a writer subsequent to Paul's day who wished to claim Paul's authority for his material."[5] In addition he suggests, ". . . the Pastorals are not exactly what they claim to be . . . ."[6] Not all who doubt the authenticity of the PE adopt such a cavalier tone, yet for the past two centuries the scholarly momentum has been with the doubters.

Despite this momentum, however, there continue to be many able defenders of Paul's authorship.[7] It is my contention that we may with good reason and great confidence receive these three letters as authentic Pauline letters. Allow me to state briefly the primary reasons given by those who reject Pauline authorship. I will then enumerate the reasons for our confidence in their

---

[4] Hanson, 7.
[5] Ibid., 11.
[6] Ibid., 23.
[7] See Appendix E for a good representation.

authenticity as having come from the Apostle Paul.

Objections to Pauline Authorship

Generally the objections to Pauline authorship of the PE fall into five basic categories.[8]

1. *The vocabulary and style of the PE are considered too distinct from those epistles deemed to be genuinely Pauline.*

> Careful scrutiny of the PE and comparison of them with other letters known to be from the pen of Paul have revealed a large number of words in the PE which are not found elsewhere in his writings. Among them is εὐσέβεια ("godliness"), found ten times in the PE and yet nowhere else in Paul's letters. It has been found that 175 words in the PE are not used elsewhere in the NT.[9] More than thirty percent of the vocabulary of 1 Timothy is not used elsewhere in the ten undisputed letters of Paul.[10] Even more telling, the critics say, is the absence in the PE of a number of particles that are frequently found in others of Paul's writings.[11] Perhaps the most influential work in this regard is P.N. Harrison's *The Problem with the Pastorals.*

2. *The level of ecclesiastical organization in the PE is considered too advanced for the time period of Paul's ministry.*

> Some argue against Pauline authorship of the PE because the level of ecclesiastical organization and structure described in the letters is deemed to be too highly refined for the time period corresponding to Paul's later years. Such an organizational order is often believed to have emerged only after the lifetime of the Apostles. Similarly, some have argued backward to understand the instructions of 1 Timothy 5 in light of the second-century church's establishment of an "order of widows."

3. *The historical setting of the PE does not fit the record of Paul's ministry in the Book of Acts.*

> The chronology and events described within the PE find no correspondence with those in the Book of Acts. For example there is no record in Acts of Paul preaching with Titus on the island of Crete (Titus 1:5). Neither is there any satisfactory way to fit Paul's appointment of Timothy to Ephesus into the record of Acts. There have been attempts to reconcile the record of Acts with the movements described in the PE. Though well-intentioned and creatively argued, in

---

[8] Kent, 39-40; Lea and Griffin, 24; Stibbs, 1166.
[9] Wilder, 38.
[10] Kent, 61.
[11] Wilder, 38-39.

the end these attempts seem to fall short of providing convincing proof.

Some have, therefore, argued that these letters were written well after Paul's time. They picture someone loyal to Paul a generation or two after his passing, a person trying to write letters which ring with Pauline authenticity, yet address issues that are current in the second century. Others have argued that the PE are comprised of fragments of genuinely Pauline documents which have been glued together by some editor's later additions.

4. *The nature of the false teaching addressed in the PE is more like that confronting the church in the second century than in Paul's lifetime.*

The heresy described in the PE is deemed to be a fully formed Gnosticism, something that did not yet exist during Paul's lifetime, but was found only in the second century. In this regard many point to the use of γνῶσις in 1 Timothy 6:20 as proof that Gnosticism was the reason for the letter. Similarly, it has been postulated that the use of the word ἀντίθεσις in 1 Timothy 6:20 is a signal that the author was writing as a polemic against the second-century heretic Marcion who used this very word as the title of one of his writings.[12] Others point to the "myths and endless genealogies" of 1 Timothy 1:4 as referencing Gnosticism's speculations regarding aeons emanating from God to man.[13] Also others look to the ascetic nature of the heresy described in 1 Timothy 4 as representative of the dualism in Gnostic thinking.[14]

5. *The theology of the PE is considered distinct from that of Paul's other letters.*

Opponents of Pauline authorship argue that the theology of these letters generally does not have the ring of Pauline doctrine found in his other epistles. There is concern, they say, because Paul does not argue against the heresy, but merely denounces it. This Paul would not do, we are told. Litfin summarizes the concerns of those who argue this line of reasoning: "Instead of developing the truth, the author was intent merely on conserving and guarding it. He was concerned with mere religion rather than theology, mere orthodoxy rather than creative thought."[15] Additionally, they say that some key Pauline elements are missing. Among them are the doctrine of the Holy Spirit, Paul's distinctive promotion of grace, and the believer's mystical union "in Christ."[16] We are also told that the writer of the PE presents righteousness not as a gift of grace, but as the goal of Christian labor. In the PE the concern is not with the imputed righteousness of salvation, but the imparted righteousness of sanctification. These, we are told, are clear indications of authorship by someone other than the Apostle Paul.

---

[12] Lea and Griffin, 28.
[13] Kent, 57.
[14] Ibid., 57-58.
[15] Liftin, 2:729.
[16] Ibid.

Evidence for Pauline Authorship

Having summarized the primary reasons set forth for doubting Pauline authorship, allow me now to advance the reasons I believe Paul wrote the PE.[17]

1. All three of these epistles claim to have been written by the Apostle Paul.

The text of the PE clearly attributes these letters to the Apostle Paul (1 Tim. 1:1; 2 Tim. 1:1; Titus 1:1). This is often brushed aside in favor of pseudepigraphy. Certainly the practice of pseudepigraphy is known in and around the first century. We know of documents from the first century and beyond which purported to be written by someone other than the actual author. One can make his own determination regarding this practice in ancient secular documents. Yet in the matter of Scripture, if these letters, which clearly claim to have been written by Paul, indeed were written by someone other than the Apostle, we must ask ourselves whether they can be trusted at all. If these letters are wrong on the matter of authorship, can we with any confidence conclude that they are right on the other matters to which they speak?

Marshall has gone to great lengths in an attempt to show that, by first-century standards, writing in Paul's name need not be taken as an inherently deceitful act.[18] He even coins a new word (allonymity or allepigraphy) since pseudonymity has become freighted with negative connotations. Yet his arguments seem unconvincing and his wordplay a needless stretch.

2. All three of these epistles have been accepted as Pauline through eighteen of the church's twenty centuries of existence.

It is only in relatively recent years that the view of pseudepigraphy has arisen and gained traction. To assert their authorship by someone other than Paul is to stand in disagreement with those who stood closest to the time of their composition. Polycarp (died ca. A.D. 135) quoted from the PE just as he did others of Paul's letters. Irenaeus quoted them as having been written by Paul (ca. A.D. 180).[19] Clement of Alexandria (ca. 155-ca. 220) referred to the PE and assigned them to Paul. Origen referred often to these letters, clearly referring to Paul as the author. Eusebius (ca. 265-ca. 339), the great historian of the early church, confirmed that the church believed the PE to have been written by Paul. The Muratorian Canon (A.D. 180-200) designates the PE as coming from Paul.[20]

As overwhelmingly solid as is the external evidence regarding Pauline

---

[17] For a more detailed defense of Pauline authorship I recommend you consult Guthrie (*New Testament Introduction*, 607-648), Mounce (xlvii-cxxix), and Towner (*The Letter to Timothy and Titus*, 3-88).
[18] Marshall, 83-84.
[19] Fee, 23.
[20] Lea and Griffin, 20; see Kent 23-37 for a fuller accounting of ancient witnesses to the authorship of 1 Timothy.

authorship of the PE, concerns have been raised on two fronts. First, the absence of the PE from the early manuscript P^{46} has raised concerns. The fact is, however, that the last seven leaves of the papyrus are missing. Based upon the print on what remains of the manuscript, some conclude that there would not have been room to include 2 Thessalonians, Philemon and the PE on the scroll. However, there are many possible explanations for their absence. Some have concluded that the further the copyist wrote the smaller his letters became, an indication perhaps that he realized he had miscalculated the space required to fit all the books on the scroll. It is estimated that he may have had enough room for all the epistles, given this tendency toward the end of what remains in our hands. It also has been suggested that leaves were added to the codex to make room for the missing epistles.[21] It has been posited further that this may have been a scroll designed to contain only Paul's letters to churches, not to individuals, which would have been placed on a separate scroll. We need not prove just what did happen to the remainder of the scroll nor what plan the copyist may have followed, only that the absence of the PE from what we do have does not prove they were not accepted as Pauline.

The second concern is that Marcion does not make mention of the PE in his list of canonical books. It is speculated that he did not know of the PE because they did not yet exist in ca. 140 when he established his canon. Yet Marcion held extreme theological views which would have provided him ample theological motivation for rejection of the PE. The fact is he also excluded Matthew, Mark, and John.[22] Thus it is not surprising that he would have excluded the PE.

The church unquestionably accepted the PE as from the Apostle Paul until 1807 when Friedrich Schleiermacher set in motion a skepticism that has dominated a good bit of the past two hundred years of scholarship. During these past two centuries there have been some who bravely stood their ground regarding Pauline authorship.[23] Mounce gladly notes what appears to be a swing back toward the Pauline authenticity of the PE among a growing number of NT scholars.[24]

3. *The historical circumstances set forth in the PE fit with what we know about Paul's life and ministry.*

Much ink has been spilt over the fact that the historical data of the PE does not seem to fit with the record of Paul's life and ministry as recorded in the Book of Acts. Yet this objection disappears if we recognize the likelihood of a second Roman imprisonment of the Apostle Paul. This has often been rejected out of hand since there is no word of Paul's release from the

---

[21] Marshall, 6.
[22] Lea and Griffin, 20.
[23] e.g., Zahn, Lightfoot, Roller, Guthrie, Kelly, Moule, Spicq, and Hiebert.
[24] Mounce, xlviii.

imprisonment he suffers as the Book of Acts closes. Yet all this seems an unnecessary and laborious attempt to avoid what seems most obvious—that the PE do not conform to the events recorded in the Book of Acts precisely because they did not happen at that time, but following the release of the Apostle Paul from his first Roman imprisonment (Acts 28:30-31).

If Paul had been executed at the end of this first Roman imprisonment, it seems obvious that Luke would have included this in his material. There appears to be no necessity to conclude anything other than Paul was released from his first Roman imprisonment in approximately 62 A.D. Though we cannot know for certain, his release may have come because of lack of evidence against him or because his accusers failed to appear at his trial. If indeed Paul was released, it would stand to reason, based on his previous history, that he again set about traveling and ministering throughout the Mediterranean world.

This in fact is precisely what the historical record of the church tells us. Paul had spoken to the Romans of his desire to preach Christ in Spain (Rom. 15:24, 28). That this in fact happened is evidenced by the testimony of the Muratorian Canon which says Paul "departed for Spain." Eusebius, the great historian of the early church, writes: "Paul is said, after having defended himself, to have set forth again upon the ministry of preaching, and to have entered the city [Rome] a second time, and to have ended his life by martyrdom. Whilst then a prisoner, he wrote the Second Epistle to Timothy, in which he both mentions his first defense, and his impending death."[25]

This period of ministry presumably stretched from 62 A.D. to 67 A.D. During this period of freedom Paul would have written 1 Timothy and Titus. Toward the end of this period of free travel and ministry Paul was arrested a second time and re-imprisoned. After his imprisonment once again in Rome he penned the letter we know as 2 Timothy.

Any reconstruction of Paul's movements and ministry during this time must be considered tentative and speculative. Yet we can also recognize that the testimony of the early church and the data of the NT provide us warrant in attempting such a reconstruction. Hendriksen, Hiebert, and Kent all provide insightful, yet tentative, reconstructions of Paul's movements and ministries during this time.[26] While these three do not agree in every detail, and while the precise details of each historical reconstruction are open to debate, there appears to be no necessity in doubting some such reconstruction of the events of Paul's later years. If these, or something close to them, are correct then the doubts cast upon Pauline authorship of the PE based upon supposed historical incongruities lose their force.

---

[25] Earle, 11:342.
[26] See Hendriksen (39-40), Hiebert (*An Introduction to the Pauline Epistles*, 322-324), and Kent (15, 47-50).

4. *The personal and historical references within the PE themselves argue against pseudepigraphy and in favor of Pauline authorship.*

There are simply too many personal references, historical references, and small nuances within the PE to understand them as the product of pseudepigraphy. For example, no disciple of Paul would have put these words in the mouth of his master: "Christ Jesus came into the world to save sinners, among whom I am foremost of all" (1 Tim. 1:15). What pseudepigraphic writer would have bothered to have included personal and mundane details such as instructing Timothy to drink a little wine for his upset stomach (1 Tim. 5:23) and the details of names and circumstances found in 2 Timothy 4:10-15, 19-21? These comments and others like them have the ring of Pauline authenticity. To conjecture a pseudepigraphic writer capable of such reconstruction and imagination is a feat both fantastic and unnecessary.

Some read these personal and historical references as evidence that a disciple of Paul, after his death, pieced together fragments of genuine letters from the Apostle to compose the documents we now call the PE. Yet this theory faces some of the same hurdles we've already confronted. Would a true disciple of the Apostle Paul, who demanded thoroughgoing truth-speaking (e.g., Eph. 4:15, 25; Col. 3:9), craft letters that were purported to be what they in fact were not? Why would such a disciple leave in these personal and historical details, if not to deceive the readers into thinking the letters were authentically from Paul's hand?

In the end, these letters are simply too personal and too historically specific to have much likelihood of arising from anyone other than the Apostle Paul himself.

5. *The PE are consistent with what we would expect from Paul in writing to two dear co-laborers in the faith, under the circumstances described in the letters.*

As stated earlier, many doubt the authenticity of the PE based upon philological studies which find many differences in style and word usage when compared with writings considered genuinely Pauline. Yet such reasoning is built on an argument from silence. Problems with such conclusions are as follows. The sample of writing we have in the PE is too small for a valid comparison. G.U. Yule, a statistician from Cambridge, has asserted that samples of at least ten thousand words are required before statistical validity of any study may be established.[27] The total number of words in the PE totals less than 3,800. We must consider also that Paul writes the PE in a different season of his life, under different circumstances, to a different audience, and for different reasons than in any of his other letters. These factors alone could adequately account for variance in style and vocabulary.

In addition, some have postulated that Paul may have employed the use of an

---

[27] Earle, 11:343.

amanuensis in some of his writings. If so, he may have been using a different companion for such a purpose during the composition of the PE. There is great debate about the level of input an amanuensis may have enjoyed (from strict dictation to a freer hand in personally framing Paul's general ideas). Yet it is possible that the stylistic differences arose because of the personality and style of the one serving the Apostle at this time. Some have put forth the possibility that Luke served as Paul's amanuensis for the PE (2 Tim. 4:11). This theory is strengthened by the fact that many key Greek words are found both in Luke/Acts and the PE, but not elsewhere in the NT.[28] While I am not arguing for Paul's use of an amanuensis in composing the PE, the possibility exists. Also it has been called a double-standard to argue that many words are non-Pauline and yet to use the words deemed genuinely Pauline to demand that the writer used authentic Pauline fragments.[29] We should also admit that a different subject matter demands a different vocabulary.[30] It is readily admitted that in many ways the subject matter of the PE is unique among Paul's writings. It seems a reasonable conclusion that a single individual writing to his best friend from his heart might use different vocabulary and style than when he composes a technical document in his workplace.

A final note of interest is that studies undertaken to compare epistles normally understood to be Pauline reveal that there are similar findings between them, thus minimizing the significance of any such findings regarding the PE.[31] Wilder notes, "Paul's letter to the Philippians contains many words that are not found in Paul's other letters nor in the whole of the NT. Do we then conclude that Philippians is pseudonymous? No scholar that I know of is willing to do so. The unique words found in Philippians, like those in the Pastorals, can be plausibly explained by Paul's specific purpose for writing these letters."[32]

6. *The theology of the PE represents that which we have come to expect from Paul's pen.*

There are those who argue that the theology of the PE appears anything but Pauline. They claim an absence of Paul's usual emphasis on the mystical union of the believer with Christ, the person, role and ministry of the Holy Spirit, and the centrality of the cross. Yet closer scrutiny of the PE reveal that all these elements are expressed within them.

Some say that the expression "in Christ" (ἐν Χριστῷ) is not used in the PE as it is in other undisputed Pauline letters. For example, Hanson says, the writer of the PE does not "seem to use the important phrase *en Christ?* ('in Christ') in the mystical way that Paul does."? Yet the writer speaks of "the promise of life that is in Christ Jesus" (2 Tim. 1:1). Does this not sound like

---
[28] Ibid.
[29] Kent, 66.
[30] Ibid.
[31] Guthrie, New Testament Introduction, 635.
[32] Wilder, 39.

the Paul we know? Furthermore, the writer speaks of God's own purpose and grace "which was granted us in Christ Jesus from all eternity" (2 Tim. 1:9). This sounds like the Paul we read in his other epistles. Does this not sound just like Paul: "all who desire to live godly in Christ Jesus will be persecuted" (2 Tim. 3:12)? Indeed, it does.

Regarding a perceived lack of reference to the person and work of the Holy Spirit, it may be observed that the PE refer to the Holy Spirit's activity in calling and empowering Timothy (1 Tim. 1:18; 4:14; 2 Tim. 1:6-7). The author makes the Holy Spirit a key part of his creedal statements (1 Tim. 3:16; Titus 3:5-6) and sees Him as active in prophecy (1 Tim. 4:1).[34]

The centrality of the cross and Christ's atoning work is sometimes deemed to be absent from the PE. Yet the author speaks of Christ's work in ransoming us (1 Tim. 2:6). He also draws attention to Christ's work in redemption (Titus 2:14).[35]

True, these and other matters may not be expressed in the same way they are sometimes spelled out in others of Paul's letters. Yet even within those letters the emphasis and expression is not as consistent as detractors would have us believe.[36] Furthermore, the fact that the PE were written out of a different season of Paul's life, from different circumstances, and for different reasons all adequately account for any differences in the expression of Paul's theology that are met here. Additionally, in writing to two personal disciples who had spent years at his side in ministry and under his personal mentoring, must we require the Apostle to repeat himself in all these matters? Any perceived absence of reference to these or other themes may be accounted for, at least in part, by the sheer familiarity of the author and recipients. Indeed, in the face of the actual evidence in the PE, Fee can say, "… for all the differences, they are still far more like Paul in these matters than otherwise."[37]

7. *The ecclesiastical structure depicted in the PE is consistent with what we have come to expect from Paul's other writings and the Book of Acts.*

Some argue for pseudepigraphy of the PE based on what they deem to be a church structure that is too highly refined for the lifetime of the Apostle Paul. Yet under careful scrutiny such arguments are found wanting. In the second century the church began to establish an organizational structure which elevated bishops (ἐπίσκοποι) over elders (πρεσβύτεροι). But in the PE the two terms are used interchangeably (e.g. 1 Tim. 3:2; Titus 1:5-7). This is in accord with what we know of Paul's pattern of usage (Acts 20:17, 28). We know that already within Paul's life and ministry he had recognized the dual

---

[33] Hanson, 3.
[34] Mounce, xci.
[35] Lea and Griffin, 36.
[36] Mounce, lxxxix.
[37] Fee, 26.

offices of elders/overseers and deacons (Phil. 1:1). Similarly, some have argued backward to understand the instructions of 1 Timothy 5 in light of the second-century church's establishment of an "order of widows."[38] Yet taken at face value these instructions represent nothing that requires a second-century setting.

8. *The problems faced and the heresy confronted in the PE sound familiar when compared with other NT writings.*

Opponents of the PE's authenticity conjecture that the heresy confronted in the letters is a fully developed, second-century Gnosticism. This, they say, betrays the writer's true context and the problems to which he hopes to apply the Apostle's authority.

Yet the data of the PE, when taken at face value, does not appear to support such a conclusion. It is true that there were already at work in the first-century Mediterranean world elements of what would become full-blown Gnosticism in the second century. But it was merely the seed form of what would become the full flower of later Gnostic teaching. The churches of Paul's day were thus battling along these lines (and others) as they sought to propagate the gospel. Yet the PE describe elements of the heresy being confronted which do not conform to what we know of second-century Gnosticism. The false teachers being confronted both in Ephesus (1 and 2 Timothy) and on Crete (Titus) were advancing a line of doctrine which appears to have been a combination of Jewish, Hellenistic, and pre-Gnostic thought.

The Jewish nature of the heresy is seen clearly in the false teacher's obsession with the Law (1 Tim. 1:7; Titus 3:9) and circumcision (Titus 1:10). Also their rabid interest in genealogies (1 Tim. 1:4; Titus 3:9) appears to have arisen from primarily Jewish roots (cf. Titus 3:9, where they are linked with "disputes about the Law"). Similarly their interest in myths was Jewish in nature (Titus 1:14).

The Hellenistic influence upon their teaching is seen in their tendency toward moral license (1 Tim. 6:5, 9; 2 Tim. 3:6; Titus 3:3). Note Paul's repeated counsel toward moral purity (1 Tim. 5:22; 6:5; 2 Tim. 2:22; 3:6; Titus 1:6, 11).

Strands of their teaching, which appear to have arisen from pre-Gnostic elements, include some selective ascetic tendencies (1 Tim. 4:3). This may have arisen from a dualistic view of the world in which the physical is equated with evil—an element of later Gnostic teaching (1 Tim. 4:3; Titus 1:15). There was also an emphasis upon "knowledge" (γνῶσις; 1 Tim. 6:20-21). They appear to have denied the resurrection of the dead (1 Tim. 1:18-20; 2 Tim. 2:18). In this they probably opted for an over-realized eschatology in

---

[38] Liftin, 2:728.

which disciples were urged to claim all their spiritual inheritance immediately, as opposed to awaiting some benefits in heaven—something akin to later Gnosticism.

Beyond this the heretics showed evidence of pride (1 Tim. 6:4), a predisposition to debate and controversy (1 Tim. 6:20), and an interest in myths and fables (1 Tim. 1:4; 4:7; 2 Tim. 4:4).

It would appear from the data that this is the very kind of trouble the Apostle Paul was forced to confront in other churches of the first century. The Jewish obsession with the Law was seen among the various Judaizing elements that worked in Galatia (Gal. 3:2, 11-12; 5:1-12) and elsewhere (Col. 2:16). The designation "the circumcision" was known in other first-century churches and Paul's letters to them (Rom. 4:12; 15:8; Gal. 2:12; Col. 4:11). Paul elsewhere confronted moral license (1 Cor. 6:12-20; Eph. 4:17ff) which had influenced believers from the Hellenistic world around them. It is standard Pauline protocol to call believers to moral purity (Eph. 4:1; Col. 1:10; 1 Thess. 2:12). In Colossae, Paul seems to have battled a similar pre-Gnostic emphasis on "knowledge" (Col. 2:8, 23) and asceticism (Col. 2:18, 23). The Corinthian believers were beset by some who insisted there was no expectation of another resurrection (1 Cor. 15:12).

In short, it appears that the heresy confronted in the PE does not demand a second-century Gnosticism, but was the very kind of false teaching confronted elsewhere by Paul in his letters to churches of the first century.

There is a comparable similarity in how Paul deals with the heresy in the PE and how he dealt with it elsewhere. In the PE Paul certainly takes decisive action against such false teaching. He names several of the key false teachers (1 Tim. 1:20; 2 Tim. 2:17-18) and even indicates his most severe discipline of two of them (1 Tim. 1:20). We are told to expect more of such opposition as the days advance (1 Tim. 4:1). He repeatedly used words such as "command" (1 Tim. 1:18; cf. 1 Thess. 4:2), "urge" (1 Tim. 1:3; 2:1; Titus 2:6; cf. Phil. 4:2; 1 Thess. 4:10), "rebuke/refute/reprove" (1 Tim. 5:20; 2 Tim. 4:2; Titus 1:13; 2:15; cf. 1 Cor. 14:24; Eph. 5:11, 13), "warning" (Titus 3:10; cf. 1 Cor. 10:11; 6:4), and "solemnly charge" (1 Tim. 5:21; 2 Tim. 2:14; 4:1; cf. 1 Thess. 4:6) when fortifying Timothy and Titus against the false teachers. As the cross-references indicate, these are words Paul used elsewhere with frequency in dealing with the churches under his charge.

Thus in both heretical content and pastoral practice, the matters confronted in the PE bear the marks of being the kind of trouble—though undoubtedly with some unique differences due to localized issues—he confronted in many of the other churches of the first century.

In the case of Ephesus, it appears that the false teaching confronted in 1 and 2 Timothy is precisely what Paul earlier had predicted would come to pass (Acts 20:28-31). Some false teachers would come from without (v.29) and

Introduction

some would arise from within the Christian community (v.30). From the data in the PE it appears that at least some of those being confronted may have arisen from the ranks of the eldership themselves. Consider the great lengths to which Paul goes in delineating the qualifications of elders/overseers (1 Tim. 3:1-7; Titus 1:6-9) and the selection of elders (1 Tim. 5:22). Similarly he provides instruction on the accountability and discipline of elders (1 Tim. 5:19-21).

The Gnostic threat to the church of the second century was most severe, threatening the very essence of the Gospel. And certainly the danger confronting the believers in Ephesus and on Crete in the first century was acute. Yet Stibbs can rightly assert, "The most striking feature is the apparent irrelevance of much of the teaching"[39] which Paul is confronting here. Paul is clearly concerned, but at least part of the problem it seems can be dealt with by simply ignoring those who propagate it. This clearly sets this problem apart from the Gnosticism of the second century. The arguments in Ephesus were "foolish and ignorant" (2 Tim. 2:23) and could be dubbed "empty chatter" (1 Tim. 6:20; 2 Tim. 2:16). On Crete the problem was "foolish controversies" which were "unprofitable and worthless" (Titus 3:9). Without minimizing the issues, Stibbs can again assert, "These teachers, therefore, were . . . wasting time on things that do not matter."[40]

9. *The practice of the early church was to reject works written out of pseudonymity.*

The early church gave no leniency in the matter of pseudepigraphic writers. Tertullian tells of elders from Asia Minor who removed a man from his post because for "love of Paul" he penned the apocryphal *Acts of Paul* which included the letter of *3 Corinthians*. The man protested that he had written from good motives, yet he was nevertheless removed from office for his offense of composing a work which "fictitiously bore Paul's name or for composing a fiction about the apostle."[41] Similarly, Eusebius, the early historian of Christianity, tells of how Serapion, who served as bishop of Antioch, denied the use of the *Gospel of Peter* because it was deemed pseudepigraphic and heretical.[42]

If the early church had any hint that the PE were pseudepigraphic they would have clearly applied similar measures against the letters and their author.[43] Rather, the entire testimony of the early church stands in favor of understanding Pauline authorship of the PE.

---

[39] Stibbs, 1167.
[40] Ibid.
[41] Wilder, 42.
[42] Ibid.
[43] Mounce, cxxiv-cxxvii.

On the whole the arguments against Pauline authorship do not outweigh the evidences for these letters authentically arising from the Apostle himself. There are, to be sure, some stylistic uniquenesses here, yet they may be accounted for based on matters like the unique nature of the recipients and their circumstances, Paul's advancing age and personal circumstances, his purpose, and the subject matter of the letters. Additionally, there may be some merit in considering the role that an amanuensis may have played in recording Paul's letters. In the end, based on the evidence, it is my conviction that we have no reason to do anything other than accept the PE as genuinely Pauline.

Recipients: To Whom Were the Pastoral Epistles Written?

The most basic—and thoroughly correct—answer is that these letters were written to Timothy and Titus, two men charged with oversight of the churches in Ephesus and on Crete. This does not mean that Timothy and Titus were the only ones expected to be exposed to the content of these three letters. On the contrary, it appears that Paul fully expected their contents to be shared with the people of the churches in these locales. Evidence of this is found in the plural "you" (ὑμῶν) employed in the final benediction of each book: "Grace be with you" (1 Tim. 6:21; 2 Tim. 4:22) and "grace be with you all" (Titus 3:15). Indeed, regarding the matters of which he wrote in 1 Timothy, the Apostle commands his protégé, "These things command and teach" (1 Tim. 4:11).

Let us then consider these two remarkable men, Timothy and Titus. We begin with Timothy. This man was clearly younger than the Apostle Paul. A deep and intimate love grew between the two. It seems Timothy held the privileged position of being the closest of all Paul's ministry companions. Just what created such bonds of love between Paul and Timothy? Timothy's father was a Gentile (Acts 16:1); his mother Eunice was Jewish. She and her mother Lois apparently came to faith in Jesus Christ and they had a profound effect upon Timothy (2 Tim. 1:5). Their foundation of teaching him the Hebrew Scriptures was an essential element in his faith in Christ at a later time and in his effectiveness in ministry for Christ (2 Tim. 3:15). Paul found Timothy to be a disciple upon his return visit to Lystra (Acts 16:1-2). During his first foray in Lystra, Paul had been taken initially for a god after healing a lame man, and then, in a remarkable turn of events, was stoned nearly to death at the hands of the Jews (Acts 14:8-20). He spent only a short time in Lystra before moving on. We have no definite word of Timothy's conversion at that time. Perhaps he had been one listening at the fringes of the crowd as Paul preached. It is possible his heart was moved and then, when he saw Paul's resolve in the face of death (2 Tim. 3:11), he put his faith in Christ. Whenever the exact starting point and whatever the final encouragement to trust in

Christ, he was no secret disciple upon Paul's return. He was known throughout his hometown (the same hometown where the Jews had stoned Paul to the point of death!) and the region as an effective disciple of Christ, advancing the cause of the Gospel for miles around (Acts 16:2). Paul wanted this young man to travel at his side in the cause of the Gospel, that he might further train and equip him for ministry (Acts 16:3). During the years and miles of travel and ministry together the bonds of love between the two grew. Paul became the spiritual father Timothy never had. Thus we find the Apostle Paul describing Timothy with the deepest affection, calling him "my beloved and faithful child in the Lord" (1 Cor. 4:17), "my true child in the faith" (1 Tim. 1:2), "my son" (1 Tim. 1:18), and "my beloved son" (2 Tim. 1:2). To others he also called Timothy "my fellow worker" (Rom. 16:21), "our brother" (2 Cor. 1:1; Col. 1:1; Philem. 1), "our brother and God's fellow-worker in the gospel of Christ" (1 Thess. 3:2), and a bond-servant of Christ Jesus (Phil. 1:1).

The Apostle said that Timothy was doing the Lord's work just as he was (1 Cor. 16:10). Indeed, Paul said that Timothy served with him in advancing the gospel "like a child serving his father" (Phil. 2:22). Timothy has come to have a reputation as a somewhat timid (2 Tim. 1:7) and sickly (1 Tim. 5:23) young man (1 Tim. 4:12). But it seems there was no one else the Apostle trusted as much as Timothy. Thus he was often entrusted with representing the Apostle Paul and conveying his heart and mind to the churches (Acts 19:22; 1 Cor. 4:17; 2 Cor. 1:19; Phil. 2:19; 1 Thess. 3:2, 6). He is listed in the opening salutation of Paul's letters on six occasions (2 Cor. 1:1; Phil. 1:1; Col. 1:1; 1 Thess. 1:1; 2 Thess. 1:1; Philem. 1). It was Timothy above all others that he wanted at his side as he faced martyrdom (2 Tim. 1:4; 4:9, 21).

Titus does not receive as much ink as Timothy, yet he was also a trusted and proven co-laborer of the Apostle Paul. A Gentile by birth, Titus was likely converted by the Apostle Paul himself. He traveled with Paul and Barnabas to Jerusalem where pressure began to mount upon Paul to have Titus circumcised. Paul refused (Gal. 2:1-3, 6-10). Titus played a key role in Paul's ministry to the church in Corinth (2 Cor. 2:13; 7:6, 13, 14; 12:18), particularly relating to the collection for the poor (8:6, 16, 23). Titus later shared in evangelistic ministries with Paul on the island of Crete and he was then left to care for the believers (Titus 1:5). He would soon join Paul in Nicopolis, after either Artemas or Tychicus had arrived in Crete to take responsibility for the pastoral work of the believers (3:12). At some later date he would go without Paul into the region of Dalmatia to do pioneer evangelism (2 Tim. 4:10). He may have eventually returned to Crete, for tradition has it that he became the first bishop of the island and died there as an old man. Titus is designated by Paul as "my true child in a common faith" (Titus 1:4). This indicates that Titus was spiritually a genuine child of the Apostle.

Occasion: What Circumstances Gave Rise to the Writing of the Pastoral Epistles?

It always helps to understand a document when you also understand the circumstances out of which it was written. Let us then briefly consider these matters with regard to the PE.

First, let us consider *the setting of the recipients*. At the time of 1 Timothy's writing Timothy appears to have been in Ephesus (1 Tim. 1:3). Similarly, Titus appears to have been on the island of Crete (Titus 1:5), left there following a tour of evangelism with the Apostle Paul. Though it is not as clearly stated, Timothy appears to have still been in Ephesus at the time Paul wrote 2 Timothy, for he writes concerning individuals who were from Ephesus in and around that time (2 Tim. 1:16-18; 4:19).

Second, we must consider *the circumstances of the Apostle Paul* himself as he wrote these letters. 1 Timothy may well have been written from Macedonia (1 Tim. 1:3), though this is by no means certain. The letter to Titus gives no indication of the location from which it was written. Because of the similarities of the two letters it seems likely it was written quite near the time of 1 Timothy's composition. 2 Timothy was written from a Roman prison (2 Tim. 1:8) where the Apostle was chained (1:16) and suffered hardship as a criminal (2:9). 2 Timothy 1:17 makes it clear that Paul was still in Rome. He was locked far within the Roman prison system, for he had been difficult to locate (1:16, 17). He was alone, except for Luke (4:11). In his hour of need he had been deserted by "all" (1:15; 4:16). Some had gone on to ministry assignments elsewhere (4:10b, 12, 20a). Another had been left helplessly sick in another place (4:20b). Paul viewed his death as imminent (4:6-8). He longed for Timothy to come to him (4:9, 21).

Precise dating of these letters is a challenge, but the following may provide a safe range for the dates of composition. 1 Timothy and Titus may have been written between A.D. 63 and 65. 2 Timothy would likely have been written sometime in A.D. 66/67.

Purpose: Why Did Paul Write the Pastoral Epistles?

What is the self-testimony regarding the purpose of these letters? 1 Timothy indicates that it was written to enable and empower Timothy in dealing with the false teachers who were at work in the church of Ephesus (1:3). The letter also is designed to explain how believers should conduct themselves as God's household (3:15). Furthermore, 1 Timothy 3:15 indicates this epistle was written in case there was a delay in Paul's return to Ephesus. This letter which arose out of a possible temporary delay has stood the changes of the passing of ages and provides us still with timeless instruction for the pastoral care of God's churches.

Titus was written to enable and empower Titus in establishing the churches on the island of Crete and in appointing elders in those churches (1:5). The Apostle furthermore is concerned to make certain the believers on Crete understand the importance of healthy doctrine (1:9, 13) and healthy living (2:1).

2 Timothy was written as a plea for Timothy to come quickly to the Apostle's side in Rome (1:4; 4:9, 21) once his replacement arrived (4:12). He longed for Timothy and also wanted his warm cloak and reading material (4:13). Beyond this, Paul's great concern was to encourage Timothy to remain faithful to Christ and the ministry of the gospel, even if this should include hardship and suffering (1:8; 2:3; 4:5). 2 Timothy is known for its depiction of Paul's final words before departing this life.

Clearly the PE were personal letters from the Apostle Paul to two intimate friends and co-laborers. Yet beyond the personal nature of the correspondence found in the PE, the letters were clearly intended to have a wider influence among the believers in Ephesus and on Crete. As already mentioned, this is evidenced by the fact that the letters conclude with a blessing: "Grace be with you" (1 Tim. 6:21; 2 Tim. 4:22) or "Grace be with you all" (Titus 3:15). In each case the pronouns are in the plural, an indication that the Apostle fully expected the contents of these letters to be known and read by more than simply Timothy and Titus. In this regard each of the letters was likely written with the intent that they would strengthen Timothy and Titus as designates of the Apostle in dealing authoritatively in the matters confronting the churches.

Theology: What Do the Pastoral Epistles Teach Us?

1 Timothy and Titus are closely related to one another. Both the content and the style hint that they may have been written near the same time. Yet the two letters are not identical in every regard. 1 Timothy seems to point to a more intimate relationship between author and recipient, while Titus is more businesslike. 1 Timothy stresses right doctrine while Titus points more heavily to right living.[44] Titus argues for right living because of its impact upon the church's ministry to the lost community in which it resides. The battle against false teaching seems more desperate in 1 Timothy than in Titus. On the other hand, 2 Timothy is warm, personal, and charged with emotion.

These three letters were written by the Apostle Paul to individuals concerning matters they faced at a particular place in a particular time. That is to say these letters were not composed as formal outlines of all that a pastor will

---

[44] Hiebert, Titus and Philemon, 8.

face and must undertake in pastoral ministry. Fee has gone to great and helpful lengths to show us that the PE are not a "church manual."[45] Yet, under the inspiration of the Holy Spirit (2 Tim. 3:16), these letters have occupied an important place in the life and ministry of the church and its spiritual leaders. As we trace how the Holy Spirit moved Paul to guide Timothy and Titus in the issues they were facing, we find in them (along with all of Scripture) an accurate, reliable, and sufficient guide for our lives and ministries.

It is not the purpose of this Introduction to detail all that the PE teach, but to prepare the reader to engage the actual text of Scripture. Yet it will be helpful to sketch in a suggestive way some of the major theological themes that will be faced in the PE. Allow the following themes both to prepare you for what you will face in the text of the PE and suggest veins of truth you may wish to mine in your own study.

> **appearing** (1 Tim. 6:14; 2 Tim. 1:10; 4:1, 8; Titus 2:13)
> **conscience** (1 Tim. 1:5, 19; 3:9; 4:2; 2 Tim. 1:3; Titus 1:15)
> **controversy/arguments** (1 Tim. 1:4, 6; 6:4, 20; 2 Tim. 2:14, 16, 23; Titus 1:10; 3:9)
> **creedal/liturgical fragments** (1 Tim. 3:16; 6:13-16; 2 Tim. 1:9, 10; 2:8, 11-13; 4:1; Titus 2:11-14; 3:4-7)
> **deception** (1 Tim. 4:1, 2; 2 Tim. 3:6, 13; Titus 1:10)
> **deposit/treasure** (1 Tim. 6:20; 2 Tim. 1:12, 14)
> **devil/demonic** (1 Tim. 3:6; 2 Tim. 2:26; 3:3)
> **entrust** (1 Tim. 6:20; 2 Tim. 1:12, 14)
> **faithful sayings** (1 Tim. 1:15; 4:9; 2 Tim. 2:11; Titus 3:8)
> **genealogies** (1 Tim. 1:4; Titus 3:9)
> **God our Savior** (1 Tim. 1:1; 2:3; Titus 1:3; 2:10; 3:4)
> **godliness** (εὐσέβεια; 1 Tim. 2:2; 3:16; 4:7, 8; 6:3, 5, 6, 11; 2 Tim. 3:5; Titus 1:1)
> **good fight** (1 Tim. 1:18; 6:12; 2 Tim. 4:7)
> **good [ἀγαθός] works** (1 Tim. 2:10; 5:10; 2 Tim. 2:21; 3:17; Titus 1:16; 3:1)
> **good [καλός] works** (1 Tim. 3:1; 5:10, 25; 6:18; Titus 2:7, 14; 3:8, 14)
> **greed** (1 Tim. 6:5; 2 Tim. 3:2, 4; Titus 1:11)
> **"guard"** (1 Tim. 5:21; 6:20; 2 Tim. 1:12, 14; 4:15)
> **ignorance of false teachers** (1 Tim. 6:4, 20; 2 Tim. 2:23; 3:7; Titus 1:5; 3:9)
> **immorality** (1 Tim. 1:19, 20; 2 Tim. 2:16, 19; 3:4, 6; Titus 1:15, 16)
> **"in Christ"** (1 Tim. 1:14; 3:13; 2 Tim. 1:1, 9, 13; 2:1, 10; 3:12, 15)
> **Jewish law** (1 Tim. 1:7; Titus 1:10, 14; 3:9)
> **learn/receive instruction** (1 Tim. 2:11; 5:4, 13; 2 Tim. 3:7, 14 [2x], Titus 3:14)
> **myths** (1 Tim. 1:4; 4:7; 2 Tim. 4:4; Titus 1:14)
> **qualifications for leadership** (1 Tim. 3:1-12; Titus 1:6-9)
> **salvation by grace, not works** (2 Tim. 1:9; Titus 3:5)
> **sound [ὑγιαίνω] doctrine/faith/teaching/words** (1 Tim. 1:10; 6:3; 2 Tim. 1:13; 4:3; Titus 1:9, 13; 2:1, 2)

---
[45] Fee, 13.

"**the faith**" (1 Tim. 1:19; 3:9; 4:1, 6; 5:8; 6:10, 12; 2 Tim. 3:8; 4:7; Titus 1:13)
"**the truth,**" (1 Tim. 2:4, 7; 3:15; 4:3; 6:5; 2 Tim. 2:25; 3:7; Titus 1:1, 14)

In addition to those themes throughout the whole of the PE, consider tracing the following themes through the individual letters. 1 Timothy: charge/commandment (1:3, 5, 18; 4:11; 5:7; 6:13, 17), guarding the faith (1:19; 3:9, 13; 4:1, 6; 6:10, 12, 21), and true doctrine (1:3, 10; 4:13, 16; 6:1, 3-4). 2 Timothy: apostasy (3:1-6; 4:3-4), memory (1:3, 4, 5, 6; 2:8; 3:14-15), and suffering/endurance (1:8, 12; 2:1, 3, 9, 10, 12; 3:10-12; 4:5). Titus: Christ as our Savior (1:4; 2:13; 3:6), good works (1:16; 2:7, 14; 3:1, 5, 8, 14; see also above under the whole of the PE), sound doctrine (1:9, 13; 2:1-2, 8), sound doctrine (1:1; 2:12), and grace (1:4; 2:11ff; 3:7, 15) leading to a godly life.

Bibliography[46]

Alford, Henry. *Alford's Greek Testament: An Exegetical and Critical Commentary*. 5 vols. Grand Rapids, Michigan: Baker Book House; reprint 1980 from the 1871 version.

Bauer, Walter. *A Greek-English Lexicon of the New Testament and Other Early Christian Literature*. William F. Arndt and F. Wilbur Gingrich. Trans. 2nd edition. Chicago: The University of Chicago Press, 1979.

Blum, Edwin. "The Apostles' View of Scripture." In *Inerrancy*, Norman L. Geisler, ed. Grand Rapids, Michigan: Zondervan Publishing House, 1980.

Brown, Colin, ed. *The New International Dictionary of New Testament Theology*. 3 vols. Grand Rapids, Michigan: Zondervan Publishing House, 1975.

Dana, H.E. and Julius R. Mantey, *A Manual Grammar of the Greek New Testament*. Toronto: The MacMillan Company, 1927, 1955.

Earle, Ralph. "1, 2 Timothy." *The Expositor's Bible Commentary*, vol. 11. Grand Rapids, Michigan: Zondervan Publishing House, 1978.

Fee, Gordon D. *1 and 2 Timothy, Titus*. New International Biblical Commentary. Peabody, Massachusetts: Hendrickson Publishers, Inc., 1984, 1988.

Friberg, Timothy, Barbara Friberg and Neva F. Miller. *Analytical Lexicon of the Greek New Testament*. Victoria, British Columbia: Trafford Publishing, 2005.

Geisler, Norman L. "A Christian Perspective on Wine-Drinking." *Bibliotheca Sacra*, January-March 1982, 50.

Grudem, Wayne A. *The Gift of Prophecy in the New Testament Today*. Westchester, Illinois: Crossway Books, 1988.

---

[46] See Appendix E for an annotated bibliography of commentaries.

Guthrie, Donald. *New Testament Introduction.* Downers Grove, Illinois: InterVarsity Press, 1990.

_____, *The Pastoral Epistles.* Tyndale New Testament Commentaries. William B. Eerdmans Publishing Company, 1957, 1980.

Hanson, A.T. *The Pastoral Epistles.* The New Century Bible Commentary. Grand Rapids, Michigan: William B. Eerdmans Publishing Company, 1982.

Harrison, P.N. *The Problem of the Pastorals (Pseudonymity and Canon).* London: Oxford, 1921.

Hendriksen, William. *Exposition of The Pastoral Epistles.* New Testament Commentary. Grand Rapids, Michigan: Baker Book House, 1957.

Henry, Matthew. *Matthew Henry's Commentary on the Whole Bible: Complete and Unabridged.* Peabody, Massachusetts: Hendrickson Publishers, Inc.; reprint 1991.

Hiebert, D. Edmond. *First Timothy.* Everyman's Bible Commentary. Chicago: Moody Press, 1957.

_____, *Second Timothy.* Everyman's Bible Commentary. Chicago: Moody Press, 1958.

_____, "Titus." *The Expositor's Bible Commentary.* Vol. 11. Grand Rapids: Zondervan Publishing House, 1978.

_____, *Titus and Philemon.* Everyman's Bible Commentary. Chicago: Moody Press, 1957.

House, H. Wayne. "Biblical Inspiration in 2 Timothy 3:16." *Biblotheca Sacra.* Vol. 137, No. 545, Jan. 1980.

_____, *Charts of Christian Theology and Doctrine.* Grand Rapids, Michigan: Zondervan Publishing House, 1992.

_____, *The Role of Women in Ministry Today.* Grand Rapids, Michigan: Baker Books, 1990.

Kelly, J.N.D., *A Commentary on the Pastoral Epistles.* New York, 1963; reprinted Grand Rapids, 1981.

Kitchen, John A. *Embracing Authority.* Ross-shire, Scotland: Christian Focus Publications, 2002.

_____, *Revival in the Rubble.* Fort Washington, Pennsylvania: CLC Publications, 2006.

Kittel, Gerhard and Gerhard Friedrich, eds. *Theological Dictionary of the New Testament.* Translated by Geoffrey Bromiley. 9 vols. Grand Rapids, Michigan: William B. Eerdmans Publishing Company, 1964-76.

Kittel, Gerhard and Gerhard Friedrich. *Theological Dictionary of the New Testament.*

Translated and abridged in one volume by Geoffrey W. Bromiley. Grand Rapids, Michigan: William B. Eerdmans Publishing Company, 1985.

Kostenberger, Andreas, J, T. Schreiner, H.S. Baldwin, eds. *Women in the Church: A Fresh Analysis of 1 Timothy 2:9-15*. Grand Rapids, Michigan: Baker Books, 1995.

Knight, George W., III. *The Pastoral Epistles*. The New International Greek Testament Commentary. Grand Rapids, Michigan: William B. Eerdmans Publishing Company, 1992.

Lea, Thomas D. and Hayne P. Griffin, Jr. *1, 2 Timothy, Titus*. The New American Commentary. Nashville: Broadman Press, 1992.

Litfin, A. Duane. "1 Timothy." In *The Bible Knowledge Commentary*. Vol. 2. Victor Books, 1983.

Lenski, R.C.H. *The Interpretation of St. Paul's Epistles to the Colossians, to the Thessalonians, to Timothy, to Titus and to Philemon*. Minneapolis: Augsburg Publishing House. Copyright 1937, Lutheran Book Concern; 1946, The Wartburg Press. Copyright assigned to Augsburg Publishing House, 1961.

Louw, J.P. and E.A. Nida, eds., *Louw-Nida Greek-English Lexicon of the New Testament Based on Semantic Domains*. 2nd. Edition (New York: United Bible Societies, 1988). Electronic version.

Marshall, I. Howard. *A Critical and Exegetical Commentary on The Pastoral Epistles*. International Critical Commentary. London: T&T Clark International, 1999, 2004.

McCalley, Chester A. *Commentary and Outline of I and II Timothy*. Kansas City: Word of Truth Cassettes and Literature, n.d.

Moo, Douglas. "What Does It Mean Not to Teach or Have Authority over Men?" In *Recovering Biblical Manhood and Womanhood*, John Piper and Wayne Grudem, eds. Wheaton, Illinois: Crossway Books, 1991.

Moule, H.C.G. *Studies in II Timothy*. Kregel Popular Commentary Series. Grand Rapids, Michigan: Kregel Publications, 1977.

Mounce, William D. *Pastoral Epistles*. The Word Biblical Commentary. Vol. 46. Nashville: Thomas Nelson Publishers, 2000.

Newman, Barclay M., Jr. *A Concise Greek-English Dictionary of the New Testament*, Copyright ©1971 by the United Bible Societies (UBS) and 1993 by Deutsche Bibelgesellschaft (German Bible Society), Stuttgart. Used by permission. MRT ASCII version reformatted, corrected, and updated in 1987 by CCAT. University of Pennsylvania. Barclay, Newman, electronic edition.

Orr, James, gen. ed. *The International Standard Bible Encyclopaedia*. Grand Rapids, Michigan: William B. Eerdmans Publishing Company, 1956.

Rienecker, Fritz. *A Linguistic Key to the Greek New Testament.* Translated by Cleon L. Rogers, Jr. Grand Rapids, Michigan: Zondervan Publishing House, 1976, 1980.

Robertson, Archibald Thomas. *Word Pictures in the New Testament.* 6 vols. Grand Rapids, Michigan: Baker Book House; reprint n.d. from 1930 Sunday School Board of the Southern Baptist Convention.

Stalker, James. *The Life of St. Paul.* Grand Rapids, Michigan: Zondervan Publishing House, 1983.

Stibbs, A.M. "1 Timothy," "2 Timothy," and "Titus." In *The New Bible Commentary: Revised.* D. Guthrie and J.A. Motyer, eds. Grand Rapids, Michigan: William B. Eerdmans Publishing Company, 1970.

Thayer, Joseph H. *Thayer's Greek-English Lexicon of the New Testament.* Peabody, Massachusetts: Hendriksen Publishers, Inc.; reprinted 2003 from the 4th edition originally published by T&T Clark, Edinburgh, 1896.

Towner, Philip H. *1-2 Timothy and Titus.* The IVP New Testament Commentary Series. Downers Grove, Illinois: InterVarsity Press, 1994.

_____, *The Letters to Timothy and Titus.* The New International Commentary on the New Testament. Grand Rapids, Michigan: William B. Eerdmans Publishing Company, 2006.

Vincent, Marvin R. *Vincent's Word Studies in the New Testament.* McLean, Virginia: MacDonald Publishing Company, n.d.

Vine, W.E. *Vine's Expository Dictionary of New Testament Words.* McLean, Virginia: MacDonald Publishing Company, n.d.

Warfield, B.B., *The Inspiration and Authority of the Bible.* Philadelphia: Presbyterian and Reformed Publishing Company, 1948.

Wiersbe, Warren W. *The Bible Exposition Commentary.* New Testament, vol. 2. Colorado Springs: Victor, 2001.

Wilder, Terry L. "A Brief Defense of the Pastoral Epistles' Authenticity." *Midwestern Journal of Theology,* 2.1. Fall 2003.

Wuest, Kenneth S., *The Pastoral Epistles in the Greek New Testament.* Grand Rapids, Michigan: William B. Eerdmans Publishing Company, 1953.

Young, Edward J., *Thy Word is Truth.* Grand Rapids, Michigan: William B. Eerdmans Publishing Company, 1957.

1 TIMOTHY

CHAPTER

1

1:1 Paul, an apostle of Christ Jesus according to the commandment of God our Savior, and of Christ Jesus, who is our hope,

The author's name ("Paul," Παῦλος) is the first word encountered, as is the case in all thirteen of Paul's NT epistles. Paul was born to the son of a Roman citizen (Acts 22:28) and was given both a Roman name ("Paul," Παῦλος) and a Hebrew name ("Saul," Σαῦλος). Early in the biblical record he is referred to by his Hebrew name (e.g., Acts 7:58; 8:1, 3; 13:1, 2, 7, 9), for he was still primarily associated with the Jewish people. When he was called and sent as a missionary to the Gentiles his Roman name became the normal way in which he was designated.

He is designated here as "an apostle" (ἀπόστολος), something he does in the opening verse of every one of his letters except Philippians, 1 and 2 Thessalonians and Philemon. The word refers to one sent with a message and endowed with the full authority of the sender in delivering it. Frequently Paul seems to employ it in the opening of a letter to make clear his authority in writing. That appears not to be the case in 2 Timothy (see comments on 2 Tim. 1:1). But that last of Paul's letters appears to contain a good deal more intimate and personal detail than does 1 Timothy and, despite the fact that this letter is addressed to an individual instead of a church, its contents were likely intended to be shared with the church (note the plural "you" in 1 Tim. 6:21). Paul, then, may note his apostolic credentials here in order to bring strength to the sometimes difficult instructions he will give in this letter concerning life in the local church. He is, of course, an apostle "of Christ Jesus" (Χριστοῦ Ἰησοῦ). That combination in that order occurs eleven times in the letter, while the reverse order ("Jesus Christ") occurs but three times (1:16; 6:3, 14). In 2 Timothy the order "Christ Jesus" is found twelve of thirteen times. In Titus it is evenly split, two cases each. The precise phrase "Paul, an apostle of Christ Jesus" (Παῦλος ἀπόστολος Χριστοῦ Ἰησοῦ) also opens the letters of 2 Corinthians, Ephesians, Colossians and 2 Timothy. If there is any significance to be found in the order of the words, "Christ Jesus" may emphasize the heavenly position of Christ as the Messiah of God, while "Jesus Christ" may emphasize the earthly personage of Jesus.

He addresses Timothy (and others who will be exposed to the contents of the letter) "according to the commandment of God our Savior" (κατ' ἐπιταγὴν θεοῦ σωτῆρος ἡμῶν). The expression is quite similar to that with which Paul opens his letter to Titus (1:3). The expression "according to the commandment" (κατ' ἐπιταγὴν) adds solemnity and authority to what the Apostle will say. The precise expression is used four other times in the NT, all by Paul (Rom. 16:26; 1 Cor. 7:6; 2 Cor. 8:8; Titus 1:3). It describes the epochal nature of God's revelation in Christ (Rom. 16:26) and the Apostle's charge in making that revelation known (Titus 1:3). It comes, then, also to be used to differentiate when the Apostle is not speaking with that same sense of authority (1 Cor. 7:6; 2 Cor. 8:8). The word "commandment" (ἐπιταγὴν) speaks of an injunction, mandate or command.[1] It bespeaks authority. It is used seven times by Paul and nowhere else in Scripture (Rom. 16:26; 1 Cor. 7:6, 25; 2 Cor. 8:8; 1 Tim. 1:1; Titus 1:3; 2:15). The preposition "according to" (κατ') combines both the notion of a standard by which something is determined and the reason for which something is done.[2] Paul does not hesitate to speak of "God our Savior" (θεοῦ σωτῆρος ἡμῶν), though he never does so again in this precise form (cf. 1 Tim. 2:3; 4:10; Titus 1:3; 2:10; 3:4). God is designated as Savior throughout the LXX (e.g., Deut. 31:15; 1 Chron. 16:35; Isa. 12:2) and Paul's usage demonstrates again his deep roots in the OT Scriptures. Additionally, Nero was demanding the confession that he was the savior and Paul's usage here may be a subtle rebuttal to that assertion being pressed upon citizens of the Roman Empire. He does not use the word "Savior" of Jesus in this letter, though he will in 2 Timothy (1:10) and Titus (1:4; 2:13; 3:6).

> **Ministry Maxim**
>
> Only one who lives under authority is ready to exercise authority.

The Apostle does go on ("and," καὶ) to speak of "Christ Jesus, who is our hope" (Χριστοῦ Ἰησοῦ τῆς ἐλπίδος ἡμῶν). The genitive form "of Christ Jesus" (Χριστοῦ Ἰησοῦ) links this to the genitive "of God" (θεοῦ) and indicates that the commandment is viewed as coming from both God the Father

---

[1] Thayer, 244.
[2] BAGD, 407.

and God the Son. He is designated as "our hope" (τῆς ἐλπίδος ἡμῶν) or, more literally, "the hope of us." The NASU translators have added "who is" for smoother English. While Christ is often connected to our hope by Paul (e.g., Eph. 2:12; 1 Thess. 1:3; 2 Thess. 2:16; Titus 2:13), He is never again specifically called "our hope" as He is here. The presence of the definite article with the noun (lit., "the hope") speaks to the unique nature of the hope which Jesus Christ brings. This hope is the foundation of all Paul's labors, as we see in 1 Timothy 4:10: "For it is for this we labor and strive, because we have fixed our hope on the living God, who is the Savior of all men, especially of believers."

Paul, as he opens this letter, presents himself as a man with authority ("apostle"), under authority ("according to the commandment of God") and taken up in anticipation ("our hope"). Jesus Christ is Paul's Master (the One who sent him as an "apostle"), Commander ("according to the commandment of . . . Christ Jesus") and Hope ("who is our hope").

> **Digging Deeper:**
> 1. In addressing a letter to a personal friend and ministry partner, why do you think Paul emphasized his authority?
> 2. Why is being under authority and filled with hope a logically necessary combination for the Christian? How might the two seem contradictory to someone steeped in a modern worldview?
> 3. What may have been going on in the experience of Paul and/or Timothy that called for the emphasis on Christ as "our hope"?

1:2 To Timothy, my true child in the faith: Grace, mercy and peace from God the Father and Christ Jesus our Lord.

The letter is addressed "To Timothy" (Τιμοθέῳ). Paul met Timothy and found him to be a disciple upon his return to Lystra (Acts 16:1-2). During the Apostle's first visit to Lystra he had been taken initially for a god after healing a lame man, and then nearly stoned to death at the hands of the Jews (Acts 14:8-20). He spent only a short time there before moving on. We have no definite word of Timothy's conversion at that time. Perhaps he had been one listening on the fringes of the crowd as Paul preached. It is possible that his heart was moved and then, when he saw Paul's resolve in the face of death (2 Tim. 3:11), he put his faith in Christ. Whenever the exact starting point and whatever the final encouragement to trust in Christ, he was no secret disciple upon Paul's return. He was known throughout his hometown (the same hometown where the Jews had stoned Paul to the point of death!) and the region as an effective disciple of Christ, advancing the cause of the Gospel for miles around (Acts 16:2). Paul wanted this young man to travel at his side in the cause of the Gospel, that he might further train and equip him for ministry (Acts 16:3).

Timothy is designated "my true child in the faith" (γνησίῳ τέκνῳ ἐν πίστει). He was not Paul's biological offspring. Timothy's mother and grandmother were Jewish (2 Tim. 1:5); his father was a Gentile (Acts 16:1). During the years and miles of travel and ministry together the bonds of love between the two grew. Paul became the spiritual father Timothy never had. It should be noted that the pronoun "my" is added by the translators, as is the definite article ("the") before "faith." Thus the phrase more literally is, "a true child in faith." This might be taken as a signal merely of the genuineness of Timothy's faith or of his relative maturity in the faith, if it were not for its position here at the opening of the letter. Paul is clearly marking out the nature of Timothy's relationship to himself. Calling Timothy "my true child in the faith" differs from 2 Timothy 1:2 where he is designated as "my beloved son." This designation here in 1 Timothy 1:2 speaks more to the character of Timothy's relationship to Paul. He was genuinely and truly Paul's child in the faith. The reference in 2 Timothy 1:2 ("beloved") is more emotional, speaking of Paul's feelings toward Timothy and befits the dire straights Paul was in as he anticipated his impending martyrdom. Here it is Timothy's standing before Paul that is in view; in 2 Timothy it is his standing within Paul's heart (cf. 1 Cor. 4:17). Here Paul, having established his authority (v.1), is now positioning Timothy to act confidently on that authority by carrying out the instructions of this letter.

The adjective "true" (γνησίῳ) generally means something genuine or sincere (2 Cor. 8:8; Phil. 4:3), but when used literally of children it means that they are legitimate, lawful or born in wedlock. The figurative extension, which applies here, is that Timothy is spiritually a genuine child of the Apostle. Paul used nearly the same expression of Titus (Titus 1:4), only here he uses the preposition ἐν instead of κατὰ (apparently for stylistic reasons only[3]) and there he adds the adjective "common" (κοινὴν). That Timothy was designated a "child" (τέκνῳ) means not that he was immature, but rather it signals the kind and quality of relationship he enjoyed with the Apostle.

> **Ministry Maxim**
>
> Grace forgives sin's debt, mercy feels sin's devastation, and peace restores sin's disorder.

Paul sends a threefold blessing to Timothy: "grace, mercy and peace" (χάρις ἔλεος εἰρήνη). This trinity of blessings begins with "grace" (χάρις; cf. 1:12, 14; 6:21). It points to the unmerited favor of God that is extended to sinners through Jesus Christ. It is

---
[3] Knight, 286.

both the initial grace by which one is saved from the penalty of sin and the ongoing daily grace for life and service above the power of sin. This "grace" forms an inclusion for this intimate letter (1:2; 6:21). The second of these extended blessings is "mercy." The word (ἔλεος) is an emotional one, pointing to the compassion of God toward those who suffer, particularly because of sin. It is the LXX's translation of the Hebrew word *hesed)*, which is the OT term to designate God's faithful, loyal covenant love. It points, therefore, both to the firm objective commitment of a covenant relationship and the subjective emotional response when one so loved is faced with adversity. Paul no doubt could sense Timothy's particular need (in his challenging ministry as pastor in Ephesus) for such faithful, compassionate love from God and extended it to him as one who had imbibed deeply of it himself. Similarly "peace" (εἰρήνη) is a reflection of Paul's Hebrew life, now fulfilled and reoriented by Christ. It is the NT equivalent of the Hebrew *shalom*. It points to the wholeness and completeness of life as it should be. Christ has brought believers objective peace *with* God the Father (Rom. 5:1) and also brings to believers the more subjective peace *of* God which results from such a standing (Phil. 4:7). In this trinity of blessings "grace" points to God's dealing with sin and guilt itself, "mercy" points to God's concern for the misery and pain that sin creates,[4] and "peace" points to the reordering of the chaos sin leaves behind.

This threefold blessing is found nowhere else in Paul's writing except 2 Timothy 1:2. The more common combination is simply "grace" and "peace" (Rom. 1:7; 1 Cor. 1:3; 2 Cor. 1:2; Gal. 1:3; Eph. 1:2; Phil. 1:2; Col. 1:2; 1 Thess. 1:1; 2 Thess. 1:2; Titus 1:4; Philem. 3). The addition of "mercy" is reserved for Timothy. It proves to us that the relationship between Paul and Timothy was unique, and thus these two letters are unique among all others in the NT.

These blessings are seen as being extended "from God the Father and Christ Jesus our Lord" (ἀπὸ θεοῦ πατρὸς καὶ Χριστοῦ Ἰησοῦ τοῦ κυρίου ἡμῶν). The close combination of "Christ Jesus our Lord" with "God the Father" is a powerful testimony to Paul's view of Christ's divinity.

Digging Deeper:
1. To whom are you a "true child in the faith"? And who is such to you?
2. Why does Paul add "mercy" to "grace" and "peace" when he opens his two letters to Timothy?

---

[4] Ibid., 66.

1:3 As I urged you upon my departure for Macedonia, remain on at Ephesus so that you may instruct certain men not to teach strange doctrines,

The sentence that runs through v.4 opens with the clause "As I urged you" (Καθὼς παρεκάλεσά σε). The verb "I urged" (παρεκάλεσα) is a compound word, coming from the verb καλέω (to call) and the prepositional prefix παρὰ (beside). Strictly speaking it means "to call alongside." It appears in all of the Apostle's letters (except Galatians) and is found frequently in the PE (1 Tim. 1:3; 2:1; 5:1; 6:2; 2 Tim. 4:2; Titus 1:9; 2:6, 15). It has a range of meaning that can swing from the softer sense of "comfort" to the sharper edge of "exhort." It is translated variously according to context by words such as "appeal" (Philem. 9, 10), "comfort" (2 Cor. 1:4, 6), "encourage" (1 Cor. 16:12), "exhort" (1 Cor. 1:10), "implore" (2 Cor. 12:8), and "urge" (Rom. 12:1). The masculine singular noun form became a title for the Holy Spirit (John 14:16, 26; 15:26; 16:7) and the Lord Jesus Christ (1 John 2:1). Here the aorist tense points to a moment in the past when in a very personal ("you," σε) encounter Paul laid this task upon Timothy. That Paul launched into specific exhortation without some word of thanksgiving (as he also did in Galatians and Titus) is a departure from his normal writing style and bespeaks the seriousness of the problems confronting Timothy and the Ephesian church.

The next clause in the original word order of the sentence is "remain on at Ephesus" (προσμεῖναι ἐν Ἐφέσῳ). A more literal rendering might be "to remain in Ephesus." The word "remain" (προσμεῖναι) is an infinitive used as the object of the verb "I urged" (παρεκάλεσά).[5] Paul's only use of the word is here and in 1 Timothy 5:5. It is a compound composed of "to" (πρός) and "remain" (μένω). The aorist tense points to Timothy's obedience at the moment the Apostle instructed him to remain at Ephesus. The preposition strengthens the idea of remaining *with* someone (Matt. 15:32; Mark 8:2) or *in* a place (Acts 18:18; 1 Tim. 1:3). It can also, then, mean figuratively to abide or continue in something like faithfulness to the Lord (Acts 11:23), the grace of God (Acts 13:43), or prayer (1 Tim. 5:5). In this case the dative "in Ephesus" marks out the location in which Timothy is to abide, but also implies the circumstances of that location in which he must remain faithful to the Lord's purposes and the Apostle's instructions.

This was to take place "upon my departure for Macedonia (πορευόμενος εἰς Μακεδονίαν). The words "upon my departure" translate the present middle participle πορευόμενος. It seems reasonable to understand the participle temporally and thus translate it as "upon my departure" (NASU) or

---
[5] Rienecker, 614.

"when I was going" (cf. NIV, NKJV, NRSV). The present tense underscores the notion that Paul was likely already on his way to Macedonia when he urged Timothy's continuance in Ephesus. Or it is possible that he charged him as he was leaving and expected him to continue there during the journeys that awaited the Apostle on that ministry trip. A more specific historical reconstruction is a venture further down the path of speculation. Though awkward in English, the sentence thus far could simply be rendered "As I urged you to remain in Ephesus when I was going to Macedonia." We do not know more about the purpose behind Paul's journey into Macedonia. Perhaps it was his intention to travel through Macedonia on his way to Dalmatia, and perhaps he had asked Titus (whom he had previously "left . . . in Crete," Titus 1:5) to catch up with him in Nicopolis (2 Tim. 4:10; Titus 3:12). Subsequent to the writing of this letter, he may have been arrested en route (perhaps in Troas, 2 Tim. 4:13) and taken to Rome, from which he would write the letter of 2 Timothy. This historical reconstruction, however, must also be considered speculative.

The purpose ("so that," ἵνα plus subjunctive) in the Apostle's assigning Timothy to remain in Ephesus is not uncertain: "you may instruct certain men not to teach strange doctrines" (παραγγείλῃς τισὶν μὴ ἑτεροδιδασκαλεῖν). The verb "you may instruct" (παραγγείλῃς) is used twelve times by the Apostle (1 Cor. 7:10; 11:17; 1 Thess. 4:11; 2 Thess. 3:4, 6, 10, 12), five of them here in 1 Timothy (1:3; 4:11; 5:7; 6:13, 17). It is a compound word from "along" (παρά) and "announce" (ἀγγέλλω). Thus its root meaning is to pass along a message to someone. It came, however, to be used of an authoritative announcement or command. Here its use signals the apostolic authority with which Timothy was to issue the appropriate instructions. The word was used in military contexts and there is strength in it. When, as here, it is followed by μὴ and an infinitive (ἑτεροδιδασκαλεῖν) it can have the sense of "forbid."[6]

The designation "certain men" (τισὶν), being the indefinite plural pronoun, is vague as to what individuals it identities, though soon enough Paul will get specific (v.20). It seems reasonable, as Fee suggests[7], that those in view may well have been elders in the Ephesian church. Paul had warned the elders of the Ephesian church that *"from among your own selves* men will arise, speaking perverse things, to draw away the disciples after them" (Acts 20:30, emphasis mine). This also might explain the extensive coverage the ministry of elders receives in this first letter—their character (3:1-7), their responsibility (5:17), and their

> **Ministry Maxim**
>
> Both forging ahead and remaining behind are essential ministry assignments.

---

[6] Friberg, 294.
[7] Fee, 40.
[8] Ibid.

discipline (5:19-20). Also the fact that Paul himself excommunicated two men (1:20) rather than calling on the church to take any such action (cf. 2 Thess. 3:14; 1 Cor. 5:1-5) may suggest as much.[8] This would in no way restrict the application of these words should a non-elder undertake any similar teaching. At this juncture all we need to know about these folk is that they "teach strange doctrines" (ἑτεροδιδασκαλεῖν). The word is found only here and 6:3. The Apostle may well have coined the word himself for this context. The compound word is comprised of "different" (ἕτερος) and "to teach" (διδάσκω). The word ἕτερος describes that which is another of a different kind. The word ἄλλος would have referred to another of a similar kind. Paul used the other in compound to indicate that this teaching had no affinity or connection to the Gospel.[9] What is "different" about this doctrine is that it "does not agree with sound words, those of our Lord Jesus Christ, and with the doctrine conforming to godliness" (6:3). Clearly there had already developed an unambiguous set of doctrines that defined the substance of Christianity.

> ### Digging Deeper:
> 1. How might the ministry assignment of remaining behind while another travels to take on new ministry frontiers emotionally affect a person?
> 2. Why do you think Paul described Timothy's ministry assignment in Ephesus in negative terms (instructing men what not to teach, rather than what to teach)?
> 3. Which seems more attractive to you, opening new ministry territory or working with an existing ministry to refine and mature the people involved in it?

1:4 nor to pay attention to myths and endless genealogies, which give rise to mere speculation rather than furthering the administration of God which is by faith.

Paul continues to expound upon the purpose statement he began in v.3. To the present tense infinitive of v.3 ("not to teach strange doctrines," μὴ ἑτεροδιδασκαλεῖν) he connects ("nor," μηδέ) another here: "to pay attention" ("to pay attention," προσέχειν). The negative particle μηδέ corresponds to the one in v.3 (μὴ). The root of the infinitive "to pay attention" (προσέχειν) is used twenty-four times in the NT, only five of which are by Paul. All of these appear in the PE, with four of those here in 1 Timothy (1:4; 3:8; 4:1, 13; Titus 1:14). It is a compound

---
[9] Kent, 77.
[10] Friberg, 333.

word comprised of "to" (πρός) and "hold" (ἔχω). When used with a dative it means to hold oneself to something (Acts 8:6) or someone (Acts 8:10).[10] First, one should not hold himself "to myths" (μύθοις). The word appears five times in the NT, four of them by Paul in the PE (1 Tim. 1:4; 4:7; 2 Tim. 4:4; Titus 1:14; cf. 2 Pet. 1:16) and always in a negative sense. The word refers to fanciful and fictitious stories that are passed off as the truth. It has been suggested that it refers to various pre-Gnostic theories that were beginning to seize upon Christian teaching and to redefine and rework it to their own perverted ends. Whether or not such elements were a part of the mix, it was primarily Jewish in nature, possessing elements that made it more appealing to those still struggling with the relationship of the Law to Christ (1 Tim. 1:7-9; Titus 1:14). Thus Paul adds ("and," καὶ) the warning about "endless genealogies" (γενεαλογίαις ἀπεράντοις). The word is used elsewhere only in Titus 3:9 where Titus is warned about "foolish controversies and *genealogies* and strife and disputes about the Law" (emphasis mine). Utilizing the text of the OT, these teachers searched for connections never meant to be made and speculated about various personages, drawing ethical implications from their esoteric speculations. The process became "endless" (ἀπεράντοις), with there always being some new place to search for a signal of some secret message. This adjective is used only here in the NT. It points to the exhausting and wearisome nature of the constant conjecture.[11] Such pursuits are worthless for those things which "have no end also have no result."[12] Those who pursue such things are "always learning and never able to come to the knowledge of the truth" (2 Tim. 3:7).

Such pursuits are of no benefit, but are only those "which give rise to mere speculation" (αἵτινες ἐκζητήσεις παρέχουσιν). The plural form of the relative pronoun "which" (αἵτινες) signals the multitudinous ways such thought finds expression. The verb means to cause, to bring about or to give rise to.[13] The present tense points to the unceasing stream of thought such pursuits bring. Those thoughts are, however, "mere speculation" (ἐκζητήσεις). The word is used only here in the NT and literally means a "seeking out." It has been variously defined as "aimless arguing,"[14] "a subject of subtle inquiry and dispute,"[15] and "useless speculation."[16]

> **Ministry Maxim**
>
> God's Word is to bring us to a specific end by a specific means, not to incite us to endless theological tail-chasing.

---

[11] Fee, 42.
[12] Knight, 74.
[13] Rienecker, 615.
[14] Friberg, 137.
[15] Thayer, 195.
[16] BAGD, 240.

Such guesswork stands in contrast ("rather than," μᾶλλον ἤ) to "the administration of God" (οἰκονομίαν θεοῦ τὴν). The noun "administration" (οἰκονομίαν) is a favorite Pauline word (1 Cor. 9:17; Eph. 1:10; 3:2, 9; Col. 1:25; elsewhere only in Luke 16:2-4). It refers to the administration of a household or the one charged with carrying out that management. Paul then used it by extension to speak of God's administration of salvation through Christ (Eph. 1:10; 3:9) or the stewardship of service laid upon an individual to further that plan (1 Cor. 9:17; Eph. 3:2; Col. 1:25). It is in the first sense that Paul uses the word here.[17] The KJV's "godly edifying" is based upon an inferior reading of the text (οἰκοδομήν instead of οἰκονομίαν, which is better attested). The genitive "of God" (θεοῦ) reveals that it is God's plan that is in view. He is the Author and ultimate Administrator of this salvation.

Knight says, "With the definite article τὴν Paul ties οἰκονομίαν with ἐν πίστει and indicates the realm in which the administration is accomplished."[18] This redemptive plan of God is worked out, not by the unending "speculation" espoused by the false teachers, but "by faith" (ἐν πίστει). This exact phrase is used eleven times in the NT, nine of which are by Paul. Eight of Paul's are in the PE, with six of those being found in 1 Timothy (1 Tim. 1:2, 4; 2:7, 15; 3:13; 4:12; 2 Tim. 1:13; Titus 3:15). The frequency of the expression in the PE underscores the fundamental danger presented by the false teaching and the threat it made to the very work of God. The preposition "by" (ἐν) probably here points to the sphere in which individuals must operate if they are to enter into and carry out the redemptive plan of God.

> **Digging Deeper:**
> 1. What did people hope to discover or prove by their "endless genealogies"? And why would this have seemed important to them?
> 2. While the false teaching confronting Timothy was unique to his first-century context in Ephesus, how does the temptation to useless speculation confront the contemporary church today?
> 3. Can you state with precision and brevity just what "the administration of God" is?

1:5 But the goal of our instruction is love from a pure heart and a good conscience and a sincere faith.

In contrast ("But," δέ) to the teaching of the false teachers (vv.3-4), Paul unveils that which he is after in his ministry. His purpose in leaving Timothy

---
[17] Thayer, 440; The NET Bible.
[18] Knight, 76.

in Ephesus was so Timothy could "instruct" (παραγγείλης) the opponents not to teach falsehoods (v.3). Now he uses the cognate noun "instruction" (τῆς παραγγελίας) to demonstrate what the appropriate teaching should produce. The noun, like the verb, is a strong word with clear undertones of authority (see on v.3; cf. Acts 5:28; 1 Thess. 4:2). The definite article sets it out as distinct and unique from the things being so freely thrown about by the false teachers. It marks this "instruction" as that which Timothy has just been charged with delivering (vv.3-4). Paul wants to set forth clearly "the goal" (τὸ . . . τέλος) of a truly Christian teaching ministry. The word describes the appointed end toward which all activity and effort is directed, the arrival at which signals all previous output has achieved its goal. The singular form and the definite article underscore that there is only one appropriate goal for a teaching ministry.

True doctrine and genuine ministry aim at and find their fulfillment in the production of "love" (ἀγάπη). This is clearly the Apostle's favorite word for "love," being his choice seventy-five times in his letters (compared to one use of the verb φιλέω in 1 Corinthians 16:2). While the word ἀγάπη existed prior to the time of Christ, His followers infused it with new meaning. (Consult Paul's discourse on love in 1 Corinthians 13.) Paul uses the word ten times in the PE, nine of which are in combination with "faith" (πίστις) (1 Tim. 1:5, 14; 2:15; 4:12; 6:11; 2 Tim. 1:13; 2:22; 3:10; Titus 2:2).

This love springs forth from a three-pronged base. First, it comes "from a pure heart" (ἐκ καθαρᾶς καρδίας). The preposition ἐκ governs all three phrases and describes that out of which love arises. Paul uses the same expression, "pure heart" (καθαρᾶς καρδίας), in 2 Timothy 2:22. Seven of Paul's eight usages of "pure" (καθαρός) are found in the PE (1 Tim. 1:5; 3:9; 2 Tim. 1:3; 2:22; Titus 1:15 [3x]). He links it not only to "heart" (καρδίας), but "conscience" (συνείδησις) as well (1 Tim. 3:9; 2 Tim. 1:3). When used literally it describes that which is devoid of any defiling elements like dirt or debris. It is used here in a moral sense. In the NT "heart" (καρδίας) describes the seat of the mind (2 Cor. 4:6), emotions (Eph. 6:22), and will (2 Cor. 9:7). The "heart" is the core and center of the individual.

Second ("and," καί), love comes from "a good conscience" (συνειδήσεως ἀγαθῆς). The word "conscience" is a compound word (συνείδησις), combining "with" (σύν) and "knowledge" (εἶδον). This is a joint-knowledge, shared with oneself. It points to self-awareness.

> **Ministry Maxim**
>
> Teaching that does not produce active, genuine, Christian love is misguided at some level.

Thus Paul speaks of "the testimony of our conscience" (2 Cor. 1:12). It is a testimony given to oneself, and then passed on to others. Paul speaks again of a "good conscience" in v.19. He can speak of "a perfectly good conscience"

(Acts 23:1), "a clear conscience" (1 Tim. 3:9; 2 Tim. 1:3), and "a blameless conscience" (Acts 24:16). The conscience is a gift from God, but has been distorted through sin. It can be "weak" through immaturity (1 Cor. 8:7), wounded through wrong (1 Cor. 8:12), "defiled" by sin (Titus 1:15), and "seared" to the point of insensitivity by repeated rebellion (1 Tim. 4:2). Only God is "good" (Mark 10:18). The conscience is, therefore, "good" (ἀγαθῆς) when it is in accord with the thoughts of God. It is thus in tune with reality; it sees as God sees. Paul would confess, "I do not even examine myself. For I am conscious of nothing against myself, yet I am not by this acquitted; but the one who examines me is the Lord" (1 Cor. 4:3b-4). Our conscience is a helpful guide only as it is conformed to the written revelation of God (2 Tim. 3:16-17).

Third ("and," καί), love arises out of "a sincere faith" (πίστεως ἀνυποκρίτου). Timothy's mother and grandmother possessed this kind of sincere faith, and Paul was certain Timothy did as well (2 Tim. 1:5). The noun "faith" (πίστεως) refers here not to the body of accepted Christian doctrine, but to the personal trust of the individual in that truth and the God who revealed it. The adjective "sincere" (ἀνυποκρίτου) refers to that which is without hypocrisy. The negation (ἀν) is added to the already compounded word (ὑπό, "under" and κρίσις, "judgment"). The noun "hypocrite" (ὑποκριτής) was commonly used to designate an actor, one playing a part that did not represent reality. A "sincere" faith is thus genuine, authentic, and without pretense. A "sincere faith" is never put on display. It functions from internal, not external, motivations.

The primary goal of our preaching and teaching ministry is not the imparting of information or merely the increase of knowledge, but the production of love. That love looks outward at others with good motives ("a pure heart"), looks inward at self in self-judgment ("a good conscience") and looks upward at God without ulterior motives ("a sincere faith"). Those who speak God's Word must seek to bring people into an authentic encounter with God through His Word. This encounter should lead to an inward examination of self before God, which in turn changes the way they look at themselves. This is the goal of all genuine Christian preaching and teaching.

> **Digging Deeper:**
> 1. Why is love the proper outcome by which a teaching and preaching ministry must be evaluated? How does this contrast with the goal of the false teachers Paul has been describing (vv.3-4)?
> 2. How might an impure heart defile any acts of love arising from it?
> 3. Why is a "good conscience" a necessary prerequisite for true love?
> 4. How would an insincere faith bring forth a failure in Christian love?

1:6 For some men, straying from these things, have turned aside to fruitless discussion,

Paul's new sentence begins with the plural relative pronoun "these things" (ὧν). Its likely referent is the "pure heart and a good conscience and a sincere faith" of v.5.[19] Next comes the vague reference to "some men" (τινες). The plural indefinite pronoun enables Paul to provide an indirect description of the false teachers, without yet naming names (cf. v.20).

The main verb "have turned aside" (ἐξετράπησαν) means to twist, turn or turn aside. In medical contexts it could speak of a joint being dislocated (cf. Heb. 12:13).[20] The aorist tense views this turning aside as history, something that had already been accomplished in the past. The passive form has the middle meaning—they wrenched themselves aside from the right path.[21] Paul uses the verb four times, all in his correspondence with Timothy (1 Tim. 1:6; 5:15; 6:20; 2 Tim. 4:4). He can employ it to speak of turning aside to follow Satan (1 Tim. 5:15) or myths (2 Tim. 4:4). Here it is "to fruitless discussion" (εἰς ματαιολογίαν) that they are turning aside to. The noun is used only here in the NT, but its cognate adjective is found in Titus 1:10. It is a compound word made up of "empty/worthless" (ματαιότης) and "word" (λόγος). It thus refers to worthless words or empty eloquence. It is, as Thayer says, "meaningless talk, empty prattle."[22] Such orations sound intellectual, spiritual and impressive, but they are devoid of meaningful content and helpful truth.

The participle "straying from these things" (ἀστοχήσαντες) represents a verb used only by Paul in the NT and used by him only in communication with Timothy. It means "to miss the mark, to swerve, to fail to aim at."[23] Rienecker says, "The word indicates 'taking no pains to aim at the right path.'"[24] Paul uses it elsewhere to speak of those who "have gone astray from the faith" (1 Tim. 6:21) or who "have gone astray from the truth" (2 Tim. 2:18). Here it is the "pure heart and a good conscience and a sincere faith" of v.5 that are left behind. The aorist tense, like the main verb, points to what has already transpired in their lives. The participle likely is used to indicate action that is

> **Ministry Maxim**
>
> Every conversation costs us something—calculate that cost carefully.

---

[19] Knight, 79.
[20] BAGD, 246.
[21] Ibid.
[22] Thayer, 392.
[23] Rienecker, 615.
[24] Ibid.
[25] Knight, 79.

antecedent to the main verb.[25] Thus it appears that some within the Ephesian church had decided that "a pure heart and a good conscience and a sincere faith" were no longer worthy goals and turned themselves aside after other ideals ("wanting to be teachers of the Law," v.7), and in so doing they "turned aside" from God's truth and into "fruitless discussion." They ended up with words aplenty, but entirely missed the goal of the Gospel. They could rattle on with endless esoteric and pious sounding words, but in the final analysis their ramblings produced nothing of any substance or worth.

1:7 wanting to be teachers of the Law, even though they do not understand either what they are saying or the matters about which they make confident assertions.

The Jewish nature of the heresy in Ephesus is clear in that the teachers were "wanting to be teachers of the Law" (θέλοντες εἶναι νομοδιδάσκαλοι). The present tense participle "wanting" (θέλοντες) points to a continuing, and as yet not entirely fulfilled, wish of the false teachers in Ephesus. The infinitive also is in the present tense indicating the continuous nature of what they want "to be" (εἶναι). That aim and longing is the status of "teachers of the Law" (νομοδιδάσκαλοι). Paul uses the word only here and Luke enjoins it in Luke 5:17 and Acts 5:34. It is a compound word comprised of "law" (νόμος) and "teacher" (διδάσκαλος). It is not known outside of the NT until the writings of the church fathers. This seems to mark out the heresy in Ephesus as primarily Jewish in nature and only peripherally, if at all, pre-Gnostic. The "myths and endless genealogies" (v.4) were thus most likely of a Jewish nature.

The remainder of the sentence represents a contrast to what they want to be. The phrase "even though they do not understand" translates just two words in the Greek (μὴ νοοῦντες). The present tense of the participle, along with the negative particle (μὴ), points to the abiding and unending nature of their ignorance. They continuously long to become teachers of the Law, but existing coterminous with their wish is their abiding ignorance. The verb (νοέω) means to perceive or understand with the mind.[26] They are living in a state of unreality. Wanting to be insightful and to play the part of the experts, they do not know what they are or what they are doing. The participle may have a concessive force, as the NASU translation indicates ("even though").[27]

> **Ministry Maxim**
>
> Eloquence can be a mask for ignorance.

---

[26] Thayer, 426.
[27] Rienecker, 615.

Two clauses express what it is they do not understand. The two are held side-by-side by use of the repetition μήτε . . . μήτε ("either . . . or"). When a previous item has been negated ("they do not understand," μὴ νοοῦντες) the use of more than one μήτε divides the items that follow into component parts.[28] First is "what they are saying" (ἃ λέγουσιν). The neuter plural relative pronoun "what" (ἃ) covers anything and everything that was coming from their mouths. Pick anything they say; they don't know what it is they are espousing. The present tense verb emphasizes the unending flow of verbiage coming from their mouths. Second is "the matters about which they make confident assertions" (περὶ τίνων διαβεβαιοῦνται). The indefinite pronoun τίνων ("the matters") is used as a substantive here. The preposition περὶ ("about which") with the genitive means something like "about," "concerning," or "with reference to." The verb "they make confident assertions about" (διαβεβαιοῦνται) is used only here and Titus 3:8. It is a compound word made up of "through" (διά) and "to confirm/verify/prove true" (βεβαιόομαι). The preposition (διά) in compound implies persistence and thoroughness in the affirmation.[29] The verb, then, comes to mean speaking confidently or strongly about something, to insist upon it.[30] It is a deponent verb—a middle/passive form, but with an active meaning. The present tense again underscores the continuous nature of their assertions. The problem is not that they speak with confidence and authority, but that they apply to error the confidence that should only be applied to truth—the same verb is used by Paul to instruct Titus to speak the truth with bold confidence (Titus 3:8). The ignorance of the false teachers in Ephesus and on Crete is a recurring theme in the PE (1 Tim. 6:4, 20; 2 Tim. 2:23; 3:7; Titus 1:5; 3:9).[31]

> **Digging Deeper:**
> 1. In what way did "wanting to be teachers of the Law" put a person in opposition to a "pure heart and a good conscience and sincere faith" (v.5)? Why was achieving both impossible?
> 2. Identify an example of when you became involved in "fruitless discussion." What motivated you during that exchange?
> 3. How can eloquence mask ignorance? What is a good indicator it has become so?

---

[28] BAGD, 519-520.
[29] Alford, 3:426.
[30] BAGD, 181.
[31] Fee, 44.

1:8 But we know that the Law is good, if one uses it lawfully,

The mention of the false teachers as desiring to be "teachers of the Law" (v.7) now leads Paul to outline what the role of the Law truly is. He does so in an extended sentence that runs to the end of v.11. He contrasts ("but," δέ) the desire of the false teachers (v.7) with the inherent value and divine purpose of the Law. He says, "We know" (Οἴδαμεν) what the inherent value of the Law is. The perfect tense has an active meaning—it is current, common knowledge. The first person plural form ("we") differentiates Paul and Timothy and those with them from the false teachers. The verb "know" (οἶδα, also used in 1:9; 3:5, 15) originally stressed the completeness of the knowledge, rather than the process of gaining that knowledge through experience or relationship (γινώσκω, not used in 1 Timothy, but employed in 2 Timothy 1:18; 2:19; 3:1).[32] Paul is completely convinced, as is Timothy and all who know the truth, regarding the value and role of the Law. What Paul knows is "that the Law is good" (ὅτι καλὸς ὁ νόμος). There is no verb, thus the more literal reading would be "that good the Law." The question is, Just what does this mean? In what sense is the Law good? The conditional clause which follows helps us answer this question: "if one uses it lawfully" (ἐάν τις αὐτῷ νομίμως χρῆται). The conditional clause (ἐάν + present subjunctive) is a third class condition which indicates the fulfillment of the action is uncertain. One may or may not use the Law lawfully. That is in question in each case and determines whether or not one derives the good benefit God intended in giving His Law. The indefinite pronoun ("one," τις) makes the reference general and sweeping—this applies to whoever might use the Law "lawfully." Paul uses καλὸς, rather than ἀγαθός, for "good." The former emphasizes that which is both intrinsically good and outwardly attractive, while the latter emphasizes that which is beneficial in its effect,[33] though the two words seem to be used interchangeably in the PE (1 Tim. 5:10).[34] Interestingly, both adjectives are used to describe the goodness of the Law in Romans 7:12, 16. The adverb "lawfully" (νομίμως; only here and 2 Tim. 2:5 in the NT) points to the irony (note the play on words) of those who were misusing "the Law" (ὁ νόμος) and yet fancied themselves as "teachers of the Law" (v.7).

What is the lawful use of the Law? The answer is given in the rest of the

> **Ministry Maxim**
>
> A straight-edge is beneficial, even if all it does is expose the crookedness of my work.

---

[32] Mounce, 32, 486.
[33] Vine, 503-504.
[34] Mounce, 32.

sentence (vv.9-11)—the Law's goodness is found in its restraint of evil. Elsewhere Paul, however, sees the Law not as a restrainer of evil, but as the agent of stirring sin up within himself (Rom. 7:8). Yet, even in that context, Paul would conclude, "So then, the Law is holy, and the commandment is holy and righteous and good" (7:12). Furthermore, he states, "But if I do the very thing I do not want to do, I agree with the Law, confessing that the Law is good" (7:16). Both passages agree that the Law is good, albeit for slightly different reasons. Thus we may conclude that Paul's statement here is accurate, though it may not expound everything about the Law that is good. The Law is good when it is used according to the purpose for which it was given (2 Tim. 3:16-17)—to reveal to "lawless" (v.9) sinners their desperate plight before holy God and to bring them to the Savior, Jesus, who can rescue them by God's grace (Gal. 3:15-4:7). The problem in Ephesus was that the false teachers were not using the Law for this purpose; on the contrary, they were using the Law as a source for "myths and endless genealogies" (1 Tim. 1:4) which resulted in "fruitless discussion" (1:6). Clearly "they do not understand either what they are saying or the matters about which they make confident assertions" (v.7).

Digging Deeper:
1. Summarize in one succinct statement what makes the Law good.
2. According to this verse, what role should the Law of God have in the life of a believer in Jesus Christ?
3. In what ways have believers in Christ often misunderstood or misused God's Law? What have been the results?

1:9 realizing the fact that law is not made for a righteous person, but for those who are lawless and rebellious, for the ungodly and sinners, for the unholy and profane, for those who kill their fathers or mothers, for murderers

The Apostle now expounds upon the lawful use of the Law (v.8) as the sentence continues from v.8 on through v.11. The participle "realizing" (εἰδώς) is the same root as the main verb that opened the sentence ("We know," Οἴδαμεν). The verb originally emphasizes the completeness or thoroughness of the knowledge. Paul is now expounding on what the believing know and hold as an axiom of faith. The words "the fact" translate τοῦτο, which should perhaps yield a translation of simply "knowing *this*." What is obvious is introduced by "that" (ὅτι), signaling that the object of this knowledge is about to be detailed. In general terms this knowledge is that "law is not made for a righteous person" (δικαίῳ νόμος οὐ κεῖται). More literally it might read "to a just [man] a law is not laid down." The adjective (δικαίῳ) is used substantively to stand for the individual it describes (thus the translation "a righteous person"). The word is used of God Himself as the "righteous Judge" (2 Tim. 4:8) and as descriptive of the qualities that should be true of an overseer in the local church (Titus 1:8). The word "law" (νόμος) is anarthrous, pointing not to a specific law(s) within the revelation given to Moses, but to the whole of that Law. It may designate that which possesses the quality of law. The verb κεῖται, translated "is not made," can be used metaphorically of something being appointed or destined.[35] It could also be used as a legal, technical term for a law that is "laid down," "existing" or "valid."[36]

Many have noted the rough parallel of Paul's list here (vv.9-10) to the Decalogue handed down by God to Moses. The first table of the Law (Exod. 20:1-11) finds only a rough equivalency with the first six of Paul's terms here (signifying, by pairs, opposition to Law, opposition to God, and opposition to that which is sacred).[37] The second table of the Law (Exod. 20:12-17) finds here a more exact parallel through the ninth commandment: "those who kill their fathers or mothers" (the fifth commandment to honor one's father and mother, Exod. 20:12), "murderers" (the sixth commandment not to murder, Exod. 20:13), "immoral men and homosexuals" (the seventh commandment not to commit adultery, Exod. 20:14), "kidnappers" (the eighth commandment not to steal, Exod. 20:15), and "liars and perjurers" (the ninth commandment not to bear false testimony, Exod. 20:16). The question arises as to why Paul did not include the tenth commandment against coveting (Exod. 20:17). In a similar representative list based on the Decalogue, he also omitted the tenth commandment (Rom. 13:9). Any answer ultimately qualifies as speculation. It is interesting that in one of Paul's key discussions as to the purpose of the Law, he identified the Law's particular effect upon himself as producing covetousness (Rom. 7:7-8).[38]

Rather than ("but," δὲ) for the righteous person, law is "for those who are lawless and rebellious" (ἀνόμοις δὲ καὶ ἀνυποτάκτοις). There is no additional verb, so it might more literally and simply read, "but to lawless and rebellious persons." Here begins a litany of ungodly people. There are fourteen designations in all running through v.10. The first eight are paired in twos and connected by the conjunction καί, subsequently the terms are simply strung together one word immediately after the previous one. All are plural—the first six are adjectives used as substantives (corresponding roughly to the first table of the Ten

---
[35] BAGD, 426.
[36] Friberg, 227.
[37] Alford, 3:306.
[38] Ibid., 3:307.

Commandments), the next seven are nouns and the final term is another adjective used as a substantive (corresponding more specifically with the second table of the Ten Commandments).

The first term, "lawless" (ἀνόμοις), is a strong one. It is used elsewhere to speak of the people of Sodom in Lot's day (2 Peter 2:8), of the antichrist (2 Thess. 2:8), and of those who crucified Jesus (Acts 2:23). The word is the common term for "law" (νόμος; just used three words prior) with the alpha privative (ἀ) prefixed for negation. The Law is for those who reject and try to throw off any law or restrictions. The second term, "rebellious" (ἀνυποτάκτοις), is used three times in the PE (1 Tim. 1:9; Titus 1:6, 10) and only one other time in the NT (Heb. 2:8). It is a compound word adjoining an alpha privative (ἀ) to negate the common verb ὑποτάσσω, which means "to arrange under" and commonly speaks of being in subjection to authority. It describes those who throw off authority and demand autonomy.

> **Ministry Maxim**
>
> As long as ungodliness exists, God's Law must be preached.

The third term is "the ungodly" (ἀσεβέσι). The adjective refers to one who is irreverent and irreligious. Paul's only other usages are in Romans 4:5; 5:6. The fourth term is "sinners" (ἁμαρτωλοῖς). Paul uses the term again in v.15 to show that all men are classified as this, even himself, and it is for just such people that Jesus died. Traditionally the Jews applied the term to Gentiles (Gal. 2:15). Paul, in another context, tied the term to the Law and proved that no one can be justified by works of the Law, but only through Jesus Christ (Gal. 2:16-17).

The fifth term is "ungodly" (ἀνοσίοις). The adjective is used only here and in 2 Timothy 3:2 in the description of the people of the last days. It refers generally to those "who impiously reject sacred obligations."[39] It has a particular emphasis upon an inward lack of piety.[40]

The sixth item is "profane" (βεβήλοις). The adjective is used three other times by Paul, all in the PE (1 Tim. 4:7; 6:20; 2 Tim. 2:16), and one time in Hebrews (12:16). It describes that which is ungodly, profane, irreligious, and vile. As such it is directed toward those things which are associated with the name of God.[41] It can describe the character of people (1 Tim. 1:9; Heb. 12:16) as well as the words that proceed from their mouths (1 Tim. 4:7; 6:20; 2 Tim. 2:16).

The seventh and eight terms are "those who kill their fathers or mothers" (πατρολῴαις καὶ μητρολῴαις). Both terms are used only here in the NT. Both

---

[39] Kittel, abidged, 734-735.
[40] Rienecker, 617.
[41] Ibid.

are compound words using either "father" (πατήρ) or "mother" (μήτηρ) combined with "to smite" (ἀλοάω). It can certainly point to the murder of one's parents, but should also be seen to include all manner of violence to and failure toward one's parents. Similarly, the ninth term is "murderers" (ἀνδροφόνοις). Here the pairing of terms ends and the single terms begin to stand alone. This term is used only here in the NT. It is a compound made up of "man" (ἀνήρ) and "murder" (φόνος).

> **Digging Deeper:**
> 1. Who do you think Paul intends to identify when he speaks of "a righteous person"? Is he pointing to some who are *actually* "righteous" or only to people who may *consider* themselves "righteous"?
> 2. Why do you think Paul constructed his list only here in rough parallel with the Ten Commandments?
> 3. Why do you think Paul may have left out the commandment about coveting?

1:10 and immoral men and homosexuals and kidnappers and liars and perjurers, and whatever else is contrary to sound teaching,

The Apostle continues his list (begun in v.9) of people for whom the Law was designed, providing here items ten through fourteen. The tenth is "immoral men" (πόρνοις). The word could be used of a male prostitute, but in the NT it appears to be used more generally of a fornicator, one who practices sexual immorality.[42] Paul used the word frequently in his correspondence with the Corinthian church (1 Cor. 5:9, 10, 11; 6:9) and the Ephesian church (Eph. 5:5; 1 Tim. 1:10). The eleventh is "homosexuals" (ἀρσενοκοίταις). This word is used elsewhere in the NT only in 1 Corinthians 6:19. It is a compound word comprised of "male" (ἄρσην; with a "strong emphasis on sex"[43]) and "bed" (κοίτη; often as a euphemism for sexual intercourse[44]). It describes one who lies sexually with a man as one would with a woman—a sodomite. The Law condemns such a one (Gen. 19; Lev. 18:22, 29; 20:13; Deut. 23:17-18) and such individuals "will not inherit the kingdom of God" (1 Cor. 6:19).[45]

The twelfth term Paul lists is "kidnappers" (ἀνδραποδισταῖς). The word is a compound, coming from ἀνδραποδίζω. This word in turn came

---
[42] BAGD, 693.
[43] Ibid., 109.
[44] Ibid., 440.
[45] DNTT, 2:569-570.

from τό ἀνδράποδον, which is compounded from "man" (ἀνήρ) and "foot" (πούς; i.e., catch by the foot).⁴⁶ It thus points to a slave, a man taken in war and sold into slavery.⁴⁷ The word refers to one who traffics in human slaves (cf. "slave traders," NIV). It is used only here in the NT. It is often wondered why Paul (and the NT writers generally) do not condemn the practice of slavery in the ancient Roman Empire. Yet here is direct condemnation of those who peddle people for profit.

The thirteenth on the list are "liars" (ψεύσταις). The devil is the first and most proficient liar and his work can be detected in every lie told (John 8:44). Finally, number fourteen, are "perjurers" (ἐπιόρκοις). The word is found only here in the NT. The compound word is made up of the preposition ἐπί and ὅρκος ("oath").⁴⁸ "The force of the prep[osition] in compound may be 'against'; i.e., one goes against his oath."⁴⁹ It thus describes one who, while under an oath to tell the truth, divulges falsehood.

Paul rounds off the list by indicating that he does not view it as exhaustive, but representative: "and whatever else is contrary to sound teaching" (καὶ εἴ τι ἕτερον τῇ ὑγιαινούσῃ διδασκαλίᾳ ἀντίκειται). The generalizing expression "whatever else" (εἴ τι ἕτερον) widens the frame of reference to show that, while truth is particular (singular form of διδασκαλίᾳ, "teaching"), the possibilities of error are endless.

The word "teaching" (διδασκαλίᾳ) is used twenty-two times in the NT, nineteen of those are by Paul and fifteen of those are in the PE (1 Tim. 1:10; 4:1, 6, 13, 16; 5:17; 6:1, 3; 2 Tim. 3:10, 16; 4:3; Titus 1:9; 2:1, 7, 10). The noun may refer to either the act of teaching or to that which is taught ("doctrine").⁵⁰ It is in this latter sense that it is used here. There may be the "doctrine of demons" (1 Tim. 4:1). But "the doctrine of God our Savior" (Titus 2:10) is "sound teaching/doctrine" (1 Tim. 1:10; 4:6; 2 Tim. 4:3; Titus 1:9; 2:1), "doctrine conforming to godliness" (1 Tim. 6:3), and "purity in doctrine" (Titus 2:7). This is the heart of Scripture's purpose (2 Tim. 3:16) and all such teaching arises from and is controlled by the Scriptures. As so often in the PE (1 Tim. 1:10; 6:3; 2 Tim. 1:13; 4:3; Titus 1:9, 13; 2:1, 2) this teaching is characterized as "sound" (ὑγιαινούσῃ). Such words are "sound" in that they are

> **Ministry Maxim**
>
> What I receive as truth, what I believe about life, and how I behave in time and space are all connected.

---
⁴⁶ Thayer, 43.
⁴⁷ Ibid.
⁴⁸ Ibid., 241.
⁴⁹ Rienecker, 616.
⁵⁰ BAGD, 191.

healthy. The word was used literally of physical health (e.g., Luke 7:10) or mental health (e.g., Luke 15:27). In the PE it is always metaphorically attached either to "faith" (Titus 1:13; 2:2), "words" (1 Tim. 6:3; 2 Tim. 1:13) or "teaching/doctrine" (1 Tim. 1:10; 2 Tim. 4:3; Titus 1:9; 2:1). The participle is used as an attributive adjective,[51] thus emphasizing the qualitative nature of the teaching. The false teachers of Ephesus were in error in their teaching and this resulted in error in their own behavior and that of those who followed their teaching. Unhealthy teaching of unhealthy "doctrine" results in sickly, unhealthy lives.

The verb "is contrary" (ἀντίκειται) is a compound made up of "against" (ἀντί) and "lay" (τίθημι). The present tense points to an ongoing, continual stance toward "sound teaching." The middle voice underscores the inward resolve that initiated and sustains the opposition.

> **Digging Deeper:**
> 1. What significance should we find in the fact that when Paul lists what is "contrary to sound doctrine" he does not list propositions and teachings, but people and their actions?
> 2. Can you describe the logical linkage of what we receive as truth, what we believe about life and how we behave in time and space?

1:11 according to the glorious gospel of the blessed God, with which I have been entrusted.

The sentence begun in v.8 now comes to its conclusion. The measure of "sound teaching" (v.10) is now detailed. That standard of measure is "according to the glorious gospel" (τὸ εὐαγγέλιον τῆς δόξης). The preposition (κατὰ) with the accusative means something like "corresponding to" or "with reference to." The expression "according to the gospel" (κατὰ τὸ εὐαγγέλιον) is used again in 2 Timothy 2:8, but there it is distinguished as "my gospel." Here it is "the glorious gospel of the blessed God" (τὸ εὐαγγέλιον τῆς δόξης τοῦ μακαρίου θεοῦ). Surprisingly, this is the only use of the noun "gospel" (εὐαγγέλιον) in 1 Timothy, but Paul will employ it liberally in 2 Timothy (1:8, 10; 2:8). The noun τῆς δόξης ("the glorious") comes next and represents a change from the accusative to the genitive case. A more literal reading would be "the gospel of the glory of the blessed God." In the PE glory (δόξα) belongs to God (1 Tim. 1:17) and Christ (1 Tim. 3:16; 2 Tim. 4:18; Titus 2:13) alone, though believers have the hope of one day sharing in His glory (2 Tim. 2:10). It is reasonable, therefore, to see the noun

---
[51] Knight, 89.

here as attributive ("the glorious gospel"), and indeed the Gospel is glorious. But it is in fact a separate noun ("the gospel of the glory") and should perhaps be read as such. The rendering "the glorious gospel," according to Guthrie, "expresses a partial truth but misses the full grandeur of the original by transferring the glory from the central figure in the drama to the drama itself."[52] Indeed, it is "the gospel of the glory of Christ, who is the image of God" (2 Cor. 4:4), and in it God "has shone in our hearts to give the Light of the knowledge of the glory of God in the face of Christ" (2 Cor. 4:6). Note, then, that "sound teaching" (v.10) is not exactly the same as the Gospel (v.11), but is in accord with it and extrapolates its practical implications and applications in a way that magnifies the glory of God.

The title "the blessed God" (τοῦ μακαρίου θεοῦ) is unique. The adjective "blessed" (μακάριος) is used of God elsewhere only in 1 Timothy 6:15. This "does not so much mean that we ascribe blessedness to God, but that all blessedness resides in him and proceeds from him."[53] There is no true blessedness to be had except that which comes in relationship to the Blessed One. A life transformed by the Gospel and conformed to the implications of the Gospel is the truly blessed life.

> **Ministry Maxim**
>
> God has inextricably bound His glory to His gospel.

Then Paul concludes the sentence by adding "with which I have been entrusted" (ὃ ἐπιστεύθην ἐγώ). The relative pronoun "which" (ὃ) points back to "gospel" (εὐαγγέλιον), with which it agrees in case (accusative), number (singular) and gender (neuter). The first person singular personal pronoun "I" (ἐγώ) is emphatic and subtly underscores that it was to Paul and not to the false teachers of Ephesus that God entrusted the Gospel. The verb "have been entrusted" (ἐπιστεύθην) is an aorist passive indicative. The aorist points to a definite moment in the past when Paul was entrusted with the Gospel by God. The passive voice reminds us that it was God who undertook this act of entrusting the Gospel to Paul. This common verb for believing is used here in the sense of entrusting something to someone (cf. Rom. 3:2; 1 Thess. 2:4; Titus 1:3).[54] Paul was ever amazed that God would entrust the ministry of the Gospel to him (1 Cor. 9:17; Gal. 2:7; 1 Thess. 2:4; 1 Tim. 2:7; 2 Tim. 1:11; Titus 1:3). The thought of this honor will launch Paul into his next section of thanksgiving (vv.12-14). By closing this opening section and this sentence with this clause, the Apostle makes both a statement about his responsibility with the Gospel and his authority in declaring and protecting it.[55]

---

[52] Guthrie, 62.
[53] Fee, 47.
[54] BAGD, 662.
[55] Fee, 47.

> **Digging Deeper:**
> 1. What is the relationship of "sound teaching" (v.10) to the "gospel" (v.11)? What does this tell us about the ministry of preaching and teaching in the church?
> 2. In what way does the Gospel reveal the glory of God?
> 3. In what sense was the Gospel entrusted to Paul and in what sense is it entrusted to us? Is there any distinction?

1:12 I thank Christ Jesus our Lord, who has strengthened me, because He considered me faithful, putting me into service,

Having just recounted that God had entrusted him with the Gospel (v.11b), Paul now springboards into thanksgiving for God's mercy and grace in bestowing that honor upon him (vv.12-17). Paul normally launches immediately into an expression of gratitude following his opening greeting (e.g., 1 Cor. 1:4ff; Phil. 1:3ff; Col. 1:3ff). Here, however, he first addressed the reason for Timothy's assignment in Ephesus (vv.3ff.), which in turn ended up launching him into thanksgiving (v.11). The word rendered "thank" (Χάριν) is the word often rendered as "grace" and which appears in the opening verses of every letter we have from Paul. It typically refers to grace, kindness or mercy. Here it has the sense of thankfulness for blessings received (cf. 1 Cor. 15:57; 2 Tim. 1:3). This gratitude is something Paul possesses (ἔχω, lit., "I have"). The present tense of the verb underscores the continual, present possession of this gratitude. Paul's expression here ("I thank," Χάριν ἔχω) reflects a classical Greek expression that he uses infrequently (elsewhere only in 2 Tim. 1:3) compared to his more usual εὐχαριστέω (e.g., 1 Cor. 1:4; Phil. 1:3; 1 Thess. 1:2).

Next, in the order of the Greek, is the phrase "who has strengthened me" (τῷ ἐνδυναμώσαντί με). It perhaps should be more literally, "I have thanks to the one who strengthened me." The articular participle is used as a substantive ("the one who"). The aorist tense looks back to the time when the strengthening was extended or bestowed. The word is used six times by Paul (Rom. 4:20; Eph. 6:10; Phil. 4:13), half of them in his correspondence to Timothy (cf. also 2 Tim. 2:1; 4:17). It is a compound word, being composed of "in" (ἐν) and "power" (δυναμόω). In the NT it always points toward moral or spiritual strength.[56] Paul personally was the object of this inward strengthening ("me," με).

Who is designated by the "who" of the substantive participle? The next clause reveals that it is none other than "Christ Jesus our Lord"

---
[56] BAGD, 263.

(Χριστῷ Ἰησοῦ τῷ κυρίῳ ἡμῶν). The exact phrase is found four other times in the NT, all by Paul (Rom. 6:23; 8:39; 1 Cor. 15:31; Eph. 3:11). The order "Christ Jesus" is used more frequently in the PE than the reverse (see discussion under 1:1). Normally Paul expressed his gratitude to God (e.g., Phil. 1:3; Col. 1:3; 2 Thess. 1:3), but here it is directed to Christ. This may indicate that his thoughts are going back to that decisive moment when Christ spoke to him while on the road to Damascus (Acts 9:1-19; 22:3-16; 26:9-18; cf. Gal. 1:11-17).

The reason Christ extended this strength to Paul was "because he considered me faithful" (ὅτι πιστόν με ἡγήσατο). The conjunction "because" (ὅτι) is used here to mark out a causal relationship (contra NIV, "that he considered me faithful"). The verb "he considered" (ἡγήσατο) means to think, consider or regard.[57] It denotes "a belief resting not on one's inner feeling or sentiment, but on the due consideration of external grounds, the weighing and comparing, of facts."[58] In the PE it is used only here and 6:1. The pronoun "me" (με) is emphatic. After all these years Paul was still dumbstruck that he, of all people, would be chosen by the Lord! God deemed Paul to be "faithful" (πιστόν). This is the adjectival form of the cognate verb encountered in v.11 (ἐπιστεύθην, "have been entrusted"). The entrusting of the Gospel to Paul there was in view of God's decision to count Paul "faithful." It means faithful, trustworthy, reliable or believing. Perhaps the sense of "trustworthy" fits the present context best. The adjective is found seventeen times in the PE (and sixteen other times by Paul in his letters), underscoring the critical importance of faithfulness in local church ministry. In the PE it describes God (2 Tim. 2:13), truth statements about Him (1 Tim. 1:15; 3:1; 4:9; 2 Tim. 2:11; Titus 3:8), ministering men (2 Tim. 2:2), ministering women (1 Tim. 3:11; 5:16), children of overseers (Titus 1:6), true teaching (Titus 1:9), all believers (1 Tim. 4:3, 10), Timothy (1 Tim. 4:12), and slave owners (1 Tim. 6:2). Paul was not saying he had been chosen for ministry because of his superior performance, but was in a state of stunned gratitude that one such as himself (cf. vv.13, 15) would be thus considered trustworthy by the Lord. This faithfulness was not something that had already arisen out of Paul's character, thus influencing God's selection of him. Rather, it was based upon the strengthening God had already extended to him (aorist tense, "who has strengthened me") in calling him to salvation and service and upon the strength He would continue to extend unceasingly to him in service (same verb in present tense, Phil. 4:13).

> **Ministry Maxim**
>
> Power for service is found in gratitude for grace.

This determination by God regarding Paul was evidenced by his "putting me

---
[57] Ibid., 343.
[58] Thayer, 276.

into service" (θέμενος εἰς διακονίαν). The participle (θέμενος, "putting") is from the simple verb meaning to put or to place. The aorist tense looks back to that decisive moment when God called Paul as an apostle. The middle voice emphasizes God's self-considered decision to place Paul in service—God's service is not a self-chosen occupation, but a matter of divine calling. This calling was "into" (εἰς, indicating the realm or sphere into which Paul was called) "service" (διακονίαν). Paul uses this noun in the PE to refer to his own ministry (1:12), Timothy's (2 Tim. 4:5) and that of Mark (2 Tim. 4:11). Elsewhere it refers to the ministry all believers are expected to render to the Lord in serving others (Eph. 4:12). Paul's use of the word "service" in this context, rather than "apostleship," is significant, for apostleship, in Paul's view, was not primarily a badge to wear and an authority to wield (though wield it he would if necessary), but a service to render. In that his apostleship was "service" rendered to the Lord, the great Apostle saw his ministry on a par with the ministry of others within the body of Christ who similarly were called to be faithful within the sphere of God's call and grace in their lives.

> **Digging Deeper:**
> 1. What happens to service when the gratitude goes out of it?
> 2. Does our faithfulness in ministry have its origin in us or in God? How does this verse speak to the issue?
> 3. What does this verse say about the significance of a divine call to ministry?

1:13 even though I was formerly a blasphemer and a persecutor and a violent aggressor. Yet I was shown mercy because I acted ignorantly in unbelief;

God entrusted Paul with the ministry of the Gospel (v.12) "even though" he had given Him no reason to do so. First in the Greek word order is "formerly" (τὸ πρότερον). It means formerly, previously or "as to the former time" (cf. Paul's only other use of this exact expression in Gal. 4:13).[59] The participle "I was" (ὄντα) is in the present tense and views the past ("formerly") in its continuous reality. The participle may be used either in a concessive (as per the NASU) or temporal sense ("when I was").[60]

What Paul had been is gathered up in three expressions, each intensifying

---
[59] Robertson, 4:563.
[60] Rienecker, 617.

even more than the former the nature of Paul's sin. He had been, first, "a blasphemer" (βλάσφημον). Paul used the word elsewhere only when he was describing the people who would characterize the last days (2 Tim. 3:2). The word is a compound. It may come from βλάξ ("sluggish," or "stupid) and φήμη ("speech," or "report"). Others believe it is a combination of βλάπτω ("harm," "hurt," or "injure") and φήμη ("speech," or "report").[61] The adjective is used here as a substantive. While Paul uses the adjective sparingly, he is more liberal with his use of the cognate verb. Interestingly, he will employ it at the end of this chapter to justify his use of the furthest extreme of church discipline (v.20). The word refers to one who speaks foolishly, injuriously or with evil intent against God. As a careful Jew and Pharisee, Paul would never have dared to knowingly slander God. He only understood himself in this light after having encountered Jesus Christ on the road to Damascus and discovering that He whom he had been persecuting is indeed God. Paul the "blasphemer" tried to force others into his own sin (Acts 26:11).

Additionally ("and," καὶ) Paul had been "a persecutor" (διώκτην). The word is found nowhere else in the NT, nor is it found in any ancient Greek writings we possess. Paul may well have invented the word for his purposes, probably from the verb διώκω ("persecute," cf. 2 Tim. 3:12),[62] in which case it would have the sense of pursuing or hunting someone down (Acts 22:5, 19). It was, in fact, Christ Himself whom Paul had been persecuting (Acts 9:4-5; 22:7; 26:14).

Paul also ("and," και) says he was "a violent aggressor" (ὑβριστήν). In the NT this word is found only here and Romans 1:30, where it describes the people of the pagan world. Rienecker says, "The word indicates one who in pride and insolence deliberately and contemptuously mistreats and wrongs and hurts another person just for hurting sake and to deliberately humiliate the person. It speaks of treatment which is calculated publicly to insult and openly to humiliate the person who suffers it."[63]

Despite ("Yet," ἀλλὰ, a strong adversative) what Paul was, he says "I was shown mercy" (ἠλεήθην). The aorist tense looks back to the moment Christ encountered Paul on the road to Damascus. The passive voice underscores the divine origin and initiative of the mercy that saved Paul. The Apostle is more prone to speak of "grace" being extended (v.14), but is not afraid to speak of "mercy" as he does here. Of the two terms, this one shows the pitying compassion in response to desperate need, whereas grace majors on the undeserved favor extended. Paul, in retrospect, looked upon himself in his former self-righteous

---

[61] Thayer, 103.
[62] Robertson, 4:563.
[63] Rienecker, 617.

Pharisaism and saw a pathetic, sinful man who had no rightful hope before a holy God. He uses the verb only here and v.16 in the PE, but he is more liberal with the use of the cognate noun (1 Tim. 1:2; 2 Tim. 1:2, 16, 18; Titus 3:5).

This mercy was extended for a specific reason ("because," ὅτι). That reason, says Paul, was that "I acted ignorantly" (ἀγνοῶν ἐποίησα). The finite verb "I acted" (ἐποίησα) is often used in the NT and refers most simply to the act of doing or making. The aorist tense may be intended to look back upon Paul's pre-Christian life as a singular whole or he may be most focused upon his persecution of the Church and be speaking specifically of his ignorance in that pursuit. The latter seems the more likely. The participle "ignorantly" (ἀγνοῶν) means to lack information, to be uniformed and thus ignorant. It appears to be a favorite of Paul's, for of the twenty-two times it is used in the NT it is either from his pen (e.g., Rom. 1:13; 2 Cor. 2:11) or placed in his mouth (Acts 13:27; 17:23) eighteen of those times. The present tense underscores the abiding state in which Paul dwelt. The Jews made a distinction between sins of ignorance (Lev. 5:15-19; 22:14; Num. 15:22-29) and those done defiantly or presumptuously (Exod. 21:14; Num. 15:30-31; Deut. 17:12). That Paul saw his prior sins in the first category is evidenced in his initial exchange with the Lord. When Christ appeared to him on the road to Damascus and asked, "Saul, Saul, why are you persecuting Me?" His answer was, "Who are you, Lord?" (Acts 9:4-5; cf. 22:7-8; 26:14-15).

> **Ministry Maxim**
>
> Ministry is not a right, but a gift based on divine mercy and grace.

Paul's actions had been undertaken in ignorance, but they were still "in unbelief" (ἐν ἀπιστίᾳ). In three of his five uses of the word, Paul speaks of the unbelief of the majority of Jews in his day (Rom. 3:3; 11:20, 23). He had once been where they are. But when his eyes were opened and his mind informed, Paul would say, "I did not prove disobedient to the heavenly vision" (Acts 26:19).

1:14 and the grace of our Lord was more than abundant, with the faith and love which are found in Christ Jesus.

In Paul's ignorant unbelief he was shown mercy (v.13), "and" (δὲ) it was not without effect. Indeed, despite how sinful Paul was, "the grace of our Lord was more than abundant" (ὑπερεπλεόνασεν δὲ ἡ χάρις τοῦ κυρίου ἡμῶν). The verb "was more than abundant" (ὑπερεπλεόνασεν) is found only here in the NT. It is a compound word made up of "over/above" (ὑπέρ) and "greatly abound" (πλεονάζω). The preposition in the compound intensifies the concept of the root verb. Thus it has a strong, intensified sense of over-abounding and overflowing.

Paul would gladly say with David, "My cup overflows" (Psa. 23:5). That with which his life was brimming was "the grace of our Lord" (ἡ χάρις τοῦ κυρίου ἡμῶν). This exact phrase appears four other times in the NT, all at the close of one of Paul's letters (Rom. 16:20; Gal. 6:18; 1 Thess 5:28; 2 Thess. 3:18). See Romans 5:20 for a similar idea. By "our Lord" Paul clearly means Jesus Christ, as the sentence will soon make clear and as the fuller title in all four of the other occurrences affirms. Paul easily passes from "mercy" (v.13) to "grace" (v.14), knowing the benevolent pair is matched perfectly and never far apart.

Paul adds "with the faith and love which are in Christ Jesus" (μετὰ πίστεως καὶ ἀγάπης τῆς ἐν Χριστῷ Ἰησοῦ). The preposition "with" (μετὰ) is used to denote "the company within which some[thing] takes place."[64] Specifically it reveals the close connection between "grace" and "faith and love," while letting the greater emphasis lie on the former.[65] Alongside the grace which God pours out in excess comes also the faith and love which grace produces. Faith (toward God) and love (toward God and man) would be impossible if not for the grace of God which He initiates in our lives. God always makes the first move.[66] "We love, because He first loved us" (1 John 4:19). Ours is always a response to grace. As Earle says, "'Grace' provided his salvation, 'faith' appropriated it, and 'love' applied it."[67] Whereas Paul previously moved in unbelief and hatred (v.13), he now moves in the realm of "faith and love."[68] Faith and love are never far apart in Paul, and this continues to be true in the PE (1 Tim. 1:5, 14; 2:15; 4:12; 6:10, 11; 2 Tim. 1:13; 2:22; 3:10; Titus 2:2; 3:15).

> **Ministry Maxim**
>
> Grace precedes faith as the sun precedes the flower.

The word "which" (τῆς) is a feminine singular, but probably refers to both "faith and love" (πίστεως καὶ ἀγάπης), which are both feminine in form. Grace, faith and love are only found "in Christ Jesus" (ἐν Χριστῷ Ἰησοῦ)— that is in the sphere and realm of relationship and proximity to Christ Jesus. The thought and expression are thoroughly Pauline, the exact expression (ἐν Χριστῷ Ἰησοῦ) being found forty-seven times in the NT, forty-six of them in Paul (nine of those in the PE: 1 Tim. 1:14; 3:13; 2 Tim. 1:1, 9, 13; 2:1, 10; 3:12, 15).

Paul has been stringing together a play on words throughout vv.11-14. Paul had been "entrusted" (ἐπιστεύθην) with the gospel (v.11), was counted

---

[64] BAGD, 508.
[65] Ibid., 509.
[66] Fee, 52.
[67] Earle, 11:354.
[68] Hiebert, *First Timothy*, 41.

"faithful" (πιστόν; v.12), had previously acted in "unbelief" (ἀπιστίᾳ; v.13), but by the grace of God in Christ he had discovered "faith" (πίστεως; v.14) and was thus to be counted as an example for "those who would believe" (πιστεύειν; v.16). Note also in this regard the "trustworthy" (πιστὸς) saying of v.15. In all this Paul's example of faith in Christ (vv.12-17) stands in stark contrast to the works orientation toward the Law of the false teachers (vv.6-7).[69]

> **Digging Deeper:**
> 1. Explain how Paul could later exercise extreme spiritual discipline (v.20) upon people who were guilty of the very thing he admits he had been guilty of before coming to faith in Christ ("a blasphemer").
> 2. What is the difference between sinning in ignorance and sinning willfully? Does God deal differently with such sins?
> 3. Which came first in Paul's understanding and experience: grace or faith? Why? What is the significance?

1:15 It is a trustworthy statement, deserving full acceptance, that Christ Jesus came into the world to save sinners, among whom I am foremost of all.

"It is a trustworthy statement" (πιστὸς ὁ λόγος) is the first example of what becomes a recurring phrase in the PE and which is not found elsewhere in the NT (1 Tim. 1:15; 3:1; 4:9; 2 Tim. 2:11; Titus 3:8). The verb is absent in the Greek text and thus it more literally reads, "Faithful the word." Confer with comments on v.14 to pick up the wordplay with "trustworthy" (πιστὸς). As the Church grew, matured through confrontation with false teachings, and transitioned to an existence without the Apostles, Paul began to employ this expression with those responsible to carry the Gospel ministry to the next generation. It served as a familiar way of identifying truth they could count on and use as a fixed point of reference. Here Paul adds (καὶ, untranslated by NASU) a second qualifying phrase: "deserving full acceptance" (πάσης ἀποδοχῆς ἄξιος). This appears with the previous phrase again in 1 Timothy 4:9. It marks out the statement which follows as not only reliable, but also as consequential. The root meaning of the adjective "worthy" (ἄξιος) came out of the marketplace and described adding weight to one side of the scales to bring the beam up to level. It thus came to describe that which is weighty or of significance. The addition of the adjective

---
[69] Mounce, 47.

"full" (πάσης; "all," "greatest," "supreme") only heightens the meaning, pointing either to an intensifying of the acceptance (complete acceptance) or to the extensive nature of the acceptance demanded (universal acceptance), or both.[70]

The aforementioned statement is "that Christ Jesus came into the world to save sinners" (ὅτι Χριστὸς Ἰησοῦς ἦλθεν εἰς τὸν κόσμον ἁμαρτωλοὺς σῶσαι). The combination "Christ Jesus" is the typical order in the PE (see on v.1). Paul says Jesus "came" (ἦλθεν). The aorist tense looks back upon the incarnation of Christ. It is at least compatible with and perhaps implies the pre-existence of Christ.[71] He thus came "into the world" (εἰς τὸν κόσμον ἁμαρτωλοὺς). The expression sounds almost Johannine (John 1:9; 6:14; 9:39; 11:27; 16:28; 18:37), perhaps reflecting the familiarity of such phrasing among the followers of Jesus because of their Master's own words (e.g., Matt. 9:13; Luke 19:10). The One who created this world (John 1:3, 10; Col. 1:16-17; Heb. 1:2) humbled Himself, took to Himself a human body and a human nature and took the form of a servant (Phil. 2:7-8), and thus came into the world He Himself had created. Jesus lived fully in this world as One who ate (Matt. 26:17), slept (Mark 1:35), walked (Matt. 4:18), talked (Matt. 22:1), was tempted (Heb. 4:15), entered into relationships (Mark 3:14) and enjoined all the normal aspects of human life.

This He did "to save sinners" (ἁμαρτωλοὺς σῶσαι). The infinitive "to save" (σῶσαι) defines Christ's mission for entering this world. The aorist tense looks to that one momentous event when the perfect life Jesus had lived in this world would be offered up on the cross for our redemption. God desires that all enter into this salvation (1 Tim. 2:4). In the PE the word is linked with arriving "at the knowledge of the truth" (1 Tim. 2:4), being called "with a holy calling" (2 Tim. 1:9), being brought into God's heavenly kingdom (2 Tim. 4:18), and "the washing of regeneration and renewing by the Holy Spirit" (Titus 3:5). The word implies our utter inability to right our own condition and our absolute need for Christ to rescue us. We must see ourselves, as He does, as "sinners" (ἁμαρτωλοὺς). The adjective is used here as substantive. Paul uses the word eight times (Rom. 3:7; 5:8, 19; 7:13; Gal. 2:15, 17; 1 Tim. 1:9). The Jewish view was that the term applied especially to the Gentiles (Gal. 2:15), but the Gospel reveals that all humans fall into this classification (Rom. 5:19). The only other use in the PE is just before this in Paul's list of vile people for whom the Law was designed (v.9).

> **Ministry Maxim**
>
> Honesty about who I am is essential to my appreciation of what Christ has done for me.

---

[70] Marshall, 397.
[71] Hiebert, *First Timothy*, 42.

Now Paul, surprisingly, adds "among whom I am the foremost of all" (ὧν πρῶτός εἰμι ἐγώ). This phrase has stirred a lot of discussion. It most simply reads, "of whom first I am." Paul's words of confession are arresting. The words "foremost of all" translate one word (πρῶτός) which means simply "first." It refers not to his rank chronologically (its most frequent meaning in the PE; 1 Tim. 2:13; 3:10; 5:4, 12; 2 Tim. 1:5; 2:6; 4:16) as the very first sinner, but rather Paul ranks himself as "the most prominent" of sinners.[72] Having spelled out in detail the kind of company he has in mind (vv.9-10), Paul makes clear where he believes he stands among this class of people. Paul chose the present tense of the verb, saying, "I am" (εἰμι), not "I was." And he further underscored his insistent declaration with the emphatic pronoun "I" (ἐγώ). Paul identified himself as the most infamous, well-known example of a sinner. Paul would tell the Corinthians, "For I am the least of the apostles, and not fit to be called an apostle, because I persecuted the church of God" (1 Cor. 15:9). To the Ephesians he had confessed that he was "the very least of all saints" (Eph. 3:8).

It should be noted that Paul did not employ the definite article, thus saying "I am *the* foremost of all" (cf. "God, be merciful to me, the sinner!," Luke 18:13), but rather left the adjective anarthrous. This does not weaken Paul's statement, but should point us in the direction he intended. Anyone who has a growing comprehension of the holiness of God will also have a commensurate growing understanding of his sinfulness before this God. The closer one comes to the light, the more dirt one sees. Paul lived so near to the heart of God that he could not help but understand the desperate need of his own heart. And let us never forget that in this confession Paul was magnifying the mercy (vv.13, 16) and grace (v.14) of God, not his own sinfulness.

> ### Digging Deeper:
> 1. In a world of many opinions and the relativistic acceptance of every voice, how can we learn from Paul's use of the phrase "a trustworthy statement, deserving full acceptance"?
> 2. In what sense could Paul rightly identify himself as "the foremost of all" sinners? How can such a view of self be healthy? How can an attempt to imitate it become unhealthy?
> 3. Why did Paul use the present tense ("I am") rather than the past tense ("I was") when speaking of himself as "the foremost" of sinners?

---

[72] BAGD, 726.

1:16 Yet for this reason I found mercy, so that in me as the foremost, Jesus Christ might demonstrate His perfect patience as an example for those who would believe in Him for eternal life.

Using the strong adversative ("Yet," ἀλλὰ) Paul again contrasts his utter sinfulness (v.15b) with God's merciful response to him and then states the purpose for which God responded to him in this way. In fact the Apostle could say it was "for this very reason" (διὰ τοῦτο)—that is to say, his position as chief of sinners—that "I found mercy" (ἠλεήθην). This indicator of purpose is picked up by the ἵνα ("so that") that follows as the specifics of that purpose are then set forth. "I found mercy" is the translation of just one word (ἠλεήθην); some have suggested the translation "I was mercied."[73] The aorist tense again looks back to that moment when Paul encountered Christ on the road to Damascus. The passive voice indicates that it was God who took the initiative and extended the mercy—it was all of grace. The word is the same one just used in v.13, the only two times the verb is used in the PE (though note the use of the cognate noun: 1 Tim. 1:2; 2 Tim. 1:2, 16, 18; Titus 3:5). The word speaks of the compassionate pity of God toward those suffering, particularly because of their sin.

This mercy was extended for a distinct purpose ("so that," ἵνα). While God's extending of mercy to Paul arose from genuine care for him as an individual, it also had a larger redemptive purpose; the Apostle majors on that purpose here. It was "in me" (ἐν ἐμοὶ), says Paul, that God was to make a spectacle of His goodness. Paul was personally ("me," ἐμοὶ) to become the sphere, arena, and stage ("in," ἐν) upon which God would parade His compassionate mercy and grace for the world to see. God selected Paul "as the foremost" (πρώτῳ). The word was just used of Paul in v.15, see the discussion of its meaning there. The KJV translates the word as "chief" in v.15, but then wrongly as "first" (in a chronological sense) here. The two occurrences so close together surely have the same meaning.

From the platform of Paul's life God purposed that "Jesus Christ might demonstrate His perfect patience" (ἐνδείξηται Χριστὸς Ἰησοῦς τὴν ἅπασαν μακροθυμίαν). The verb "demonstrate" (ἐνδείξηται) is thrust forward to place emphasis upon it. Of the eleven times Paul uses the verb, four appear in the PE (1 Tim. 1:16; 2 Tim. 4:14; Titus 2:10; 3:2). It means to show, demonstrate or prove something, either by words or actions.[74] The aorist tense views God's extension of mercy to Paul as an event taking place at a specific moment of time in the past. The middle voice (in which it always appears in the NT) emphasizes here that Christ did this to fulfill His own purpose and to hold forth His own glory.[75] The

---

[73] Lea and Griffin, 76; Lenski, 525.
[74] Thayer, 213.

subjunctive voice couples with the ἵνα at the head of the clause to form a purpose statement. The active agent is "Jesus Christ." The translators have reversed the order of the Greek text which has "Christ Jesus" (Χριστὸς Ἰησοῦς), the far more common order in the PE (see on v.1).

It is "His perfect patience" (τὴν ἅπασαν μακροθυμίαν) which Christ showed in Paul. The adjective "perfect" (ἅπασαν) is in the attributive position, emphasizing the qualitative nature of the patience in view. The adjective appears thirty-four times in the NT, but only twice in Paul (Eph. 6:13; 1 Tim. 1:16). It has here the sense of not merely "all," but of "the whole mass"[76] or immensity[77] of His patience. Because of the magnitude of Paul's sin before God, his case required the whole measure of God's mercy and thus could stand as an example of the extent to which a merciful God holds back His wrath against sinners. The word "patience" (μακροθυμίαν) has the definite article and is used by Paul in ten of its fourteen NT appearances. It is often used of human patience (2 Cor. 6:6; Eph. 4:2; Col. 3:12; 2 Tim. 3:10; 4:2), but also of God's (Rom. 2:4; 9:22), as here. Predictably, such patience is produced only by the indwelling Holy Spirit (Gal. 5:22; Col. 1:11). The word generally refers to a longsuffering endurance in the face of indignities and injuries by others. Here it reflects the divine reserve in responding to us in the holy wrath that our actions and attitudes justly evoke.

In all of this, God's dealings with Paul were used "as an example" (πρὸς ὑποτύπωσιν). The preposition "as" (πρὸς) with the accusative can point to the purpose of something, which is how it seems to function here. The word translated "an example" (ὑποτύπωσιν) is used only two times in the NT, both in the PE (1 Tim. 1:16; 2 Tim. 1:13). It described an outline or sketch such as an artist might draw up before beginning the final work of art. In literature it pointed to the rough draft drawn up before the final exposition was composed.[78] In how God dealt with Paul he was not only extending mercy to the Apostle personally, but sketching an outline for others of all time to observe how he deals with sinners. Paul was God's prototype of mercy to sinners. This example was held forth "for those who would believe in Him for eternal life" (τῶν μελλόντων πιστεύειν ἐπ' αὐτῷ εἰς ζωὴν αἰώνιον).

> **Ministry Maxim**
>
> A major part of my life's purpose is to point to God's patience.

Paul is the prototype "for those who would believe" (τῶν μελλόντων πιστεύειν).

---

[75] Alford, 3:93.
[76] Ibid., 3:309.
[77] Marshall, 402.
[78] Rienecker, 639.
[79] Marshall, 402; Knight, 103.

The present participle (τῶν μελλόντων) and the present infinitive (πιστεύειν) are a pariphrasis (a longer form of expression in place of a shorter form of expression) for the future participle.[79] The future tense could hint at the doctrine of particular election, but that is probably to read into this statement a debate that must be answered in other passages. Paul probably points forward to those who would in fact "believe" as the future unfolds. The future tense may have an iterative sense, pointing to case after case of salvation to sinners stretching on to the future horizon[80]—each one after the pattern of Paul's salvation. To "believe" (πιστεύειν) is to rest one's trust savingly upon Christ and His finished work of redemption. Indeed, such faith is "in Him" (ἐπ' αὐτῷ). The preposition "in" (ἐπ') with the dative pictures the faith resting upon a solid and enduring foundation.[81] The antecedent of the singular personal pronoun "Him" (αὐτῷ) is "Jesus Christ" (Χριστὸς Ἰησοῦς). The object of saving faith is the Person of Christ Himself and the work of redemption wrought in Him. The outcome of such faith is "for eternal life" (εἰς ζωὴν αἰώνιον). The phrase "eternal life" (ζωὴν αἰώνιον) is one more likely to come from John's pen (16 times; e.g., John 3:15, 16, 36; 1 John 3:15; 5:11), but is not uncommon to Paul (Rom. 2:7; 5:21; 6:22; Gal. 6:8) or the other NT writers (Acts 13:48; Jude 21). The word "life" (ζωὴν) is used in the NT "of the supernatural life of God and Christ, which the believers will receive in the future, but which they enjoy here and now."[82] Indeed we are able even now to experience something of that "life in the blessed period of final consummation."[83] It is "eternal" (αἰώνιον) in that it is the life of Him who is Himself eternal (v.17; 6:16). It is the life that will characterize and make up our eternal home, and that is ours even now in a foretaste of heaven on earth. Mercy indeed!

> ### Digging Deeper:
> 1. What do I forfeit when I lose a sense of the magnitude of God's mercy to me as a sinner?
> 2. Reflect back over the course of your life—how has God demonstrated "His perfect patience" with you? Be specific.
> 3. How would you feel about the major contribution of your life being to serve as an example of God's patience with sinners?

---

[80] Lenski, 526.
[81] Guthrie, 66; Hiebert, *First Timothy*, 44.
[82] BAGD, 341.
[83] Ibid., 340.

1:17 Now to the King eternal, immortal, invisible, the only God, be honor and glory forever and ever. Amen.

The Apostle's review of what he had been (vv.13, 15) and God's merciful and gracious response (vv.12, 13b, 14, 16) produced a burst of praise from his heart that found expression through his pen. This doxology is beautifully expressive of Paul's theology and worship (cf. other Pauline doxologies: Rom. 11:36; 16:27; Gal. 1:5; Phil. 4:20; Eph. 3:21; and briefer examples in 1 Tim. 6:16; 2 Tim. 4:18). The postpositive conjunction δέ ("Now") opens the way out of the previous discussion (vv.12-16) and launches Paul into praise. This worship is directed "to the King eternal" (τῷ δὲ βασιλεῖ τῶν αἰώνων). The mention of "eternal life" in v.16 may have led Paul to begin his praise with this title for God. The definite article makes clear the solitariness and uniqueness of God. Paul will use the word "king" in the plural in just a few lines (2:2) in order to call for prayer for the kings of the earth, but at the close of the letter he will use the word again to emphasize that God is "the King of kings and Lord of lords" (6:15). He is here "the King eternal," or more literally "the King of the ages." The expression is comprised of a plural noun and its definite article (τῶν αἰώνων). That it refers to eternity is clear in that Paul will again employ the word at the end of the verse to say "forever and ever" (τοὺς αἰῶνας τῶν αἰώνων) or, more literally, "the ages of the ages." He declares God to be not merely sovereign in the present—the most powerful and controlling Being at the moment—but to be the only sovereign ruler of any and every moment of all eternity in either direction! God is in complete control—always. God is the King who deserves the absolute submission of every creature ever to be infused with being. The unfolding ages and all they contain are the work of His sovereign hand, representing the outworking of His sovereign will, and they are headed toward the full revelation of His sovereign glory.

God is "immortal" (ἀφθάρτῳ). The word describes that which is not liable to death, corruption or decay. Paul uses the word only four times in the NT. He elsewhere employs the word to speak of the glory of God (Rom. 1:23), the reward the believer hopes to gain through his life's service (1 Cor. 9:25), and the resurrection body believers will receive at the return of Christ (1 Cor. 15:52). Peter uses the word three times, to speak of the believer's reward (1 Peter 1:4), the Word of God (1:23), and the nature of personal character (3:4). A different noun (ἀθανασία) is used three times by Paul to describe a similar thought (1 Cor. 15:53, 54; 1 Tim. 6:16), though its emphasis is "unable to die." Indeed, God "alone possesses immortality" (ὁ μόνος ἔχων ἀθανασίαν; 1 Tim. 6:16). God was, is, and always will be the sovereign Ruler of all things—and He will never die and His sovereignty will never fade, spoil, diminish or be minimized in any way.

God is "invisible" (ἀοράτῳ). The word appears five times in the NT, four of those in Paul's writings. God's attributes are "invisible," yet they "have been clearly seen, being understood through what has been made" (Rom. 1:20). Jesus Christ is "the image of the invisible God" (Col. 1:15) and He created all things "visible and invisible" (Col. 1:16). Moses found courage to leave Egypt and persevere on the road through the wilderness because he was "seeing Him who is unseen" (Heb. 11:27). In a world where "seeing is believing," we must remember that invisibility is not necessarily unreality. There is a reality that resides beyond the seen, and God is sovereign there as well.

Indeed, He is "the only God" (μόνῳ θεῷ). The adjective μόνος is used seven times in the PE (1 Tim. 1:17; 5:13; 6:15, 16; 2 Tim. 2:20; 4:8, 11). God is the "only Sovereign" (1 Tim. 6:15) and "alone possesses immortality" (6:16). He is "the only wise God" (Rom. 16:27). Some later manuscripts have "the only wise God" here also (cf. KJV), but they probably represent an attempt by copyists to conform it to Romans 16:27. Paul's Jewish monotheism is still firmly in place (Deut. 6:4), despite his new awareness of the divinity of Jesus Christ (Col. 1:19; 2:9-10; Titus 2:13). The exclusivity of God may not be popular in today's cultural climate, but He nevertheless remains singular and solitary as "the only God."

> **Ministry Maxim**
>
> Knowing who God is (v. 17) and who I am (vv. 13-16) are the dual lenses that keep reality clearly in focus.

The sentence contains no verb in the Greek, so the translators have rightly inserted "be" in order to make for better reading in English. It is "honor and glory" (τιμὴ καὶ δόξα) which is rightly rendered to God. The former word ("honor," τιμή) could denote the price or value of something (e.g., Matt. 27:6, 9; Acts 4:34; 5:2, 3; 1 Cor. 6:20). It came to be used for the honor or reverence that signifies the value of a person. At the pinnacle of all who deserve honor stands God alone (1 Tim. 6:16). The latter word ("glory," δόξα) probably arose from the verb δοκέω which means "to seem." It meant then an opinion or judgment that was made, and in the Bible always a positive one. Thus the word pointed to praise, honor and glory.[84] "Honor is the esteem and reverence, and glory is the ascription of our praise as we see and adore all his excellencies."[85] This "honor and glory" is God's due "forever and ever" (εἰς τοὺς αἰῶνας τῶν αἰώνων), or more literally, "unto the ages of the ages." No greater expression for eternity could be found in the Greek language (Gal. 1:5; Phil. 4:20; 2 Tim. 4:18). He who is "King of the ages" will throughout all the ages deserve all "honor

---

[84] Thayer, 155.
[85] Lenski, 528.

and glory." The Apostle's doxology concludes with a reverberating "Amen" (ἀμήν). Paul often ended his expressions of praise in this way (cf. Rom. 1:25; 9:5; 11:36; 16:27; Gal. 1:5; Eph. 3:21; Phil. 4:20; 1 Tim. 1:17; 6:16). When so used it means something like "so it is," "so be it" or "may it be fulfilled."[86] All who read (or heard) these words would be moved to reciprocate with an affirming "Amen."

> **Digging Deeper:**
> 1. Can you describe in your own words just what this expression of praise asserts about the sovereignty ("the King") of God?
> 2. How would it change your day if you were able to maintain throughout it an understanding and awareness of all this prayer spoke about God?

1:18 This command I entrust to you, Timothy, my son, in accordance with the prophecies previously made concerning you, that by them you fight the good fight,

By "This command" (Ταύτην τὴν παραγγελίαν) Paul is referring back to the imperative he laid upon Timothy in v.3 ("remain on at Ephesus so that you may instruct certain men not to teach strange doctrines") and then expanded upon through to v.7. This indicates that Paul's words in vv.8-17 have been parenthetical, but not without purpose. There, in the face of false teachers who wanted to be teachers of the Law (v.7), he explained the Law's appropriate use (vv.8-11) and then set himself forth as the supreme example of salvation by grace, not Law-observance (vv.12-17). But now Paul returns to the primary point he had been making—the purpose for Timothy's continuing ministry in Ephesus. The word "command" is used by Paul only two other times, one of those being in v.5 (cf. also 1 Thess. 4:2). The cognate verb, however, is found in Paul's actual command to Timothy in v.3 (cf. also 1 Tim. 4:11; 5:7; 6:13, 17). Both the verb and the noun have strong overtones of authority. Here, as in v.5, the noun is accompanied by the definite article, which serves to make definite the command that is in view.

This imperative Paul could say again in the present tense, "I entrust to you" (παρατίθεμαί σοι). Paul uses the verb only two other times in the NT, one of those being his later instruction to Timothy about handing off the ministry to succeeding generations (2 Tim. 2:2; cf. also 1 Cor. 10:27). Paul was

---
[86] Thayer., 32.

asking Timothy there to do the very thing he had already done with him. In essence Paul was asking Timothy there simply to follow the pattern of ministry he had employed with him. The verb means simply "place beside" or "place before," but in the middle voice, as here, it carries the sense of entrusting or committing something to someone for safekeeping.[87] The term came out of the world of banking where people placed their wealth on deposit at a bank and into the care of another.[88] The cognate noun is used in the NT only by Paul in his correspondence with Timothy and becomes important as well as he develops this theme with his protégé in ministry (1 Tim. 6:20; 2 Tim. 1:12, 14). The transfer of trust and responsibility was personal ("you," σοι). Paul, as it were, looks Timothy directly in the eye as he makes his point, calling him "Timothy, my son" (τέκνον Τιμόθεε). Paul often referred to Timothy as his "son" (1 Cor. 4:17; Phil. 2:22; 1 Tim. 1:2, 18; 2 Tim. 1:2; 2:1). He did the same with Titus (Titus 1:4), but clearly Timothy held a special place in his heart. Paul appeals to the warmth of that relationship now as he lays the seriousness of these responsibilities upon him. The word "my" is supplied by the translators. The noun "son" is in the vocative case making it a form of direct address so that a literal translation might be "son Timothy."

Paul made clear that he was entrusting these responsibilities to Timothy "according to the prophecies previously made concerning you" (κατὰ τὰς προαγούσας ἐπὶ σὲ προφητείας). The responsibilities the Apostle was laying upon Timothy were believed to be in appropriate measure to what the Spirit of God had previously indicated about him (κατὰ, "according to"). The participle "previously made" (τὰς προαγούσας) means most simply "to lead before," but also came to signal previous action.[89] These words previously spoken had been uttered "concerning you" (ἐπὶ σὲ). The preposition ἐπὶ ("concerning") is used "to introduce the person . . . by reason of whom . . . someth[ing] happens."[90] Timothy personally

> **Ministry Maxim**
>
> Ministry is a battle—count the cost and know your charge.

stood under the brilliant light of the prophetic words spoken ("you," σὲ). What was said is classified as "prophecies" (προφητείας). We are not told precisely when or in what context these "prophecies" were made, but it may well have been at the time of Timothy's consecration to ministry: "Do not neglect the spiritual gift within you, which was bestowed on you through prophetic utterance [the only other use of the noun in the PE] with the laying on of hands by the presbytery" (1 Tim. 4:14). The content of these "prophecies" may have

---

[87] Friberg, 298.
[88] Robertson, 4:565.
[89] Ibid., 400.
[90] Ibid., 298.

given some indication of the kind of ministry in which God would use Timothy or the sort of spiritual gifts God had invested in him. Acts 13:1-3 may provide the best example of the kind of event being described here.

As to the purpose of the prophecies, Paul adds, "that by them you fight the good fight" (ἵνα στρατεύῃ ἐν αὐταῖς τὴν καλὴν στρατείαν). The use of ἵνα ("that") signals a purpose clause. The clause employs a verb (στρατεύῃ, "you may fight") and its cognate noun (στρατείαν, "fight"). The verb is a present middle subjunctive. The present tense points to the ongoing nature of being in the service of the King and fighting His battles. Indeed the word looks not to a single battle, but to the whole of what it means to be a soldier. The verb appears in the NT only in the middle voice, which points to the inward nature of the spiritual conflict and the determination to engage it. The subjunctive mood sets the action one step away from reality, where the actuality of the conflict depends upon Timothy's determination to enter the battle. Later Paul will call on Timothy to "Suffer hardship with me, as a good soldier of Christ Jesus" (2 Tim. 2:3) and will remind him that "No soldier in active service [the participial form of the verb used here] entangles himself in the affairs of everyday life, so that he may please the one who enlisted him as a soldier" (2:4). Such military imagery is common in Paul's writings (2 Cor. 6:7; 10:3-5; Eph. 6:10-18; 1 Thess. 5:8-9; 1 Tim. 6:12; 2 Tim. 2:3-4). The battle here envisioned is "good" (καλὴν). The adjective describes that which is "in every respect unobjectionable, blameless, excellent."[91] The notion of "the good fight" (τὴν καλὴν στρατείαν) is a recurring theme for Paul in his correspondence with Timothy (1 Tim. 6:12; 2 Tim. 4:7). We are reminded that a struggle for truth is an inevitable part of this life. The notion of the perfectly tranquil existence in this life is a fantasy. The decision to enter the struggle on the side of truth is a moral decision with profound and far-reaching implications for this life and the next. We are also reminded just how powerful and long lasting words spoken at the Spirit's leading can be—they may carry the power to keep and encourage in battles on fields of service not yet even imagined. We do well to remember our call to ministry and the affirmation of God's people as they affirmed God's call upon us.

> ### Digging Deeper:
> 1. What has been entrusted to you? Who entrusted it to you? What does this require of you?
> 2. What do the Apostle's words tell us about the power of speaking to others about their place in God's kingdom?
> 3. What does the imagery of combat bring to the understanding of living a life of ministry? What are we fighting for? What are we fighting over?

---

[91] Ibid., 400.

1:19 keeping faith and a good conscience, which some have rejected and suffered shipwreck in regard to their faith.

The sentence continues from the previous verse. The opening participle "keeping" (ἔχων) indicates how one may "fight the good fight" (v.18), which in turn pointed back to the command of v.3 and regards the importance of protecting the truth. The present tense points to a continual or habitual commitment to this "keeping." The word is a general one which means "have," "hold" or "possess." Here it has the sense of an inner possession such as a characteristic, capability or emotion.[92] That which is to be thus kept are "faith and a good conscience" (πίστιν καὶ ἀγαθὴν συνείδησιν). The former (πίστιν, "faith") probably here has the sense of active trust. Here surely it is the truth as it is in Christ (v.3) that such trust is pictured as resting upon (v.5). The latter (ἀγαθὴν συνείδησιν, "a good conscience") has already been referred to as the goal of Paul's teaching of the truth (v.5, see comments there). The use of these two terms again, after Paul used them so pointedly in v.5, underscores that the Apostle is writing with intention and purpose, not haphazardly or at a whim (find these two in combination again in 3:9). Guthrie is correct, "The Christian leader must personally possess the spiritual qualities he would enforce."[93]

The "keeping" of these two treasures is not an optional hobby, but a matter of life and death. It is these very things "which some have rejected" (ἥν τινες ἀπωσάμενοι). The singular feminine relative pronoun ἥν ("which") agrees in gender and number with its antecedent (ἀγαθὴν συνείδησιν, "a good conscience"). The indefinite pronoun τινες ("some") is also plural in number, underscoring that such abandoning of the faith is not an isolated incident, but is something Paul has witnessed multiple times. Those in Paul's mind are described as those who "have rejected" (ἀπωσάμενοι) the treasure that is to be kept. The word is a strong one, meaning to push something away from one's self or to push it aside. It speaks of the repudiation and rejection of that thing.[94] It is a violent and intentional rejection that is pictured.[95] The word is used of the response of the Israelites to Moses' leadership (Acts 7:27, 39) and of the Jews to the preaching of the Word of God by Paul and Barnabas (Acts 13:46). It is also used to say God did not thus "reject" the Israelites (Rom. 11:1-2). The strong word emphasizes what weighs

> **Ministry Maxim**
>
> The slide from a good conscience to a shipwrecked faith is greased by a lack of vigilance.

---

[92] BAGD, 332.
[93] Hiebert, *First Timothy*, 46.
[94] Rienecker, 618.
[95] Guthrie, 68.

in the balance as one hears and proclaims the Word of God. Defining theology is not a sport, but more akin to handling high explosives. Careful and deliberate choices must be made which affect life now and forever.

Indeed those who thus "rejected" the truth also "suffered shipwreck in regard to their faith" (περὶ τὴν πίστιν ἐναυάγησαν). The one follows the other as the night the day. The preposition περὶ is used here in the sense of "with regard to" or "with respect to."[96] The precise expression περὶ τὴν πίστιν is found only three times in the NT, all in the PE (1 Tim. 1:19; 6:21; 2 Tim. 3:8). For the second time in this verse Paul uses the noun "faith" (πίστιν). As it does earlier in the verse, it probably carries here the sense of personal trust in Christ, though certainly that trust must rest upon the true doctrine of Christ ("the faith"). The definite article (τὴν) is found in this instance and functions as a possessive pronoun, thus the translation "their."[97] The verb "suffered shipwreck" (ἐναυάγησαν) is used only twice in the NT. It is a compound word arising from ναυαγός, which in turn is composed of "ship" (ναῦ) and "to break" (ἄγνυμι).[98] In 2 Corinthians 11:25 the Apostle used it literally to say "three times I was shipwrecked." To this could be added Paul's final shipwreck in route to his first Roman imprisonment (Acts 27:27-44). Thus four times Paul had experienced literal shipwreck and could say "a night and a day I have spent in the deep" (2 Cor. 11:25b). This enabled him to use the verb here as a powerful and descriptive metaphor for turning from true faith in Christ.

A "good conscience" is the possession of one who actively and knowingly is walking in accord with the will of God as revealed by the word of God. To have "rejected" a "good conscience" is to have knowingly compromised the will of God. Such a compromise is the precursor to a total "shipwreck" of one's faith. Most of those who have abandoned their "faith," could, with a bit of investigation, trace that departure not to unresolved intellectual difficulties, but to some significant moral compromise.

> **Digging Deeper:**
> 1. What attitudes and actions are involved in "keeping" a good conscience?
> 2. What choices and/or actions are involved when a person rejects a good conscience?
> 3. See if you can enumerate the downward steps from a good conscience to a shipwrecked faith.

---

[96] BAGD, 645.
[97] Robertson, 4:566.
[98] Thayer, 423.

1:20 Among these are Hymenaeus and Alexander, whom I have handed over to Satan, so that they will be taught not to blaspheme.

The sentence begun in v.18 continues on through verse 20 in the Greek text. "Among these" is the translation of the simple genitive relative pronoun ὧν, which indicates that the two men named here were a part of a larger group.[99] The verb "are" (ἐστιν) is in the present tense to show that the problem was current at the time of Paul's writing. The Apostle has been dealing in generalities and principles until now, but here he becomes explicit by naming two from an apparently larger group of apostates. "Hymenaeus" ('Υμέναιος) is known to us only here and 2 Timothy 2:17. By the time Paul wrote his second letter to Timothy the error Hymenaeus was propagating was "saying that the resurrection has already taken place" (2 Tim. 2:18). Whether that was his particular error at the time of 1 Timothy is unclear. In 2 Timothy he is paired with an individual named Philetus. In both places Hymenaeus is mentioned first and this may be an indicator that he was a leader of the false teaching that was finding a hearing in the Ephesian church. The fact that he is mentioned again in 2 Timothy, but with a different partner, points out the power, persuasion, and persistence of the man. His cohort here is "Alexander" ('Αλέξανδρος). He may be the one designated "Alexander the coppersmith," who Paul later marked out as one who "did me much harm" and of whom he said, "the Lord will repay him according to his deeds" (2 Tim. 4:14, see comments there), but it is uncertain given the popularity of the name "Alexander." It is unlikely that he is the same Alexander as mentioned in Acts 19:33. Whoever these men were, they and those who stood with them illustrate the truth of Paul's prediction in Acts 20:29-30.

Paul refers to these two as those "whom I have handed over to Satan" (οὓς παρέδωκα τῷ σατανᾷ). The verb is a compound made up of "alongside of" (παρά) and "to give" (δίδωμι), and has the sense of "to give over" or "to hand over" something to someone else. It is used frequently both by Paul and the other writers of the NT. Paul uses it of decisive, epochal exchanges. He uses it to describe people giving themselves over to sin (Eph. 4:19) and God's turning over of depraved man to the compounding consequences of their wickedness (Rom. 1:24, 26, 28). It is used to describe Christ being given over to death for our sakes (Rom. 4:25; 8:32; 1 Cor. 11:23b; Gal. 2:20; Eph. 5:2; 5:25) and His eventual turning over of the kingdom to the Father (1 Cor. 15:24). It can describe both people being given over to a teaching (Rom. 6:17) and teaching being turned over to a succeeding generation (1 Cor. 11:2, 23a; 15:3). The closest parallel to our passage is the usage in 1 Corinthians 5:5

---

[99] Knight, 110.

where the Apostle speaks of his decision: "to deliver such a one to Satan for the destruction of his flesh, so that his spirit may be saved in the day of the Lord Jesus." Here the verb is in the aorist tense, describing an action Paul has already taken in the past. In view of the similar case in 1 Corinthians 5:1-5 where Paul exhorts the congregation to act with him in his absence, it is likely that Paul had similarly acted in concert with the Ephesian congregation in this action against these two false teachers. Paul is reminding Timothy (and the believers of Ephesus) of what has been done, so that they might enforce the past action and take similar action when necessary in the future.

Just what does this decisive deliverance of a sinning one into Satan's hands mean and to what end was it done? This appears to be the furthest extremity on the continuum of church discipline. One starts down that continuum in quiet places and in personal conversations between just two people (Matt. 18:15), but, if change is not forthcoming, the dealings become increasingly more intense and more public (Matt. 18:16). Other steps along this path may be derived from reflection upon passages such as these: Matt. 18:15-20; Luke 17:1-4; Rom. 16:17-18; 1 Cor. 5:1-13; 2 Cor. 2:5-11; Gal. 6:1-5; 1 Tim. 5:19-21; 2 Tim. 2:23-26; Titus 2:15; 3:10-11. One has passed through many conversations, tears and pleadings before reaching this final step. Delivering one over to Satan may mean that, when all else as failed, the individual in question is finally allowed to go the way he has determined to go. No more efforts will be made to dissuade him and turn him back. As God turned depraved humanity over to the compounding consequences of self-chosen sin (Rom. 1:24, 26, 28), so the church may be required to grant a defiant one his or her wishes. He will be allowed to wander at will and without restraint into the dangerous territory he has chosen—which is pictured as the domain of Satan, who is "the ruler of this world" (John 12:31; 14:30; 16:11; cf. 1 John 5:19), "the god of this world" (2 Cor. 4:4), and "the spirit that is now at work in the sons of disobedience" (Eph. 2:2). The safety and security of the fellowship of believers is withdrawn and the protecting influence of the truth abandoned. The evil one will now be allowed to have his way with the defiant one. Commentators debate whether this is understood to include excommunication. Practically speaking, it is hard to picture thus delivering one over to Satan without such a step being included. The similar actions in 1 Corinthians 5 appear to have included this: ". . . in order that the one who had done this deed might be removed from your midst . . . Remove the wicked man from among yourselves" (vv.2, 13, NASB).

The goal at every stage of discipline is redemptive and not punitive: "so that they may be taught not to blaspheme" (ἵνα παιδευθῶσιν μὴ βλασφημεῖν). The

> **Ministry Maxim**
>
> Truth that is not protected is truth that is not truly believed.

use of ἵνα with the subjunctive verb marks this out clearly as a purpose clause, defining the target at which all decisions and actions are aimed. The verb "they will be taught" (παιδευθῶσιν) is one which describes the discipline a parent takes with his or her child for the purposes of training and bringing him to maturity. The word has a breadth of emphasis which includes both severe punishment and redemptive instruction. Paul uses it to describe judgment by the Lord (1 Cor. 11:32) on the one hand and the gentle ways of grace on the other (Titus 2:12). Paul later demanded that such a balance be embodied by Timothy in his dealings with opponents (2 Tim. 2:25). The inherent strength of the term is evident in our present passage, without losing the loving heart behind the actions it describes. Paul's goal has been that these two would learn "not to blaspheme" (μὴ βλασφημεῖν). These false teachers did not wish to leave the church; indeed, they wanted to lead it. They did not want to abandon all talk of Christ; they wanted to redefine what belief in Christ meant. They were seeking to be "teachers of the Law" of God, but "they do not understand either what they are saying or the matters about which they make confident assertions" (v.7). This amounts to blasphemy, according to the Apostle. Paul sees how we conduct ourselves in business (1 Tim. 6:1) and marriage (Titus 2:5) as having potential to arouse blasphemy, so we ought not be surprised that teaching untruth regarding God and His ways would thus be categorized. Paul classified himself as a former "blasphemer" (v.13), apparently for misrepresenting the truth. The infinitive is in the present tense, pointing to the ongoing propagation of these false notions of God and His truth by these false teachers.

> **Digging Deeper:**
> 1. What challenges confront the leadership of a church when it comes to expressing and enforcing genuine church discipline?
> 2. Can you articulate in a way that would make sense to today's average church member how church discipline is a redemptive, not a punitive, act?
> 3. What does it mean to hand someone over to Satan? What kind of behavior would call for such an extreme act?

CHAPTER

2

2:1 First of all, then, I urge that entreaties and prayers, petitions and thanksgivings, be made on behalf of all men,

The Apostle now changes direction. Having stated his purpose for writing and expounded upon it in chapter 1, he now takes up the proper decorum of the people of God as the household of God. "First of all, then, I urge" (Παρακαλῶ οὖν πρῶτον). The verb ("I urge," Παρακαλῶ) is thrust forward to the head of the sentence for emphasis. The verb is the familiar (109 times in the NT) compound made up of the verb καλέω (to call) and the prepositional prefix παρά (beside). Paul has already used it in 1:3 (see comments there) and will use it again frequently throughout the PE (1 Tim. 1:3; 2:1; 5:1; 6:2; 2 Tim. 4:2; Titus 1:9; 2:6, 15). The particular form he uses here (present active indicative, first person singular) is used by Paul (e.g., Rom. 15:30; Philem. 9-10) or comes from his mouth (Acts 24:4; 27:34) in sixteen of its twenty uses in the NT. He often takes it up at times when he is drawing moral implications from previous teaching (e.g., Rom. 12:1; 1 Cor. 4:16; Eph. 4:1). The conjunction οὖν ("then") is inferential—drawing a conclusion from what has been previously stated. The thought seems to be that, given the sad state of affairs in the Ephesian church and its false teaching, here are the things that the people of God ought to focus upon. The Apostle's exhortation is of ultimate importance, "First of all" (πρῶτον πάντων). The adverb often denotes that which is first chronologically (1 Tim. 3:10; 5:4; 2 Tim. 1:5; 2:6). It also, as we have seen in 1:15-16, can designate that which is preeminent in rank or importance. This seems to be the idea here. While the adverb (πρῶτον, "first") puts this exhortation at the head of the line, the genitive adjective (πάντων, "of all") ranks all others behind it. Of all the exhortations Paul will deliver in this letter, prayer ranks first in importance. Paul is urging Timothy—and through him the Ephesian believers—that their greatest priority is that of prayer. He urges not merely reactive prayer, but to excel in proactive prayer. Pray first. Pray always. Pray through.

> **Ministry Maxim**
>
> Prayer is always priority one in any strategy for ministry.

Paul urges that such prayers "be made" (ποιεῖσθαι). While in the English translation the words are pushed toward the end of the sentence, in the Greek text the infinitive is placed before the substantives describing prayer. This emphasizes the responsibility of the individual in making such prayers. The present tense calls for continual action and is not out of line with Paul's other exhortations to ongoing prayer (e.g., Rom. 12:12; Eph. 6:18; Col. 4:2; 1 Thess. 5:17). The middle voice emphasizes the subject taking action upon itself, thus the inward nature of the decision of prayer is underscored.

Paul describes the prayer called for with four substantives. The first is "entreaties" (δεήσεις). Rienecker reports, "The verb from which the noun is derived had the meaning 'to chance upon,' then 'to have an audience w[ith] a king,' to have the good fortune to be admitted to an audience, so to present a petition. The word was a regular term for a petition to a superior and in the papyri it was constantly used of any writing addressed to the king."[1] The next word is "prayers" (προσευχὰς). This and the first word are found together again in 1 Timothy 5:5 and in reverse order in Ephesians 6:18 and Phil. 4:6. This is a more general word, but describes making a more specific supplication.[2] The third word is "petitions" (ἐντεύξεις). The only other time this word is used in the NT is in 4:5, though Paul uses the verbal cognate in Romans 8:27, 34; 11:2 (cf. also the same verb in compound in Rom. 8:26). The word literally describes "falling in with" or "meeting with" someone, thus a coming together or a meeting for the purpose of talking or conversing. The word then became descriptive of the petition or supplication that might be made at such a meeting.[3] The word is thus "not properly intercession in the accepted sense of that term, but rather approach to God in free and familiar prayer."[4] Of these first three words, Thayer comments that, "in combination, δέησις gives prominence to the expression of personal need, προσευχή to the element of devotion, ἔντευξις to that of childlike confidence, by representing prayer as the heart's converse with God."[5] To these the word "thanksgivings" (εὐχαριστίας) is added. The word

---

[1] Rienecker, 618-619.
[2] BAGD, 172.
[3] Thayer, 218.
[4] Vincent, 4:216.
[5] Thayer, 126.

describes prayer with a particular emphasis on the gratitude expressed. Paul consistently underscores the appropriateness of thankfulness (e.g., Eph. 5:20; Phil. 4:6; Col. 1:12; 2:7; 3:17; 4:2; 1 Thess. 5:18) and he particularly sees the power of gratitude in the face of the false teaching at Ephesus (1 Tim. 1:12; 4:3-4).

Such prayers are to be made "on behalf of all men" (ὑπὲρ πάντων ἀνθρώπων). The preposition ὑπέρ, when following a request for prayer, means "for, in behalf of, for the sake of someone or someth[ing]."[6] The scope of prayer is as broad as the sea of humanity itself. All the needs, relationships, sins, triumphs, possibilities and actualities of humanity should be borne up before God in prayer. Those within the family of God should be held before God with all the promises of God on our lips. Those separated from God and without hope in this world or the next should be our special concern as we call out to God. Such prayer is the church's first duty. The greatest antidote for a church mired in internal conflict—as the Ephesian church clearly was—is to lift its eyes off of itself and to look again upon the needs of those without Christ around them. After all, God "desires all men to be saved" (v.4) and Christ "gave Himself as a ransom for all" (v.6). The church should have as first priority that which is most heavily upon God's heart.

Digging Deeper:
1. What keeps the modern church from making prayer the "First of all" its priorities?
2. Why was prayer Paul's number one antidote for the division that was tearing the Ephesian church apart?
3. How does the command of prayer "on behalf of all men" challenge the way we normally pray?

2:2 for kings and all who are in authority, so that we may lead a tranquil and quiet life in all godliness and dignity.

The Apostle now continues the sentence from v.1 by naming some of the "all men" who are to be prayed for. Specifically he calls "for kings and all who are in authority" (ὑπὲρ βασιλέων καὶ πάντων τῶν ἐν ὑπεροχῇ ὄντων) to be prayed for. The preposition ὑπέρ is used with the same meaning as in v.1. By "kings" (βασιλέων) Paul would include Roman emperors. Nero was currently on the throne. There is but one true King (1:17; 6:15), but Paul recognized that

---

[6] BAGD, 838.

He sets up earthly kings with a measured, earthly, delegated authority (Rom. 13:1). Thus we should call upon the true King who alone possesses absolute sovereignty to work His will through the earthly king who has been given a measured sovereignty. Paul broadens out the reference by adding, "and all who are in authority" (καὶ πάντων τῶν ἐν ὑπεροχῇ ὄντων). The noun "authority" (ὑπεροχῇ) occurs only here and 1 Corinthians 2:1 in the NT. It describes a place of prominence and authority and was used in secular Greek to describe the prominent position of a leading person.[7] This would broaden out the field of prayer to include not only the one at the pinnacle of earthly leadership, but all who are thrust forward in one arena or another of human endeavor.

The purpose ("so that," ἵνα + subjunctive) of such prayer is now set forth. The goal is that "we may lead a tranquil and quiet life" (ἤρεμον καὶ ἡσύχιον βίον διάγωμεν). Two adjectives are used to describe the qualitative nature of the life desired. The first ("tranquil," ἤρεμον) is used only here in the NT. It describes that which is quiet and peaceful. The second ("quiet," ἡσύχιον) appears elsewhere only in 1 Peter 3:4. It has been suggested that the former denotes a quietness which arises from a void of outward disturbance, while the latter describes peace that arises from within a person. Thus the first would describe the one "who is withdrawn from outward disturbances," while the second describes "the composed, discreet, self-contained man, who keeps himself from rash doing."[8] The word translated "life" (βίον) is used by Paul only here and in 2 Timothy 2:4. The word βίος refers to life as it relates to this earthly world as opposed to ζωή which tends to be used in reference to spiritual life (cf. 1 Tim. 1:16). The former is used by Paul only twice; the latter thirty-seven times. Paul is telling us to pray so that the details of getting along with everyday life may be undertaken without undue hassle and resistance. We are to pray that "we may lead" (διάγωμεν) such a life. The verb is a compound word meaning "through" (διά) and "to lead" (ἄγω). It is used elsewhere in the NT only in Titus 3:3 where the participial form is rendered "spending our life." Here the present tense points to one's life as it continuously unfolds. The subjunctive mood is used with the preposition ἵνα to form the purpose clause. The Apostle firmly believed that a praying church could affect national policy and cultural climate. The goal was not simply a hassle-free life, but one devoid of offense to others that would inhibit our fulfillment of taking salvation to all people (vv.4-6).

In Titus 3:3 when the verb was used it was preceded by a prepositional phrase made up of ἐν and two nouns, describing the sphere in which unregenerate life is

---

[7] BAGD, 841.
[8] Vincent, 4:217.

First Timothy 2

passed. Here the same preposition is combined with two different nouns (plus the adjective "all," πάσῃ) in a prepositional phrase describing the ideal life toward which Christians are to pray: "in all godliness and dignity" (ἐν πάσῃ εὐσεβείᾳ καὶ σεμνότητι). The first noun ("godliness," εὐσεβείᾳ) is the first of ten times Paul uses the word in the PE (1 Tim. 2:2; 3:16; 4:7, 8; 6:3, 5, 6, 11; 2 Tim. 3:5; Titus 1:1). The Apostle does not employ the word outside of the PE. It generally describes the outward evidences of a genuine faith in and reverence for God (1 Tim. 2:2; 3:16; 4:7, 8; 6:3, 6, 11; Titus 1:1). False teachers often imitated it for selfish ends (1 Tim. 6:5; 2 Tim. 3:5), but here Paul has the real thing in mind. The second noun ("dignity," σεμνότητι) is used in the NT only by Paul in the PE (1 Tim. 3:4; Titus 2:7). Here the word applies to all believers, in 3:4 it

> **Ministry Maxim**
>
> Pray for earthly peace, not so that you might be comfortable, but that you might be fruitful.

applies to overseers, and in Titus 2:7 it is used of young men. The adjective is used to speak of what should characterize deacons (1 Tim. 3:8), their wives (3:11), and older men (Titus 2:2). The word pictures the kind of dignity, gravity, majesty or sanctity which would mark a person as worthy of respect.[9] Proper reverence for God ("godliness," εὐσεβείᾳ) leads to proper respect of others ("dignity," σεμνότητι). The adjective "all" (πάσῃ) underscores the completeness of these two qualities as the aim of the believer.[10] These two qualities enable the church to fulfill her mission. An atmosphere of peace makes the best soil for the growth of these virtues; therefore the people of God must pray.

Our prayer should be that we might live daily lives free of the controversies and conflicts that might arise with people of power—not so we can be comfortable, but so that we might outwardly, fully and appropriately evidence the inward reality of our faith relationship with God through Christ.

> **Digging Deeper:**
> 1. What specific requests do you imagine the Apostle Paul's prayers for Nero would have included?
> 2. What is the goal in praying for those who rule over us on this earth?
> 3. How is it that proper reverence for God ("godliness") leads to proper respect for others ("dignity")?

---

[9] Thayer, 573.
[10] Hiebert, *First Timothy*, 52.

2:3 This is good and acceptable in the sight of God our Savior,

The precise expression "This is good" (τοῦτο καλὸν) is found again in 1 Corinthians 7:26, albeit in a different context. The demonstrative pronoun "This" (τοῦτο) refers back to the kind of prayer called for in vv.1-2. Specifically it probably looks to the universal prayer concern of v.1, given that the relative clause of v.4 develops God's concern for the salvation of all men. The adjective "good" (καλὸν) is used forty-one times by Paul, twenty-four of them are in the PE. It is used to refer to, among other things, "the good fight" (1 Tim. 1:18; 6:12; 2 Tim. 4:7), "a good servant" (1 Tim. 4:6), "the sound [good] doctrine" (1 Tim. 4:6), "the good confession" (1 Tim. 6:12, 13), "a good soldier" (2 Tim. 2:3), and "good deeds" (Titus 2:7, 14; 3:8, 14). The exact expression "acceptable in the sight of" (ἀπόδεκτον ἐνώπιον) is found again in 1 Tim. 5:4. The adjective "acceptable" is found only in these two passages, but see the kindred noun ἀποδοχή ("acceptance") in 1:15 and 4:9 and the adjective εὐπρόσδεκτος ("acceptable") in Romans 15:16, 31; 2 Cor. 6:2; 8:12; 1 Peter 2:5. The word "in the sight of" (ἐνώπιον) is used often in the PE (1 Tim. 2:3; 5:4, 20, 21; 6:12, 13; 2 Tim. 2:14; 4:1). As Guthrie well states, being "acceptable in the sight of God" is "the ultimate standard for all Christian worship."[11] Too often in a consumer-minded church His pleasure takes a backseat to that of the people gathered in His name.

> **Ministry Maxim**
>
> The pleasure of God is the measure of all true worship of God.

The precise phrase "of God our Savior" (τοῦ σωτῆρος ἡμῶν θεοῦ) is found only in the PE, most of those in Titus (1 Tim. 2:3; Titus 1:3; 2:10; 3:4; cf. 1 Tim. 1:1; 4:10). It reminds us that God is the point of origin and initiator of salvation and that we are the recipients of His undeserved grace and love.

2:4 who desires all men to be saved and to come to the knowledge of the truth.

The singular relative pronoun "who" (ὅς) refers to "God our Savior" in v.3. He "desires all men to be saved" (πάντας ἀνθρώπους θέλει σωθῆναι). By positioning "all men" (πάντας ἀνθρώπους) at the head of the sentence, Paul placed the emphasis upon it. God is the Savior of "all men" (πάντων ἀνθρώπων; 4:10) and thus the "all men" (πάντων ἀνθρώπων; 2:1) of our prayers must match the "all men" of His desire (πάντας ἀνθρώπους). The adjective "all" (πᾶς) is found six times in this chapter alone (vv.1 [twice], 2 [twice], 4, 6, 8, 11), underscoring

---
[11] Guthrie, 71.

the sweeping nature of God's concern. This is probably intended to stand in contrast to a tendency among the false teachers toward exclusivist claims. The verb "desires" (θέλει) is in the present tense, stressing the ongoing, continuous nature of God's desire. The infinitive "to be saved" (σωθῆναι) is in the aorist tense, pointing to the moment of salvation. The passive voice underscores that God must do the saving and man can be rescued only by divine initiative.

Does "desires" (θέλει) point to God's wish or God's will? That is to say, Does it indicate what God purposes and chooses or what He prefers and longs for? The range of the word's usage encompasses both poles of meanings.[12] Thus this verse alone will not provide the definitive answer to the question. We must build our theology from a larger base of Scriptural evidence. What we do know is that, for some reason which only divine wisdom can completely understand, God has linked the universal provision of Christ's sacrifice (vv.5-6) and His universal concern for the salvation of all people (v.4) with the obedience of His people to ask for their salvation (v.1). Why would He thus arrange things? We do not know. How can His sovereignty be tied so intimately to our responsibility? We do not know. What we do know is this: God places upon His people the responsibility to pray for the salvation of all people and He in some way (which remains a mystery to us) links the reality of their entrance into salvation with the obedience of His people in prayer. When we pray for the salvation of others we share in the purpose and passion of God. Thus in one sense, prayer is primarily about conforming our will to God's will, even more than changing the circumstances concerning which we call upon Him.

God also ("and," καί) desires all people "to come to the knowledge of the truth" (εἰς ἐπίγνωσιν ἀληθείας ἐλθεῖν). Apart from Christ we are held under the lie (Rom. 1:18, 25) propagated by the ultimate liar, the devil (John 8:44; 2 Tim. 2:26). The goal of our salvation in Christ is to deliver us fully into the truth (1 Tim. 2:7; 3:15; 4:3; 6:5; 2 Tim. 2:15, 18, 25; 3:7, 8; 4:4; Titus 1:1, 14). It is interesting, therefore, to take note of how often in the PE Paul addresses the problem of lying among the false teachers (1 Tim. 1:10; 4:2; Titus 1:12) and that he stresses that God is One "who cannot lie" (Titus 1:2). The phrase "knowledge of the truth" (ἐπίγνωσιν ἀληθείας) is used only in the PE. Paul used it in 2 Timothy 2:25 when Paul gave the rationale for the instructions he issued on dealing with those who are agitators in the church (vv.24-26):

> **Ministry Maxim**
>
> Our praying is not done until it has reached the far horizon of God's concern.

"if perhaps God may grant them repentance leading to the knowledge of the truth [ἐπίγνωσιν ἀληθείας]." It is used to describe the condition of some women

---

[12] BAGD, 354-355; Thayer, 285-287; Kittel, abridged, 318-320; DNTT, 3:1018ff.

in the church who were under the deception of false teachers: "always learning and never able to come to the knowledge of the truth [ἐπίγνωσιν ἀληθείας]" (2 Tim. 3:7). The Apostle used it again when he told Titus why he was writing to him: "for the faith of those chosen of God and the knowledge of the truth [ἐπίγνωσιν ἀληθείας] which is according to godliness" (Titus 1:1). The word for "knowledge" (ἐπίγνωσιν) is a compound word (ἐπὶ, "upon" and γνῶσις, "knowledge") which intensifies the root and points to fullness of knowledge. The infinitive "to come" (ἐλθεῖν) is in the aorist tense, pointing to a definite and personal arrival at the goal.

> **Digging Deeper:**
> 1. In what way would our corporate worship be transformed if we truly made its measure the pleasure of God, rather than the pleasure of the people?
> 2. Explain how the breadth of God's concern is to govern the breadth of our praying.
> 3. Why has God so intimately linked the salvation of lost people to the praying of His people?

2:5 For there is one God, and one mediator also between God and men, the man Christ Jesus,

The Apostle now gives the reason behind his exhortation to prayer. The "For" (γὰρ) is explanatory.[13] Paul's clarification of God's desire for all peoples rests upon four foundational truths (vv.5-6). The first is *the singularity of God*: "For there is one God" (εἷς γὰρ θεός). The verb is absent, but understood (lit., "For one God"). Even with his understanding of Christ's divinity (Titus 2:13), Paul was still staunchly monotheistic (cf. 1 Cor. 8:4-6; Eph. 4:6). So was Jesus (Mark 12:29), who claimed "I and the Father are one" (John 10:30). "Hear, O Israel! The LORD is our God, the LORD is one!" (Deut. 6:4). Paul saw no contradiction when he declared Jesus to be God and when He declared "there is one God." If there is only one God, then He must be the God of all.[14] Kent says, "If there are many gods, men could be left to their own. But since there is only one God, and He desires all to be saved, then prayer to Him for all men is in order."[15]

The second foundational truth is *the exclusivity of Christ*: "one mediator also between God and men" (εἷς καὶ μεσίτης θεοῦ καὶ ἀνθρώπων). The noun

---
[13] Marshall, 428.
[14] Mounce, 87.
[15] Kent, 100.

"mediator" (μεσίτης) is used in the NT only in Galatians 3:19, 20, Hebrews 8:6; 9:15; 12:24. It comes from the adjective μέσος ("middle") and thus refers to one who operates between or as a "middle man" for two parties.[16] Christ did not mediate in order to produce a compromise between an angry God and a failing humanity. Rather, He served as God's representative to a lost and rebellious race.[17] God sent His Son to establish a new covenant (Heb. 8:6; 9:15; 12:24), the terms of which were graciously and unilaterally met from God's side. The adjective "one" (εἷς) makes clear that there are not many paths to God, but one exclusive way (John 14:6; Acts 4:12). The saints of old longed for such security (Job 9:33) and now we may live in it. Only Christ mediates between God and man. No angel, saint, or god exists which can serve as an intermediary between God and man. We must come to God through His appointed way (Christ) or we cannot come at all.

The third foundational truth is *the humanity of Christ*: "the man Christ Jesus" (ἄνθρωπος Χριστὸς Ἰησοῦς). Christ could stand "between God and men" (θεοῦ καὶ ἀνθρώπων) because he was a "man" (ἄνθρωπος). The noun is anarthrous—not "*the* man," but "*a* man" or "*a* human being." The lack of the article stresses the qualitative nature of Christ's humanity. Jesus was a man unlike any other, for He never sinned (2 Cor. 5:21; Heb. 4:15) and was fully divine (Col. 1:19; 2:9). Yet His ability to mediate rests upon the fact that He could, as fully divine, represent God and, as fully human, He could stand in our stead (Phil. 2:7; Heb. 2:14, 17; 4:15-16). Additionally, Paul may have been alluding to Christ as the second Adam (Rom. 5:12-21; 1 Cor. 15:21-22, 45-49), the Head of a new race of redeemed people.[18]

> **Ministry Maxim**
>
> The universatality of God's love is never at odds with the exclusivity of God's Son.

God's heart is for the salvation of "all men" and "all men" are welcome, but they must come in God's "one" appointed way. There is not a plurality of paths to God, but only one. God is one. There is but "one mediator." The universality of God's desire finds expression not in multiculturalism, but in the singularity and exclusivity of Christ as the only way to God.

2:6 who gave Himself as a ransom for all, the testimony given at the proper time.

The fourth foundational truth (cf. comments on v.5) is *the sacrifice and sufficiency of Christ*: "who gave Himself as a ransom for all"

---

[16] Robertson, 4:568.
[17] NET Bible.
[18] Lea and Griffin, 91.

(ὁ δοὺς ἑαυτὸν ἀντίλυτρον ὑπὲρ πάντων). The articular participle "who gave" (ὁ δοὺς) is used as a substantive and refers to Christ Jesus (v.5b). The aorist tense could view Jesus' incarnation, life and death as one whole event or it may look more specifically at the events of the cross. The active voice underscores that ultimately it was Jesus' decision to give Himself up in death for us. The reflexive pronoun "Himself" (ἑαυτὸν) adds emphasis to the fact that Jesus took action upon Himself—He gave, and His gift was Himself. The word underscores the totality of Christ's giving. He gave all He was and all He had.

It was "as a ransom" (ἀντίλυτρον) that Jesus gave Himself. This noun is found only here in the NT. It is a compound comprised of ἀντί ("over against" and thus "corresponding to") and λύτρον ("means of release"). But here the preposition in compound suggests some kind of exchange taking place, since it comes in the NT often to have the sense of "instead of" or "in the place of."[19] The word describes, according to Thayer, "what is given in exchange for another as the price of his redemption, ransom."[20] The uncompounded noun is found in Mark 10:45: "For even the Son of Man did not come to be served, but to serve, and to give His life a ransom for many" (cf. the parallel in Matt. 20:28). Paul's words here likely reflect a reminiscence of that saying of Jesus. The cognate verbal forms are found in Luke 24:21, Titus 2:14, and 1 Peter 1:18. This provision, says Paul, was universal or "for all" (ὑπὲρ πάντων). This exact pairing of words was used in v.1 to describe the breadth of prayers God demands of us: "on behalf of all" (ὑπὲρ πάντων; cf. 2 Cor. 2:14-15). The breadth of our prayers must match the breadth of Christ's sacrifice. The preposition ὑπὲρ describes that which is done on behalf of another or for the sake of someone else.[21] Paul only uses this preposition four times in the PE and three of them are found here in 1 Timothy 2 (vv.1, 2, 6). In the other use Paul says Christ "gave Himself for us to redeem us" (ἔδωκεν ἑαυτὸν ὑπὲρ ἡμῶν, ἵνα λυτρώσηται ἡμᾶς; Titus 2:14). Paul uses "for *us*" (ὑπὲρ ἡμῶν) thirteen times in his writings, while he says "for *all*" (ὑπὲρ πάντων) seven times. The combination of the prefixed preposition ἀντί ("instead of") and the preposition ὑπὲρ ("on behalf of") underscore, and make unavoidably clear, the substitutionary nature of Christ's atoning work.

Paul then adds a final phrase whose exact function is the matter of some debate: "the testimony given at the proper time" (τὸ μαρτύριον καιροῖς ἰδίοις).

> **Ministry Maxim**
>
> The *one* and *only* God gave His Son as the *singular* way to Him precisely because He loves *all* people.

---

[19] Rienecker, 619.
[20] Thayer, 50.
[21] BAGD, 838.

First Timothy 2

Just what connection does this phrase have to what precedes? Does Paul speak of a testimony given about Christ's work given by another (v.7)? Or does he refer to the work of Christ itself as a testimony to God's love and grace (vv.3-4)? Why does Paul use the plural καιροῖς ἰδίοις (lit., "proper times") rather than the singular?

It appears that the whole of this final expression stands in apposition to what is stated in vv.5-6a. The identity of "the testimony" (note the use of the definite article, marking out the unique and singular nature of this testimony) is likely, given the context, to point to Christ's death as a testimony to the gracious and loving nature of God (vv.3-4), but not far behind is the implicit requirement to lift our voices to proclaim this testimony to all peoples (v.7). The precise expression ("proper times") is used again by in the NT only in 1 Timothy 6:15 and Titus 1:3. The word for "time" (καιροῖς) views time as an occasion or event—a favorable moment. Its plural form may well be used as a singular, gathering up the entirety of our Lord's life and viewing it as a whole.[22] The adjective "proper" (ἰδίοις) speaks of that which belongs to or is peculiar to an individual or thing.[23]

Digging Deeper:
1. Why are the singularity of God and the exclusivity of Christ not welcome news to the popular culture?
2. How is the breadth of God's concern for humanity misrepresented in multiculturalism? How would it be more accurately represented in a right understanding of the Gospel of Jesus Christ?
3. How does the sacrifice and sufficiency of Christ, rightly understood, transform the singularity of God and exclusivity of Christ into truly good news? How can we better communicate it as such to the people of our day?

2:7 For this I was appointed a preacher and an apostle (I am telling the truth, I am not lying) as a teacher of the Gentiles in faith and truth.

The preposition and relative pronoun ("For this," εἰς ὅ) signal that for which Paul was appointed (cf. 2 Tim. 1:11a), the antecedent being "the testimony" (τὸ μαρτύριον) in v.6b. Paul says he was appointed to three roles in regards to the Gospel. The same three are stated again in 2 Timothy 1:11, though he

---
[22] Guthrie, 182.
[23] BAGD, 369.

inserts two phrases here that are absent in the later passage. The verb and emphatic personal pronoun are also identical in both passages (ἐτέθην ἐγώ). The verb is a simple one, meaning to put or to place. In this case Paul was placed officially in relationship to the Gospel in the roles he is about to describe. The aorist tense points to a specific action that had taken place in the past. The passive voice indicates that this appointment was an honor bestowed by God upon Paul. He makes this emphatic: "I [ἐγώ] was appointed." Paul's appointment to Gospel service arose not from personal assertiveness, but from divine initiative.

The first role is that of a "preacher" (κῆρυξ). The word was used secularly to describe one sent by a king, magistrate, or other civil or political ruler to deliver an official message. The words herald, ambassador, and messenger convey something of the meaning. The individual was, for the task before him, vested with the authority of the one sending him. To hear the herald proclaim the message was tantamount to having heard the king himself. To defy the messenger was to defy the one who sent him. The one delivering the message had no power to alter the message and was held responsible for the clarity and purity with which the message was conveyed. The herald was thus both under authority and vested with authority. This word was then employed by the Christians to describe the function of one who heralds the good news of Christ. It is an authoritative proclamation, one for which the one speaking it will be held accountable and one for which the listener will be held responsible as well.

The second role Paul held with regard to the Gospel was that of "apostle" (ἀπόστολος). Like "preacher" the word "apostle" describes one sent out by another with official authority. The word "apostle," however, focuses more on the mission to be accomplished, while "preacher" focuses on the message to be delivered. As an Apostle, Paul joined the small band of Jesus' first disciples, although it came "as to one untimely born" (1 Cor. 15:8). Paul was thus under the commission of Christ Himself to go forward in His name and establish communities of faith centered on Him.

Finally, Paul was also, with regard to the Gospel, "a teacher" (διδάσκαλος). Paul applies this term to himself only here and in 2 Timothy 1:11. These last two roles are designated as specific spiritual gifts given to the church (1 Cor. 12:28, 29; Eph. 4:11). A "preacher" proclaims; a "teacher" explains. One announces; the other expounds. One calls for response, the other for understanding. Yet both are necessary to the advancement of the Gospel and Paul undertook both. All three nouns are anarthrous, emphasizing the qualitative nature of the role and actions of each. All three roles are an expression of the one divinely given ministry which had been entrusted to Paul. He was pulling three strands from one rope to help us examine the constituent parts of one whole calling which had been laid upon him. We thus discover that the Gospel is something that must be announced ("preacher"), enforced ("apostle"), and explained ("teacher").

Here, following "apostle," Paul adds the seemingly parenthetical comment "(I am telling the truth, I am not lying.)" (ἀλήθειαν λέγω οὐ ψεύδομαι). A nearly identical statement is found in Romans 9:1, except that there Paul inserts "in Christ" (ἐν Χριστῷ). Paul's negation ("not," οὐ) is absolute and categorical.[24] Paul has shown that, in times of conflict or self-defense, he will confirm that in giving his testimony he is "not lying" (οὐ ψεύδομαι; Rom. 9:1; 2 Cor. 11:31; Gal. 1:20). It appears that the statement is intended to be taken with what follows ("a teacher of the Gentiles"), rather than what precedes.[25] This accords with the paragraph's emphasis upon the universal provision of Christ and thus the universal nature of the Gospel's call and ministry. That Paul would feel the need to so emphatically underscore the truthfulness of such a universal application of the Gospel probably betrays the exclusivist nature of the false teachers and their message in Ephesus.

Also here, following "teacher," he adds "of the Gentiles in faith and truth" (ἐθνῶν ἐν πίστει καὶ ἀληθείᾳ). That Paul believed himself uniquely called as the Apostle to the Gentiles is abundantly witnessed to throughout his writings (e.g., Acts 9:15; 22:21; 26:17-18; Rom. 11:13; 15:16; Gal. 1:16; Eph. 3:8). The expression "in faith" (ἐν πίστει) is a favorite of Paul in the PE (1 Tim. 1:2, 4; 2:7, 15; 3:13; 4:12; 2 Tim. 1:13; Titus 3:15). Paul uses it also in Galatians 2:20; it is found elsewhere in the NT only in James 1:6 and 2:5. It seems reasonable, therefore, that we allow the greater usage of this expression, particularly in 1 Timothy, to explain its meaning here. It seems probable that the phrase was a part of his correction of the false teaching being spread in Ephesus. The false teachers were seeking to be "teachers of the Law" (1:7), espousing "myths and endless genealogies, which give rise to mere speculation" (1:4a). But "the administration of God . . . is by faith" (ἐν πίστει, 1:4b). Paul makes clear that the false teachers are operating in another sphere, one outside of relationship to God and His truth. In fact "truth" (ἀληθείᾳ) is another of Paul's favorite topics in the PE (2:4, 7; 3:15; 4:3; 6:5; 2 Tim. 2:15, 18, 25; 3:7, 8; 4:4; Titus 1:1, 14). The "knowledge of the truth" by all men is God's great desire (1 Tim. 2:4). The church is to be "the pillar and support of the truth" (3:15). Christians

> **Ministry Maxim**
>
> A call to ministry comes always by divine initiative, not by personal assertiveness.

---

[24] Thayer, 408.
[25] Fee, 67; Hiebert, *First Timothy*, 56; Marshall, 434.

are those "who believe and know the truth" (4:3). Unbelievers are those who are "deprived of the truth" (6:5). False teachers are those "who have gone astray from the truth" (2 Tim. 2:18), "oppose the truth" (3:8), and "turn away from the truth" (Titus 1:14). Their followers are "never able to come to the knowledge of the truth" (2 Tim. 3:7). If they are ever to be right, God must "grant them repentance leading to the knowledge of the truth" (2:25). Servants of God must accurately handle "the word of truth" (2:15), for in the last days people "will turn away their ears from the truth" (4:4). Thus Paul can summarize his whole ministry as being "for the faith of those chosen of God and the knowledge of the truth which is according to godliness" (Titus 1:1).

While the similarities of this verse and 2 Timothy 1:11 are remarkable, these two basic differences make Paul's statement here the more solemn, but the statement in 2 Timothy the more personal.

> **Digging Deeper:**
>
> 1. In what sense do preachers both live under and wield authority?
> 2. Can you articulate the distinctions between preaching and teaching?
> 3. Why does Paul feel the need to defend his truthfulness? In what circumstances might a servant of God similarly feel the need today?

2:8 Therefore I want the men in every place to pray, lifting up holy hands, without wrath and dissension.

The Apostle now draws a conclusion from all he has said about prayer (vv.1-7). The postpositive conjunction (οὖν, "Therefore") is inferential, gathering up the previous discussion and distilling its appropriate outcome. This conclusion relates to Paul's desire, for he says "I want" (βούλομαι). The verb used here (βούλομαι) is different from the one just used to describe God's "desires" (θέλω, v.4). Thayer says the distinction between the two is that "the former seems to designate the will which follows deliberation, the latter the will which proceeds from inclination."[26] That is to say βούλομαι expresses more strongly than θέλω the "deliberate exercise of the will."[27] θέλω is used five times more frequently in the NT, thus it would seem to signal Paul had a good reason for selecting βούλομαι here.[28] Thus we may conclude that Paul is not

---
[26] Thayer, 286.
[27] Vine, 301, 1240-1241.
[28] Thayer, 286.

expressing here a "wish" that the believers may fulfill to make him happy, but an authoritative apostolic conclusion and command based upon a strong theological basis (vv.1-7). Compare Paul's use of the same verb elsewhere in the PE (1 Tim. 5:14; 6:9; Titus 3:8).

The infinitive "to pray" (προσεύχεσθαι) is cognate to the noun "prayers" (προσευχή) of v.1, another signal that Paul is gathering up the whole of his discussion in vv.1-7 and laying down an authoritative application of it. The present tense underscores the unceasing nature of the praying that is thus demanded. The middle voice stresses that one must make a volitional choice (act upon himself) in order to live an acceptable life of prayer. This is required of "the men in every place" (τοὺς ἄνδρας ἐν παντὶ τόπῳ). The Apostle is addressing the adult males in the congregation. The noun ἀνήρ is used rather than ἄνθρωπος when wishing to make a distinction between males and humans generally. Soon enough he will give extensive counsel to the women (vv.9-15), but his instruction here is focused upon the men of the congregation. Note also the use of the definite article to make his intention all the more clear.

The Apostle's instructions here were not confined to one locality. This is more than a mere remedy for the adverse local conditions in Ephesus. Rather, this applies to the men "in every place" (ἐν παντὶ τόπῳ). A decision regarding the intended scope of this phrase not only helps us understand the Apostle's aim in this verse, but sets the stage for understanding the scope of his instructions for women in vv.9ff. He could have in mind merely every house church in Ephesus where believers gathered. But the context seems to point to a broader, more universal intent. Throughout vv.1-7 Paul has had a universal application in mind, indicated by his repeated use of πᾶς ("all," six times in vv.1, 2, 4, 6). The logical connection made between those verses and this by οὖν ("Therefore") indicates that Paul has not changed his focus. Paul's intent in writing the entire letter is "so that you will know how one ought to conduct himself in the household of God" (3:15). This broadens the scope of teaching beyond Ephesus, to how people in every place are to conduct themselves in the church.[29] The *occasion* of this letter may have arisen from local factors in Ephesus, but the *content* of Paul's counsel was not unique to Ephesus alone. Surely God wants these truths about prayer to be found universally among men in God's church. Surely he intends that women everywhere not dress seductively (vv.9-10). The same expression ("in every place," ἐν παντὶ τόπῳ) is used elsewhere by Paul to represent various places, locations and conditions as opposed to one locality (1 Cor. 1:2; 2 Cor. 2:14; 1 Thess. 1:8). This is a command issued by an Apostle of the Lord Jesus Christ and is universally applicable wherever God's people gather for worship.

---

[29] Mounce, 107.

Men should lead the congregational prayer life. Clearly Paul did not prohibit women from praying in the congregation (1 Cor. 11:5, 13). But he did lay the burden of leadership in prayer upon the males. How seldom this is true in our congregations! We need men of prayer to step to the fore and lead the whole of God's people consistently, passionately, purposefully into the presence of God.

Paul adds a participial phrase to explain how he wants the men to pray. The participle "lifting" (ἐπαίροντας) is in the present tense, underscoring that the action should be the abiding nature of the way the men lead in public prayer. That which is to be lifted are "holy hands" (ὁσίους χεῖρας). Standing with hands upraised in prayer was the ancient custom for public worship (e.g., Psa. 28:2; 63:4; 141:2; 143:6). Certainly this is not being prescribed as the only acceptable posture for prayer. Scripture also describes other postures such as falling prostrate (Num. 16:22), kneeling (Psa. 95:6), and bowing the head to the ground (2 Chron. 20:18), among others. It is, however, likely that standing with hands raised to God was the most common posture for public prayer, thus Paul speaks of it here (cf. Luke 24:50; James 4:8). The hands raised before God must be "holy" (ὁσίους). That is to say, they must represent an entire life that has been lived as holy to the Lord. Not just any man may lead in public prayer, but the one who is living his life in accord with God's will. The word describes the pious, pure, and clean action which is in accordance w[ith] God's command."[30] It is only upon God (Acts 2:27; Rev. 15:4; 16:5) and His Son (Acts 2:27; 13:34-35; Heb. 7:26) that the word may be perfectly set. Paul uses it here, however, to describe that which is offered up to Him in worship. In Paul's only other use of the word, it is used to describe the kind of life that should be true of an overseer (Titus 1:8).

> **Ministry Maxim**
>
> That which adversely affects a church's prayer life attacks her at the very essence of her existence.

Such prayers and hands are to be lifted before God "without wrath and dissension" (χωρὶς ὀργῆς καὶ διαλογισμοῦ). The word "without" (χωρὶς) is an adverb that means "separately" or "apart." It is used in the NT as a preposition with the genitive, combining to mean "without" in the sense of "making no use of, having no association with, apart from, aloof from, etc."[31] Here there are two genitives that follow. The first is "wrath" (ὀργῆς). The word is a powerful one. Thayer says it derives from ὀργάω which means "to teem, denoting an internal motion, especially that of plants and fruits swelling with juice."[32] Unresolved conflicts fester and eventuate in bitterness. The churning resentment eventually

---

[30] Rienecker, 620.
[31] Thayer, 675.
[32] Ibid., 452.

erupts upon the surface and destroys those in its path. Forgiveness is a necessary prerequisite to effective prayer (Matt. 5:23-24; 6:14-15; Mark 11:25; Col. 3:8; Eph. 4:31-32).[33]

The second genitive is "dissension" (διαλογισμοῦ). The word is a compound: "through" (διά) and "thought" (λογισμός). It came to describe "a thinking back and forth, deliberation."[34] But it also came to be descriptive of disputing, arguing or even doubting.[35] While, in connection with prayer, the word could point to doubting (cf. KJV), it seems more likely, due to its close proximity to "wrath" (ὀργῆς), that it means something more like "disputing" or "arguing."

The point may well be that the current false teaching and the division it created was keeping the church from being the very thing it should have been. It may also be intended to say that those who divide themselves away from the church as Paul founded it (through their false teaching) are not fit to lead in public worship. That which undercuts the church's prayer life attacks her very essence.

> **Digging Deeper:**
> 1. Why is it significant to see these instructions about prayer as more than simply Paul's wish for one church, but rather as God's divine will for all churches?
> 2. While there is no single acceptable posture for approaching God, what significance does posture play in prayer and worship?
> 3. How does disunity affect the prayer life of a church? How might the prayer life of a church help deal with problems of dissension?

2:9 Likewise, I want women to adorn themselves with proper clothing, modestly and discreetly, not with braided hair and gold or pearls or costly garments,

Paul now shifts attention away from the males ("the men," τοὺς ἄνδρας, v.8) to the "women" (γυναῖκας). While the word can be used to describe "wives," it seems here that it refers to females in general (note the absence of the definite article). What the Apostle prescribes for women in some way corresponds ("likewise," ὡσαύτως) to the instruction he has just given the men (v.8). Six of Paul's eight usages of this adverb occur in the PE (Rom. 8:26; 1 Cor. 11:25; 1 Tim. 2:9; 3:8, 11; 5:25; Titus 2:3, 6). In most of those instances it occurs, as it does here,

---
[33] Marshall, 445.
[34] Rienecker, 620.
[35] BAGD, 186.

in a listing of instructions or qualities for various groups. The correspondence between this verse and the one that precedes it is not to be found in the specific instructions given, but in the fact that just as the Apostle has authoritative instruction for the men (v.8), so too he has authoritative instruction for the women (vv.9-15). There is no main verb in this sentence. The NASB, NASU and NIV see the previous verb from verse 8 ("I want," Βούλομαι) continuing its influence here. Thus the context continues to outline the conduct of God's people during public worship (vv.8-15) and that within the broader context of their conduct as they relate to one another generally (3:15).

The issue here is how women are "to adorn themselves" (κοσμεῖν ἑαυτάς). The present infinitive matches the present infinitive of the last verse ("to pray," προσεύχεσθαι) and supports the notion that "I want" (βούλομαι) is the verb governing both statements. The verb "adorn" (κοσμεῖν) came from the noun κόσμος ("world"), describing the ordered world. It has the root idea of placing things in order or arranging things and then to adorn or ornament something.[36] Our word *cosmetic* comes from this root. Paul's only other use of the word comes when he told Titus that bondservants should "adorn the doctrine of God our Savior in every respect" (Titus 2:10). The word seems, then, to refer to drawing out the natural beauty of a thing by ordering and arranging it to look its best. Peter used it in a similar context where, after instructing women that "Your adornment [κόσμος] must not be merely external—braiding the hair, and wearing gold jewelry, or putting on dresses," he then told of how "in former times the holy women also, who hoped in God, used to adorn [ἐκόσμουν] themselves, being submissive to their own husbands" (1 Peter 3:3, 5). The appropriate adornment is, as Peter states it, "the hidden person of the heart, with the imperishable quality of a gentle and quiet spirit, which is precious in the sight of God" (v.4). Here, the present tense stresses the continual and ongoing nature of how women are "to adorn themselves." The reflexive pronoun ("themselves," ἑαυτάς) is a feminine plural form which marks out the females as a group.

Paul becomes more specific, saying that a woman's adornment should be "with proper clothing" (ἐν καταστολῇ κοσμίῳ). The noun ("clothing," καταστολῇ) is a compound word, being made up of "down" (κατά) and "robe" (στολή). Most simply it means "a lowering" or "a letting down," and thus "a garment let down" or a "gown."[37] It came also then to describe "deportment, outward, as it expresses itself in *clothing* . . . as well as inward . . . and prob[ably] both at the same time."[38] Paul has both clothing (v.9) and conduct (v.10) in mind here.

---

[36] Thayer, 356.
[37] Ibid., 337.
[38] BAGD, 419.

The word reminds us that, regardless of our gender, the outward says something about the inward. Whatever women do with the outward should be "proper" (κοσμίῳ). This adjective also derives from κόσμος. It describes that which is "well-arranged, well-ordered, moderate, modest."[39] Note the play on words: women are "to adorn [κοσμεῖν] themselves with proper [κοσμίῳ] clothing."

Paul adds a further explanatory word, stating both positively and negatively what he had in mind by "to adorn themselves with proper clothing." Positively, it means dressing "modestly and discreetly" (μετὰ αἰδοῦς καὶ σωφροσύνης). The translators of the NASU have failed to include a translation of the preposition μετὰ, which might be rendered "with." First, women are to behave "modestly" (αἰδοῦς). The word is used only here in the NT. Rienecker says, "The word connotes fem[inine] reserve in matters of sex. In the word is involved an innate moral repugnance to the doing of the dishonorable. It is 'shamefastness' which shrinks from overpassing the limits of womanly reserve and modesty, as well as from dishonor which would justly attach thereto."[40] The heart of the word is seen as Thayer contrasts αἰδώς with its synonym, αἰσχύνη: "αἰδώς is prominently objective in its reference, having regard to others; while αἰσχύνη is subjective, making reference to oneself and one's actions . . . It is often said that αἰδώς precedes and prevents the shameful act, αἰσχύνη reflects upon its consequences in the *shame* it brings with it' (Cope, Aristotle, rhet. 5, 6, 1). αἰδώς is the nobler word, αἰσχύνη the stronger; while 'αἰδώς would always restrain a good man from an unworthy act, αἰσχύνη would sometimes restrain a bad one.'"[41] Secondly, women should behave "discreetly" (σωφροσύνης). The word is found twice in Paul (here and v.15) and once as reported from his lips by Luke (Acts 26:25). "It stands basically for perfect self-mastery in the physical appetites and as applied to women it too had a definitely sexual nuance. It is habitual inner self-government, w[ith] its constant reign on all the passions and desires."[42]

> **Ministry Maxim**
>
> One's outward deportment says something about one's inward disposition.

What motivated these instructions? Was Paul countering specific teaching by the false teachers in Ephesus? Or was he addressing a wider problem known in the churches? He may have used these two words in view of the fact that the false teachers preyed upon "weak women weighed down with sins, led on by various impulses" (2 Tim. 3:6b). Paul warned of the woman "who gives herself to wanton pleasure" (1 Tim. 5:5) and he instructed Timothy to refuse

---

[39] Rienecker, 620.
[40] Ibid.
[41] Thayer, 14.
[42] Rienecker, 620.

young widows from the official listing, "for when they feel sensual desires in disregard for Christ, they want to get married' (1 Tim. 5:11). There may well have been a breech in propriety by the false teachers with some women in the church. This must be stopped, and the women were to do their part in restoring decency to the male/female relationships within the church. On the other hand, we should not make too much of the connection to the false teaching. There was an ascetic side to the false teaching as well (1 Tim. 4:3). Also it seems unlikely that the false teachers were instructing men to be angry while in prayer (cf. v.8). It is widely confirmed in both Hellenistic and Jewish writings that the excesses Paul denounces in this verse were common cultural problems for women who were given either to the excesses of wealth or to impure and immoral motives (or both). We cannot quickly dismiss the Apostle's instruction by relegating it to a bygone day which no longer exists.

Negatively stated, their dress is "not to be with" (μὴ ἐν) four different items. The first is "braided hair" (πλέγμασιν). This noun is used only here in the NT. It refers to "anything entwined, woven, braided."[43] Here, the reference is to hair that is braided or interwoven in elaborate fashion with various substances in order to create a stylish impression. The plural indicates that Paul is not condemning one hairstyle, but points to any of a multitude of attempts at some elaborate hair style. Neither ("and," καὶ) are women to adorn themselves with "gold" (χρυσίῳ). The word is used by Paul only here in the NT, though Luke puts it in his mouth in Acts 20:33 ("I have coveted no one's silver or gold or clothes"). Peter uses the word three times, once in similar instructions to women (1 Peter 3:3; cf. also 1:7, 18). Neither ("or," ἢ) were they to use "pearls" (μαργαρίταις). This word too is used by Paul only here, but Jesus' usage (Matt. 7:6; 13:45-46) underscores the value the ancients placed upon pearls. In Revelation the Apostle John sees the great harlot adorned with pearls (Rev. 17:4; 18:12, 16; cf. the New Jerusalem in 21:21). Rienecker says, "Pearls were considered to have had the topmost rank among valuables and were considered to be three times more valuable than gold. Pearls were esp[ecially] prized by women who used them to adorn their hair, to hang them on their fingers, to use them as earrings, or to use them to decorate their garments and even their sandals."[44] Finally, ("or," ἢ) Paul instructs women not to adorn themselves with "costly garments" (ἱματισμῷ πολυτελεῖ). Both the noun and adjective are used only here by Paul. However, the noun is found in that same Acts 20:33 statement by Paul ("I have coveted no one's silver or gold or clothes"). Clearly Paul viewed clothing as one means used by people to exalt themselves socially. Perhaps this was instilled in him early in life, seeing as his

---

[43] BAGD, 667.
[44] Rienecker, 621.

hometown of Tarsus was renown in the weaving trade and its garments were known the world over for their quality.[45] The noun "garments" (ἱματισμῷ) is in the singular, pointing to purchasing one very expensive garment in order to make a statement socially. The noun itself could point to clothing more commonly, as it is used of what Jesus wore (Luke 9:29; John 19:24). But here it is specifically called "costly" (πολυτελεῖ). The adjective is used only two other times in the NT. Once it is used to speak of the "costly perfume" broken and poured over Jesus (Mark 14:3). Peter also employed the word in his instructions to women on how to adorn themselves, but used it positively, speaking of "the imperishable quality of a gentle and quiet spirit, which is precious [πολυτελές] in the sight of God" (1 Peter 3:4).

A woman of godly virtue avoids dress, hairstyling, makeup and other adornment that is either extravagant or erotic, or both. She avoids making statements with her outward adornment that are either lavish or sensual. In fact, she avoids making a statement by her outward adornment at all. What both Paul and Peter prescribe is that Christian women are to operate from a valuation of beauty that is different from the world's valuation. Women should aim at beauty, but at the right kind of beauty. Neither Apostle is calling for women to be frumpy.

Lenski helpfully says, "Paul is not insisting on drab dress. Even this may be worn with vanity; the very drabness may be made a display. Each according to her station in life: the queen not being the same as her lady in waiting, the latter not the same as her noble mistress. Each with due propriety as modesty and propriety will indicate to her both when attending divine services and when appearing in public elsewhere."[46]

> **Digging Deeper:**
> 1. What authoritative standard might be determined to be "proper" when it comes to dress, makeup and hairstyling? How is that determination arrived at? Is it the same in all generations, in all places, and in all cultures?
> 2. In a world of constantly changing fashion and in a congregation of multiple generations, what challenges confront the church which seriously seeks to train its women—young and old; mature disciples and new converts—in proper deportment?
> 3. How can a local church effectively train its women in these matters without falling into legalism?

---

[45] Ibid.
[46] Lenski, 560.

2:10 but rather by means of good works, as is proper for women making a claim to godliness.

As Paul continues the sentence he uses the strong adversative ("but rather," ἀλλά) to contrast what should not be a woman's means of adornment (v.9) with what should rightfully adorn her life. The English translation inverts the word order of this part of the sentence in Greek (though cf. KJV and ESV). The relative singular pronoun ὅ points to that "which" is the right adornment of a woman's life. The plural noun "women" (γυναιξὶν) marks out what the Apostle says is true for all females. The concern is that which "is proper" (πρέπει). The verb is found seven times in the NT (Mark 3:15; Heb. 2:10; 7:26), four of those in Paul (1 Cor. 11:13; Eph. 5:3) and two of those in the PE (1 Tim. 2:10; Titus 2:1). It describes that which is proper, suitable or fitting for a given context.[47] It reminds us that there is right and wrong, light and darkness, black and white. In fashion some things are not "proper" and other things are. If a woman is "making a claim to godliness" (ἐπαγγελλομέναις θεοσέβειαν), her whole life should be brought into submission to that claim, including her clothing, hairstyles, and jewelry. God, not Paris or New York, sets the standard for such a woman's deportment. The participle "making a claim" (ἐπαγγελλομέναις) normally has the sense of making a promise (e.g., Rom. 4:21; Gal. 3:19; Titus 1:2), but here it means to "profess," or to "lay claim to," or to "give oneself out as an expert in someth[ing]."[48] It has a similar sense in 1 Timothy 6:21. Here the present tense stresses the continual nature of the claim being made. It is found in the middle voice in all its fifteen NT usages (except Gal. 3:19 which has the passive sense). What she is claiming is "godliness" (θεοσέβειαν). The noun is used only here in the NT and points to religion, piety, devotion, reverence or fear of God.

Such women should be adorned "by means of good works" (δι' ἔργων ἀγαθῶν). The clause is saved for the end of the sentence in order to place the emphasis upon it.[49] The preposition (διά) with the genitive describes the means by which something takes place. It relates this prepositional phrase to the infinitive "adorn" (κοσμεῖν, v.9b) as does the prepositional phrase initiated by ἐν ("with") in v.9.[50] The exact expression ("good works,"

> **Ministry Maxim**
>
> Overdone efforts at outward adornment are often over-compensation for inward emptiness.

---

[47] Rienecker, 653.
[48] BAGD, 281.
[49] Knight, 136-137.
[50] Marshall, 451.

ἔργων ἀγαθῶν) is found in Acts 9:36 where Dorcas is described as "abounding with deeds of kindness [ἔργων ἀγαθῶν] and charity which she continually did." The theme of "good works" is a rich vein running throughout the PE. The standard of "good works" is one of the criteria by which widows were to be judged worthy of being put on the church's support list (1 Tim. 5:10). In 2 Timothy the theme continues (2:21; 3:17) and it is prominent in Titus (3:1). Paul often points in the same direction using the adjective καλός instead of ἀγαθός (1 Tim. 3:1; 5:10, 25; 6:18; Titus 2:7, 14; 3:8, 14). The former points to that which is aesthetically good or beautiful, while the latter points to that which is morally, ethically, and spiritually good[51], thus making it the more appropriate adjective to use in this discussion. Mounce summarizes by saying, "Jesus gave himself to prepare a people zealous for good deeds (Titus 2:14), and therefore believers should pursue them (2 Tim. 2:21; Titus 3:1, 8, 14), equipped by Scripture (2 Tim 3:17)."[52] The plural noun "works" (ἔργων) emphasizes that, while Paul has named several ways in which improper adornment may express itself (v.9b), there are an infinite variety of ways for a godly woman's goodness of heart to find expression. Paul later gave some specific examples of what this infinite variety of "good works" might look like in a woman's life: bringing up children, showing hospitality, washing the feet of believers, and assisting those in distress (1 Tim. 5:10).

A woman who seeks to please God aims for beauty that exudes from within, adding a beautiful adornment to her physical person. Too often for both men and women an inward emptiness is betrayed by overdone efforts to compensate with outward adornment. As Peter says, a godly woman's adornment is to be "the hidden person of the heart, with the imperishable quality of a gentle and quiet spirit, which is precious in the sight of God" (1 Peter 3:4).

Digging Deeper:
1. In what way do one's actions ("works") adorn or detract from one's beauty?
2. By what criteria are one's works to be judged "proper"? Is there some standard beyond personal opinion and interpretation?
3. How would you explain inward beauty that arises from godliness to a young woman fully immersed in contemporary culture?

---

[51] Mounce, 32.
[52] Ibid., 115.

2:11 A woman must quietly receive instruction with entire submissiveness.

Paul now continues on the theme of women in the context of the local church's life of worship (vv.9-15). He has shifted from the plural "women" (γυναῖκας, v.9) to the singular "A woman" (Γυνὴ), now specifying each and every woman individually instead of all women as a class. The verb "must . . . receive instruction" (μανθανέτω) is in the present tense, stressing the ongoing and continuous nature of the action called for. The imperative mood makes compliance obligatory. In the first-century context it might be considered somewhat remarkable that the Apostle so strongly demanded that women be learners (though it must be admitted that the emphasis here is not on the fact that women are to learn, but *how* they should learn).[53] Learning is a consistent theme throughout the PE, as evidenced by the fact that the verb is used seven times (1 Tim. 2:11; 5:4, 13; 2 Tim. 3:7, 14 [2x], Titus 3:14). It refers to learning something through the instruction of another.[54] The women in the Ephesian church were constantly learning from the false teachers (2 Tim. 3:7, note the present tense) and from the larger fellowship (1 Tim. 5:13). They were to have no less of an opportunity to learn from those proclaiming the truth. On the curriculum would be "to practice piety" (1 Tim. 5:4) and "to engage in good deeds to meet pressing needs" (Titus 3:14), among other things. As Timothy had learned from Paul (2 Tim. 3:14), so the women should have the opportunity to learn from Timothy and the other teachers in the Ephesian church.

Two prepositional phrases outline the sphere in which this apostolic command is to be carried out. The prepositional phrase ἐν ἡσυχίᾳ (lit., "in silence") is translated simply "quietly." It is placed between the subject ("A woman") and the main verb ("must . . . receive instruction") in order to highlight its importance. The same word is repeated at the end of v.12, signaling that this is a major part of the point Paul is making. The noun "silence" (ἡσυχίᾳ) is used four times in the NT (Acts 22:2; 2 Thess. 3:12; 1 Tim. 2:11, 12). It carries the notion of the quietness and rest of an "undisturbed life" (2 Thess. 3:12) and, at other times, of silence and the absence of noise (Acts 22:2).[55] The two uses of the cognate adjective (ἡσύχιος) tend toward the former meaning (2 Tim. 2:2; 1 Peter 3:4; in the latter Peter counsels women to aim for a "quiet [ἡσυχίου] spirit"). The cognate verb (ἡσυχάζω) is found five times in the NT. It can mean complete "silence" (Luke 14:4), but also a quietness in contrast to confusion and controversy (Acts 11:18; 21:14; note that in both instances the quietness

---
[53] Ibid., 119.
[54] BAGD, 490.
[55] Ibid., 349; Thayer, 281.

was accompanied by verbal statements) and peacefulness about life (1 Thess. 4:11). Given the close proximity to the use of the adjective in v.2 ("quiet life"), here, as with the whole word-group, the emphasis seems to be toward the quietness [without necessarily total silence] of a life free from contention, confusion, controversy and self-assertion. This learning should happen in the sphere (ἐν) of such quietness, undisturbed. Women are not to become embroiled in the controversies of leadership and doctrinal debate, but to come to worship with a heart quieted by the peace of Christ and attuned to the Spirit of Christ through the Word of God taught by the leadership of the church. That this was not merely a command of expediency given to overcome a problem unique to Ephesus is clear from Paul's similar instruction to the church in Corinth: "The women are to keep silent in the churches; for they are not permitted to speak, but are to subject themselves, just as the Law also says. If they desire to learn anything, let them ask their own husbands at home; for it is improper for a woman to speak in church" (1 Cor. 14:34-35). Timothy, because of his relationship to the Corinthian church and assistance to Paul in ministry there (1 Cor. 4:17; 16:10; 2 Cor. 1:1, 19), would have been well aware of this instruction.[56] There Paul used the stronger word "silence" (σιγάω), specifying the absence of talk. This practice was natural for Paul and other Jewish believers, for it was the practice in the Jewish synagogue that women were not permitted to speak.[57]

Similarly the Apostle instructs that this learning should take place "with entire submissiveness" (ἐν πάσῃ ὑποταγῇ). Again he is describing the sphere in which (ἐν) the learning is to take place. Paul places the imperative between the two prepositional phrases ("quietly" [ἐν ἡσυχίᾳ] and "with entire submissiveness" [ἐν πάσῃ ὑποταγῇ]) to indicate that the latter phrase modifies and explains the former phrase. In other words, what Paul means by "quietly" is "with entire submissiveness."[58] The sphere of such learning is described here as "submissiveness" (ὑποταγῇ). Its cognate verb (ὑποτάσσω) is a compound from "under" (ὑπό) and "appoint" or "order" (τάσσω). It is a word that bespeaks authority and submission. It was a military word which described the ranks of soldiers arranging themselves under the leadership of their commander. Similarly the noun means "subjection, subordination, obedience."[59]

> **Ministry Maxim**
>
> Submission and authority are the twin-threads from which God has woven the fabric of relationships.

The command is not for mindless submission, the surrender of independent

---

[56] Lenski, 561.
[57] Rienecker, 438.
[58] Lenski, 562; cf. Mounce, 119.
[59] BAGD, 847.

thought or abandoning personal discernment. Nor does this imply a second-class rank for women within the church. Rather it assumes the fuller teaching of Scripture regarding the absolute authority of God and how He has chosen to delegate measured portions of that authority in certain institutions (e.g., government, church, home) and to certain people within those institutions (rulers, elders, husbands/fathers) for the illustrating of the respective roles of the Trinity in the purposes of redemption (1 Cor. 11:3) and for the outworking of His redemptive plan among humanity. Women are not the sole subjects of such authority, for every life comes under some such authority in some sphere (e.g., all believers to one another [Eph. 5:21], citizens to their rulers [Rom. 13:1-7; Titus 3:1], wives to husbands [Eph. 5:22; Titus 2:5], children to parents [Eph. 6:1; 1 Tim. 3:4]; slaves to their masters [1 Tim. 6:1-2; Titus 2:9], and the younger to the older [1 Peter 5:5]). Authority and submission are part of the fabric of life as God has created it for us. Such authority is always relative, for only God possesses absolute authority. Such authority is always accountable to God's absolute authority, and each one will answer to Him for their use of the authority He has delegated. The Apostle here makes clear that God intends the leadership within the local church to be comprised of qualified males (cf. 1 Tim. 3:1-7; Titus 1:6-9). The women of the congregation, like the non-elder males, are to follow the lead of those God-given leaders (Heb. 13:17).[60]

The adjective "entire" (πάσῃ) underscores the all-encompassing nature of the submission that is required. It stresses that the submission in view must go to "the highest degree."[61] It also is another bit of evidence that Paul has in mind here the women in the context of the church at worship, not individual wives and their relationships to their husbands.

Digging Deeper:

1. At the time of its writing, did this command show Paul to be a liberator or a repressor of women? Why?
2. Do you think the Apostle intended the qualification "quietly" as a restriction or a protection for those to whom it is addressed?
3. Why does the idea of "submissiveness" draw such strong reactions today? What does that say about us?

---

[60] For a fuller discussion of the issues surrounding authority, consult the author's *Embracing Authority*.
[61] BAGD, 631.

2:12 But I do not allow a woman to teach or exercise authority over a man, but to remain quiet.

The conjunction δέ ("But") is left untranslated by many English translations (e.g., NIV, ESV, NRSV). It can have either a continuative sense ("and," cf. NKJV) or an adversative sense ("But," KJV, NASB, NASU). In favor of the adversative force is that Paul has made a positive statement in v.11 ("a woman . . . must receive instruction") and now contrasts that with a prohibition ("I do not allow a woman to teach"). The subject "woman" (γυναικὶ) is still in the singular form and without the definite article, thus considering womanhood generally.[62] The concern is her liberty "to teach" (διδάσκειν). Paul has used the same verb in the PE to describe what Timothy is to do (1 Tim. 4:11; 6:2), what he is to train "faithful men" to do (2 Tim. 2:2), and what false teachers wrongly do (Titus 1:11). There is a sense in which all the members of the body teach one another "with psalms and hymns and spiritual songs" (Col. 3:16) when they worship, but as it is used here there is an official sense attached to the word. The content was sacred (2 Thess. 2:15) and the duty divinely given (Rom. 12:6-7). The word, along with its cognate nouns (διδασκαλία and διδάσκαλος), is used in the PE to point to authoritative teaching of God's truth.[63] Here the word is thrust forward to the head of the sentence in order to place emphasis upon it. This activity ("to teach") Paul says "I do not allow" (οὐκ ἐπιτρέπω) women to exercise in the gathered congregation. The adverb chosen (οὐκ, "not") makes this prohibition absolute and categorical.[64] The verb (ἐπιτρέπω) means simply to permit or allow something.[65] It is used eighteen times in the NT. Outside of Paul's writings it is always used either of permission granted by a governing authority (John 19:38; Acts 21:39, 40; 26:1; 27:3; 28:16), Jesus (Matt. 8:21; Mark 5:13; Luke 8:32 [2x]; 9:59, 61), God (Heb. 6:3) or Moses as God's appointed leader (Matt. 19:8; Mark 10:4). Paul uses it three times. Once he uses it of divine permission (1 Cor. 16:7). His two other usages are here and in 1 Corinthians 14:34 when he says in a similar context, "The women are to keep silent in the churches; for *they are not permitted* to speak, but are to subject themselves, just as the Law also says" (emphasis added). This confirms that the permission Paul speaks of here is not a matter of personal opinion, but of apostolic command. The first person singular form points not merely to Paul personally, but rather to him as God's appointed Apostle. The present tense of the verb points not to what Paul is concluding in just this one circumstance at this particular moment ("I am not permitting,"

---

[62] Knight, 140.
[63] Moo, 185.
[64] Thayer, 408.
[65] Rienecker, 621.

as per Fee[66] and others), but what he habitually and regularly holds as the apostolic standard in all churches. Indeed, Paul's other usages of the first person singular present indicative (Rom. 12:1, 3; 1 Cor. 4:16; 2 Cor. 5:20; Gal. 5:2, 3; Eph. 4:1; 1 Thess. 4:1; 5:14; 2 Thess. 3:6; 1 Tim. 2:1, 8) demonstrate "that he uses it to give universal and authoritative instruction or exhortation (cf. especially Rom. 12:1; 1 Tim. 2:8)."[67]

Similarly Paul does not allow a woman "to exercise authority" (οὐδὲ αὐθεντεῖν). The word is found only here in the NT, which presents a challenge for ascertaining its meaning. Studies show that it can mean both "to have authority over and to domineer."[68] Some immediately determine that the prohibition is against a woman being domineering over a man, not in exercising authority over him. Thus they contend that the prohibition is not against exercising authority *per se*, but against the abuse of authority. However, the first meaning given by BAGD is "to have authority" and the second is "to domineer . . . over someone."[69] Thayer lists only the meaning "to govern . . . exercise dominion over . . ."[70] Studies by George W. Knight III and H.S. Baldwin have taken into account the broad usage of the word in extra-biblical Greek writings and have concluded that, to use Baldwin's own words, "In analyzing this material it becomes evident that the one unifying concept throughout is that of authority."[71] Those instances that are closest to this passage in both time and nature demonstrate that "'have authority over' or 'dominate' (in the neutral sense of 'have dominion over,' not in the negative sense 'lord it over')" is the meaning.[72] The present tense, as with the previous infinitive ("to teach," διδάσκειν), points to Paul's abiding decision.

The prohibition here is indicated by the use of the conjunction οὐδέ. Some have tried to assert that the conjunction is used when combining two ideas to make one single idea (hendiadys). This would combine the two infinitives into "teaching in a domineering manner."[73] The 143 usages of οὐδέ in the NT, however, reveal that such a usage is either non-existent or used so seldom as to be of no influence here. Thomas Edgar concludes, "The evidence is amazingly one-sided. There is not one instance of the 143 occurrences . . . which function as a hendiadys."[74] The conjunction "is used to join similar ideas and intensify

---

[66] Fee, 72.
[67] Knight, 140.
[68] DNTT, 3:1066.
[69] BAGD, 121.
[70] Thayer, 84.
[71] Quoted in House, *The Role of Women in Ministry Today,* 32; see also Baldwin's "A Difficult Word: αὐθεντέω in 1 Timothy 2:12," and "Appendix 2: αὐθεντέω in Ancient Greek Literature," in *Women in the Church: A Fresh Analysis of 1 Timothy 2:9-15,* A. Kostenberger, T. Schreiner, H.S. Baldwin, eds. (Grand Rapids: Baker Books, 1995), 65ff, 269ff respectively.
[72] Moo, 186.
[73] Philip Barton Payne, cited in House, *The Role of Women in Ministry Today,* 45-46.
[74] quoted in House, *The Role of Women in Ministry Today,* 47.

the concepts,"⁷⁵ but not to present one singular idea. This leads us to realize that while authoritative teaching and exercising authority in the church are closely related to one another, they may not always be identical. Authority may be exercised in ways other than teaching.⁷⁶ The conjunction requires that since "to teach" is viewed as a positive action (not "to teach false doctrine," which would have called for ἑτεροδιδασκαλέω instead of διδάσκω, cf. 1 Tim. 1:3; 6:3), so too must "exercise authority" be viewed as a positive action ("exercise authority") and not as "domineer over" or some such notion.⁷⁷

This prohibition against women teaching and exercising authority is not universal, but is restricted to their relationship with "men" (ἀνδρός). The noun serves as the object of both "to teach" (διδάσκειν) and "exercise authority" (αὐθεντεῖν). That this points to "men" in general in the church, rather than to each woman's husband, is clear from the larger context of this chapter. Women are instructed elsewhere to teach one another (Titus 2:3-4) and the ministry of women teaching children is commended (2 Tim. 1:5; 3:15). This does not prohibit women from speaking at all, for women are allowed to pray and to prophesy (1 Cor. 11:5) in the public services of the church. On the distinction between teaching and prophecy consult Wayne Grudem's *The Gift of Prophecy in the New Testament and Today*.

The Apostle's instruction to women is that they not teach or exercise authority in the gathered church as a whole, "but to remain quiet" (ἀλλ' εἶναι ἐν ἡσυχίᾳ). The adversative "but" (ἀλλ') is a strong one, stressing the absolute nature of the contrast. A third infinitive ("to remain," εἶναι) is added in contrast to the first two and points to what Paul does "permit" in the churches. The present tense here also stresses the abiding and constant nature of Paul's apostolic determination. The prepositional phrase ἐν ἡσυχίᾳ ("quiet") is repeated verbatim from v.11 (the only two instances of this exact expression in the NT) and rounds out the use of the literary device of inclusion. This helps fill out our understanding of vv.11-12. With the opening statement ("quietly," ἐν ἡσυχίᾳ) of v.11 matching exactly the closing statement ("quiet," ἐν ἡσυχίᾳ) of v.12, we are signaled that

> **Ministry Maxim**
>
> Grasping after authority leaves you with an armload of troubles.

what is sandwiched between these two statements probably relates to one another as well. Thus "entire submissiveness" (v.11) corresponds to "teach or exercise authority over a man" (v.12). The submissiveness called for in v.11 is specifically detailed in v.12 as not teaching men in the gathered church or

---
⁷⁵ House, *The Role of Women in Ministry Today*, 47.
⁷⁶ Moo, 187.
⁷⁷ Kostenberger, 103.

exercising authority over them.

These verses raise many questions concerning their appropriate application in the church today. One lesson we learn is that standing before God's people with God's Word and speaking on His behalf is a far more serious matter than perhaps many Christians understand. Something unique from all other human communication is taking place in those instances. When we reduce the significance of God's Word being taught to God's people, we open the door to sentiments such as "What's the big deal?" concerning any divine restrictions upon that act. Not only must we answer the individual questions that arise from the Apostle's words here, but we must reexamine our understanding and attitude toward the proclamation of God's Word when His people gather for worship. What are we expecting to take place in those moments?

By way of specific application we again assert that women may pray and prophesy (the term being rightly understood) among God's gathered people (1 Cor. 11:5). Women are charged with teaching one another (Titus 2:3-4) and are commended for teaching children (2 Tim. 1:5; 3:15). A married woman may serve alongside her husband in private counsel and instruction (Acts 18:26). Any restrictions imposed here by the Apostle are not statements regarding the worth of women, for he elsewhere asserts in the strongest terms the equality of women and men before God as creatures of dignity, worth, significance and spiritual standing (Gal. 3:28). The members of the Trinity, who are co-equal in glory and divinity, each functioned within particular roles for the outworking of redemption (1 Cor. 11:3; Eph. 1:3-14). Similarly, and in a reflection of that equality and diversity within the Godhead, God has ordained that male and female, created equal in dignity and worth, will best fulfill His redemptive purposes and most beautifully reflect His own nature by fulfilling distinct, though equally significant, roles within the church and home.

Digging Deeper:

1. Does our worth arise out of what we can *do* (our ability to perform) or out of who we *are* (by design and intrinsic worth)? Does then a person lose worth if they are unable to perform some particular task (i.e., if I can't do what you do, I am not worth as much as you)?
2. Is the divine commission to "exercise authority" a burden or a privilege? Is it a goal one should aim to achieve or a divine assignment one can only receive?
3. In what way do these instructions change the way we should perceive the very nature of teaching the gathered body of believers?

2:13 For it was Adam who was first created, and then Eve.

The Apostle now provides a twofold foundation for his statements regarding women in the gathered church (vv.13-14). The conjunction γὰρ ("For") signals that a causal statement is being made. The Apostle takes us all the way back to the beginning of the human race and establishes a pre-Fall reason for his instructions regarding women in the congregation. He says "it was Adam who was first created, and then Eve" (᾿Αδὰμ γὰρ πρῶτος ἐπλάσθη, εἶτα Εὔα).

Adam (᾿Αδὰμ) is mentioned nine times in the NT, seven of those in Paul's writings (Rom. 5:14 [2x]; 1 Cor. 15:22, 45 [2x]; 1 Tim. 2:13, 14). Paul points to Adam as the head of the race and as the one who brought death upon humanity through his sin (Rom. 5:14; 1 Cor. 15:22). Adam is contrasted with Christ who is known as the "last Adam" (1 Cor. 15:22, 45). But here there is no mention of his sin, for Paul takes us further back, to a time prior to Adam's creation-marring choice. We have here not injunctions based upon the realities of a fallen race living in a sin-cursed world, but commands that date to the time when God still pronounced everything He made as "good" (Gen. 1:4, 10, 12, 18, 21, 25). Upon the creation of the man and the woman, He pronounced it all "very good" (Gen. 1:31). In God's good pleasure it was Adam "who was first created" (πρῶτος ἐπλάσθη). The verb means "to form" or "to mold" something, particularly as it relates to working with some substance like clay or wax.[78] We get our word "pliable" from this root. It is the word the LXX chooses in Genesis 2:7, 8, 15, 19 to describe the creation of Adam.[79] In the only other NT usage of the word, Paul speaks of God being the Potter and we being the clay (Rom. 9:20). God formed Adam from the dust of the earth (Gen. 2:7), thus the word is appropriate here. But it is also appropriate, for in Paul's other use he conjures up another OT image: "On the contrary, who are you, O man, who answers back to God? The thing molded will not say to the molder, 'Why did you make me like this,' will it?" (Rom. 9:20; reflecting for example Isa. 29:16; 45:9; 64:8; Jer. 18:1-6; Lam. 4:2). If we squirm under Paul's instruction here, we are reminded of the sovereignty of the Potter in fashioning humanity (both male and female) according to His own plan. It was His will to make man "first" (πρῶτος). Adam is not mentioned here as "first" in the human race, but rather "first" in relationship to the creation of Eve. The word functions here not as an adverb, but as a predicate adjective (i.e., Adam was created "the first").[80] Adam was created "then Eve" (εἶτα Εὔα). Paul always uses the adverb εἶτα ("then") with its temporal significance, signifying what is next in

---

[78] Thayer, 515.
[79] Knight, 143.
[80] Thayer, 555; Knight, 143; Lenski, 565.8

time (1 Cor. 15:5, 7, 24; 1 Tim. 2:13; 3:10). Eve is mentioned by name in the NT only here and in 2 Corinthians 11:3.

Paul has used similar argumentation in another context: "For man does not originate from woman, but woman from man; for indeed man was not created for the woman's sake, but woman for the man's sake" (1 Cor. 11:8-9). Apart from these NT applications of the Scriptural record of God's order of creation (Gen. 2:7, 20-23), one might conclude that the order carries no special or abiding significance. But the Apostle Paul's Spirit-directed application confirms what was in God's heart as He formed the first male and female as He did. The female's equal share in the redemption purchased by Christ and in the liberation wrought by Christ (Gal. 3:28) does not abolish or substantively change God's intended design for the sexes as established in creation. Rather, salvation in Christ restores both male and female to a place where they are able to fulfill those God-designed roles. The order of creation communicates something significant and enduring about the roles the male and female are to fulfill in accomplishing God's good, pleasing and perfect will.

> **Ministry Maxim**
>
> God's original intention was no mere convention but a reflection of His protection.

2:14 And it was not Adam who was deceived, but the woman being deceived, fell into transgression.

The Apostle now introduces a second (καὶ, "And") reason for his instruction regarding women teaching and exercising authority (v.12). This reason moves out of the pre-Fall state of creation (v.13) to the Fall itself where "it was not Adam who was deceived" (Ἀδὰμ οὐκ ἠπατήθη). The statement is terse and emphatic, the negation absolute and categorical (οὐκ, "not").[81] The verb means to deceive, cheat or mislead someone with something.[82] The passive voice signals that Adam was not thus deceived by another. The aorist tense is used to point to an event or a moment of deception. There was no such event or moment in Adam's experience. Paul's only other use of the verb was also in communication with the church in Ephesus: "Let no one deceive [ἀπατάτω] you with empty words, for because of these things the wrath of God comes upon the sons of disobedience" (Eph. 5:6).

On the contrary (δέ, "but") "the woman, being deceived, fell into transgression" (ἡ δὲ γυνὴ ἐξαπατηθεῖσα ἐν παραβάσει γέγονεν). Eve is now simply designated "the woman" (ἡ . . . γυνή). The definite article marks her out

---
[81] Thayer, 408.
[82] BAGD, 408.

specifically, whereas the same noun without the article appears in vv.9, 10, 11, 12, referring generally to all the women who have come behind her. Paul marks her out not simply as distinct from all other women, but as *the* woman—the first, the prototype, the head of all women. As such Eve "fell into transgression" (ἐν παραβάσει γέγονεν). The noun "transgression" pictures sin in relation to law, as an overstepping of a known requirement. God had given Adam clear instruction concerning what he could and could not eat (Gen. 2:16-17). It is equally clear that this instruction had come to Eve and she understood it, for the serpent questioned God's word to her face and she recounted God's requirement (Gen. 3:1-3). Whether God delivered the commandment to the woman directly or mediated it through Adam, she understood what He had demanded. The verb ("fell," γέγονεν) is used over 650 times in the NT and carries a broad range of meaning. Generally it means "to be" or "to become." Some have translated it as "became a transgressor" (ESV, NRSV) or "became a sinner" (NIV), but that seems to miss the force of ἐν παραβάσει ("into transgression"). Perhaps a translation such as "has come into transgression" catches something of the meaning as well. The verb is in the perfect tense, signaling that it is an abiding state of transgression into which Eve came.

Eve came into this state by "being deceived" (ἐξαπατηθεῖσα). The participle is a compound form of the verb used of Adam earlier in the sentence: "out of" (ἐκ) and "deceived" (ἀπατάω). The preposition in compound has a strengthening effect upon the verb. While Adam was not deceived (ἀπατάω), Eve was *utterly* deceived (ἐξαπατάω). The passive voice points back to the serpent as the deceiver (Gen. 3:1, 4-5). The aorist tense recalls the decisive moment of her being led astray (Gen. 3:6). That one act led to an abiding state of transgression. In the only other use of the name "Eve" (outside of v.13) in the NT, Paul also spoke of her being deceived (2 Cor. 11:3).

> **Ministry Maxim**
>
> Deception was and is at the root of the confusion regarding God's design for both genders.

Adam was apparently with Eve when she was deceived (Gen. 3:6). We might infer that he failed to take the leadership necessary to dispel the deception and to dispense with the serpent. While Eve was deceived (Gen. 3:13), Adam knowingly transgressed God's command. Eve knew she was violating God's command, but was deceived regarding the nature of God (Gen. 3:5) and His promised judgment (Gen. 3:4). Adam knew God's nature and the inevitability of judgment, yet he followed his wife's lead anyway (Gen. 3:6b). Paul was not attempting to relieve Adam of responsibility, for he traced the universal effects of the Fall back to him (Rom. 5:12-21). But Eve's deception by the serpent and her subsequent enticement of Adam into sin were a powerful influence upon

Adam. The serpent slyly bypassed Adam, the head of the couple (by virtue of his being created first, v.13), and addressed the woman directly. She bypassed the natural order of leadership—by listening to the serpent and refusing to direct him back to the man—and Adam allowed her to do so. Having fallen into sin herself, she enticed Adam to follow her lead ("Because you have listened to the voice of your wife," Gen. 3:17). God indicated that the aftermath of such decisions would be a continuing struggle for leadership outside of God's appointed, pre-Fall design (Gen. 3:16b). A single act can become a lasting legacy. For the protection of both sexes and for the preservation of the church, the Apostle appeals here for a wise return to the God-ordained order of leadership.

Clearly Eve's deception is seen as a warning to both sexes: "But I am afraid that, as the serpent deceived Eve by his craftiness, your minds will be led astray from the simplicity and purity of devotion to Christ" (2 Cor. 11:3). We do well to heed this warning as we wrestle with the complexities of the issues and the emotions that surround the role of women in the gathered church.

> ### Digging Deeper:
> 1. What abiding significance does the Apostle place upon the order of the creation of man and woman?
> 2. Why does it seem, with regard to gender roles within the church, that Eve's deception was more significant than Adam's rebellion?
> 3. In what way is deception still at the root of the controversy over the roles of men and women in the church?

2:15 But women will be preserved through the bearing of children if they continue in faith and love and sanctity with self-restraint.

By means of a mild contrast ("But," δέ) Paul holds out hope for women. Deciding just what the nature and content of this hope is has been a matter of some debate through the centuries. Generally the options fall out along these lines, with variations on these basic options by various interpreters: 1) women receive spiritual salvation through giving birth. The problem, of course, is that salvation is a matter of grace, not of works. Also, not all women are physically capable of giving birth. 2) Women will be kept safe through the painful and sometimes life-threatening process of birthing a child. The problem is that many women have died in childbirth. It would then be inferred that those women had not continued "in faith and love and sanctity with self-restraint," a strained line of reasoning to be sure. 3) Women are saved (as are men, but women are the subject presently) through "*the* childbearing" (the definite article exists in the original, pointing to the birth of Messiah, Gen. 3:15). That is to say, women are saved by the one, ultimate and promised Child to be born into the world, the Lord Jesus Christ (Gal. 4:4). This understanding requires "the bearing of children" (τῆς τεκνογονίας) to refer to the product of childbearing (the Child), rather than its normal sense as a reference to the process of childbearing. It nowhere else has such a meaning.[83] 4) Women may be saved despite the curse of bearing children (reading διά ["through"] as attendant circumstances, rather than as means or instrument). This sees "the bearing of children" as pointing to the curse of Genesis 3:16. However, the curse was not "the bearing of children" *per se*, but "the bearing of children" *with pain*. 5) Women are saved, not by grasping after a role that God has not ordained for them (i.e., teaching and exercising authority in the church, v.12), but in accepting their divinely appointed role of womanhood (the whole of which is here spoken of through the representative act of childbearing).

None of the options is without its challenges. Yet it seems that the last of these options may be the Apostle's point in this context. He says that women "will be preserved" (σωθήσεται). The verb means "will be saved" and is used throughout the PE of the spiritual deliverance that comes through faith in Christ and by the grace of God (1 Tim. 1:15; 2:4; 4:16; 2 Tim. 1:9; 4:18; Titus 3:5) and we should retain the meaning here. Thus the translation "preserved" (rather than the normal "saved") may be misleading. The future tense looks forward to the final deliverance into the full hope of eschatological salvation. The passive voice views another as acting upon the woman. The singular form carries over from the previous verse and is literally "she will be saved," though by the end of the verse the shift will be made to the plural.

Understanding in just what sense Paul thus means that women will be saved is a matter of some stern debate. It is said to take place "through the bearing of children" (διά τῆς τεκνογονίας). Normally the preposition διά would be used to indicate the means by which something happens or the instrument through which something happens, but here it seems to denote attendant circumstances. In other words, women are saved not *by* bearing children, but *while* bearing children.[84] That is to say, women are saved, not by grasping after a role God has not created them for (teaching and exercising authority in the church, v. 12), but rather as they gladly fulfill the role God has created for them. Women are not saved "by means of" child-bearing, but by Christ. But they, like men, are saved by Christ as they rely upon Him and fulfill the role He has created them for. That role is "the bearing of children" (τῆς τεκνογονίας, "child-bearing"). The entire phrase is represented in the Greek text by a noun and its definite article.

---

[83] Marshall, 468.
[84] BAGD, 180.

The noun occurs only here in the NT, but see its cognate verb used in 1 Timothy 5:14 (τεκνογονεῖν, "bear children"). The definite article may particularize the reference to not one singular birth (i.e., a reference to Messiah), but to the singular role of child-bearing, which is awarded by God to women. It probably has reference not only to physically bearing the child into the world, but the entire process of birthing and raising the child up to maturity.[85] Employing the literary device of synecdoche, Paul likely gathers up the whole of a woman's role and references it here by mention of one prominent part of that role.[86] Women are not mere "baby factories." In God's plan a woman's role is rich, broad, and powerfully influential. That influence is first and fundamentally exercised in the bringing of the next generation into the world, nurturing them in the ways of God, and deploying them into the world to serve God.

Women are saved as they accept God's call upon their lives and gladly fulfill it, only "if they continue in faith and love and sanctity with self-restraint" (ἐὰν μείνωσιν ἐν πίστει καὶ ἀγάπῃ καὶ ἁγιασμῷ μετὰ σωφροσύνης). The condition (ἐὰν plus the aorist subjunctive) is a class three condition, meaning that its fulfillment is undetermined as to certainty, but it is probable. For the sake of argument Paul accepts that such conditions will likely be met, but for the sake of application he does not make such certainty absolute. The condition requires that women must "continue in" (μείνωσιν ἐν) certain qualities. The verb means to abide, remain, continue, stay put, live or dwell. The number has changed from the singular to the plural, indicating that Paul has had in mind all along to make the particular example of Eve (vv.13-14) apply to all women (v.15). The preposition ("in," ἐν) describes the sphere or realm in which the continuance must be worked out.

The first three items listed in the condition are said to continue in is that of "faith" (πίστει). It is one of Paul's favorite words, being used by him 142 times in his writings, thirty-three of those being in the PE. One is saved by grace, "through faith" (διὰ πίστεως; Rom. 3:22; Gal. 2:16; Eph. 2:8; Phil. 3:9; 2 Tim. 3:15). Little wonder Paul lists it first here. No woman is saved simply by fulfilling a role, but through explicit faith in Jesus Christ. The second item is "love" (ἀγάπῃ). This too is one of the Apostle's favorite words, being found seventy-five times in his writings, with ten of those in the PE. These first two qualities are paired often in Paul (e.g., 1 Cor. 13:2, 13; Gal. 5:6, 22; Eph. 1:15; Col. 1:4; 1 Thess. 3:6; 2 Thess. 1:3; 1 Tim. 6:11; 2 Tim. 2:22; Philem. 5). One might have expected Paul to make the third pair in the list "hope" (ἐλπίς; e.g., 1 Cor. 13:13), but instead we find here "sanctity" (ἁγιασμῷ). The word is used only by Paul in the NT, being found eight times (Rom. 6:19, 22; 1 Cor. 1:30;

---

[85] Marshall, 468.
[86] Lea, 102.

1 Thess. 4:3, 4, 7; 2 Thess. 2:13; 1 Tim. 2:15). This noun refers to holiness, consecration or sanctification. It may refer to the process of becoming holy or, and more often, the resulting state of being sanctified or consecrated.[87] Each woman (as with each man) must place her trust in Christ and consecrate the whole of her life to Him, dedicating herself to actively fulfilling His will for her as a woman and as an individual. These three ("faith and love and sanctity") must co-exist in each woman along "with self-restraint" (μετὰ σωφροσύνης). This noun is found but three times in the NT, once from Paul's lips (Acts 26:25) and twice from his pen (1 Tim. 2:9, 15). See on v.9 for the word's meaning. Paul's use of the noun on either end of his discussion of women's roles in the congregation (vv.9, 15) is an example of the literary device of inclusion and it holds the entire discussion together thematically. It also underscores the contextual support for our understanding of this verse.

One might ask why Paul would spend so much time on the women's role (vv.9-15) and comparatively little upon that of the men (v.8). The answer probably lies in that the false teachers were misguiding the women concerning their role—teaching them that marriage was to be spurned (1 Tim. 4:3; cf. Paul's counsel in 5:11, 14) and likely also that motherhood lacked the dignity and priority of other forms of leadership. This does not limit the application of the Apostle's words as culturally irrelevant to our society, for he did not instruct the women regarding what was merely prudent in their present context, but what God has established from creation (v.13). Rather it underscores that the answer is to return to God's original design for humanity whenever challenges confront the church. God has not denigrated the woman's value or diminished the woman's role. Rather He has elevated it and dignified it. The influence of a woman is broader and fuller than what simply takes place in a local congregation. It begins from a child's earliest days, continues throughout all those days and in all the places through which she goes with that child. She is the molder of hearts and minds and lives as a constant, unceasing presence and teacher of her children. She is not limited to the hours that a congregation may gather together for worship; she is released to exert her influence twenty-four hours a day, seven days a week for as long as her children are at her side. Then she deploys them strategically into the world in hopes that her influence will compound and spread far beyond where her single voice might have been heard had she taken up a position in the church which God has not afforded

> **Ministry Maxim**
>
> A mother's influence often out-distances that of church leaders in actually advancing the purposes of God.

---

[87] BAGD, 9.

her. As Hendriksen well says, "It is his will that the woman should influence mankind 'from the bottom up' (that is, by way of *the child*), not 'from the top down' (that is, not by way of *the man*)."[88] In the end we may discover that the influence of the mother will have far outdistanced that of the father or church leader.

> **Digging Deeper:**
> 1. Does the phrase "the bearing of children" *exhaust* the extent of a woman's role or *represent* the whole of a woman's role? What difference does this make in understanding God's intent in v.15?
> 2. Why do people often perceive this as demeaning to women? What are they missing when they adopt such an understanding?
> 3. How may eternity reveal the seemingly hidden power and influence of mothers?

---

[88] Hendriksen, 111.

CHAPTER

3

3:1 It is a trustworthy statement: if any man aspires to the office of overseer, it is a fine work he desires to do.

We encounter here for the second time a phrase that becomes stock jargon in the PE: "It is a trustworthy statement" (Πιστὸς ὁ λόγος; 1 Tim. 1:15; 3:1; 4:9; 2 Tim. 2:11; Titus 3:8). The verb is absent in the Greek text and thus it more literally reads, "Faithful the word." See the comments on 1:15. The expression is used here to signal a transition in the letter. It points forward to the words in v.1b; not backward to the saying in 2:15, as some have supposed. Paul moves from instruction about the proper role of men and women in the congregational life (2:8-15) to instruction about the qualification for proper leadership of the church (3:1-13).

The trusted word begins with a conditional clause: "if any man aspires to the office of overseer" (Εἴ τις ἐπισκοπῆς ὀρέγεται). The condition is of the first class, being assumed true (i.e., the Apostle assumes for the moment that there are those within the church who would aspire to leadership). The indefinite pronoun τις ("any man") is general and broadens the possibilities out as widely as possible.[1] The combination of "if anyone" (Εἴ τις) is found frequently in the PE (1 Tim. 1:10; 3:1, 5; 5:4, 8, 16; 6:3; Titus 1:6). Soon enough the qualities of those who qualify for leadership will be enumerated, but at present all comers are considered. What we do know is that the person "aspires" (ὀρέγεται) to leadership. The verb occurs only two other times in the NT. Paul uses it in 6:10 to describe those who long for wealth. The writer of Hebrews employs it to describe the longing of God's people for heaven (11:16). The word has the sense of stretching out, reaching out or striving after

---

[1] BAGD, 220.

something.² The present tense views this as more than a passing interest, but as a continuing desire that lives within the individual. The middle voice is used in all three NT usages and may point to the inward nature of the longing.

That which is longed after is "the office of overseer" (ἐπισκοπῆς). The word is used only four times in the NT. It can have the meaning of a "visitation," either in a good sense (Luke 19:44) or a negative one (Jer. 10:15, LXX; 1 Peter 2:12).³ It came also, then, to describe the position or office of one who oversees or has charge of something (Acts 1:20), which is clearly its meaning in the present context. The noun ἐπίσκοπος ("overseer") is used to refer to the individual "overseer(s)" (e.g., v.2; Phil. 1:1; Titus 1:7), while the present noun is used to describe the position of an overseer as an office. The singular form here indicates that there is but one office, though it is filled normally by a plurality of "overseers" (Acts 20:28; Phil. 1:1).⁴ The terms "overseer" (ἐπίσκοπος) and "elder" (πρεσβύτερος) are both used to describe one office and are used interchangeably (Acts 20:17, 28; Titus 1:5, 7). The distinction is often made by saying that "overseers" (ἐπίσκοπος) describes the duty of the office, while "elders" (πρεσβύτερος) depicts the honor and dignity of the office. The use of the word ἐπίσκοπος ("bishop," KJV) in the sense of a hierarchical office that oversees a dioceses of churches is an invention of the second century and not in Paul's mind.

> **Ministry Maxim**
>
> No one should lead God's people who doesn't desire to do so.

Assuming that the condition is true, the Apostle then says, "it is a fine work he desires" (καλοῦ ἔργου ἐπιθυμεῖ). The expression is more literally, "a good work he desires." Good works is a recurring theme of the PE, and the combination of καλός and ἔργον is found also in 5:10 and 6:18. The combination of ἀγαθός and ἔργον is also found (e.g., 1 Tim. 2:10; 2 Tim. 2:21; 3:17; Titus 1:16; 3:1). The adjective καλός points to that which is aesthetically good or beautiful, while ἀγαθός points to that which is morally, ethically, and spiritually good.⁵ See on 2:10 for further information on the theme of good works in the PE. The noun "work" (ἔργου) is in the singular form to match the noun ἐπισκοπῆς ("the office of an overseer") and gathers up all the various duties and obligations of the office and views them as one work. The Apostle here commends the office, not necessarily the individual's desire for it.⁶ Perhaps the image of overseers/elders had suffered because of

---

² Friberg, 284.
³ BAGD, 299.
⁴ Mounce, 168.
⁵ Ibid., 32.
⁶ Fee, 79.

the false teachers who may have arisen from within the ranks of the elders (Acts 20:30). Paul wishes to elevate the office and work of an overseer/elder. It is this work which the one under consideration "desires" (ἐπιθυμεῖ). Paul uses this verb four other times, always of a negative desire (Rom. 7:7; 13:9; 1 Cor. 10:6; Gal. 5:17). The noun ἐπιθυμία is found six times in the PE, always in a negative sense (1 Tim. 6:9; 2 Tim. 2:22; 3:6; 4:3; Titus 2:12; 3:3). It can be used in a good sense as well, however (e.g., Matt. 13:17; Luke 22:15). It is a strong compound word made up of "upon" (ἐπί) and "to be angry" (θυμέω). It points to the intensity of the desire the prospective overseer may feel. It appears that such leadership positions were coveted by both men (i.e., false teachers) and women (2:13) in the Ephesian congregation. But the desire to be an overseer by itself does not qualify one for the office. Such a desire is a good initial signal to check for the qualifications that follow. An overseer should desire to serve in this way, but the desire may be found also among those who do not meet the qualifications that will be enumerated momentarily.

> **Digging Deeper:**
> 1. What might motivate an individual to desire the office of overseer/elder? Are all such motivations pure?
> 2. Why is the desire to serve as an overseer/elder a good starting point, but not a sufficient qualification in itself for such service?
> 3. How might the office of overseer/elder have become unattractive to the men in your congregation? Why is that?

3:2 An overseer, then, must be above reproach, the husband of one wife, temperate, prudent, respectable, hospitable, able to teach,

Having introduced the office ("the office of overseer," ἐπισκοπῆς, v.1), the Apostle now addresses the qualifications necessary of each officer ("An overseer," τὸν ἐπίσκοπον; lit., "*the* overseer"). He continues logically from the one to the other ("then," οὖν). The evidence seems to point to a plurality of leadership (i.e., multiple overseers/elders in each church), though the singular form is used here in a generic sense to designate "the category of those who give oversight to and teach the church."[7] The term used here is

---
[7] Knight, 155.

a compound word comprised of "over" (ἐπί) and "a watchman or observer" (σκοπός). The root noun is used in the NT only in Philippians 3:14 when he employs it to say, "I press on toward the *goal* [i.e., that which one set his eye upon] for the prize of the upward call of God in Christ Jesus" (emphasis mine). Thus as an "overseer" the elder is charged with watching over the whole of the congregation—not only to protect the congregation as a whole and its individual members, but also to guard the purpose and mission of the church.

The Apostle's concern here is with what each overseer "must be" (δεῖ). The word points to the compulsion of necessity according to what is fitting.[8] It "speaks of logical necessity according to the binding needs of the circumstances."[9] The present tense points to what is continually required. Paul files off fourteen qualifications of an overseer (vv.3b-6) before using the same verb again in v.7 ("must have," δεῖ) when a fifteenth qualification is listed. Here in v.2 the present tense infinitive "be" (εἶναι) also points to the continuous nature of the qualities looked for.

The first qualification is that the overseer must be "above reproach" (ἀνεπίλημπτον). The adjective is used only three times in the NT, all of them here in 1 Timothy. Later it is used of widows (5:7) and of Timothy himself (6:14). The word means literally "not to be laid hold of,"[10] in the sense that no ground of accusation may be found within a person. "The word implies not only that the man is of good report, but that he is deservedly so."[11] It has the sense of "inviolable" or "unassailable."[12] The point is not simply that no one has found a ground for accusation against the man, but that no such ground exists to be found (we might say there are no skeletons in his closet). By this Paul probably means basically the same thing he required of elders/overseers on Crete when twice he used the word ἀνέγκλητος ("above reproach," Titus 1:6-7) and here when he required it to be true of deacons (1 Tim. 3:10). It is likely that Paul begins his list with this word because he saw it as an overarching term under which the others could rightly be gathered up.

Next, an overseer must be "the husband of one wife" (μιᾶς γυναικὸς ἄνδρα), or, more literally, "an of one woman man." Just what this means in specific terms has been the topic of vociferous and volatile debate. This qualification stands not only for overseers, but also for deacons (1 Tim. 3:12). Paul also required this be true of the leaders of the church on Crete (Titus 1:6). It is obvious that this refers to a male and establishes the office of

---

[8] BAGD, 172.
[9] Rienecker, 622.
[10] Friberg, 55.
[11] Rienecker, 622.
[12] Kittel, abridged, 496.

overseer as a position of male leadership. Beyond this, some of the suggested options are: 1) the overseer must be married, 2) a married overseer must never divorce, 3) a married overseer must never remarry after a divorce, 4) an overseer who is a widower must never remarry, 5) an overseer must not be a polygamist (he must be married to only one wife at a time), 6) an overseer must be faithful to the wife he has, not a man of wandering eyes or adulterous relationships.

If number 1 was Paul's intent, it seems an odd way to express it. Few would say that when Paul later demands that the overseer keep "his children under control" (v.4), he is insisting that an overseer must have at least two children.[13] Besides, Paul was single and considered himself as an overseer/elder (1 Cor. 7:7-8, 32-35; 9:1-5). Paul surely did not intend these words to restrict a widower from serving as an elder, nor would remarriage disqualify him (#4), since elsewhere he teaches that the death of a spouse frees a believer to remarry (Rom. 7:1-3; 1 Cor. 7:8-9; 1 Tim. 5:14). Clearly number 5 should be true, but polygamy was a rare occurrence in the pagan culture of the day and would not likely have required space in such a list. And, as Fee shows, it would not fit the nearly identical expression when applied to widows (1 Tim. 5:9).[14] Number 6 should also be true, but is this all that the Apostle intended here? The greatest energy in contemporary debate has centered on numbers 2 and 3. The answer to these two options requires a good deal of exegesis in other passages (such as Matt. 5:31-32; 19:1-12; Mark 10:1-12; Luke 16:18; 1 Cor. 7:10ff) and solving the larger debate of the place of divorce and divorce and remarriage within the church generally. But for further discussion see our comments on Titus 1:6.

The overseer must also be "temperate" ($\nu\eta\phi\acute{\alpha}\lambda\iota o\nu$). The word is used only three times in the NT. This quality was also required of the women in v.11 and of the "older men" of Crete (Titus 2:2). It literally means "holding no wine." Strictly speaking it referred originally to abstinence from alcoholic beverages. However, the word then came to be used more broadly to describe self-control in the appetites and desires generally.[15] Paul's use of the word in Titus 2:2 in the context of some concern about gluttony and drunkenness (1:12 and 2:3) may indicate that he intends the word to retain some of its original, literal meaning.[16] But here the issue of alcohol seems to be addressed more directly in v.3 ("not addicted to wine"). Thus, without entirely losing the literal sense, it probably tends here toward the broader, more general, meaning.

An overseer should also be "prudent" ($\sigma\acute{\omega}\phi\rho o\nu\alpha$). The word is used in the

---

[13] Knight, 157.
[14] Fee, 80.
[15] Rienecker, 622.
[16] Marshall, 240.

NT only here and in Titus (1:8; 2:2, 5). It means prudent, thoughtful, and self-controlled.[17] It describes a person "as having ability to curb desires and impulses so as to produce a measured and orderly life *self-controlled, sensible*."[18] This same quality is to characterize all older men (Titus 2:2), and the older women are to possess this quality and teach the younger women to do the same (2:5).

An overseer is also to be "respectable" (κόσμιον). This adjective comes from the noun κόσμος (the ordered world). It describes that which is "well-arranged, well-ordered, moderate, modest."[19] Its only other use is found in 1 Timothy 2:9 where it describes a woman's "proper" (κοσμίῳ) clothing. Thus an overseer's entire life must be under control, ordered under the larger mission of living a life of honor to God and ministry to others.

The overseer must also be "hospitable" (φιλόξενον). The word is used elsewhere in the NT only in Titus 1:8 and 1 Peter 4:9. The compound word strictly means "stranger-loving," being made up of φίλος ("love") and ξένος ("strange" or "foreign"). This is an interesting shift from the more common, and perhaps more expected, brotherly-love (φιλαδελφία), which is often called for by the churches. With "hospitable" there is no payback, no family obligation, no blood-lines to make one feel obligated. There is no earthly human reason to love the stranger. Yet just such a practical expression of love for strangers is made the obligation of all believers (Rom. 12:13; 1 Tim. 5:10; Heb. 13:2; 1 Peter 4:9). While required of all, church leaders are to lead the way in showing the body of Christ how to do so. Finally, this was a vivid and regular part of Hebrew society. Community residents were almost under obligation to take in the traveling stranger who stopped in the city for a night of rest. But hospitality has fallen on hard times in a day when privacy and individuality are valued above community.

> **Ministry Maxim**
>
> When it comes to spiritual leaders, go with character over giftedness every time.

Then the overseer must also be "able to teach" (διδακτικόν). Paul shifts here from required character qualities to a required skill. The word is found elsewhere only in 2 Timothy 2:24 where its meaning is expanded by what follows in vv.25-26. Paul later instructs, "The elders who rule well are to be considered worthy of double honor, especially those who work hard at preaching and teaching" (1 Tim. 5:17). The Apostle strikes a similar note when he instructs Titus regarding the qualifications of an elder: "holding fast the faithful word

---

[17] BAGD, 802.
[18] Friberg,373.
[19] Rienecker, 620.

which is in accordance with the teaching, so that he will be able both to exhort in sound doctrine and to refute those who contradict" (Titus 1:9) Similarly here this qualification may have in view not only the instruction of the faithful in what is true, but the correction of the false teachers and their followers regarding what they have erroneously set forth (cf. 1 Tim. 6:3-5). Thus the emphasis may not be on the ease with which one speaks in front of people, but on the ability to know and understand truth and its implications along with cogently reasoning through arguments and presenting a clear understanding and application of those truths so others understand them. Overseers were charged with teaching in the congregation (1 Tim. 5:17), but apparently others were also allowed to teach (2 Tim. 2:2) and is seems here that the prospective overseer's ability to teach would be evident prior to his being placed in the office.[20]

Digging Deeper:
1. Is it legitimate to view these qualifications for overseers as an ideal for all Christian manhood? Why or why not?
2. In practical terms how might a local church employ this list of qualifications as they select or recognize those whom God is lifting up as overseers?
3. Why is there only one skill-related qualification among many character-related qualifications? What does this tell us?

3:3 not addicted to wine or pugnacious, but gentle, peaceable, free from the love of money.

An overseer must be "not addicted to wine" (μὴ πάροινον). The word is a compound made up of "beside" (παρά) and "wine" (οἶνος).[21] It thus describes one who sits too long over his wine, thus drinking to excess and becoming drunk. Every usage of the word in Hellenistic Greek or Jewish literature describes one addicted to wine.[22] The concern here is not whether an overseer should practice total abstinence, but the matter of drunkenness and addiction. The same requirement is held forth for the elders of Crete (Titus 1:7); these are the only two uses of this word in the NT.

Neither is an overseer to be "pugnacious" (μὴ πλήκτην). In its most

---
[20] Marshall, 478.
[21] Thayer, 490.
[22] DNTT, 1:514.

literal sense the word depicts "a striker." Our word "pugnacious" is thus related to the word "pugilist" (i.e., boxer). It describes one who wants to use physical force to settle disagreements. As we apply this, however, we need not think only of physical striking, but also of any form of physical intimidation or violence employed to win an argument, make a point or manipulate others. God's work is not accomplished through such means. The word is also listed in the qualifications for eldership in Titus 1:7. The fact that in both contexts this word about physical violence is mentioned in connection with alcohol's influence may speak to the nature of alcohol's effects upon the human mind and underscores why its use is discouraged.

The Apostle next used the strong adversative ("but," ἀλλὰ) to mark the utter distinction between the two negative qualities just spoken of and the two positive qualities he is about to enumerate. Thus he adds that an overseer is to be "gentle" (ἐπιεικῆ). The word "gentle" (ἐπιεικεῖς) is a compound made up of "over" (ἐπί) and "reasonable" (εἰκός). The preposition in compound intensifies the meaning. It "denotes a humble, patient steadfastness, which is able to submit to injustice, disgrace, and maltreatment without hatred and malice, trusting in God in spite of it all."[23] The adjective is found only five times in the NT, three of them in Paul's writings (Phil. 4:5; 1 Tim. 3:3; Titus 3:2; James 3:17; 1 Peter 2:18). The noun form is found in Acts 24:4 and 2 Corinthians 10:1, the latter of these holding forth Christ as the model of this virtue.

An overseer is also to be "peaceable" (ἄμαχον). This word and the previous one both appear together also in Titus 3:2 (the only other NT appearance of this word). This word comes from the root μάχη (rendered "quarrels" in 2 Tim. 2:23 and "disputes" in Titus 3:9) and is negated by the addition of the alpha privative. In secular Greek writings it meant "not to be withstood" or "invincible." In the NT it means not to fight or, stated positively, to be "peaceable."[24]

> **Ministry Maxim**
>
> Controlling one's self is the precursor to commanding the respect of others.

Additionally, an overseer is to be "free from the love of money" (ἀφιλάργυρον). This adjective appears elsewhere in the NT only in Hebrews 13:5. The word is a compound made up of "love" (φιλ-) and "silver" (ἄργυρος) with the alpha privative for negation. Thus the word demands that no greediness be found in an overseer. The same word without the alpha privative is used to describe both the Pharisees of Jesus' day and the people of the last days as "lovers of money" (Luke 16:14; 2 Tim.

---

[23] Rienecker, 485.
[24] Thayer, 31.

3:2).[25] In the Apostle's instructions to Titus about the qualifications for overseers, he said they must be "not fond of sordid gain" (Titus 1:7) and he will demand the same of deacons momentarily (1 Tim. 3:8). Peter demanded that elders serve "not for sordid gain" (1 Peter 5:2). Clearly spiritual leadership gives opportunity for greed to grow in a man's heart. In Ephesus there were those who thought "that godliness is a means of gain" (1 Tim. 6:5) and in Crete there were those "teaching things they should not teach for the sake of sordid gain" (Titus 1:11). In this matter Paul had set an example among the elders of Ephesus (Acts 20:33). The positive quality that delivers from this cancerous covetousness is contentment, as is clear from Hebrews 13:5 (the only other occurrence of this word in the NT) and 1 Timothy 6:6-10.[26]

The Apostle demands that those who lead God's church must demonstrate self-control in their appetites ("not addicted to wine"), relationships ("not . . . pugnacious, but gentle, peaceable"), and material desires ("free from the love of money").

Digging Deeper:

1. What non-alcoholic abuses might be included under the prohibition "not addicted to wine"?
2. Beyond sheer physical violence, how might an individual fail the test of being "pugnacious"?
3. How does ministry provide a context for temptation regarding money and material things?

3:4 He must be one who manages his own household well, keeping his children under control with all dignity

The first portion of the Greek clause reads simply "the one whose house" (τοῦ ἰδίου οἴκου). The presence of the definite article singles out the man's own home (and thus his family) as the object of his management. It is not his business to manage other people's homes, but in his own home and family his leadership must be seen clearly. Later in the chapter, "house" (οἶκος) will become "the household of God (οἴκῳ θεοῦ, 3:15), a rich metaphor for the family of God. The phrase "one who manages" represents a participle (προϊστάμενον). The Greek text does not begin a new sentence

---

[25] Mounce, 177.
[26] Knight, 160.

here, so the expression "*He must* be" has been added by the translators to provide smooth English. A more literal translation would place a comma at the end of verse 3 and render the participle here "managing his own household well." The participle is in the present tense, pointing to an abiding and continuous exercise of such leadership. The middle voice pictures the overseer acting upon himself in order to take the lead in his home. Such leadership always takes initiative. In the present middle form the word means to "*put oneself (responsibly) at the head, lead, direct, rule*"[27] and thus "to be over, to superintend, preside over."[28] There is a clear sense of authority in the word. The verb is used eight times in the NT, all by Paul. Six of those are in the PE and four of those are here in 1 Timothy and have reference to the ministry of overseers (1 Tim. 3:4, 5, 12; 5:17). Indeed, it is used to describe the leadership an elder gives to the church as a whole (5:17), and thus the statement of 3:5 (where the verb is again repeated) makes a good deal more sense. He is to exercise this leadership "well" (καλῶς). The word points to what is fitting, appropriate and beautiful. This is not heavy-handed leadership. There is no dictatorial right implied here. The father/overseer understands those in his home and is fully engaged with its daily life and leads those allotted to his charge with understanding (1 Peter 3:7) and wisdom. Three of the four times καλῶς is found in the PE, it is connected to προΐστημι,[29] signaling something of the nature of the leadership required in the church.

> **Ministry Maxim**
>
> A man must control himself before he can control his children.

The second clause explains something of this leadership: "keeping his children under control with all dignity" (τέκνα ἔχοντα ἐν ὑποταγῇ, μετὰ πάσης σεμνότητος). The word "children" (τέκνα) is plural—not to demand that an overseer must have multiple children, but that if he has children (no matter the number), he must relate to them in the prescribed way. The participle "keeping" (ἔχοντα) means most basically "having" or "holding." The present tense demands that this action be taken repeatedly or habitually. It should be the normal course of his relationship to his children that he should have them "under control" (ἐν ὑποταγῇ) or, more literally, "in submission." The noun is used in the NT only three other times, all of them by Paul (2 Cor. 9:13; Gal. 2:5; 1 Tim. 2:11). It means "subjection, subordination, obedience."[30] See on 1 Timothy 2:11 for more detail regarding its meaning. It is

---

[27] Friberg, 329.
[28] Thayer, 539.
[29] Mounce, 178.
[30] BAGD, 847.

important to recognize that God does not single out just women (1 Tim. 2:11) and children (3:4) for this submission, but enjoins all believers to live thus under Christ through the Gospel (2 Cor. 9:13). The preposition (ἐν) describes the sphere in which the children are to live in relationship to their father. The parenting in view is not a dictatorial plotting of each step a child must take, but the maintaining of a broader sphere of submission and obedience that often allows them freedom of choice within that sphere. The result is to be, "children who believe, not accused of dissipation or rebellion" (Titus 1:6).

This parenting mandate the father/overseer must carry out "with all dignity" (μετὰ πάσης σεμνότητος). The word dignity (σεμνότητος) is used only three times in the NT, all of them by Paul in the PE (1 Tim. 2:2; 3:4; Titus 2:7). The word is applied here to overseers in their fatherly role, in 2:2 to all believers, and in Titus 2:7 of young men. The cognate adjective is used to speak of what should characterize deacons (1 Tim. 3:8), their wives (3:11), and of older men (Titus 2:2). The word pictures the kind of dignity, gravity, majesty or sanctity which would mark a person as worthy of respect.[31] Does Paul call for the "dignity" to be characteristic of the children ("his children obey him with proper respect," NIV; cf. NRSV) or of the father (as with NASU and ESV)? Given its application as the maturity aimed at by all God's people, it would be more appropriate to see it as here applied to the father/overseer.[32] The adjective "all" (πάσης) is used to underscore the all-encompassing nature of this respectable lifestyle. Not only is the overseer to keep his children "under control," but he is likewise to keep himself under control as he deals with them—a proposition that is sometimes equally challenging. In doing so he becomes one worthy of respect; not only from his children, but also from the watching world around him.

Digging Deeper:
1. Why is there a connection between a man's leadership of his home and his leadership in the church?
2. Does this put an elder at the mercy of his children?
3. How should a church respond when an elder's child(ren) is/are not under control?

---

[31] Thayer, 573.
[32] Mounce, 179.

3:5 (but if a man does not know how to manage his own household, how will he take care of the church of God?),

In something of a parenthetical statement the Apostle now gives the justification for the requirement set forth in v.4. The postpositive conjunction δέ is translated here as an adversative ("but"), yet in most modern English translations it is taken as introducing an explanatory statement ("for," e.g., ESV, NKJV, NRSV, NLT; untranslated in NIV). Friberg says it is used "most commonly to denote continuation and further thought development, taking its specific sense from the context."[33] Paul is advancing the thought of v.4 and it seems appropriate to translate it as "for" or to leave it untranslated. The conditional statement (εἰ + present indicative) is of the first class, assuming that it is true, in this case for the sake of argument. The supposition is that "a man [τις, more lit., "anyone"] does not know how to manage his own household" (τοῦ ἰδίου οἴκου προστῆναι οὐκ οἶδεν). The main verb is "know" (οἶδεν). The perfect tense is active in meaning. The verb (οἶδα, also used in 1:8, 9; 3:15) originally stressed the completeness of the knowledge, rather than the process of gaining that knowledge through experience or relationship (γινώσκω, not used in 1 Tim., but employed in 2 Tim. 1:18; 2:19; 3:1).[34] It is negated by οὐκ, indicating an individual who is devoid of the knowledge under consideration. Such knowledge relates to "his own household" (τοῦ ἰδίου οἴκου). The phrase is thrown forward for emphasis and contrasted with "the church of God," which will lead the next clause. The close interplay between these two expressions in this context highlights the growing use of the metaphor of a home/household/family to describe the church (Heb. 3:2-6; 10:21; 1 Peter 2:5; 4:17). Paul will make this connection explicit in v.15. The particular failure in view is that of "how to manage" (προστῆναι) his home and family. This is the same basic verb found in the previous verse, this time as an aorist indicative (see there for meaning).

> **Ministry Maxim**
>
> The life you live in private determines the ministry you can have in public.

With the protasis in place, the apodosis is now "how will he take care of the church of God?" (πῶς ἐκκλησίας θεοῦ ἐπιμελήσεται). The designation "the church of God" (ἐκκλησίας θεοῦ) is unique to Paul (1 Cor. 1:2; 10:32; 11:16; 2 Cor. 1:1; Gal. 1:13; 1 Thess. 2:14; 2 Thess. 1:4). In Acts 20:28 he refers to "the church of God" (τὴν ἐκκλησίαν τοῦ θεοῦ) while addressing the elders of this same church. Here the nouns are anarthrous, emphasizing "that this is a

---
[33] Friberg, 104.
[34] Mounce, 32, 486.

general principle about an 'overseer's' relationship to any church."³⁵ The genitive ("of God," θεοῦ) reminds us that the church is God's and He determines who may lead it. The verb "will . . . take care of" (ἐπιμελήσεται) is rare, used elsewhere in the NT only to describe the action of the good Samaritan toward the waylaid man, both in terms of personal care (Luke 10:34) and in the command he gave to the innkeeper, having made financial provision for the man (v.35). The verb is a compound and the preposition (ἐπί) in compound points either to the "direction of the mind toward the object cared for"³⁶ or the direction of the care itself toward something or someone.³⁷ In either case the two are not far apart. This word coupled with "manage" (προϊστάμενον) reveals the balance sought in the ministry of overseers. The office of overseer clearly carries authority, but it is to be carried out in tender care. "Paul intended that the church leader exhort his people to obedience not by ruling them with a heavy hand but by showing the care and compassion of a servant-leader (1 Pet 5:1-4)."³⁸

The Apostle indicates clearly that one's performance in the private sphere has consequence for one's fitness to lead in the more public sphere of ministry. Additionally, God's call to leadership not only affects the man who accepts it, but his family as well. A man's acceptance of the mantel of leadership in the church brings new expectation upon and exposure to his family.

Digging Deeper:

1. If the elder's ability to lead his home is part of his requirement to lead the church, how public should his family life be? When does that become unfair to his wife and children?
2. How can a church distinguish between the challenges of family life that confront everyone and an inability of an elder to lead his home effectively?
3. Who in the church should determine whether an individual elder meets this qualification?

3:6 and not a new convert, so that he will not become conceited and fall into the condemnation incurred by the devil.

The Apostle adds (the "and" is not represented in the Greek text and has been added by the translators) that an overseer be "not a new convert" (μὴ νεόφυτον).

---
³⁵ Knight, 163.
³⁶ Thayer, 240.
³⁷ Robertson, 4:573.
³⁸ Lea and Griffin, 112.

The noun is used only here in the NT and is the source of our English word neophyte. It means literally "newly-planted," being a compound word from νέος ("new," "fresh," "young") and φύω ("grow"). It is used here metaphorically to describe one who is a recent convert to Christ. The negation ("not," μὴ) demands that overseers be found from another, more mature group of disciples—those who have walked with Christ and proven themselves faithful. It appears that this means something similar to what Paul will require of deacons in v.10: "These men must also first be tested; then let them serve . . . if they are above reproach." By this time the church in Ephesus had been in existence for ten[39] to twelve[40] years. This same requirement was not given to Titus for the much younger church on Crete (Titus 1:6-9), apparently because all the believers were new in their faith. Yet Paul's instructions here to Timothy reflect the greater wisdom whenever it is possible.

The reason is stated negatively ("so that . . . not," ἵνα μὴ) and might be translated "lest" (cf. NASB). The concern is that if such a neophyte is thrust too quickly into leadership, "he will . . . become conceited" (τυφωθεὶς). The word means literally to wrap or fill with smoke. In the NT it is used figuratively and always in the passive voice. It comes, then, to describe one who is puffed up with pride or blinded by pride and conceit.[41] The word is used only three times in the NT, all by Paul. He directly applies it to the false teachers in Ephesus (1 Tim. 6:4) and more generally to the people who will characterize the last days (2 Tim. 3:4).

If an overseer falls prey to such pride, he would "fall into the condemnation incurred by the devil" (εἰς κρίμα ἐμπέσῃ τοῦ διαβόλου). Pride was the original sin and that which introduced evil into creation. The devil actively seeks to draw others into his pit. The main verb is "fall" (ἐμπέσῃ). It is used literally to describe falling into a pit (Matt. 12:11; Luke 6:39) and metaphorically of falling into the hands of robbers (Luke 10:36). Paul uses the word three times, once to speak of falling into temptation (6:9) and twice to speak of falling into judgment with the devil (3:6, 7). The only other NT use is in the dire warning, "It is a terrifying thing to fall into the hands of the living God" (Heb. 10:31). Here the aorist tense may see this fall as taking place at a point of time. The subjunctive mood removes the anticipated action one step from certainty, holding it out as a possibility depending upon other factors.

> **Ministry Maxim**
>
> Time does not equal maturity, but maturity always takes time.

---

[39] Mounce, 181.
[40] Kent, 130.
[41] Thayer, 633.

The previous participle ("he will . . . become conceited," τυφωθεὶς) points then to the conditions necessary for such a fall to transpire. Such a fall would be "into the condemnation incurred by the devil" (εἰς κρίμα . . . τοῦ διαβόλου). The definite article ("the," τοῦ) with "devil" (διαβόλου) makes clear it is the person of the devil that is under consideration (cf. 1 Tim. 3:7; 2 Tim. 2:26) and not some human slanderer (cf. usages in the PE without the definite article: 1 Tim. 3:11; 2 Tim. 3:3; Titus 2:3).[42] The genitive form means simply "of the devil" and could refer to the condemning accusations the devil casts upon one who falls to pride, but more likely it refers to the judgment that was passed on the devil for his own pride and into which he drags those who similarly succumb to hubris (cf. Isa. 14:12-15).[43] The translators of the NASU have pointed us in this direction with their rendering. The false teachers in Ephesus had grown proud (1 Tim. 6:3-4) and the Apostle said we could expect such arrogance to characterize the people of the last days (2 Tim. 3:4). Taking the lead can plant a seed that, when watered with self-conscious reflection, gives rise to the noxious weeds of self-importance. Younger believers should be spared this dangerous trial.

Digging Deeper:

1. What is it about the office and ministry of overseer/elder that makes its members particularly vulnerable to pride?
2. How long must a person be a believer before they are no longer considered a "new convert"?
3. Does Paul here require the mere passage of time or a growing maturity over time?
4. Why would a newer believer be more vulnerable to the pitfalls of pride than an older believer?

3:7 And he must have a good reputation with those outside the church, so that he will not fall into reproach and the snare of the devil.

The conjunction δέ ("and") serves as a continuative to move the discussion along to the final qualification for overseers, a list which began in v.2. As he did to begin the list, Paul uses "must" (δεῖ) to close the enumeration of these qualifications. See the discussion on v.2 for this word's meaning and implications. By

---

[42] Hiebert, *First Timothy*, 67.
[43] Ibid.

using the term as bookends to bracket the whole of the list, the Apostle is underscoring that these qualifications were not given merely as good advice, but as compulsory and authoritative. The Greek text contains the conjunction καὶ, which is left untranslated by the NASU, but might be rendered "also" (NIV).

The overseer is required to "have a good reputation" (μαρτυρίαν καλὴν ἔχειν). The present tense of the verb points to a present and abiding action. He does now possess and has for some time had such a reputation. To have "a good reputation" is to have lived such a life that those under consideration would bear witness (μαρτυρίαν) in a way that what they say would be fitting (the emphasis of καλὴν, cf. the comments on v.4) with the faith one possesses. This is to be true "with those outside the church" (ἀπὸ τῶν ἔξωθεν). The expression is more literally "from the ones outside," with "the church" being added by the translators for clarification. The Apostle regularly showed concern for the witness of believers to those outside the church (1 Cor. 10:32; Col. 4:5; 1 Thess. 4:12; 1 Tim. 5:14; 6:1; Titus 2:5, 8, 10; 3:2, 8).[44] Despite the Apostle's constant concern for "those outside," we should not lose sight of the fact that they were indeed on the "outside" looking in on the benefits of the salvation found in Christ. Only a radical regeneration could bring them *in* to enjoy the love and grace of God that is in Christ. It was to that end that Paul was concerned for proper leadership within the church.

The purpose of this qualification is then stated—not in terms of the benefit to the watching world, nor even to the church at large—but to the individual being considered for the office of overseer: "so that he will not fall into reproach and the snare of the devil" (ἵνα μὴ εἰς ὀνειδισμὸν ἐμπέσῃ καὶ παγίδα τοῦ διαβόλου). The negative purpose ("so that . . . not," ἵνα μὴ) might also be rendered "lest." The verb "fall" (ἐμπέσῃ) is the same one just used in v.6, which see for further details. The aorist tense sees the fall as a sudden event taking place at a moment in time, while the subjunctive mood holds the action as a possibility, the reality of which depends upon other factors. Such a fall would be "into reproach" (εἰς ὀνειδισμὸν). The noun has the sense of "reviling, disgrace, insult."[45] It is used five times in the NT, twice by Paul. In order to save us, Christ took upon Himself the reproaches that justly fell upon us for what we were and what we had done (Rom. 15:3). So we should willingly take on the reproaches that unjustly come to us because of our standing with Christ (Heb. 10:33; 11:26; 13:13). But here the "reproach" is that which would come upon one

> **Ministry Maxim**
>
> The mantel of leadership looks strangely like a bull's eye to the devil.

---

[44] Marshall, 484.
[45] BAGD, 570.

who now counts himself as a believer. A potential overseer should have a good reputation with the unbelievers around him or else he might become the object of their reproaches: not because of his faith in Christ, but because of some discernable fault in himself.

Likewise ("and," καὶ), a potential overseer who does not enjoy a good reputation with the unbelieving might fall into "the snare of the devil" (παγίδα τοῦ διαβόλου). The word "snare" (παγίδος) was used in a literal sense of a trap or snare employed in catching birds.[46] It became a metaphorical way of describing the dangers of temptation in this life (Luke 21:35). Such traps may include the pursuit of wealth (1 Tim. 6:9) and false doctrine (2 Tim. 2:26). There is no definite article here, so it more accurately is "*a* snare of the devil." We know that the evil one pursues and hunts believers in general (1 Peter 5:8), but here it is clear that he especially pursues the downfall of those in leadership. To accept a role of leadership in Christ's church is to invite the devil's attack. It would be unwise to place someone in such a position that already has vulnerabilities in his witness to the unbelieving world. The designation "devil" (τοῦ διαβόλου) marks him out as a slanderer. The definite article marks him out specifically as "*the* slanderer." The genitive is a subjective genitive, meaning that the snare is one set by the devil. The devil, through his pride, fell into condemnation and wishes to drag others into it with him (v.6). As one condemned, he in turn majors in slander though accusation and condemnation (Zech. 3:1-3; Rev. 12:10).

> **Digging Deeper:**
> 1. Just what does having "a good reputation" with unbelievers mean?
> 2. Does it mean they speak well of you and your commitment to Christ or does it mean that, whether or not they like you and your faith, they have to admit that you do stand for Christ?
> 3. What is the danger in church leadership falling "into reproach" with the unbelieving world?
> 4. In what way would a poor reputation with unbelievers make a person vulnerable to "the snare of the devil"?

3:8 Deacons likewise must be men of dignity, not double-tongued, or addicted to much wine or fond of sordid gain,

The Apostle now transitions from discussing overseers (vv.1-7) to considering "Deacons" (Διακόνους). The noun is used twenty-nine times in the NT,

---
[46] Ibid., 602.

twenty-one of which are found in Paul. It often has the general sense of a servant, helper or minister (e.g., Matt. 20:26; Rom. 15:8; 1 Tim. 4:6). It came, however, to be used also to designate a second office within the maturing church (Phil. 1:1), and is thus translated here "Deacons." While the overseers/elders focused their ministry upon leadership and teaching, the deacons seem to center their ministry upon serving the physical needs of the congregation, especially the disadvantaged (such as widows, cf. Acts 6:1-7). While the Acts 6 passage does not yet employ the title "Deacons" of the seven men chosen to serve the needs of widows, the related noun διακονία is used twice (vv.1, 4) and the verb διακονέω is used once (v.2). These men may have filled an embryonic role which the church grew to see as essential in all their congregations, making way for this second office within the local church. The NT does not define the role of deacon as clearly as it does that of the overseer/elder. There appears to be no parallel office within the Jewish synagogue. It is possible that in the outworking of the life and ministry of the church such ministry became obviously essential and that the office grew and was defined to some extent by the existing needs within the local churches. While many of the qualifications laid upon the overseers are repeated here for deacons, noticeably absent is "able to teach" (1 Tim. 3:2). The emphasis upon service enables the one who fills this role to free the overseers/elders to focus on their prescribed ministries of leadership and teaching.

As the Apostle prepares to list qualifications for service as a deacon, he uses the adverb "likewise" (ὡσαύτως) to head the list. It describes action being taken in a manner which is similar or undertaken in the same way. The link is clearly back to what has been said regarding overseers; the question remaining, just what exactly does it look back to? Since there is no main verb in this sentence, the likelihood is that it looks back to "must be" (δεῖ . . . εἶναι) in v.2 (and cf. v.7).[47] The NASU seems to represent such a view, as the translators have inserted "must be" (cf. also ESV, NKJV, NLT, NRSV).

The first qualification required of deacons is to be "men of dignity" (σεμνούς). The word describes that which is worthy of respect or honor, a person who is noble and dignified.[48] "The word denotes moral earnestness, affecting outward demeanor as well as interior intention."[49] The adjective and its cognate noun reveal that this quality should be true of our thoughts (Phil. 4:8) and the result of prayer (1 Tim. 2:2). Such should be true of overseers (1 Tim. 3:4), deacons (1 Tim. 3:8), deaconesses (3:11), and Paul's representative (Titus 2:7).

---

[47] Lenski, 594.
[48] Ibid., 747.
[49] Rienecker, 619.

Deacons must be "not double-tongued" (μὴ διλόγους). The adjective is a compound word comprised of δίς (twice) and λόγος (something said).[50] It is used only here in the NT. It means to say the same thing twice with the intent to communicate two different things on each occasion, and to thus be hypocritical, insincere and deceitful.[51] The negation ("not," μὴ) then means that the idea could be either "not saying one thing while thinking another" or "not saying one thing to one man and a different thing to the next."[52] The deacon must be a man whose "yes" means "yes" and whose "no" means "no" (Matt. 5:37). He says what he means and he means what he says. His words are reliable and he stands behind them.

Nor is he to be "addicted to much wine" (μὴ οἴνῳ πολλῷ προσέχοντας). The participle (προσέχοντας) means "turning or holding one's mind to someone or something" and thus "occupying one's mind with something."[53] It is used negatively of a preoccupation with myths (1 Tim. 1:4; Titus 1:14) and "deceitful spirits" (1 Tim. 4:1). It is used positively of a commitment to "public reading of Scripture" (4:13). The deacon is not to find himself constantly thinking about his next drink. By saying "much wine" (οἴνῳ πολλῷ), Paul does not categorically rule out the drinking of alcohol. In a world which struggled to provide clean, safe drinking water, alcohol was used as a purifying agent. It could have, in small amounts, some medicinal purposes (1 Tim. 5:23). Paul used the same expression in giving the ideals for older women (Titus 2:3), though there he employed a different verb. He also required overseers (1 Tim. 3:2; cf. 3:3; Titus 1:7), older men (Titus 2:2), and the wives of deacons (1 Tim. 3:11) to be "temperate." The believer is not to allow himself to come under the controlling influence of alcohol (or any other thing), but is commanded to be controlled by the Holy Spirit (Eph. 5:18).

> **Ministry Maxim**
>
> Serving to enable others to serve is a double-service.

Nor is the deacon to be "fond of sordid gain" (μὴ αἰσχροκερδεῖς). The same requirement was set forth for overseers in Titus 1:7 and the synonym ἀφιλάργυρος ("free from the love of money") was applied to elders in 1 Timothy 3:3. The term αἰσχροκερδῶς ("sordid gain") is found in reference to elders in 1 Peter 5:2.[54] Our present adjective is a compound made up of "shameful" (αἰσχρός) and "gain" (κέρδος). In Titus 1:11 the two words are

---

[50] Mounce, 199.
[51] Friberg, 117.
[52] Kelly, quoted in Rienecker, 623.
[53] Friberg, 333.
[54] Knight, 292.

separated, but used in union to describe the opponents of the Gospel on Crete ("for the sake of sordid gain"). Since spiritual leaders are in view in the NT usages, the word may refer to those who adjust their teaching or use their ministry to manipulate people of means to give gifts to them. The ministry of deacon may involve the handling of resources intended for the disadvantaged, thus giving opportunity for and leaving a vulnerability to such sin. Judas is an example of one such failure (John 12:6; 13:29).

> **Digging Deeper:**
> 1. In our contemporary setting how can deacons serve to free elders to fulfill their role?
> 2. How might a local church be impoverished in its corporate spiritual life without a strong deacon ministry?
> 3. Why is it sometimes difficult to find men to fill the role of deacon?

3:9 but holding to the mystery of the faith with a clear conscience.

The noun "mystery" (τὸ μυστήριον) was used in Paul's day by the mystery religions to speak of their secret teachings which were available only to the initiated and which were veiled to all others. Paul used the term in a variety of ways. He spoke of "this mystery" (Rom. 11:25), "the mystery" (Rom. 16:25; Eph. 3:3), or "a mystery" (1 Cor. 2:7; 15:51). Paul used it to point to something which had been previously veiled by God from humanity: "the administration of the mystery which for ages has been hidden in God" (Eph. 3:9), "the mystery which has been hidden from the past ages and generations" (Col. 1:26a). But that which was once veiled by God "has now been manifested to His saints" (Col. 1:26b). In His perfect plan, "God willed to make known what is the riches of the glory of this mystery among the Gentiles" (Col. 1:27). As Ralph Earle states it, "Today the word *mystery* implies knowledge withheld; in the Bible it indicates truth revealed."[55] The issue becomes, just what is the content of this mystery? Paul states this in a variety of ways. He speaks of the mystery which is "Christ in you, the hope of glory" (Col. 1:27) or "Christ Himself" (Col. 2:2). At various times it is called "the testimony [lit., "mystery"] of God" (1 Cor. 2:1), "the mysteries of God" (1 Cor. 4:1), "the mystery of His will" (Eph. 1:9), "the mystery of Christ" (Eph. 3:4; Col. 4:3), "the mystery of the gospel" (Eph. 6:19), and soon enough he will call it "the mystery of godliness" (1 Tim. 3:16).

Here "the mystery" (τὸ μυστήριον) is made definite by the use of the

---
[55] Earle, 11:367.

article. Its content is defined as "of the faith" (τῆς πίστεως). The use of the definite article here points to "*the* faith"–that is, the content of the Gospel of Jesus Christ. The genitive gives the content or substance of the mystery under consideration.[56]

This Gospel the deacon must be "holding . . . with a clear conscience" (ἔχοντας . . . ἐν καθαρᾷ συνειδήσει). The participle "holding" (ἔχοντας) here has the sense of "keep" or "preserve."[57] It points to that which must be happening as the other qualities (v.8) are found to be true as well. The present tense points to a constant or habitual action. This, says the Apostle, must be done "with a clear conscience" (ἐν καθαρᾷ συνειδήσει). When the preposition ἐν is found with the dative "the primary idea is *within, in, withinness*, denoting static position or time[58]," but the various nuances of meaning are vast and the individual context rules in determining each case. The exact expression "a clear conscience" (καθαρᾷ συνειδήσει) was used by Paul again in 2 Timothy 1:3, where he links it with how he served God. The word translated "conscience" is a compound word (συνειδήσει), combining "with" (συν) and "knowledge (εἶδον)." Such awareness is a joint-knowledge, shared with oneself. It is a self-awareness. Thus Paul can speak of "the testimony of our conscience" (2 Cor. 1:12). Conscience is a testimony given to oneself, and then passed on to others. The Apostle speaks of "a good conscience" (1 Tim. 1:5, 19), "a perfectly good conscience" (Acts 23:1), and "a blameless conscience" (Acts 24:16). Such a conscience is a gift from God, but can be distorted through sin. One's conscience can be "weak" through immaturity (1 Cor. 8:7), wounded through wrong (1 Cor. 8:12), "defiled" by sin (Titus 1:15), and "seared" to the point of insensitivity by repeated rebellion (1 Tim. 4:2). It is "clear" when it is free from dirt, filth, and that which would befoul it. This is not a demand for sinlessness, but for a conscience that is "clear" because one has walked in humility, quickly confessing and turning from any sin that comes to one's attention. Our conscience is a helpful guide only as it is conformed to the written revelation of God (2 Tim. 3:16-17). The false teachers in Ephesus had already rejected such a conscience (1 Tim. 1:5-6, 19-20),[59] so Paul makes certain those serving as deacons will not have done so.

> **Ministry Maxim**
>
> There is a direct correlation between one's conscience and one's grip on the faith.

---

[56] Rienecker, 623.
[57] BAGD, 332.
[58] Friberg, 147.
[59] Fee, 87.

> **Digging Deeper:**
> 1. In what sense could Paul rightly call the Gospel a mystery?
> 2. Why the imagery of "holding" the faith? What does this tell us about thus trusting Christ?
> 3. What happens to a person's service when their conscience is not clear?

3:10 These men must also first be tested; then let them serve as deacons if they are beyond reproach.

The sentence begins with the καὶ οὗτοι δὲ. The translators of the NASU have left the postpositive δὲ untranslated, rendering the καὶ with "also." The NASB has translated both, beginning the sentence, "And let these also" (cf. ESV, NRS). Hiebert says, "The 'also' indicates that the deacons, no less than the elders, must be tested before being placed into office. (The testing of the elders, although not stated before, is self-evident from the requirements laid down concerning them.)"[60] The demonstrative pronoun οὗτοι ("These") is plural and points back to the deacons under consideration in vv.8-9. The Apostle demands that they "must . . . first be tested" (δοκιμαζέσθωσαν πρῶτον). The verb has both the sense of testing (2 Cor. 13:5) and approving (Phil. 1:10) something, or approving something after testing. It was used in the world of metallurgy to describe the scrutiny employed to test the genuineness of metal. As such, then, it was used to describe both the scrutiny itself and the resulting approval of the genuine article.[61] The present tense imperatival form demands that the action be taken repeatedly—such testing should extend over an indefinite period of time. This likely does not refer to a formal period of testing, but to the ongoing witness of such a candidate in the midst of the church.[62] In this way the requirement is not unlike that for overseers which required that candidates not be new converts (v.6; cf. 1 Tim. 5:22). This testing should always take place when selecting deacons in the local congregation. The passive form is represented by the NASB with "let . . . be tested" (note the change in the NASU; cf. also ESV, KJV, NLT, NRS). The testing is to take place "first" (πρῶτον), that is to say, before they begin their service as deacons. The exact nature of the testing is not spelled out, but it would certainly at least have to do with determining whether the requirements laid out here (vv.8-12) are met in each individual being considered for the office of deacon. Strangely, no such examination is mentioned for elder/overseers. Yet, as already mentioned, it does

---
[60] Hiebert, *First Timothy*, 69.
[61] Thayer, 154.
[62] Hiebert, *First Timothy*, 70.

appear to be assumed, for how else could the church determine whether the individual candidates met the requirements the Apostle laid down for them (vv.2-7)?

If they have been so examined, "then let them serve as deacons" (εἶτα διακονείτωσαν). The adverb εἶτα ("then") is used in a temporal way, indicating a time sequence in what is next.[63] The verb (διακονέω) is often translated generally with words like "serve" or "minister" (e.g., Matt. 4:11; Luke 10:45). Originally it described waiting upon tables (e.g., Matt. 8:15; Luke 10:40; 12:37; John 12:2). In fact it is the word used in the context of the original need that gave rise to what may have been the forerunners of the NT deacons (Acts 6:2). But because the context here is clearly centered on the overall ministry of deacons (vv.8-9), and because it is the verbal cognate of the noun διάκονοι ("deacons," v.8), it is here translated "let them serve as deacons." The same verb will be used again in v.13. Here the present tense imperative calls for continual, unceasing action.

> **Ministry Maxim**
>
> Those who lead will be tested, so test them carefully before they lead.

This service should take place "if they are beyond reproach" (ἀνέγκλητοι ὄντες). The translators have determined that the participle (ὄντες) should be translated as a conditional statement ("if they are"). This probably captures the sense well, though it might simply be translated "being beyond reproach." The adjective (ἀνέγκλητοι, "beyond reproach") is the same one used as a requirement for overseers in Titus 1:6, 7 (cf. the synonym in 1 Tim. 3:2). The word strictly means not having been called up or arraigned before a judge.[64] It then has the sense of being without charge or accusation, and thus irreproachable.[65] In the only other NT usages it describes the state in which all believers will stand before God at Christ's return (1 Cor. 1:8; Col. 1:22). The term is likely used here to summarize all the other qualifications mentioned regarding deacons (vv.8-9, 12).

Digging Deeper:
1. What dangers can be avoided by testing and approving candidates before they are placed in positions of leadership within the local church?
2. If the testing demanded by Paul is not formal, what then makes up the test? Who administers the test? What is the standard against which someone is tested?

---

[63] BAGD, 233-234.
[64] Friberg, 54.
[65] Rienecker, 623.

3:11 Women must likewise be dignified, not malicious gossips, but temperate, faithful in all things.

The Apostle makes an unannounced and unanticipated transition away from the qualifications for deacons (vv.8-10). He will return momentarily to that discussion (vv.12-13), but at present he is concerned with "Women" (γυναῖκας). Paul has already proven in this letter that the word can describe *women* generally (2:9, 10, 11, 12, 14) and a man's *wife* specifically (3:2). Indeed, in the next verse he will use it in the latter sense (cf. also 5:9). The question then becomes. In which sense does he use it here? Is he addressing the wives of deacons or female deacons (i.e., deaconesses)?

In favor of understanding the meaning generally to refer to "women" (and thus female deacons or deaconesses) are the following arguments. 1) The use of the adverb ὡσαύτως ("likewise") parallels its use in v.8. There it introduced deacons as a new category of church office separate from, but comparable to, the office of overseer. Similarly it here introduces the office of deaconess as separate from, but comparable to that of deacon. 2) The qualifications set forth here, though briefer, are comparable to those set forth for deacons. 3) The Apostle sets forth no special requirements for the wives of overseers. It seems odd, then, that he would do so here for the wives of deacons. 4) Phoebe is elsewhere referred to as a deacon (Rom. 16:1). It seems reasonable to conclude that Paul sets forth here the requirements for such female servants. 5) This sentence is dependent upon "must be" (δεῖ ... εἶναι) from v.2, just as v.8 was. This too suggests that Paul was intending to start a new discussion on a new category of worker. 6) There was as yet no feminine form of the word διάκονος (servant, deacon), so the Apostle would not have had the option of using such a word. Thus he chose the more general term (γυνή, woman), knowing he would be understood in his reference. 7) If Paul's intent had been to refer to the wives of the deacons, he would have likely used either the definite article or a pronoun to connect them as such to the deacons. But neither of these is present in the Greek text (despite the "*their* wives" of the ESV, KJV, NIV, NLT). 8) Some argue that Paul has limited women's involvement in ministry (2:11-15) and that this means he is unlikely to designate here a church office for women. However, the role of deacons did not apparently carry the same responsibility as overseers with regard to teaching and authoritative oversight. Thus it would hold to reason that neither would the role of the deaconesses. Paul, rather than holding women out of ministry, often commended them for their service to God and the church (e.g., Rom. 16:1-4, 6, 12).

The following arguments are set forth in favor of understanding the meaning of the word to refer to the "wives" of deacons. 1) Paul surrounds this sentence with qualifications regarding deacons (vv.8-10, 12-13). It seems unlikely he would introduce a new category of worker only to return to the previous office he had been discussing. It is more reasonable, it is argued, to believe he parenthetically refers to the wives of deacons here. 2) If a new office is under consideration, one would expect more detail regarding the qualifications for such an office. The women in view here are treated only briefly, something more to be expected if wives of deacons are under consideration. 3) There is no mention here as to the marital status of the women under consideration, something that is done elsewhere in the PE when a church office is under consideration (vv.2, 12; Titus 1:6). This would seem to support the notion that the women under consideration are already married to the deacons discussed in vv.8-10, 12-13.[66] 4) The fact that no definite article or pronoun is found with "women" (γυναῖκας) is answered by the fact that throughout the pericope Paul speaks of people anarthrously.[67] 5) The same word (γυνή) is used in the next verse with the clear meaning "wives." 6) Because Paul has limited the role of women in ministry (2:11-15), it seems unlikely that he is here designating them for a church office.

The following versions support the translation "wives": ESV (marginal note, "*Wives*, or *Women*"), KJV, NEB (marginal note, "Deaconesses"), NIV (marginal note, "deaconesses"), NLT (marginal note, "Or *the women deacons*"), TEV (marginal note, "Their wives; or Women helpers"). The following support the translation "women": Amplified, JB, NASB and NASU (marginal note, "I.e., either deacons' wives or deaconesses"), NRSV (marginal note, "Or *Their wives*, or *Women deacons*").

While any conclusion must be tentative, in the end the evidence, it seems to this author, falls out more strongly in favor of a translation of "women" (rather than "wives"). The more ancient interpreters generally viewed it as such[68] and the majority of modern scholars concur. Paul probably had in mind some level of recognized female servants within the local church—perhaps a prototype of what in due

> **Ministry Maxim**
>
> Female servants of the Lord are often the strength of a church's ministry.

time would become the full-blown office of deaconess. While a deacon's wife might fulfill this role, it is doubtful that she was required to do so.

These women have their own set of qualifications, and these stand both in contrast to the qualities some women in the Ephesian church displayed (1 Tim. 5:11-15; 2 Tim. 3:6-7) and parallel to the requirements for deacons (1 Tim.

---

[66] Knight, 171.
[67] Ibid., 172.
[68] Hiebert, *First Timothy*, 70.

3:8-9). They must be "dignified" (σεμνάς). The same requirement was just placed on deacons (see discussion on v.8), though the feminine form of the word is used here.

A second requirement is to be "not malicious gossips" (μὴ διαβόλους; cf. "not double-tongued" for deacons, v.8). In the only other use of the expression, Paul called on Titus to require this of all older women on Crete (Titus 2:3). The word translated "malicious gossips" is more literally "devils." The masculine singular form of the word is always used of the devil himself. Robertson suggests "she-devils" as a translation.[69] The word means "slanderer." The masculine plural is also used in 2 Timothy 3:3 to describe what will be true of both males and females generally in the last days. Jesus told the unbelieving Jews, "You are of your father the devil, and you want to do the desires of your father . . . Whenever he speaks a lie, he speaks from his own nature, for he is a liar and the father of lies" (John 8:44). Similarly, Satan is called "the accuser of our brethren . . . who accuses them before our God day and night" (Rev. 12:10). Those who in like fashion falsely accuse and slander others are operating in the devil's realm and advancing his cause. It is sad how often conversation in "Christian" circles can slip into such talk.

The third qualification is "temperate" (νηφαλίους; "but" is not found in the Greek text and is added by the translators of the NASU). The word is used elsewhere in the NT only to describe the qualifications for overseers (see discussion above on v.2) and older men on Crete (Titus 2:2). It possibly retains here more of its original sense ("holding no wine") since it might be seen as standing in parallel with the qualification for deacons which requires him to be not "addicted to much wine" (v.8).

The fourth and final qualification is that these women be "faithful in all things" (πιστὰς ἐν πᾶσιν; perhaps parallel to the requirements of v.9 for deacons[70]). The adjective means trustworthy, reliable or believing. Perhaps the sense of "trustworthy" fits the present context best. The adjective is found seventeen times in the PE (and sixteen times by Paul in his other letters), underscoring the critical importance of faithfulness in local church ministry. In the PE it describes God (2 Tim. 2:13), truth statements about Him (1 Tim. 1:15; 3:1; 4:9; 2 Tim. 2:11; Titus 3:8), ministering men (2 Tim. 2:2), ministering women (1 Tim. 3:11; 5:16), children of overseers (Titus 1:6), true teaching (Titus 1:9), all believers (1 Tim. 4:3, 10), Timothy (1 Tim. 4:12), and slave owners (1 Tim. 6:2). The trustworthiness of these women must be "in all things" (ἐν πᾶσιν). This prepositional phrase becomes a favorite of the Apostle in the PE: "understanding in everything" (2 Tim. 2:7), "sober in all

---

[69] Robertson, 4:575.
[70] Knight, 172.

things" (2 Tim. 4:5), "subject . . . in everything" (Titus 2:9), and "adorn the doctrine of God our Savior in every respect" (Titus 2:10). As Kent says, "She must be faithful to her husband, to her family, to Christ, and to the church."[71] Unfaithfulness in one area is an indicator of a potential weakness in another (Luke 16:10). Life cannot be compartmentalized. Private life does affect public ministry. Only those who are faithful in little are to be entrusted with the "much" of ministry within the church (19:17).

> **Digging Deeper:**
> 1. In your estimation, does this verse refer to the wives of deacons or to female deacons? Why?
> 2. Why do you suppose the Apostle felt it necessary to emphasize the four qualities he did here in regard to these women? What might this say about the potential vulnerabilities or dangers of their service and position?
> 3. What significance should we find in the fact that "faithfulness" is so often a requirement of someone involved in ministry?

3:12 Deacons must be husbands of only one wife, and good managers of their children and their own households.

Paul returns to the discussion of "Deacons" (διάκονοι; vv.8-10) after a parenthesis to deal with the female servants of v.11. He sets forth here the domestic qualifications for such servants. The present tense imperative "must be" (ἔστωσαν) demands that they "be" continually in the prescribed state. Knight points out that, "The imperative ἔστωσαν substitutes for δεῖ εἶναι, which has been understood since its appearance in v.2."[72] That state is "husbands of only one wife" (μιᾶς γυναικὸς ἄνδρες; lit., "one woman men"). This is the precise statement applied to overseers (v.2), except that the final noun ("men," ἄνδρες) is plural rather than singular ("man," ἄνδρα). See the discussion on v.2.

> **Ministry Maxim**
>
> A man's home life and ministry will always follow similar lines of trajectory.

In addition they must be "good managers of their children" (τέκνων καλῶς προϊστάμενοι). The requirement to be "good managers" (καλῶς προϊστάμενοι) is identical to the demand for overseers in v.4,

---
[71] Kent, 137.
[72] Knight, 173.

except that the case and number of the noun have changed from accusative singular to nominative plural. See the discussion on vv.4-5. There it was "his own household" (τοῦ ἰδίου οἴκου) he was to manage well; here it is their "children" (τέκνων). This does not require deacons to have children, only to manage them well if they do. That his point is the same is seen in that the Apostle immediately adds ("and," καὶ) "their own households" (τῶν ἰδίων οἴκων) here as well.

3:13 For those who have served well as deacons obtain for themselves a high standing and great confidence in the faith that is in Christ Jesus.

Paul now gives an explanation (γὰρ, "for") for the qualifications for deacons he has just set forth (vv.8-10, 12). He is discussing the male deacons, for he uses the masculine plural form of the definite article along with the participle in a substantive way ("those," οἱ). Nevertheless, the argument he makes surely would apply to the female servants of v.11 as well, just as it would the overseers of vv.2-7. The concern here is "those who have served well as deacons" (καλῶς διακονήσαντες). The verb is the same one used in v.10 and thus likely means here, as there, "serve as deacons." See the discussion on v.10. It is possible, however, that Paul had in mind a more general reference to the service of all who are named as servants of the church in this chapter. Elsewhere in the NT the word describes service generally. Though it likely is intended to describe the service of deacons (given the immediate context), the promise of this verse would no doubt apply to all who have been discussed in this chapter as serving God's church. This service has been rendered "well" (καλῶς). The adverb was used to describe the good management of the home by both the overseer (v.4) and the deacon (v.12). Now it characterizes the whole of the deacon's service. Such service is fitting, appropriate and beautiful according to the need of the moment and the individuals involved.

The aorist tense of the participle ("served well as deacons") points to the length of time in which the deacon has served as such.[73] Those who thus serve will "obtain for themselves a high standing" (βαθμὸν ἑαυτοῖς καλὸν περιποιοῦνται). The verb is found only three times in the NT (Luke 17:33; Acts 20:28; 1 Tim. 3:13) and always in the middle voice, which is used reflexively. To this is added the reflexive pronoun "themselves" (ἑαυτοῖς) to underscore that their actions in good service are destined to come back upon themselves in the form of rewards. The present tense of the verb points to the fact that they "are obtaining" this reward in a continual, ongoing sense. As Mounce states it, "The linear aspect of the verb ... indicates that Paul is describing an ongoing process. It is not so much that by being a good deacon

---

[73] Hiebert, *First Timothy*, 71.

a person will receive rewards; it is in the actual doing of the service that one daily acquires a better standing before the people and more confidence in one's faith."[74] The verb here means to achieve, gain or acquire for oneself.[75]

That which is gained is twofold. First, deacons gain "a high standing" (βαθμὸν). The word is used only here in the NT. It originally spoke of stairs or steps (e.g., 1 Sam. 5:5, LXX).[76] It could also refer to a base or foundation, as of a pedestal. It began, over time, to be used metaphorically also, as it is here. Some have seen this as a step up to the office of overseer for those who have proven themselves as deacons. This, however, seems to miss Paul's point here and has no support from anywhere else in Scripture. It could be understood here to refer to a special standing in the sight of God or of some level of reputation or influence gained among the congregation.[77] In light of the second part of this twofold blessing, it probably refers to the reputation of standing gained among the congregation.

> **Ministry Maxim**
>
> Serving well in the past builds confidence for serving well in the future.

Secondly ("and," καὶ), deacons gain "great confidence" (πολλὴν παρρησίαν). The noun is a compound made up of πᾶς (all) and ῥῆσις (speaking). It literally means "to say it all." It thus came to describe boldness, openness and confidence. Such confidence is magnified even more for it is "great" (πολλὴν). It is not confidence in any and all areas, but "in the faith that is in Christ Jesus" (ἐν πίστει τῇ ἐν Χριστῷ Ἰησοῦ). This prepositional phrase, in fact, governs both "a high standing" and "great confidence." The exact expression is found only here in the NT, but the prepositional phrase "in faith" (ἐν πίστει) is found eleven times in the NT, nine of those in Paul and all but one of those in the PE (Gal. 2:20; 1 Tim. 1:2, 4; 2:7, 15; 3:13; 4:12; 2 Tim. 1:13; Titus 3:15). The fuller expression here is closest to the similar statement in 2 Timothy 1:13. This could describe confidence toward God (Eph. 3:12) or in service and witness to others (2 Cor. 3:12; Phil. 1:20; Philem. 8).[78] The latter would be more in parallel with the first of these two rewards, the later would provide a balancing reward before both God and man. The fact that this confidence is said to be "in faith" (without the definite article, contra "in *the* faith that is in Christ Jesus", NASU, emphasis added) probably points it to the individual's personal faith (cf. NIV, "great assurance in their faith in Christ Jesus"). It also seems more likely that the qualifying prepositional phrase ("in Christ Jesus") would point to the individual's personal faith.[79]

---

[74] Mounce, 205.
[75] Rienecker, 624.
[76] Robertson, 4:575.
[77] Rienecker, 624.
[78] Fee, 89.
[79] Lea and Griffin, 119.

> **Digging Deeper:**
> 1. How does "These men must also first be tested" (v.10) prior to their appointment relate to obtaining through their faithful service "a high standing" in the eyes of the congregation?
> 2. How does a track record of faithful service rightly build a servant's image in the eyes of his congregation?
> 3. How does a track record of faithful service over time engender greater confidence in Christ for facing future ministry challenges?

3:14 I am writing these things to you, hoping to come to you before long;

The Apostle reveals here his intent to visit Timothy soon (v.14) and the purpose of this letter (v.15). Just where Paul was as he penned this letter is not entirely clear, but his intent to make his way to Timothy speedily underscores both the severity of the issues in Ephesus and his love for the young man. The expression "these things" (Ταῦτά) is used in PE (4:6, 11, 15; 5:7, 21; 6:2, 11; cf. 2 Tim. 1:12; 2:2, 14; Titus 2:14, 15; 3:8) primarily to designate the things that have preceded.[80] Thus Paul is probably making reference to the instruction of chapters 1-3, rather than what he will now write in chapters 4-6, though surely this would not be excluded. Paul has not directly addressed Timothy since 1:3, 18,[81] but will now begin to do so much more regularly (4:12, 14, 15, 16; 5:23; 6:11, 13, 14, 21). The participle "hoping" (ἐλπίζων) is probably used concessively to mean something like "even though I hope."[82] The expression "before long" (ἐν τάχει) is used eight times in the Bible, twice by Paul (Rom. 16:20; 1 Tim. 3:14). It means "without delay," "at once," or "speedily."[83] Did Paul make it to Ephesus as planned? We cannot be certain, but he called on Titus about this time to join him in Nicopolis for the winter (Titus 3:12). Perhaps Paul planned on a quick trip to Ephesus, then returning to Nicopolis where he would meet Titus.[84]

> **Ministry Maxim**
>
> One's pen and one's presence can work together powerfully in ministry.

---

[80] Mounce, 219.
[81] Marshall, 505.
[82] Ibid.; Fee, 91; Knight, 179.
[83] Friberg, 376.
[84] Lenski, 605.

3:15 but in case I am delayed, I write so that you will know how one ought to conduct himself in the household of God, which is the church of the living God, the pillar and support of the truth.

Despite his best intentions to leave post haste (v.14), Paul was as yet uncertain of the speed with which he might make his departure. The sentence continues with the conjunction δέ ("but") used as a mild adversative. The Apostle knew that certain contingencies could come up and delay his departure, so he says, "in case I am delayed" (ἐὰν . . . βραδύνω). The condition created by the conjunction and the present subjunctive is undetermined as to its fulfillment, speaking of what is probable, but as yet uncertain. The verb ("I am delayed," βραδύνω) is used only here and 2 Peter 3:9.

In view of his possible delay in arrival at Ephesus, Paul has written regarding his purpose for penning this letter (ἵνα, "so that"). The translators rightly assume the verb "I write," though it is missing from the Greek text. The line literally reads, "in order that you may know how it is necessary in God's house to live" (ἵνα εἰδῇς πῶς δεῖ ἐν οἴκῳ θεοῦ ἀναστρέφεσθαι). The verb "you may know" (εἰδῇς) is a defective perfect with a present tense meaning. It (οἶδα, also used in 1:8, 9; 3:5) originally stressed the completeness of the knowledge, rather than the process of gaining that knowledge through experience or relationship (γινώσκω, not used in 1 Tim., but employed in 2 Tim. 1:18; 2:19; 3:1).[85] Rienecker says, "The word was used to describe 'know how'; i.e., the possession of knowledge or skill necessary to accomplish a desired goal."[86] The second person singular form points to Timothy as the intended possessor of this knowledge. That which should be so thoroughly known is how one "ought" (δεῖ) to live. The word points to the compulsion of necessity according to what is fitting.[87] As in vv.2, 7 it here also "speaks of logical necessity according to the binding needs of the circumstances."[88] The present tense points to what is continually required.

That which is of such necessity is how one should "conduct himself" (ἀναστρέφεσθαι). It is a compound word comprised of "up" (ἀνά) and "turn" (στρέφω). It can have the sense of "to turn upside down." But the passive form (as here) can have a reflexive nuance that describes turning back and forth in a place and thus means "to live" or "to stay." Then figuratively it can describe moral conduct and mean "to act," "to behave," or "to live."[89] Paul uses the verb only three times (2 Cor. 1:12; Eph. 2:3; 1 Tim. 3:15). The lack of a clear subject for the verb has given rise to a debate about whether this is intended more generally (how members of the church generally should conduct themselves)

---

[85] Mounce, 32, 486.
[86] Rienecker, 624.
[87] BAGD, 172.
[88] Rienecker, 622.
[89] Friberg, 52.

or specifically (how Timothy should conduct himself). The knowledge was to be Timothy's (second person singular, "you may know"), but this could well have been so he could instruct the congregation as to their appropriate behavior. The context has focused on the involvement of the larger congregation (vv.1-13), thus it is probably best to understand it more widely. The present tense of the present verb describes that which should be the continual way of life in "the household of God" (ἐν οἴκῳ θεοῦ). Now we know at least in part why the Apostle required the overseer to be one who "manages his own household well" (3:4). Indeed, Paul hinted at the church as "the household of God" earlier when he queried, "if a man does not know how to manage his own household, how will he take care of the church of God?" (3:5). Similarly he required deacons be "good managers of their children and their own households" (3:12). Churches met in homes (Rom. 16:5; 1 Cor. 16:19; Col. 4:15; Philem. 2), so it was not a stretch to consider them a new family and collectively describe them as the occupants of a home. He demanded to this same church that Gentiles are now a part of "God's household" (οἰκεῖοι τοῦ θεοῦ; Eph. 2:19). He called the church "the household of faith" (τοὺς οἰκείους τῆς πίστεως) in Galatians 6:10. The imagery intended here is not that of a building ("house of God," KJV), but of a family ("God's family," JB). The purpose of the letter is not to outline how to behave when "in church," but to describe what is proper conduct for a member of God's family.[90]

> **Ministry Maxim**
>
> The church thrives when divine love, life, and truth exist in dynamic balance.

The relative pronoun and verb ("which is," ἥτις ἐστὶν) lead to a further description of "the household of God." Another way to speak of the same entity is "the church of the living God" (ἐκκλησία θεοῦ ζῶντος). Paul transitions naturally from "household" (οἴκῳ) to "church" (ἐκκλησία), much as he does in Ephesians 2:19-20 and above in 1 Timothy 3:5. The use of the noun without the definite article identifies this as the assembled local body of believers, rather than the universal church as a whole.[91] Elsewhere Paul speaks of "sons of the living God" (Rom. 9:26) and "the Spirit of the living God" (2 Cor. 3:3). He says "we are the temple of the living God" (2 Cor. 6:16; cf. also Heb. 3:12; 10:31; 12:22; Rev. 7:2). Later Paul will designate God as the One who "gives life to all things" (1 Tim. 6:13). The expression here emphasizes the church as a dynamic body, an entity alive with the presence of God. He does exist and He rewards those who diligently seek Him (Heb. 11:6). He watches over and engages His people. The imagery of God's people as the temple of His dwelling is hinted at here and developed more fully elsewhere (1 Cor. 3:16; 6:19; 2 Cor.

---

[90] Fee, 92.
[91] Mounce, 222.

6:16; Eph. 2:20-22 [note the proximity of the imagery of "God's household" in Eph. 2:19 in a way similar to the use of the two metaphors here]).

Yet another way of describing the church is "the pillar and support of the truth" (στῦλος καὶ ἑδραίωμα τῆς ἀληθείας). The word "pillar" (στῦλος) was used literally to speak of a pillar or column in a building ("cf. 1 Kings 17:15ff, where two pillars are named Jachin and Boaz, i.e., 'he shall establish' and 'in it is strength.'"[92]). It was used metaphorically to designate an important person (Gal. 2:9).[93] Here the notion is that the church is the entity which holds high the truth of God in this world. The word "support" (ἑδραίωμα) describes a foundation, buttress or bulwark.[94] The two words combine to designate the church as the bastion of truth. Both nouns are anarthrous ("a pillar" and "a support"). Mounce observes, "The church is only part of God's defense. God is not dependent on the established church, in Ephesus or anywhere, to protect the proclamation of Christ."[95] He goes on to quote Hort, "There are few passages of the New Testament in which the reckless disregard of the presence or absence of the article has made wider havoc of the sense than this. To speak of either an Ecclesia or the Ecclesia, as being the pillar of the truth, is to represent the truth as a building, standing in the air supported on a single column."[96] The definite article with the noun ("the truth," τῆς ἀληθείας) designates the Gospel and the doctrines God has revealed with it ("the content of Christianity as the absolute truth"[97]). If the church does not propagate and protect the Gospel, who will?

The church is a place of warmth and belonging ("the household of God"), a place alive with the presence of God ("the church of the living God") and a place of proclamation and instruction ("the pillar and support of the truth"). The church is to be a place of belonging, abounding and believing.

Digging Deeper:

1. In what way does v.14 illustrate a healthy interdependence of one's pen and one's presence in ministry?
2. What value comes from understanding Christ's church as a family?
3. How does the church appropriately serve as "the pillar and support of the truth" without becoming legalistic and brittle?

---

[92] Knight, 181.
[93] BAGD, 772.
[94] Rienecker, 624.
[95] Mounce, 222.
[96] Ibid.
[97] BAGD, 35.

3:16 By common confession, great is the mystery of godliness: He who was revealed in the flesh, Was vindicated in the Spirit, Seen by angels, Proclaimed among the nations, Believed on in the world, Taken up in glory.

The Apostle now moves to close this lengthy discussion of conduct and roles within the local church (2:1-3:15). The connective καὶ is not represented in the NASU (though cf. "And" of the NASB). "By common confession" (ὁμολογουμένως) translates an adverb that is found only here in the NT. It means "confessedly," "undeniably," or "most certainly."[98] It is used to remove doubt and establish common ground.

That which is universally agreed upon is that "great is the mystery of godliness" (μέγα ἐστὶν τὸ τῆς εὐσεβείας μυστήριον). Just what this identifies has been a matter of some debate. Paul typically uses the word "mystery" (μυστήριον) to describe that which has previously been concealed, but of late has been revealed (cf. "the mystery which has been hidden from the past ages and generations, but has now been manifested to His saints" Col. 1:26). Paul has just spoken of "the mystery of the faith" (v.9). The noun "godliness" (τῆς εὐσεβείας) is used extensively by Paul in the PE (1 Tim. 2:2; 3:16; 4:7, 8; 6:3, 5, 6, 11; 2 Tim. 3:5; Titus 1:1). The Apostle does not employ the word outside of the PE. It generally describes the outward evidences of a genuine faith in and reverence for God (1 Tim. 2:2; 3:16; 4:7, 8; 6:3, 6, 11; Titus 1:1). False teachers often imitated it for selfish ends (1 Tim. 6:5; 2 Tim. 3:5), but here Paul has the real thing in mind. Though there are many imitations, genuine spirituality is a new revelation from God. In v. 9 "the mystery of the faith" refers more directly to the body of truth. Here "the mystery of godliness" includes the notion of that body of truth, but goes further to include the life rightly lived in response to it. Indeed, to Titus Paul will speak of "the knowledge of the truth which is according to godliness" (Titus 1:1). Thus Paul is here expanding upon the notion of the church as "the pillar and support of the truth" (v.15).

That revelation is centered in a Person: "He who" (ὅς). There has been debate about the genuineness of this reading. Some manuscripts have "God" (θεός) or "the God" (ὁ θεός). Others have the neuter "which" (ὅ). The presence of the word "God" (θεός) is explainable as an attempt by a scribe to magnify Christ and clarify what may have seemed ambiguous grammar in the original. The addition of the definite article (ὁ θεός) was probably a later effort to improve upon the improvement in grammar. If "God" (θεός) was original, by what explanation would a scribe have reverted to the more general "He" (ὅς)? The neuter "which" (ὅ) could easily have become, by omission of the final letter, the masculine "He"

---
[98] Ibid., 569.

(ὅς). The Alexandrian and Western texts support the use of the masculine relative pronoun ("He," ὅς), and this is clearly to be considered the original text.[99] Thus, the great mystery of godliness is centered in a Person. The fact that the relative pronoun has no antecedent has been a stumbling block to some. However, what follows appears to be a hymn, or fragment thereof, and thus a quotation of it would lead to a break in the grammar. Christ is the center and core of true religion and godliness. "God willed to make known what is the riches of the glory of this mystery among the Gentiles, which is Christ in you, the hope of glory" (Col. 1:27). Indeed, "Christ is all" (Col. 3:11). Paul told the Galatians that it was his commitment to "labor until Christ is formed in you" (Gal. 4:19). The practical spirituality and "godliness" that is desired for all believers (2:2) and demanded of leaders in the church is based not upon a new ethic, but a dynamic Person.

> **Ministry Maxim**
>
> Godliness is based, not on a new ethic, but on the Person of Jesus Christ.

What Paul now says centers on the Person of Christ and unfolds in six lines, giving an outline of Christ's saving work and thus of our Christian faith and confession. Analysis of these six lines has yielded in some cases one six-line hymn (KJV, NASB), three sets of two lines (NIV), or two sets of three lines (GNB). Some have tried to see a chronological arrangement, but, while there appears at first to be some such progression from line to line, overall this seems to force the issue and lead away from the author's intent. Five of the six (except line three) end in a prepositional phrase using ἐν ("in" or "by"). All six lines use verbs in the aorist passive third person singular form.

The first line points to the incarnation with the words, "He who was revealed in the flesh" (ὃς ἐφανερώθη ἐν σαρκί). The Second Person of the Trinity took to Himself a human body in order to obtain our salvation (John 1:14). The verb describes making something visible or manifest. It is in the aorist tense, pointing not simply to His birth, but to the whole of Christ's earthly pilgrimage as one event. The passive voice describes His obedience to the Father, who made Christ known to the world through His Son's obedience. The statement here presupposes the preexistence of Christ (cf. also 1:15).[100] Paul uses the same verb elsewhere in the PE to speak of Christ's incarnation (2 Tim. 1:10; Titus 1:3). He also uses it to speak of the second coming of Christ (Col. 3:4) and of the present manifestation of Christ through His people (2 Cor. 2:14; 4:10, 11). Christ is God "in the flesh" (ἐν σαρκί). The theological term "incarnation" is from the Latin meaning literally "in flesh," the precise statement the Greek

---

[99] NET Bible.
[100] Guthrie, 89.

text has here (ἐν σαρκί).[101]

The intent of the second line is less clear. Christ, says the Apostle, "Was vindicated in the Spirit" (ἐδικαιώθη ἐν πνεύματι). What did Paul mean by "Spirit"? Did he refer to Christ's human spirit, the Holy Spirit, or His own divine nature? The first option is supported by the fact that the noun lacks the definite article and would hold a strict parallelism with the first line ("in flesh" vs. "in spirit"). The last option would be viewed as contrasting Christ's divine nature ("in spirit") with His human nature ("in flesh"). Viewing it as a reference to the Holy Spirit would appear to point to those events—like His baptism (Matt. 3:15-17), resurrection (Rom. 1:4; 8:11; 1 Peter 3:18), and ascension (John 16:7)—when the Holy Spirit manifestly vindicated the claims of Christ. This would require reading the preposition ἐν as indicating the means by which the vindication is made—a different use of the preposition than in the first line (where it indicates place).[102]

Perhaps Paul had in mind something of all three of these ideas. The Holy Spirit was visibly manifest at Christ's baptism as the Father spoke to declare that Christ was indeed the Son of God. Christ lived His life by the power of the Holy Spirit, thus performing miracles which vindicated His claims to a divine nature. His resurrection from the dead was the ultimate declaration in the spiritual realm (1 Peter 3:18) that He was "the Son of God with power" (Rom. 1:4). The verb is used often by Paul to speak of justification (e.g., Rom. 3:4, 20, 24, 26, 28, 30). Here it is used in the sense of God (or in this case specifically Christ) being proved right (cf. also Rom. 3:4) and thus vindicated.[103]

The third line describes the onlooking angels as Christ carried out His earthly work. He was "Seen by angels" (ὤφθη ἀγγέλοις). Angels seemed to minister in special ways to Christ at times during His earthly sojourn: at His birth (Luke 2:13), temptation (Matt. 4:11; Mark 1:13), in the garden (Luke 22:43), and at His resurrection (e.g., Matt. 28:2, 5; Luke 24:23). We know also that salvation is a marvel to the angels and that these are "things into which [they] long to look" (1 Peter 1:12). This is the only one of the lines lacking the preposition ἐν and instead employs the dative case of the noun. The verb (ὁράω) with the person being appeared to is used regularly in the NT to describe Christ's post-resurrection appearances (Luke 24:23; Acts 9:17; 1 Cor. 15:5-8).[104] If this is the intention here, then the angels could be considered either fallen (Col. 2:15) or unfallen (Heb. 1:6; 1 Peter 1:12).[105] The first three lines thus may present Christ in His incarnation, resurrection and glorification.[106]

---

[101] Earle, 11:370.
[102] Knight, 185.
[103] BAGD, 198.
[104] Fee, 94.
[105] Lea, 126.
[106] Fee, 94.

In the fourth line the Apostle says Christ was "Proclaimed among the nations" (ἐκηρύχθη ἐν ἔθνεσιν). Christ's final commissioning of His disciples was to "make disciples of all the nations [τὰ ἔθνη]" (Matt. 28:19). Jesus was a Jew. That the Gentiles would be included in the salvation He wrought was a wonder and a scandal to the Jews (Eph. 2:11-22). Having just spoken of "the mystery of the faith" (v.9) and "the mystery of godliness (v.16a), Paul elsewhere spoke of "the mystery of Christ" (Eph. 3:4) and revealed that this mystery is "that the Gentiles are fellow heirs and fellow members of the body, and fellow partakers of the promise in Christ Jesus through the gospel" (v.6). Proclamation to these Gentile "nations" was Paul's peculiar calling as "an apostle of the Gentiles" (Rom. 11:13; cf. 1 Tim. 2:7). So thorough was the preaching of the Gospel from Ephesus that Luke could say, "all who lived in Asia heard the word of the Lord, both Jews and Greeks" (Acts 19:10). The verb "Proclaimed" (ἐκηρύχθη) describes the official activity of a herald. What is thus "Proclaimed" is an authoritative message. Ralph Earle comments, "It will be noted that what was preached was not a theory or even a creed, but a Person. Paul declared, 'We preach Christ' (1 Cor. 1:23)."[107]

Christ, of whom the proclamation was made according to the previous line, was "Believed on in the world" (ἐπιστεύθη ἐν κόσμῳ). Paul's opponents in Ephesus could say, "not only in Ephesus, but in almost all of Asia, this Paul has persuaded and turned away a considerable number of people" (Acts 19:26). Little wonder that such faith should be found even among the Gentiles, for "faith comes from hearing, and hearing by the word of Christ" (Rom. 10:17).

Finally, the hymn describes Christ as "Taken up in glory" (ἀνελήμφθη ἐν δόξῃ). If one is looking for a chronological progression to the hymn, this appears to frustrate those efforts by referring back to the ascension of Christ. Indeed, the verb is used elsewhere to describe Christ's ascension back to heaven (Mark 16:19; Acts 1:2, 11, 22). This may be a reference, however, not simply to the act of Christ's ascension, but to His resulting and present session "in glory." As such it would enfold the truths of Christ's resurrection (Luke 24:26), ascension (Acts 1:9) and the anticipation of His glorious return (Luke 21:27).[108] This sixth stanza forms a fitting climax to the whole of the hymn, which began with the humiliation of Christ's incarnation and ends with His glorification in heaven.

One might justly wonder where the death of Christ and the doctrine of the cross are in this hymn. They are assumed, but one would expect Paul not to leave so central a doctrine for assumption. Paul may have quoted only a portion of the hymn and perhaps we may conclude that the remainder of the original would

---

[107] Earle, 11:370.
[108] Kent, 142.

have mentioned the cross. The purpose for the inclusion of the hymn-fragment at this point may be that: 1) it further enlarges upon the "truth" of which the church is "the pillar and support" (v.15, which in turn gives justification for the instructions regarding the church and its leaders in chapters 2-3) and 2) it prepares for the coming defense against the false teachers now loose in Ephesus (4:1ff). Mounce wisely observes, "While it is easy to become lost in the exegetical minutiae of the hymn, its central purpose should not be lost: the gospel is about Christ, it is a mystery revealed, and the opponents are wrong."[109]

> **Digging Deeper:**
> 1. What is the value of shared common confessions by God's people? What, if any, danger is found in their use?
> 2. What is the significance of the six lines of truth selected by the Apostle Paul in this confession?
> 3. How can these six truths both guide the church in its leadership (chapters 2-3) and guard it in its battles with opponents (chapter 4)?

---

[109] Mounce, 225.

CHAPTER

4

4:1 But the Spirit explicitly says that in later times some will fall away from the faith, paying attention to deceitful spirits and doctrines of demons,

The Apostle launches in a new direction. He has spoken of the church as "the pillar and support of the truth" (3:15) and then, through what was probably an early hymn, stated something of that Gospel truth (3:16). Now, in contrast ("But," δέ), Paul speaks of the conditions in which the church must hold and protect that truth. The conjunction δέ may be a mild adversative (as here) or it may be used in a resumptive manner ("Now," ESV, RSV, NRSV). NIV chooses not to translate it at all.

The Apostle asserts that "the Spirit explicitly says" (Τὸ ... πνεῦμα ῥητῶς λέγει) something. The adverb ("explicitly," ῥητῶς) means something like "expressly," "clearly," "unmistakably," or "in express terms."[1] It is used only here in the NT. This is unique language to Paul, signaling that what he says is of the utmost importance. Just *how* and to *whom* (Paul or other prophets) the Spirit has made this known is not clear, but *what* ("that," ὅτι) He has spoken is now delineated. The present tense of the verb indicates this is a message the Holy Spirit had given more than once and continued to speak it even as Paul wrote. The coming apostasy was spoken of by OT prophets (Dan. 7:25; 8:23), Jesus (Matt. 24:4-12; Mark 13:22), and Apostles (2 Thess. 2:3-12; 2 Peter 3:3; 1 John 2:18; Jude 18).[2] The Spirit was continuing to press this point home even as Paul wrote to Timothy.

The message concerns what takes place "in later times" (ἐν ὑστέροις καιροῖς).

---

[1] Rienecker, 625.
[2] Hiebert, *First Timothy*, 142-143.

Elsewhere in the PE the Apostle speaks of "the proper time" (1 Tim. 2:6; 6:15; Titus 1:3), "difficult times" (2 Tim. 3:1) in the last days, and a "time" when people will flout sound teaching (2 Tim. 4:3). Paul also uses the noun to speak of his impending death (2 Tim. 4:6). Only here, however, does he speak of "later times." The adjective "later" (ὑστέροις) designates that which is behind or after in time or space.[3] It is used only here by Paul. The noun "times" (καιροῖς) points to a period of time, not to the passing of time.[4] These are part of what Paul elsewhere calls "the last days" (2 Tim. 3:1). These "last days" inaugurated with the coming of Christ and continue until His glorious return (Acts 2:16-17; Heb. 1:2; 1 John 2:18). We now live in these "last days" which will include some "times" (apparently still future at the time of Paul's writing) when "some will fall away from the faith" (ἀποστήσονταί τινες τῆς πίστεως). The verb is a compound word from ἀπό (from, away from) and ἵστημι (to stand). It has a range of meaning from withdraw to fall away in the sense of apostasy. It is the latter sense that is used here. The middle voice points to each individual acting upon himself and thus the inward nature of the departure. The future tense sets it before Paul as he writes, but it is clearly a present danger to Timothy and the church in Ephesus. What will be manifestly and overwhelmingly true in the end is often met in sporadic and less intensive ways throughout church history (cf. 1 John 2:18; 4:3).

The departure is made "from the faith" (τῆς πίστεως). The definite article points to the body of truth that is in Christ—to Christian doctrine—with which Paul was entrusted as an Apostle (2:7), the knowledge of which is God's goal in salvation (2:4), and of which the church is to be "the pillar and support" (3:15). This will be true not of all, but only of "some" (τινες), though at times the proportion may seem large (Mark 13:20). The departure of these folk would prove they had never really been a part of the church which is the "pillar and support of the truth." As the Apostle John wrote, "They went out from us, but they were not really of us; for if they had been of us, they would have remained with us; but they went out, so that it would be shown that they all are not of us" (1 John 2:19).

A participial phrase is introduced ("paying attention," προσέχοντες), apparently to define how or when or in what way such folk will "fall away." The root is used twenty-four times in the NT, only five of which are by Paul. All Paul's uses appear in the PE, with four of those here in 1 Timothy (1:4; 3:8; 4:1, 13; Titus 1:14). It is a compound word comprised of "to" (πρός) and "hold" (ἔχω). It means "turning or holding one's mind to someone or something" and thus "occupying one's mind with something."[5] Four of Paul's five

---
[3] Friberg, 394.
[4] Mounce, 544.
[5] Friberg, 333.

usages are negative: giving attention to "myths and endless genealogies" (1 Tim. 1:4), "much wine" (3:8), "deceitful spirits and doctrines of demons" (4:1), and "Jewish myths and commandments of men" (Titus 1:14). Only in 1 Timothy 4:13 is it attached to something positive, "the public reading of Scripture, to exhortation and teaching." Here the present tense views this as a habitual pattern of life (cf. "addicted," 3:8). Those of whom Paul writes find themselves repeatedly caught up in listening to two things. First, there is listening "to deceitful spirits" (πνεύμασιν πλάνοις). The adjective "deceitful" (πλάνοις) originally meant wandering and roving[6] and then came to describe that which is deceptive, deceiving or seducing.[7] It is used only five times in the NT, twice by Paul (Matt. 27:63; 2 Cor. 6:8; 1 Tim. 4:1; 2 John 7 [twice]). That these are "spirits" (πνεύμασιν) points to demonic beings who operate in and through others who infiltrate the church and espouse false teachings. They have wandered from their divinely appointed station and service and now seek to seduce humans into doing the same. Paul warned the elders of this very church that such influencers would come into their midst from the outside (Acts 20:29) and would even arise from the midst of the elders themselves (v.30). The second ("and," καὶ) concern is "doctrines of demons" (διδασκαλίαις δαιμονίων). The noun "doctrines" (διδασκαλίαις) is used nineteen times by Paul (only two other usages in the NT, Matt. 15:9; Mark 7:7) and fifteen of those are in the PE (1 Tim. 1:10; 4:1, 6, 13, 16; 5:17; 6:1, 3; 2 Tim. 3:10, 16; 4:3; Titus 1:9; 2:1, 7, 10). It may refer to either the act of teaching or to that which is taught ("doctrine").[8] It is in this latter sense that it is used here. There may be, as here, the "doctrine of demons." Yet there Paul speaks also of "the doctrine of God our Savior" (Titus 2:10), "sound teaching/doctrine" (1 Tim. 1:10; 4:6; 2 Tim. 4:3; Titus 1:9; 2:1), "doctrine conforming to godliness" (1 Tim. 6:3), and "purity in doctrine" (Titus 2:7). The teaching Paul has in mind here comes from "demons" (δαιμονίων). The word is used frequently throughout the Gospels, but Paul uses it five times in only three verses (1 Cor. 10:20-21; 1 Tim. 4:1). It refers to those fallen angels who have rebelled and now serve Satan. Till now in this letter Paul has been speaking in guarded terms about this spiritual warfare (1 Tim. 2:14; 3:6-7), but now states clearly the conflict we are in and the demonic influences that stand behind all false teaching (2 Cor. 4:4; 11:3, 13-14). Such a demonically

> **Ministry Maxim**
>
> The devil is not against doctrine; he is against *true* doctrine.

---

[6] Thayer, 515.
[7] Rienecker, 625.
[8] BAGD, 191.

inspired departure from the faith continued to be a grave concern of the Apostle Paul in his second letter to Timothy (2 Tim. 2:16-18; 3:13; 4:3-4).[9]

> **Digging Deeper:**
> 1. From what specific teachings do we find people falling away today?
> 2. What teachings are they embracing instead?
> 3. While exercising caution, how might one nevertheless accurately identify the work of deceitful spirits today?
> 4. Is there anything you can identify today that could justly bear the title "doctrines of demons"?

4:2 by means of the hypocrisy of liars seared in their own conscience as with a branding iron,

It is true, as Paul had earlier informed the believers in Ephesus, that "our struggle is not against flesh and blood, but against the rulers, against the powers, against the world forces of this darkness, against the spiritual forces of wickedness in the heavenly places." (Eph. 6:12). Yet the prepositional phrase "by means of the hypocrisy of liars" (ἐν ὑποκρίσει ψευδολόγων) reveals that while the source and origin of the false teaching is demonic (v.1b), the agents are human (cf. 1 John 4:1). The word "hypocrisy" (ὑποκρίσει) is used only six times in the NT and only two of those are by Paul. His other use designates the actions of Peter and Barnabas and the others who withdrew from table fellowship with the Gentile believers of Galatia out of fear of other Jews' scorn (Gal. 2:13). In the Gospels it is applied to the Pharisees (Matt. 23:28; Mark 12:15; Luke 12:1). The word originally described an actor on stage, wearing a mask and playing the part of someone else. In the NT the word is always negative, referring to a person pretending to be one thing while in actuality being something quite different. The preposition ἐν ("by") is used to describe the means (NASU) or instrument (e.g., ESV, NIV) through which the action takes place. The noun "liars" (ψευδολόγων) is used only here in the NT. It is a compound word from "false" (ψευδής) and "word" (λόγος). It implies a knowing deception rather than an unwitting misleading.

Such folk are "seared in their own conscience as with a branding iron" (κεκαυστηριασμένων τὴν ἰδίαν συνείδησιν). Just one word in Greek is represented by the English "seared . . . as with a branding iron"

---
[9] Fee, 97-98.

(κεκαυστηριασμένων). It is used only here in the NT. Used literally, it describes the application of a red-hot iron to the skin, as in the case of a slave being marked as property by his owner. Its figurative use here could mean that such folk are marked as belonging to Satan by the falsehood being burned into their very consciences ("branded with the devil's sign," NEB), or it could refer to the resulting state, a place of insensitivity where the nerve-endings have been destroyed (i.e., a conscience that no longer is functional or reliable; cf. "seared as with a hot iron," NIV). We get our word *cauterize* from this word (cf. Eph. 4:19). Either figurative meaning is possible. The context may point to the former meaning, but the latter seems a preferable understanding. The perfect tense points to an abiding state; they were so branded at a point in the past (when they believed the false doctrine) and they continue to be thus branded even now. The passive voice pictures them as being acted upon by another—the demonic spirits that operate through them.

> **Ministry Maxim**
>
> My conscience is only as reliable as its adherence to the truth.

This takes place "in their own conscience" (τὴν ἰδίαν συνείδησιν). Paul has already spoken in this letter quite frequently of the "conscience" (συνείδησις; 1:5, 19; 3:9). The word "conscience" is a compound word (συνείδησις), combining "with" (σύν) and "knowledge" (εἶδον)." This is a joint-knowledge, shared with oneself. It points to self-awareness. Thus Paul speaks of "the testimony of our conscience" (2 Cor. 1:12). It is a testimony given to oneself, and then passed on to others. Paul speaks again of a "good conscience" in v.19. He can speak of "a perfectly good conscience" (Acts 23:1), "a clear conscience" (1 Tim. 3:9; 2 Tim. 1:3), and "a blameless conscience" (Acts 24:16). The conscience is a gift from God, but is distorted through sin. It can be "weak" through immaturity (1 Cor. 8:7), wounded through wrong (1 Cor. 8:12), "defiled" by sin (Titus 1:15), and, as here, "seared" to the point of insensitivity by embracing falsehood. This they have done to their "own" (ἰδίαν) conscience, signaling that their embrace of the false doctrines worked an inward tragedy in their own lives, a tragedy they now wish to compound by passing it on to others. The adjective ("own," ἰδίαν) in the attributive position, tucked between the noun and its definite article, ascribes a quality to the noun. The conscience is only as reliable as its adherence to the truth.[10] Thus when these folk abandoned the truth, their conscience was scrambled and disabled and became unreliable. We damage ourselves deeply when we embrace false teaching.

False teachers' words are untrue, their appearances are insincere, and their consciences are unreliable.

---

[10] Kent, 146.

> **Digging Deeper:**
> 1. How do we admit that "our struggle is not against flesh and blood," and yet deal compassionately and wisely with the human agents through which the evil one works?
> 2. Does the expression "the hypocrisy of liars" mean that the false teachers know they are teaching falsehoods? What difference does our answer make?
> 3. Is a "seared . . . conscience" totally disabled? Or can a portion of one's conscience be disabled by belief in a particular area?

4:3 men who forbid marriage and advocate abstaining from foods which God has created to be gratefully shared in by those who believe and know the truth.

Until now we have caught only small glimpses of the nature of the heresy in Ephesus. The false teachers were caught up in "myths and endless genealogies, which give rise to mere speculation" (1:4). They wanted "to be teachers of the Law" (1:7). They may have touted themselves as liberators of women (2:8-15), even while preying upon them inappropriately (2 Tim. 3:6-7). Later we will discover that they held to some form of over-realized eschatology, proclaiming that the resurrection had already taken place (2 Tim. 2:18). Now Paul more clearly names some tenets of the false teachers. They practiced and proclaimed a false asceticism, for they were "men who forbid marriage" (κωλυόντων γαμεῖν). The present tense probably points to a regular practice or the consistent teaching of the false teachers. Paul counseled single people to remain unmarried, as apparently he was, if they were so gifted (1 Cor. 7:8). But if not gifted with celibacy then they should marry, but only to a believer (v.9). There are, he recognized, certain advantages to being unmarried (vv.26-34). But he said, "if you marry you have not sinned" (v.28). Paul recognized the sensual vulnerabilities of younger widows (1 Tim. 5:11) and urged them to marry (5:14), but to do so only in the Lord. The Essenes were among other sects who forbade marriage at that time. Gnosticism would later promote similar false teachings. Perhaps already the seeds for such full-grown Gnosticism were being planted. Teachings of a celibate priesthood smack of the same error. Strangely this is an error that sect and cult leaders have continued to make throughout the ages (e.g., Shakers).

Additionally they "advocate abstaining from foods" (ἀπέχεσθαι βρωμάτων). The verb ("abstaining," ἀπέχεσθα) is a compound word made up of "from" (ἀπό) and "to hold" (ἔχω). In the middle voice, as it is here, it means to "hold oneself off" from something,[11] to "keep away" or to "abstain."[12] The present tense probably points here to a repeated and perhaps habitual pattern of fasting from certain foods for supposedly spiritual reasons. It is used by Paul only four other times (Phil. 4:18; 1 Thess. 4:3; 5:22; Philem. 15). It is difficult to determine the exact intent of the infinitive form. Most commentators settle on calling this an example of zeugma (a figure of speech where one word is understood to refer to two or more other words, but must be understood in different senses in each case) and suggest we should simply read in a verb like "forbid."[13]

The plural noun "foods" (βρωμάτων) describes solid food generally (as opposed to liquids), not just "meats" (KJV). These "foods" from which they hold themselves back are those "which God has created" (ἃ ὁ θεὸς ἔκτισεν). The relative pronoun "which" (ἃ) is connected to the noun "foods," apparently not to both "marriage" and "foods." Paul does not answer the first error here, perhaps believing he has said enough in regards to marriage already (2:11-15; 3:2, 4-5, 11-12) and will yet encourage younger widows to remarry (5:14). Interestingly the definite article is found with "God" (ὁ θεὸς), so the rendering would literally be "the God" (i.e., "the one and only God"). The verb ("has created," ἔκτισεν) is used to point to God as the Creator (Rom. 1:25) and that which He originally created (1 Cor. 11:9; Eph. 3:9; Col. 1:16). He also employs it to speak of the new creation which takes place through an individual's spiritual rebirth (Eph. 2:10; 4:24; Col. 3:10) as well as the formation of the church itself (Eph. 2:15). The aorist tense looks back to the beginning of each thing God made. Paul is attacking the dualistic notion that physical matter is inherently evil or defiling. God, the only Creator of all that is, made these foods and set them before us "to be gratefully shared in" (εἰς μετάλημψιν μετὰ εὐχαριστίας). God created these, most literally, "for reception" (εἰς μετάλημψιν).[14] Eating these things was God's intent from the beginning. The noun is used only here in the NT. It is a compound from "with" (μετά) and "receiving" (λῆμψις). This reception was designed to be "with gratitude" (μετὰ εὐχαριστίας). The noun for thanksgiving (εὐχαριστία) is used again in the next verse. Thankfulness is a big deal for Paul, for in thirteen of the noun's fifteen NT usages it comes either from his pen (e.g., Col. 2:7; 4:2; 1 Tim. 2:1; 4:3-4) or from his mouth (Acts 24:3). A prayer of thanksgiving

> **Ministry Maxim**
>
> Understanding the implications of God's grace follows personal trust in God's grace.

---

[11] Thayer, 57.
[12] BAGD, 85.
[13] Knight, 190; Marshall, 542.
[14] Robertson, 4:579.

before eating was common Jewish practice, was the habit of Jesus (e.g., Matt. 15:36; Mark 8:6), and is assumed by the Apostle Paul (Rom. 14:6; 1 Cor. 10:16, 30).

Such glad reception of these foods will only happen "by those who believe and know the truth" (τοῖς πιστοῖς καὶ ἐπεγνωκόσι τὴν ἀλήθειαν). The truth is a major concern of Paul in this letter (2:4, 7; 3:15; 4:3; 6:5), in his next letter to Timothy (2 Tim. 2:15, 18, 25; 3:7, 8; 4:4), and in his letter to Titus as well (Titus 1:1, 14). In the PE it is found, as here, with the definite article in 1 Timothy 3:15; 6:5 and 2 Timothy 2:15, 18; 3:8; 4:4 (cf. also Titus 1:14). The combination of "who believe and know" (τοῖς πιστοῖς καὶ ἐπεγνωκόσι) this truth is interesting. Only one definite article holds the two together closely. The former, "those who believe" (τοῖς πιστοῖς), uses the adjective and definite article as a substantive. It points thus to those who have placed personal trust in the truth and the Christ who embodies it. The latter, "know" (ἐπεγνωκόσι), is a perfect active participle. The word is a compound, made up of "upon" (ἐπί) and "to know" (γινώσκω). The preposition in compound is perfective and points to a full and complete knowledge. The perfect tense points to knowledge at which one arrived at a point in time and in which the person still stands. The participle is used also as a substantive, meaning "those who have come to know fully." See 1 Timothy 2:4; 2 Timothy 2:25; 3:7 and Titus 1:1 for other combinations of "know" (ἐπίγνωσις) and "truth" (ἀλήθεια) in the PE (cf. also 2 John 1). There is a hint that not all who thus "believe" (πιστοῖς) necessarily also "know" (ἐπεγνωκόσι). This was certainly the case in Corinth (1 Cor. 8:7). This may not be dissimilar from Paul's later testimony to Timothy regarding what "I have believed and I am convinced" (2 Tim. 1:12) or his reminder about what "you have learned and become convinced of" (3:14). Is Paul saying that not all who have come to faith in Christ have as yet started to grasp fully the implications of the doctrine of grace?

> **Digging Deeper:**
> 1. Why have leaders of some cults and sects been drawn to forbidding marriage?
> 2. What motivates cult leaders to teach false asceticism?
> 3. Why does the Apostle speak of those who both "believe" and "know" the truth? Is there a distinction between knowing and believing? If so, what are the implications?

4:4 For everything created by God is good, and nothing is to be rejected if it is received with gratitude;

Paul now explains his statement in v.3 (ὅτι, "For"). The truth is "everything created by God is good" (πᾶν κτίσμα θεοῦ καλὸν). The singular noun κτίσμα designates that which is the product of God's creative activity ("creature"). The adjective πᾶν ("everything), when used with a single anarthrous noun, "emphasizes the individual members of the class denoted by the noun."[15] There is an echo of the Genesis account of creation where God stopped after each day of creation and observed what He had done to be "good" (Gen. 1:4, 10, 12, 18, 21, 25, 31). Such a reference, in view of the false teacher's desire to be "teachers of the Law" (1 Tim. 1:7), may be an intentional ploy to remove the ground of their argumentation from them. By "good" Paul may well mean not merely "good" in a general sense, but "good for food" (Gen. 2:9). The Mosaic dietary restrictions have been abolished by Christ. Jesus, by Mark's own commentary, "declared all foods clean" (Mark 7:19). God commanded Peter, "Get up, Peter, kill and eat!" (Acts 10:13) when he was shown in a dream a sheet full of all kinds of animals. Then He spoke again saying, "What God has cleansed, no longer consider unholy" (Acts 10:15). The primary point was the acceptance of the Gentiles by God through grace, but this point was made through the clarification of previous dietary restrictions under the Mosaic Law. Paul would then later tell the believers in Colossae, "no one is to act as your judge in regard to food or drink" (Col. 2:16). Indeed, such ascetic practices give an appearance of godliness, but in fact stand opposed to God's grace and yield no benefit. "These are matters which have, to be sure, the appearance of wisdom in self-made religion and self-abasement and severe treatment of the body, but are of no value against fleshly indulgence" (Col. 2:23).

> **Ministry Maxim**
>
> Spiritual distinctions in diet are a false use of God's Word.

Paul adds (καὶ, "and"), therefore, that "nothing is to be rejected" (οὐδὲν ἀπόβλητον). The adjective is used only here in the NT, but it comes from a related compound verb made up of "from" (ἀπὸ) and "throw" (βάλλω). This is already the third ἀπό–compounded verb in this chapter (ἀποστήσονται, "fall away," v.1; ἀπέχεσθαι, "abstaining," v.3) and a fourth is coming in v.9. The negation is categorical and absolute (οὐδὲν, "nothing").[16] There is no food which can be thrown off as unfit for spiritual reasons "if it is received with gratitude" (μετὰ εὐχαριστίας λαμβανόμενον). The exact phrase "with gratitude"

---
[15] Knight, 191.
[16] Thayer, 408, 462.

(μετὰ εὐχαριστίας) is repeated from v.3. It is used elsewhere only in Philippians 4:6 (though cf. Acts 24:3). The participle is used in a conditional sense (λαμβανόμενον, "if it is received"). The passive voice views that food as being acted upon by the one who will partake of it.

4:5 for it is sanctified by means of the word of God and prayer.

A further reason (γὰρ, "for") that every kind of food can be "received with gratitude" (v.4) is now set forth. The food under consideration "is sanctified" (ἁγιάζεται). The present tense describes the continuous status of the food once the means are applied. The passive voice means that the food is acted upon by another, presumably the one who is about to consume it. The word is often translated "holy" and designates a thing separated from one purpose and set apart to another, special purpose. There is behind the word the notion of ritual cleanness or uncleanness. This sanctification takes place "by means of" (διὰ) two things.

The first of these is "the word of God" (λόγου θεοῦ). There is some debate about just what the Apostle means by this phrase. It could be: (1) a further reference back to Genesis 1 (cf. comments on v.4) and the creative word of God and His evaluation of all He made as "good" (cf. Gen. 1:31), thus meaning something like, "By virtue of the fact it was brought into being by the creative word of God." (2) It could refer to Scripture being read and prayer being offered before a meal. (3) It could describe the Word of God as those specific passages wherein Jesus and the Apostles declared all Mosaic ceremonial laws trumped and all foods pronounced clean. (4) It could refer to the Gospel message (as the expression often does in the PE; e.g., 2 Tim. 2:19; Titus 1:3; 2:5) which delivers one from the bondage of Law keeping (of which ceremonial food laws are but one example) and into the liberty that is in Christ. (5) It could refer to a prayer into which the Word of God is woven as part of its fabric.

> **Ministry Maxim**
>
> God's truth and blessing set apart any meal as a holy event to be enjoyed fully and freely.

The second (καὶ, "and") means of sanctifying food for consumption is "prayer" (ἐντεύξεως). The only other use of this noun occurs in 1 Timothy 2:1, though Paul uses the verbal cognate (Rom. 8:27, 34; 11:2; cf. also the same verb in compound in 8:26). The word literally describes "falling in with" or "meeting with" someone, thus a coming together or a meeting for the purpose of talking or conversing. The word then became descriptive of the petition or supplication that might be made at such a meeting.[17] The word is thus "not properly intercession in the accepted sense of that term, but rather approach to God in free and familiar prayer."[18]

Paul told the Romans, "I know and am convinced in the Lord Jesus that nothing is unclean in itself; but to him who thinks anything to be unclean, to him it is unclean" (Rom. 14:14). Does this sanctify the kind of good generally (this kind of stuff is ok for Christians to eat)? Or does it deal with the specific portion of food set before a person at that moment?

> **Digging Deeper:**
> 1. What do these two verses do to those—even in the Christian camp—who would like to make dietary restrictions a spiritual/biblical matter?
> 2. Of the options presented, which do you think most accurately describes what Paul meant by "by means of the word of God"?

4:6 In pointing out these things to the brethren, you will be a good servant of Christ Jesus, constantly nourished on the words of the faith and of the sound doctrine which you have been following.

By "these things" (Ταῦτα) Paul presumably means the whole of what has gone before in the epistle, though it may be restricted to vv.1-5 regarding false asceticism and the true nature of God's creation or perhaps all of 2:1-4:5. He uses the same demonstrative pronoun in vv.11, 15 and his focus appears to be broader than just the immediate context.[19] The verb "pointing out" (ὑποτιθέμενος) is a compound word from "under" (ὑπό) and "to place" (τίθημι). It is found elsewhere in the NT only in Romans 16:4 where it is used literally to refer to those who "risked their own necks" for Paul's sake. Here, in the middle voice, it is used metaphorically to describe suggesting, teaching or making something known.[20] It is a purposeful, but gentle, presentation as opposed to a stern imperative. The present tense underscores the repetitive nature of the instruction needed. The participial form may be used as a condition[21] ("If you keep pointing out these things") or it may be a participle of means[22] ("By means of pointing out these things you will be . . ."). This is done

---

[17] Thayer, 218.
[18] Vincent, 4:216.
[19] Mounce, 248.
[20] BAGD, 848.
[21] Riencecker, 626.
[22] Mounce, 248.

"to the brethren" (τοῖς ἀδελφοῖς). The noun is used frequently by Paul (133 times), but only four of those appear in the PE (1 Tim. 4:6; 5:1; 6:2; 2 Tim. 4:21). While the word is masculine, it was used to refer to the total population of the church, both male and female.

In carrying out the action of the participle, the Apostle tells Timothy, "you will be a good servant of Christ Jesus" (καλὸς ἔσῃ διάκονος Χριστοῦ Ἰησοῦ). Paul earlier combined "good" (καλός) and "serve" (διακονέω) in the phrase "those who have served well as deacons" (καλῶς διακονήσαντες; 3:13). He uses the expression more broadly here. Such service is by appointment only (1 Tim. 1:12). The adjective "good" (καλός) describes that which is "in every respect unobjectionable, blameless, excellent."[23] The future tense of the verb points to the time when Timothy has passed on this teaching faithfully. The middle voice emphasizes the intrinsic, inward nature of the goodness.

Being such a servant Timothy will be "constantly nourished" (ἐντρεφόμενος). It is a compound word from "in" (ἐν) and "nourish" or "feed" (τρέφω). It is found only here in the NT. It can have the literal sense of feeding someone on something or can be used metaphorically to describe bringing up a child and training them in something.[24] The participle is in the present tense, stressing continuous action, and indicates the manner by which Timothy is to become "a good servant of Christ Jesus."[25] If the form is passive it means something like "educated in," if middle it means "nourish yourself on."[26] See 2 Timothy 3:14-17 for a similar emphasis.

That which Timothy is to feed continually upon are "words" (τοῖς λόγοις). This is described by two qualifying genitive phrases. They are, firstly, "the words of the faith" (τοῖς λόγοις τῆς πίστεως). The combination of πιστὸς ὁ λόγος ("a trustworthy statement") is found throughout the PE (1 Tim. 1:15; 3:1; 4:9; 2 Tim. 2:11; Titus 3:8). The words are also found in combination to describe teaching that is in conformity to apostolic teaching ("the faithful word which is in accordance with the teaching," Titus 1:9). The definite article with the noun points to *the* faith," the Gospel message with its body of truth. Secondly ("and," καὶ), these are words "of the sound doctrine" (τῆς καλῆς διδασκαλίας). The word "doctrine" (διδασκαλίας) is used twenty-two times in the NT, nineteen of those are by Paul and fifteen of those are in the PE (1 Tim. 1:10; 4:1, 6, 13, 16; 5:17;

> **Ministry Maxim**
>
> He who does not feed himself will be unable to feed others.

---

[23] BAGD, 400.
[24] Ibid., 269.
[25] Lea and Griffin, 133.
[26] Marshall, 549.

6:1, 3; 2 Tim. 3:10, 16; 4:3; Titus 1:9; 2:1, 7, 10). The noun may refer to either the act of teaching or to that which is taught ("doctrine").[27] It is in this latter sense that it is used here. As Paul has just stated, there may be "doctrine of demons" (1 Tim. 4:1). But "the doctrine of God our Savior" (Titus 2:10) is "sound teaching/doctrine" (1 Tim. 1:10; 4:6; 2 Tim. 4:3; Titus 1:9; 2:1), "doctrine conforming to godliness" (1 Tim. 6:3), and "purity in doctrine" (Titus 2:7). This is the heart of Scripture's purpose (2 Tim. 3:16) and all such teaching arises from and is controlled by the Scriptures. Paul, in this chapter, is especially concerned for such teaching in Timothy's life and ministry (vv.1, 6, 13, 16). Here such teaching is described as "sound" (καλῆς). It is the adjective just used to describe everything God created (v.4) and the kind of servant Timothy is called to be (v.6). If one is to be a "good [καλὸς] servant of Christ Jesus," one must feed on "sound ["good," καλῆς] doctrine."

These are not new words to Timothy, for Paul says they are words "which you have been following" (ᾗ παρηκολούθηκας). The verb is a compound word, made up of "beside" (παρά) and "follow" (ἀκολουθέω). Paul will use it in 2 Timothy 3:10 to tell Timothy "you followed my teaching, conduct, purpose, faith, patience, love, perseverance." It is used of the meticulous research Luke gave himself to before writing his Gospel (Luke 1:3; cf. also Mark 16:17). The preposition in compound gives the basic sense of "following beside" something. Then it comes to mean "follow closely." It describes following along with the mind, to understand and then to make that thing one's own.[28] It may also have become a technical term relating to the intimate relationship of a disciple to his master.[29] The perfect tense describes Timothy as having started to follow this truth in the past and as having continued to do so right up to the present time.

See 2 Timothy 3:10-16 for a fuller development of these ideas.

> ### Digging Deeper:
> 1. Why is nourishing oneself on the Word of God so critical to being "a good servant of Christ Jesus"?
> 2. Is there a distinction to be made between "the words of the faith" and "the sound doctrine"? Why do you suppose the Apostle used both expressions?
> 3. What does the verb "you have been following" imply about one's relationship to the Word of God?

---

[27] BAGD, 191.
[28] Ibid., 619.
[29] Rienecker, 647.

4:7 But have nothing to do with worldly fables fit only for old women. On the other hand, discipline yourself for the purpose of godliness;

In contrast ("But," δέ) to nourishing and training himself on the truth (v.6), Timothy is to "have nothing to do" (παραιτοῦ) with what the false teachers are espousing. The present imperative (the first of twelve such commands in vv.7, 11-14) demands that action be taken repeatedly and habitually. The word has a broad range of meaning, from request (Mark 15:6), to decline (1 Tim. 5:11), to a strong rejection, as here.[30] Paul uses the word four times, all in the PE, and always in the present middle imperative form. He counsels that at times certain conversations (1 Tim. 4:7; 2 Tim. 2:23), widows (1 Tim. 5:11), and rebels (Titus 3:10) must be rejected. What does this tell us about the demands of pastoral ministry? The use here is similar to its use in 2 Timothy 2:23 where Paul tells Timothy, "refuse foolish and ignorant speculations" (cf. also Titus 3:10).

That which is to be rejected is placed first in the sentence for emphasis. It is "worldly fables fit only for old women" (τοὺς ... βεβήλους καὶ γραώδεις μύθους). More literally it might read "worldly and womanish myths." The noun and its definite article are separated by some distance, with two adjectives and the connective καὶ (as well as the postpositive δέ) in between. By placing the adjectives in the attributive position Paul is emphasizing the qualitative nature of these "fables." The word translated "fables" (μύθους; from which we get our word "myth") is used five times in the NT, four of those by Paul in the PE (1 Tim. 1:4; 4:7; 2 Tim. 4:4; Titus 1:14; cf. 2 Peter 1:16). It is always used in a negative sense. The word refers to fanciful and fictitious stories that are passed off as the truth. It has been suggested that it refers to various pre-Gnostic theories that were beginning to seize upon Christian teaching and to redefine and rework it to their own perverted ends. Whether or not such elements were a part of the mix, it was primarily Jewish in nature, possessing elements that made it more appealing to those still struggling with the relationship of the Law to Christ (1 Tim. 1:7-9; Titus 1:14). Thus in 1 Timothy 1:4 Paul adds a warning about "endless genealogies" (γενεαλογίαις ἀπεράντοις).

Here the myths are designated, first of all, as "worldly" (βεβήλους). This adjective is also used only five times in the NT and four of those by Paul in the PE (1 Tim. 1:9; 4:7; 6:20; 2 Tim. 2:16; cf. Heb. 12:16). It describes that which is ungodly, profane, irreligious, and vile; as such it is directed toward those things which are associated with the name of God.[31] It can describe the

---
[30] BAGD, 616.
[31] Ibid.

character of people (1 Tim. 1:9; Heb. 12:16) as well as the words that proceed from their mouths (1 Tim. 4:7; 6:20; 2 Tim. 2:16). Secondly, the myths are denoted as "fit only for old women" (γραώδεις). The word is used only here in the NT. Other translations are "silly" (ESV), "gullible" (NET), "old wives' tales" (NIV, NLT, NRSV) and "old wives' fables" (KJV). The word describes that which is characteristic of old women.[32] It was used frequently in philosophical circles of the day. Indeed, "It is the sarcastic epithet which was frequent in philosophical polemic and conveys the idea of limitless credulity."[33]

> **Ministry Maxim**
>
> Sometimes a resolute refusal to enter or continue a conversation is a sign of wisdom.

In contrast or "On the other hand" (δέ) Paul has a better pattern of behavior for Timothy. The Apostle commands Timothy, "discipline yourself" (Γύμναζε δὲ σεαυτόν). The verb is used by Paul only here, though it appears also in Hebrews 5:14; 12:11; 2 Peter 2:14. We derive our word *gymnasium* from this root. In the secular Greek world it literally referred to an athlete exercising naked.[34] All restraint was removed in order to give freedom of movement and to maximize the opportunity of attaining one's goal. It is used metaphorically here (note the contrast with "bodily discipline" in v.8) to speak of the self-discipline of exercising and training oneself in spiritual pursuits. The present tense imperative demands that the action be taken repeatedly or habitually. Paul makes clear the object of this discipline by using the singular reflexive pronoun ("yourself," σεαυτόν). Paul may have used such rugged, manly imagery in a purposeful contrast to the "fables fit only for old women."[35]

This self-discipline has a specific target, it is "for the purpose of godliness" (πρὸς εὐσέβειαν). The preposition with the accusative speaks "of the result that follows a set of circumstances."[36] The noun "godliness" (εὐσεβείᾳ) is used ten times by Paul in the PE (1 Tim. 2:2; 3:16; 4:7, 8; 6:3, 5, 6, 11; 2 Tim. 3:5; Titus 1:1). He does not use the word outside of the PE. It generally describes the outward evidences of a genuine faith in and reverence for God. False teachers often imitated it for selfish ends (1 Tim. 6:5; 2 Tim. 3:5), but here Paul has the genuine article in mind. Paul is not a slacker morally, as the false teachers in Ephesus may have concluded because he opposed their ascetic system of rules. Rather he was a man of tremendous self-discipline aimed like a laser at the goal of true godliness.

---

[32] Ibid., 167.
[33] Kelly, quoted in Rienecker, 626.
[34] Friberg, 102.
[35] Guthrie, 95.
[36] BAGD, 710.

> **Digging Deeper:**
> 1. What does the fact that Paul uses such a strong word ("have nothing to do with") only in counsel to pastors of local churches tell us about the demands of pastoral ministry?
> 2. Can you identify some conversations that might arise within the context of your ministry that would fit the description here and should thus be rejected?
> 3. Is Paul guilty of sexism by referring to some fables as "fit only for old women"? Why or why not?

4:8 for bodily discipline is only of little profit, but godliness is profitable for all things, since it holds promise for the present life and also for the life to come.

Paul now explains ("for," γὰρ) the command to "discipline yourself for the purpose of godliness" (v.7b). He compares the profitability of "bodily discipline" with "godliness." His first concern is "bodily discipline" (ἡ . . . σωματικὴ γυμνασία). The noun "discipline" (γυμνασία) is used only here in the NT, but it is the cognate of the verb used in v.7. The adjective "bodily" (σωματικὴ) is used only here and in Luke 3:22 where the Holy Spirit is said to have descended upon Christ "in bodily form like a dove." The adjective in the attributive position—tucked between the noun and its definite article—emphasizes the qualitative nature of the discipline under consideration.

Just what does Paul have in view here? The noun concerns the gymnasium and the physical preparation of athletes for competition. The context, however, concerns the severe asceticism of the false teachers in Ephesus (vv.3-5). It seems the context should rule here. Paul is not suddenly debating the merits of physical exercise over spiritual disciplines. Rather his comment grows directly out of the matter of the false teachers' promotion of a false asceticism in Ephesus (vv.3-7). Paul would not say that bodily discipline is of no value at all, for he practiced it in appropriate measure (1 Cor. 9:27; 2 Cor. 11:27). But out of balance it takes the emphasis off the more important matter—the inward life of godliness.

For this reason Paul says bodily discipline "is only of little profit" (πρὸς ὀλίγον ἐστὶν ὠφέλιμος). A literal translation is "to little is profit." The expression "of little" (πρὸς ὀλίγον) is found elsewhere only in James 4:14 where it means "a little while." Here the time element is not in view because it is contrasted later in the sentence by "all things" (πρὸς πάντα).[37] The verb

---
[37] Ibid., 564.

"is" (ἐστὶν) is in the present tense and stresses the continuous worth of the discipline in view. The noun "profit" (ὠφέλιμος) is used only four times in the NT, all of them in the PE (1 Tim. 4:8 [2x]; 2 Tim. 3:16; Titus 3:8). It has the sense of helpful, beneficial, useful or advantageous.[38] The relative benefit of such bodily discipline is inconsequential.

In contrast ("but," δὲ) is the value of "godliness" (ἡ . . . εὐσέβεια). The word is often found in the PE and was just used in the previous verse where Timothy is charged with disciplining himself "for the purpose of godliness." Here it has the definite article, marking it out as unique, unlike the feigned "godliness" of the false teachers (1 Tim. 6:5; 2 Tim. 3:5). It "is profitable" (ὠφέλιμός ἐστιν). The noun is the same one just used in the first part of the verse. Again the present tense verb "is" underscores the continuous nature of the benefit. In contrast to the "little" benefit of bodily discipline is that godliness is profitable "for all things" (πρὸς πάντα; or perhaps "in every way"[39] or "in all directions"[40]).

This superior profitability is "since it holds promise" (ἐπαγγελίαν ἔχουσα). The participle "holds" is translated as having concessive force. The present tense points to the continuous connection of "godliness" and the "promise." The only other use of the noun "promise" (ἐπαγγελίαν) in the PE is also connected to "life" (2 Tim. 1:1). As there so also here the genitive designates the content of the promise. Here the promise is "for the present life and also for the life to come" (ζωῆς τῆς νῦν καὶ τῆς μελλούσης). The expression is more compact in Greek: "of life, the now and the to come." The word "life" (ζωή), as Mounce explains, "denotes not mere existence but has a richer, fuller meaning, describing an abundant type of life that is promised to those in Christ."[41] Usually in the PE the word "life" (ζωή) is accompanied by the adjective "eternal" (αἰώνιος; 1 Tim. 1:16; 6:12; Titus 1:2; 3:7). It is a life that is to be experienced in "the present" (τῆς νῦν) and even more fully in *the life* to come" (τῆς μελλούσης). The adverb "now" (νῦν) is elsewhere found in the PE with the definite article (1 Tim. 6:17; 2 Tim. 4:10; Titus 2:12), always in the expression "this present world" (αἰών). This stands in contrast to "the life to come" (τῆς μελλούσης). The participle is used as a substantive ("the future"). The continuous nature of that life as "coming" is stressed through the present tense.

> **Ministry Maxim**
>
> Discipline follows values, never the other way around.

---

[38] BAGD, 900.
[39] Fee, 104.
[40] Guthrie, 95.
[41] Mounce, 253.

Some see in this saying a shadow of Jesus' statement in Luke 18:29-30: "And He said to them, 'Truly I say to you, there is no one who has left house or wife or brothers or parents or children, for the sake of the kingdom of God, who will not receive many times as much at this time and in the age to come, eternal life.'"[42]

> **Ministry Maxim**
>
> When words capture our beliefs and values they guide our lives.

4:9 It is a trustworthy statement deserving full acceptance.

We meet here once again the Apostle's expression, "It is a trustworthy statement" (πιστὸς ὁ λόγος). It appears five times in the PE and nowhere else in the NT (1 Tim. 1:15; 3:1; 4:9; 2 Tim. 2:11; Titus 3:8). In fact the full sentence is a repeat from 1 Timothy 1:15 (which see). It can point to that which follows (1 Tim. 1:15; 3:1; 2 Tim. 2:11), but here it appears to point to that which precedes it (vv.7-8) as in Titus 3:8 (contra. NIV and NEB). This understanding seems correct because the conjunction "For" (γὰρ) in v.10 seems to offer an explanation, not a faithful saying, and the nature of v.8b seems more like a proverbial saying than the content of v.10.

> **Digging Deeper:**
> 1. Why is discipline the answer to the conversations spoken of in v.7a?
> 2. How does Paul's comparison of bodily discipline and discipline for godliness teach us about the relative value of what is important to this world?
> 3. Does the church today generally and heartily accept this notion of discipline and its value system (v.9)? What evidence do you offer for your answer?

4:10 For it is for this we labor and strive, because we have fixed our hope on the living God, who is the Savior of all men, especially of believers.

Paul gives the reason "For" (γὰρ) his confidence in the previous statement (vv.7-9). The words "it is for this" (εἰς τοῦτο) might be more literally "to this." The "this" (τοῦτο) refers back to the "promise" inherent in "godliness" in v.8. Two actions are made "for this" goal (the two verbs are found in combination

---
[42] Knight, 201.

also in Col. 1:29). First, says the Apostle, "we labor" (κοπιῶμεν). The second person singular (v.7) has now become the first person plural ("we"). This was not a solitary struggle for Paul, but one fought together with other believers. This verb stresses the wearisome nature of the toil. Paul uses it in 2 Timothy 2:6 to describe "the hard-working farmer." It might apply to the ministry of local church leadership generally (1 Thess. 5:12), to preaching specifically (1 Tim. 5:17), or, as here, to striving after godliness in one's personal life (1 Tim. 4:10). Paul knew from experience what it meant to work to the point of weariness (1 Cor. 4:12; 15:10; Gal. 4:11; Phil. 2:16; Col. 1:29; 1 Tim. 4:10). The present tense underscores the habitual, unending nature of the toil. Paul also ("and," καὶ) says that "we . . . strive" (ἀγωνιζόμεθα). The reading of the KJV ("suffer reproach") is less likely, being based on inferior manuscript evidence. The verb we meet here, when used literally, can describe either competing for a prize in an athletic contest (1 Cor. 9:25) or engaging another in a battle with weapons (John 18:36). When it is used figuratively, it often has the sense of contending or struggling with great effort against difficulties or dangers generally (Col. 1:29; 1 Tim. 4:10) or of striving after something with strenuous zeal (Luke 13:24; Col. 4:12).[43] Paul uses it to summarize the entire nature of his battle in this life, "I have fought the good fight" (2 Tim. 4:7). It is related to our words "agony" and "agonize." Here, too, the present tense stresses the continual action. The middle voice pictures the inward nature of the agonizing battle and effort. Both verbs can have athletic overtones (the former in Phil. 2:16 and the latter in 1 Cor. 9:25). Given the context (v.8), this may be the imagery the Apostle intends here as well.

The motivating factor ("because," ὅτι) behind this, says Paul, is that "we have fixed our hope on the living God" (ἠλπίκαμεν ἐπὶ θεῷ ζῶντι). The verb is in the perfect tense, emphasizing this hope as an abiding state entered at some point in the past and continuing to the present moment. Paul uses the verb four times in this letter to speak of hope (1 Tim. 3:14; 4:10; 5:5; 6:17). What fear cannot do, hope achieves. It draws out agonizing, striving effort in the anticipation of achieving godliness. This hope is set, not upon a dead idol, but "on the living God" (ἐπὶ θεῷ ζῶντι). At Lystra Paul called the adoring crowds who were about to offer sacrifice to them to "turn from these vain things to a living God" (Acts 14:15). Quoting Hosea 1:10, Paul told the Romans that the Gentiles would be called "SONS OF THE LIVING GOD" (Rom. 9:26). He told the Corinthians that they were living letters written "with the Spirit of the living God" (2

> **Ministry Maxim**
>
> Hope is the motivator behind all great human effort and achievement.

---
[43] Thayer, 10.

Cor. 3:3). He reminded the Thessalonians that they had turned "from idols to serve a living and true God" (1 Thess. 1:9). Paul has just referred to "the church of the living God" (1 Tim. 3:15). The title "the living God" is a favorite in Hebrews as well (Heb. 3:12; 9:14; 10:31; 12:22; cf. also Rev. 7:2). Because He is "the living God," He is able to make and keep a "promise for the present life and also for the life to come" (1 Tim. 4:8).

The living God is the One "who is the Savior of all men" (ὅς ἐστιν σωτὴρ πάντων ἀνθρώπων). The singular relative pronoun ("who," ὅς) points back to "the living God" just spoken of. The noun "Savior" is used often in the PE, being found ten times, while Paul uses it only two times elsewhere (Eph. 5:23; Phil. 3:20). He refers to God as our Savior (1 Tim. 1:1; 2:3; 4:10; Titus 1:3; 2:10; 3:4) slightly more than He does to Jesus as our Savior (2 Tim. 2:10; Titus 1:4; 2:13; 3:6). Here He is called the Savior "of all men" (πάντων ἀνθρώπων), emphasizing the universal sufficiency of the Father's saving plan through Christ. Indeed, as the believing Samaritans confessed, Jesus is "the Savior of the world" (John 4:42). He is, as John the Baptist declared, "the Lamb of God who takes away the sin of the world" (John 1:29). The Father sent the Son "to be the Savior of the world" (1 John 4:14). "For God so loved the world, that He gave His only begotten Son" (John 3:16a). "He Himself is the propitiation for our sins; and not for ours only, but also for those of the whole world" (1 John 2:2). Jesus "gave Himself as a ransom for all" (1 Tim. 2:6) because the Father "desires all men to be saved" (v.4).

The Apostle Paul, however, quickly adds "especially of believers" (μάλιστα πιστῶν). The adverb ("especially," μάλιστα) is the superlative of the adverb μάλα. It designates "the highest point in the extent of something" and means something like "most of all," "especially," or "above all."[44] With this clause the Apostle moves from the universal scope of the *sufficiency* of Christ's sacrifice ("the Savior of all men") and narrows the field regarding the limited scope of its *efficiency* ("especially of believers"). Indeed, only "believers" (πιστῶν) will experience the saving grace of God, for salvation comes to "everyone who believes" (Rom. 1:16). The righteousness of God comes "through faith in Jesus Christ for all those who believe" (Rom. 3:22). To be saved we must "believe in Him for eternal life" (1 Tim. 1:16). While God's love extends to the entire world and Christ's sacrifice is sufficient for all, it is clearly efficient only for those who believe. Paul stresses the essential nature of faith placed in the person of Christ when he questions the Romans: "How then will they call on Him in whom they have not believed? How will they believe in Him whom they have not heard? And how will they hear without a preacher?" (Rom. 10:14).

---

[44] Friberg, 252.

> **Digging Deeper:**
> 1. If God is "the Savior" and salvation is entirely of His doing, why do we have to "labor and strive"?
> 2. What does it mean to *fix* one's hope on something?
> 3. Did Jesus die for the whole world or only for the elect? Upon what do you base your answer?

4:11 Prescribe and teach these things.

This terse sentence serves to summarize and apply all that has been said in vv.1-10, as well as to open the way for more personal encouragements to Timothy himself (vv.12-16). It returns to the notion of "pointing out these things" in v.6 and seals here the idea started there with two imperatives (numbers three and four of the twelve present tense imperatives in vv.7, 11-16). The identity of "these things" (ταῦτα) is probably wrapped up in the whole of the discussion from v.1 and repeats the same word from v.6. There may, however, be special emphasis upon the soteriological thoughts of v.10.

Regarding "these things" Paul makes two demands of Timothy. With two present tense imperatives Paul succinctly demands regular, ongoing compliance with his orders ("Keep on prescribing" and "keep on teaching"). He turns from the first person plural ("we," v.10) and returns again to the second person singular throughout vv.11-16. The verb "Prescribe" (Παράγγελλε) is used twelve times by the Apostle (1 Cor. 7:10; 11:17; 1 Thess. 4:11; 2 Thess. 3:4, 6, 10, 12), five of them here in 1 Timothy (1:3; 4:11; 5:7; 6:13, 17; and cf. the cognate noun in 1:5, 18). It is a compound word from "along" (παρά) and "announce" (ἀγγέλλω). Thus its root meaning is to pass along a message to someone. It came, however, to be used of an authoritative announcement or command. Here its use signals the apostolic authority with which Timothy was to issue the appropriate instructions. The word was used in military contexts and there is strength in it. It is found in this same present imperative form three times in this letter. Timothy is to command the people regarding the matters here (vv.1-10), widows (5:1-7), and the instability of trusting riches (6:17).

> **Ministry Maxim**
>
> Every imperative should stand on clear reasoning and every instruction should be based on appropriate authority.

The second command is to "teach" (δίδασκε). The emphasis here is not on command, but instruction. The same form of the verb is used in 1 Timothy 6:2 and paired with a different verb regarding right attitude and behavior of slaves ("teach and preach," δίδασκε καὶ παρακάλει). Paul does not allow a woman to "teach" in the gathered assembly (1 Tim. 2:12). Timothy is to teach "faithful men who will be able to teach others also" (2 Tim. 2:2). The false teachers on Crete were "teaching things they should not teach" (Titus 1:11).

The combination here of "Prescribe" (with its emphasis upon authoritative command) and "teach" (with its emphasis upon instruction) reminds us that in Christian ministry all demands should have cogent reasoning behind them and all instruction should be backed by an appropriate urgency and authority.

> **Digging Deeper:**
> 1. Timothy had a direct link to Paul, but how does the pastor of today speak with authority?
> 2. What does the combination of "prescribe" and "teach" communicate about the speaking ministry of the pastor?

4:12 Let no one look down on your youthfulness, but rather in speech, conduct, love, faith and purity, show yourself an example of those who believe.

Continuing in a more personal exhortation, the Apostle demands, "Let no one look down on your youthfulness" (Μηδείς σου τῆς νεότητος καταφρονείτω). The negation "no one" (Μηδείς) is used as a substantive and makes the prohibition absolute. The expression "your youthfulness" is more literally "of you the youth" (σου τῆς νεότητος). The noun does not specify an age, but a person of 30 or 40 years of age could still be considered a youth.[45] We do not know Timothy's precise age. Yet if he first traveled with the Apostle Paul during his second missionary journey (Acts 16:1ff) in approximately A.D. 49-50 and it is approximately at the time of the writing of 1 Timothy, it is probable that Timothy was at least thirty years of age.[46] Many of the elders in the Ephesian congregation would have been much older than this. Many had probably been personally trained by the Apostle Paul himself (Acts 19:1-41; 20:17-38). The combination of their age, Timothy's relative youthfulness and the long legacy of the "former pastor" could easily have led some to "look down on" Timothy

---
[45] Rienecker, 627.
[46] Kent, 155.

and his leadership. Titus, who may have been older and who served a congregation of primarily newer believers, did not face quite this same situation and thus we find no parallel command given to him.[47] It could also have been the false teachers who were discounting Timothy because of his age. Soon enough Paul will counsel Timothy regarding how to conduct himself with each age group (5:1ff). Whatever the reason, the prohibited action here is letting someone "look down on" (καταφρονείτω) Timothy. It is a compound word made up of "down" (κατά) and "to think" (φρονέω). It has the sense of to despise, scorn or treat with contempt.[48] The present tense imperative calls for repeated and vigilant action. For a similar concern regarding Timothy see 1 Corinthians 16:11 (cf. Titus 2:15).

In stark contrast ("but," ἀλλὰ), Paul says, "show yourself an example" (τύπος γίνου). The way not to let others "look down on your youthfulness" is not primarily through confrontation, but through exemplification. The present tense of the imperative "Let no one look down" is expressive of the continuous labor over time necessary to "show yourself an example." This command is fulfilled not by demands for respect, but through ongoing godliness of life. The noun "example" (τύπος) originally referred to the mark left by a blow or an impression made under pressure. Then it described a copy or an image and came to refer to a type, pattern or model. Here the sense is that of being an example or pattern in the moral life.[49] Mounce says, "The word picture it paints is a mold that should be pressed into the lives of others so that they attain the same shape."[50] The pastor's life is to be a model of all the Scripture calls the flock to be. The same word was used similarly of Titus (Titus 2:7). The verb "show yourself" (γίνου), in its most basic form, means "become." The present tense imperative again demands constant action ("keep on becoming"[51]). A young pastor wins the respect of his congregation one day at a time as he continually lives out his life before them. Over time they behold what he is and come to respect him. The middle voice puts the onus on Timothy to "become" such an example. The meaning is something like "make yourself become an example," and thus the translation "show yourself" is a fair rendering. Specifically, the aim is to be an example "of those who believe" (τῶν πιστῶν). The adjective with its definite article is used substantively. The genitive can mean either an example "of those who believe" or an example "for the believers" (NIV). The parallel form in 1 Peter 5:3 ("examples to the flock") shows that the genitive can have the latter meaning. Surely both are true—the pastor

---

[47] Mounce, 259.
[48] BAGD, 420.
[49] Ibid., 829-830.
[50] Mounce, 259.
[51] Robertson, 4:580-581.

must be an example of a believer and to the believers. The pastor is first and fundamentally one of the believers. His life must model what it means to be a disciple of Jesus Christ. Then also he is called in a special sense to the ministry, and his life must additionally bear the marks of one called and commissioned uniquely as an under-shepherd. He is to model what all believers should be. The authoritative command called for in v.11 must be backed up by an unfolding life of personal devotion to God lived out before the people.

The specifics of this example are spelled out by five prepositional phrases, all beginning with "in" (ἐν). The preposition describes the sphere in which Timothy's example is to be found. The KJV's "in spirit" is not attested by the best manuscripts and should not be included. These qualities concern both the outward ("speech" and "conduct") and inward ("love, faith and purity") life. First his example is to be "in speech" (ἐν λόγῳ). The word λόγος has a broad and varied usage in the NT. Here it refers simply to speaking or one's conversation.[52] The pastor must guard his teaching and preaching (v.16). Yet it is not simply in the pulpit or when the pastor is "on," but also in his everyday conversations over seemingly mundane and inconsequential matters that he must set an example.

The example also it is to be in "conduct" (ἐν ἀναστροφῇ). The noun is cognate to the compound verb ἀναστρέφω which means "up" (ἀνά) and "to turn" (στρέφω). The verb can then mean "to turn upside down," "to turn back," or "to turn oneself around."[53] The noun has the sense of "turning about in place" and thus comes to describe a way of life or one's conduct or behavior.[54] The noun is used only two more times by Paul, both where he speaks of "your former manner of life" (Gal. 1:13; Eph. 4:22). Peter has an affinity to the word, using it eight times in his letters (1 Peter 1:15, 18; 2:12; 3:1, 2, 16; 2 Peter 2:7; 3:11). The pastor, at whatever age, should stand as an example of one whose life has been turned around and is now in pursuit of God.

> **Ministry Maxim**
>
> Disrespect is overcome fundamentally not through confrontation, but exemplification.

He should also be an example in "love" (ἐν ἀγάπῃ). This rich word describes that love which can only be found in Christ Himself (1 Tim. 1:14) and is sent into our hearts by His Spirit (2 Tim. 1:7). Such love is the goal of all true preaching and teaching (1 Tim. 1:5) and all truth is to be held in love (2 Tim. 1:13). In this Paul was an example (2 Tim. 3:10). Such love is to be the pursuit of every child of God, no matter his age (1 Tim. 4:12; Titus 2:2) or gender (1 Tim. 2:15; 6:11). The pastor is to set an example in his personal pursuit of such love (1 Tim. 6:11; 2 Tim. 2:22).

---

[52] BAGD, 477.
[53] Thayer, 42.
[54] Friberg, 52.

The Apostle surely has both the vertical ("YOU SHALL LOVE THE LORD YOUR GOD WITH ALL YOUR HEART, AND WITH ALL YOUR SOUL, AND WITH ALL YOUR MIND," Matt. 22:37) and the horizontal ("YOU SHALL LOVE YOUR NEIGHBOR AS YOURSELF," v.39) in view.

The pastor also is to be an example in "faith" (ἐν πίστει). Paul uses this noun thirty-three times in the PE. The emphasis here is not so much on "the faith" as a body of truth (e.g., 1 Tim. 4:6), but upon faith as personal trust in the God who gives that body of truth. The word could possibly be understood in the passive sense of "faithfulness," but faith (πίστις) and love (ἀγάπη) are found in combination ten times in the PE (1 Tim. 1:5, 14; 2:15; 4:12; 6:2, 11; 2 Tim. 1:13; 2:22; 3:10; Titus 2:2) and when found together the noun normally points to personal trust. One cannot possess true faith without having come in contact with divine love. True faith will always issue in an expression, however imperfect it may be, of divine love in and through that life. Love and faith are inseparable.

And finally this example is to be in "purity" (ἐν ἁγνείᾳ). Rienecker says, "The word covers not only chastity in matters of sex, but also the innocence and integrity of heart which are denoted by the related noun in 2 Corinthians 6:6 . . . The word refers to purity of act and thought."[55] The only other use of the word in the NT is in 1 Timothy 5:2 where Timothy is to treat "the younger women as sisters, in all purity."

Paul is addressing Timothy personally in these exhortations, yet he does so within the context of his ministry as pastor in Ephesus. Not surprisingly the five areas in which the Apostle calls Timothy to excel as an example are the very areas in which the false teachers have failed. In their "speech" they are among those "advocating a different doctrine" that "does not agree with sound words" (1 Tim. 6:3). They "teach strange doctrines" (1 Tim. 1:3). Indeed, "their talk will spread like gangrene" (2 Tim. 2:17). In their "conduct" they, on the one hand, practice a false asceticism (1 Tim. 4:3); on the other hand they have no qualms about fleecing the flock (1 Tim. 6:5, 9-10). They enter "disputes about words" and give vent to "envy, strife, abusive language, evil suspicions" (1 Tim. 6:4). With regard to "love" they are among those who are "lovers of self, lovers of money" (2 Tim. 3:2) and are "lovers of pleasure rather than lovers of God" (3:4). In "faith" they have "suffered shipwreck in regard to their faith" (1 Tim. 1:19). They are among those who "fall away from the faith" (4:1), have "wandered away from the faith" (6:10) and "gone astray from the faith" (6:21). In so doing they "upset the faith of some" (2 Tim. 2:18). They prove themselves to be "rejected in regard to the faith" (3:8). In regards to "purity" they "enter into households and captivate weak women" (2 Tim. 3:6), perhaps even targeting younger widows who are struggling with their sensual desires (1 Tim. 5:11).

---

[55] Rienecker, 627.

> **Digging Deeper:**
> 1. At what age is one past the vulnerability of being looked down upon by another because of age?
> 2. How is long-term example an answer to the immediate problem of disrespect? How is that helpful? How is that frustrating?
> 3. Why do you suppose Paul mentioned the five areas of example that are enumerated here? What area of life might these fail to cover?

4:13 Until I come, give attention to the public reading of Scripture, to exhortation and teaching.

The Apostle gives Timothy instruction regarding what is to happen "Until I come" (ἕως ἔρχομαι). The temporal conjunction ἕως usually means "Until." Here it is found with the present indicative when one would have suspected the aorist subjunctive (cf. also Mark 6:45; Luke 19:13; John 21:22).[56] The sense here could be "While I am coming."[57] The net difference in meaning is not major. The statement does tell us that Paul had every intention of returning to Ephesus (1 Tim. 3:14) and that Timothy was to act in his stead in the intervening time. Timothy had Paul's apostolic backing for his ministry in Ephesus.

Paul commands Timothy to "give attention" (πρόσεχε). The word is used twenty-four times in the NT. Only five of those uses are by Paul, and of which appear in the PE. Four of those are here in 1 Timothy (1:4; 3:8; 4:1, 13; Titus 1:14). It is a compound word comprised of "to" (πρός) and "hold" (ἔχω). It means "turning or holding one's mind to someone or something" and thus "occupying one's mind with something."[58] It is used negatively of a preoccupation with myths (1 Tim. 1:4; Titus 1:14) and "deceitful spirits" (1 Tim. 4:1), as well as addiction to alcohol (1 Tim. 3:8). Here we find the lone positive use in the PE. It means to "occupy oneself with, devote or apply oneself to."[59] The present tense imperative demands that the action be undertaken repeatedly. The verb "implies previous preparation in private."[60]

That to which Timothy's attention is to be given is indicated by three nouns with their definite articles in the dative case. The definite articles are significant, indicating some well-known feature in the congregation. First is "the public reading of Scripture" (τῇ ἀναγνώσει). It is more literally and

---
[56] Thayer, 268.
[57] Robertson, 4:581.
[58] Friberg, 333.
[59] BAGD, 714.
[60] Guthrie, 97.

simply, "the reading." It is a compound word made up of "again" (ἀνά) and "knowledge" (γνῶσις). It refers to the Jewish custom of reading the Scriptures aloud in the synagogue as the other two NT references indicate (Acts 13:15; 2 Cor. 3:14). Thus nearly all English translations go beyond the bare translation "the reading" and make some reference to "public" and "Scripture" as well. That which was read, following the synagogue custom, would have been the OT Scriptures. Clearly by this time some portions of what we now know as the NT were becoming available, and were viewed as Scripture (1 Tim. 5:18 refers to Matt. 10:10 and Luke 10:7 as "the Scripture says"; cf. 2 Peter 3:15-16) and would have been included as well. Paul instructed that his letters be read (Col. 4:16; 1 Thess. 5:27; cf. Rev. 1:3). In an age before the printing press and in illiterate societies the "public reading of Scripture" had a vital part in the congregation's discipleship. In an era when large parts of the world have multiple translations of the Scriptures available and vast portions of the populace own multiple copies of the Scriptures, it is sad to see so few carry a Bible to public worship nor ever refer to it during the service. Sadder still is the worship service where the Bible is seldom used or ever seen.

> **Ministry Maxim**
>
> A pastor should be "addicted" to the Scriptures.

Second is "exhortation" (τῇ παρακλήσει). The noun is used only here in the PE, but it is the cognate noun of the oft-used verb παρακαλέω (1 Tim. 1:3; 2:1; 5:1; 6:2; 2 Tim. 4:2; Titus 1:9; 2:6, 15). It is a compound word meaning "alongside" (παρά) and "to call" (καλέω). The meaning of the word ranges from comfort to admonition. Here it describes the more official "powerful hortatory discourse"[61] typical among the Jews in their synagogues (Acts 13:15) and of the church when the local assembly of believers comes together for worship (Rom. 12:8).

Third is "teaching" (τῇ διδασκαλίᾳ). The exact form is found in 1 Timothy 4:16, 2 Timothy 3:10, and Titus 1:9; 2:7. It may refer to either the act of teaching or to that which is taught ("doctrine").[62] There may be the "doctrine of demons" (1 Tim. 4:1). But "the doctrine of God our Savior" (Titus 2:10) is "sound teaching/doctrine" (1 Tim. 1:10; 4:6; 2 Tim. 4:3; Titus 1:9; 2:1), "doctrine conforming to godliness" (1 Tim. 6:3), and "purity in doctrine" (Titus 2:7). Paul held forth this "teaching" to Timothy (2 Tim. 3:10). This is the heart of Scripture's purpose (2 Tim. 3:16) and all our teaching is to arise from and be controlled by the Scriptures. Such a ministry requires careful attention (1 Tim. 4:13), perseverance, and meticulous study (4:16), if our "doctrine will not

---

[61] Thayer, 483.
[62] BAGD, 191.

be spoken against" (6:1). These terms remind us that by God's design preaching and teaching are never completely distinct from one another. The verbal forms of these latter two words are found in 1 Tim. 6:2 in the imperative mood, demanding that Timothy use the contents of this letter in these ways.[63]

One might have expected the order to be "public reading of Scripture," then "teaching" and finally "exhortation." It is probable, however, that Paul was simply holding the three before Timothy without thought to the logical order of their use in preaching and teaching. "Probably Paul does not mean for the exhortation to precede the instruction, but the reverse in actual public work. Exhortation needs teaching to rest it upon, a hint for preachers today."[64] The pastor "must *read and exhort*, that is, read and expound, read and press what he read upon them; he must expound it both by way of exhortation and by way of doctrine; he must teach them both what to do and what to believe."[65] The heart of the local church's worship is the reading of Scripture followed by an exposition of those Scriptures, which includes both doctrinal instruction and personal appeal and application. This is not all that should take place during public worship, but this should be at the heart of it all. This should occupy the mind and heart of the pastor. He should be "addicted" (to use the translation of the same verb in 3:8) to the teaching and preaching of the Scriptures.

> **Digging Deeper:**
> 1. Do widespread literacy and the broad availability of the Scriptures alter the need to "give attention to the public reading of Scripture"?
> 2. What is the distinction between "exhortation" and "teaching"? How should both be a part of what takes place in corporate worship?
> 3. Why do you think the reading of Scripture has become less common in the worship of Christian churches? What is the effect?

4:14 Do not neglect the spiritual gift within you, which was bestowed on you through prophetic utterance with the laying on of hands by the presbytery.

The Apostle issues a strong prohibition: "Do not neglect" (μὴ ἀμέλει). The negative particle (μὴ) "denies the thought of the thing, or the thing according to the judgment, opinion, will, purpose, preference, of someone (hence, as we

---
[63] Fee, 108.
[64] Robertson, 4:581.
[65] Henry, 2355.

say technically, indirectly, hypothetically, subjectively)."[66] The present imperative with the negative particle normally demands that action now in progress be stopped. It may be that Paul uses this expression not as an indication of some neglect on Timothy's part, but as an example of the literary device *litotes*, a positive command set forth in negative terms.[67] The verb is used only here by Paul (cf. Matt. 22:5; Heb. 2:3; 8:9).

That which is not to be neglected is "the spiritual gift within you" (τοῦ ἐν σοὶ χαρίσματος). Most literally this is "the in you gift," the preposition and personal pronoun being tucked between the noun and its definite article in order to stress the personal and inward nature of Timothy's gift. This sounds similar to what Paul would later say to Timothy when he reminded him "to kindle afresh the gift of God which is in you through the laying on of my hands" (2 Tim. 1:6). We find there the same word for "spiritual gift" (χάρισμα) and the expression "in you" (ἐν σοὶ). The noun is used seventeen times in the NT, sixteen of those by Paul. It can refer to the free gift of salvation in Christ (Rom. 5:15, 16; 6:23), to divine enablements worked out in the believer by the Holy Spirit (Rom. 12:6; 1 Cor. 1:6; 12:4, 9, 28, 30, 31; 1 Peter 4:10), and more generally of favor extended (2 Cor. 1:11). Jesus, just before He ascended, spoke of "the promise of My Father" (Luke 24:49). Shortly afterward that promise was referred to more specifically as "the gift of the Holy Spirit" (Acts 2:38). It might be more accurate to say that the gift to which Paul refers here is the Holy Spirit Himself. The contextual connection of "gift" and the Spirit in 2 Timothy 1:6 (cf. vv.7, 14) and elsewhere (Rom. 1:11; 1 Cor. 1:7; 12:4, 31) seems to confirm this. The Spirit is the gift. We often speak of a spiritual gift as the ability to "do" something, treating it almost as an objective thing we possess. It seems more in keeping with the teaching of Scripture to see the Spirit as the gift and the newly imparted ability as simply the way the Holy Spirit sovereignly chooses to express Himself through the individual. A spiritual gift is simply the Holy Spirit being Himself uniquely through an individual believer. All believers receive the Holy Spirit (Rom. 8:9; Titus 3:5). The Holy Spirit chooses how He expresses Himself in and through the individual. The arena in which this gift works is "in" (ἐν) Timothy. This "spiritual gift" is not simply an outward ability to "do," but an inward relationship to be cultivated ("Do not neglect"; cf. 2 Tim. 1:6).

Since all believers receive the Holy Spirit at the time of conversion (Rom. 8:9; Titus 3:5), how can Paul speak of that "which was bestowed on you through prophetic utterance with the laying on of hands by the presbytery" (ὃ ἐδόθη σοι διὰ προφητείας μετὰ ἐπιθέσεως τῶν χειρῶν τοῦ πρεσβυτερίου)? As a "gift" it must be that "which is given" (ὃ ἐδόθη). The aorist tense looks back

---

[66] Thayer, 408.
[67] Kent, 158.

to the moment of the event the Apostle describes. Just when that was is not stated. It was likely at Timothy's initial commissioning into ministry. The passive voice underscores the free and gracious nature of the gift as coming from God himself. The pronoun "you" (σοι) identifies this as a personal and individual bestowment to Timothy Himself. Something uniquely special, intimate and personal took place between God and Timothy at that moment. This took place "through prophetic utterance" (διὰ προφητείας). The preposition ("through," διὰ) usually indicates the means by which the action takes place, but it can also point to agency, and attendant circumstances.[68] The only other use of the noun in the PE is when Paul entrusts a command to Timothy "in accordance with the prophecies previously made concerning you" (1 Tim. 1:18). Here, as there, the content of these "prophecies" may have given some indication of the kind of ministry in which God would use Timothy or the way the Spirit would express Himself through Timothy in ministry. Acts 13:1-3 may provide the best example of the kind of event being described here. It is not that Timothy received the Holy Spirit for the first time at this moment, but that the Spirit sovereignly expressed at that moment how He would work in and through Timothy in ministry in the future. The Spirit made this known at that moment through a prophetic utterance given to one of those present.

> **Ministry Maxim**
>
> Neglect of the Holy Spirit's work *in* you affects His work *through* you.

This took place "with the laying on of hands by the presbytery" (μετὰ ἐπιθέσεως τῶν χειρῶν τοῦ πρεσβυτερίου). The preposition ("with," μετὰ) speaks of that which accompanies the action. Timothy's spiritual gift did not come "through" the laying on of hands, but its arrival was accompanied by the laying on of hands. The singular noun "the presbytery" (τοῦ πρεσβυτερίου) is used as a collective, viewing the elders as one whole entity. In 2 Timothy 1:6 Paul spoke only of his hands being laid upon Timothy ("through the laying on of my hands"), but that may have been due to the personal nature of that letter. Rather than two different occasions in view, it seems more likely that Paul had been joined by the presbytery in laying hands upon Timothy. During the transitional days of the church's early preaching, Luke pictures the bestowment of the Holy Spirit as coming upon new converts through the laying on of hands (Acts 8:17-18; 19:6). Yet we know that every believer is indwelt by the Holy Spirit (Rom. 8:9; 1 Cor. 12:13). So in what sense did Paul impart the Holy Spirit and His gifting to Timothy through the laying on of hands? When Timothy put his faith in Christ, the Holy Spirit indwelt him, as He does all believers. But as the Holy Spirit shaped Timothy's life it became clear that He

---

[68] Mounce, 261-262.

was calling him into ministry. As God's people recognized this calling, they affirmed it through the laying on of hands. As they did so, God the Holy Spirit revealed through His people, via a prophetic utterance, the way He would work through Timothy in ministry. The modern practice of ordination may find some echo here, but also may contain elements that go well beyond what Paul describes.

> **Digging Deeper:**
>
> 1. In what unique ways does the Holy Spirit express Himself through you in ministry to others?
> 2. How may a person neglect the Holy Spirit's work *in* his/her life? How will this affect the work of the Holy Spirit *through* his/her life?
> 3. What value may there be in the Holy Spirit's witness to the community of believers concerning His work in and through your life?

4:15 Take pains with these things; be absorbed in them, so that your progress will be evident to all.

Paul now issues two more present tense imperatives (numbers nine and ten of the twelve such commands used in vv.7, 11-16) and then gives the purpose behind them. "Take pains with these things" (ταῦτα μελέτα) represents a mere two words in the Greek text. By "these things" (ταῦτα) Paul probably means Timothy's personal life (v.12), ministry of Scripture (v.13), and spiritual gift (v.14). The verb can speak of the attention of the mind (cf. KJV, "meditate upon") or of practicing something.[69] It is probably in this latter sense it is used here, with a meaning of practicing, cultivating or taking pains with something.[70] This may be a continuation of the athletic imagery of vv.7-10. The former meaning can also have a negative connotation, meaning to plot, conspire, or premeditate.[71] It is used in this sense in the only other NT use (Acts 4:25; cf. Mark 13:11). The present tense imperative demands the action be taken repeatedly or habitually.

Secondly, Paul demands Timothy to "be absorbed in them" (ἐν τούτοις ἴσθι). The identification of "them" (τούτοις) is the same as "these things" in the previous clause. The preposition "in" (ἐν) pictures Timothy immersing himself in these matters. Indeed, the verb demands literally that he "*be* in them" ("absorbed" is added by the translators for smoother reading). Once again the

---
[69] Fee, 109.
[70] BAGD, 500.
[71] Friberg, 257.

present tense imperative demands that this is ever to be Timothy's continuous habit. Robertson suggests that Paul's meaning is not far from our phrase "being up to our ears" in work.[72] Guthrie comments, "The mind is to be as immersed in these pursuits as the body in the air it breathes."[73] As a fish lives and moves and has its being in water, as the bird is made for the sky and the worm for the earth—so we must *be* in these things, indeed, we must be *in* these things.

The purpose ("so that," ἵνα + present subjunctive) behind issuing these two commands is the hope that Timothy's "progress will be evident to all" (σου ἡ προκοπὴ φανερὰ ᾖ πᾶσιν). All eyes are on Timothy. The pronoun ("your," σου) is emphatic by its position. The people are watching him for "progress" (ἡ προκοπή). The word is used elsewhere in the NT only in Philippians where it speaks of progress "of the gospel" (1:12) and "in the faith" (1:25). The use of the cognate verb demonstrates that the word can be used both positively (Luke 2:52; Rom. 13:12; Gal. 1:14) and negatively (2 Tim. 2:16; 3:9, 13), for "not every 'advance' is also 'growth'."[74] The noun is used here in a positive sense. Perhaps the concentration of the negative usage in 2 Timothy 2:16; 3:9, 13 indicates the false teachers in Ephesus were promising a unique "progress" for their followers.[75] The word was a favorite of Stoic philosophers, used to speak of a student's progress in their philosophic studies,[76] so it might naturally be borrowed by the false teachers for their purposes as well. If this be the case then Paul is here making a powerful statement about the superiority of the Gospel over their false teaching and is calling Timothy to demonstrate that superiority in his own life and action. The presence of the definite article may point to "*the* progress" that every congregation looks for in their minister. The kind of growth Paul and the church hope for in Timothy is that which "will be evident" (φανερὰ ᾖ). The adjective describes that which is manifest, evident, clear, and plain. And this is to be obvious, not merely to a few discerning folk, but "to all" (πᾶσιν).

> **Ministry Maxim**
>
> Invisible discipline results in observable growth.

It is rare for churches to expect their pastor to be perfect, but they do want us to grow. Our responsibility is to make *visible* progress in our personal godliness (v.12), in our preaching and teaching (v.13), and in our particular area of gifting (v.14). The Apostle's words imply that we do not arrive on the scene already in possession of all we will need throughout the course of our ministry. We each must grow into our ministries. It further intimates that a

---

[72] Robertson, 4:582.
[73] Guthrie, 98.
[74] DNTT, 2:130.
[75] Mounce, 264.
[76] Rienecker, 628.

humble, educable attitude is essential for any servant of God. Nearly as dangerous as the absolutely unteachable spirit is the selectively teachable one—the individual who does not claim perfection, but who has chosen who is capable of helping him grow and who is not. A wise pastor can learn something valuable from nearly every circumstance and congregant.

> **Digging Deeper:**
> 1. What are some practical actions wrapped up in the command to "Take pains in these things"?
> 2. Specifically what kind of demonstrable, outward evidence will people see in their pastor when he is growing?
> 3. Agree or disagree: the pastor who grows himself will grow his people? Why or why not?

4:16 Pay close attention to yourself and to your teaching; persevere in these things, for as you do this you will ensure salvation both for yourself and for those who hear you.

The final two of the twelve imperatives (vv.7, 11-16) appear here. As with verse 15 the imperatives here lead the way, followed by a clause which provides justification for the commands (γὰρ, "for"). First the Apostle demands of Timothy, "Pay close attention" (ἔπεχε). When used intransitively, the verb describes the mental processes of fixing one's attention on something, observing or taking note of something. Here in the present tense the imperative demands of Timothy a constant state of readiness, being alert to or watching out for something.[77] Just what Timothy is to give such careful study to is comprised of two things: "to yourself and to your teaching" (σεαυτῷ καὶ τῇ διδασκαλίᾳ). Just what does the Apostle mean by giving such heed to "yourself"? Self-absorption is not the answer, but what is? The use of this reflexive pronoun throughout the PE may give some hints. Elsewhere Paul demands of Timothy, "discipline yourself for the purpose of godliness" (1 Tim. 4:7), "keep yourself free from sin" (5:22), and "Be diligent to present yourself approved to God as a workman who does not need to be ashamed, accurately handling the word of truth" (2 Tim. 2:15). Similarly he exhorted Titus, "in all things show yourself to be an example of good deeds" (Titus 2:7). He may well have also intended the self-awareness necessary to keep body, mind, and emotions in a healthy balance. The second area to be of Timothy's concern is "to your teaching" (τῇ διδασκαλίᾳ). See v.13

---
[77] Friberg, 161.

for the meaning of this noun so oft used in the PE.

Again the Apostle demands, "persevere in these things" (ἐπίμενε αὐτοῖς). The verb is a compound, composed of "upon" (ἐπί) and "remain" (μένω). The preposition in compound "is directive indicating the concentration of the verb's action upon some object."[78] That object is "these things" (αὐτοῖς), a reference to paying close attention to "yourself" and to "your teaching," and perhaps also a backward glance to the imperatives of vv.7-15 as well.[79] Once again the present imperative demands action that is to be undertaken repeatedly or habitually.

> **Ministry Maxim**
>
> Ministry is not the means to fill your well, but arises out of a well already filled by and with Jesus.

Now Paul justifies his two commands by using "for" (γάρ) to express the reason behind them. That reason is that "as you do this you will ensure salvation both for yourself and for those who hear you" (τοῦτο γὰρ ποιῶν καὶ σεαυτὸν σώσεις καὶ τοὺς ἀκούοντάς σου). The main verb ("will ensure salvation," σώσεις) could be rendered more literally "you will save." The future tense looks forward to the final fulfillment of all that salvation is to mean. Of course only God can save, and He does through His Son Jesus Christ. Yet as the conveyor of that saving message, Timothy is seen as having a key role. This happens "as you do this" (τοῦτο ... ποιῶν), referring to the imperatives in the first part of the verse. This salvation will be "both for yourself and for those who hear you" (καὶ σεαυτὸν ... καὶ τοὺς ἀκούοντάς σου). It is easier to understand how Timothy's fulfillment of the commands would bring salvation to those who hear him, for it would ensure that he as the messenger remained a trustworthy conduit of the good news. It is more difficult to see how it would also "save" himself since Paul so universally condemns any place for works in salvation. While it is true that Paul allows no place for works in salvation (2 Tim. 1:9; Titus 3:5), it is also true that he consistently holds forth true salvation as producing good works (Titus 2:14; 3:8, 14). Thus if Timothy would fail to fulfill these key components of his call, he would be proving that the "salvation" he claimed was not a true salvation (1 Cor. 9:27). As Hiebert wisely comments, "We are not saved by our faithful performance of our duties, but the faithful performance of our duties is the sphere within which our salvation is realized. A pastor unfaithful in doctrine and morals is saving neither himself nor his congregation."[80]

The current chapter has spanned from the evil nature of the last days (v.1)

---

[78] Rienecker, 628.
[79] Knight, 210; Mounce, 265.
[80] Hiebert, *First Timothy*, 89.

to Timothy's own personal, private life and disciplines (vv.7, 11-16). This underscores the pivotal nature of the pastor's personal and private life in enabling him to walk closely with God and in fulfilling the demands of his calling. Our outward service flows from the well of inner spiritual reality. Never use the ministry to try to fill the well. Only Christ can do that and as He does He enables us to fulfill the calling He places upon us.

Digging Deeper:
1. Just what should the command to "Pay close attention to yourself" look like in your life and ministry?
2. How has self-absorption influenced our society, the church, and pastoral ministry? How does Paul's command help or hinder in these challenges?
3. In what sense does obedience to these commands "ensure salvation . . . for yourself"?

CHAPTER

5

5:1 Do not sharply rebuke an older man, but rather appeal to him as a father, to the younger men as brothers,

The Apostle now shifts his emphasis significantly. He turns away from exhortations to Timothy regarding his own life and ministry (4:11-16) and addresses Timothy's response to various groups within the church. First he addresses his response broadly to various age and gender categories (vv.1-2), then widows (vv.3-16), elders (vv.17-25), slaves (6:1-2), and finally to the false teachers and those who would follow them (6:3-10).

The word translated "an older man" (Πρεσβυτέρῳ) is the same one used to speak of elders (1 Tim. 5:17, 19; Titus 1:5). That it here refers more generally to a male of advanced age is clear from the context where others, both male and female, are addressed according to their age. The feminine form of the word is found in the next verse to speak of "the older women" (πρεσβυτέρας). Both are adjectives used as comparatives. The fact that Paul speaks in the singular form of "an older man" when the other three classes are in the plural form indicates that he is employing the singular here in a generic sense.[1]

Paul instructs Timothy, "Do not sharply rebuke" (μὴ ἐπιπλήξῃς) such a man. The verb is a compound made up of "upon" (ἐπί) and "strike" (πλήσσω). Most literally, then, it means "to inflict with blows,"[2] "to strike," or "beat upon."[3] It came then to be used metaphorically of reproving or rebuking someone sharply.[4] This Timothy is "not" (μὴ) to do toward men of advanced age. The combination of the negation and the aorist subjunctive verb combine to

---

[1] Knight, 213.
[2] Friberg, 166.
[3] Thayer, 241.
[4] Friberg, 166.

suggest that the action has not yet taken place and that it should not take place.⁵ In stark contrast ("but," ἀλλὰ) to such an approach, Timothy is to "appeal to him as a father" (παρακάλει ὡς πατέρα). While Timothy is not to beat an older man verbally, it does not mean that the conduct of older men is beyond censure. The verb is a familiar one, used often in Paul and already encountered in 1 Timothy (1:3; 2:1). It is a compound word comprised of "beside" (παρὰ) and "to call" (καλέω). Most literally, it means "to call alongside." It has a range of meaning that can swing from the softer sense of "comfort" to the sharper edge of "exhort." According to each context it is variously translated with words such as "appeal" (Philem. 9, 10), "comfort" (2 Cor. 1:4, 6), "encourage" (1 Cor. 16:12), "exhort" (1:10), "implore" (2 Cor. 12:8), or "urge" (Rom. 12:1). The present tense imperative calls for action to be undertaken repeatedly and consistently. Such men are to be thus addressed "as a father" (ὡς πατέρα). That is to say we should do so with respect and deference because of their age and standing in the Christian community. Paul clearly views the church as the household of God (1 Tim. 3:5, 15; cf. Matt. 12:49-50; Mark 3:31-35; 10:30; Luke 8:21), as will become even more clear in his instructions regarding older women and the younger members of both genders (v.1b-2). True, Paul told Timothy, to "Let no one look down on your youthfulness" (1 Tim. 4:12a), but he is to reciprocate with appropriate respect as well.

> **Ministry Maxim**
>
> Respect is never out of order, especially when confronting trouble.

Similarly, this same approach (the clause assumes the verb used in the previous clause as does v.2) should be taken "to the younger men" (νεωτέρους). The adjective can mean simply new or fresh, but here is used as a substantive and thus means those younger than the "older men" already mentioned (v.1).⁶ Eight of the eleven appearances of the noun in the NT are found in Paul. Of those eight, five are found in the PE. The feminine form of the word appears in the next verse to speak of "younger women" (νεωτέρας), and later in the chapter to speak of "young widows" (vv.11, 14). Paul uses it similarly in writing to Titus about "young women" and "young men" (Titus 2:4, 6). This time the comparison is to them "as brothers" (ὡς ἀδελφούς). Paul is liberal with his use of this noun (133 times in his letters), but only four of those appear in the PE (1 Tim. 4:6; 5:1; 6:2; 2 Tim. 4:21). The word in this case points to the common life and purpose they share in Christ. Though different from a relationship with "an older man," respect should still govern such a relationship.

---

⁵ Rienecker, 628.
⁶ BAGD, 536.

> **Digging Deeper:**
> 1. Since some of the false teachers in Ephesus were older than Timothy (apparently elders of the church), how would this work out as he endeavored to answer and silence the false teaching?
> 2. Practically speaking, how can censure be communicated without also communicating disrespect, particularly when it flows from younger to older?
> 3. While the verb "appeal" describes how to confront both an "older man" and "younger men," how might it appear different outwardly with each?

5:2 the older women as mothers, and the younger women as sisters, in all purity.

The Apostle continues his instructions to Timothy regarding relationships with individuals of various age and gender within the church. Next are "the older women" (πρεσβυτέρας). The term is the feminine plural form of the masculine singular adjective rendered "older man" in v.1. The feminine form is found only here in the NT. As in v.1 this adjective is used as a comparative. Here too, as in the second case in v.1, the verb "appeal" (παρακάλει) is understood as governing these two cases. These "older women" Timothy is to address "as mothers" (ὡς μητέρας). This presumes an approach which is rich with respect and deference. Timothy had a rich heritage from his mother and grandmother. Paul knew this and appealed to him on this basis in his second letter (2 Tim. 1:5). Indeed he reminded Timothy "that from childhood you have known the sacred writings which are able to give you the wisdom that leads to salvation through faith which is in Christ Jesus" (2 Tim. 3:15). A wealth of vivid memories would have informed Timothy's mind as to the Apostle's intent when he read these words. We see something of Paul's attitude in this regard when, in writing to the Christians of Rome, he said, "Greet Rufus, a choice man in the Lord, also his mother and mine" (Rom. 16:13).

Next are "the younger women" (νεωτέρας). Here also we have a feminine plural adjective used as a comparative (cf. τὰς νέας used in a similar way in Titus 2:4). The same form will be used momentarily in vv.11, 14 to speak of "younger" widows. These Timothy was to treat "as sisters" (ὡς ἀδελφάς). Paul set an example in this regard, speaking of "our sister Phoebe" (Rom. 16:1). The Apostle is not calling for the use of the word as a title (e.g., "sister Phoebe" or "brother Timothy"), but is calling upon Timothy to shape his relationships toward individuals after the pattern of healthy family relations.

The vulnerability to sensual temptations for some of the younger widows was heightened because of the loss of their spouses (1 Tim. 5:11). The false teachers operating in Ephesus were of the sort to exploit this vulnerability (2 Tim. 3:6). For these reasons Paul will soon give special instructions to these younger widows in order to "give the enemy no occasion for reproach" (1 Tim. 5:14). Probably motivated by this, Paul adds the tag "in all purity" (ἐν πάσῃ ἁγνείᾳ). Rienecker says, "The word covers not only chastity in matters of sex, but also the innocence and integrity of heart . . . The word refers to purity of act and thought."[7] The only other use of the word in the NT is in 1 Timothy 4:12 where it is found in a list of virtues in which Timothy is to show himself an example of those who believe. The adjective "all" (πάσῃ) is added to heighten the urgency and ratchet up Timothy's vigilance in this regard. Paul instructed Titus to have the older women teach the younger women (Titus 2:4). Mounce wisely observes, "If this verse is used to clarify the present passage, to treat younger women as sisters means keeping some degree of separation, presumably to guard against the possibility of sin and the damaging of one's reputation and therefore that of the church."[8] Though pastors may fall into sin in any one of a million directions, it seems from experience that covetousness (1 Tim. 6:5-11), pride (2 Tim. 3:2) and this temptation to sensuality (1 Tim. 4:12) form the treble hook with which the devil trolls the waters of pastoral ministry, seeking to snare pastors unaware.

> **Ministry Maxim**
>
> The impulse to be the "savior" of the wounded woman is likely not from God.

Digging Deeper:
1. What would an "appeal" to your mother look like? How should this be duplicated in working through difficulties with an older woman in your church?
2. How can this be done without being manipulated?
3. Practically speaking, what safeguards are implicit in Paul's command to relate to younger women "as sisters, in all purity"?

5:3 Honor widows who are widows indeed;

The Apostle now begins an extended section (vv.3-16) devoted to "widows" (Χήρας). To modern Western Christian minds this seems an inordinant amount

---
[7] Rienecker, 627.
[8] Mounce, 270.

of coverage. Yet widows were a constant concern in the Mosaic Law (e.g., Deut. 24:17-21), and the NT reflects the same concern (e.g., Acts 6:1; 9:39-41; James 1:27). In many cases today the governmental authorities have taken over what was often the exclusive domain of religious entities in the ancient world. We do well to study carefully these instructions and examine our current ministry as churches to these unique and often needy women.

The noun "widows" (Χήρας) is a feminine form arising from the masculine adjective "bereft" (χῆρος).[9] Paul uses the word ten times, nine of them in this chapter. The imperative "honor" (τίμα) is in the present tense demanding repeated or continuous action. It means first to estimate or fix a value on something (e.g., Matt. 27:9) and then by extension, to honor or revere someone.[10] It is used repeatedly in the command to honor one's father and mother (Matt. 15:4, 6; 19:19; Mark 7:10; 10:19; Luke 18:20) and then of honor given to God (Matt. 15:8; Mark 7:6; John 5:23; 8:49). It can have the extended sense in which such honor is made manifest through material or financial provision (e.g., Acts 28:10). The noun form is used similarly, for in v.17 it describes that which appears to be financial or material support and again in 6:1 of that which amounts to esteem or respect.[11] The noun and verb form the theme of this latter part of the letter: honor to widows (v.3), elders (v.17), and masters (6:1). In the present context where Paul has just instructed Timothy to treat "older women as mothers" (v.2), he combines in this word the notion of honoring father and mother and doing so through a tangible expression of physical and material support. We are to "honor" widows by calculating their worth and then tangibly expressing that worth through financial and/or material aid. Such women are not "charity cases," but deserving of support in light of the exemplary lives they have lived.

> **Ministry Maxim**
>
> At times honor must be not only an attitude shown, but assistance given.

However, this support is not for every woman who has lost her husband. It is reserved for those "who are widows indeed" (τὰς ὄντως χήρας). This time the noun has the definite article, to contrast the anarthrous usage that began the sentence. Tucked between the definite article and noun is the adverb rendered "indeed" (ὄντως). The adverb is akin to and arose from the present participle of εἰμί ("to be"). Used with a noun it serves to attest the genuineness of something and is thus translated "real," "true," or "indeed."[12] Cf. the combination of this adverb and noun again in vv.5, 16. Just what Paul means by this will

---
[9] Thayer, 668.
[10] BAGD, 817.
[11] Fee, 115.
[12] Friberg, 283.

be made clear throughout vv.4-16. Such women would include those whose husbands have died and who have no children or grandchildren to care for them (vv.4, 16). She is truly alone in this world, except for God (v.5a). She will have maintained her purity (v.6) and focused her energies on seeking God (v.5b). She will be a woman sixty years of age or older and thus unlikely to be of a marriageable age (vv.9, 11-14). Additionally, she must be known for her service to others, her child-rearing, and her hospitality (v.10). She must be circumspect in both conduct (vv.11-12) and speech (v.13).

5:4 but if any widow has children or grandchildren, they must first learn to practice piety in regard to their own family and to make some return to their parents; for this is acceptable in the sight of God.

The financial and material part of the honor called for in v.3 does have a condition placed upon it. The conjunction "but" (δέ) indicates a contrast. The condition (εἰ + present indicative) is assumed true for the sake of argument. Should the widow have any "children or grandchildren" (τέκνα ἢ ἔκγονα), the responsibility for her care is theirs. The latter word is used only here in the NT and refers to descendents more generally. It is a compound word from "out of" (ἐκ) and "be born" (γίνομαι). However, here "grandchildren" probably represents the thought well. The KJV translated it "nephews" in a day when that word meant something different than it does today. Note that, "they must . . . learn" (μανθανέτωσαν). The subject ("they") is "children and grandchildren," not the widows themselves. That this is so is seen in that the verb is plural and so also must be the subject ("children and grandchildren"). Additionally, what sort of logic would make a widowed woman's care for her children and grandchildren a "return to [her own] parents"? Learning is a consistent theme throughout the PE, as evidenced by the fact that the verb is used seven times (1 Tim. 2:11; 5:4, 13; 2 Tim. 3:7, 14 [2x], Titus 3:14). It refers to learning something through the instruction of another.[13] The present tense imperative indicates that this is a lesson to be learned again and again. It should not pass us by that fulfilling such responsibility does not come naturally to us, but is a learned virtue. Who, we might ask, provides the instruction? Perhaps it is the church itself through its leadership, who explains the Biblical basis for this familial responsibility, exhorts the children to begin practicing it, and perhaps even refuses to provide care for the widow which the children and grandchildren are capable, but perhaps reticent, to provide for. Of course, should the family do all they can and the widow still be in need, the church would gladly step in with assistance.

Just what is to be learned is expressed in two parallel clauses, both

---

[13] BAGD, 490.

employing a present tense infinitive and the second more fully explaining the first. They "must first learn to practice piety in regard to their own family (μανθανέτωσαν πρῶτον τὸν ἴδιον οἶκον εὐσεβεῖν). By "their own family" (τὸν ἴδιον οἶκον) Paul means the widowed mother or grandmother. The adverb "first" (πρῶτον) indicates that the church is not unwilling to be of assistance to such a widow, but that they will not act until the responsibilities of her family have been fulfilled. Such familiar care is designated as "to practice piety" (εὐσεβεῖν). This verbal form is found elsewhere only in Acts 17:23; however, the cognate noun (εὐσέβεια, "godliness") is used to express a major concern of Paul in this letter (1 Tim. 2:2; 3:16; 4:7, 8; 5:4; 6:3, 5, 6, 11) and throughout the PE (2 Tim. 3:5; Titus 1:1), as is the adverb (2 Tim. 3:12; Titus 2:12). It generally describes the outward evidences of a genuine faith in and reverence for God. Though the false teachers often imitated it for selfish ends (1 Tim. 6:5; 2 Tim. 3:5), the reality of such godliness is often seen in the more mundane responsibilities of life such as unselfishly and sacrificially providing support for aging and needy family members (cf. James 1:27). Jesus denounced the Pharisees for their refusal to aid their aging parents because their resources had been given to God (Matt. 15:3-6; Mark 7:8-13). As Robertson aptly comments, "No acts of 'piety' toward God will make up for impiety toward parents."[14] Reflect upon the remarkable example of Ruth with Naomi (Ruth 2) and of Jesus with Mary in His dying hours (John 19:26). The present tense infinitive calls for action that is repeated and continual.

> **Ministry Maxim**
>
> A failure in piety toward my parents is a failure in piety toward God.

The second thing to be learned is added ("and," καὶ) to the first. It is expressed in the statement that they "make some return to their parents" (ἀμοιβὰς ἀποδιδόναι τοῖς προγόνοις). The word "return" (ἀμοιβὰς) is used only here in the NT, but was common in the Greek of Paul's day. It refers to recompense, repayment or some form of return for benefits that have been received.[15] The infinitive "to make some" (ἀποδιδόναι) is a compound word comprised of "from" (ἀπὸ) and "give" (δίδωμι). It carries the idea of giving away, giving up or giving out.[16] It has the connotation of paying something back, either paying back a debt owed (e.g., Matt. 5:26), or positively rewarding (2 Tim. 4:8) or negatively recompensing (2 Tim. 4:14) someone for something. Here the positive sense is emphasized. The present tense again points at continual action. This return is to be made "to their parents" (τοῖς προγόνοις). The noun is used

---

[14] Robertson, 4:584.
[15] Friberg, 46.
[16] BAGD, 90.

elsewhere in the NT only in 2 Timothy 1:3 where Paul refers to his "forefathers." It describes simply those born before someone else. It thus refers to one's parents, forefathers or ancestors.[17] The definite article is employed here to make clear the specific progenitors indicated: "their parents." Clearly children owe their parents. We are in their debt. Paul says in another place and in another context that "children are not responsible to save up for their parents, but parents for *their* children" (2 Cor. 12:14b). Parents are generally expected in Scripture to strive to pass something along to their children, but it is also true that children are then expected to care for their aging parents.

An explanatory statement is added, "for this is acceptable in the sight of God" (τοῦτο γάρ ἐστιν ἀπόδεκτον ἐνώπιον τοῦ θεοῦ). The use of "for" (γάρ) signals that Paul is providing some justification for these demands. The antecedent of the pronoun "this" (τοῦτο) is found in the two infinitives: "to practice piety" and "to make some return." The exact expression "acceptable in the sight of" (ἀπόδεκτον ἐνώπιον) was found previously in 1 Timothy 2:3. The adjective "acceptable" is found only in these two passages, but see the kindred noun ἀποδοχή ("acceptance") in 1:15 and 4:9 and the adjective εὐπρόσδεκτος ("acceptable") in Romans (15:16, 31), 2 Corinthians (6:2; 8:12), and 1 Peter 2:5. The expression "in the sight of God" (ἐνώπιον τοῦ θεοῦ) is used by Paul ten times (Rom. 14:22; 1 Cor. 1:29; 2 Cor. 4:2; 7:12; Gal. 1:20; 1 Tim. 5:4, 21; 1 Tim. 6:13; 2 Tim. 2:14; 4:1). Paul's charges to Timothy personally were also made using the same expression (1 Tim. 5:21; 6:13; 2 Tim. 4:1). This expression often served as an attestation of a statement made (Gal. 1:20), an attitude held (Rom. 14:22) or an action undertaken (1 Tim. 5:4). It is often used to solemnify a statement. This final explanatory statement likely reflects the fifth commandment. Clearly children's concern should be toward their parents, but even beyond that it should be set upon God's pleasure. A child's loving care of an aging or destitute mother should be an expression of love for her and for God.

> **Digging Deeper:**
> 1. In what way has the plight of widows changed in our contemporary context when compared to first-century Ephesus? How does this affect application of the Apostle's words today, if at all?
> 2. When and how should "honor" of our parents become tangible, practical, and material?
> 3. Practically speaking, how can a church encourage negligent children to help an aging parent so that the church can direct their support to others without children available to assist?

---

[17] Ibid., 704.

5:5 Now she who is a widow indeed and who has been left alone, has fixed her hope on God and continues in entreaties and prayers night and day.

The conjunction δέ ("Now") is used in a resumptive way to specifically spell out the marks of one "who is a widow indeed" (ἡ . . . ὄντως χήρα). The same phrase is used in vv.3 and 16. See the discussion just above. Immediately connected ("and," καί) to the phrase is "who has been left alone" (μεμονωμένη). The word is used only here in the NT. It means to make solitary or, as it is rendered here, to be left alone.[18] The passive voice sees the action as being pressed upon the widow from outside herself (i.e., through the death of her husband). The perfect tense sees this as an abiding state in which she finds herself. She is thus the opposite of the widow considered in v.4, who has children or grandchildren who can care for her.

What fits this woman for the classification of "a widow indeed" is not simply that she is utterly alone, but also a twofold spiritual set to her focus. First, she "has fixed her hope on God" (ἤλπικεν ἐπὶ θεόν). Her hope is set upon (ἐπί, "on") God because there are no children or relatives to which she may look. God has made many promises regarding His care for the desolate and the widow (e.g., Deut. 10:18; 14:29; Psa. 68:5; Mal. 3:5), so her hope is rightly placed.[19] The perfect tense of the verb pictures her decision at a point in the past to hope in God and describes it as continuing unceasingly down to the present time. It matches the perfect tense of the preceding participle ("who has been left alone"). Such a settled resolve is the practice of all believers, "we have fixed our hope on the living God" (4:10). So she

> **Ministry Maxim**
>
> Fixed hope and continuous prayer are the twin handles by which desperate people hold fast to God.

is seen as applying the hope that is characteristic of all believers to the uniquenesses of her plight as a widow, much as the rich are urged to set their hope on God and not their riches (6:17).

A second ("and," καί) mark of such a widow is that she "continues in entreaties and prayers" (προσμένει ταῖς δεήσεσιν καὶ ταῖς προσευχαῖς). The verb is a compound made up of "to" (πρός) and "continue" (μένω). It is used by Paul elsewhere only in 1:3 to describe Timothy's charge to "remain on at Ephesus." The preposition strengthens the idea of remaining *with* someone (Matt. 15:32; Mark 8:2) or *in* a place (Acts 18:18; 1 Tim. 1:3). It can also, then, mean figuratively to abide or continue in something like faithfulness to

---

[18] BAGD, 528.
[19] Hiebert, *First Timothy*, 92.

the Lord (Acts 11:23), the grace of God (13:43), or prayer (1 Tim. 5:5). Here the widow is pictured as faithfully continuing on "in entreaties and prayers" (ταῖς δεήσεσιν καὶ ταῖς προσευχαῖς). Both words were used in 2:1 where they were joined with two other words descriptive of prayer. See there for the meaning of these words. Here both nouns have the accompanying definite article, indicating specific "entreaties and prayers" are in view. Perhaps it was set times for prayer that were kept by these women. The latter noun is found again with the definite article in Acts 2:42 to describe that which all the believers devoted themselves to. It seems that the earliest believers may have continued the Jewish practice of keeping set, rhythmic hours for prayer, although now those prayers were in Jesus' name and were empowered by the Holy Spirit. It may be that this widow is a regular at such times of prayer. This notion is strengthened by the added explanatory phrase "night and day" (νυκτὸς καὶ ἡμέρας). The order of "night" before "day" represents the Semitic understanding of a day beginning at the going down of the sun.[20] The expression does not demand that the widow never ceased to pray, but that prayer was characteristic of her life at all times (cf. Rom. 12:12; Eph. 6:18; Col. 4:2; 1 Thess. 5:17). Paul used the exact expression to remind the Thessalonian believers of how he and his missionary team did not demand their money, but rather worked "night and day" to provide for their personal needs (1 Thess. 2:9; 2 Thess. 3:8). In connection with prayer he told the same believers, "we night and day keep praying most earnestly that we may see your face" (1 Thess. 3:10) and he would later say to Timothy, "I constantly remember you in my prayers night and day" (2 Tim. 1:3). Anna serves as an example of what the Apostle has in mind (Luke 2:36-38).

5:6 But she who gives herself to wanton pleasure is dead even while she lives.

The words "she who gives herself to wanton pleasure" represent only a single participle and its definite article in the Greek text (ἡ . . . σπαταλῶσα). The conjunction δέ introduces a contrast ("But") to the godly widow just described in v.5. The participle is used as a substantive and serves as the subject of the sentence. The word is used elsewhere in the NT only in James 5:5 ("You have . . . led a life of wanton pleasure"). It describes living luxuriously, voluptuously, or in indulgence.[21] The woman in view has abandoned herself to pleasure and comfort.[22] The word may here have sensual overtones. The present tense pictures

---

[20] Mounce, 282.
[21] BAGD, 761.
[22] Rienecker, 629.

this as a habitual lifestyle she has adopted. Guthrie suggests that perhaps she has turned to immoral living in order to support herself.[23] If such were the case, where prayer and piety would have cast her upon God for His aid (v.5), she has chosen rather to use her body as her last asset. It seems more likely, however, that what is described here is enlarged upon in vv.11-13. In such a case the widow in view may be using the material support of the church to finance her profligate lifestyle.[24]

The main verb, "is dead" (τέθνηκεν), is used elsewhere of literal death (e.g., Matt. 2:20; Luke 7:12; John 19:33), but here pictures the spiritual death of the widow who has abandoned God's path. It is found throughout the NT, as here, only in the perfect tense, pointing to the abiding state of the one dead. This is true "even while she lives" (ζῶσα). The participle pictures this as contemporaneous action.[25] She is spiritually dead at the same time that she is physically alive (cf. John 11:25; Rev. 3:1). The person, of whatever gender and marital status, who has given himself or herself over to a life of unbridled pleasure is a walking corpse. They think they are "living it up,"[26] when in fact they are only advancing down the path of death. Solomon warned his sons of the adulteress, "For her house sinks down to death and her tracks lead to the dead; none who go to her return again, nor do they reach the paths of life." (Prov. 2:18-19). The man who goes with such a woman to her lair, "does not know that the dead are there, that her guests are in the depths of Sheol" (Prov. 9:18).

> **Ministry Maxim**
>
> The one who chases pleasure is a dead man running.

Digging Deeper:

1. Why did the early church refuse to place widows on their care list if they had children or grandchildren available? What does this say to us today?
2. Practically speaking, how does one "fix" his or her hope on God?
3. Why are grieving, wounded people vulnerable to looking simply for comfort and pleasure, rather than God's will? How can God's people help them in such needs and at such times?

---

[23] Guthrie, 101.
[24] Mounce, 283.
[25] Rienecker, 629.
[26] Knight, 219.

5:7 Prescribe these things as well, so that they may be above reproach.

Paul commands Timothy to "Prescribe these things as well" (καὶ ταῦτα παράγγελλε). What Paul refers to by "these things" (ταῦτα) will include his instructions regarding widows and their families in vv.3-6. These matters Timothy is to "Prescribe" (παράγγελλε). This verb is one of Paul's favorites in this letter (1:3; 4:11; 5:7; 6:13, 17; cf. also the cognate noun in 1:5, 18) and he uses it seven more times elsewhere (1 Cor. 7:10; 11:17; 1 Thess. 4:11; 2 Thess. 3:4, 6, 10, 12). It is a compound word from "along" (παρά) and "announce" (ἀγγέλλω). Thus its root meaning is to pass along a message to someone. In time it came to speak of an authoritative announcement or command. Here its use signals the apostolic backing with which Timothy was to issue these instructions regarding widows. The word was used in military contexts and there is strength in it. It is found in this same present imperative form three times in this letter. Timothy is to command the people regarding the false teachers and their teaching (vv.1-10), widows and their care (5:1-7) and the instability of trusting riches (6:17). The present tense imperative calls for repeated or continuing action. The instructions are to be taught again and again, as long as they are needed. The words "as well" (καὶ) indicate that, though urgent, these instructions form but a part of the larger body of material the Apostle wishes Timothy to pass along to the believers in Ephesus.

The purpose ("so that," ἵνα) behind these instructions is now spelled out. That purpose is that "they may be above reproach" (ἀνεπίλημπτοι ὦσιν). The adjective ("above reproach," ἀνεπίλημπτοι) is used only three times in the NT, all of them in this letter. Paul has already called for overseers to be "above reproach" (3:2) and soon enough he will do the same to Timothy personally (6:14). The word means literally "not to be laid hold of,"[27] in the sense that no ground of accusation may be found within a person. It has the sense of "inviolable" or "unassailable."[28] See on 3:2 for a fuller description of the word. The verb "might be" (ὦσιν) is the present active subjunctive of the simple verb εἰμί ("to be"). The subjunctive mood is used to indicate that the reality is a possibility, but it will depend upon Timothy's faithfulness in teaching these matters and upon the choices and actions of the widows and their offspring.

> **Ministry Maxim**
>
> The hardships of life do not exempt any of us from living "above reproach."

---

[27] Friberg, 55.
[28] Kittel, abridged, 496.

> **Digging Deeper:**
> 1. In practical terms, how can a pastor today speak authoritatively ("Prescribe") to so many broad and diverse circumstances, relationships, and needs?
> 2. Is a life "above reproach" a realistic goal for people as deeply wounded and challenged by the hardships of life as these widows?
> 3. Of all the things a woman in such circumstances would have to be concerned about, what would have to happen within her to have her leading concern be to live "above reproach"?

5:8 But if anyone does not provide for his own, and especially for those of his household, he has denied the faith and is worse than an unbeliever.

What should Timothy make of one who would resist his teaching in these matters (cf. especially v.4)? The conjunction "But" (δέ) signals a contrast. The conditional statement (εἰ + present indicative) is assumed true. Paul may have known of some in the Ephesian church who were shirking their duty toward their mothers or grandmothers and were trying to lay it upon the church. The indefinite pronoun ("anyone," τις) makes a wide sweep to consider any and all who might forsake these familial responsibilities. The verb (προνοεῖ) is a compound word comprised of "before" (πρό) and "to perceive/think" (νοέω). It thus means to think of beforehand and then, by extension, to make provision for or take care of. It is used elsewhere in the NT only by Paul, and then only twice (Rom. 12:17; 2 Cor. 8:21). It is negated by οὐ ("not"), signaling an absolute or categorical negation. The verb pictures one who has failed to take his responsibilities to account prior to earning his wages. So when the income is received, he has made no mental notation that a part of it must go to the welfare of others for whom he is responsible.

Those who are thus neglected are first described as "his own" (τῶν ἰδίων). Paul then goes further and says, "and especially for those of his household" (καὶ μάλιστα οἰκείων). The former is a broader word, including any and all who might fall within the circle of his responsibilities. Yet the presence of the definite article draws a circle around those and distinguishes them from other needy folk for whom he is not responsible. The latter expression is more restrictive. It is "especially" (μάλιστα) concerned with a more limited circle. It is the superlative of the adverb μάλα. It describes "the highest point in the extent of something" and means something like "most of all," "especially," or "above all."[29] Paul uses this adverb eight times (Gal. 6:10; Phil. 4:22; Philem. 16), five of them here in the PE. He uses it to distinguish "believers" from "all men" (1 Tim. 4:10), elders who "work hard at preaching and teaching" from a larger number of "elders who rule well" (5:17), "the parchments" from "the books" (2 Tim. 4:13), and "those of the circumcision" from "many rebellious men" (Titus 1:10). Here he distinguishes those within "his household" (οἰκείων). The adjective is used only two other times in the NT (Gal. 6:10; Eph. 2:19). In both of those instances it refers to the church as God's family or household. Here the relation is through bloodlines, not faith. By "his own," Paul probably refers to one's extended family and by "his household" his more immediate family.

The Apostle describes those who give no forethought to their responsibility to support family with two phrases. First, he says "he has denied the faith" (τὴν πίστιν ἤρνηται). The noun "faith" (πίστις) is found thirty-three times in the PE. It is accompanied by the definite article, as here, sixteen times in the PE (1 Tim. 1:19; 3:9, 13; 4:1, 6; 5:8; 6:10, 12, 21; 2 Tim. 1:5; 2:18; 3:8, 10; 4:7; Titus 1:13; 2:2). Of those sixteen, seven are accompanied by negative statements such as "suffered shipwreck in regard to" (1 Tim. 1:19), "fall away from" (4:1), "denied" (5:8), "wandered away from" (6:10), "gone astray from" (6:21), "upset" (2 Tim. 2:18), and "rejected in regard to" (3:8). On the other hand, seven times they are accompanied by some positive statement, such as "holding to" (3:9), "great confidence in" (3:13), "nourished on the words of" (4:6), "fight the good fight of" (6:12), "you followed" (2 Tim. 3:10), "kept" (4:7), and "may be sound in" (Titus 1:13). Those who fail to provide for their own fall into the former camp. His is not a failure in his profession of the faith, but in his conformity to it in behavior. The latter, in the Apostle's mind, is as bad as the former. He is among those who "profess to know God, but by their deeds they deny Him, being detestable and disobedient and worthless for any good deed" (Titus 1:16).

> **Ministry Maxim**
>
> Practical love is always proof of personal faith.

Secondly ("and," καὶ), Paul says such a one "is worse than an unbeliever" (ἔστιν ἀπίστου χείρων). The adjective "unbeliever" (ἀπίστου) simply adds an alpha privative to the common noun for faith (πίστις) in order to negate it. Such a person may appear highly religious and may even take the name "Christian." Yet he is unbelieving and his deeds tell the truth even when his words do not. Its only other use in the PE is in Titus 1:15 where Paul warns Titus of "those who are defiled and unbelieving." But here the one under consideration is "worse" (χείρων) even than that. The adjective is the comparative

---

[29] Friberg, 252.

of κακός ("evil"). He is evil and growing more so every day.

Jesus asked, "For if you love those who love you, what reward do you have? Do not even the tax collectors do the same? If you greet only your brothers, what more are you doing than others? Do not even the Gentiles do the same?" (Matt. 5:46-47). Indeed, He demanded that more was required of true believers: "you are to be perfect, as your heavenly Father is perfect" (v.48).

> **Digging Deeper:**
> 1. Who in your life would fall within the circle of your "own"? Who then would qualify as your own "household"?
> 2. In what way have you included their welfare and support in your financial and future plans?
> 3. In what sense would a shirker in this regard be "worse than an unbeliever"? What exactly is "worse"—their character or their condemnation?

5:9 A widow is to be put on the list only if she is not less than sixty years old, having been the wife of one man,

Paul continues the discussion of widows, but now shifts his focus. In vv.3-8 he seems to have been concerned primarily with moving any family to action. In vv.9-16 he seems to be more concerned with when and how the church ought to get involved with the care of "A widow" (Χήρα). It is the same noun we've been confronted with in vv.3-5 and which we will again face in vv.11, 16. The words "is to be put on the list" (καταλεγέσθω) translate but one Greek word. This is the word's only occurrence in the NT. It is a compound word, comprised of "down" (κατά) and "to speak" (λέγω). It means to select someone for a group, to enlist or enroll them.[30] Here it refers to a recognized roll of widows who will be officially recognized as such and likely thus approved to receive the financial aid of the church. It is unlikely, as some have asserted, that Paul here establishes or recognizes an order of widows who were expected to render ministry benefits to the church in exchange for their support. The present tense imperative calls for continuous action. The passive voice pictures the woman being placed on the list by others, perhaps the elders. The qualifications for being placed upon such a list are now outlined.

A widow may be placed on this list "only if she is not less than sixty years

---
[30] BAGD, 413.

old" (μὴ ἔλαττον ἐτῶν ἑξήκοντα γεγονυῖα). The phrase is more literally, "not less than sixty years old having become." The verb is in the perfect tense, signaling the arrival at a settled state. The reason for this qualification may be that she is well beyond child-bearing years and thus unlikely to remarry as Paul will counsel younger widows (v.14). Additionally, she may be considered less likely to give in to "sensual desires" (v.11) and abandon her station in life. Widows younger than sixty years of age may well have been expected to work and provide her own support.

In addition she must have been "the wife of one man" (ἑνὸς ἀνδρὸς γυνή). She is literally to have been "a one man woman." This is similar to the requirement for elders and deacons requiring each man to be "husband of one wife" (3:2, 12; Titus 1:6). The statement there is also more literally "a one woman man" (μιᾶς γυναικὸς ἄνδρα; 3:2). See on 3:2 for the discussion of various meanings of that phrase. It is worth noting that, while many argue that "husband of one wife" must surely refer to not allowing a polygamist to be an elder, few argue that the thought here is of a widow not having been married to more than one man at a time. Paul required the widow to have been true to the husband to which she is now widowed, if she is to be financially supported by the church. It is thus assumed that there might be some widows within the church who did not have children or extended family to care for them who were nevertheless refused support from the church because of past indiscretions. It is possible that some younger widows may have received a measure of support from the church without being on the official listing of widows, but we have no evidence in support of that notion.

> **Ministry Maxim**
>
> Conditions for help do not necessarily constitute a failure in grace.

5:10 having a reputation for good works; and if she has brought up children, if she has shown hospitality to strangers, if she has washed the saints' feet, if she has assisted those in distress, and if she has devoted herself to every good work.

To the previous two conditions set forth in v.9 for widows who will be supported by the church (age and marital faithfulness), Paul now adds a third, "having a reputation for good works" (ἐν ἔργοις καλοῖς μαρτυρουμένη). Again the widow's past life comes under scrutiny in making a decision about present support. The verb translated "having a reputation" (μαρτυρουμένη) means simply "bear witness," but here it is in the passive voice giving it the sense of "be well spoken of" or "be approved."³¹ The present tense points to a consistent witness from others concerning the widow. She must be well known "for good works" (ἐν ἔργοις καλοῖς). Paul is especially concerned for good works in the PE (1 Tim. 2:10; 3:1; 5:10, 25; 6:18; 2 Tim. 2:21; 3:17; Titus 1:16; 2:7, 14; 3:1, 8, 14). Good works do not save (2 Tim. 1:9; Titus 3:5), but they do witness to the genuineness of one's salvation (Titus 2:14).

Now in a series of five conditional statements Paul sets forth examples of what is meant by "good works." All five conditional statements (εἰ + aorist indicatives) are first class conditions, assuming the reality of what is set forth. First, consider "if she has brought up children" (εἰ ἐτεκνοτρόφησεν). The verb is used only here in the NT. It requires more than the physical ability to reproduce, but also the additional skills of nurture and discipline that will aid the children in reaching maturity both physically and spiritually.³² Surely the Apostle has in view, not a woman's ability to conceive and deliver children into the world (and thus perhaps exclude the barren widow), but, assuming her ability physically to bear children, her ability to raise her children responsibly. As the church determines a widow's status for support, they must ask, "Where then are her children in this hour of need?"

Second, the church must consider "if she has shown hospitality to strangers" (εἰ ἐξενοδόχησεν). This verb too is found only here in the NT. Hospitality was a major component of the early church's ministry (Rom. 12:13; Heb. 13:2; 1 Peter 4:9). Paul required a proclivity toward hospitality essential enough to require it of overseers (1 Tim. 3:2; Titus 1:8). In a day when Christians were scattered by persecution, and when apostles, evangelists and preachers were spreading out across the globe with the Gospel, hospitality was a vital component of the fulfillment of Christ's great commission (Matt. 28:19-20). A widow was to have excelled in the ministry of hospitality if she was to receive financial support from the church.

> **Ministry Maxim**
>
> Good works have a way of coming back to us even in this life.

Third, the church must ponder "if she has washed the saints' feet" (εἰ ἁγίων πόδας ἔνιψεν). This is connected to the previous ministry of hospitality. When guests were welcomed into her home, she was to have lead the way in service and care by gathering water and a towel and bowing low to wash their feet. This was a symbol of acceptance and welcome, as well as a physical act of refreshing for the visitors. Jesus had set the example in this humble service and His people are to follow in His steps (John 13:1-17). Paul was not referring to foot washing as an established ordinance in the church,

---

[31] BAGD, 493.
[32] Ibid., 808-809.

but as a practical act carried out in the mundane events of each day. By using the plural form of the noun "saints'" (ἁγίων), Paul is employing a familiar NT expression that refers to believers in Jesus Christ generally, not a specific order or class of believers.

Fourth, the church must consider "if she has assisted those in distress" (εἰ θλιβομένοις ἐπήρκεσεν). The verb (ἐπήρκεσεν, "she has assisted") is used only here and in v.16 where it appears twice. It is a compound word made up of "on" (ἐπί) and "be enough/sufficient" (ἀρκέω). At root it means something like "to avail" or "to be strong enough for."[33] It came to refer to warding off something from someone and then by extension to coming to their aid or relief.[34] The aorist tense looks back to her past actions. Those she thus assists are "those in distress" (θλιβομένοις). The word means to press upon or crowd, to press together, compress and make narrow. Thus is comes to mean, as it does here, to oppress or afflict.[35] The present tense pictures this as an ongoing state of life. The passive voice sees the victim being pressed between a rock and a hard place by outside forces. The participle is used in a substantive way ("those in distress"). The widow who will be supported by the church needs to be one who took up the plight of those overwhelmed and pressed by life's circumstances and/or oppressed by others. How has she responded to those who were in the distress she now finds herself in?

Finally, the church must determine "if she has devoted herself to every good work" (εἰ παντὶ ἔργῳ ἀγαθῷ ἐπηκολούθησεν). Now the Apostle adds a sweeping generalization to sum up all previous matters. Fee is correct, "This last item suggests that the list is merely representative of her godliness, not definitive of her duties."[36] The word for "work" (ἔργῳ) is the same as used to start the verse. The adjective "good" (ἀγαθῷ) is different, but little difference in meaning is probably intended. The adjective "all" (παντὶ) is added to gather up and include any expressions of good that were within her power to perform. The verb is a compound, comprised of "on" (ἐπί) and "follow" (ἀκολουθέω). The preposition in compound is directive ("after")[37] or perfective ("to devote oneself").[38] The idea of following after then comes to have the sense of being devoted to something, that something being indicated by the dative case.[39] The word is used elsewhere in Mark 16:20, 1 Peter 2:21, and 1 Timothy 5:24, where some people's sins "follow after" them. The aorist tense again looks back upon the widow's past record.

---

[33] Thayer, 229.
[34] Friberg, 159.
[35] BAGD, 362.
[36] Fee, 120.
[37] Rienecker, 630.
[38] Mounce, 289.
[39] BAGD, 282.

Guthrie sees a progression in these concerns, from care for family, to fellow believers (hospitality and foot washing), to the destitute and strangers.[40]

> **Digging Deeper:**
> 1. Was it just to withhold financial and material help from some widows because of their past?
> 2. How do the Apostolic conditions for support of widows grate against current cultural understandings of justice?
> 3. How do these conditions relate to the doctrine of grace?

5:11 But refuse to put younger widows on the list, for when they feel sensual desires in disregard of Christ, they want to get married,

"But" (δὲ), in contrast to enrolling the godly, elderly widows like those mentioned in v.10, Timothy is to "refuse" (παραιτοῦ) certain other widows. The verb has a broad range of meaning, from making a request (Mark 15:6), to declining an offer (Luke 14:18-19), to strongly rejecting someone or something (1 Tim. 4:7; 2 Tim. 2:23; Titus 3:10).[41] Though the other usages in the PE employ the fullest strength of the word, it seems that something gentler is intended here, without losing any of the strength behind the word. Paul uses the word four times, all in the PE and always in the present middle imperative form (1 Tim. 4:7; 5:11; 2 Tim. 2:23; Titus 3:10). The present imperative demands action that is taken repeatedly or, perhaps here, consistently. The middle voice pictures Timothy and the church leadership making the inward determination of who is and is not enrolled on the list of widows. Those to be thus refused are "younger widows" (νεωτέρας . . . χήρας). The adjective is the same one used earlier in vv.1-2 when referring to "younger men" and "younger women" (cf. similar usage in Titus 2:4, 6). It is comparative and refers to those who are "younger" than those widows over "sixty years old" (v.9). It is also further defined by their ability to marry and bear children (v.14).[42]

The Apostle now goes on to explain ("for," γὰρ) just why this strong refusal is mandated against enrolling such widows. The verb ("they feel sensual desires," καταστρηνιάσωσιν) is used only here in the NT. It is a compound made up of "against" (κατά) and "to live sensually" (στρηνιάω). The root word, minus the preposition, is found only in Revelation 18:7, 9. The aorist tense sees these desires welling up at a point in time. The temporal particle

---
[40] Guthrie, 102.
[41] BAGD, 616.
[42] Knight, 225.

("when," ὅταν) makes the time general and can be translated "whenever." The subjunctive mood signals that the reality of the situation depends upon external circumstances (i.e., the right man, the right moment, the right mood). When a certain combination of events comes together, such widows may be overcome by their desires. These desires stand in opposition to the call "of Christ" (τοῦ Χριστοῦ) on their lives. BAGD translates, "they feel sensuous impulses that alienate them from Christ."[43] This does not mean that sexual desire is necessarily ungodly, for He created us as sexual beings. The full understanding of this awaits the rest of the sentence in v.12 and an understanding of what it means to "set aside their previous pledge."

Note that the bait to which the women respond is "they want to get married" (γαμεῖν θέλουσιν), not that they want to indulge in sex outside of marriage. The meaning of the verb ("they want," θέλουσιν) ranges from "wish" to "will," depending upon the context. The false teachers were "wanting [θέλοντες] to be teachers of the Law" (1:7) and God "desires [θέλει] all men to be saved" (2:4). The meaning here is closer to the former than the latter. That which they wish for is "to get married" (γαμεῖν). The false teachers were apparently forbidding marriage (1 Tim. 4:3), but they also were preying upon vulnerable women (2 Tim. 3:6). As Mounce concludes, "This suggests that the Ephesian heresy was not a well-formulated doctrine but rather a collection of loosely associated ideas without internal consistency."[44] These women may have been vulnerable from the social, sexual, and financial pressures of life. They may then have found themselves susceptible to the powerful personalities of the false teachers and the false security of their legalistic teaching. Yet they found this admiration putting them in conflict with their inward desires, resulting in a conflicted state of mind (i.e., wanting to marry when the leaders they admire preach against it).

> **Ministry Maxim**
>
> Leaders may be required to make decisions others will consider cold or insensitive.

5:12 thus incurring condemnation, because they have set aside their previous pledge.

A younger widow's wish to marry results in "incurring condemnation" (ἔχουσαι κρίμα). The participle ("incurring," ἔχουσαι) means simply "to have" or "to hold," but then has its nuances flavored by the immediate context in which it is found. The present tense points to ongoing or continuous action. The participle describes action which is contemporaneous with the main verb

---

[43] BAGD, 419.
[44] Mounce, 290-291.

("wishes," v.11), though "it specifically includes the results of the widows' desire to remarry."[45] That which she thus brings upon herself is "condemnation" (κρίμα). The same word describes that in which the devil finds himself and which someone may, because of pride, be vulnerable to if elevated too quickly to the status of elder (3:6). So also here the devil attacks (cf. 5:15). The noun describes a judicial verdict, usually negative in nature, after evaluation and judgment. It can also be used of the actual condemnation and punishment that follows the decree.[46] The KJV's "damnation" may communicate more than the Apostle intended in this context, although he does view those guilty of these actions as having "turned aside to follow Satan" (v.15).

Paul now explains how ("because," ὅτι) young widows might fall into this state. This would be because "they have set aside their previous pledge" (τὴν πρώτην πίστιν ἠθέτησαν). Strictly speaking, the verb means "regard as nothing" or "set aside." Regarding legal statutes it can mean "annul" or "declare invalid."[47] The aorist tense views the act as a singular event, happening at a point in time. Suddenly, because of the unexpected opportunity to marry, the widow declares what she said before to be of no consequence and she accepts the new marriage proposal. That which she thus rejects is "their previous pledge" (τὴν πρώτην πίστιν), or, more literally, "their first faith." Just what this means has been a matter of some discussion by commentators. Those who view the list of widows as a class of women who, when accepted, are placed on a list for full support in return for services rendered to the church, believe this to be a "pledge" never to again marry, but to remain faithfully a widow in service to God and the believers. They find support for this from the example of Anna (Luke 2:36-37). Evidence for such an arrangement in the church, however, cannot be substantiated prior to the second century. The noun πίστις ("pledge") can be used in the sense of "solemn promise," "oath," or "troth," but it is a relatively rare occurrence.[48] By far its more common meaning is simply "faith." Fee has helpfully outlined three possible meaning for πίστις here. First, it may mean "pledge" and refer to a commitment made by the widow to remain unmarried and serve the Lord and the church. It is, in such a case, tantamount to a vow of celibacy. Second, it may mean "pledge" and refer to her vows to her first, and now dead, husband. This views Paul's words "the wife of one man" (v.9) as meaning the widow may have been married only one

> **Ministry Maxim**
>
> Even the most resolute can give way under life's pressures.

---

[45] Ibid., 292.
[46] BAGD, 450.
[47] Friberg, 36.
[48] BAGD, 662.

time. Third, it may be taken in its most common sense and mean simply "faith" and refer to the Christian faith and the widow's personal trust in Christ.[49] The first possibility would stand opposed to Paul's instructions for younger widows to remarry (v.14) and is thus unlikely. The second possibility reads in a practice that cannot be substantiated until at least the second century and is thus unlikely as well. The third view uses the noun as it is used in every other instance in the PE and in the vast majority of cases throughout the NT. This meaning would be the way most people would be expected to have understood the word and seems to be the best option.

Similarly, the adjective πρῶτος can mean "previous," but is more commonly translated "first." It would seem that by "their first faith," Paul intends their Christian faith, not a pledge to remain unmarried. Requiring such a pledge would seem to contradict the Apostle's command to have them remarry (v.14). It would make better sense of the circumstances and the fuller teaching of Scripture to view these young widows as bereft and destitute and lonely, when an opportunity arises to remarry. The only problem is that the man is unbelieving. Paul says that in such circumstances these young widows will face a severe test of faith. Will they remain true to Christ and hold out for a Christian husband or will they rush into the first opportunity for earthly security and love? Culturally, a woman would be expected to adopt the religious faith of her husband, and thus, if she marries an unbeliever, she would be seen as leaving her faith in Christ.[50] This view seems be supported by Paul's instructions to the Corinthians that those widowed may remarry, "only in the Lord" (1 Cor. 7:39). Thus the issue is remaining true to Christ, not true to a vow the church required of them. Paul's practical instruction to younger widows would be to find a Christian husband, settle down, and raise a family (v.14). Until then, they should work to support themselves as they are able. No doubt the church would have been of some sporadic support, as necessary, but these younger widows were not placed on the list for permanent support because of their opportunities for self-support and remarriage.

> ### Digging Deeper:
> 1. Were the Apostle's instructions regarding permanent support of younger widows insensitive or wise? Or something else entirely? Why?
> 2. How can the church and its leadership help guard younger widows in their vulnerability to life's pressures and temptations?
> 3. Why is it that previous commitments can easily cave in under pressure? What can non-widows learn from these verses?

---

[49] Fee, 121-122.
[50] Marshall, 600.

5:13 At the same time they also learn to be idle, as they go around from house to house; and not merely idle, but also gossips and busybodies, talking about things not proper to mention.

Paul's concern with younger widows is not simply their desire to marry, but (δέ, a conjunction the functions as a continuative and is left untranslated by the NASU) "At the same time" (ἅμα) they "also" (καὶ) face other temptations. The entire opening formula (ἅμα δὲ καὶ) is found also in Philemon 22. The adverb ἅμα ("At the same time") describes a coincidence of action—while the younger widows find themselves struggling with sensual desires and wishing to get married (v.12), they also face the temptations listed here. These struggles are in addition (καὶ, "also") to the ones they already face. The deck is stacked against them. All of this is emphasized in order to set the table for the command to marry, raise a family and keep a home in v.14.

The problem is that if the church simply provides all these able bodied-women need, "they . . . learn to be idle" (ἀργαὶ μανθάνουσιν). They have energy and time and both of those need to be focused rightly. The verb, interestingly, is the same one Paul would later use to describe some women in the congregation "always learning" but never coming to the knowledge of the truth (2 Tim. 3:7). But he also will use it of Timothy's learning in the things of God (v.14). He has already used it to demand that women "must quietly receive instruction" (1 Tim. 2:11) and that children or grandchildren of widows must "learn to practice piety" by caring for them (5:4). The Apostle used it to tell Titus that people "must also learn to engage in good deeds" (Titus 3:14). It refers to learning something through the instruction of another.[51] In this case it would be the church who is teaching them to be idle because they have removed the necessity of work from those who are able to perform it. The present tense of the verb indicates that they are continuously learning these things. The translators have rightly inserted "to be," though no corresponding verb is in the original text. The adjective rendered "idle" (ἀργαὶ) is used as a substantive, the first of three such adjectives in this verse (cf. "gossips and busybodies"), all of which are parallel and dependent upon "learn" (μανθάνουσιν).[52] It ranges in meaning from unemployed to lazy to useless and unproductive.[53] It is used in Titus 1:12 to describe the Cretans as "lazy gluttons." It is used by Jesus to describe

> **Ministry Maxim**
>
> Hard work is not only productive, but protective.

---

[51] BAGD, 490.
[52] Mounce, 294.
[53] BAGD, 104.

the unemployed and thus idle men standing around the marketplace waiting for an offer of employment (Matt. 20:3, 6).

This idleness is learned "as they go around from house to house" (περιερχόμεναι τὰς οἰκίας). The verb is found only two other times in the NT (Acts 19:13; Heb. 11:37) and is a compound comprised of "around" (περί) and "to come/go" (ἔρχομαι). It has the sense, then, of "wander about," "rove," or "go from place to place."[54] The present tense indicates repeated or habitual action. The middle voice pictures the subjects acting upon themselves. The participle could be intended temporally ("*while* they go around"), instrumentally ("*by* going around"), or as pointing out a result ("*with the result that* they go around").[55] The place, in this case, is literally "the houses" (τὰς οἰκίας). Just what houses are intended is not made clear, but it could have been the homes of other idle widows who, because of the church's full financial support, had significant portions of time on their hands. Or it may have been the homes of other women who had responsibilities upon them and were being distracted from their duties by these idle widows who dropped in.

Whatever the actual circumstances, these widows were "not merely idle" (οὐ μόνον δὲ ἀργαὶ). The same adjective is used as earlier in the sentence. The negation is absolute and categorical (οὐ, "not").[56] No, the problem was much bigger than just this. Paul uses the strong adversative to signal the contrast ("but," ἀλλὰ). They "also" (καὶ) had become "gossips and busybodies" (φλύαροι καὶ περίεργοι). These two adjectives are used as substantives, as was the previous adjective (ἀργαὶ, "idle"). The first word (φλύαροι, "gossips") is used only here in the NT. It is akin to the verb φλύω, which means "to boil up" or "to throw up bubbles." Thayer adds, "since bubbles are hollow and useless things, [it means] 'to indulge in empty and foolish talk.'"[57] It describes people who spew out whatever comes to their minds.[58] The second word (περίεργοι, "busybodies") at root means to be overly careful and taking needless trouble. It came to be used then of paying too close attention to things that were not one's business. Thus it describes people who pay "attention to things that do not concern" them and are meddlesome or curious to a sinful degree.[59] The word is used elsewhere in the NT only in Acts 19:19 where it is translated "magic." This may seem an odd combination of meanings, but magic is simply the pursuit of one who has become curious about special powers, odd happenings, and matters of

---

[54] Friberg, 308.
[55] NET Bible.
[56] Thayer, 408.
[57] Ibid., 655.
[58] Rienecker, 630.
[59] BAGD, 646.

the occult. These widows, however, were not accused of being dabblers in the occult, but of simply sticking their noses into other people's business. Indeed, they were "talking about things not proper to mention" (λαλοῦσαι τὰ μὴ δέοντα). The participle describes the activity of the "gossips and busybodies." The present tense describe repeated and continuous activity. That which they speak is, literally, "the not necessary things" (τὰ μὴ δέοντα).[60] The participle represents an impersonal verb which means "it is necessary," "one must," or "one has to."[61] It appears here with the article and is used as a substantive ("necessary things"). The negation (μὴ, "not") reverses the meaning and indicates those things which are unnecessary in discussion. Since, as Fee points out, the speech of these women sounds very much like that of the false teachers themselves (foolish, 1 Tim. 1:6; empty, 6:20; ignorant, 1:6-7; 4:7; 6:4), it may be that the "things not proper to mention" may be the heresy itself.[62] Perhaps more than simply wasting time and talking nonsense, they were becoming conduits for the spread of the falsehood. Certainly the false teachers were targeting such women (2 Tim. 3:6). The problem here is identified as Satanic in nature (v.14), just as was the falsehood itself (1 Tim. 4:1).[63]

This picture is of women with too much time on their hands (because the church had taken on their full support) and who end up congregating with one another and, one thing leading to another, before you know it they have made things their business that are none of their business and they have begun to talk about things that simply are not necessary to talk about. At the least, these were women who enjoyed, as Marshall states it, "the subsidized leisure to become nuisances."[64] At worst, they were advancing the spread of falsehood.

Digging Deeper:

1. In what sense may idleness be a breeding ground for all kinds of temptation?
2. How would you answer the charge that Paul is being sexist in attributing these temptations to younger widows?
3. In what way may these temptations confront anyone with too much time on his/her hands?

---

[60] Robertson, 4:586.
[61] Friberg, 104.
[62] Fee, 122.
[63] Mounce, 295.
[64] Marshall, 601.

5:14 Therefore, I want younger widows to get married, bear children, keep house, and give the enemy no occasion for reproach;

By using the inferential conjunction ("Therefore," οὖν) Paul is signaling his move toward a conclusion. For the reasons outlined in vv.11-13, the Apostle expresses his ruling regarding "younger widows" (νεωτέρας). The same adjective is used of "younger men" (v.1; cf. Titus 2:6), "younger women" (v.2; cf. Titus 2:4), and "younger widows" (v.11). In v.11 the noun "widows" (χήρας) is found with it, here it is absent (though the translators have added it for clarity). The context, however, makes clear that it is "younger widows" that are under discussion. Paul says "I want" (Βούλομαι) three things to be true for these "younger widows." The present tense expresses the continuous nature of Paul's desire. The middle voice points to the inward nature of the desire. He uses the same verb and form in 1 Timothy 2:8 to express what he desires for men generally and in Titus 3:8 to speak of what he wants from Titus personally. He uses the participial form in 1 Timothy 6:9. The word points more to the Apostle's will than his wish. See on 1 Timothy 2:8 for more on this verb.

That which Paul desires to be true of the younger widows is set forth in four present tense infinitives. The first is "to get married" (γαμεῖν). Paul uses the verb nine times in 1 Corinthians 7 and three times in 1 Timothy (4:3; 5:11, 14). He uses it nowhere else. Here he uses it to describe the false teachers who "forbid marriage" (4:3) and the younger widows as those who "want to get married" (5:11). In 1 Corinthians 7 the Apostle counsels against marriage without strictly forbidding it. But here, in view of the false teacher's overly strict asceticism and the younger widow's desire to marry, he now determines that marriage would be best in most cases. This is in accord with Paul's counsel to the Corinthians that "it is better to marry than to burn" (7:9).

> **Ministry Maxim**
>
> Righteous living is the most strategic kind of spiritual warfare.

The second infinitive indicates that Paul wants the younger widows to "bear children" (τεκνογονεῖν). The word is found only here in the NT, but see the cognate noun in 1 Timothy 2:15 ("the bearing of children," τῆς τεκνογονίας). Earlier the Apostle indicated that women do not find their salvation by grasping after positions of authority and instruction in the church, but in fulfilling their primary, God-given role of raising and nurturing the next generation (cf. discussion on 1 Tim. 2:15). He points here again to the same role rather than the spreading of falsehood (5:13).

The third infinitive spells out the Apostle's desire for the younger widows to "keep house" (οἰκοδεσποτεῖν). This word is found only here in the NT. It is a compound word comprised of "house" (οἶκος) and "rule" (δεσποτέω). This is a remarkable statement for the Apostle to make. The word "house" (οἶκος) has been used to describe an elder who "manages his own household well" (1 Tim. 3:4) as a signal that he is fit to lead the church (v.5). It is similarly used of deacons (v.12). It refers to "the household of God" (1 Tim. 3:15) over which God himself rules. The word "rule" (δεσποτέω) is that from which our words "despot" and "despotism" come. The cognate noun of "lord/master" (δεσπότης) has been used in the PE of the master of a slave (1 Tim. 6:1, 2; Titus 2:9) and God as "Master" of His servants (2 Tim. 2:21). In the Gospels the ruler of the household is always the man (e.g., Matt. 13:27; 21:33; Mark 14:14).[65] For some, the first two infinitives may sound to denigrate women to a secondary role. This third infinitive, however, was a radical validation of the lofty significance of their role and position in society.

Paul now adds the fourth infinitive, "give" (διδόναι). There is, however, a negation, for what the widows are to "give" is "no occasion" (μηδεμίαν ἀφορμὴν). This fourth infinitive is parallel to the previous three, though "in meaning it is dependent on them in the sense that, if the first three things are done . . . then 'no occasion for reproach' is left to be given."[66] The noun "occasion" (ἀφορμὴν) is used seven times in the NT, all by Paul (Rom. 7:8, 11; 2 Cor. 5:12; 11:12 [2x]; Gal. 5:13; 1 Tim. 5:14). Strictly speaking, it refers to the starting point or base of operations for an expedition.[67] It came then to be used more broadly of any kind of occasion or opportunity. Opportunity is to be withheld from "the enemy" (τῷ ἀντικειμένῳ). The participle with the definite article is used in a substantive way. It is a compound made up of "against" (ἀντί) and "lay" (τίθημι). The participle is used elsewhere as a substantive by Paul and is translated "adversaries" (1 Cor. 16:9), "opponents" (Phil. 1:28), and the one "who opposes" (2 Thess. 2:4). The verb was used in the indicative in 1 Timothy 1:10 to describe whatever "is contrary" to sound teaching (cf. Paul's only other use in Gal. 5:17). Here the present tense views the opponents as those who are always looking for an occasion "for reproach" (λοιδορίας χάριν). The noun "reproach" (λοιδορίας) is used elsewhere in the NT only by Peter ("insult for insult," λοιδορίαν ἀντὶ λοιδορίας, 3:9). It refers to "verbal abuse intended to injure someone's reputation."[68] Those vulnerable to gossip (v.13) may, by their own indiscretions, become victims of such talk (v.14). The rumor mill is ruthless. The preposition χάριν is used to indicate the goal of their activity (cf. Titus 1:5, 11).[69] The adversary may well be Satan

---

[65] Hiebert, *First Timothy*, 99.
[66] Knight, 228-229.
[67] Friberg, 84.
[68] Ibid., 248.
[69] BAGD, 877.

himself (v.15; cf. Rev. 12:10), but it seems likely that his activity would be seen and heard through secondary, human sources. There are always those who, at the devil's bidding, are looking for opportunity to destroy the testimony of believers.

5:15 for some have already turned aside to follow Satan.

Now Paul adds an explanation ("for," γάρ) regarding his instructions in v.14. The fact is "some have already turned aside" (ἤδη γάρ τινες ἐξετράπησαν). The indefinite plural pronoun ("some," τινες) indicates that an undesignated number of unidentified widows have given the opportunity for reproach that Paul was concerned about (v.14). This had "already" (ἤδη) happened. The adverb points to what is currently underway. Though the location of these widows is not indicated, it was presumably a real-time problem facing Timothy in Ephesus. Though the Apostle leaves the identity general ("some," τινες), these widows had faces and names that Timothy could likely have identified. The problem is that they had "turned aside" (ἐξετράπησαν). The verb means to twist, turn, or turn aside. In medical contexts it could speak of a joint being dislocated (cf. Heb. 12:13).[70] The aorist tense views this turning aside as something that had been already accomplished in the past. The passive form has the middle meaning—they wrenched themselves aside from the right path.[71] Paul uses the verb four times, all in his correspondence with Timothy (1 Tim. 1:6; 5:15; 6:20; 2 Tim. 4:4). He can employ it to speak of turning aside to follow "fruitless discussion" (1 Tim. 1:6), "worldly and empty chatter" (6:20), or myths (2 Tim. 4:4). Here their turning aside is "to follow Satan" (ὀπίσω τοῦ σατανᾶ). With the genitive the adverb ὀπίσω ("to follow") is used as a preposition and means "after" or "behind." Thus the concern is that these widows have "turned aside after Satan." Interestingly, Jesus used the word in His call to His disciples, "Follow Me" (Matt. 4:19; Mark 1:17), a demand that requires taking up one's cross (Matt. 10:38; Mark 8:34; Luke 9:23; 14:27) and denying self (Matt. 16:24; Mark 8:34; Luke 9:23). Notably, Jesus also used it when He rebuked Peter, saying, "Get behind Me, Satan" (Matt. 16:23; Mark 8:33). Again, Jesus said, "No one, after putting his hand to the plow and looking back, is fit for the kingdom of God." (Luke 9:62).

> **Ministry Maxim**
>
> Selfish choices are tantamount to aiding and abetting the enemy.

The picture, then, is a graphic one. These young widows made a profession of faith in Christ and pledged their obedience to Him. When, in their vulnerable

---

[70] Ibid., 246.
[71] Ibid.

state, the first eligible, though unbelieving, man showed interest, they abandoned their discipleship (i.e., commitment to marry only in the faith) and took out after him (see discussion above on v.12). This, says Paul, was the work of Satan. The Apostle is not reticent to point out the activity of the evil one in the PE (1 Tim. 1:20; 2:14; 3:6-7; 4:1; 2 Tim. 2:26).

> **Digging Deeper:**
> 1. Exactly how does the Apostle see Christian marriage saving such widows from potential "reproach"?
> 2. In what way does the word "keep house" (οἰκοδεσποτεῖν) elevate a woman's status rather than denigrate it?
> 3. In what way does Satan get his work done through gossips? Who then is to blame for the resulting destruction—the devil or the gossips?

5:16 If any woman who is a believer has dependent widows, she must assist them and the church must not be burdened, so that it may assist those who are widows indeed.

Paul now moves to conclude his concerns regarding widows. Having addressed the problem of younger widows (vv.11-15), he now returns to the previous concern that the family members of widows are to take up their care and relieve the church so they can care for those widows who are truly destitute (vv.4, 8).

The conditional statement is assumed true (εἴ + present indicative). There are some women in the church who were able to care for the widows in their family. The matter is left general in nature by using the indefinite feminine adjective (τις, "any woman"). Yet not just all women are the concern, but any woman "who is a believer" (πιστή). The adjective is used as a substantive. Many manuscripts have πιστὸς ἢ before πιστή, with the resulting meaning "any man or woman that believeth" (KJV). This, however, appears suspiciously like an attempt to "improve" the text by making it conform to v.4 and giving apparent equity of responsibilities between men and women.[72] Furthermore, intimate ministry by a man—single or married—to a widow could lead at least to awkwardness and at worst to impropriety.[73] Paul is not dictating behavior to society in general, but to the church. Similarly, it is not all believing women he speaks to, but to any who "has dependent widows" (ἔχει χήρας). The word

---
[72] NET Bible.
[73] Mounce, 298.

"dependent" has been added by the translators based on the context. It captures the intent well, but the statement is literally "has widows." Paul has previously laid the responsibility for support upon children and grandchildren (v.4), but now he appears to widen the circle of responsibility to any extended family member.

Regarding any such woman Paul issues two commands. First, "she must assist them" (ἐπαρκείτω αὐταῖς). The verb is used twice here and the only other usage is in v.10 (which see) where it was used to outline the qualifications of which widows would receive support—namely the widows who had "assisted those in distress." Now the same verb is used to describe the ministry this widow should receive in her advanced age. What she has made a habit of giving she is now to receive herself. The believing relatives of the true widow should see that her life becomes proof of Jesus' statement: "Give, and it will be given to you. They will pour into your lap a good measure—pressed down, shaken together, and running over. For by your standard of measure it will be measured to you in return" (Luke 6:38).

> **Ministry Maxim**
>
> When we care for our own family, we care for the whole church.

By "she" Paul means the believing woman who has an aged widow in her family. The present tense imperative demands repeated or continual action; the woman is to take on the ongoing support of the dependent widow in her family. The feminine plural personal pronoun (αὐταῖς, "them") looks back to the feminine plural noun "widows" (χήρας).

When this is done not only will the widow be supported and the woman fulfill her duty (vv.4, 8), but additionally (καί, "and") the second command will be fulfilled: "the church must not be burdened" (μὴ βαρείσθω ἡ ἐκκλησία). The verb appears six times in the NT, three of them in Paul (Matt. 26:43; Luke 9:32; 21:34; 2 Cor. 1:8; 5:4; 1 Tim. 5:16). It means to be weighed down and thus burdened.[74] It was used often in secular writing of the day, as it is here, in the context of financial concerns.[75] The negative (μή, "not") with the present tense imperative demands that action already in progress be stopped. The passive voice pictures the church being burdened by something outside itself; in this case, one of its own members who should be supported by capable family members.

The purpose (ἵνα + subjunctive, "so that") behind all this is that the church ("it") "may assist those who are widows indeed" (ταῖς ὄντως χήραις ἐπαρκέσῃ). The combination of noun and adverb ("widows indeed," ταῖς ὄντως χήραις) is repeated from vv.3, 5. See on v.3 for what qualifies a widow as such. The verb

---

[74] Friberg, 87.
[75] Mounce, 298.

"assist" (ἐπαρκέσῃ) is the same one used previously in this verse (and in v.10).

> **Digging Deeper:**
> 1. How far down the family line does the responsibility to care for widowed relatives go?
> 2. Have government welfare programs changed the responsibility of families and churches toward widows? If so, in what way?
> 3. How should the church collectively respond to members who do not adequately care for widowed family members?

5:17 The elders who rule well are to be considered worthy of double honor, especially those who work hard at preaching and teaching.

Paul now turns from his extended instructions regarding widows (vv.3-16) to another extended section, this time regarding elders (vv.17-25). Taking up this topic, as with the teaching regarding widows, probably betrays the fact that there was a foundational flaw in the eldership of the church in Ephesus. The false teachers may well have made entry into the eldership or perhaps had arisen from within the elders themselves. Paul had earlier warned them that this would be the case: "I know that after my departure savage wolves *will come in among you*, not sparing the flock; and *from among your own selves* men will arise, speaking perverse things, to draw away the disciples after them" (Acts 20:29-30, emphasis added). Paul earlier set forth the standards for elders (1 Tim. 3:1-7). He now deals with matters of their compensation and accountability.

Paul begins on a positive note, with "The elders who rule well" (Οἱ καλῶς προεστῶτες πρεσβύτεροι). The adjective was used in v.1 to speak of an "older man" and in v.2 to speak of "older women," but here it is clear that "elders" as leaders are in view. The word "elders" (πρεσβύτερος) originally spoke of men of advanced age, but in regard to leadership it is a carry over from the Jewish roots of the church. In the synagogue, elders were the leaders. The word then came to refer to the leaders of the church rather than simply the chronological age of an individual. Paul speaks for the first time in this letter of the office of elders (cf. 4:14), though he does so also in Titus 1:5. In chapter 3 the Apostle referred to individuals in this same office as "overseers." The terms "overseer" (ἐπίσκοπος) and "elder" (πρεσβύτερος) are both used to describe one office and are used interchangeably (Acts 20:17, 28; Titus 1:5, 7). The title "overseers" (ἐπίσκοπος) may describe the duty of the office, while "elders" (πρεσβύτερος) depicts the honor and dignity of the office. In this present case the adjective is accompanied by the definite article and is used as a substantive.

In the attributive position—tucked between the definite article and the adjective—is the qualifying phrase "rule well" (καλῶς προεστῶτες). The verb means to "*put oneself (responsibly) at the head, lead, direct, rule*"[76] and thus "to be over, to superintend, preside over"[77] (emphasis original). There is a clear sense of authority in the word. The verb is used eight times in the NT, all by Paul. Six of those are in the PE and four of those are here in 1 Timothy and have reference to the ministry of elders/overseers (1 Tim. 3:4, 5, 12; 5:17). Here it has in view the leadership the elders give to the church as a whole (5:17). This is leadership that elders must first and always demonstrate within their own homes (1 Tim. 3:4, 5; cf. the same requirement of deacons in 3:12). The perfect tense of the participle indicates that they began this ministry of leadership at some point in the past and have continued faithfully in it to the present time. This leadership must be exercised "well" (καλῶς). The word points to what is fitting, appropriate, and beautiful. Elders are not permitted to exercise heavy-handed leadership. There is no dictatorial right implied here. The elder is to live with and among and for those in his charge. Three of the four times καλῶς is found in the PE, it is connected to προΐστημι,[78] signaling something of the nature of the leadership required in the church (1 Tim. 3:4, 12; 5:17). Apparently not all the elders in Ephesus were exercising their office in this manner.

Those elders who were ruling well, says Paul, "are to be considered worthy of double honor" (διπλῆς τιμῆς ἀξιούσθωσαν). The verb ("are to be considered worthy," ἀξιούσθωσαν) is a present tense imperative and thus demands action that is repeated or continuous. The passive voice indicates that it is not the elders themselves who are to calculate thus, but those outside them; perhaps either the larger body of elders or the congregation itself. It means to consider worthy or deserving.[79] Paul uses the verb elsewhere only in 2 Thessalonians 1:11 where he is concerned that "God will count you worthy of your calling." The centurion sent word to Jesus, saying, "I did not even consider myself worthy to come to You" (Luke 7:7; cf. other NT usages, Acts 15:38; 28:22; Heb. 3:3; 10:29). The use of this verb here is likely due to the presence of its cognate adjective in the statement of Jesus to be cited in the next verse (Matt. 10:10; Luke 10:7).

Just what "double honor" (διπλῆς τιμῆς) means has been a matter of some debate. The noun ("honor," τιμῆς) could denote the price or value of some-

---
[76] Friberg, 329.
[77] Thayer, 539.
[78] Mounce, 178.
[79] BAGD, 78.

thing (e.g., Matt. 27:6, 9; Acts 4:34; 5:2, 3; 1 Cor. 6:20). It came to be used for the honor or reverence that signifies the value of a person. The use of the noun "honor" reveals that ultimately all "honor" belongs to God (1 Tim. 1:17; 6:16), yet slaves are instructed to give "all honor" (πάσης τιμῆς) to their masters (6:1). Believers exist and serve to bring "honor" to God (2 Tim. 2:20) and we are exhorted to be "a vessel for honor, sanctified, useful to the Master, prepared for every good work" (v.21). Clearly the word most often has the sense of esteem, respect and reverence. Yet it can also refer to financial compensation, or, as some might put it, an "honorarium."[80] That is has this meaning here seems likely because of the context where Paul has discussed at length which widows are to be financially supported by the church (vv.3-16) and because of the quotations that follow in v.18. The adjective "double" (διπλῆς) means either twofold or double. It is used only three other times in the NT. Jesus used it to tell the scribes and Pharisees regarding a disciple of theirs, "you make him twice as much a son of hell as yourselves" (Matt. 23:15). In Revelation 18:6 the angel used it twice to say of Babylon, "give back to her double according to her deeds; in the cup which she has mixed, mix twice as much for her." By double could mean "honor and honorarium" (i.e., respect and financial support), double pay (over the other elders who do not rule well), twice as much financial support as the enrolled widows (cf. vv.3-16)[81] or respect because of the office he holds and respect for the excellence of his work.[82] Regarding the last option, nothing in the context supports the idea of respect simply for the office, even if the work done in that office is deficient. Viewing this as double a widow's portion seems unlikely. The second seems unlikely in that elders who are not "ruling well" are unlikely to be deserving of any financial support and more likely to be candidates for discipline by the other elders (vv.19-20). This leaves the sense of "double honor," meaning both respect and financial remuneration for their ministry.

The Apostle adds, "especially those who work hard at preaching and teaching" (μάλιστα οἱ κοπιῶντες ἐν λόγῳ καὶ διδασκαλίᾳ). The adverb ("especially," μάλιστα) is the superlative of the adverb μάλα. It is "the highest point in the extent of something" and means something like "most of all," "especially," or "above all."[83] Paul uses it in the PE to single out "believers" from among "all men" (1 Tim. 4:10), one's "household" from one's "own" (5:8), "parchments" from "books" (2 Tim. 4:13), and "those of the circumcision" from a larger body of "rebellious men, empty talkers and deceivers" (Titus 1:10). Paul is here singling out certain elders from among the larger

---

[80] Ibid., 818.
[81] Robertson, 4:587-588.
[82] Kent, 176.
[83] Friberg, 252.

body of elders. But is this a subset of the elders as a whole or of those elders "who rule well"? In other words does Paul intend a twofold division of the elders or a threefold division (all elders, elders who rule well, elders who work hard at preaching and teaching)? A twofold division seems more likely and in that case "especially" (μάλιστα) might be better rendered "namely."[84] Those "who rule well" are designated as "those who work hard" (οἱ κοπιῶντες). The verb means to labor to the point of weariness and exhaustion. The exact expression is found elsewhere in the NT only in Jesus' invitation to all "who are weary" (Matt. 11:28). The participle with the definite article is used as a substantive. The present tense views the action as ongoing and repeated and continual. Paul used the word to describe the labors of a farmer (2 Tim. 2:6) and to describe his own ministry (1 Tim. 4:10). The arena ("in," ἐν) of this ongoing, wearying toil is "preaching and teaching" (λόγῳ καὶ διδασκαλίᾳ). The two nouns are found together again in 1 Timothy 4:6; 6:3; Titus 1:9; Hebrews 5:12. Both words are found often in the PE and are keys in dealing with the false teachers and their false doctrine that is being faced in Ephesus and on Crete. The former word (λόγος) is used regularly to designate a "trustworthy statement" (1 Tim. 1:15; 3:1; 4:9; 2 Tim. 2:11; Titus 3:8), "sound words" (1 Tim. 6:3; 2 Tim. 1:13), and "the faithful word" (Titus 1:9). It designates "the word of God" (1 Tim. 4:5; 2 Tim. 2:9; Titus 2:5), the "words of the faith" (1 Tim. 4:6), and "the word of truth" (2 Tim. 2:15). This word is to be preached (2 Tim. 4:2). It can refer to Paul's own preaching and teaching (2 Tim. 4:15) and the Gospel (Titus 1:3). It can also be used of the words of the false teachers (2 Tim. 2:17). The latter word (διδασκαλία) is used twenty-two times in the NT, nineteen of those are by Paul and fifteen of those are in the PE (1 Tim. 1:10; 4:1, 6, 13, 16; 5:17; 6:1, 3; 2 Tim. 3:10, 16; 4:3; Titus 1:9; 2:1, 7, 10). The noun may refer to either the act of teaching or to that which is taught ("doctrine").[85] It is in the former sense that it is used here, without losing the emphasis on correct content. There may be the "doctrine of demons" (1 Tim. 4:1). But "the doctrine of God our Savior" (Titus 2:10) is "sound teaching/doctrine" (1 Tim. 1:10; 4:6; 2 Tim. 4:3; Titus 1:9; 2:1), "doctrine conforming to godliness" (1 Tim. 6:3), and "purity in doctrine" (Titus 2:7). This is the heart of Scripture's purpose (2 Tim. 3:16), and all such teaching arises from and is controlled by the Scriptures.

Some conclude that Paul has in mind here two classes of elders: ruling elders and teaching elders. This reads more into this sentence than is justified.

> **Ministry Maxim**
>
> Faithful preachers should be respected and remunerated.

---

[84] Marshall, 612.
[85] BAGD, 191.

All elders were expected to teach and all were called upon to preside over the congregation—each was an "overseer" who was "able to teach" (3:2; cf. 2 Tim. 2:24). Furthermore, it may be said that "preaching and teaching" is a primary means (among others) by which the elders watch over and lead the flock. Paul does elevate the ministry of the Word of God. All ministry is significant and important, but accurate study and proclamation of God's Word is paramount and indispensable. All elders must be "able to teach," but some elders will preach and teach more than others. Such ministry is exacting and exhausting. It should be compensated by both respect and remuneration.

> **Digging Deeper:**
> 1. What evidences mark a man as an elder who rules well?
> 2. How might "double honor" for some elders strain relationships with other elders?
> 3. What current cultural factors—both Christian and secular—discourage hard work in preaching and teaching?

5:18 For the Scripture says, "You shall not muzzle the ox while he is threshing," and "The laborer is worthy of his wages."

Paul now supports his assertion in v.17 ("For," γὰρ) by quoting "the Scripture" (ἡ γραφή). This is Paul's standard formula for introducing a quotation from the OT (Rom. 4:3; 9:17; 10:11; 11:2; Gal. 3:8, 22; 4:30). Paul uses the same noun (minus the definite article) in 2 Timothy 3:16 when he says "All Scripture is God-breathed" (NIV). The verb "says" (λέγει) is in the present tense, indicating that the power and voice of the Scripture is contemporary and current.

The first citation says, "YOU SHALL NOT MUZZLE THE OX WHILE HE IS THRESHING" (βοῦν ἀλοῶντα οὐ φιμώσεις). This is a quotation of Deuteronomy 25:4. The same passage is quoted also in 1 Corinthians 9:9 where the Apostle is clearly discussing a minister's right to financial support from those to whom he ministers. This confirms that the understanding of "honor" (τιμῆς) in v.17 should include financial or tangible remuneration. The statute appears to have been intended, in its original context, quite literally as governing an animal and its owner, though its implications surely were intended to be applied more broadly. It is used by the Apostle in a metaphorical sense and applied to Christian workers. Paul does not expound upon the application of this quote here; read 1 Cor. 9:7-14 for what he probably has in mind here.

To this Paul adds ("and," καί) a second quotation. The coordinating conjunction holds the two quotations in parallel. Now he says, "The laborer is worthy of his wages" (ἄξιος ὁ ἐργάτης τοῦ μισθοῦ αὐτοῦ). This is an exact representation of Jesus' words in Luke 10:7 (and Matt. 10:10 is nearly verbatim as well). It appears that Paul was quoting from Luke's Gospel. Some debate the dates of composition for Luke's Gospel and this letter, calling into question the possibility that Paul could be quoting from Luke here. The dates are not impossible, even if they are beyond absolute proof. If Paul is not quoting directly from Luke's Gospel, he may have received the information directly from Luke (note their close association as evidenced in the "we" sections of Acts; cf. also Col. 4:14; 2 Tim. 4:11; Philem. 24; though ἡ γραφή usually refers to what is written), from a common source that predated both Luke's Gospel and this letter of Paul, or from a oral tradition in the church regarding Jesus' statement (though, again, ἡ γραφή usually refers to that which is written). In Paul's similar argumentation in 1 Corinthians 9, in which we have noted, he also quoted Deuteronomy 25:4 (v.9) when he added the statement, "So also the Lord directed" (v.14). Perhaps he had this very statement of Christ in mind there, though he does not quote it directly as he does here. It is of great importance that the Apostle holds this statement of Christ in parallel with a citation of OT Scripture. It provides clear indication that the Apostles accepted what we know as the canonical NT writings as authoritative Scripture (cf. 2 Peter 3:15-16).

> **Ministry Maxim**
>
> Both mercenary ministers and miserly congregations dishonor Christ.

Paul denounced both mercenary ministers (1 Tim. 3:3, 8; Titus 1:5, 11) and miserly congregations.

> **Digging Deeper:**
> 1. What significance is to be found in Paul placing an Old Testament quotation next to a quotation of Christ and referring to them both as "the Scripture"?
> 2. By what kind of hermeneutic can Paul make application of an agricultural directive concerning livestock to those in service in the church?

5:19 Do not receive an accusation against an elder except on the basis of two or three witnesses.

Paul's concern turns now from elders who do well (vv.17-18) to those who may do evil (vv.19-22). In this verse the Apostle issues a prohibition and then qualifies it. The prohibition is, "Do not receive an accusation against an elder" (κατὰ πρεσβυτέρου κατηγορίαν μὴ παραδέχου). The adjective "elder" (πρεσβυτέρου) is used as a substantive here. It is employed here not in the sense of advanced age only (vv.1-2), but in reference to the office of leadership within the local church (vv.17-18). The noun "accusation" (κατηγορίαν) was a technical term from the legal world for a charge or accusation. It is used only three times in the NT. Pilate, concerning Jesus, asked the crowds, "What accusation do you bring against this Man?" (John 18:29). Paul used the word to tell Titus that elders must have children who are "not accused of dissipation or rebellion" (Titus 1:6). The picture is of someone bringing a charge of sin against an elder. The individual may be someone from among the people of the church, the eldership itself, the false teachers, or perhaps even from the surrounding community. Whoever brings the charge, Paul instructs Timothy, "Do not receive" (μὴ παραδέχου) it. The verb is used six times in the NT (Mark 4:20; Acts 15:4; 16:21; 22:18; Heb. 12:6), but Paul uses it only here. It is a compound word comprised of "from/beside" (παρά) and "receive" (δέχομαι). The present tense imperative with the negation ("not," μὴ) usually demands that action now in progress be stopped. This may mean that the eldership in Ephesus was being torn apart by unsubstantiated accusations, rumor, and innuendo. Paul here, then, provides a process whereby elders can be held accountable, but in a reasonable and verifiable way.

Paul then qualifies the prohibition with "except on the basis of two or three witnesses" (ἐκτὸς εἰ μὴ ἐπὶ δύο ἢ τριῶν μαρτύρων). The expression behind "except" (ἐκτὸς εἰ μὴ) is used also in 1 Corinthians 14:5; 15:2. The regulation of "two or three witnesses" (δύο ἢ τριῶν μαρτύρων) is derived from the principle given to Moses in Deut. 17:6; 19:15. Any accusation expecting serious consideration must be "on the basis of" (ἐπὶ)[86] multiple witnesses. This would serve to limit, if not eliminate entirely, frivolous accusations and needless harm to reputations and ministries. A well-formulated plot to spoil an innocent man's ministry could still possibly succeed, it is true. Yet the difficulty of achieving such success would be greatly increased. There are, however, some sins which by their very nature are unlikely to be exposed and judged appropriately by this strict limitation (e.g., some sexual sins). Thus we must recognize that there are other valid forms of evidence beyond multiple eye witnesses that on occasion must be taken into consideration if justice is to be done and the church is to be protected. Great wisdom and discernment is needed is such cases.

> **Ministry Maxim**
>
> To plan for a problem is to defuse much of its power.

All of this serves to make the point that leadership does not get a pass on accountability. In fact their accountability is greater and the repercussions of

---

[86] BAGD, 286.

any sin may be more severe. Every local church must proactively establish the method by which church discipline will be carried out, including how accusations against those in leadership will be handled, who leads this process, and who determines the outcome and hands down a judgment (v.20). To wait until a problem arises is to open the church and its leaders to temptations of partiality and compromise (v.21).

> **Digging Deeper:**
> 1. Why is it necessary to have a process for accountability for leaders in place *before* an accusation arises?
> 2. Explain the wisdom in requiring two or three witnesses before entertaining an accusation against a leader.
> 3. Describe a scenario where this requirement might actually inhibit justice.

5:20 Those who continue in sin, rebuke in the presence of all, so that the rest also will be fearful of sinning.

"Those who continue in sin" (Τοὺς ἁμαρτάνοντας) refers to elders, as the context makes clear (vv.17-19), not to church members generally. The participle and its definite article are used as a substantive. The present tense points to ongoing action, thus "continue in" is a good translation. This assumes the process standing behind v.19—that an accusation has been received by multiple witnesses, an investigation has been carried out discreetly, the individual interviewed, and guilt determined. Yet in the face of all this, the elder continues to hold to his sinful pattern of behavior, speech, or thinking. When an elder remains in a state of sin, the other elders are to 'rebuke" him (ἔλεγχε). Of Paul's eight uses of this verb, five of them appear in the PE (1 Tim. 5:20; 2 Tim. 4:2; Titus 1:9, 13; 2:15). It means to correct with the connotation of refuting.[87] It describes exposing another's position with overwhelming proof so that they are brought to the point of conviction of sin.[88] In the PE Paul uses it to describe part of the regular ministry of preaching (2 Tim. 4:2). Titus was to exercise it generally in his ministry because of the obstinate nature of the Cretans (Titus 1:13; 2:15). It is used also in Titus of exposing the faulty thinking of opponents (Titus 1:9). Here, as a present tense imperative, the demand is for ongoing or continuous action. This probably does not mean that there are repeated public rebukes toward the sinning elder, but that, once the rebuke

---
[87] BAGD, 249.
[88] Rienecker, 647.

has been made, the ongoing stance of the elders and church is to be opposition to and rebuke of the sin, until it is repented of. The second person singular form may point to Timothy as the leader of the elders as they collectively take this action, with him serving as their spokesman. This rebuke is to take place "in the presence of all" (ἐνώπιον πάντων). This combination is used six other times in the NT (Luke 8:47; 14:10; Acts 6:5; 19:19; 27:35; Rom. 12:17). The preposition itself is found over ninety times in the NT. It probably derives from the expression ὁ ἐν ὦπι ὤν ("in the eye of"). The phrase was compressed by usage, became one word, and thus described the one who is in the eye of someone else.[89] By "all" (πάντων) Paul probably refers to the whole congregation (Matt. 18:17; Rom. 16:17; 1 Cor. 5:4; 2 Cor. 2:6; 2 Thess. 3:6, 14; 3 John 9-10), not simply the whole of the elders. This presumes that the prior steps of confrontation personally (Matt. 18:15) and by a smaller group (Matt. 18:16) have already been carried out. These should have been undertaken in the spirit of Galatians 6:1-5.

> **Ministry Maxim**
>
> A rebuke that is not successful in dealing with the offender may be effective in the life of an onlooker.

These painful steps are to be undertaken with a specific purpose in mind (ἵνα, "so that"). The intent is that "the rest also will be fearful" (καὶ οἱ λοιποὶ φόβον ἔχωσιν). By "the rest" (οἱ λοιποὶ) the Apostle surely means the whole of the congregation, not simply the other elders. If the rebuke has been before the church then the effect would necessarily be as well. Certainly the elders should learn fear through this, but so should all the members of the church. This fear is in addition to ("also," καὶ) that evoked in the sinning elder. The words "will be fearful" (φόβον ἔχωσιν) are more literally "have fear." The verb is a present tense pointing to an ongoing or continuous action. The subjunctive mood couples with the previous ἵνα to indicate purpose. The noun "fear" (φόβος) is used in the PE only here. Paul uses it on occasion of ordinary, human fears (1 Cor. 2:3). He also uses it of the fear we have been delivered from (Rom. 8:15). But Paul more often employs the word to speak of the fear of God (Rom. 3:18; 2 Cor. 5:11; 7:1; 2 Cor. 7:11; Eph. 5:21; 6:5; Phil. 2:12) and even of appropriate fear toward earthly, God-ordained authorities (Rom. 13:7). It would seem that the fear of the Lord is what Paul has in mind in this context (cf. v.21). The Apostle knows "The fear of the LORD is a fountain of life, that one may avoid the snares of death" (Prov. 14:27) and that "by the fear of the LORD one keeps away from evil" (Prov. 16:6b; cf. 23:17). The goal of the OT requirement of two or three witnesses (v.19; cf. Deut. 19:15) was that "The rest will hear and be afraid, and will never again do such an evil thing among you" (Deut. 19:20).

---

[89] Robertson, 4:589; Thayer, 219.

> **Digging Deeper:**
> 1. Why would the Apostle demand that a sinning elder be rebuked "in the presence of all" the congregation?
> 2. What contemporary realities make obeying these instructions even more challenging than they might have been in the first century?

5:21 I solemnly charge you in the presence of God and of Christ Jesus and of His chosen angels, to maintain these principles without bias, doing nothing in a spirit of partiality.

That Paul is serious is clear, for he says, "I solemnly charge you in the presence of God and of Christ Jesus" (Διαμαρτύρομαι ἐνώπιον τοῦ θεοῦ καὶ Χριστοῦ Ἰησοῦ). The entire expression is used again by Paul in 2 Timothy 4:1. In 2 Timothy 2:14 Paul commands Timothy, regarding his teaching the church the truth, to "solemnly charge them in the presence of God" (cf. also 1 Tim. 6:13). The Apostle Paul had issued a similar charge to the Thessalonian believers regarding sexual purity (1 Thess. 4:6). The verb is used frequently by Luke (Luke 16:28; Acts 2:40; 8:25; 10:42; 18:5; 20:21, 23, 24; 23:11; 28:23). Here the present tense verb emphasizes the ongoing nature of the charge. It is a deponent verb, thus the middle/passive form has an active meaning. "The first person singular form gives the charge a direct and forceful quality and conveys the fact that the charge is given by Paul in his apostolic authority (cf. 1:1)."[90] The word can speak of bearing a solemn witness or testimony to something (e.g., Acts 20:21, 23, 24; 23:11; 28:23); however, here it means to charge, warn, or adjure (cf. 1 Tim. 4:6; 5:21; 2 Tim. 2:14).[91]

Paul's charge is made all the more solemn by the building up of the atmosphere in which it is made, prior to actually leveling the charge. Paul charges Timothy "in the presence of God and of Christ Jesus" (ἐνώπιον τοῦ θεοῦ καὶ Χριστοῦ Ἰησοῦ). The expression "in the presence of" is the translation of the same word just encountered in v.20 (ἐνώπιον; see there for more on this word). The kind of discipline demanded in vv.19-20 is to be undertaken with the clear knowledge that the whole church (v.20) and the whole of heaven (v.21) are watching. It is one of the Apostle's favorite ways for making assertions and oaths which call upon God (Gal. 1:20; 1 Tim. 5:21; 6:13; 2 Tim. 2:14).[92] It is significant that God and Jesus are mentioned together in such close connection. The two Persons are here held together by one definite article. Paul closely links Father and Son, they who

---
[90] Knight, 452.
[91] BAGD, 186.
[92] Ibid., 270.

are one in essence, yet distinct in Personhood.

The presence of God is not simply something apocalyptic, but is a present reality. Paul declared to the Athenians, "in Him we live and move and exist" (Acts 17:28a). Yes, "now we see in a mirror dimly, but then face to face" (1 Cor. 13:12). And, yes, one day we will stand before His unveiled presence and be assayed by His searching eyes of omniscience. But it is equally true that He is all of that at the present moment as well, if we will have eyes to discern it. All that He will be then, He is now. Paul had been "caught up to the third heaven" (2 Cor. 12:2), into the very presence of God Himself. The Apostle called Timothy to live and minister now in the awareness that he did so in the presence of the One who one day will be unveiled in all His magnificence and glory.

To this already solemn assembly, Paul adds, "and of His chosen angels" (καὶ τῶν ἐκλεκτῶν ἀγγέλων). This noun is set apart from the reference to the Father and Son by having its own definite article, marking the distinction between God and His creatures.[93] Some angels rebelled against God and sided with Lucifer. They were "angels who did not keep their own domain, but abandoned their proper abode" (Jude 6). "God did not spare [these] angels when they sinned, but cast them into hell and committed them to pits of darkness, reserved for judgment" (2 Peter 2:4). By "chosen" (ἐκλεκτῶν) Paul refers to angels who did not join in the rebellion and are now constituted "holy angels" (Mark 8:38; Luke 9:26; Rev. 14:10). Paul believed that angels are beholding life unfold here on earth (1 Tim. 3:16). He said that he and the other Apostles had become "a spectacle to the world, both to angels and to men" (1 Cor. 4:9; cf. 11:10). This most serious charge is leveled in the combined presence of God the Father, God the Son, and the angels who worship and serve them (Heb. 1:6) and expedite the will of God among His people on earth (Heb. 1:14).

> **Ministry Maxim**
>
> An awareness of the presence of God is the greatest antidote to partiality.

The solemn charge itself is "to maintain these principles without bias" (ἵνα ταῦτα φυλάξῃς χωρὶς προκρίματος). This is more literally, "in order that these things you may keep without prejudice." The ἵνα points to the content of the charge.[94] The "these things" (ταῦτα) surely points to the directions regarding elders (vv.17-20) and probably focuses primarily upon vv.19-20. The verb ("maintain," φυλάξῃς) describes protecting something entrusted to you so that it is unharmed.[95] It is used in the PE to alternate between a responsibility laid on Timothy (1 Tim. 6:20; 2 Tim. 1:14; 4:15) and one God takes up

---

[93] Hiebert, *First Timothy*, 103.
[94] Knight, 238.
[95] BAGD, 868.

(2 Tim. 1:12). Here the former is in view. This action is to be taken "without bias" (χωρὶς προκρίματος). The word "without" (χωρὶς) is an adverb that means "separately" or "apart." It is used in the NT as a preposition with the genitive, combining to mean "without" in the sense of "making no use of, having no association with, apart from, aloof from, etc."[96] The noun "bias" (προκρίματος) is used only here in the NT. It is a compound word made up of "before" (πρό) and "judgment" (κρίμα). Thus it describes something that takes place "as the result of a prior unjustified decision."[97] Paul adds a subordinate participial clause to show that this action must be undertaken "doing nothing in a spirit of partiality" (μηδὲν ποιῶν κατὰ πρόσκλισιν). The combination of μηδὲν ποιῶν ("doing nothing") forms a universal negative—nothing at all of the sort should take place.[98] The preposition (κατὰ) is used here with a meaning that combines "in accordance with" and "because of."[99] The noun "partiality" (πρόσκλισιν) also is used only here in the NT. It is a compound word from the verb προσκλίνω, which is comprised of "toward" (πρός) and "to incline" (κλίνω). It thus describes inclining toward something, and then came to describe partiality.[100] Paul emphatically affirms that there is no partiality with God (Rom. 2:11; Gal. 2:6; Eph. 6:9; Col. 3:25) and thus there must not be any among those who lead His church.

> **Digging Deeper:**
> 1. Do you go about your daily responsibilities with a sense of the "presence of God and of Christ Jesus and of His chosen angels"?
> 2. Why do you think Paul went to such great lengths to build up the solemn nature of this charge? What must this say about the powerful pull of partiality?
> 3. In what way are you tempted toward bias and partiality?

5:22 Do not lay hands upon anyone too hastily and thereby share responsibility for the sins of others; keep yourself free from sin.

Two prohibitions and one command are laid down in this verse. The first prohibition is, "Do not lay hands upon anyone too hastily" (χεῖρας ταχέως μηδενὶ ἐπιτίθει). The present tense imperative ("lay hands upon," ἐπιτίθει) with negation (μηδενὶ) demands that action that is now in progress be stopped. The verb is a

---
[96] Thayer, 675.
[97] Friberg, 329.
[98] Knight, 239.
[99] BAGD, 407.
[100] Rienecker, 632.

compound comprised of "upon" (ἐπί) and "to lay" (τίθημι). In the early days of the church, the Apostles laid hands on those charged with organizing the distribution to widows (Acts 6:6) and prayed for them. The act of laying hands on someone is often associated with healing (9:12, 17; 28:8). Paul and Barnabas were set apart by the church leadership in Antioch for their missionary ministry (13:3). It is associated with the reception of the Holy Spirit (8:17, 19; 19:6). Paul speaks of the gift Timothy received when the elders laid their hands upon him (1 Tim. 4:14; cf. 2 Tim. 1:6). Here it seems to be used in a way similar to the consecration of those organizing the ministry to widows (Acts 6:6) and the setting apart of Paul and Barnabas for missionary service (13:3). This is not to be done "hastily" (ταχέως). The adverb describes that which is quick, fleet, or speedy.[101]

There is debate regarding just what this act ("lay hands") refers to. 1) This could refer to lifting a man to the position of elder too quickly after his conversion (1 Tim. 3:6). 2) It could refer to lifting a man to the position of elder without sufficient time to examine his life, character and reputation (1 Tim. 3:10). 3) It could refer to hastily welcoming a sinning, former elder back into the position he once held (1 Tim. 5:20). The immediate context may appear at first to support the last view. The Apostle has just outlined how to go about disciplining sinning elders (1 Tim. 5:19-21). The situation in Ephesus was apparently volatile. The false teachers seem to have arisen from within the ranks of the elders themselves (Acts 20:30). He may then be warning against too quickly accepting a man back into the office of elder after he has failed there previously. Such a return is not ruled out, but the process is governed by time and careful examination. The fact is, however, that there is no evidence to suggest that the early church laid hands upon sinning, but now repentant, elders as they restored them to office. Such a practice cannot be verified prior to the third century. What can be verified is that the early church did lay hands upon people when commissioning them to service or to an office of leadership in the church. Therefore, it seems more likely that this is a reference to hasty appointment of immature and/or untried men (i.e., options 1 and 2 above). In practice and application the principle would then apply as well to the restoration of elders who had lapsed into sin but were now repentant, though this is unlikely to be the immediate purpose of the statement.

> **Ministry Maxim**
>
> Time tells the reality of repentance.

The second prohibition complements the first, "and thereby share responsibility for the sins of others" (μηδὲ κοινώνει ἁμαρτίαις ἀλλοτρίαις). More literally this is, "Do not share sins of others." Again the present tense imperative with negation implies that action that is already underway is to be

---

[101] Thayer, 616.

stopped. The verb means to share or to have a share in something,[102] in this case "the sins of others" (ἁμαρτίαις ἀλλοτρίαις). If the first prohibition was primarily against the appointment of immature and untried men, then this is simply pointing out that those who appoint men to office are responsible to some degree for their performance in that office. If the previous prohibition referred to the restoration of a fallen elder, then the sins referred to here may relate more specifically to the past sins of the elder which may again come to fruition if repentance is not complete. The Apostle John was concerned that believers might share in the sins of false teachers because "the one who gives him a greeting participates [κοινωνεῖ] in his evil deeds" (2 John 11). The participation here in 1 Timothy 5:22 comes via the laying on of hands too hastily. If false teaching is not exposed and repentance is not thorough, the elder will again fall into sin and those who too quickly restored him to the ministry of leadership will share in the responsibility for those sins he commits. Verse 24 reminds us that all is not as it sometimes seems, but v.25 reminds us that time and careful observation soon enough reveal reality.

Following the two prohibitions comes the command, "keep yourself free from sin" (σεαυτὸν ἁγνὸν τήρει). The verb "keep" (τήρει) can mean to guard or keep watch over something; to keep blameless or protect a thing. The present tense imperative demands that action be taken continually or repeatedly. It gives the sense of "keep on keeping yourself" pure. Paul will use the same verb at the end of his life to say, "I have kept the faith" (2 Tim. 4:7). The adjective "free" (ἁγνὸν) describes being chaste and modest. It originally referred to ritual cleanness, but over time its emphasis shifted to the moral realm. The second person singular reflexive pronoun ("yourself," σεαυτὸν) lifts Timothy's eyes off the false teachers, erring elders, and manifold problems facing the church in Ephesus. He is to watch himself and his life that he might remain in a position to lead in these matters of appointment to office, church discipline, and the judgments necessary to deal with the false teaching and to solidify the eldership.

> **Digging Deeper:**
> 1. What length of time keeps us from being "too hasty" in these matters?
> 2. In what sense would these who had previously laid hands on now erring elders "share responsibility" for their sins?
> 3. Why is the exhortation to "keep yourself free from sin" appropriate in this context of dealing with sinning leaders (cf. Gal. 6:1b)?

---

[102] BAGD, 438.

5:23 No longer drink water exclusively, but use a little wine for the sake of your stomach and your frequent ailments.

This verse serves as a parenthetical thought, spurred by the exhortation to "keep yourself free from sin" (v.22b). In vv.24-25 Paul will return to the primary line of thinking regarding the selection and discipline of elders (vv.22). Paul, not wanting to be misunderstood as supporting an ascetic approach to sanctification (something he has charged the false teachers with, cf. 1 Tim. 4:3), adds this note. He was motivated also by the knowledge that Timothy had been ailing physically in some way, perhaps from some water-borne bacteria that the alcohol content of wine would purify. We should note that the introduction of this sentence at this point in the discussion seems a bit jarring—something which commentators have puzzled over for centuries. This, however, provides one of the best arguments for Pauline authorship, for surely no later forger would have introduced something so apparently foreign to the context.

He commands, "No longer drink water" (Μηκέτι ὑδροπότει). The present tense imperative with the negation demands that action now in progress be stopped. The verb is used only here in the NT. It means simply to drink water. But here it seems to be heightened to mean drink water *only*, thus the translators have added the word "exclusively." It probably looks to this practice as part of "an abstemious way of life."[103] The verb is negated by the adverb translated "No longer" (Μηκέτι). If this be the case, it appears there were some misguided scruples that motivated Timothy's stance regarding wine drinking. The Apostle clearly understood the dangers of alcohol. He demanded that overseers and deacons not be "addicted to wine" (1 Tim. 3:3, 8). He told Titus to make sure the older women were not "enslaved to much wine" (Titus 2:3). He instructed the people of this very church, "do not get drunk with wine, for that is dissipation, but be filled with the Spirit" (Eph. 5:18). He saw drinking as a potential way of causing harm to another's faith (Rom. 14:21). It is possible that Timothy was trying to live out something like a Nazarite vow in which he abstained from all alcohol (Num. 6:2-4; cf. Luke 1:15).

Now the Apostle appears to make a sudden change of course. In contrast to a teetotaling lifestyle (ἀλλὰ, "but"), Paul now commands Timothy to "use a little wine" (οἴνῳ ὀλίγῳ χρῶ). To what was Paul referring when he used the noun "wine" (οἴνῳ)? The term can refer to both fermented grape juice and to grape juice that it not yet fully fermented (Rev. 19:15). The alcohol content of wine today is much higher than the drinking wine used in the NT. Research reveals that in the ancient world wine was mixed with water as a purifying agent. The reported ratios of water to wine vary, but the average is between

---

[103] BAGD, 832.

three and four parts water to one part wine.[104] Geisler reports that "in the ancient world water could be made safe in one of several ways. It could be boiled, but this was tedious and costly. Or it could be filtered, but this was not a safe method. Or some wine could be put in the water to kill the germs – one part wine with three or four parts water."[105] What is sold as wine today has the alcohol content of what was to the Biblical writers "strong drink" (e.g., Lev. 10:9; Prov. 20:1; 31:4; Isa. 5:11) and thus would have thus been strictly off limits for those who wanted to please God.

Note that Paul counsels Timothy to "use" (χρῶ) the wine. The wine was to serve Timothy's purposes. He was to be in control of it, rather than it being in control of him (Eph. 5:18). And it was only "a little" (ὀλίγῳ) that was to be thus employed. This points to the practice of diluting the wine with water for the purpose of purifying the latter.

Clearly pure water/wine for drinking was the issue, for the instructions are given "for the sake of your stomach and your frequent ailments" (διὰ τὸν στόμαχον καὶ τὰς πυκνάς σου ἀσθενείας). Here the preposition διὰ ("for the sake of") is used with the accusative case and points to the purpose for using "a little wine." That purpose points to "your stomach" (τὸν στόμαχον). The noun is used only here in the NT. Originally it may have referred to the throat, but in the later writers it refers to the stomach.[106] Here it is more literally and simply, "the stomach." Timothy was apparently having digestive tract issues which drinking purified liquid free of bacteria would aid. Additionally (καὶ, "and") Paul gave this order for the sake of "your frequent ailments" (τὰς πυκνάς σου ἀσθενείας). The singular personal pronoun (σου, "your") designates this as Timothy's personal problem. These troubles are called "ailments" (ἀσθενείας). The word means "weakness" generally, a meaning which Paul represents with most of his twelve usages (Rom. 6:19; 8:26; 1 Cor. 2:3; 15:43; 2 Cor. 11:30; 12:5, 9 [2x], 10; 13:4; Gal. 4:13; 1 Tim. 5:23). The word can, however, refer to weakness in the sense of physical sickness. Paul said he preached the Gospel to the Galatians because of "a bodily illness" (ἀσθένειαν τῆς σαρκὸς; Gal. 4:13). The presence of the definite article (τὰς) here points to the specific problem Timothy was suffering. These illnesses were a "frequent" (πυκνάς) problem for Timothy. This adjective designates something which occurs often or on numerous

> **Ministry Maxim**
>
> Faith and medicine are not necessarily at odds with one another.

---

[104] Geisler, 50.
[105] Ibid., 51.
[106] Thayer, 590.

occasions.[107] Timothy's ministry is suffering because of his repeated struggle with ill-health. The remedy is not difficult; Paul prescribed a therapy through the medicinal uses of "a little" wine, the alcohol of which would kill off the bacteria which were causing Timothy's stomach troubles and ailments.

This hardly serves as a permission slip for social drinking. It does provide permission for survival-drinking. Wine drinking in the NT was not stylish, but may have been primarily for health reasons. Paul's instruction here was for physical, not fashionable, reasons. When it became a "right" to be demanded, the Apostle's counsel was to surrender that "right" for the sake of one's brother (Rom. 14:17-21; 1 Cor. 10:31-33). It is worth noting that by this parenthetical note the Apostle sanctions the use of medical means as a legitimate way of dealing with physical sickness.[108] While surely he prayed for Timothy's healing, he also suggested a course of action which would deal with the physical cause of those symptoms.

> **Digging Deeper:**
> 1. What evidence in this sentence points us away from making it a permission slip for social drinking?
> 2. How does this verse speak to our decisions about using medical means to address illness?

5:24 The sins of some men are quite evident, going before them to judgment; for others, their sins follow after.

Paul now returns to the line of thought he left after v.22—the selection and discipline of elders (vv.17-22). The concern before the parenthetical thought of v.23 had been not to select and commission elders hastily, lest one share in their sins. In this light he closes the discussion in this verse and the next with general, almost proverbial, statements,[109] to underscore how time reveals the truth about people's sins (v.24) and good works (v.25). Not all is as it seems to be at first glance.

Paul speaks broadly and universally, "The sins of some men" (Τινῶν ἀνθρώπων αἱ ἁμαρτίαι). He leaves for Timothy the application of these principles to the specific matter of selection of elders in Ephesus. "The sins" (αἱ ἁμαρτίαι) are multiple (plural). Paul uses this otherwise fre-

---
[107] Rienecker, 632.
[108] Kent, 181.
[109] Marshall, 624.

quent noun only two times in 1 Timothy, here and v.22—providing the link that connects the discussion on either side of the parenthetical thought of v.23 (cf. the only use of the cognate verb ἁμαρτάνω in v.20).[110] The sins are personal ("of some men," Τινῶν ἀνθρώπων) and specific (the definite article, αἱ). Also they "are quite evident" (πρόδηλοί εἰσιν). The verb is in the present tense and points to what is continuously true of these sins. The adjective ("quite evident," πρόδηλοί) is used only here and v.25 by Paul (cf. the only other NT use in Heb. 7:14). It is a compound word made up of "before" (πρό) and "clear/plain/evident" (δῆλος). It means "openly evident, known to all, manifest."[111]

These sins, says Paul, are "going before them to judgment" (προάγουσαι εἰς κρίσιν). The present tense of the participle underscores the ongoing march of these sins toward judgment day. It is a compound made up of "before" (πρό) and "to go" (ἄγω). The prepositional phrase in the accusative ("to judgment," εἰς κρίσιν) indicates that toward which the advance is made. The picture is of one's sins around one's neck as a millstone, dragging him toward the judgment that waits after an exit from this world. Or perhaps the sins are seen as racing ahead and awaiting him at the finish line after departure from this physical world. Such a person dies only to be greeted at the judgment by the sins he committed in this life and the discerning eye of the Judge. It is "Christ Jesus, who is to judge the living and the dead" (2 Tim. 4:1). Paul possessed a hope that these folk know nothing about: "in the future there is laid up for me the crown of righteousness, which the Lord, the righteous Judge, will award to me on that day; and not only to me, but also to all who have loved His appearing" (2 Tim. 4:8). Some want to make this "judgment" a human one, by Timothy or the body who select elders. The argument is that if these sins only become evident on judgment day, how does that help Timothy now in the selection of elders? The answer is that all human judgment is only discerning, accurate and wise if it is in conformity with what will be revealed in the last day. As Paul so often does, he is counseling that choices now be made in light of what will be seen then to be reality (Rom. 8:24-25; 1 Cor. 13:12; 2 Cor. 4:18; 5:7).

> **Ministry Maxim**
>
> Assumptions in the selection of leaders can be disastrous.

In contrast there is a different experience "for others" (τισὶν δὲ). In their case, "their sins follow after" (καὶ ἐπακολουθοῦσιν) them. The subject of the verb is still "the sins" (αἱ ἁμαρτίαι) of the first part of the verse. The verb is a compound, comprised of "on" (ἐπί) and "follow" (ἀκολουθέω). Paul's only other use of this verb is in v.10 (but cf. Mark 16:20 and 1 Peter 2:21). The contrast to

---

[110] Knight, 241.
[111] Thayer, 538.

the previous people is found in this—it is obvious that some are sinners and everyone knows that their sins race ahead of them and await them when they die. They are, therefore, clearly unfit to serve as elders. Haste in this decision is not a problem (v.22). There are, however, others whose sins are not immediately obvious. Their sins trail behind them and surprise everyone at the judgment. Haste in selection of elders in such a case may prove disastrous. Time (v.22), testing (1 Tim. 3:10), and prayer with fasting (Acts 14:23) will give every good opportunity to gain God's direction in these matters.

> **Digging Deeper:**
> 1. Some sins are obvious and would render a man obviously unsuitable for the office of elder, but practically speaking how are we to discern "their sins that follow after"?
> 2. Is Paul counseling cautious discernment in the selection of elders or a wary eye upon those who already are elders?

5:25 Likewise also, deeds that are good are quite evident, and those which are otherwise cannot be concealed.

What Paul is about to say in some way corresponds to what he has just set forth in v.24 (ὡσαύτως καὶ, "Likewise also"; cf. same expression in 1 Cor. 11:25; 1 Tim. 2:9). Six of Paul's eight usages of this adverb (ὡσαύτως, "likewise") occur in the PE (Rom. 8:26; 1 Cor. 11:25; 1 Tim. 2:9; 3:8, 11; 5:25; Titus 2:3, 6). There is something that is true of both "the sins of some men" (v.24) and "deeds that are good" (v.25). That similarity is found in that just as "the sins of some men are quite evident" (v.24), some good works are also "quite evident" (πρόδηλα, same word as in v.24). Also, some sins "follow after" those who commit them (v.24) and eventually become known, though now they are unseen. Similarly there are some good works which "cannot be concealed" (κρυβῆναι οὐ δύνανται) forever, though at present they are inconspicuous.

The concern in the first part of the verse is "deeds that are good" (τὰ ἔργα τὰ καλὰ). The combination of καλός ("good") and ἔργον ("works") forms a main theme of the PE (1 Tim. 3:1; 5:10, 25; 6:18; Titus 2:7, 14; 3:8, 14). Good deeds are not the basis of salvation (Titus 3:5), but they are an evidence of its reality (3:8). We are to be "rich in good works" (1 Tim. 6:18) and "zealous for good deeds" (Titus 2:14). If this is true, these good works will generally be "quite evident" (see v.24 for this word).

The concern in the latter part of the verse is "those which are otherwise" (τὰ ἄλλως ἔχοντα). The definite article (τὰ) and participle (ἔχοντα) are in the neuter plural form to correspond to τὰ ἔργα ("deeds") in the first part of the verse. The present tense underscores the abiding nature of these deeds. The adverb ἄλλως ("otherwise") is used only here in the NT and refers generally to that which is of another sort.[112] But does this mean they are different from "good deeds" (i.e., evil works)? Or does this mean that they are different in that they are not "quite evident" (i.e., good works not presently obvious)? The former is possible grammatically, but the latter seems the more likely given the parallel of v.24. This makes v.24 speak of "sins" and all of v.25 a reference to "deeds that are good." The whole expression is literally, "Those which have it otherwise"[113] or "the things having otherwise."[114]

> **Ministry Maxim**
>
> Good and evil are both ultimately self-revealing.

The expression "cannot be concealed" (κρυβῆναι οὐ δύνανται) is a strong one. The negation (οὐ δύνανται, "can not") is absolute and categorical (cf. same combination in Rom. 8:8; 1 Cor. 2:14; 10:21; 12:21; 15:50; 2 Tim. 2:13). The present tense verb (δύνανται) emphasizes the notion of continual action. The infinitive "be concealed" (κρυβῆναι) is in the aorist tense, pointing to the event of an attempted concealment. The passive voice negates the possibility of anyone acting upon these good deeds to keep them covered up forever. "But there is nothing covered up that will not be revealed, and hidden that will not be known" (Luke 12:2; cf. Matt. 10:26; Mark 4:22; Luke 8:17).

Just as haste in selecting elders (v.22) may lead to appointing unworthy men (v.24), so also it may lead to missing some fine, highly qualified men whose qualities are not immediately evident (v.25). The wise Christian leader avoids both pitfalls by taking his time and praying thoroughly over the selection of elders.

> **Digging Deeper:**
> 1. According to vv.24, 25 in what way are evil deeds and "deeds that are good" alike?
> 2. What do these two verses teach us about the reliability of first impressions?

---

[112] Thayer, 29.
[113] Robertson, 4:590.
[114] Mounce, 320.

CHAPTER

6

6:1 All who are under the yoke as slaves are to regard their own masters as worthy of all honor so that the name of God and our doctrine will not be spoken against.

The Apostle has addressed various age and gender categories (5:1-2), widows (5:3-16), and elders (5:17-25). Now he speaks to "All who are under the yoke as slaves" ("Οσοι εἰσὶν ὑπὸ ζυγὸν δοῦλοι, vv.1-2) before he will turn one final time to address the matter of the false teachers and those who would follow them (vv.3-10). "All" ("Οσοι) represents a plural relative pronoun which has the meaning of "as many as." It is used to indicate "those who belong to a particular class or group."[1] In this case it is the totality of those "who are under the yoke as slaves." The verb ("are," εἰσὶν) is in the present tense, underscoring the present, ongoing reality of those who are slaves. The noun "slaves" (δοῦλοι) referred to those who had sold themselves into slavery, generally for economic reasons. They had willingly given themselves up to the will of another, albeit under negative conditions. The word "bond-slave" better captures the meaning, though this does not communicate to contemporary audiences as it once did. It is only in Biblical translation and in early American history that the word "servant" has been substituted for "slave."[2] Paul uses the noun literally to speak of those who are enslaved to earthly masters (e.g., Eph. 6:5-8; Col. 3:11, 22-25; Titus 2:9). He used it as a negative image for slavery to sin (Rom. 6:16, 19-20) and to men (1 Cor. 7:23). He could use it to speak of one who is "Christ's slave" (1 Cor. 7:22; Eph. 6:6) and of a slave to righteousness (Rom. 6:19). It thus became a title which he gladly applied to himself (Rom.

---

[1] Rienecker, 632.
[2] BAGD, 205.

1:1; Gal. 1:10; Titus 1:1) and others (Phil. 1:1; Col. 4:12). This is a title all who serve Christ should be glad to take (2 Tim. 2:24). He could even say he was a bond-slave of others, for Christ's sake (2 Cor. 4:5). Ultimately, the image is dignified and elevated by the fact that Christ willingly took ". . . the form of a bond-servant" (Phil. 2:7).

Here, of course, Paul is speaking of slavery in the literal sense. It was thus considered a "yoke" (ζυγὸν). Strictly speaking the noun referred to a crossbeam or crossbar.[3] A "yoke" was a wooden beam placed across the necks of oxen or other beasts of burden in order to bind them to one another and harness them for labor. The image of slavery being a yoke is found also in Galatians 5:1 where the two nouns are again combined. Here one is pictured as "under" (ὑπὸ) the yoke. All this serves to demonstrate the demeaning nature of first-century slavery, a lot which made a slave little more than an animal. However, Jesus and Paul used the idea spiritually and elevated the notion (not the practice of slavery) in the process. In Galatians 5:1 the imagery is of one "subject again to" (ἐνέχεσθε) the yoke of slavery. Jesus used the word in His famous invitation, "Take my yoke (τὸν ζυγόν μου) upon you and learn from Me, for I am gentle and humble in heart, and YOU WILL FIND REST FOR YOUR SOULS. For My yoke [ὁ . . . ζυγός] is easy and My burden is light." (Matt. 11:29-30). Luke puts the word in Peter's mouth when he addressed the leaders in Jerusalem saying, "Now therefore why do you put God to the test by placing upon the neck of the disciples a yoke [ζυγὸν] which neither our fathers nor we have been able to bear?" (Acts 15:10). The only other use of the noun in the NT is in Revelation 6:5 where the root idea of a crossbeam or crossbar is transferred to the imagery of "a pair of scales."

Those who find themselves in this social and physical condition "are to regard their own masters as worthy of all honor" (τοὺς ἰδίους δεσπότας πάσης τιμῆς ἀξίους ἡγείσθωσαν). The concern is not a slave's outlook upon the institution of slavery in general nor upon the master of another slave and his treatment of those in his service, but upon "their own masters" (τοὺς ἰδίους δεσπότας). The noun "master" (δεσπότας) is used of the owners of slaves (1 Tim. 6:1-2; Titus 2:9; 1 Peter 2:19). We derive our word *despot* from this word. But it is used also of God (Luke 2:29; Acts 4:24) and of Jesus Christ (2 Peter 2:1; Jude 4; Rev. 6:10) with a different connotation. A slave is to adopt a determined outlook of mind (ἡγείσθωσαν, "are to regard") toward his earthly master. The verb means to think, consider, or regard.[4] It is used elsewhere in the PE only in 1 Timothy 1:12. It denotes "a belief resting not on one's inner feeling or sentiment, but on the due consideration of external grounds, the weighing and

---

[3] Friberg, 186.
[4] BAGD, 343.

comparing, of facts."⁵ This is not left as an option, as the imperative mood reveals. The present tense demands this be the continual and abiding attitude of mind. That specific pattern of thinking which is demanded is "as worthy of all honor" (πάσης τιμῆς ἀξίους). In the PE Paul sees "honor" (τιμῆς) as something due supremely to God (1 Tim. 1:17; 6:16). Elders who serve well should receive "double honor" (1 Tim. 5:17). Every believer should aim to be a "vessel for honor" in service to his Lord (2 Tim. 2:20-21). In this context the word points to an attitude of mind which reveals itself in obedience and service offered with a willing heart. This should be offered in undiluted form (πάσης, "all"). A grudging obedience is not in view, for the slave should make up his mind to see his earthly master as "worthy" (ἀξίους) of this offering. The root meaning of the adjective came out of the marketplace and described adding weight to one side of the scales to bring the beam up to level. It thus came to describe that which is weighty or of significance.

This determination to look upon one's earthly master with honor has a definite purpose. It is "so that the name of God and our doctrine will not be spoken against" (ἵνα μὴ τὸ ὄνομα τοῦ θεοῦ καὶ ἡ διδασκαλία βλασφημῆται). This may be an allusion to Isaiah 52:5 (cf. its use in Rom. 2:24). The reason is stated negatively ("so that . . . not," ἵνα μὴ) and might be translated "lest" (cf. NASB). The concern is to protect two precious treasures. The first is "the name of God" (τὸ ὄνομα τοῦ θεοῦ). For Paul, putting one's trust in Christ is tantamount to naming "the name of the Lord" (2 Tim. 2:19). Indeed, we must "CALL ON THE NAME OF THE LORD" to be saved (Rom. 10:13). "God highly exalted [Christ], and bestowed on Him the name which is above every name, so that at the name of Jesus EVERY KNEE WILL BOW, of those who are in heaven and on earth and under the earth" (Phil. 2:9-10). As believers everything we do is to be done in the name of the Lord Jesus (Col. 3:17). The name of God represents His character and reputation. Everything we are as believers is wrapped up in the name of our God.

The second (καὶ, "and") treasure to be guarded is "our doctrine" (ἡ διδασκαλία). The expression is more simply, "the doctrine." The word "doctrine" (διδασκαλία) is used twenty-two times in the NT, nineteen of those are by Paul and fifteen of those are in the PE (1 Tim. 1:10; 4:1, 6, 13, 16; 5:17; 6:1, 3; 2 Tim. 3:10, 16; 4:3; Titus 1:9; 2:1, 7, 10). The noun may refer to either the act of teaching or to that which is taught ("doctrine").⁶ It is in this latter sense that it is used here. There may be "doctrine of demons" (1 Tim. 4:1). But "the doctrine of God our Savior" (Titus 2:10) is "sound teaching/doctrine" (1 Tim. 1:10; 4:6; 2 Tim. 4:3; Titus 1:9; 2:1), "doctrine conforming to godliness"

---

⁵ Thayer, 276.
⁶ BAGD, 191.

(1 Tim. 6:3), and "purity in doctrine" (Titus 2:7). This is the heart of Scripture's purpose (2 Tim. 3:16) and all such teaching arises from and is controlled by the Scriptures. The word is used in a similar context (instruction to slaves) in Titus 2:10 where it is modified and explained by the additional clause "of God our Savior" (τὴν τοῦ σωτῆρος ἡμῶν θεοῦ).[7] Thus the term can refer to the Gospel itself. Perhaps this is its usage here. Thus, even in his instruction to slaves, the Apostle is never far away from the concern over false teachers and the honor and purity of the truth of the Gospel in and through Ephesus.

We guard God's name and truth so that they "will not be spoken against" (βλασφημῆται). The verb means to slander or to speak lightly or injuriously of sacred things.[8] The present tense sees this as an ongoing concern. The passive voice pictures the slave's earthly master acting upon the name and truth of God. If a slave lived dishonorably the disgrace was naturally transferred also to the One he claimed as his ultimate Master. This must never be allowed to happen. Suffering wrong with an upright attitude for the sake of Christ's name and truth is a price all who are slaves of Christ must be willing to pay (1 Peter 3:17). This negative purpose clause may indicate that v.1 primarily is concerned for Christian slaves under non-Christian masters, whereas v.2 specifically concerns "Those who have believers as their masters." It is also possible that v.1 is to be understood more generally of all slaves, since even the relationship of a Christian slave to a Christian master would affect the evangelistic thrust of the church.

> **Ministry Maxim**
>
> Our common mission is more important than my individual circumstances.

It is troublesome to some that the Apostle does not here (or elsewhere) explicitly denounce slavery. Several points should be borne in mind. First, Paul knew that the Gospel contained the truths that would eventually topple the sinful practice of slavery. Some estimate that as many as half of all adults in the Roman Empire were slaves. A sudden overturning of the institution of slavery would have created a chaos in which the mission and message of the church would have been swallowed and perhaps lost. Yet by preaching the Gospel, Paul was unleashing the truth that would bring down the institution of slavery from the inside. Second, Paul is addressing a local situation in a specific church, not writing a far-ranging philosophy of Christianity and its social implications. This is clear in that he is concerned for the individual response of slander and blasphemy that would take place if slaves did not live in a Christ-honoring relationship to their masters. Third, Paul grounds this appeal

---

[7] Knight, 246.
[8] Rienecker, 654.

on different grounds than he does in his instructions regarding other social institutions. For example, when he teaches on the Christian marriage, he sets the teaching on the foundation of Christ and the church (Eph. 5:31). When he teaches that children should obey their parents, he sets it on the foundation of the fifth commandment (Eph. 6:1-3).[9] However, when he speaks here of a slave's attitude and response to his master, he places it on pragmatic ground—that the Gospel and its God "will not be spoken against." The instructions on marriage and family are set on unchanging ground. The instructions to slaves are set on situational and pragmatic ground. Throughout the PE Paul is concerned for the honor of God and the evangelistic edge of the church's ministry (1 Tim. 5:14; Titus 2:5, 8). This continues to be the case here with slavery as well. For all believers, regardless of social station in life, missional concerns are to govern our choices and responses to the hardships and advantages of life.

Digging Deeper:
1. Why didn't Paul seek to abolish slavery?
2. Why did Paul seem to spend more time talking to those who were slaves about their behavior than to masters regarding theirs?
3. What do the Apostle's instructions tell us about the relationship of our circumstances to our mission?

6:2 Those who have believers as their masters must not be disrespectful to them because they are brethren, but must serve them all the more, because those who partake of the benefit are believers and beloved. Teach and preach these principles.

Paul now clearly addresses "Those who have believers as their masters" (οἱ δὲ πιστοὺς ἔχοντες δεσπότας). The NASU leaves the postpositive conjunction δὲ untranslated (cf. the NASB where it is translated "And"). "Those who have" (οἱ ... ἔχοντες) translates a present active participle used as a substantive. The present tense underscores this as their ongoing state. Sandwiched between the definite article and the participle is the adjective πιστοὺς ("believers," as in 1 Tim. 4:3, 10; 5:16). These believers serve "as their masters" (δεσπότας). See on v.2 for this word. The slaves "must not be disrespectful to them" (μὴ καταφρονείτωσαν). It is a compound word made up of "down" (κατά) and "to think" (φρονέω). It has the sense of despise, scorn, or treat with contempt.[10]

---

[9] Knight, 242.
[10] BAGD, 420.

Paul used the same word to tell Timothy, "Let no one look down on your youthfulness" (1 Tim. 4:12). The present tense imperative with the negation (μὴ) demands that action already underway be discontinued. Perhaps Christian slaves were looking down upon their Christian masters because they believed that devotion to Christ should compel their masters to free them from their servitude. Such slaves must not take this view of their masters "because they are brethren" (ὅτι ἀδελφοί εἰσιν). This could be understood as explaining the ground for their bad attitudes ("As believers our masters should free us!") or the reason they should not despise their masters ("Don't despise them for they are your brothers!"). Paul uses the noun "brethren" (ἀδελφοί), either in the singular or plural, 133 times in his letters. Yet he uses it only four times in the PE (1 Tim. 4:6; 5:1; 6:2; 2 Tim. 4:21). This may be due to the fact that the letters are addressed to individuals rather than whole churches. Paul is counseling Christian slaves to view their new spiritual relationship to their masters, not as something that places the onus upon the masters (to free the slaves), but as something that places new responsibility upon themselves (as even more responsible to be a benefit to their brother/masters). How easily we interpret the direction of responsibility to flow toward ourselves rather than from ourselves!

In stark contrast ("but," ἀλλὰ) to being "disrespectful" to their believing masters, Christian slaves "must serve them all the more" (μᾶλλον δουλευέτωσαν). At times Paul employs the verb negatively to describe slavery to sin (Rom. 6:6), the Law (7:6), our appetites (16:18), idols (Gal. 4:8), and "weak and worthless elemental things" (4:9). He also uses it positively in the sense of "service" to the Lord (Rom. 12:11; 14:18; Eph. 6:7; Col. 3:24; 1 Thess. 1:9), to one another (Gal. 5:13), in the furtherance of the Gospel (Phil. 2:22), and here of service to an earthly master (1 Tim. 6:2). Here it is in the present active imperative form which demands action be taken continually. The adverb μᾶλλον can be used to describe a preferred choice ("rather than") and has this meaning in its other two uses in the PE (1 Tim. 1:4; 2 Tim. 3:4), but here it has its more normal sense as it points to a "higher point in the extent of something" ("all the more").[11] The positive-minded service of the slave to his master should be all the greater because of their bond in Christ.

As the first imperative was followed by a ὅτι clause, so is this one. Their over-and-above service is justified "because those who partake of the benefit are believers and beloved" (ὅτι πιστοί εἰσιν καὶ ἀγαπητοὶ οἱ τῆς εὐεργεσίας ἀντιλαμβανόμενοι). Some make this refer to the slaves, who would benefit from the service of a Christian master. This seems an unlikely turn of the emphasis, however. This refers to the masters and the masters under consideration first (according to the word order of the Greek text) "are believers and beloved" (πιστοί εἰσιν καὶ ἀγαπητοί).

---

[11] Friberg, 252.

The first adjective ("believers," πιστοί) is the same one used earlier in this verse and should be taken in the same sense (i.e., "believers" rather than "faithful"). The second adjective ("beloved," ἀγαπητοί) is used elsewhere in the PE only in 2 Timothy 1:2 where Paul calls Timothy "my beloved son." Since these instructions are intended to guide and correct slaves in their conduct, the one who considers the master "beloved" must first of all be the Lord Himself, rather than the slave. But the disciple must become like his Master and adopt His view of this earthly master. Secondly, these masters are "those who partake of the benefit" (οἱ τῆς εὐεργεσίας ἀντιλαμβανόμενοι). The participle and its definite article (οἱ . . . ἀντιλαμβανόμενοι) are used as a substantive ("those who partake"). It is from a compound word comprised of "on behalf of" (ἀντί) and "to take/receive" (λαμβάνω). The word can mean to devote oneself to something, in which case this would be a reference to slaves who devote themselves to benefiting their masters.[12] The word can also mean to perceive or to notice (i.e., perhaps therefore to enjoy or benefit by) something. While this appears to stretch the meaning of the word, it seems to conform better to the context here and makes this a reference to the masters rather than the slaves.[13] This is how most major English translations understand the word.

> **Ministry Maxim**
>
> The gospel calls me to own my responsibilities before I argue for someone else's.

In the attributive position, tucked between the definite article and participle, is the expression "of the benefit" (τῆς εὐεργεσίας). This declares that which is enjoyed by the masters. The noun is used elsewhere in the NT only in Acts 4:9 where it describes the healing enjoyed by a lame man. Here the slave is put in the position of doing good to his master. Convention would have viewed the master in the position of power which would enable him to do good to the slave. The Gospel makes the weak strong and the strong weak.

The final statement of the verse is probably intended to be taken with what precedes rather than what follows (in contrast to the UBS division of the text): "Teach and preach these principles" (Ταῦτα δίδασκε καὶ παρακάλει). The demonstrative pronoun (Ταῦτα, "these things") is used similarly in 1 Timothy 4:11; 2 Timothy 2:14 and Titus 2:15. In all cases it refers to what has just been said, rather than to what is about to be said.[14] Thus by "these principles" (Ταῦτα) Paul gathers up all the preceding instructions to various age groupings (5:1-2), widows (5:3-16), elders (5:17-25), and slaves (6:1-2) and underscores one more time how essential it is that Timothy train the people in these matters.

---

[12] BAGD, 74.
[13] Ibid.
[14] Knight, 247; Marshall, 637-638.

This sentence sounds very much like 1 Timothy 4:11 (cf. 2 Tim. 2:14; Titus 2:15). With two present tense imperatives the Apostle succinctly demands regular, ongoing compliance with his orders ("keep on teaching" and "keep on preaching"). The first command is to "Teach" (δίδασκε). The same form of the verb is used in 1 Timothy 4:11, where it is paired with a different verb. There it is the second of the two commands; here it leads the pair. Paul does not allow a woman to "teach" in the gathered assembly (1 Tim. 2:12). Timothy is to build into "faithful men who will be able to teach others also" (2 Tim. 2:2). The false teachers on Crete were "teaching things they should not teach" (Titus 1:11). The second command is to "preach" (παρακάλει). It is a compound word, coming from the prepositional prefix παρά (beside) and the verb καλέω (to call). Strictly speaking it means "to call alongside." It appears in all of the Apostle's letters (except Galatians) and is found frequently in the PE (1 Tim. 1:3; 2:1; 5:1; 6:2; 2 Tim. 4:2; Titus 1:9; 2:6, 15). It has a range of meaning that can swing from the softer sense of "comfort" to the sharper edge of "exhort." It is translated variously according to context by words such as "appeal" (Philem. 9, 10), "comfort" (2 Cor. 1:4, 6), "encourage" (1 Cor. 16:12), "exhort" (1 Cor. 1:10), "implore" (2 Cor. 12:8), and "urge" (Rom. 12:1). The masculine singular noun form became a title for the Holy Spirit (John 14:16, 26; 15:26; 16:7) and the Lord Jesus Christ (1 John 2:1).

> **Digging Deeper:**
> 1. Why does Paul argue that slaves of believing masters should serve them all the more diligently because they are brothers?
> 2. Why do you think Paul does not counsel believing masters regarding their treatment of their slaves, especially those which are fellow-believers?
> 3. What should we make of Paul's logic that always puts the responsibility on the believer being addressed regardless of their station or circumstances?

6:3 If anyone advocates a different doctrine and does not agree with sound words, those of our Lord Jesus Christ, and with the doctrine conforming to godliness,

The final two commands of v.2 were a signal that the Apostle was completing a section of thought. Now he begins his last major thrust of the epistle—a final word about the false teachers (vv.3-10). This verse is comprised of an extended conditional clause which will come to us in two parts. The remainder of his thought will be picked up in vv.4-5. The condition ("If," εἰ + present indicative) is of the first class, signaling that the matters are determined as to their fulfillment. False teachers were active in the Ephesian church as the Apostle penned this letter and both Paul and Timothy knew it to be so. The protasis of the conditional statement includes all of v.3, with the apodosis being found in vv. 4-5.[15] The concerns to be expressed are broad and will cover "anyone" (τις) who fits the description advanced here. What sets such a one apart is that he "advocates a different doctrine" (ἑτεροδιδασκαλεῖ). The word is used elsewhere in the NT only in 1:3, signaling that Paul is utilizing the rhetorical device of inclusion to open and close the letter and thereby set forth the primary concern in its writing.[16] The word is comprised of "different" (ἕτερος) and "to teach" (διδάσκαλος). The word ἕτερος describes that which is another of an altogether different kind. It stands in contrast to the imperative "Teach" (δίδασκε) in the previous verse.[17] The word ἄλλος would have referred to another of a similar kind. Paul used ἕτερος in compound to indicate that this teaching had no affinity or connection to the Gospel.[18]

The kind of thing that is "different" about the teaching of these folk is explained in the rest of the verse. Such a one not only teaches strange doctrines, but additionally ("and," καὶ) he "does not agree with sound words" (μὴ προσέρχεται ὑγιαίνουσιν λόγοις). This is the only place in the NT where μὴ ("not") appears with a verb in the indicative mood, an expression found in classical Greek.[19] The verb ("agree with," προσέρχεται) appears eighty-six times in the NT, but this is the sole use by the Apostle Paul. Its usual meaning is "come to" or "go to." It can also have a more specialized meaning of "turn to" or "occupy oneself with." Here it approaches that meaning as it points to acceding to or agreeing with something to which one has given his attention.[20] The verb is negated ("not," μὴ) and thus points to that which one has personally rejected. That which is rejected is "sound words" (ὑγιαίνουσιν λόγοις). The participle "sound" (ὑγιαίνω) becomes one of Paul's favorite themes in writing to Timothy and Titus. Eight of the twelve NT occurrences of the word appear in the PE. The word was used literally of physical (e.g., Luke 7:10) or mental health (e.g., Luke 15:27). In the PE it is always metaphorically attached either to "faith" (Titus 1:13; 2:2), "teaching/doctrine" (1 Tim. 1:10; 2 Tim. 4:3; Titus 1:9; 2:1) or, as here, to "words" (1 Tim. 6:3; 2 Tim. 1:13). The participle is used as an attributive

---

[15] Mounce, 336.
[16] Marshall, 638.
[17] Ibid.
[18] Kent, 77.
[19] Mounce, 337.
[20] BAGD, 713.

adjective,[21] thus emphasizing the qualitative nature of the words under consideration. These words are, more specifically, "those of our Lord Jesus Christ" (τοῖς τοῦ κυρίου ἡμῶν Ἰησοῦ Χριστοῦ). The genitive could be subjective, referring to words directly from Jesus. This would be a signal that the sayings of Jesus were already being gathered into a collection(s). Specific examples might include what we find in 1 Timothy 5:8 and Acts 20:35 (cf. Acts 16:7; 1 Cor. 11:23). Or this could be an objective genitive which would point to words about the Lord Jesus (cf. 1 Cor. 1:18; 2 Tim. 1:8; 1 John 4:14; 5:11-12).[22] The Apostles, those who had personal contact with Jesus Himself, were the authoritative conveyors of His message. The latter seems the more likely, but in either case clearly the standard of measure in the early apostolic church was Jesus and His preaching and teaching. All else was calibrated from Him and His instruction. The full designation "our Lord Jesus Christ" (τοῦ κυρίου ἡμῶν Ἰησοῦ Χριστοῦ) signals that Paul is calling out the authority of Jesus and underscoring that the false teachers have no intention of submitting themselves to Him.[23]

Not only do the words of the false teachers not conform to "sound words" and to those of the Lord Jesus, but these words also ("and," καὶ) do not agree "with the doctrine conforming to godliness" (τῇ κατ' εὐσέβειαν διδασκαλίᾳ). The expression is more literally, "the according-to-godliness doctrine." The expression "according to godliness" (κατ' εὐσέβειαν) is used by Paul in opening his letter to Titus (Titus 1:1). The preposition κατὰ ("according to") with the accusative points toward the end aimed at or the goal toward which a thing tends.[24] The noun "godliness" (εὐσέβεια) is used by Paul often in the PE, but never outside of them. It generally describes the outward evidences of a genuine faith in and reverence for God (1 Tim. 2:2; 3:16; 4:7, 8; 6:3, 6, 11; Titus 1:1). False teachers often imitated it for selfish ends (1 Tim. 6:5; 2 Tim. 3:5), but here Paul has the real thing in view. The prepositional phrase is the attributive position, tucked between the noun and its definite article. This emphasizes the nature of the "doctrine" as such. Fifteen of the twenty-one times the noun "doctrine" (διδασκαλίᾳ) is found in the NT are here in the PE. See on v.1 for more on this important word. Clearly "doctrine" is not merely a philosophical debate detached from real life. A major test of its rightness is in the life that it produces.

> **Ministry Maxim**
>
> True doctrine produces personal holiness and spiritual health.

The Apostle's words here make clear that by this time there had developed

---

[21] Knight, 89.
[22] Robertson, 4:592.
[23] Knight, 250.
[24] Thayer, 329.

a clear set of doctrines that defined the substance of Christianity. Paul clearly viewed some propositions as false and some as true. The false were to be stood against as those things which were deadly in their influence and those which are true were to be propagated and their life-giving effect felt in as many lives as possible.

> **Digging Deeper:**
> 1. Is Paul being narrow to demand that "different doctrine" is dangerous?
> 2. What instruction does this verse give to our pluralistic age in which truth is deemed relative?
> 3. What does this verse teach us about the marks of true doctrine?

6:4 he is conceited and understands nothing; but he has a morbid interest in controversial questions and disputes about words, out of which arise envy, strife, abusive language, evil suspicions,

The protasis of the conditional clause has been advanced in v.3, now in vv.4-5 the apodosis is set forth. Assuming the truth of the "if" clauses in v.3, a conclusion is drawn about anyone who "advocates a different doctrine" (v.3). Paul says, "he is conceited" (τετύφωται). The word is used only three times in the NT, all in the PE (1 Tim. 3:6; 6:4; 2 Tim. 3:4). It means literally to wrap or fill with smoke. In the NT it is used figuratively and always in the passive voice. By extension it comes, then, to describe one who is puffed up with pride or blinded by pride and conceit.[25] The perfect tense indicates that this had become an abiding state. This was the trap the devil fell into and he loves to drag others into it with him (1 Tim. 3:6). It is one of the characteristics of people in the last days (2 Tim. 3:4). This verb is modified by a participle and its negation: "understands nothing" (μηδὲν ἐπιστάμενος). The participle points to the arena of his conceit—he thinks he possesses insight when he does not. This is another signal Paul is returning to the theme on which he opened the letter, for in 1:7 he said the false teachers were those "wanting to be teachers of the Law, even though they do not understand either what they are saying or the matters about which they make confident assertions." They reproduced after their own kind, for among their followers were those who were "always learning and never able to come to the knowledge of the truth" (2 Tim. 3:7). Ignorance begets ignorance; arrogance begets arrogance.

In utter contrast (ἀλλὰ, "but") "he has a morbid interest" (νοσῶν). This

---
[25] Thayer, 633.

begins a second, contrasting participial clause that parallels, while standing in opposition to, the first. This too is in the present tense, underscoring the ongoing nature of the action and contrasting the perfect tense of the main verb. The word is used only here in the NT. It means "to be sick" and stands in contrast to the healthy ("sound") words of v.3. It is used here to describe an "ailment of the mind,"[26] a "morbid craving for someth[ing]."[27] This unhealthy interest is manifest in an obsession with two issues. First, "controversial questions" (περὶ ζητήσεις). The noun is found seven times in the NT. Three of those are here in the PE (1 Tim. 6:4; 2 Tim. 2:23; Titus 3:9). Strictly speaking, the word means "seek." It arose from the Greek philosophical quest for wisdom (cf. Acts 17:27 and 1 Cor. 1:22 for the concept). In the NT it can describe arguments, word battles, and disputes.[28] Second (καὶ, "and") are "disputes about words" (λογομαχίας). This is a compound word comprised of "words" (λόγοι) and "a fight" (μάχη).[29] It is used only here in all of Greek literature (though compare the cognate verb in 2 Tim. 2:14). It describes a "war of words." Friberg says it signals "a dispute revolving around the meaning or use of words."[30] Both words return us to a common theme throughout the PE. In his second letter Paul will counsel Timothy to "refuse foolish and ignorant speculations [ζητήσεις]" (2 Tim. 2:23). Likewise, he will command Titus to "avoid foolish controversies [ζητήσεις]" (Titus 3:9). The false teachers "pay attention to myths and endless genealogies" (1 Tim. 1:4; cf. Titus 3:9). They occupied themselves with "worldly fables fit only for old women" (1 Tim. 4:7). In a moment the Apostle will warn Timothy to avoid "worldly and empty chatter and the opposing arguments of what is falsely called 'knowledge'" (1 Tim. 6:20; cf. 2 Tim. 2:14, 16-18; Titus 1:14).

Such debates are a problem not merely for the damage they do in themselves, but because they lead to further problems. This is made clear through the expression "out of which arise" (ἐξ ὧν γίνεται). The connective "out of which" (ἐξ ὧν) is used elsewhere only in Acts 15:29, Romans 9:5, and 1 Corinthians 15:6. Five nouns (running into v.5) are used to signal just what it is that arises from these sick, twisted discussions. First is "envy" (φθόνος). The noun is used to describe unregenerate humanity (Rom. 1:29; Titus 3:3) and is one of the deeds of the sinful nature (Gal. 5:21). It is what motivated those who delivered over Jesus to be killed by the Jewish religious leaders (Matt. 27:18; Mark 15:10). Second is "strife" (ἔρις). This too is listed with the previous word as one of the marks of unregenerate humanity (Rom. 1:29) and as

---

[26] Ibid, 429.
[27] BAGD, 543.
[28] DNTT, 3:532.
[29] Fee, 141.
[30] Friberg, 248.

one of the deeds of the flesh (Gal. 5:20). In fact, in all but one of its NT usages it is listed with a word for envy.[31] James was correct, "What is the source of quarrels and conflicts among you? . . . You are envious and cannot obtain; *so* you fight and quarrel" (James 4:1-2). It was a major problem in the church at Corinth (1 Cor. 1:11; 3:3; 2 Cor. 12:20). This was a part of the problem on Crete as well (Titus 3:9). Third is "abusive language" (βλασφημίαι). We derive our word "blasphemy" from this word, and it can have the connotation when used of speech directed against God (e.g., John 10:33). When directed at persons, however, it can also refer to slander or, as here, more generally to "abusive language." This is the only occurrence of the noun in the PE, but the adjective and verb forms are used in both the sense of blasphemy against God (1 Tim. 1:13, 20; 6:1; Titus 2:5) and speech against humans (2 Tim. 3:2; Titus 3:2). Fourth is "evil suspicions" (ὑπόνοιαι πονηραί). The noun "suspicions" (ὑπόνοιαι) is found only here in the NT. It is a compound word made up of "under" (ὑπό) and "to perceive/understand" (νοέω). The preposition in compound "suggests the idea of thoughts making their way up into the mind."[32] The thoughts of concern here are "evil" (πονηραί). The adjective can be used generally to refer to that which is bad, in poor condition, spoiled, or worthless. Here, however, it probably carries the ethical sense of wicked, evil, bad, base, worthless, vicious, and degenerate.[33] The combination of these two words probably means something like "evil conjectures" or "false suspicions."[34]

> **Ministry Maxim**
>
> Ignorance and arrogance are seldom separated.

6:5 and constant friction between men of depraved mind and deprived of the truth, who suppose that godliness is a means of gain.

The fifth and final noun in the series that began in v.4 is "constant friction" (διαπαρατριβαὶ). The word is a triple compound made up of "through" (διά), "beside" (παρά), and "friction" (τριβή). It is found only here in the NT. The simple compound παρατριβή means "irritation" or "friction."[35] The second preposition in compound (διά) intensifies the meaning and adds a sense of either thoroughness or mutualness about the action.[36] Thus it means "mutual

---

[31] Knight, 251.
[32] Rienecker, 633.
[33] BAGD, 690.
[34] Ibid., 846.
[35] Ibid., 187.
[36] Robertson, 4:592.

irritation" or "constant friction/arguing."[37] Clearly the false teachers cannot even agree or get along with one another. Their arrogance ("conceited," v.4) foils all attempts at mutuality in living.

The noun "men" (ἀνθρώπων) modifies the final word in the list ("constant friction," διαπαρατριβαὶ). Three attributive participles now conclude the sentence, describing these people who so irritate one another.[38] First is that they are "men of depraved mind" (διεφθαρμένων ἀνθρώπων τὸν νοῦν). The participle "depraved" (διεφθαρμένων) is a compound comprised of "through" (διά) and "to ruin/corrupt/spoil" (φθείρω). It is used six times in the NT (Luke 12:33; 2 Cor. 4:16; 1 Tim. 6:5; Rev. 8:9; 11:18 [2x]). It means to spoil, ruin or utterly destroy.[39] That which is so thoroughly corrupted is the "mind" (τὸν νοῦν) of these false teachers. It refers to the ability to reason and think. The definite article specifies that it includes the whole realm of their reasoning. It is "a person's inner disposition, the moral and intellectual capacity to make a decision."[40] Paul will again call these false teachers "men of depraved mind" (2 Tim. 3:8), though using a different verb to do so. Of the problem people on Crete, the Apostle will say that "both their mind and their conscience are defiled" (Titus 1:15). Our living arises from our thinking and when the thinking is so thoroughly confused, the living cannot but be spoiled. The perfect tense of the participle here underscores the abiding nature of their depraved thinking. The passive voice probably pictures these people being acted upon by another, perhaps (as will be seen in the next passive participle as well) the evil one is to be understood as behind this corruption and robbery.

Second, they are also ("and," καὶ) men "deprived of the truth" (ἀπεστερημένων τῆς ἀληθείας). The participle is a compound word, from "from" (ἀπό) and "to rob" (στερέω). It means to steal or to rob someone (Mark 10:19; 1 Cor. 6:7-8; 7:5; James 5:4).[41] Here it is in the passive voice indicating they are the one who has been robbed. The genitive noun "of the truth" (τῆς ἀληθείας) signifies that which has been stolen from them. The articular noun is used elsewhere in the PE to designate the truth of the Gospel as it is in Christ (1 Tim. 3:15; 2 Tim. 2:15; 4:4). The perfect tense indicates that they abide in a state in which they are robbed of the truth. Paul does not signify who stole the truth from them. As in the previous participle Paul could simply be viewing them being robbed by the falseness of their ideas (i.e., they were robbed of the truth by the opposing lies they believed). Ultimately it is the liar and father of lies (John 8:44) that has defiled their minds and defrauded them

---

[37] Friberg, 111.
[38] Mounce, 340.
[39] Friberg., 113.
[40] Mounce, 340.
[41] BAGD, 99.

of the truth (1 Tim. 3:6, 7; 4:1; 2 Tim. 2:26). To have had the truth stolen from them seems to indicate that at one time and in some way they had a relationship to the truth. Paul earlier had warned the elders of this church, "from among your own selves men will arise, speaking perverse things, to draw away the disciples after them" (Acts 20:30). This may give credence to the notion that at least some core of these false teachers were from among the elders themselves. This does not necessitate that they were necessarily regenerate at one time, but only that they came within the orbit of the truth of the Gospel and subsequently disavowed it by embracing a false and hybrid gospel.

The third participial phrase tells us these are men "who suppose that godliness is a means of gain" (νομιζόντων πορισμὸν εἶναι τὴν εὐσέβειαν). The participle can describe having something in common use or, in the passive voice, "be the custom" (Acts 16:13).[42] Then it also comes to mean suppose, think, or presume.[43] It seems here to point to thinking that has settled into an assumption. It is a pattern of thinking that is unexamined because it is presumed true. The present tense sees this as an ongoing and uninterrupted pattern of their thoughts. The particular pattern of thought is designated by use of an infinitive phrase, "that godliness is a means of gain" (πορισμὸν εἶναι τὴν εὐσέβειαν). Paul has used the noun "godliness" (τὴν εὐσέβειαν) ten times in the PE (1 Tim. 2:2; 3:16; 4:7, 8; 6:3, 5, 6, 11; 2 Tim. 3:5; Titus 1:1). The Apostle does not employ the word outside of the PE. It generally describes the outward evidences of a genuine faith in and reverence for God (1 Tim. 2:2; 3:16; 4:7, 8; 6:3, 6, 11; Titus 1:1). As we note here, false teachers often imitated it for selfish ends (1 Tim. 6:5; cf. 2 Tim. 3:5). It

> **Ministry Maxim**
>
> Not all doctrinal debate is motivated by love of the truth.

appears elsewhere in Paul with the definite article in 1 Timothy (3:16; 4:8; 6:6). The noun "a means of gain" (πορισμὸν) is used only here and in v.6 in the NT. The present tense of the infinitive ("is," εἶναι) reveals this as their default mode of thinking. Clearly the false teachers in Ephesus were motivated by greed and were charlatans using their doctrine to bilk the believers of their funds. This is not to say that the false teachers did not sincerely believe what they taught, but it is to underscore that their motives were not purely doctrinal.

The KJV has wrongly inverted the order, confusing the subject: "supposing that gain is godliness." The noun "godliness" (τὴν εὐσέβειαν), however, is accompanied by the definite article and is thus to be preferred as the subject of the sentence over the noun "gain" (πορισμὸν). The correct order is, "who suppose that godliness is a means of gain." The KJV also adds, "from such

---

[42] Ibid., 541.
[43] Friberg, 272.

withdraw thyself." However, the manuscript evidence for the addition of this phrase is too slight to concur with its inclusion.

The suggestion of Fee, that we compare vv.3-5 with the qualifications for leaders of the church (1 Tim. 3:2-12), is a good one.[44]

> **Digging Deeper:**
> 1. Describe the symbiotic relationship between ignorance and arrogance.
> 2. What is the inevitable fruit of hairsplitting debates? Why is this necessarily so?
> 3. What is the connection between depravation of the truth and depravity of the heart?

6:6 But godliness actually is a means of great gain when accompanied by contentment.

The postpositive conjunction δέ is used here as an adversative, to show the contrast between the religious clutch-and-grab mentality of the false teachers (v.5) and what true "godliness" is like. The subject is "godliness" (ἡ εὐσέβεια; see on v.5 for this word). The false teachers in Ephesus used religion as a cover for their greed (v.5). They "put on" religiously in order to "get ahead" financially. Their "godliness" was a ploy to bilk people of their money. But, says Paul, godliness "is a means of great gain" ("Εστιν δὲ πορισμὸς μέγας). The verb is placed at the head of the sentence for emphasis.[45] The NASU seeks to represent this emphasis in English through the addition of the word "actually." The present tense of the verb sets this forward as continually true. The noun "gain" (πορισμὸς) is also used in the previous verse (which see), though here it is used in a metaphorical way. It is now magnified by the adjective "great" (μέγας). Godliness *is* a boon—"when accompanied by contentment" (μετὰ αὐταρκείας). The noun "contentment" (αὐταρκείας) is used only here and 2 Corinthians 9:8 in the NT (but note the cognate adjective in Phil. 4:11). It is a compound word comprised of "self" (αὐτός) and "be enough/sufficient" (ἀρκέω, used in v.8). It describes "a perfect condition of life, in which no aid or support is needed"[46] or "as [the] ability to

> **Ministry Maxim**
>
> Godliness + contentment = true wealth.

---

[44] Fee, 142.
[45] Hiebert, *First Timothy*, 112.
[46] Thayer, 84.

supply the necessities of life without help from others" and thus "self-sufficiency" or "adequacy."[47] The Stoic and Cynic philosophers of the day used the word to declare self-sufficiency a crowning virtue. Paul, however, transformed the word for Christ's purposes. But as Paul used the word here it meant "a mind contented with its lot,"[48] and, thus, "contentment." Paul had achieved this state of mind personally, for he could say, "I have learned to be content in whatever circumstances I am" (Phil. 4:11). This is, as Fee states it, "not *self*-sufficiency but *Christ*-sufficiency"[49] (for cf. Phil. 4:13). Indeed, Paul would say, "And God is able to make all grace abound to you, so that always having all sufficiency [αὐτάρκειαν] in everything, you may have an abundance for every good deed" (2 Cor. 9:8). The combination ("with," μετὰ) of godliness and contentment is the Apostle's definition of true wealth. The preposition μετὰ ("with") is used "to show a close connection betw[een] two nouns, upon the first of which the main emphasis lies."[50] Thus "godliness" is the key virtue and when it is combined "with" (μετὰ) contentment, true wealth is attained. Godliness that is not dependent upon circumstances—in this case cash flow, bank balances, or stock market performances—for genuine wealth. Such godliness is not achieved by keeping a constant eye on the market, but only by setting one's eyes upon Christ.

> **Digging Deeper:**
> 1. What would godliness look like if it lacked contentment? Would it still be godliness?
> 2. Is contentment possible without godliness? Why?
> 3. Is godliness plus contentment a "means" of gaining something else? If so, what is that thing? Or are godliness and contentment the "gain" itself?

6:7 For we have brought nothing into the world, so we cannot take anything out of it either.

The conjunction γὰρ ("For") signals that what we encounter here is in some way an explanation or cause behind Paul's statement in v.6. The fact is, "we have brought nothing into the world" (οὐδὲν γὰρ εἰσηνέγκαμεν εἰς τὸν κόσμον). The verb is a compound made up of "into" (εἰς) and "bring" (φέρω). Paul uses it only here, though Luke likes it (Luke 5:18, 19; 11:4; 12:11; Acts 17:20; cf. Matt. 6:13;

---
[47] Friberg, 81.
[48] Thayer, 85.
[49] Fee, 143.
[50] BAGD, 509.

Heb. 13:11). The preposition in compound then stands alone to emphasize "into" what nothing is being led (εἰς τὸν κόσμον, "into the world"). The aorist tense looks to that moment when we are birthed into this world. The first person plural form, here and throughout the verse, brings Paul himself into the discussion with Timothy and any others who might be touched by these words. It gives a proverbial flair to the statement. This is a universal fact. By "the world" (τὸν κόσμον), Paul means simply this present physical creation in which we live out our lives (1 Tim. 1:15). The negative pronoun οὐδέν ("nothing") is absolute and categorical in its negation.[51] Additionally, it is put to the front of the sentence to emphasize it further. When we are birthed we bring nothing, *absolutely nothing*, with us into this world.

This being established, Paul says, "so we cannot take anything out of it either" (ὅτι οὐδὲ ἐξενεγκεῖν τι δυνάμεθα). The form is awkward and commentators are divided on how to understand the conjunction ὅτι. It usually points to a causal relationship, but that seems a strange and strained meaning here. The awkwardness of the expression has led to variations in the Greek texts. Most agree that ὅτι is the correct reading. It seems here to signal more of a result or of a consecutive step that follows on the first. A translation of "so that" may then be most appropriate here.[52]

By "we cannot" (οὐδὲ ἐξενεγκεῖν) Paul is pointing to the utter inability or powerlessness any one of us has. The negation is again, as in the first line, absolute and categorical. The present tense of the verb points to this ongoing and unending inability. The middle voice emphasizes the inward, innate nature of this inability. By our very nature as mortal beings we are unable to take any of our "stuff" beyond the grave. That which we are powerless to do is to "take anything out of it either" (ἐξενεγκεῖν τι). The indefinite neuter pronoun (τι, "anything") covers anything in the material or financial realm that one might name. The infinitive "take ... out" (ἐξενεγκεῖν) is a compound comprised of "out/from" (ἐκ) and "bring" (φέρω). Paul selected this word to answer the similar compound in the first part of the sentence. The root word is identical in both cases and the two prepositions used in compound contrast one another: εἰς ("into") and ἐκ ("out/from"). The aorist form points to that point in time when we pass out of this life. We will not, at that moment, be able to do anything about all that we leave behind. It cannot go with us and we cannot continue to control it here.

> **Ministry Maxim**
>
> Our beginning and ending should in some way govern our living in between.

The point of this verse is one made repeatedly throughout the Scriptures. Job

---
[51] Thayer, 408, 462.
[52] BAGD, 589.

declared, "Naked I came from my mother's womb, and naked I shall return there. The LORD gave and the LORD has taken away. Blessed be the name of the LORD" (Job 1:21). "As he had come naked from his mother's womb, so will he return as he came. He will take nothing from the fruit of his labor that he can carry in his hand. This also is a grievous evil—exactly as a man is born, thus will he die. So what is the advantage to him who toils for the wind?" (Eccl. 5:15-16). "For when he dies he will carry nothing away; his glory will not descend after him" (Psa. 49:17). "But God said to him, 'You fool! This very night your soul is required of you; and now who will own what you have prepared?' So is the man who stores up treasure for himself, and is not rich toward God" (Luke 12:20-21).

All this being true, Fee is arrestingly concise and to the point: ". . . material gain is irrelevant—and greed is irrational."[53]

> **Digging Deeper:**
> 1. What about our estate in the beginning and ending of life should influence our living in between? Why?
> 2. Why do you suppose this simple truth is so often repeated throughout the Scriptures?

6:8 If we have food and covering, with these we shall be content.

Having surveyed the destitution of our beginning and end to life (v.7), Paul now speaks to what our attitude should be while in this life. The conjunction δέ is left untranslated by the NASU. Other English translations translate it, though doing so in various ways: "And" (KJV, NASB), "But" (ESV, NET, NIV, NRSV), "So" (NLT). It seems best to understand it as a mild adversative which contrasts the utter destitution with which we enter and exit this life (v.7) with the daily provision in this life (v.8).

The conditional clause in English represents a participle in the Greek, "If we have" might be rendered simply "having" (ἔχοντες). That which is under consideration is "food and covering" (διατροφὰς καὶ σκεπάσματα). Both words are used only here in the NT, making it somewhat difficult to know just what Paul had in mind. Both are plural. The first word, "food" (διατροφὰς), is a compound made up of "through" (διά) and "nourishment/food" (τροφή). It refers to "support" or "sustenance" generally.[54] The second word, "covering" (σκεπάσματα), refers to "anything that serves as a cover and hence as a protection."[55] Thus it could refer

---
[53] Fee, 143.
[54] BAGD, 190.
[55] Ibid., 753.

either to shelter or to clothing. Many scholars believe that in this case it is more likely to refer to clothing,[56] though there is not universal agreement.[57] But perhaps the plural form suggests both clothing and shelter.[58] The two nouns together seem to point to sufficient food and clothing for each day. This combination is found throughout the Scriptures as comprising the basic needs of man (Gen. 28:20; Deut. 8:3-4; Prov. 27:23-27; Matt. 6:25-33).

Assuming that these basic necessities of life are in our possession, "with these we shall be content" (τούτοις ἀρκεσθησόμεθα). The demonstrative plural pronoun "these" (τούτοις) refers clearly to the "food and covering" just spoken of. The verb "shall be content" (ἀρκεσθησόμεθα) is a cognate to the root that is compounded to make the noun in v.6 (αὐταρκείας, "contentment"). The verb is used by Paul only here and in 2 Corinthians 12:9. It can mean to be enough, to be sufficient, or to be adequate. Here the passive voice gives it the sense of to be satisfied or to be content with.[59] The future tense anticipates what shall be the case for the godly. While not an imperative in form, it carries a suggestive sense of authority.

> **Ministry Maxim**
>
> A list of the "essentials" is closer to nothing that I wish it to be.

Agur was wise: "Keep deception and lies far from me, give me neither poverty nor riches; feed me with the food that is my portion, that I not be full and deny You and say, 'Who is the LORD?' Or that I not be in want and steal, and profane the name of my God" (Prov. 30:8-9). Jesus taught us to pray, "Give us this day our daily bread" (Matt. 6:11). He counseled us, "Do not worry then, saying, 'What will we eat?' or 'What will we drink?' or 'What will we wear for clothing?' For the Gentiles eagerly seek all these things; for your heavenly Father knows that you need all these things. But seek first His kingdom and His righteousness, and all these things will be added to you" (6:31-33).

Digging Deeper:

1. Why do you think Scripture consistently draws the line of essentials at "food and covering"?
2. What might you wish to add to the list of essentials?
3. How would you feel about having only "food and covering"?

---

[56] Friberg, 350; Thayer, 577.
[57] BAGD, 753.
[58] Knight, 254-255.
[59] BAGD, 107.

6:9 But those who want to get rich fall into temptation and a snare and many foolish and harmful desires which plunge men into ruin and destruction.

The conjunction δέ ("But") is used as an adversative to contrast the contented folk in v.8 with "those who want to get rich" (οἱ δὲ βουλόμενοι πλουτεῖν). The present middle participle is used as a substantive ("those who want"). The same verb is used three other times in the PE, each to express the will of the Apostle (1 Tim. 2:8; 5:14; Titus 3:8). It tends to express will more than wish (cf. comments on 2:8). It means "to will deliberately" or "to have a purpose."[60] The present tense indicates that those under consideration set their will continually to get rich. The middle voice bespeaks a deep, inner drive after that state. These are folks who have determined "to get rich" (πλουτεῖν) and have set their will to achieve their goal. Paul will use the word again in v.18 to speak of being "rich in good works."

Those who set themselves on being rich "fall into" (ἐμπίπτουσιν εἰς) many dangers. Paul uses the verb only two other times, both of which have to do with falling "into the condemnation incurred by the devil" (1 Tim. 3:6) or "into reproach and the snare of the devil" (v.7). It is used literally to describe falling into a pit (Matt. 12:11; Luke 6:39) and metaphorically of falling into the hands of robbers (Luke 10:36). The only other NT use is in the dire warning, "It is a terrifying thing to fall into the hands of the living God" (Heb. 10:31). Here the present tense pictures this as what regularly or normally happens to those seeking to get rich.[61]

Three pitfalls are mentioned as dangers "into" (εἰς) which such people might fall. First is "temptation" (πειρασμὸν). The word can mean either "test/trial" or "temptation." God may allow our faith to be "tested" (James 1:2-3), but God never tempts us (1:13). In this case the temptation is self-inflicted for they have set their hearts on being rich (Psa. 62:10). The temptation of riches is to "trust" in them (49:6; 52:7). God guarantees that "He who trusts in his riches will fall" (Prov. 11:28a). The second pitfall is "a snare" (παγίδα). Paul uses the word two other times in the PE, both to speak of "the snare of the devil" (1 Tim. 3:7; 2 Tim. 2:26). Thus the evil one is likely understood as behind this temptation of wealth. It was used in a literal sense of a trap or snare employed in catching birds.[62] It became a metaphorical way of describing the dangers of temptation in this life (Luke 21:35). The third pitfall is "desires" (ἐπιθυμίας). The word points to any strong and overwhelming desire. It can refer to everything from the desire to be

---

[60] Thayer, 105.
[61] Rienecker, 634.
[62] Ibid., 602.

told what one wants to hear (2 Tim. 4:3) to illicit sexual desire (1 Thess. 4:5). False teachers thrive on those who never rise above their bondage to such impulses (2 Tim. 3:6). We all once lived under the control of such desires (Titus 3:3), but the grace of God teaches us to deny them (Titus 2:12). Paul told Timothy to flee them (2 Tim. 2:22). The emphasis is often sexual, but goes far beyond just that to include covetousness (1 Tim. 6:9) and misguided religious impulses (2 Tim. 4:3). These "desires" are numerous (πολλὰς, "many"). The decision to pursue wealth opens a Pandora's Box from which rushes a host of lusts which are "foolish and harmful" (ἀνοήτους καὶ βλαβεράς). The former word means to be without understanding or thought. It is used in Romans 1:14 as the opposite of "wise" (σοφός). In its only NT usage by someone other than Paul it is applied to the two disciples with whom the resurrected Jesus walked on the road to Emmaus. It described their darkened, unenlightened view of the redemptive events and their relationship to the prophecies of Scripture (Luke 24:25). The Apostle used the word to describe the Galatians who were ready to depart from grace and return to the works of the Law (Gal. 3:1, 3). He used it in Titus 3:3 to describe our state before conversion. Interestingly, there he also says we were "enslaved to various lusts," the latter word of which is the same as our word "desires" [ἐπιθυμίαις] here. The word "harmful" (βλαβεράς) is used only here in the NT. That which is embraced in hopes of pleasure is injurious in the end.

> **Ministry Maxim**
>
> That which promises pleasure may be injurious in the end.

Indeed, these are pleasures "which plunge men into ruin and destruction" (αἵτινες βυθίζουσιν τοὺς ἀνθρώπους εἰς ὄλεθρον καὶ ἀπώλειαν). The plural form of the relative pronoun "which" (αἵτινες) agrees with "many . . . desires" (ἐπιθυμίας πολλὰς) and reaffirms the multitudinous forms these yearnings can take. The plural noun "men" (τοὺς ἀνθρώπους) picture the numerous victims who fall prey to the lure of riches. The verb "plunge" (βυθίζουσιν) is used elsewhere in the NT only to speak of a boat sinking into the sea (Luke 5:7). It is a graphic word which pictures these desires as weights that drag a man down into the sea and drown him.[63] That "into" (εἰς) which these people are immersed to their own peril is "ruin and destruction" (ὄλεθρον καὶ ἀπώλειαν). The former word ("ruin," ὄλεθρον) is used three other times in the NT, all by Paul. He employs it to speak of the destruction of one's physical body in death (1 Cor. 5:5), of the destruction wrought upon the earth at the time of Christ's coming (1 Thess. 5:3), and of the "eternal destruction" experienced in hell (2 Thess. 1:9). There is always a religious connotation to the word.[64] The latter

---

[63] Rienecker, 634.
[64] Friberg, 280.

word ("destruction," ἀπώλειαν) is even stronger. The antichrist is called "the son of destruction" (ὁ υἱὸς τῆς ἀπωλείας, 2 Thess. 2:3). The same phrase is used to call Judas "the son of perdition" (ὁ υἱὸς τῆς ἀπωλείας, John 17:12). The word is used to speak of the destruction awaiting one down the broad path (Matt. 7:13). It pictures the lot of those who go to hell (Rev. 17:8, 11). Peter used the word five times in rapid succession in his description of false prophets, speaking of both the current destructiveness of their ways and teaching (2 Peter 2:1) and of the eschatological judgment awaiting them (2 Peter 2:1, 3; 3:7, 16). Thayer says the word describes "the destruction which consists in the loss of eternal life."[65]

The sellout often required to build a winning financial portfolio ultimately brings about loss and destruction. In the rush for wealth and the pipedream of accumulated goods one loses something far more valuable, something which he can never recover. The pursuit of riches is a baited hook, a concealed trap, and a sinking ship. The longing to get rich is dangerous for the temptations it makes us vulnerable to, the snares it lays for us, and the destruction it assures us. Solomon was right, "A faithful man will abound with blessings, but he who makes haste to be rich will not go unpunished" (Prov. 28:20).

Digging Deeper:
1. Why is the danger for those who "want" to get rich rather than simply those who do indeed get rich?
2. Can you describe several contemporary illustrations of this verse?
3. How might this look when true of someone in "the ministry"?

6:10 For the love of money is a root of all sorts of evil, and some by longing for it have wandered away from the faith and pierced themselves with many griefs.

Paul now gives the reasons v.9 is true (γὰρ, "For"). He does so by first quoting from a well-known proverb (attested in both Jewish and Greek writings). The problem is "the love of money" (ἡ φιλαργυρία)—not simply "money" itself (as the verse has often been misquoted to say). The noun is used only here in the NT, but it is akin to the adjective φιλάργυρος ("lovers of money") which he uses in 2 Timothy 3:2 (as opposed to "lovers of God," 2 Tim. 3:4). This is a compound word made up of "love" (φίλος) and "silver/money" (ἀργύριον). The definite article serves to set it in a class to itself. This love of

---

[65] Thayer, 71.

money "is" (ἐστιν) a continual problem. The present tense points to the ever-present problem it proves to be to humanity. It is "a root of all sorts of evil" (ῥίζα γὰρ πάντων τῶν κακῶν). The noun "root" (ῥίζα) is used in the NT both literally (e.g., Matt. 13:6, 21; Mark 11:20) and metaphorically (e.g., Rom. 11:16-18; Heb. 12:15). It is used here in the latter sense. The big question seems to be whether it should be understood as definite ("the root," KJV, NKJV, NET, NLT, RSV) or more generally ("a root," ESV, NASB, NIV, NRSV). It is not accompanied by a definite article, but it is placed at the head of the sentence for emphasis, which might lend itself to a sense of definiteness. To say that the love of money is "the" sole root of evil is simply not true. But we must not lose the emphatic nature of "root" when we translate "a root." It is not the sole root of evil, but it is one among a few root sins. A root is that which is generally hidden, but which gives life to much stalk and foliage above ground. The presenting problem is "of all sorts of evil" (πάντων τῶν κακῶν) or, more literally, "of all the evils." But the presenting problem is seldom the root problem. The foliage and flowers may come in many shapes and colors, but they trace their life back to a single root. The noun is in the plural (κακῶν, "evils"). The presence of the definite article (τῶν, "the") pictures all the possible evils gathered into one and considered as a class. Should πάντων be understood in the sense of "every/all" evil (KJV, NET) or "all sorts/kinds of" evil (ESV, NASU, NASB, NIV)? Does it intend us to look at each and every evil or simply a vast variety of evil? To view it in the former sense would make this an example of hyperbole—an intentional exaggeration to make a point, for clearly there are expressions of evil that also find their root in other root sins such as pride. The Apostle's point is to lay bare the fundamental nature of covetousness and the far-reaching ramifications of indulging in it. Given that Paul has just spoken of "many" (πολλὰς) desires awakened by the determined pursuit of riches,[66] and that he will finish this sentence speaking of "many" (πολλαῖς) griefs caused by the love of money, it seems likely that he uses πάντων here in the sense of "all sorts of" evil.

Paul asserts that "some by longing for it" (ἧς τινες ὀρεγόμενοι) have destroyed their lives. The relative pronoun ἧς ("it") refers to "the love of money" (ἡ φιλαργυρία), or probably simply to money itself for it is hard to picture someone longing for "the love of money."[67] The indefinite pronoun (τινες, "some") broadens the case out to anyone who might take out after riches, but it is also Paul's normal way of referring to the false teachers in Ephesus.[68] The participle "longing for" (ὀρεγόμενοι) represents a verb that

---

[66] Knight, 258.
[67] Marshall, 652.
[68] Mounce, 347.

occurs only two other times in the NT. Paul uses it in 3:1 to describe those who desire to serve as an overseer. The writer of Hebrews employs it to describe the longing of God's people for heaven (11:16). The word has the sense of stretching out, reaching out, or striving after something.[69] The present tense views this as more than a passing interest, but as a continuing desire that lives within the individual. The middle voice is used in all three NT usages and may point to the inward nature of the longing. The participial form is used in a causal sense, giving the ground or reason why two disastrous things take place.[70]

The first is some "have wandered away from the faith" (ἀπεπλανήθησαν ἀπὸ τῆς πίστεως). The verb (ἀπεπλανήθησαν, "have wandered away") is used only one other time in the NT, where it describes attempts of false Christs and false prophets in trying to "lead astray" the elect (Mark 13:22). It is a compound word from ἀπό ("from") and πλανάω ("lead astray"). The uncompounded root is used often of deception, leading astray, and misleading (e.g., 2 Tim. 3:13; Titus 3:3). The preposition in compound gives direction to the wandering. The word signifies more than aimless wandering, but an intentional misleading—something signaled by the passive voice of the verb. Someone else has incited their going astray. Indeed, it is "from the faith" (ἀπὸ τῆς πίστεως) that they go forth. The preposition ἀπό ("from") is the same one compounded with the verb and stresses the direction of the deception. In the PE "the faith" (τῆς πίστεως), with the presence of the definite article, normally refers to the saving Gospel of Jesus Christ and all the truths which make it up (1 Tim. 3:9; 4:1, 6; 5:8; 6:10, 12, 21; 2 Tim. 3:8; 4:7; Titus 1:13). The Pharisees's love of money kept them from the faith (Luke 16:14) and this lust for wealth characterizes fallen humanity as time goes by (2 Tim. 3:2). Little wonder overseers must be free of "the love of money" (1 Tim. 3:3). "You cannot serve God and wealth" (Matt. 6:24).

> **Ministry Maxim**
>
> Covetousness opens a Pandora's Box full of trouble.

The second (καὶ, "and") negative effect is that some have "pierced themselves with many griefs" (ἑαυτοὺς περιέπειραν ὀδύναις πολλαῖς). The verb (περιέπειραν, "pierced") is used only here in the NT. It is a compound word comprised of περί ("around") and πείρω ("pierce"). It means "to pierce through" as with a spike[71] or to "impale."[72] The aorist tense views the action as a singular event. The moment they give in to a lust for money they impale themselves. The reflexive pronon ἑαυτοὺς ("themselves"), in contrast to the passive voice of the previous verb, pictures this as self-inflicted pain. By giving

---

[69] Friberg, 284.
[70] Knight, 258.
[71] Newman, electronic edition.
[72] Friberg, 309.

in to the deception of another they are driving a stake through their own hearts. That which they impale themselves upon is "many griefs" (ὀδύναις πολλαῖς). The word can point to mental distress.[73] It is used elsewhere only in Romans 9:2 (one variant has it in Matt. 24:8 as well) where it describes Paul's unceasing grief over the hardness of his fellow Jews to the Gospel. The cognate verb is found in Luke (2:48; 16:24-25) and Acts 20:38. Mounce says, "The word group describes an intense, deeply felt pain."[74] Much sorrow, regret and unhappiness pierces to the deepest recess of a man's life when he takes out after money.

> **Digging Deeper:**
> 1. How does the common misquotation of the first part of this verse confuse its understanding?
> 2. How might this single verse serve as a commentary on modern American life?

6:11 But flee from these things, you man of God, and pursue righteousness, godliness, faith, love, perseverance and gentleness.

The Apostle now changes direction dramatically. He thrusts the second person singular personal pronoun "you" (Σὺ) to the front of the sentence for emphasis. He is leaving the false teachers behind and is beginning an extended section of personal exhortations to Timothy as he prepares to close the letter. The conjunction δέ ("But") is used as an adversative and signals the transition as well. This opening device (Σὺ δέ, "But . . . you") is used by Paul several more times in the PE as a way to contrast Timothy or Titus from the ungodly and false teachers around them (2 Tim. 3:10, 14; 4:5; Titus 2:1). In contrast to the character, nature, and behavior of the false teachers just described here, Paul calls Timothy "man of God" (ὦ ἄνθρωπε θεοῦ). The expression is akin to the OT designation for a prophet (e.g., 1 Sam. 2:27; 2 Kings 1:9) or another anointed leader (e.g., Deut. 33:1; Neh. 12:24, 36). Perhaps the Apostle is emphasizing for Timothy the prophetic nature of his ministry in Ephesus—the fact that he may have to stand alone on the Word of God like the prophets did. Or perhaps this is Paul's way of reminding Timothy that he ministers according to God's call, not personal convenience. Paul can also speak more generally of "the man of God" (2 Tim. 3:17). The interjection ὦ has been left untranslated here, but means something like "O!" It is an expression of

---

[73] BAGD, 555.
[74] Mounce, 348.

exclamation here used in a personal address (cf. Matt. 15:28; Acts 1:1; 18:14; 27:21). Paul will address Timothy with it again in v.20.

Paul lays down two commands for Timothy, "flee" (φεῦγε) and "pursue" (δίωκε). Both "flee" and "pursue" are present tense imperatives, requiring that action be taken repeatedly or habitually. The two are butted against one another in the original text, highlighting the contrasting direction of each. Both will be used in the same way later in 2 Timothy 2:22. The things to be pursued stand on a moral continuum opposite of the things to be fled. These actions cannot be taken singly. One cannot flee without pursuing, nor pursue without fleeing. The combination is not dissimilar to Paul's concept of "putting off" and "putting on" used elsewhere (Eph. 4:22-24; Col. 3:8-17).

Timothy is first to "flee from these things" (ταῦτα φεῦγε). The word "flee" (φεῦγε) can be used absolutely to describe literal flight from one place to another (cf. Matt. 2:13; 8:33; Mark 14:50; Acts 27:30). It also is used in a moral sense when accompanied with an accusative that designates the thing to be fled from.[75] The accusative is found in "these things" (ταῦτα). This may refer to the particular problem of the lust for wealth found among the false teachers (vv.5-10). It may refer to all the pitfalls and temptations of the false teachers (vv.3-10). Or it may also gather up the whole of the false teaching that has been exposed throughout the letter.

> **Ministry Maxim**
>
> To flee one thing is to pursue another; to pursue something is to flee something else.

A positive direction is now set in distinction from the negative flight ("and," δέ). That which Timothy is to "pursue" (δίωκε) is set forth in a list of six nouns. Three of these also appear in 2 Timothy 2:22. First is "righteousness" (δικαιοσύνην). The believer is justified and thus declared righteous by God (Rom. 3:21-26). He then stands in the righteousness of Christ as a free gift (Rom. 5:2). In what sense, then, does the believer need to pursue righteousness? Paul probably has in mind the believer's conformity to the character of Christ Himself. Paul's concern here is the imparted righteousness of sanctification, not the imputed righteousness of justification.

Second is "godliness" (εὐσέβειαν). This noun is used ten times by Paul in the PE (1 Tim. 2:2; 3:16; 4:7, 8; 6:3, 5, 6, 11; 2 Tim. 3:5; Titus 1:1). He does not use the word outside of the PE. It points to the outward evidences of a genuine faith in and reverence for God (1 Tim. 2:2; 3:16; 4:7, 8; 6:3, 6, 11; Titus 1:1). The false teachers tried to mimic godliness to gain an advantage (1 Tim. 6:5; 2 Tim. 3:5), but here Paul uses it with the real thing in view.

The third pursuit of Timothy is to be "faith" (πίστιν). It can describe the

---

[75] BAGD, 856.

body of truth the church has embraced (1 Tim. 3:9; 4:1, 6; 6:10, 12). It also describes an individual's personal trust in the God of that truth (2 Tim. 1:5; 3:15). It is in this latter sense that Paul employs it here.

Timothy is also to pursue "love" (ἀγάπην). This love is the result of the Spirit's presence and power in a believer's life (2 Tim. 1:7) and is to mark a believer in all situations, especially divisive ones (1:13). It is the goal in all Paul's teaching (1 Tim. 1:5). Both love and faith had been modeled for Timothy by Paul (2 Tim. 3:10) and he is to become an example of the same to others (1 Tim. 4:12).

Fifth is "perseverance" (ὑπομονήν). This is a compound word comprised of "under" (ὑπό) and "stay" (μονή). It means then to "remain under." It pointed then to a patient endurance which held out long under difficulty with hope and courage. Here too Timothy had observed and followed Paul's example (2 Tim. 3:10). This was to be a quality particularly exemplified in the older men (Titus 2:2).

Finally is "gentleness" (πραϋπαθίαν). The word is found only here in the NT. It is a compound that seems to be a combination of πραΰς ("gentle") and cognate of πάσχειν ("to suffer"). It may, therefore, connote gentleness in the midst of suffering.[76] It seems to put particular emphasis upon a meekness of temperament and feelings while facing wrong. Not only does the man of God remain steadfastly under the pressures inherent in doing God's will ("perseverance"), but he does so with the right attitude and spirit.[77]

It is often noted that these six virtues break neatly into three pairs: "righteousness" and "godliness" represent God-honoring conduct, "faith" and "love" designate the essential virtues of the Christian life, and "perseverance" and "gentleness" picture the right response to opponents of the Gospel. There may also be a progression from one's orientation to God ("righteousness" and "godliness") to one's inward virtues ("faith" and "love") to one's outward response to difficult people ("perseverance" and "gentleness").[78]

Digging Deeper:

1. In what way is fleeing also pursuing and pursuing also fleeing?
2. In practical terms in your own life, what does it mean to "flee" from these dangers?
3. What steps can you take to "pursue" consistently these six qualities?

---

[76] Mounce, 354.
[77] Kent, 193.
[78] Mounce, 354.

6:12 Fight the good fight of faith; take hold of the eternal life to which you were called, and you made the good confession in the presence of many witnesses.

To the two previous imperatives (v.11), Paul now adds two more. The first is "Fight the good fight of faith" (ἀγωνίζου τὸν καλὸν ἀγῶνα τῆς πίστεως). The imperative itself (ἀγωνίζου, "Fight") is again in the present tense, demanding action be taken repeatedly. If this sounds familiar it is because the Apostle made a similar statement in 1 Timothy 1:18: "fight the good fight." There, however, the Greek word is different. It is from a militaristic background. The word here, while in English sounding the same, is different and conveys more of an athletic metaphor. Paul used the same word we confront here when, at the end of his life, he told Timothy, "I have fought the good fight" (τὸν καλὸν ἀγῶνα ἠγώνισμαι, 2 Tim. 4:7). Actually the verb "fight" (ἀγωνίζου) when used literally can describe either competing for a prize in an athletic contest (1 Cor. 9:25) or engaging another in a battle with weapons (John 18:36). When it is used figuratively it often has the sense of contending or struggling with great effort against difficulties or dangers generally (Col. 1:29; 1 Tim. 4:10), or of striving after something with strenuous zeal (Luke 13:24; Col. 4:12).[79] It is matched here by its cognate noun "fight" (ἀγῶνα), which can speak of an athletic contest such as a race (Heb. 12:1), but more often speaks of a conflict, struggle, or fight for the Gospel (Phil. 1:30; Col. 2:1; 1 Thess. 2:2).[80] It seems more likely that Paul intends here the imagery of an athletic event than that of a soldier at war. In other contexts Paul pictured a boxer locked in his contest (1 Cor. 9:26), and he similarly used the imagery of a runner (2 Tim. 4:7, "I have finished the course"). Athletic imagery is a favorite of Paul. The words used here describe not just the outward engagement of such a fight, but also the inward turmoil inherent in such conflict. Our English words "agonize" and "agony" are derived from this verb and noun. Indeed, the middle voice of the verb may emphasize the inward nature of this struggle.

This fight is "good" (καλὸν). While the love of money is "evil" (κακός, v.10), the fight of faith and the confession of faith (end of the sentence) are "good" (καλὸς). Paul chose καλὸς, rather than ἀγαθός, for "good." The former emphasizes that which is both intrinsically good and outwardly attractive, while the latter emphasizes more that which is beneficial in its effect,[81] though the two words seem to be used interchangeably in the PE (1 Tim. 5:10).[82] Life as we know it now is an agony. We need to be certain the agony which we

---

[79] Thayer, 10.
[80] BAGD, 15.
[81] Vine, 503-504.
[82] Mounce, 32.

embrace is the "good" agony. What makes this fight good is that it is "of faith" (τῆς πίστεως). The presence of the definite article would call for a translation "of the faith" (ESV, NIV, NRSV). This identifies what is being fought for ("for the true faith," NLT), not simply how the fight is being waged ("of faith"). The context justifies this emphasis as well. One day when faith shall be sight, the agony will fall away like the husk from the wheat. Many will find that all they possessed in this life was the husk of agony and struggle. The believing will find that when the agony of this life falls away, life eternal continues forever, free from the battles of this world.

Not surprisingly, then, the second imperative is "take hold of the eternal life to which you were called" (ἐπιλαβοῦ τῆς αἰωνίου ζωῆς, εἰς ἣν ἐκλήθης). The verb is a compound made up of ἐπί ("upon") and λαμβάνω ("take hold of"). It means to take hold of something in order to make it one's own.[83] That which is grasped after, unlike the riches the false teachers were grasping after (vv.5-10), is "the eternal life" (τῆς αἰωνίου ζωῆς). We are to believe in Christ for eternal life (1 Tim. 1:16), and thus we come to possess the hope of eternal life (Titus 1:2; 3:7). The word "life" (ζωή) is used in the NT "of the supernatural life of God and Christ, which the believers will receive in the future, but which they enjoy here and now."[84] Even now we are able to experience something of that "life in the blessed period of final consummation."[85] It is "eternal" (αἰώνιον) in that it is the life of Him who is Himself eternal (1 Tim. 1:17; 6:16). The "fight" is not eternal, but "life" is. It is the life that will characterize and make up our eternal home, and that is ours now in a foretaste of heaven on earth. This is what Timothy is called to "take hold of." While the previous imperative ("Fight") is in the present tense and points to the ongoing struggle in this life, the aorist tense of this command ("take hold of") points to a singular event. One takes hold of eternal life now not through an ongoing struggle, but through a decisive act of faith. It may also have in view the final and full experience of eternal life in eternity when one takes hold of this life most fully and finally. Eternal life is a gift given to us by God (Rom. 6:23), but He requires a human response of faith ("take hold") to appropriate the gift personally. The response of faith does not negate the free nature of the grace in which the gift is extended to us. Eternal life as experienced in the present is mingled with striving agony, but one day it will be void of the struggle and be perfect rest. This is a life, Paul can say to Timothy, "to which you were called" (εἰς ἣν ἐκλήθης). The

> **Ministry Maxim**
>
> The "fight" of faith won't last forever, but the "life" of faith will.

---

[83] BAGD, 295.
[84] Ibid., 341.
[85] Ibid., 340.

feminine singular relative pronoun "which" (ἥν) conforms to its antecedent, "the eternal life." We are called *into* (εἰς) this life, not just "to" this life. We are immersed in and surrounded by this life. This life of eternity becomes the very atmosphere in which we live and move and have our being. And this is our privilege by calling (ἐκλήθης). The individual is called (second person singular). It is only His grace that has brought us within the sound of the Gospel's call. The only other use of the verb in the PE is in 2 Timothy 1:9. Being called, we exist no longer for ourselves but with a divine purpose and hope.

The coordinating conjunction καὶ ("and") holds in parallel to the previous verb another aorist indicative verb: "you made the good confession" (ὡμολόγησας τὴν καλὴν ὁμολογίαν). The verb is a compound word, constructed from "together" (ὁμοῦ) and "to say" (λέγω). Its basic root meaning is "to say the same thing." Here it has the sense of to declare something publicly.[86] Its only other use in the PE is in Titus 1:16. The direct object is the cognate noun with its definite article and an adjective: "the good confession" (τὴν καλὴν ὁμολογίαν). The noun is used by Paul only here, v.13 and 2 Corinthians 9:13. A literal translation here might be, "you confessed the good confession" (just as "fight the good fight" at the beginning of the sentence represented a verb and cognate noun). For "good" (καλὴν) see just above in this same verse. It is "good" in that it is an affirmation of belief in the Gospel that offers eternal life. Paul perfectly balances the truth of divine sovereignty and initiative ("to which you were called") with the truth of human responsibility and response ("you made the good confession"). This confession of faith was made "in the presence of many witnesses" (ἐνώπιον πολλῶν μαρτύρων). The word "in the presence of" (ἐνώπιον) is used often in the PE (1 Tim. 2:3; 5:4, 20, 21; 6:12, 13; 2 Tim. 2:14; 4:1), always with reference to the presence or sight "of God," except in 1 Timothy 5:20 and here. The expression "many witnesses" (πολλῶν μαρτύρων) is used only here and 2 Timothy 2:2 in the NT.[87] Here it probably refers to those present at Timothy's baptism where he would have made a public confession of faith in Christ.

Digging Deeper:
1. How does this verse balance divine sovereignty and human responsibility in salvation?
2. What does this verse teach us about the nature of this life's struggles?
3. What hope does this verse hold out to us in the battles of this life?

---

[86] Ibid., 568.
[87] Knight, 264.

6:13 I charge you in the presence of God, who gives life to all things, and of Christ Jesus, who testified the good confession before Pontius Pilate,

In the Greek text the sentence the Apostle begins here does not come to completion until the end of v.16. He sets the context of his charge here (v.13), expresses the content of the charge in v.14a, then establishes the duration for the action (v.14b) and transitions into a moving doxology (vv.15-16).

Paul's opening command is "I charge" (παραγγέλλω). Paul uses the verb five times in this letter (1:3; 4:11; 5:7; 6:13, 17). It is a compound word from "along" (παρά) and "announce" (ἀγγέλλω). The essence of the root word is to pass along a message to someone. Over time it began to carry more weight and was used of an authoritative announcement or command. The word is employed in military settings and has strength to it. The second person singular personal pronoun (σοι, "you") is found in many manuscripts, but is missing from some of the most important and earliest. One would expect it to be present given the context, which gives good reason to consider that a "correction" was made by scribes who added it. It is likely to be unoriginal, but the context seems to demand understanding this as a directive to Timothy even without it.

This apostolic command is set before Timothy "in the presence of" two witnesses. It is issued "in the presence of God" (ἐνώπιον τοῦ θεοῦ). The similar expression "in the presence of many witnesses" (ἐνώπιον πολλῶν μαρτύρων) was just used in v.12. Six of the PE's eight usages of ἐνώπιον ("in the presence") are connected with "of God" (1 Tim. 2:3; 5:4, 21; 6:13; 2 Tim. 2:14; 4:1). To set the charge "in the presence of God" was to solemnify it and mark its seriousness. Indeed, He is the God "who gives life to all things" (τοῦ ζῳογονοῦντος τὰ πάντα). The verb means either to give life to (make alive) or to keep/preserve life (Luke 17:33; Acts 7:19).[88] Both nuances may be present here. The present tense does not look back upon the events of original creation, but describes the ongoing providential, life-giving and life-preserving care of God in the present time. Paul told the Athenians, "He Himself gives to all people life and breath and all things" (Acts 17:25; cf. 14:17). Jesus declared, "He causes His sun to rise on the evil and the good, and sends rain on the righteous and the unrighteous" (Matt. 5:45). Indeed, "In whose hand is the life of every living thing, and the breath of all mankind" (Job 12:10; cf. Psa. 104:27-30). The "all things" (τὰ πάντα) encompasses every animate object in the universe. All things are dependent upon God's continual, sustaining providence. In even more sweeping fashion Paul gathered up all of creation, animate and inanimate, and told the Colossian

---
[88] BAGD, 341.

Christians, "by Him [Christ] all things were created, *both* in the heavens and on earth, visible and invisible, whether thrones or dominions or rulers or authorities— all things have been created through Him and for Him" and he went on to add, "and in Him all things hold together" (Col. 1:16, 17b). Paul, as it were, was taking Timothy by the arm and ushering him into the presence of the God who controls his every breath and who commands his next heartbeat, and there, before His face, he issued this charge.

But it was not only "in the presence of God," but also (καὶ, "and") "of Christ Jesus" (Χριστοῦ Ἰησοῦ). Paul similarly combines both the presence of God and of Christ Jesus in his charges to Timothy in 1 Timothy 5:21 and 2 Timothy 4:1. Paul designates Christ as He "who testified the good confession before Pontius Pilate" (τοῦ μαρτυρήσαντος ἐπὶ Ποντίου Πιλάτου τὴν καλὴν ὁμολογίαν). Though similar to the expression in the previous verse, there is a difference here. Paul substitutes a different verb—τοῦ μαρτυρήσαντος ("who testified") for ὡμολόγησας (lit. "confessed")—while retaining the same adjective and noun (τὴν καλὴν ὁμολογίαν, "the good confession"). The aorist participle looks back to the historical event. This took place "before Pontius Pilate" (ἐπὶ Ποντίου Πιλάτου). The preposition is not to be understood temporally ("in the time of"), but in the sense of "in the presence of." It was commonly used in this way in the legal world when lawsuits were being laid down.[89] Apparently the reference is to Jesus' answer to Pilate's question: "Are You the King of the Jews?" (Matt. 27:11; Mark 15:2; Luke 23:3; John 18:33-37). To this question Jesus answered, "It is as you say" (Matt. 27:11; Mark 15:2; Luke 23:3; cf. John 18:37), or more literally and simply, "You say" (σὺ λέγεις). To this concise answer John adds that Jesus indicated that He rules over a kingdom which is not of this world (John 18:36). When asked again if He was indeed a king, Jesus replied that this was true and that He came "to testify [μαρτυρήσω, the same verb used here in 1 Tim. 6:13] to the truth" (John 18:37). Perhaps this is the reason for the verb change here. Jesus did not simply "confess the good confession" (v.12), but He gave a witness to the kind of confession His followers would be called to make. He provided His disciples with the prototypical confession by what He said before Pilate. He affirmed the truth even though it cost Him His life. And the God "who gives life to all things" raised Him from the dead as His seal of approval placed upon Him (Rom. 1:4). So too Timothy can keep this charge and continue to "confess the good confession" knowing that no matter what the outcome—even if death—God will raise him up to eternal life in His presence forever.

> **Ministry Maxim**
>
> All Jesus requires of me He has already demonstrated for me.

---

[89] BAGD, 286.

6:14 that you keep the commandment without stain or reproach until the appearing of our Lord Jesus Christ,

The Apostle now sets down the content of the "charge" begun in v.13. The infinitive "that you keep" (τηρῆσαί σε) can mean to guard or keep watch over something; to keep blameless or protect a thing. The infinitive is used to express the object of the verb "I charge" (v.13).[90] The singular personal pronoun (σε, "you") emphasizes the personal and direct nature of this responsibility as it is placed upon Timothy. That which is to be protected is "the commandment" (τὴν ἐντολὴν). The noun describes a "prescribed rule in accordance with which a thing is done."[91] The definite article and singular form make this a clear reference to a specific command. Discerning just what is intended, however, has become something of a challenge. It could refer to: 1) 1 Timothy 1:3 as the singular purpose for the letter: "As I urged you upon my departure for Macedonia, remain on at Ephesus so that you may instruct certain men not to teach strange doctrines," 2) all the injunctions Paul has set upon Timothy throughout the letter, viewing them as one collective whole, 3) the exhortations of vv.11-12 viewed as a collective whole, 4) the supposed baptismal confession alluded to in v.12, 5) a charge made at Timothy's ordination, 6) the whole of the Gospel and all it contains and intends, 7) a command to Timothy to press on in his own life and ministry (cf. 4:16).[92] Though the debate will continue, it seems best to understand it "collectively, of the whole body of the moral precepts of Christianity"[93] or "the whole Christian religion . . . thought of as . . . a new law."[94]

> **Ministry Maxim**
>
> I have not fully kept my charge until I stand in God's presence.

This is to be carried out in such a way and with such thoroughness that the commandment is kept free of two things. The following two adjectives modify "the commandment" (τὴν ἐντολὴν) rather than "you" (σε). First it is to be kept "without stain" (ἄσπιλον). The word is formed from the alpha privative (for negation) and the word σπίλος (spot/blemish). The word is used four times in the NT. It refers to Jesus as "a lamb unblemished and spotless [ἀσπίλου]" (1 Peter 1:19). James exhorts us to keep ourselves "unstained" by the world (James 1:27). Similarly Peter exhorts us to be found "spotless" at the returning of Christ (2 Peter 3:14). Second, the commandment is to be kept without "reproach" (ἀνεπίλημπτον). This too is formed by use of an alpha privative. The word is used only two other times in the NT, both in

---
[90] Rienecker, 634.
[91] Thayer, 218.
[92] Fee, 151.
[93] Thayer, 218.
[94] BAGD, 269.

this letter. It is used first as the overarching term to describe all the qualifications required of overseers (1 Tim. 3:2). In the other occurrence it is used following some of the instructions regarding widows (1 Tim. 5:7). The word means literally "not to be laid hold of,"[95] in the sense that no ground of accusation may be found. It has the connotation of "inviolable" or "unassailable."[96]

This keeping is to endure "until the appearing of our Lord Jesus Christ" (μέχρι τῆς ἐπιφανείας τοῦ κυρίου ἡμῶν Ἰησοῦ Χριστοῦ). The preposition (μέχρι, "until") carries here a temporal sense (unlike its only other occurrence in the PE, 2 Tim. 2:9). The word "appearing" (ἐπιφανείας) is used only by Paul in the NT and in every instance he uses it exclusively of Christ's second coming (2 Thess. 2:8; 1 Tim. 6:14; 2 Tim. 4:1, 8; Titus 2:13), except for 2 Timothy 1:10 where it refers to Christ's first advent. In secular Greek the word was familiar in descriptions of the glorious appearing of their mythical, pagan gods.[97] The word was rescued and endued with new meaning by the Apostle for the cause of truth. The exact phrase "of our Lord Jesus Christ" (τοῦ κυρίου ἡμῶν Ἰησοῦ Χριστοῦ) is used in v.3 and a total of thirty-four times in the NT (twenty-seven of those by Paul). The full designation is used here to underscore the authority and majesty of the Lord, adding solemnity to the charge and expectation to our watching and waiting. It is of note that the Apostle calls Timothy to keep this commandment "until the appearing of our Lord Jesus Christ" rather than something like "until you die." It appears that Paul is expecting the Lord's return prior to Timothy's passing, or, if not, that the commandment is of sufficient gravity that it must be kept well beyond Timothy's life unto the very end of this age. Timothy is dealing with matters larger than himself and whose importance will outlast this life.

Paul underscores that we live our lives here in accountability ("keep the commandment") and that our charge is both demanding ("without stain or reproach") and life-long ("until the appearing of our Lord Jesus Christ").

Digging Deeper:

1. Does the vision of God in His universal and absolute sovereignty and providence (v.13) govern your view of your circumstances today?
2. What is the relationship of Christ's "confession before Pontius Pilate" (v.13) to the "good confession" (v.12) we are called to make?
3. In specific terms what does keeping "the commandment" (v.14) require of you today?

---

[95] Friberg, 55.
[96] Kittel, abridged, 496.
[97] DNTT, 3:317.

6:15 which He will bring about at the proper time—He who is the blessed and only Sovereign, the King of kings and Lord of lords,

The relative pronoun ἣν ("which") refers back to "the appearing" in v.14. This coming "He will bring about" (δείξει). The verb means to point out, to show, or to make known.[98] The future tense sets the action down the road from the time of Paul's writing. Indeed, this revelation will be made known "at the proper time" (καιροῖς ἰδίοις). This precise phrase will be used two more times in the PE and nowhere else in the NT (1 Tim. 2:6; Titus 1:3; but cf. Gal. 6:9 where it is singular). The word for "time" (καιρός) views time as an occasion or event—a fixed or favorable moment. Being in the plural form it may indicate that Paul views all moments as gathered up and anticipating their climactic head in Christ's return. The adjective "proper" (ἰδίοις) speaks of that which belongs to or is peculiar to an individual or thing.[99] In Titus 1:3 the "proper time" refers to Christ's first advent with all its saving effects, and in 2 Timothy 2:6 it refers more specifically to His passion and the subsequent witness it has evoked. Here the reference is forward to the time of Christ's return. The first advent of Christ took place "when the fullness of time came" (Gal. 4:4), so we can be confident the timing of His second advent will be no less precise.

There is much discussion about who the "He" is. Is this a reference to Christ or to God the Father? In favor of understanding this as a reference to Christ is the fact that He is the one just mentioned (v.14). In favor of understanding this as a reference to God the Father is the fact that elsewhere, by Jesus' own admission, the timing of His return is something only the Father knows: "But of that day and hour no one knows, not even the angels of heaven, nor the Son, but the Father alone" (Matt. 24:36; cf. Mark 13:32; Acts 1:7). It is true that Jesus is called "the King of kings and Lord of lords" (Rev. 17:14; 19:16), but the designation originated as a statement for God in the OT (Deut. 10:17; Psa. 136:3). Verse 16 says that He is the one "whom no man has seen or can see," but clearly people have seen Jesus Christ; that was the very point of His incarnation. Additionally "eternal dominion" is ascribed to Him (v.16). We know that at the end of time there will come a moment "when He [Christ] hands over the kingdom to the God and Father, when He has abolished all rule and all authority and power" and "When all things are subjected to Him, then the Son Himself also will be subjected to the One who subjected all things to

> **Ministry Maxim**
>
> Only as we submit to God's rule do we enter and enjoy His blessedness.

---

[98] BAGD, 172.
[99] Ibid., 369.

Him, so that God may be all in all" (1 Cor. 15:24, 28). When all the evidence is fully considered it appears that we should probably understand "He" as a reference to God the Father.

The Apostle now launches on an extended doxology extolling the greatness of God through the use of seven statements (vv.15-16). Much of what we find here echoes the language of the Hellenistic Jewish synagogue, with which Paul was so familiar. God "is the blessed and only Sovereign" (ὁ μακάριος καὶ μόνος δυνάστης). Paul has already designated Him as "the blessed God" (τοῦ μακαρίου θεοῦ; 1 Tim. 1:11). The adjective "blessed" (μακάριος) is applied to God in only these two passages. The only other use in the PE is his reference to "the blessed hope" of Christ's return (Titus 2:13). The word has a wide range of meaning—from "happy" to "blessed." In what sense can this be said to be true of God? God alone possesses within Himself all that is necessary for His complete, contented happiness. God did not create the worlds out of loneliness or a deficit of some kind. Before creation God resided in complete self-sufficiency and self-satisfaction. Now since creation He continues as the only such being. All others derive their blessedness from their proximity and relationship to Him. God is the source of all true blessedness for His creation.

He is also (καὶ, "and") the "only" (μόνος) one of His kind. The adjective is found seven times in the PE (1 Tim. 1:17; 5:13; 6:15, 16; 2 Tim. 2:20; 4:8, 11). God is "the only God" (1 Tim. 1:17) and He "alone possesses immortality" (6:16). Elsewhere He is named "the only wise God" (Rom. 16:27). Paul's Jewish monotheism remains unchanged (Deut. 6:4), even with his new understanding of Jesus as divine (Col. 1:19; 2:9-10; Titus 2:13). There is but one God. Such divine exclusivity is not popular in the current cultural climate, but the facts remain unchanged—God remains singular and solitary as the "only Sovereign." The position of both adjectives between the definite article and the noun emphasizes the qualitative nature of "the . . . Sovereign" (ὁ . . . δυνάστης) under consideration. The noun occurs only two other times in the NT (Luke 1:52; Acts 8:27). It designates "one who is in a position to command others."[100] We derive our word "dynasty" from this root. It thus designates a ruler, potentate, or sovereign. Only God is ultimately in this position. All other authorities derive their authority from Him.[101] Only God dispenses blessedness. Blessedness is found only in proximity to Him. Only as we submit to His rule do we enter and enjoy His blessedness.

He only is "the King of kings and Lord of lords" (ὁ βασιλεὺς τῶν βασιλευόντων καὶ κύριος τῶν κυριευόντων). In the OT God is designated as "the God of gods and the Lord of lords" (Deut. 10:17; cf. Psa.

---

[100] Friberg, 121.
[101] See the author's *Embracing Authority* for more on this topic.

136:3). As mentioned previously, in Revelation Jesus is designated with these words (17:14; 19:16). He is, as Robertson puts it, "the King of those who rule as kings."[102] They receive their limited sovereignty from Him who is absolute and universal in His. They answer to Him who alone is absolute and universal in His reign. "The king's heart is like channels of water in the hand of the LORD; He turns it wherever He wishes" (Prov. 21:1). The God from whom and in whose presence this "charge" (v.13) is laid upon Timothy is in complete and sovereign control of the universe. Thus the keeping of the "commandment" (v.14) is not as burdensome as it might first appear.

> **Digging Deeper:**
> 1. How does the knowledge that God has "the proper time" in hand help you in your responsibilities today?
> 2. In what sense is God "blessed"?
> 3. What is the significance of the word "only" in speaking of God as the "only Sovereign"?

6:16 who alone possesses immortality and dwells in unapproachable light, whom no man has seen or can see. To Him be honor and eternal dominion! Amen.

The sentence begun in v.13 now comes to a conclusion. It is God "who alone possesses immortality" (ὁ μόνος ἔχων ἀθανασίαν). The participle with the definite article (ὁ . . . ἔχων, "who . . . possesses") is used as a substantive referring to God.[103] The present tense underscores this as His continual nature. The noun "immortality" (ἀθανασίαν) is used only here and 1 Corinthians 15:53, 54 in the NT. It is comprised of the alpha privative (for negation) and θάνατος ("death").[104] It describes one who is not able to die.[105] The use of μόνος ("alone") may well be a polemic against the Emperor worship which found such ready acceptance in Ephesus. In his earlier doxology (1:17) Paul declared God to be the "immortal" King, using an adjective from a different word group (ἀφθάρτω; cf. Rom. 1:23; 1 Cor. 9:25; 15:52; 1 Peter 1:4, 23; 3:4). God alone is untouched by sin and is therefore the only immortal being in the universe. His rule cannot and will not be threatened by death. He possesses within Himself the power and prerogative of self-existence. All

---
[102] Robertson, 4:595.
[103] Knight, 270.
[104] Robertson, 4:595.
[105] Rienecker, 635.

others are contingent and dependent upon Him, but He Himself depends upon no one and nothing.

Beyond this God "dwells in unapproachable light" (φῶς οἰκῶν ἀπρόσιτον). The metaphor of "light" (φῶς) is one often connected with God (e.g., Psa. 27:1; 36:9; Isa. 9:2; John 1:4). Indeed, "God is Light, and in Him there is no darkness at all" (1 John 1:5). Here, however, Paul, rather than saying "God is Light," says God "dwells" (οἰκῶν) in light. The participle is again used as a substantive and the present tense speaks of what God does continually and unceasingly.[106] The word "unapproachable" (ἀπρόσιτον) is made up of an alpha privative ("not") and προσιεναι ("to go to").[107] Exactly why the light in which God dwells is designated as "unapproachable" is not stated. God is likened elsewhere to the sun in its glory (e.g., Psa. 104:2; Hab. 3:4; Rev. 1:16). Indeed, of the final state the Apostle John says, "And there will no longer be any night; and they will not have need of the light of a lamp nor the light of the sun, because the Lord God will illumine them; and they will reign forever and ever" (Rev. 22:5). Thus it would appear that the light in which God is here said to dwell is "unapproachable" in the same sense in which the writer to the Hebrews says, "our God is a consuming fire" (Heb. 12:29). The light of the sun is the physical giver of life to our planet, but too close a proximity to the sun quickly renders all life null and void. Its rays warm us from an appropriate distance, but they would consume us if presumptuously encroached upon.

God is the One "whom no man has seen or can see" (ὃν εἶδεν οὐδεὶς ἀνθρώπων οὐδὲ ἰδεῖν δύναται). The relative pronoun ὃν ("whom") refers to God the Father. The first verb (εἶδεν, "has seen") is in the aorist tense, pointing to a particular event in time. The negation is absolute and categorical (οὐδεὶς, "no").[108] It rules out all humans (ἀνθρώπων, "man"). The second verb (δύναται, "can") speaks of the power of capacity or ability.[109] The negation is again

> **Ministry Maxim**
>
> The awesomeness of God's character underscores the seriousness of His command.

set forth in the strongest terms (οὐδὲ). The present tense of the verb gives the sense that the subject is never at any time able to see God. The middle voice stresses that there is nothing within a person to enable him to see God. The infinitive (ἰδεῖν, "see") tells us just what is impossible. The verb is again aorist to picture even one moment, one glance. This seems to be a reflection

---
[106] Knight, 270.
[107] Thayer, 70.
[108] Ibid., 408.
[109] Friberg, 121.

of God's words to Moses: "You cannot see My face, for no man can see Me and live!" (Exod. 33:20). The Hebrews believed one cannot see God and survive. Some, having encountered God, marvel that they did not die (Gen. 32:30; Deut. 5:24; Judg. 6:22; 13:22; Isa. 6:5; Rev. 1:17). Jesus said, "No one has seen God at any time" (John 1:18a; cf. 6:46). Paul said of Jesus, "He is the image of the invisible God" (Col. 1:15). Indeed, the great news of the incarnation is that Jesus "has explained Him" (John 1:18b). He told Philip, "He who has seen Me has seen the Father" (14:9b) and on another occasion He declared, "He who sees Me sees the One who sent Me" (12:45). The hope of the believer is to behold God (Matt. 5:8; Heb. 12:14; 1 John 3:2; Rev. 22:4), but as finite creatures we will never be able to look completely upon and comprehend the essence of Him who alone is infinite.[110]

The Apostle brings the doxology to a close with the exalted affirmation: "To Him be honor and eternal dominion!" (ᾧ τιμὴ καὶ κράτος αἰώνιον). The expression lacks the verb, but this gives a terse punch to its expressiveness. The dative form of the relative pronoun gives us "to Him" (ᾧ), a reference again to God the Father. The word "honor" (τιμὴ) was used to denote the price or value of something (e.g., Matt. 27:6, 9; Acts 4:34; 5:2, 3; 1 Cor. 6:20). Over time it came to describe the honor or reverence that was due to a person. This word was used in Paul's opening doxology of this letter (1:17). While there it was coupled with "glory" (δόξα), here it is matched (καὶ, "and") with "dominion" (κράτος). The word denotes "the possession of force or strength that affords supremacy or control."[111] "The word refers to strength regarded as abundantly effective in relation to an end to be gained or dominion to be exercised."[112] It is often used in doxological statements (1 Peter 4:11; 5:11; Jude 25; Rev. 1:6; 5:13). This dominion is "eternal" (αἰώνιον). The adjective was just used in v.12 in the expression "eternal life" (τῆς αἰωνίου ζωῆς) and is found thus in the PE (1 Tim. 1:16; Titus 1:2; 3:7) and elsewhere. It describes the opposite of that which is temporary and transitory.[113] It thus refers to that which is eternal or everlasting.

As in 1:17, the Apostle's song of praise finds a fitting crescendo with a echoing "Amen" (ἀμήν). He often concluded his doxologies in this way (cf. Rom. 1:25; 9:5; 11:36; 16:27; Gal. 1:5; Eph. 3:21; Phil. 4:20; 1 Tim. 1:17; 6:16). In such contexts it means something like "so it is," "so be it," or "may it be fulfilled."[114] Every reader (or listener) would likewise be moved to affirm these words with their own "Amen."

---

[110] Hiebert, *First Timothy*, 120.
[111] Friberg, 236.
[112] Rienecker, 523-524.
[113] Friberg, 39.
[114] Thayer, 32.

> **Digging Deeper:**
> 1. When Paul says that God *alone* "possesses immortality," what does he imply about our hope of *eternal* life?
> 2. Why should we find the fact that God dwells in "unapproachable light" to be good news?
> 3. Explain how "no man . . . can see" God and yet our great hope is that "we will see Him just as He is" (1 John 3:2)?

6:17 Instruct those who are rich in this present world not to be conceited or to fix their hope on the uncertainty of riches, but on God, who richly supplies us with all things to enjoy.

After a parenthesis (vv.11-16) Paul now returns to the topic of riches. Previously (vv.5-10) he was concerned about "those who want to get rich" (v.9). Now he addresses the matter of "those who are rich."

The command "Instruct" (παράγγελλε) is the same word used in v.13 when Paul told Timothy "I charge you." See there for more on the word. It is a present tense imperative which demands that action be taken repeatedly. Such instruction is not a one-and-done matter. As vv.6-10 reveal, the grip of materialism is strong and the way to true stewardship will be strewn with much instruction and learning. The second person singular form puts this obligation upon Timothy as the pastor of the church. This instruction is to be aimed at "those who are rich" (Τοῖς πλουσίοις). The adjective with the definite article is used as a substantive. Paul uses the word only two other times, both metaphorically: of the riches of Christ in His preincarnate state (2 Cor. 8:9) and of God as "rich in mercy" (Eph. 2:4). But here it is wealth "in this present world" (ἐν τῷ νῦν αἰῶνι) which Paul has in view (in contrast to "the future" [τὸ μέλλον], v.19). The precise phrase is used elsewhere only in Titus 2:12 where the grace of God calls us "to deny ungodliness and worldly desires and to live sensibly, righteously and godly in the present age." In 2 Timothy 4:10 we will discover that Demas loved "this present world" (τὸν νῦν αἰῶνα) so much that he deserted Paul. The noun "world" (αἰῶνι) means more literally "age." It is frequently used in the expression "forever and ever" (εἰς τοὺς αἰῶνας τῶν αἰώνων; e.g., 2 Tim. 4:18) or "unto the ages of the ages." But in contrast, here it is "the now age" (τῷ νῦν αἰῶνι) that is of concern. Paul wants Timothy to address those who are well supplied in the currency of the present ruling culture and worldview. That same currency may mean nothing in the next "age," but his concern at the moment is to single out those who don't realize that and are prideful in their present place. Jesus was similarly concerned for those who are "not rich toward God" (Luke 12:21).

Timothy is to teach them two things not to do (by use of two infinitives) and one thing to do. First, these people are "not to be conceited" (μὴ ὑψηλοφρονεῖν). The word is found only here in the NT (and as a variant in Rom. 11:20). It comes from ὑψηλοφρονέω, which in turn comes from ὑψηλός ("high") and φρήν ("thinking").[115] The present tense infinitive demands that this never become their self-evaluation. The true standard of measure for a person's worth stands outside of the values and possessions of this age. Thus one who believes himself better than another who has less of this world's goods is fundamentally living in deception. Second, they are not "to fix their hope on the uncertainty of riches" (μηδὲ ἠλπικέναι ἐπὶ πλούτου ἀδηλότητι). Paul has used this verb form three other times in this letter. He speaks of his personal hope of coming to see Timothy soon (1 Tim. 3:14), of the Christian's hope as fixed on the living God (4:10), and of the widow's hope as similarly fixed upon God (5:5). All except the first of these is in the perfect tense, underscoring the hope as settled and fixed upon a particular object. Here, instead of one's hope being placed decisively upon God (1 Tim. 4:10; 5:5), the concern is about trusting "the uncertainty of riches" (πλούτου ἀδηλότητι). The noun "riches" (πλούτου) describes simply "the possession of many earthly goods."[116] In such gain there is an inherent "uncertainty" (ἀδηλότητι). This word appears only here in the NT. It comes from the adjective which means "unseen, unobserved, not manifest" or "indistinct."[117] There is a hidden side to the accumulation of wealth. It appears to provide stability and to steady one's life, but in fact the riches themselves are volatile and unstable. The Scriptures repeatedly sound this warning (Psa. 39:6; Prov. 27:24; Eccl. 5:13-14; Matt. 6:19; James 5:1-2). "Do not weary yourself to gain wealth, cease from your consideration of it. When you set your eyes on it, it is gone, for wealth certainly makes itself wings like an eagle that flies toward the heavens" (Prov. 23:4-5).

> **Ministry Maxim**
>
> A key to stewardship is never to confuse the gift and the Giver.

With a strong adversative (ἀλλ', "but") the Apostle makes clear that instead of fixing our hope on riches, we should set it "on God" (ἐπὶ θεῷ). Paul

---
[115] Thayer, 11.
[116] BAGD, 674.
[117] Rienecker, 635.

used this with the preceding verb previously in 1 Timothy 4:10 (cf. also 5:5; 2 Cor. 1:10). He only is the Rock (Psa. 18:2). Any other foundation is shifting sand (Matt. 7:26-27; 1 Cor. 3:11; cf. 1 Tim. 6:19). Yet Timothy is not simply to demand that people set their hope upon God in some vague, general way. Rather he is to set God before the people as the One "who richly supplies us with all things to enjoy" (τῷ παρέχοντι ἡμῖν πάντα πλουσίως εἰς ἀπόλαυσιν). The participle and its definite article (τῷ παρέχοντι, "who . . . supplies") is used as a substantive, further enlarging upon the God just described. Paul uses the verb two other times in the PE (1 Tim. 1:4; Titus 2:7). It is a compound word made up of "beside" (παρά) and "to hold" (ἔχω). Here it has the simple meaning of "to grant" or "to show something to someone."[118] The present tense underscores that God is a continual giver. This giving is not in a broad sense only, but to "us" (ἡμῖν) personally; not in a limited sense, but "with all things" (πάντα); not in a meager way, but "richly" (πλουσίως). This richness comes to us not simply that we might be a conduit to pass it along to others, but "to enjoy" (εἰς ἀπόλαυσιν) personally. This is likely an intentional jibe both at the severe ascetics of the false teachers (1 Tim. 4:3-5; 5:23) and the hedonism of some of their followers (5:6). God is not anti-pleasure. God is not promoting an other-worldly mindset in which we are unable to embrace and enjoy His created order here. God intends us to enjoy what He has made and providentially supplies to us (Eccl. 5:18-19). But we must not be blinded by pleasure. We must ever look to and trust the Giver rather than the gift.

Note the word play that has taken place in this verse and continues into the next. This is about those who are rich (πλουσίοις) and their riches (πλούτου) and how God richly (πλουσίως) gives those gifts to them. In v.18 these same people are told to be rich (πλουτεῖν) in good works.[119]

> **Digging Deeper:**
> 1. By what standard should we judge whether we are "rich in this present world"? Are you?
> 2. What is the connection between riches and conceit?
> 3. How can we enjoy all that God gives us without being seduced into putting our hope in those riches?

---

[118] BAGD, 626.
[119] Knight, 273; Mounce, 367.

6:18 Instruct them to do good, to be rich in good works, to be generous and ready to share,

The sentence continues from v.17 through v.19 in the Greek text. Three more infinitives are added to the previous two from v.17 to explain more fully what it is Timothy is to "Instruct those who are rich in this present world" about. The translators have added "Instruct them" here in order to make for smoother reading. All three infinitives are in the present tense, pointing to continuous action. These then round out into four requirements laid upon the rich. These form two pairs.

Timothy is to teach the rich "to do good" (ἀγαθοεργεῖν). The word is used elsewhere in the NT only in Acts 14:17 where it is used of God in His giving rains and crops even to pagan people. The rich should view their wealth as a God-given gift and trust—one from which they are to multiply the goodness of God's heart poured out through their own hands. The adjective ἀγαθός is used often in the PE to speak of good works (1 Tim. 2:10; 5:10; 2 Tim. 2:21; 3:17; Titus 3:1). In the next breath he will do the same with the adjective καλός.

Indeed, Paul goes on to say that Timothy is also to teach them "to be rich in good works" (πλουτεῖν ἐν ἔργοις καλοῖς). The infinitive has just been employed in v.9. Note again the play on words. Here we have "to be rich" (πλουτεῖν), which has assonance with "those who are rich" (πλουσίοις), "riches" (πλούτου), and "richly" (πλουσίως) in v.17. The One who richly supplies all things has made the wealthy rich for the purpose that they might then become "rich in good works." As Paul uses the adjective ἀγαθός to point to good works, so too he uses καλός (1 Tim. 3:1; 5:10, 25; 6:18; Titus 2:7, 14; 3:8, 14). Good works do not save us (Titus 3:5), but they do fairly represent the reality of our salvation (Titus 2:14; 3:8). Here the plural noun "works" (ἔργοις) points to a multiplicity of deeds and expressions. The wealthy believer is to be rich "in good works" and the works themselves must be rich in nature, substance, and number.

> **Ministry Maxim**
>
> I must help the rich make certain they are truly rich.

Timothy is further to teach the rich "to be generous and ready to share" (εὐμεταδότους εἶναι, κοινωνικούς). Both adjectives are found only here in the NT. The former is a triple compound made up of εὐ (well), μετά (with), and δίδωμι (give). It means "sharing well," "generous," and "ready to impart."[120] The latter is akin to the better-known noun κοινωνία ("fellowship"). It may have, then, the sense of "ready and apt to form and maintain communion and

---
[120] Riencecker, 635.

fellowship."[121] In this sense it might demand that rich believers "share their hearts as well as their money."[122] Paul praised the Macedonians for their example of generosity in giving first themselves and then their material possessions (2 Cor. 8:1-5). Note the use of the cognate verb in 1 Timothy 5:22.

Note well Jesus' example: "For you know the grace of our Lord Jesus Christ, that though He was rich, yet for your sake He became poor, so that you through His poverty might become rich" (2 Cor. 8:9). True wealth is found in relationships and employing one's physical possessions to enhance those relationships.

6:19 storing up for themselves the treasure of a good foundation for the future, so that they may take hold of that which is life indeed.

Timothy is to "Instruct" (v.17a) those in his charge to take the actions already outlined in five infinitive phrases (vv.17-18) with the understanding that they are thus "storing up" (ἀποθησαυρίζοντας) something. The word is used only here in the NT. It is a compound comprised of ἀπό ("from") and θησαυρίζω ("store up"). The idea is that of taking something from one place and storing it up for another. While we cannot take worldly possessions with us when we die, we may use them now in such a way that we store up from this world something different—and better—for the next. The concept is sometimes called transmutation—turning one substance into another. In this case it involves turning the currency of this world into the currency that has value in the next. This participle qualifies all of the previous infinitives (vv.17-18), and describes what one is doing for oneself as one does good to others. As the wealthy choose not to be conceited or to fix their hope on riches, but rather on God (v.17) and as they do good, become rich in good works and prove ready to share (v.18) they are continuously (present tense) transmuting their present riches into riches that will matter after leaving this present world. While the wealthy are called to use what they possess for the welfare of others, they are thus also doing something "for themselves" (ἑαυτοῖς). The reflexive pronoun pictures their action as rebounding into their own laps as a matter of course. The wealthy who are truly wise delay present personal gratification for future personal blessing. That which they are storing up for themselves is "a good foundation" (θεμέλιον καλὸν). The word

> **Ministry Maxim**
>
> The only place we can cash-in this world's goods for the next world's currency is in this life.

---
[121] Hiebert, *First Timothy*, 122.
[122] Earle, 11:388.

"foundation" (θεμέλιον) describes the foundation under a building, upon which the superstructure rests. Paul will use it again in 2 Timothy 2:19 to speak of "the firm foundation of God." It is used metaphorically elsewhere by Paul to speak of the foundation of the church, which is Jesus Christ (Rom 15:20; 1 Cor 3:10-12). In another place Paul sees the apostles and prophets as being part of the foundation, but even then Christ is the cornerstone of that foundation (Eph. 2:20). Here, however, the foundation is a more personal one. It is "good" (καλὸν) in that it is solid and lasting, in contrast to "the uncertainty of riches" (v.17).[123] It proves reliable, safe, and steady, not merely in this world, but also "for the future" (εἰς τὸ μέλλον). Here the neuter participle is used as a substantive and refers to "an unlimited extent of time to come" (i.e., "the future").[124] The present tense describes it as ever and always looming before us. There is never a time in this life that we ought not to be preparing for the future.

In all this Paul is sounding very much like Jesus: "Do not store up for yourselves treasures on earth, where moth and rust destroy, and where thieves break in and steal. But store up for yourselves treasures in heaven, where neither moth nor rust destroys, and where thieves do not break in or steal; for where your treasure is, there your heart will be also" (Matt. 6:19-21; cf. 19:21; Luke 12:21; 12:33-34; 18:22).

Paul urges this be done for a specific purpose (ἵνα, "so that"). That purpose is "that they may take hold of that which is life indeed" (ἐπιλάβωνται τῆς ὄντως ζωῆς). Paul's only other use of the verb is in v.12 where he demanded that Timothy "take hold of the eternal life" to which God had called him. It is a compound word made up of ἐπί ("upon") and λαμβάνω ("take hold of"). It means to take hold of something in order to make it one's own.[125] The aorist tense points to a definite act. The middle voice (in which all nineteen of its NT usages appear) underscores the inward nature of this act. The adverb (ὄντως, "indeed") is akin to and arose from the present particle of εἰμί ("to be"). Used with a noun it serves to attest to the genuineness of something and is thus translated "real," "true," or "indeed."[126] Paul used it three times in chapter 5 to speak of those who are "widows indeed" (5:3, 5, 16). In the attributive position (here tucked between the noun and its definite article) it denotes the quality or kind of "life" (τῆς . . . ζωῆς) under consideration—a life found not in the mere enjoyment of riches (though such enjoyment is not illegitimate, v.17), but in the delight of using them for the glory of God and the good of others. Some late manuscripts replace this word with "eternal" (cf. KJV), but ὄντως is surely the correct reading, though

---

[123] Ibid., 11:389.
[124] Friberg, 257.
[125] BAGD, 295.
[126] Friberg, 283.

the reference is indeed to eternal life. The word "life" (ζωῆς) is used in the NT "of the supernatural life of God and Christ, which the believers will receive in the future, but which they enjoy here and now."[127] This is "eternal life" (1 Tim. 1:16; 6:12; Titus 3:7), which is promised us in Christ Jesus (2 Tim. 1:1) and brought to light in His Gospel (1:10). This life is the great hope of every believer (1 Tim. 4:8; Titus 1:2). Living a generous life now in Jesus' name gives great confidence for the next life—not because the good works merit eternal life, but because they evidence its present reality and presence.

> **Digging Deeper:**
> 1. How would you go about convincing someone rich in this world's goods to use them generously for the purposes of God and eternal life?
> 2. How can being generous enable us to experience more fully that which is "life indeed"?
> 3. When calculated on a global scale, you likely live within the top few percentage points of the world's wealthiest people—what do these verses mean to you?

6:20 O Timothy, guard what has been entrusted to you, avoiding worldly and empty chatter and the opposing arguments of what is falsely called "knowledge" —

As Paul moves to close the letter, he now turns his attention to Timothy directly. He uses the vocative (Ὦ Τιμόθεε, "O Timothy") as a means of arresting Timothy's attention and heightening the urgency of what he is about to convey (cf. 1:18). The Apostle closes with what amounts to a summation of the entire letter in one sentence.[128] Picking up on themes developed throughout the letter he gathers up the whole of his purpose and expresses it one last time in succinct fashion.

Paul issues the command to "guard" (φύλαξον). The verb describes protecting something entrusted to you so that it is kept unharmed.[129] It is used in the PE primarily of a responsibility laid on Timothy (1 Tim. 5:21; 6:20; 2 Tim. 1:14; 4:15), but also can speak of something God does (2 Tim. 1:12). The aorist imperative adds to the urgency and demands that action be undertaken at once and brought to "effective accomplishment."[130] That which is to be thus

---
[127] BAGD, 341.
[128] Kent, 201.
[129] BAGD, 868.
[130] Hiebert, *First Timothy*, 123.

kept is "what has been entrusted to you" (τὴν παραθήκην). The noun is found only two other times in the NT (2 Tim. 1:12, 14; always with the definite article). In 2 Timothy 1:12 the expression is literally "my deposit" or "the deposit of me" (τὴν παραθήκην μου). There is debate as to whether it refers to what Timothy had left for safe keeping with God or to what God had entrusted to Timothy (see discussion at 2 Tim. 1:12). Two verses later in 2 Timothy 1:14 (τὴν καλὴν παραθήκην, lit. "the good deposit") it clearly refers to a deposit given to Timothy, as it also does in the present context. Timothy is a steward and guardian. That "deposit" is the Gospel and all its accompanying truth contained in the Scriptures.

As Timothy is thus guarding the good deposit entrusted to Him by God, he is to be "avoiding" (ἐκτρεπόμενος) certain dangers. Four of the five occurrences of this verb are in the PE (1 Tim. 1:6; 5:15; 6:20; 2 Tim. 4:4; Heb. 12:13). It means to twist, turn, or turn aside. In medical contexts it could speak of a joint being dislocated (cf. Heb. 12:13).[131] The present tense points to a continual vigilance against such a turning way. The passive voice has a middle sense to it[132] and thus indicates that Timothy himself is responsible (by God's grace, of course) to keep himself from these wrong paths. Paul can use the word to speak of turning aside to follow Satan (1 Tim. 5:15) as well as engaging in "fruitless discussions" (1 Tim. 1:6) and "myths" (2 Tim. 4:4). The Apostle's concern here is more in keeping with the last two of those. The participle may carry some imperatival overtones.[133]

Timothy is to keep clear of two dangers. The first is "worldly and empty chatter" (τὰς βεβήλους κενοφωνίας). The nearly identical expression appears in 2 Timothy 2:16 where Paul warns Timothy again, "But avoid worldly and empty chatter [τὰς δὲ βεβήλους κενοφωνίας], for it will lead to further ungodliness." The noun (τὰς... κενοφωνίας, "empty chatter") is found only in these two passages in the NT. It is a compound word formed by κενός ("empty") and φωνὴ ("voice"). It points simply to talk that has no real content. It is comprised of empty words strung together into a vacuous babble. There is always plenty of sound, but never any point. The adjective (βεβήλους) is used three other times by Paul (1:9; 4:7; 2 Tim 2:16) and once in Hebrews (12:16). It describes that which is ungodly, profane, irreligious, and vile. It can describe the character of people (1 Tim. 1:9; Heb. 12:16) as well as the words that proceed from their mouths (1 Tim. 4:7; 6:20; 2 Tim. 2:16). That there is one particular example of such talk in Paul's mind is clear from his use of the definite article (τὰς).[134] Paul has in mind the specific problems, people, conversation, and teaching going on

---

[131] BAGD, 246.
[132] Ibid.
[133] Knight, 276-277; Mounce, 371.
[134] Mounce, 526.

in Ephesus at the time. Yet history repeats itself and falsehood has carried these same marks wherever it has shown up throughout the history of the church.

To this Paul adds (καί, "and") a second danger to be avoided, "the opposing arguments of what is falsely called 'knowledge'" (ἀντιθέσεις τῆς ψευδωνύμου γνώσεως). The noun rendered "the opposing arguments" (ἀντιθέσεις) is the word from which we derive our word *antithesis*. It is used only here in the NT. It is a compound comprised of ἀντί ("against") and τίθημι ("to place").[135] It describes that which is an opposition, objection, or contradiction. It was a "a technical term in debate for the counter proposition" and thus "describes the heresy as self-defeating."[136] Paul is surely describing that which is set forth by the false teachers in Ephesus in opposition to the Gospel and the Scriptures. Because there is but one definite article before κενοφωνίας ("empty chatter"), the adjective βεβήλους ("worldly") may also qualify this noun as well.[137] This is further qualified by the noun/adjective combination: "of what is falsely called 'knowledge'" (τῆς ψευδωνύμου γνώσεως). The false teachers claim to have "knowledge" (τῆς ... γνώσεως). Twenty-three of this noun's twenty-nine appearances in the NT are in Paul, but this is its only use in the PE. The opponents laid claim to a secret, superior knowledge known only to them and their followers (cf. 1 Cor. 1:10-4:21; 8:1-13; Col. 2:1-10). The reasoning was that the Apostles, like Paul, were fine—as far as they went—but for true "knowledge" and enlightenment people should follow these new, more advanced teachers. In this the false teachers were in some sense similar to the Gnostics who would arise in the second century. But this is knowledge which is "falsely called" (ψευδωνύμου). The compound word is made up of ψευδής ("false") and ὄνομα ("name").[138] We derive our word *pseudonym* (a fictitious or pen name) from this word. What the false teachers and their followers dub "knowledge" is not knowledge at all, but a deception (1 Tim. 1:7; 2 Tim. 2:23). Thus Timothy is to avoid all such conversation and teaching.

> **Ministry Maxim**
>
> Falsehood usually has plenty of sound, but seldom any point.

6:21 which some have professed and thus gone astray from the faith. Grace be with you.

This pseudo-"knowledge" (v.20b) is something "which some have professed" (ἥν τινες ἐπαγγελλόμενοι). The feminine singular relative pronoun ἥν

---
[135] Thayer, 50.
[136] Mounce, 371.
[137] Knight, 277; Mounce, 371.
[138] Mounce, 372.

("which") clearly finds its antecedent in the "knowledge" (τῆς ... γνώσεως) of v.20b. The participle "have professed" (ἐπαγγελλόμενοι) normally means something more like making a promise (e.g., Rom. 4:21; Gal. 3:19; Titus 1:2), but here it means to "profess," to "lay claim to," or to "give oneself out as an expert in someth[ing]."[139] It has a similar sense in 1 Timothy 2:10. The present tense stresses the present profession these people make and continue to cling to. It is found in the middle voice in all its fifteen NT usages (except Gal. 3:19 which has the passive sense). The plural form underscores that the false teachers have succeeded in drawing away at least several to follow them. But those who professed this false doctrine have "thus gone astray from the faith" (περὶ τὴν πίστιν ἠστόχησαν). The main verb is used only three times in the NT, all of them in the PE (1 Tim. 1:6; 6:21; 2 Tim. 2:18). The repetition of this otherwise rare verb underscores that Paul opens and closes this letter with the same concern (1:6; 6:20). It means "to miss the mark, to swerve, to fail to aim at."[140] Rienecker says, "The word indicates 'taking no pains to aim at the right path.'"[141] The plural form plus the plural indefinite pronoun τινες ("some") again indicate that more than one has gone down this false path. The aorist tense underscores what has already transpired. In a decisive moment they left the path of truth and defected to falsehood in the name of "knowledge." The direction they have chosen moves away "from the faith" (περὶ τὴν πίστιν). The exact phrase appears also in 1 Timothy 1:19 and 2 Timothy 3:8. The preposition περὶ ("from") is used here in the sense of "with regard to" or "with respect to."[142] The noun and the definite article (τὴν πίστιν, "the faith") together point to the body of truth which conveys the saving grace of God in Christ. The definite article serves to specify the one and only faith through which one might be rescued from sin and its judgment.

> **Ministry Maxim**
>
> Every day I deal with matters of truth and error, life and death, heaven and hell.

The great Apostle closes his letter as he began it (1:2)—with the extension of grace: "Grace be with you" (Ἡ χάρις μεθ' ὑμῶν). The exact expression also closes the books of Colossians (4:18) and 2 Timothy (4:22). The verb is assumed and must be supplied by the reader. Paul used the definite article with "grace" (Ἡ χάρις). Though Paul opens and closes each of his NT letters with this noun, the grace the Apostle extended to Timothy (and the congregation in Ephesus) was not the typical beneficence of cultural custom, but the unique grace that comes only from God the Father through Jesus Christ by the power

---

[139] BAGD, 281.
[140] Rienecker, 615.
[141] Ibid.
[142] BAGD, 645.

First Timothy 6

of the Holy Spirit. Paul employed the plural pronoun (ὑμῶν, "you")—as he also did in closing 2 Timothy and Titus—which is an indicator that while this was a personal letter addressed to Timothy, he expected it to be shared publicly with the entire congregation.

The final "Amen" (KJV) is not found in the most significant manuscripts and surely was a later addition.

And thus this great letter concludes. The Gospel stands, though its enemies rage. The church goes on, though falsehood finds a home and voice even from within its number. At the center of the battle is a solitary individual, called of God to guard the trust of truth delivered in the Gospel of the Lord Jesus Christ. The Apostle Paul has sought to encourage, exhort, and strengthen Timothy to be faithful in this high calling. All today who find themselves in the thick of this same battle will find in the words of this ancient, but ever-living letter, the same grace for this epic struggle of truth and error, life and death, heaven and hell.

> **Digging Deeper:**
> 1. Why does the Apostle demand "avoiding"—rather than confronting—the falsehood faced by the church?
> 2. How can we expose pseudo-knowledge for what it is?
> 3. According to v.21, what is at stake in our faithfulness in these matters?

2 TIMOTHY

CHAPTER

1

1:1 Paul, an apostle of Christ Jesus by the will of God, according to the promise of life in Christ Jesus,

The author's name is the first word encountered. He identifies himself as "Paul" (Παῦλος), using his Roman name, as opposed to Saul, his Jewish name. Both names were likely his from birth, but once he answered God's call as Apostle to the Gentiles, he seems to have used the Gentile moniker exclusively (Acts 13:9). James Stalker notes, "… as if to mark that he had become a new man and taken a new place, he was no longer called by the Jewish name of Saul, which up to this point he had borne, but by the name of Paul, which has ever since been his designation among Christians."[1] He is thus, as he faces the close of his life and ministry, identified fully with Christ's salvation and call upon his life.

The rest of the verse goes on to establish firmly the reality of his situation. His physical circumstances are a Roman prison (2:9)—not a house arrest like his first imprisonment (Acts 28:30-31), but a dank, dark dungeon. He suffers (1:12; 2:3, 9), has been abandoned by what seems to be all associates (1:15; 4:16; though Luke is with him, 4:11), is chained (2:9), and has gone through his first defense (4:16). So isolated is he that even his closest associates have had a hard time finding him (1:17). He fully expects that he will soon perish (4:6). Tradition holds that Paul was executed by beheading sometime shortly after the writing of this letter.

Yet note how he presents himself and his circumstances! He is "an apostle of Christ Jesus" (ἀπόστολος Χριστοῦ Ἰησοῦ). The word "apostle" (ἀπόστολος) refers to one sent with a message and endowed with the full authority of the

---

[1] Stalker, 68.

sender in delivering it. The outworking of this commission has landed Paul now in this dungeon. Paul the author often referred to his apostleship to establish his authority in the face of opposition or internal division. Yet Timothy needs no such authentication of Paul. It is possible that Paul cites his apostleship here not to enforce his authority, but to commission Timothy with apostolic authority to move forward with the ministry of the Gospel in his absence. Yet it seems closer to the point that Paul cites his apostleship here not to enforce his authority, but to authenticate his circumstances. He wants Timothy to know his imprisonment and eventual death are no accident, but a part of his ambassadorship for "Christ Jesus" (Χριστοῦ Ἰησοῦ). Of the thirteen times this combination is found in the letter, it is in this order (rather than "Jesus Christ") twelve of those times (the one exception is 2:8). Among the writers of Scripture only Paul uses this order (though see the slightly different form in Acts 24:24). He employs it eighty-nine times, in every letter he penned except 2 Thessalonians. The special import of this order is not easily discernable. Moule comments, "this Pauline order breathes a certain feeling of worshipping while intimate *affection* towards the blessed Lord."[2]

This divine commissioning was "by the will of God" (διὰ θελήματος θεοῦ). This same expression is used in the salutations in 1 Corinthians 1:1, 2 Corinthians 1:1, Ephesians 1:1, and Colossians 1:1. Romans has Paul "called *as* an apostle" (1:1) and 1 Timothy has Paul an Apostle "according to the commandment of God our Savior" (1:1). The preposition "by" (διὰ) signals the "efficient cause"[3] of Paul's apostleship and, by extension, all that comes from it. The point here is that his apostleship is directly from the hand of God, and that all the events that have flowed from fulfilling that role are also from the hand of God—including his current imprisonment. This not only is the fact, but it is likely stated here to steady Timothy, who no doubt was worried about Paul. The only other use of the word "will" (θέλημα) in the PE is in 2 Timothy 2:26 where it refers to the will of the devil, underscoring that we are in a spiritual battle, as surely Paul's circumstances prove. Yet in that battle the only will that has controlling influence over a submissive believer's life is that of his Master.

Paul adds that his apostleship is also "according to the promise of life in Christ Jesus" (κατ' ἐπαγγελίαν ζωῆς τῆς ἐν Χριστῷ Ἰησοῦ). The expression "promise of life" (ἐπαγγελίαν ζωῆς τῆς) reminds one of Paul's instruction in 1 Timothy 4:8. There it is godliness which holds forth this "promise of life" and Paul makes clear that this means not only the present earthly life, but also the coming eternal life. The genitive designates the content of the promise. The thing promised is "life" (ζωῆς), a word which in the New Testament

---
[2] Moule, 30.
[3] BAGD, 180.

points to the supernatural life of God which believers enjoy now and will fully enter into in eternity (as 1 Tim. 4:8 makes explicit).[4] Paul makes this life specific by utilizing the definite article: a promise of *the* life that is in Christ Jesus. The preposition "according to" (κατ') points to the goal and purpose of his apostleship.[5] Paul was sent in order to make clear that in Christ we find the realization of eternal life. That the promised life is realized "in Christ Jesus" is a classically Pauline expression. The preposition "in" (ἐν) reveals that the source of such life is Christ Jesus and that such life only becomes actual experience in the sphere of a relationship with Him.[6] The expression "in Christ Jesus" occurs elsewhere in 2 Timothy (1:9, 13; 2:1, 10; 3:12, 15). So intimate is this connection that Paul can speak of "Christ, who is our life" (Col. 3:4). This mystical union of Christ and the believer is at one and the same time the great perplexity of the philosopher and the great delight of the child of God.

> **Ministry Maxim**
>
> God's promise of and ability to give me "life" is not hampered by the particulars of my current ministry assignment.

Paul awaits execution (4:6). It is the salvation of God (by which he is now "Paul," no longer Saul), the call of God ("an apostle"), and the will of God that have landed him in this dungeon with a death-sentence upon him. Nevertheless, while facing death, Paul is fixated—not upon his impending beheading, but upon the "promise of life in Christ Jesus"!

1:2 To Timothy, my beloved son: Grace, mercy and peace from God the Father and Christ Jesus our Lord.

Paul designates the recipient of the letter—"Timothy, my beloved son" (Τιμοθέῳ ἀγαπητῷ τέκνῳ). This differs from 1 Timothy where he is called "my true child in the faith." Such a designation speaks more to the character of Timothy's relationship to Paul. He was genuinely and truly Paul's son in the faith. This reference ("beloved") is more emotional, speaking of Paul's feelings toward Timothy. The former describes Timothy's standing before Paul; the latter his standing within Paul's heart (cf. 1 Cor. 4:17).

Just what created such bonds of love between these two? Timothy was not Paul's biological offspring. Timothy's Jewish mother and grandmother will be designated in v.5. His father was a Gentile (Acts 16:1). Paul found Timothy to be a disciple upon his return to Lystra (Acts 16:1-2). During Paul's first visit to Lystra he had been taken initially for a god after healing a lame man, and

---

[4] Knight, 364.
[5] Lea and Griffin, 180.
[6] Rienecker, 637.

then stoned nearly to death at the hands of the Jews (Acts 14:8-20). He spent only a short time there before moving on. We have no definite word of Timothy's conversion at that time. Perhaps he had been one listening at the fringes of the crowd as Paul preached. It is possible his heart was moved and then, when he saw Paul's resolve in the face of death (2 Tim. 3:11), he put his faith in Christ. Whenever the exact starting point and whatever the final encouragement to trust in Christ, he was no secret disciple upon Paul's return. He was known throughout his hometown (the same hometown where the Jews had stoned Paul to the point of death!) and the region as an effective disciple of Christ, advancing the cause of the Gospel for miles around (Acts 16:2). Paul wanted this young man to travel at his side in the cause of the Gospel, that he might further train and equip him for ministry (Acts 16:3). During the years and miles of travel and ministry together the bonds of love between the two grew. Paul became the spiritual father Timothy never had.

Out of the depths of his heart for Timothy Paul extends a threefold blessing. The trinity of blessings begins with "grace" (χάρις; cf. 1:3, 9; 2:1; 4:22). It points to the unmerited favor of God that is extended to sinners through Jesus Christ. It is both the initial grace by which one is saved from the penalty of sin and the ongoing daily grace for life and service above the power of sin. This "grace" forms an inclusion for this intimate letter (1:2; 4:22). The second of these extended blessings is "mercy." The word (ἔλεος; cf. 1:16, 18) is an emotional one, pointing to the compassion of God toward those who suffer, particularly because of sin. It is the LXX's translation of the Hebrew word *hesed,* which is the OT term to designate God's faithful, loyal covenant love. It points, therefore, both to the firm objective commitment of a covenant relationship and the subjective emotional response when one so loved is faced with adversity. Paul, no doubt, could sense Timothy's particular need (in his concern for his spiritual mentor and in his challenging ministry as pastor in Ephesus) for such faithful, compassionate love from God and extended it to him as one who had imbibed deeply of it himself. Similarly "peace" (εἰρήνη; cf. 2:22) is a reflection of Paul's Hebrew life, now fulfilled and reoriented by Christ. It is the NT equivalent of the Hebrew *shalom.* It points to the wholeness and completeness of life as it should be. Christ has brought us objective peace *with* God the Father (Rom. 5:1) and also brings to us the more subjective peace *of* God that results from such a standing (Phil. 4:7). In this trinity of blessings "grace" points to God's dealing with sin and guilt itself, "mercy" points to God's concern for the misery and pain that sin creates,[7] and

> **Ministry Maxim**
>
> No circumstance—no matter how difficult—can render me incapable of giving.

---

[7] Knight, 66.

"peace" points to the reordering of the chaos sin leaves behind.

This threefold blessing is found nowhere else in Paul's writing except 1 Timothy 1:1 (cf. 2 John 3). The more common combination is simply "grace" and "peace" (Rom. 1:7; 1 Cor. 1:3; 2 Cor. 1:2; Gal. 1:3; Eph. 1:2; Phil. 1:2; Col. 1:2; 1 Thess. 1:1; 2 Thess. 1:2; Titus 1:4; Philem. 3). The addition of "mercy" is reserved for Timothy. It proves to us that the relationship between Paul and Timothy was unique, and thus these two letters are unique among all others in the NT. It also proves that despite Paul's extreme hardship, nothing had really changed as he regarded his relationship to Timothy. It was still a relationship of giving. Paul's straits had not incapacitated him. When he could have been demanding, he was still giving. It was almost as if he were saying, "Here, Timothy, take some of this grace, mercy, and peace that God keeps giving me. It's too much. I've got more than I need. You have some. I know you are worried. I know you are concerned. You enjoy some of God's provision too." Such an attitude in the face of certain death is remarkable. Only one who has lived in God's "grace, mercy and peace" can be so willing a giver when under duress.

Indeed, these opening lines reveal a man of unearthly attitude. His present circumstances have not changed who he is (He is "Paul," no longer Saul), his calling ("apostle"), God's will ("by the will of God"), his hope ("according to the promise of life"), nor his focus ("Timothy," i.e., others). To have lived so consistently by God's "grace, mercy and peace" enabled Paul to realize that even the dire circumstances of his Roman imprisonment were not inconsistent with his calling, incidental to the plan of God, irredeemable as to the promises of God, nor incapacitating as to the ministry of God through his life.

Digging Deeper:

1. How does Paul's attitude in the face of such extreme adversity help me as I face my own current trials?
2. What do Paul's words tell me about what God will provide me as I trust Him in my most dire moments?
3. How can Paul's relationship to Timothy guide me in touching the lives of others around me today

---

1:3 I thank God, whom I serve with a clear conscience the way my forefathers did, as I constantly remember you in my prayers night and day,

As Paul is accustomed to doing, after his salutation he immediately moves into an expression of thanksgiving (every letter except Galatians, 1 Timothy, and Titus). This expression, however, is different. He normally uses the word εὐχαριστέω ("I thank"), while here he uses Χάριν ἔχω ("I have thanks"). It must be acknowledged, however, that he employs the same wording in 1 Timothy 1:12. The gratitude which Paul possesses is directed to God. Paul uses the definite article when he designates God (lit., "to the God"). The present tense verb points to this gratitude toward God as a continual possession.

Just what or who is Paul thankful for? Technically he does not say until the end of the sentence arrives in v.5: "the sincere faith within you." Between this statement of his gratitude and the identification of the object of his gratitude, Paul speaks concerning who this God is and the state of heart in which he serves Him. It is clear that the God he worships is the same God his "forefathers" (προγόνων) served. Paul did not view his faith in Christ as a change of deities, but as the fulfillment of all the promises and prophecies of the Hebrew Scriptures. The verb "I serve" (λατρεύω) is not the normal word for service. It points rather to performing religious service in acts of worship. The root is most frequent in Hebrews where it points to the service of worship under the old covenant (9:9; 10:2; 13:10) or to one's present service through Christ (9:14; 12:28), as well as to the true worship in heaven (8:5). As such, Paul again views this worship not as a new religion, but as the fulfillment of that faith inaugurated by his forefathers. The present tense of the verb shows that Paul views the whole of his life as a continual act of such worship. Even prison has not interrupted Paul's service to the Lord; for true service is not simply a matter of doing, but of being. Whatever God has us doing at the moment, we can do it as an act of worship from a pure heart. Paul makes this clear by saying that he renders such service "with a clear conscience" (ἐν καθαρᾷ συνειδήσει). The preposition (ἐν) points to the sphere in which such worship is rendered—in the arena of "a clear conscience."[8]

Just what does Paul mean by "a clear conscience"? It is a compound word (συνειδήσει), combining "with" (σύν) and "knowledge" (εἶδον)." This is a joint-knowledge, shared with oneself. It points to self-awareness. Thus Paul speaks of "the testimony of our conscience" (2 Cor. 1:12). It is a testimony given to oneself, and then passed on to others. He uses it in combination with "clear" (καθαρᾷ) also in 1 Timothy 3:9. He can speak of "a good conscience" (1 Tim. 1:5, 19), "a perfectly good conscience" (Acts 23:1), and "a blameless conscience" (Acts 24:16). The conscience is a gift from God, but is distorted through sin. It can be "weak" through immaturity (1 Cor. 8:7), wounded through wrong (1 Cor. 8:12), "defiled" by sin (Titus 1:15), and "seared" to the point of insensitivity by repeated rebellion (1 Tim. 4:2). It is "clear" when it is free from dirt, filth, and that which would befoul it. Paul was not sinless (1

---

[8] Rienecker, 637.

Tim. 1:13, 15). His conscience was "clear" because he had walked in humility, quickly confessing and turning from any sin that came to his attention. He refused to entertain sin knowingly. He had sought to live uprightly and in purity before all people. A "clear conscience" frees the way for peace to fill our hearts and confidence to empower our service. Yet Paul would also confess, "I do not even examine myself. For I am conscious of nothing against myself, yet I am not by this acquitted; but the one who examines me is the Lord" (1 Cor. 4:3b, 4). Our conscience is a helpful guide only as it is conformed to the written revelation of God (cf. 2 Tim. 3:16-17).

The phrase "the way my forefathers did" (ἀπὸ προγόνων) is literally "from forefathers." In fact the word order is "whom I serve from my forefathers in a clear conscience." Paul is not downplaying the radical change brought to his life when he met Christ Jesus (cf. Gal. 1:13-16). Rather he is saying that in meeting Jesus, far from abandoning the God of his fathers, he entered into the fulfillment of faith that Abraham, Moses, David and the other forefathers held. Perhaps the NIV captures the intent: "whom I serve, as my forefathers did." Paul saw himself standing in a long line of the faithful. He had not given up his Jewishness when he came to faith in Christ, but he had completed and fulfilled it. Opponents claimed the Hebrew Scriptures as their backing (1 Tim. 1:7; 2 Tim. 2:23-26; Titus 3:9), but Paul was saying that he stood in the fulfillment of all that those Scriptures pointed to.

> **Ministry Maxim**
>
> There is a direct correlation between the condition of my conscience and the health of my ministry.

Paul's gratitude comes to expression in his repeated times of prayer. Pharisees followed a regimented schedule of prayer. This would have been Paul's long habit. It was likely not abandoned when converted, but harnessed now for his growing communion with the Lord Jesus. The adjective "constantly" (ἀδιάλειπτον) does not point to unceasing activity, but to its repetition. It was used of repeatedly paying taxes, a bothersome cough, and the regular bearing of fruit.[9] Thus the reference is to Paul's regular, habitual practice of calling out to God in prayer. At such times Paul said, "I . . . remember you." More literally it is "I have the concerning you remembrance" (ἔχω τὴν περὶ σοῦ μνείαν). This begins a series of statements about memory ("recall," v.4; "mindful," v.5; "remind," v.6). Reminiscence is not unexpected as one nears the end of life. This highlights the pathos and rich personal nature of Paul's present letter. The word used here (μνείαν) points to the mental act of consciously calling something to mind. It was Paul's practice to bring Timothy to mind every time he went before

---

[9] Rienecker, 637.

God in prayer. This was common practice for Paul with the many he had ministered to or knew of (Rom. 1:9; Eph. 1:16; Phil. 1:3; 1 Thess. 1:2; Philem. 4). The word "prayers" (δεήσεσίν) points to the expressing of a need.[10] Amazing! Paul, facing his own death, has made it his regular habit to take up Timothy's needs and take them to the Father! Such was his practice "night and day" (νυκτὸς καὶ ἡμέρας). The genitive form denotes time, "by night and by day." The normal Hebrew calculation saw the day begin at sunset. Paul apparently had set times of prayer which he consecrated to God. Paul never failed in these times to call Timothy and his needs to mind and then deliver them up to God in prayer.

1:4 longing to see you, even as I recall your tears, so that I may be filled with joy.

In the Greek text, the sentence begun in verse 3 runs on through verse five. The "longing" (ἐπιποθῶν) is expressed through a present participle. The present tense indicates the ongoing and continuous nature of Paul's yearning for Timothy. The participial form points to attendant circumstances—Paul's prayers are accompanied by an intense inner longing for Timothy.[11] The word is a strong one, describing an intense longing after something (2 Cor. 5:2) or someone (Rom. 1:11; 2 Cor. 9:14; Phil. 1:8; 2:26; 1 Thess. 3:6). The preposition (ἐπι) in the compound word gives direction to the yearning.[12] Paul then employs an infinitive (ἰδεῖν), with the aorist tense pointing to a yearning for a meeting at a point in time with his beloved protégé. The infinitive points out what it is Paul longed for—"to see you."

This longing is fed by a recollection of their tearful parting at some point in the past. The perfect passive participle ("I recall") points to a continuing state of recollection. The memories began to flood Paul's mind at some point in the past and have continued to do so right up to the moment of writing. The passive voice indicates that these memories are not from mental effort, but are pressed upon Paul's heart by another. What was the active cause of these recurring memories? God? Paul's circumstances? His deep loneliness? This participle provides the next link in the theme of memory ("remember," v.3; "mindful," v.5; "remind," v.6).

What Paul recalled were Timothy's "tears" (τῶν δακρύων). We are not able to place precisely the time or circumstances of such a tearful parting. Timothy's tears were previously illustrated in the response of the elders of the Ephesian church in Acts 20:37, but the most recent parting we are aware of between the Apostle and him is in 1 Timothy 1:3. These tears may have been

---

[10] Mounce, 469.
[11] Marshall, 692.
[12] Rienecker, 637.

shed by Timothy at that time or at some subsequent parting that may have occurred. Paul had taught Timothy and the elders at Ephesus to minister through tears (Acts 20:19, 31).

The purpose ("so that," ἵνα) of Paul's longing is that he "may be filled with joy" (χαρᾶς πληρωθῶ). Paul, the unselfish servant, is also in touch with his own needs and is not afraid to express them. The aorist tense points to an anticipated meeting when, in a moment of time, Paul's sorrowful heart will experience a flood of joy. The passive voice reveals that Paul views such a surge of joy as an involuntary and spontaneous response of his heart to Timothy's arrival. Such joy would be a gift from God Himself (Rom. 15:13).[13] The subjunctive mood shows that the experience would depend upon Paul's prayers being answered and Timothy actually arriving on the scene in Rome. This is the only mention of joy in the PE, underscoring that ministry is difficult business and often fraught with more tears than cheers. Paul would soon make clear just how deep his loneliness ran (2 Tim. 1:15; 4:16) and how bitter the pain of betrayal (4:10a) and persecution (4:14) had been. Little wonder he would plead, "Make every effort to come to me soon" (4:9) and "Make every effort to come before winter" (4:21)! These earnest longings for fellowship with Timothy form another inclusion for the letter.

> **Ministry Maxim**
>
> Ministry requires me to endure and to embrace the emotional demands of both tears and joy.

Digging Deeper:

1. Of the different kinds of conscience (see comments under v.3), which is my conscience most like? Why?
2. What steps can I take to train my conscience to be an accurate and reliable guide?
3. How does the pattern and regularity of Paul's praying challenge me regarding my communion with the Lord?
4. How can praying for the needs of others during our own time of crisis help us with our own needs?
5. What relationship(s) in your life has as much emotion behind it as that of Paul and Timothy? How has that affected your prayer ministry for that person?

---

[13] Knight, 368.

1:5 For I am mindful of the sincere faith within you, which first dwelt in your grandmother Lois and your mother Eunice, and I am sure that it is in you as well.

Here, at the end of the sentence that began in v.3, Paul identifies the object of his thanksgiving. "I am mindful" (ὑπόμνησιν λαβών) is more literally, "I have received a remembrance." The aorist tense of the verb indicates a point in time when Timothy's sincere faith came to Paul's mind. Perhaps some specific event sparked this memory in Paul, though it is left unstated, if it did.[14] The participial form functions in a causal sense, thus the "For" that heads the verse in English. The noun translated "mindful" (ὑπόμνησιν) is used only here and 2 Peter (1:13; 3:1). It can be used in an active sense of the act of remembering, but also, as here, in a passive sense to refer to the receiving of such a remembrance.[15]

That which is remembered is Timothy's "sincere faith" (τῆς ἐν σοὶ ἀνυποκρίτου πίστεως). The order of the phrase is more literally "the in you sincere faith." The preposition, personal pronoun, and adjective are sandwiched between the definite article and its noun. This word order emphasizes the qualitative nature of Timothy's faith as "sincere" (ἀνυποκρίτου) This adjective refers to that which is without hypocrisy. What it designates is thus genuine, authentic, and without pretense. Such faith is never simply on display. It functions from internal—not external—motivations. Such a faith had been Paul's goal in all his teaching and throughout his ministry (1 Tim. 1:5). Perhaps, here at the end of his life and amid so much unfaithfulness (2 Tim. 2:18; 3:8), Paul took special comfort in the fact that his ministry had produced at least one such faithful individual (3:10). Timothy's faith stood in stark contrast to that of the greater portion of Christians in Asia Minor (2 Tim. 1:15), others generally (4:16), and Hymenaeus, Philetus (2:17) and Demas in particular (4:10).

This sincere faith of Timothy "first dwelt" in his mother and grandmother. Elsewhere Paul speaks of the Holy Spirit (Rom. 8:11; 2 Tim. 1:14), God (2 Cor. 6:16), the word of Christ (Col. 3:16), and sin (Rom. 7:17) as dwelling in us. Nowhere else, however, is faith described as dwelling in us. The picture of our lives as a dwelling where faith comes to make itself at home is descriptive of the nature of belief in Christ. The word (ἐνῴκησεν) is a compound meaning "in" (ἐν) and "dwell" (οἰκέω). This dwelling took place "first" (πρῶτον) in Timothy's mother and grandmother. This adjective serves in an adverbial way here.[16] It points to the priority of one thing over others, whether by virtue of time, space, or sequence.

In what sense, then, was the faith of Lois and Eunice prior to Timothy's?

---
[14] Earle, 11:394.
[15] Marshall, 693.
[16] Knight, 369.

When Paul came to Lystra he found both Timothy and his mother to be disciples of Christ, with no indication as to which one may have come to faith in Christ first (Acts 16:1). Had they become followers of Christ during one of Paul's earlier brief visits to their city (Acts 14:6-23)? It would appear that, if they had, Paul was not aware of it until his return (Acts 16:1). Is this, then, a reference to their Jewish faith or to their Christian faith?

Paul saw his Christian faith as an extension and fulfillment of his Jewish faith (Acts 24:14). At the head of this sentence he stated that he served God "with a clear conscience the way [his] forefathers did" (v.3). Paul will tell Timothy "that from childhood you have known the sacred writings which are able to give you the wisdom that leads to salvation through faith which is in Christ Jesus" (3:15). Clearly Timothy was not a Christian believer from childhood, else the record of Acts is called into question. It seems probable that Paul was stressing the devout nature of Lois and Eunice and that from his earliest days they had endeavored to inculcate into Timothy the true faith of Israel, which is now fulfilled in Jesus. However, it is worth noting that Eunice's marriage to a Gentile (Acts 16:1) would seem to indicate that she, at least at that time, was not practicing an orthodox Jewish faith.[17] In this Paul was encouraging Timothy that like himself (1:3); he too must be faithful to that which was now the fulfillment of his ancestral faith.

Paul was convinced that this faith, whatever its exact point of origin, dwelt in Timothy too: "and I am sure that it is in you as well" (πέπεισμαι δὲ ὅτι καὶ ἐν σοί). The conjunction δὲ has no adversative force here.[18] The verb (πέπεισμαι) is used again in v.12 (its only other use in the PE) and points toward trust, reliance, conviction, confidence, and assurance. The perfect tense indicates the thorough and complete nature of Paul's assurance regarding the reality of Timothy's faith. The verb's passive voice shows Paul as having been overcome by the many proofs of Timothy's faith. The miles and ministry shared together brought proof upon proof of his young protégé's genuine reliance upon Christ. In Paul the conjunction ὅτι frequently follows this verb, as here, and points to "that" which is the object of such conviction (Rom. 8:38; 14:14; 15:14; 2 Tim. 1:12).

This final clause is literally, "and I have been convinced that [it dwells] also in you." A verb is assumed, and it seems reasonable to understand it to be "dwells" (ἐνῴκησεν) from the earlier clause.[19]

> **Ministry Maxim**
>
> Beyond mere professionalism, the demands of ministry require the authenticity, reality, and believability of my personal faith.

---

[17] Guthrie, 124-125.
[18] Mounce, 472.
[19] Knight, 369.

O that our faith might be so *authentic* ("the sincere faith") and *personal* ("within you") that it might be *utterly convincing* to all who encounter us ("I am sure that *it is* in you as well")!

> **Digging Deeper:**
> 1. What outward evidences mark a person's faith as truly "sincere"?
> 2. Do we need to attempt consciously to produce these evidences? Or would the conscious effort somehow taint the sincerity of them?
> 3. What encouragements does the example of Lois and Eunice give to mothers and grandmothers today (cf. 3:14-15)? Particularly single mothers, as Eunice probably was?

1:6 For this reason I remind you to kindle afresh the gift of God which is in you through the laying on of my hands.

"For this reason" (δι' ἣν αἰτίαν) is a strong causal statement (cf. its use in 1:12; Titus 1:13). It is probably to be linked to "the sincere faith within you" in v.5 (also a feminine singular), though some connect it more generally to the whole of Paul's thanksgiving (vv.3-5). Because of the genuineness of Timothy's faith (v.5) he brings this additional reminder. Only an authentic faith will endure such paternal reminding. An unauthentic faith might take offense at such an intrusion. The verb "I remind" (ἀναμιμνῄσκω) is the fourth such word along this theme (cf. "remember," v.3; "recall," v.4; "mindful," v.5), all from the same root. This same compound word is used to describe how Timothy had once been the personal embodiment of reminder to the Corinthian believers (1 Cor. 4:17) and how Titus, in turn, had been reminded fondly of their obedience (2 Cor. 7:15). The preposition in compound (ἀνά) may serve to emphasize the causative nature of the action.[20] Here the verb is a present tense, probably as a simple statement of Paul's present intention.

The reminder was designed to move Timothy to action (ἀναζωπυρεῖν, "to kindle afresh"). This represents a compound word meaning "again" or "up" (ἀνά) and "kindle a fire" (ζωπυρεῖν). The exact force of the preposition in compound is debated, some minimizing it and others emphasizing it. The word occurs only here in the NT. In the ancient world a fire was in need of regular stoking, lest it burn down. Paul's encouragement to Timothy should not be read as a sign that his faith was slipping, but as a call to the attention we all must give to our spiritual state (cf. a similar metaphor in 1 Thess. 5:19).

---
[20] Rienecker, 638.

Marshall is right, "the gift of the Spirit is clearly to be understood as something dynamic and not static."[21] It is purely a gift, but a gift to which we must respond and a relationship which we must cultivate. It is this continuous (present tense) spiritual cultivation, common to all believers, that Paul calls Timothy to now. This is a healthy reminder that even those in spiritual leadership, as Timothy was, are not exempt from the waning of spiritual health and intensity that comes from inattention and distraction. If anything, those in spiritual leadership are to be the more zealous and careful because the state of their spiritual health doubly affects those they lead.

The object of such intense and constant personal attention is "the gift of God" (τὸ χάρισμα τοῦ θεοῦ). What is the exact identification of this "gift of God"? Does it refer to salvation, a spiritual gift, the Holy Spirit Himself, the Gospel or something else entirely? The word "gift" (τὸ χάρισμα) can be used to refer to eternal life (Rom. 6:23), generally to other spiritual endowments from God (e.g., 2 Cor. 1:11), and even God's dealings with Israel (Rom. 11:29). For Luke "the promise of My Father" (Luke 24:49), spoken of by the soon-to-be-ascended Jesus, became more specifically "the gift of the Holy Spirit" on the day of Pentecost (Acts 2:38). It seems likely that the gift to which Paul refers here is to be identified as the Holy Spirit Himself. The contextual connection of "gift" and the Spirit here (cf. vv.7, 14) and elsewhere (1 Cor. 1:7; 12:4, 31; Rom. 1:11) seem to confirm this. The Spirit is the gift. We often speak of a spiritual gift as the ability to "do" something, treating it almost as an objective thing we possess. It seems more in keeping with the teaching of Scripture to see the Spirit as the gift and the newly imparted ability as simply the way the Holy Spirit expresses Himself through the individual. A spiritual gift is simply the Holy Spirit being Himself uniquely through an individual believer. All believers receive the Holy Spirit (Rom. 8:9; Titus 3:5), though the Holy Spirit sovereignly chooses the manner in which He works through the individual.

> **Ministry Maxim**
>
> I must constantly cultivate my relationship with the Holy Spirit, for ministry cannot be accomplished apart from Him.

Some may object that the Holy Spirit cannot be kindled like a fire, that as God He cannot be affected by human action. God the Spirit is sovereign. "The wind blows where it wishes and you hear the sound of it, but do not know where it comes from and where it is going; so is everyone who is born of the Spirit" (John 3:8). He does as He pleases and no man can stay His hand. Yet the Holy Spirit is a Person. He is relational and has condescended to associate with us on a relational basis. As we respond to Him, He reciprocates with us. "Draw near to

---

[21] Marshall, 696.

God and He will draw near to you" (James 4:8a). He places the responsibility of moral choice upon us and expects us to use that capacity to cultivate a warm, intimate relationship of love and obedience with him.

This gift, Paul says to Timothy, "is in you" (ὅ ἐστιν ἐν σοί). The arena of operation for the Holy Spirit's work was "in" (ἐν) Timothy. We often speak of "having" a spiritual gift, as if it is our possession. Here, however, it is almost pictured as the gift "having" Timothy—a particularly apt designation since the gift is ultimately the Holy Spirit. The inward life must always be the object of our most careful attention. The Christian life and ministry are not about presentation or show, but about substance.

The means by which this gift was bestowed was "through the laying on of my hands" (διὰ τῆς ἐπιθέσεως τῶν χειρῶν μου). In an important earlier passage Paul warned Timothy, "Do not neglect the spiritual gift within you, which was bestowed on you through prophetic utterance with the laying on of hands by the presbytery" (1 Tim. 4:14). We note that, in this laying on of hands, Paul was apparently a part of a larger body of believers. Perhaps he refers only to himself here because of the personal nature of 2 Timothy. We also discover that the laying on of hands was accompanied by a "prophetic utterance" (cf. 1 Tim. 1:18; 4:14). Apparently there had been a clear message from the Holy Spirit to those laying their hands upon Timothy to separate him to ministry. That message indicated the nature of the way He would operate ("gift") through him in ministry. Paul's own call to missionary ministry provides a helpful parallel (Acts 13:1-3).

During the transitional days of the church's early preaching, Luke pictures the bestowment of the Holy Spirit as coming upon new converts through the laying on of hands (Acts 8:17-18; 19:6). Yet we know that every believer is indwelt by the Holy Spirit (Rom. 8:9; 1 Cor. 12:13). So in what sense did Paul impart the Holy Spirit and His gifting to Timothy through the laying on of hands? When Timothy put his faith in Christ, the Holy Spirit indwelt him, as He does all believers. But as the Holy Spirit shaped Timothy's life it became clear that He was calling him into ministry. As the larger body of God's people recognized this calling, it was affirmed through the laying on of their leader's hands. As they did so, God the Holy Spirit revealed through that body the way He would work through Timothy in ministry.

Digging Deeper:
1. Am I open to "the ministry of reminder" from other believers?
2. What is there in me that resists such reminders?
3. What is the condition of the fire of God's Spirit in my heart?
4. What practical steps can I take to "kindle afresh" that relationship?

1:7 For God has not given us a spirit of timidity, but of power and love and discipline.

"For" (γὰρ) is causal and gives the reason Timothy should "kindle afresh the gift of God which is in" him (v.6). The very nature of the Holy Spirit—the gift itself—is reason enough. Paul begins with the negative and moves to the thrice-stated positive. By speaking of "a spirit" does Paul intend us to understand a reference to the Holy Spirit, our own spirit, or some quality of our inner life? The noun is anartharous, leading some to translate "a spirit" (i.e., not the Holy Spirit). This is, however, not demanded by the absence of the definite article. Many English translations opt for a lower case "s" (e.g., KJV, RSV, NIV, NASB). It seems best to view this as a reference to the quality of life produced either by the neglect of ("a spirit of timidity")—or the influence of ("power and love and discipline")—the Holy Spirit in a believer's life. The connection of "gift" (χάρισμα, v.6) and "spirit" (πνεῦμα, v.7) almost universally point to the Holy Spirit (cf. 1 Tim. 4:14). In this regard the conjunction that heads this verse (γὰρ) is a powerful link between the two verses. Paul's use here of a "not . . . but" argumentation is a common one for him. When he employs this line of reasoning he often does so to contrast that which is not of the Holy Spirit ("of slavery," "of the world," "of timidity") with that which is (cf. Rom. 8:15; 1 Cor. 2:12).[22] Additionally, the fact that Paul will draw this extended line of reasoning to a close by an explicit reference to the Holy Spirit (v.14) makes it likely that He is beginning on the same note. So, should "spirit" be spelled with a lower or upper case "s"? Probably the lowercase is correct, but with the understanding that "power and love and discipline" are only produced by the presence of the Spirit (v.6).

This "spirit" was, in Paul's understanding, "given." The aorist tense points to a definite time—potentially either Timothy's conversion or his consecration to ministry. The former is supported by the fact that all believers receive the same Spirit at conversion (Rom. 8:9), the latter by this passage's close connection to 1 Timothy 4:14 and its description of Timothy's consecration to ministry. Paul told Timothy this spirit was given to "us." Does this refer only to Paul and Timothy (and perhaps others like them in ministry), or does it refer to all believers? Paul was writing a personal letter, so his immediate reference was to Timothy and himself. He probably, however, designates themselves ("us") not as clergy, but as believers in Christ Jesus.

Life under the control of the Spirit is not characterized by "timidity" (δειλίας). The word is a strong one, used only here in the NT, and never in a good sense. The rendering "timidity" is considered to be too weak. It points to cowardice and the abandonment of responsibilities due to fear. Does this mean

---

[22] Fee, 226-227.

Timothy was a naturally fearful individual? Perhaps he was, but his reputation as such has been overstated. This word speaks to more than timidity, but to the terrorizing fear that causes one to turn tail and run when faced with a battle. Ephesus was home to many enemies of the Gospel. Paul had nearly lost his life there (Acts 19:23-41; 1 Cor. 15:32). False teachers, pagan unbelievers, and disgruntled Christians all served to make Timothy's pastoral ministry a beachhead against the works of the evil one (2 Tim. 2:26). Paul was not accusing Timothy of such cowardice, but was fortifying him against its very real possibility.

This is not at all the Spirit's way of working in the believer. The contrast is a significant one, marked by the strong adversative (ἀλλὰ). Paul identifies three ways the Spirit manifests Himself in the willing believer. The first is "power" (δυνάμεως). The word points to the ability to do (live godly, 3:5) or endure (suffer hardship, v.8). The second is "love" (ἀγάπης). This is the first fruit of the Spirit (Gal. 5:22). It is the way in which we must guard the truth (1:13). It is that which we must pursue (2:22). It is something we may observe in others and then imitate (3:10). The third is "discipline" (σωφρονισμοῦ). This is the only occurrence of the word in the NT (though see its cognates in Rom. 12:13; 1 Tim. 2:9, 15; 3:2; Titus 1:8). It is variously translated as "discipline" (NASB), "self-discipline" (NIV, NRSV), "self-control" (ESV), and "a sound mind" (NKJV). It literally means "making understanding or wise" and thus also "admonition." By extension it then describes the resulting state of discretion, moderation, and discipline.[23]

> **Ministry Maxim**
>
> The fearful impulse to quit is never from God.

The believer, then, rather than giving way to fear, is to be animated ("power"), motivated ("love"), and dictated by the Spirit ("discipline") in all thoughts, words, and actions. In this way Paul believes Timothy will be equal to any pressure brought upon him.

Digging Deeper:

1. In what way are you tempted to abandon your responsibilities and take an easier course? What/who is the motivating power behind such a drive?
2. What do you need the Holy Spirit to enable you to do or endure? Have you asked Him for such power?
3. In what relationship do you most need the Holy Spirit to love another person through you?
4. If the Holy Spirit was allowed to manifest "discipline" in your life, what would that look like on a daily basis?

---

[23] Kittel, abridged, 1152.

1:8 Therefore do not be ashamed of the testimony of our Lord or of me His prisoner, but join with me in suffering for the gospel according to the power of God,

"Therefore" (οὖν) links logically back to verse seven (and generally to all of vv.3-7) and the description of how the Holy Spirit manifests Himself in the believer's life through "power and love and discipline." If it is true that the believer has inherited such a "spirit," then he should "not be ashamed" (μὴ οὖν ἐπαισχυνθῇς). The negative particle (μὴ) with the aorist tense verb points to the prohibition of an action contemplated, but not necessarily yet begun.[24] The verbal form may be either the subjunctive or imperative mood. The imperatival form would hold it in parallel with the aorist imperative ("join with me in suffering") coming later in the sentence,[25] though even if a subjunctive[26] it would have imperatival force.

The same verb occurs in v.12 to describe Paul's lack of shame in obediently trusting Christ and in v.16 to hold forth Onesiphorus as one who was not ashamed of Paul. The Apostle employs it also in Romans 1:16 where he makes his famous declaration: "For I am not ashamed of the gospel, for it is the power of God for salvation to everyone who believes, to the Jew first and also to the Greek." Perhaps this statement rang in the Apostle's ears even as he wrote to Timothy. There also may be a link to the daunting warning of Jesus when He used the same root twice, "For whoever is ashamed of Me and My words, the Son of Man will be ashamed of him when He comes in His glory, and the glory of the Father and of the holy angels" (Luke 9:26). The word can point to either justified shame/guilt over sin (Rom. 6:21) or unjustified embarrassment over something like the Gospel (Rom. 1:16). Here the latter is in view.

> **Ministry Maxim**
>
> Bind a man with cords of love and he will never again be free to do his own will.

Paul enumerated two things Timothy was not to be ashamed of. The first is "the testimony of our Lord" (τὸ μαρτύριον τοῦ κυρίου ἡμῶν). This could be a subjective genitive (i.e., "the testimony our Lord gave"), but the context makes clear this is an objective genitive (i.e., "the testimony about our Lord"). After the fuller "Christ Jesus our Lord" (v.2), the designation "our Lord" is clearly a reference to Jesus, not God the Father. The word "testimony" (μαρτύριον) is one from which we get our word martyr; however, here it points not so much to death for Christ, but to the preaching of the Gospel concerning Christ (cf. 1 Tim. 2:6). In the first century there was, from the perspective of

---

[24] Rienecker, 638.
[25] Fee, 227; Marshall, 702.
[26] Knight, 372; Rienecker, 638.

the unbelieving, plenty for one to be "ashamed" of regarding the Gospel of Christ. The notion that God became man, was offered as a substitutionary sacrifice for the sins of the world upon the cross, risen from the dead and ascended to heaven was foolishness to the Greek mind (Acts 17:18, 32;1 Cor. 1:18-25). Yet it is in this apparent foolishness and weakness that God delights to demonstrate His wisdom and power (1 Cor. 1:26-31).

The second object of which Timothy was not to be ashamed is "of me His prisoner" (ἐμὲ τὸν δέσμιον αὐτοῦ). By this does Paul mean "me, a prisoner for Jesus' sake" or "me, one taken captive by Jesus Christ"? The former was true (2 Tim. 1:16; 2:9), but the reference here is to the latter.[27] Paul explicitly says that he is "His" (αὐτοῦ) prisoner, the pronoun pointing to its antecedent "the Lord" (τοῦ κυρίου).[28] Paul's heart had been taken captive by Christ the Lord, so much so that no matter what obedience brought his way—even imprisonment—he was first and foremost a captive of Christ (cf. Eph. 3:1; 4:1; Philem. 1, 9). Bonds of love always hold more firmly than shackles of iron. Such a perspective on Christ's Lordship not only sustained Paul in prison, but it would have heartened Timothy in his troubles as well.

Using a strong adversative (ἀλλὰ), Paul called Timothy to another path. The Apostle commanded him to "join with me in suffering for the gospel." The entire phrase "join with me in suffering" is a translation of but one Greek word (συγκακοπάθησον). It is a compound word composed of three parts: suffer (πάσχειν), evil (κακὸς), and with (σὺν).[29] It means either "suffer together with" or "take your share in suffering."[30] The aorist imperative form demands that action be taken at once. Paul uses the same verb and form again in 2:3 when he commands Timothy, "Suffer hardship with me, as a good soldier of Christ Jesus."

> **Ministry Maxim**
>
> My ability to endure is never measured by my self-resolve, but by the Spirit of God dwelling in me.

Who is Timothy being called to suffer with here? The translators of the NASU added "me," though it is not in the Greek text. Given the personal nature of the letter, Paul's history of suffering for the Gospel, his present imprisonment and impending execution, and Paul's repeated exhortations to Timothy throughout the letter to carry on the ministry of the Gospel, it seems likely that this is the correct assumption.

This urgent suffering is "for the gospel" (τῷ εὐαγγελίῳ). This is a dative of advantage (i.e., "for the sake of the gospel"). This implies that Timothy

---

[27] Litfin, 2:750; Knight, 373; Lea and Griffin, 190.
[28] Knight, 373.
[29] Marshall, 480.
[30] Rienecker, 638.

would suffer both for his identification with the Gospel as a believer and for his proclamation of that Gospel as a minister. In Paul's correspondence with Timothy the "gospel" is also mentioned by name in 1 Timothy 1:11 and 2 Timothy 1:10 and 2:8.

The theme of suffering begins here and becomes a thread woven throughout the letter (e.g., 1:12; 2:3, 9, 10; 3:10-12; 4:5).

Timothy was not left to his own devices to cope with the pressures of the Gospel ministry. Rather, Paul called him to suffer "according to the power of God" (κατὰ δύναμιν θεοῦ). Paul has just referred to the power the Spirit manifests in the believer's life (vv.6-7), and he calls upon Timothy to bear up in proportion to the God whose Spirit dwells within him. The measure of our endurance is never our self-resolve, but the Spirit of God dwelling in us.

Certainly Paul's words would have come to Timothy's mind during his own later imprisonment (Heb. 13:23). Paul's words here were not wasted, for Timothy later proved true despite the ignominy of incarceration for Christ.

1:9 who has saved us and called us with a holy calling, not according to our works, but according to His own purpose and grace which was granted us in Christ Jesus from all eternity,

The sentence begun in v.8 continues on now through v.11; the exhortation of v.8 is now braced with theological support. Paul employs two aorist participles in a substantive way. The word "who" represents the translation of this first participle (i.e., "the one who has saved us") and points back to the powerful "God" in v. 8. This God has done two things for both Paul and Timothy. The first is that He "has saved us" (τοῦ σώσαντος ἡμᾶς). Paul uses the verb (σῴζω) often to describe the redemptive activity of God. Given Paul's current circumstances and impending death, it seems an interesting choice of words here. Yet Paul will employ it again at the end of the letter to speak of how God was ready to save him into His heavenly kingdom (4:18), even if through death. The second participle reminds us that God has "called us" (καλέσαντος). Since this calling was common to both Paul and Timothy, it would appear Paul was referring to the call to faith in Christ which God issues to every believer, rather than his own unique calling as an apostle (cf. only other use of the verb in the PE in 1 Tim. 6:12). This broadens the application and calls us all to listen more carefully. Both of these participles are in the aorist tense and point to action which had already taken place in the lives of Paul and Timothy. The Apostle enlarges on the second participle by adding a cognate noun and a dative adjective, God has called us "with a holy calling" (κλήσει ἁγίᾳ). There is debate as to whether this should be understood as a dative of means ("with a holy calling," as here) or as a dative of instrument ("to a holy life," NIV). Both are true. "A holy God issues a holy call for believers to live a holy life."[31]

This salvation and calling are "not according to our works" (οὐ κατὰ τὰ ἔργα ἡμῶν). The preposition "according to" (κατὰ) is used first in a negative clause here and then, separated by a strong adversative (ἀλλὰ), in a positive statement concerning the basis upon which this salvation and calling do come to us as believers. In both cases the preposition is followed by an accusative noun which yields the meaning "according to."

That salvation and calling are "not according to our works" is a classically Pauline statement (cf. Gal. 2:16; Eph. 2:9; Titus 3:5). Paul uses the word "works" (ἔργον) with a broad spectrum of meaning. On the one hand, he employs it to describe human works as an inadequate basis for salvation (Eph. 2:9); and on the other hand, as the holy product of a life so saved (Eph. 2:10). That same breadth of meaning finds expression here in 2 Timothy as well, both in the negative (1:9) and in the positive (2:21; 3:17).

In contrast (ἀλλὰ) and positively stated, our salvation and calling are "according to His own purpose and grace" (κατὰ ἰδίαν πρόθεσιν καὶ χάριν). The word "purpose" (πρόθεσιν) is a compound word meaning to set before or to set forth. It describes a premeditated plan.[32] This sense of pre-planning for our salvation and calling is made emphatic by the words "from all eternity" (πρὸ χρόνων αἰωνίων). Paul uses this word ("purpose," πρόθεσιν) to describe the redemptive purpose of God that has been in place from before time (Eph. 1:11; 3:11). He works this plan out in the lives of individual people, calling some into a saving relationship (Rom. 9:11) and this always apart from their "own works." This purpose governs all things (Eph. 1:11), including the lives of God's people and is our ground of assurance amid life's confusion (Rom. 8:28). Only once does Paul employ the word to describe something other than God's own purpose (2 Tim. 3:10). That this was God's own independent, sovereign, decision, uninfluenced by "our works," is made clear through the adjective "His own" (ἰδίαν). It stands in marked contrast to "our [ἡμῶν] works."[33]

> **Ministry Maxim**
>
> My first calling is to my relationship with Christ. If I fail in this calling I can never succeed in my ministry calling.

This eternal purpose is coupled here with "grace" (χάριν). That God would choose before our existence—and thus before our ability to do anything

---

[31] Mounce, 483; cf. Knight, 374.
[32] Kittel, abridged, 1180.
[33] Mounce, 483.

to influence His decision—to act redemptively in our lives (Rom. 9:11) is by definition an act of "grace." Paul opened (1:2) and closed (4:22) this letter by holding forth God's grace to Timothy. In Paul's mind this "grace" is always a thing given ("granted," τὴν δοθεῖσαν). The aorist passive verb looks to a point in the past (aorist tense) when God chose to set His grace upon us (passive voice). Paul has already used the same word to speak of what God has and has not given us in the gift of the Spirit (v.7). Elsewhere in this letter Paul speaks of God giving mercy (1:16, 18), understanding (2:7), and repentance (2:25). This purpose and grace, along with its attendant blessings like mercy, understanding and repentance, are extended to us "in Christ Jesus" (ἐν Χριστῷ Ἰησοῦ). This exact phrase shows up forty-six times in Paul's letters. Paul uses the same idea many more times through similar phrases such as "in Christ" and "in the beloved." The expression describes faith as a transference of a person's entire being into the realm of relationship to Christ. In that sphere of existence God's saving purpose and grace are realized and made actual in our experience.

Of equal significance to Paul is the timing of God's determination to extend this purpose and grace to us—"from all eternity." The expression (πρὸ χρόνων αἰωνίων) is most literally "before times eternal." The same wording is used in Titus 1:2. The intent is to point to a decision made prior to the creation of the world and implies the pre-existence of Christ (cf. Eph. 1:4; 3:11; Rev. 13:8; 17:8). Out of eternity—before we were or anything else was—God in His grace determined to save us by His grace through the sacrifice of Jesus Christ. Let all creation stand in awe of such love!

Digging Deeper:

1. Why might a person be tempted to be "ashamed of the gospel" today? How does that compare with why first-century Christians might have been so tempted?
2. How can we suffer "according to the power of God"? Doesn't suffering imply a loss of power? How would suffering "according to the power of God" look differently than some other way of suffering?
3. How does clarity about the calling of God on our lives help us in suffering for the Gospel? How does ambiguity in this area make us vulnerable in suffering?
4. What difference does it make that God's purpose and grace were set on you "from all eternity"?

1:10 but now has been revealed by the appearing of our Savior Christ Jesus, who abolished death and brought life and immortality to light through the gospel,

God's purpose and grace were extended to us from eternity past (v.9), "but" (δέ) Paul says that what had been reality from eternity "has been revealed" (φανερωθεῖσαν) to us in time and space. The temporal adverb "now" (νῦν) stands in direct contrast to "from all eternity" (πρὸ χρόνων αἰωνίων) in v.9. The verb is aorist in tense, pointing to the historical reality in past time of this revelation. This points to the incarnation of Jesus Christ, His life as a whole, and especially to His death and resurrection as a revelation of God's purpose and grace. The passive voice indicates that it was God the Father making a revelation of His grace through Christ as He obeyed His Father's will. The participle functions in parallel with "was granted" (v.9), both of them modifying "purpose and grace."

This revelation took place "by the appearing of our Savior Christ Jesus" (διὰ τῆς ἐπιφανείας τοῦ σωτῆρος ἡμῶν Χριστοῦ Ἰησου). The preposition (διὰ) with the genitive points to the means of the revelation. The word "appearing" (ἐπιφανείας) is used only by Paul in the NT and on all other occasions he uses it exclusively of Christ's second coming (2 Thess. 2:8; 1 Tim. 6:14; 2 Tim. 4:1, 8; Titus 2:13). The word was one familiar to Greeks, as they employed it to describe the glorious appearing of their pagan gods.[34] Writing to Timothy in Ephesus, a hotbed of pagan worship, Paul no doubt took up the word in a polemic against the false gods of the Greeks and against the tendency toward Emperor worship. There is here an emphasis on the pre-existence of Christ.[35] This and naming Jesus as "Savior" in such close proximity to God the Father "who has saved us" (v.9) underscores the divinity of Jesus and the intimacy of Father and Son in the purposes of God. Paul is comfortable referring to both God the Father (1 Tim. 1:1; 2:3; 4:10) and Jesus Christ (Eph. 5:23; Phil. 3:20; Titus 1:4; 2:13; 3:6) as Savior.

During His appearance upon earth, Christ is said to have accomplished two things. These are put before us by two aorist participles set apart by the μέν ... δέ construction ("on the one hand . . . on the other hand"). The two participles describe for us the effect of Christ's redemptive work. First, stated negatively, Christ "abolished death" (καταργήσαντος μὲν τὸν θάνατον). The verb describes not the obliteration of something, but the breaking of its power.[36] It refers to the annulling of power, the rendering of something inoperative. Thus as Paul speaks

---
[34] DNTT, 3:317.
[35] Mounce, 484.
[36] Rienecker, 638.

of death being "abolished," he means not that it is non-existent any longer, but that its power has been broken. Death is now powerless to do what it once did.

The question arises as to just what Paul means here by "death." Does he refer to physical death, to spiritual death, or to both? Paul views death's defeat as an accomplished fact (aorist tense). Death is the great terror of humanity. The devil is said to have "had the power of death," but Christ died and rose to "render powerless" (same verb as here) the evil one (Heb. 2:14). The evil one does not cease to exist, but his power has been broken. Jesus rose from the dead to render physical death powerless over Himself, and one day at His return, when He raises the bodies of all those who died in faith, He will forever render physical death powerless (1 Cor. 15:26, same verb again). However, here Paul views death as an already defeated, if not obliterated, foe. The fact that its defeat is mentioned in the same breath as our having received life indicates that he is here viewing primarily the spiritual death which now no longer holds any power over the believer.[37]

> **Ministry Maxim**
>
> I must never be ashamed to speak the Gospel, for when I do God is pulling back the temporal veneer of this world and unveiling the core of reality.

The second effect of Christ's appearing, stated positively, is that He has "brought life and immortality to light" (φωτίσαντος δὲ ζωὴν καὶ ἀφθαρσίαν). The verb can be used to describe the bringing to light of something previously existent, but hidden from view (cf. 1 Cor. 4:5).[38] A new day has dawned with the appearing of Christ and the accomplishment of His redemptive work. As the sun of salvation arose, the light revealed two things previously beyond the sight of human understanding. The first is "life" (ζωή). The word points to spiritual life, rather than simply physical existence. This spiritual life was in existence prior to its unveiling to us, but only now through Christ has it come within the orbit of human experience. The word forms a rich vein of truth throughout the PE. It is "eternal life" (1 Tim. 1:16; 6:12; Titus 1:2; 3:7), enjoyed already in the present and more fully in eternity (1 Tim. 4:8). It is "life indeed" (6:19). This life is that which the Father long ago promised His own (2 Tim. 1:1). Jesus' appearance in human flesh manifested this life; indeed He Himself is the life (John 11:25; 14:6; Col. 3:4). The second, and related, thing brought to light by Christ is "immortality" (ἀφθαρσίαν). The word refers to incorruptibility, the state of not being subject to decay. Being so closely related to "life," it helps define just what life is referred to—that "life" which is never subject to death and its decay (cf. 1 Cor. 15:54). This too is the very quality of God's own life (1 Tim. 1:17), now shared with His people through Christ.

---

[37] Knight, 376.
[38] BAGD, 873.

Such "life and immortality" is put in the center of the spotlight "through the gospel" (διὰ τοῦ εὐαγγελίου). The preposition (διὰ) with the genitive points to the means by which light is thrown upon "life and immortality." This "gospel" is synonymous with "the testimony of our Lord" which, at the head of this sentence, Paul urged Timothy not to be ashamed of (v.8). Jesus' incarnation and redemptive work have revealed "life and immortality," and when we declare the Gospel message of Christ it is a revelatory experience for those who hear.[39]

1:11 for which I was appointed a preacher and an apostle and a teacher.

Paul now brings the sentence begun in v.8 to a close. The mention of the Gospel (v.10b) spurs Paul to make mention of his role in relationship to the good news. He saw himself as related to the Gospel in three roles. To each of these he says he "was appointed" (εἰς ὃ ἐτέθην ἐγώ). The verb is a simple one, meaning to put or to place. In this case Paul was placed officially in relationship to the Gospel in the roles he is about to describe. The aorist tense (like every verb in the sentence, vv.8-11) makes this a definite past action and the passive voice signals that this was an honor bestowed upon Paul by God Himself. He makes this emphatic: "I [ἐγώ] was appointed." Paul's appointment to Gospel service arose not from personal assertiveness, but from divine initiative. The verb also signals that Paul was telling Timothy not merely that he was placed in relationship to the Gospel as "a preacher and an apostle and a teacher," but also that he had been placed into the circumstances into which those roles had taken him, including his present imprisonment and his impending martyrdom.[40]

The preposition and relative pronoun (εἰς ὅ) signal that "for which" Paul was appointed, the antecedent of εἰς being "the gospel" (τοῦ εὐαγγελίου) in v.10b.

Paul was appointed to three roles with regard to the Gospel. The first is that of a "preacher" (κῆρυξ). The word was used secularly to describe one sent by a king, magistrate, or other civil or political ruler to deliver an official message. The words herald, ambassador, and messenger convey something of the meaning. The individual was, for the task before him, vested with the authority of the one sending him. To hear the herald proclaim the message was tantamount to having heard the king himself. To defy the messenger was to defy the one who sent him. The one delivering the message had no power to alter the message and was held responsible for the clarity and purity with

---
[39] Knight, 376.
[40] Lea and Griffin, 193.

which the message was conveyed. The herald was thus both under authority and vested with authority. This word was then employed by the Christians to describe the function of one who heralds the good news of Christ. It is an authoritative proclamation, one for which the speaker will be held accountable and one for which the listener will be held responsible as well.

The second role Paul held with regard to the Gospel was that of "apostle" (ἀπόστολος). Like "preacher" the word "apostle" describes one sent out with official authority by another. The word "apostle," however, focuses more on the mission to be accomplished, while "preacher" focuses on the message to be delivered. As an Apostle, Paul joined the small band of Jesus' first disciples, although it came "as to one untimely born" (1 Cor. 15:8). Paul was thus under the commission of Christ Himself to go forward in His name and establish communities of faith revolving around Christ.

> **Ministry Maxim**
>
> Absolute certainty of my call *to* ministry is essential to my faithfulness *in* ministry.

Finally, Paul was also, with regard to the Gospel, appointed "a teacher" (διδάσκαλος). Paul applies this term to himself only here and in 1 Timothy 2:7. These last two are designated as specific spiritual gifts given to the church (1 Cor. 12:28, 29; Eph. 4:11). A "preacher" proclaims, a "teacher" explains. One announces, the other expounds. One calls for response, the other for understanding. Yet both are necessary to the advancement of the Gospel and Paul undertook both. All three roles are an expression of the one divinely given ministry which was entrusted to Paul. He was pulling three strands from one rope to help us examine the constituent parts of one whole calling which had been laid upon him. We thus discover that the Gospel is something that must be announced ("preacher"), enforced ("apostle"), and explained ("teacher").

Why are these roles mentioned in this order? Does the order suggest a particular significance? Certainly the Gospel must be proclaimed ("preacher") before it can be explained ("teacher"). Lenski believes, "It is well to note that 'apostle' is placed between 'herald' and 'teacher.' We take this to mean that Paul is not stressing his office as one that is distinct and higher than Timothy's."[41] There is some thought that the term "apostle" can at times be used more generically, as descriptive of a broader circle than simply the thirteen Apostles (e.g., Rom. 16:7; 1 Thess. 2:6). Even if that is the case elsewhere, it seems unlikely here given Paul's emphatic reference to himself (ἐγώ). Whatever deduction is made, it must fit the context not only here, but also in 1 Timothy 2:7 where the same order is found. The fact is that from a human standpoint, Paul the "preacher" had been stopped, Paul the "apostle" had been confined,

---

[41] Lenski, 765-766.

and Paul the "teacher" had been silenced. Yet, as Paul would soon add, "the word of God is not imprisoned" (2:9b).

The nearly identical expression in 1 Timothy 2:7 adds two phrases not found here: "(I am telling the truth, I am not lying)" follows "apostle" and "of the Gentiles in faith and truth" follows "teacher." Most manuscripts include "of the Gentiles" here in 2 Timothy 1:11 following the word "teacher," but it was likely an attempt by later copyists to conform the latter to the former.[42] These differences make Paul's earlier statement the more solemn, but this one the more personal. All three nouns are anartharous, emphasizing the qualitative nature of the role and actions of each. The emphasis here is not on Paul, nor even the roles he plays with regard to the Gospel, but upon the Gospel itself. It is this Gospel to which Timothy also is called, though perhaps not in the same apostolic sense as Paul.

In this extended sentence Paul was telling Timothy what the Gospel is worth. The Gospel is beyond value because in it our painful past is swallowed up by God's glorious future (v.9a), our weakness is swallowed up in God's wise will (v.9b-10), and our present aimlessness is swallowed up in God's gracious appointment (v.11).

> **Digging Deeper:**
> 1. How would sharing the Gospel with someone you know be a "revelation" or a bringing "to light," if they already know the facts of the Gospel? Is there something more than the simple facts of the Gospel that is necessary to make it a "revelation" to someone? What is that "something"?
> 2. How does the word "preacher" change the way you view sharing the Gospel with people you know?
> 3. Do you tend to be more of a "preacher" or a "teacher" when it comes to how you share the Gospel with others?

1:12 For this reason I also suffer these things, but I am not ashamed; for I know whom I have believed and I am convinced that He is able to guard what I have entrusted to Him until that day.

A new sentence begins,[43] but not without connections to what precedes it. "For this reason" (δι' ἣν αἰτίαν) is a strong causal statement which we have already encountered in v.6 (cf. Titus 1:13). In this case it points back to the

---
[42] Knight, 377.
[43] Ibid., 378.

Gospel and the circumstances resulting from Paul's divine appointment in its service. For the Gospel Paul can declare, "I also suffer these things" (καὶ ταῦτα πάσχω). It is more literally, "also these things I suffer." The "also" (καὶ) points to his current sufferings as either in addition to the things he had previously suffered for the Gospel (e.g., 2 Cor. 4:8-11; 11:23-27) or in addition to his divine appointment to serve in the Gospel ministry there has come the call to suffer in it as well. Either is possible, but the latter connects more directly with v.11. Just what "these things" (ταῦτα) are is not yet specified. We shall discover that it means "chains" (v.16) and impending death (4:6). Perhaps Paul believed Timothy to be aware of his present conditions or he left it to his sanctified imagination. The word "suffer" (πάσχω) points generally to what one experiences, but it most often has a dark shade of meaning pointing to negative circumstances and the pain they cause. This same root was found in compound in v.8 where Paul exhorted Timothy to "join with me in suffering [συγκακοπάθησον] for the gospel." The verb here is in the present tense stressing the ongoing nature of Paul's sufferings.

Despite his sufferings ("but," the strong adversative ἀλλὰ), Paul can say "I am not ashamed" (οὐκ ἐπαισχύνομαι). This also is in the present tense. The present and ongoing nature of Paul's sufferings is matched by a continuous absence of shame. Not for a moment did Paul feel chagrined for having followed Christ. The form may be either the middle or passive voice. Probably the former is correct, stressing the inward quality of this absence of shame. Three of the five times Paul uses this word are found in this chapter (vv.8, 12, 16), a fact that stresses the extent to which humanly speaking Paul had sunk to his lowest point. He had used it in his famous thematic statement for the epistle to the Romans, "I am not ashamed of the gospel" (Rom. 1:16). Paul proved that same sentiment was still true now at the end of his life (v.8). The specific shame he repudiated here was that of being imprisoned for this Gospel. The word can denote legitimate shame (Rom. 6:21), but most often Paul linked it with a negative particle in statements repudiating unwarranted shame (e.g., Rom. 1:16; 2 Tim. 1:8, 12, 16).

Paul went on to explain the reasons ("for," γὰρ) why he was untouched by shame. It was, in the first case, because the Apostle could say, "I know whom I have believed" (οἶδα γὰρ ᾧ πεπίστευκα). "I know" is a defective perfect, having a present tense meaning. He is in continuous possession of this knowledge. The verb (οἶδα, also used in 1:12, 15; 2:23; 3:14, 15) stresses the completeness of the knowledge, rather than the process of gaining that knowledge through experience or relationship (γινώσκω, used in 1:18; 2:19; 3:1).[44]

The specific knowledge that delivers from shame is not informational, but

---

[44] Mounce, 32, 486.

relational. It is the knowledge of God—His Person and character—that has thus liberated Paul. The relative pronoun "whom" (ᾧ) does not have a clear antecedent. Does it point to God or to Christ? Paul probably had in mind the former. Ultimately, since the Father and Son have both been mentioned by Paul and since they work in concert in redemption, we need not press for more precision.

Paul had "believed" (πεπίστευκα) God. The word is one of Paul's favorites. Here the emphasis seems to be upon his trust in God. The verb is in the perfect tense, stressing that at a point in the past Paul chose to trust God and he continues to abide in that state of trust. Nothing in all God's dealings with him has moved Paul to question the trust he has placed in Him. This underscores that belief is only as good as the character of the one trusted. It also reminds us that shame is not overcome by looking to yourself or your circumstances, but to the God who created you and controls your circumstances. A solid grasp of the character of God disables many of our most disquieting problems.

Paul's second reason for feeling no shame is that "I am convinced" (πέπεισμαι). The word means "to convince someone to believe something and to act on the basis of what is recommended."[45] It has already been encountered as "sure" in v.5. The perfect tense verb is paired with "I believe," here too stressing that at some point in the past Paul had become convinced and stood so still. The passive voice indicates that something (experiential evidences of God's faithfulness?) or someone (the work of the Holy Spirit?) has built a case in his heart for this conviction regarding God's trustworthiness. It is not sufficient to believe facts about God's character and nature; we must also be convinced of them in regard to our personal needs.

Just what it is Paul was convinced of is set forth in an explanatory clause. Paul was convinced "that" (ὅτι) God "is able" (δυνατός ἐστιν). The word points to the overwhelming power and ability of God. When Paul was weakest he never lost sight of the greatness of God's power (cf. 2 Cor. 12:9-10). The particular angle of God's power that was in Paul's view was His ability "to guard" (φυλάξαι). The word describes protecting something entrusted to you so that it is unharmed.[46] Paul had already laid this responsibility upon Timothy (1 Tim. 6:20) and soon would again (2 Tim. 1:14). However, here it is God who does the protecting (cf. 2 Thess. 3:3).

Just what is it that God is able and willing to guard? Answering that question has proven to be a difficulty for commentators. The short answer is "what I have entrusted to Him." Literally it is simply "my deposit" or "the deposit of me" (τὴν παραθήκην μου). Does this, however, refer to something Paul entrusted to God (i.e., himself, his ministry) or something God entrusted to

---

[45] Louw and Nida, Electronic version.
[46] BAGD, 868.

Paul (i.e., the Gospel)? The list of defenders for either option is impressive. The only other times the word is used are in 1 Timothy 6:20 and 2 Timothy 2:14. In 1 Timothy it clearly points to a deposit given to Timothy ("O Timothy, guard what has been entrusted to you"). 2 Timothy 1:14 refers to "the treasure which has been entrusted to you." These clearly point to a deposit/treasure given by God to Timothy. Thus previous usage and context seem to favor seeing this as a deposit given by God to Paul (i.e., the Gospel). This would make the greater concern here the ongoing ministry of the Gospel after Paul's death. If this makes Paul more concerned over the welfare of the Gospel than his own personal and eternal wellbeing, then it sounds all the more Pauline. This does not rule out the implied issue of God's ability to protect what Paul had committed to Him. In the end perhaps Lock has the best take of all: "The life which at first was God's deposit with us becomes our deposit with God."[47]

> **Ministry Maxim**
>
> While God demands my faithfulness, the success of the Gospel ultimately rests with Him, not me.

God's faithful keeping continues "until that day" (εἰς ἐκείνην τὴν ἡμέραν). Both Paul and Timothy seemed to know the identity of "that day," for Paul quickly used the same phrase again in v.18 without further specification. He is more specific later in the letter when he says, "in the future there is laid up for me the crown of righteousness, which the Lord, the righteous Judge, will award to me on that day" (4:8a). Thus "that day" refers to the day in which Paul will stand before Christ for judgment and reward regarding his ministry (1 Cor. 3:12-15). The preposition εἰς with the accusative is used temporally and means "up to which something continues."[48] Right up till all things are judged and set right, God guards His Gospel.

Timothy and other believers with him would have likely worried not only for Paul's welfare in prison, but may have been fretful about the future of the Gospel should the great Apostle die. This fear is what Paul alleviated by recounting the faithful keeping-power of God with regard to the Gospel. The truth, purpose, and mission of God are always bigger than one person, even so great a person as the Apostle Paul. Ultimately God does not need us. He does, however, privilege us with participation in and sacrifice for what He is doing. When we prove ourselves faithful in that which God exercises His faithfulness, we are moving in the stream of God's eternal purposes and are guaranteed success regardless of the appearance of earthly outcomes. We are also reminded that we will all die trusting Christ for some things not yet realized in personal experience. Not all we trust Christ for will be resolved

---

[47] Walter Lock, quoted in Earle, 11:397.
[48] BAGD, 228.

in this life—we will have to be like the people of old who died believing the promises (Heb. 11:13).

> **Digging Deeper:**
> 1. How does knowing God personally and deeply help to fend off feelings of shame when hardships come for having followed Him?
> 2. How do we move from having simply "learned" something to the place where we are also "convinced" of it? Why are both important in the Christian life?
> 3. The Gospel and mission of God are bigger than any one person (no matter how great he may be)—how does knowing this help us in serving Him?

1:13 Retain the standard of sound words which you have heard from me, in the faith and love which are in Christ Jesus.

The word translated "the standard" (ὑποτύπωσιν) comes first in the sentence for emphasis. No definite article is found in the Greek text. The word described an outline or sketch such as an artist might draw up before beginning the final work of art. In literature it pointed to the rough draft drawn up before the final exposition was composed.[49] It thus suggests that what Timothy had heard from Paul was authoritative, but not entirely detailed. Paul did not hand off to Timothy an intricate legal code prescribing behavior in any and every situation, but rather the broad shape of the living truth, which if embraced and guarded would lead him into the knowledge of God's will in each and every situation he might encounter. By extension, then, the word came to describe a model, pattern, or example. The only other time the word is found in the NT is 1 Timothy 1:16: "Yet for this reason I found mercy, so that in me as the foremost, Jesus Christ might demonstrate His perfect patience as an example [ὑποτύπωσιν] for those who would believe in Him for eternal life."

This standard is made up "of sound words" (ὑγιαινόντων λόγων). Such words are "sound" in that they are healthy. The word was used literally of physical (e.g., Luke 7:10) or mental health (e.g., 15:27). In the PE it is always metaphorically attached either to "faith" (Titus 1:13; 2:2), "words" (1 Tim. 6:3; 2 Tim. 1:13) or "teaching/doctrine" (1 Tim. 1:10; 2 Tim. 4:3; Titus 1:9; 2:1). In this context, then, the word emphasizes the truthfulness,

---
[49] Rienecker, 639.

accuracy or correctness of the words. They beget health by transmitting truth and a correct view of reality. These "sound words" are those which proclaim, explain, and expound upon "the gospel" and "the testimony of our Lord" (vv.8, 10).

This standard Timothy is commanded to "Retain" (ἔχε). The word means simply "to have" or "to hold." But these general sounding words can carry weighty intent as the traditional wedding vows indicate: "to have and to hold until death do you part." The gravity of this command is captured in a variety of ways by differing translations: "Hold fast" (KJV, NKJV), "keep" (NIV, NJB), "Follow" (ESV, RSV), "Hold" (NRSV). This present imperative (demanding action be undertaken continuously or repeatedly) is teamed with the command to "guard" (v.14), which underscores the seriousness of Paul's charge here.

Paul made specific which "words" he meant. They were the ones "which you have heard from me" (ὧν παρ' ἐμοῦ ἤκουσας). In a moment he will charge Timothy with the transference of these words to succeeding generations of godly men (2:2), but for now he is reminding him of the identity and source of those words which give life (cf. 1 Tim. 4:6; 2 Tim. 3:10). Paul is not discounting that others have had a profound influence upon Timothy's understanding of the Gospel (1:5; 3:14), but his concern here is with the purity of the message in the face of the false teachers of Ephesus.

> **Ministry Maxim**
>
> It is possible to protect the truth and yet fail in ministry.

The seriousness of the charge to protect the truth does not justify any means in the battle. This is to be done "in the faith and love which are in Christ Jesus" (ἐν πίστει καὶ ἀγάπῃ τῇ ἐν Χριστῷ Ἰησοῦ; cf. 1 Tim. 1:14). The prepositional phrase describes the spirit or atmosphere in which (ἐν) Timothy was to protect the truth of the Gospel.[50] The words "the faith" point to Timothy's attitude toward God and His word, while "love" refers to his attitude toward both God and man.[51] We are well reminded that a significant part of protecting the truth is *how* we protect the truth. It is possible to protect a doctrine, but lose the debate. This "faith and love" are found only "in Christ Jesus." Only through union with Christ and a constant abiding in Him will we not only hold to the truth, but allow the truth to hold us.

If the truth is to live on from generation to generation, orthodoxy must always define itself ("retain the standard of sound words"), reproduce itself ("which you have heard from me"), and examine itself ("in the faith and love which are in Christ Jesus").

---

[50] Knight, 381.
[51] McCalley, 42.

1:14 Guard, through the Holy Spirit who dwells in us, the treasure which has been entrusted to you.

Paul now picks up two words he has already used in v.12 to underscore Timothy's Gospel responsibility ("Guard" and "the treasure which has been entrusted to you"). The aorist imperative "Guard" (φύλαξον) stresses the urgency of Paul's command and demands that the assigned action be undertaken at once. This is paired also with the present imperative "Retain" (ἔχε) in verse 13 to highlight Timothy's responsibility. What Paul assured Timothy God will "guard" (v.12), Timothy is now charged to "guard" himself (vv.13-14), by the power of the Holy Spirit. Here is the dynamic interplay of divine sovereignty and human responsibility!

What Timothy is to protect is literally "the good deposit" (τὴν καλὴν παραθήκην) which has been elongated into "the treasure which has been entrusted to you" by the NASU. The expression is thrust to the head of the sentence for emphasis. The noun is used only here, v.12 and 1 Timothy 6:20. In verse 12 it was literally "the deposit of me" and it was difficult to determine if Paul meant something God entrusted to his care or something he entrusted to God's keeping. Here the former is clearly in view. The word points to something placed on deposit with another for safekeeping. The definite article (τὴν) and the adjective "good" (καλὴν) clearly make this a reference to the Gospel and its teaching (cf. "the standard of sound words you have heard from me," v.13). Elsewhere in the PE Paul uses this adjective and speaks of, among other things, "the good fight" (1 Tim. 1:18; 6:12; 2 Tim. 4:7), "a good servant" (1 Tim. 4:6), "the sound [good] doctrine" (1 Tim. 4:6), "the good confession" (1 Tim. 6:12, 13), "a good soldier" (2 Tim. 2:3), and "good deeds" (Titus 2:7, 14; 3:8, 14).

> **Ministry Maxim**
>
> God does what only He can do as I, in reliance upon the Holy Spirit, do what He requires me to do.

This work is of such a nature that human ability alone will not succeed. Thus it is to be carried out "through the Holy Spirit" (διὰ πνεύματος ἁγίου). The preposition "through" (διὰ) identifies the means or, more specifically, the personal agent by whom Timothy will be enabled.[52] It is the Holy Spirit "who dwells in us" (τοῦ ἐνοικοῦντος ἐν ἡμῖν). The present participle points to the continuous nature of the Spirit's indwelling. The verb is used elsewhere to describe faith (2 Tim. 1:5), the Word of God (Col. 3:16), the Holy Spirit (Rom. 8:11), and God Himself (2 Cor. 6:16) dwelling in or among His people. The prepositional phrase "in us" (ἐν ἡμῖν) is in the plural. Some take this as a reference to a ministry of the Holy

---

[52] Knight, 382.

Spirit unique to leaders like Paul and Timothy. It more likely points to the fact that all believers are thus indwelt by the Holy Spirit (Rom. 8:9; 1 Cor. 12:13).

Paul began by speaking of Timothy's personal responsibility in the Gospel and the accompanying aid of the Spirit (vv.6-7) and now he returns to this same place. God calls us to take responsibility in His work, but as we step forward in obedience the work is done by Him. ". . . it is God who is at work in you, both to will and to work for His good pleasure" (Phil. 2:13). Having exhorted Timothy to vigilance in the ministry of the Gospel (vv.6-14), Paul now produces examples which, on the one hand, Timothy must avoid (v.15) and, on the other hand, which he is to emulate (vv.16-18).

> **Digging Deeper:**
> 1. How can the way in which we protect the truth either help us or hinder us in that responsibility?
> 2. If God has already promised to guard the Gospel (v.12), why then does He call us to do so (v.14)?
> 3. Why do we need the Holy Spirit to guard the Gospel successfully?
> 4. From what or whom must we protect the Gospel?

1:15 You are aware of the fact that all who are in Asia turned away from me, among whom are Phygelus and Hermogenes.

Paul now begins a new paragraph. He does so in order to produce two negative examples (v.15), along with one positive example (vv.16-18), of the kind of fidelity to the Gospel he has been pressing upon Timothy (vv.6-14). To this end Paul tells Timothy "You are aware of the fact" (Οἶδας τοῦτο; lit., "You know this"). The same word was encountered in v.12 when Paul said, "I know whom I have believed" (cf. also 2:23; 3:14, 15). It stresses the completeness of the knowledge Timothy possesses. The verb is a defective perfect with a present tense meaning—Timothy was in present and continuous possession of this knowledge.

That which Timothy knew was "that all who are in Asia turned away from me" (ὅτι ἀπεστράφησάν με πάντες οἱ ἐν τῇ 'Ασίᾳ). This is a reference not to the continent of Asia, but to the Roman province by that name. It covered much of what would be modern-day western Turkey. It was a hotbed of Paul's apostolic ministry. Its leading and capital city was Ephesus, where Timothy pastored as Paul wrote this letter. Paul invested three years of concentrated ministry in that city and region (Acts 20:31), longer than any other one location. So thorough was the saturation of the Gospel across the province at that time that Luke could write, "all who lived in Asia heard the word of the Lord, both Jews and Greeks" (19:10). During that season the Gospel had made such inroads into the pagan culture that one of their number could testify, "You see and hear that not only in Ephesus, but in almost all of Asia, this Paul has persuaded and turned away a considerable number of people, saying that gods made with hands are no gods at all" (19:26). Indeed, Paul apparently had found a favorable hearing for the Gospel even among some of the ruling class (19:31). Yet for all this widespread ministry and profound impact, Paul could say "all" in that region had "turned away" from him. The expression drips with heartache.

> **Ministry Maxim**
>
> Abandonment and loneliness in ministry usually *feels* more total than it really is.

What should we make of Paul's use of "all"? It clearly is a hyperbole, for he immediately produces an example of one who had not deserted him (vv.16-18). Timothy himself and the others he greets (4:19) also prove that Paul's "all" is not to be taken literally. It clearly *felt* as if "all who are in Asia" had abandoned him. Some trusted colleagues had either defected (2 Tim. 4:10a) or had been deployed to other ministries (4:10b). Paul would say again at the close of the letter, "At my first defense no one supported me, but all deserted me" (4:16a). Emotions often color our perception and our language. God recognizes this by including statements like these in Scripture.

All these, Paul said, "turned away from me" (ἀπεστράφησάν). The word describes the rejection or repudiation of someone.[53] The aorist tense points to a time in the past when the turning away occurred. But does this mean they abandoned Paul personally or that they defected from the faith altogether? Or could it refer to both? At the least a defection from Paul is in view. The Apostle does say that they turned away from "me" (με). Perhaps it had been the heat of persecution that had turned back the majority from standing with Paul during his preliminary hearing (2 Tim. 4:16). The verb (ἀποστρέφω), however, is used elsewhere in the PE only of apostasy from Christ (2 Tim. 4:4; Titus 1:14). To describe the personal desertion of 2 Timothy 4:10, Paul used another word.[54] It is unlikely that all Christians in Asia renounced Christ. It seems more probable that they distanced themselves from the Apostle of Christ. In so doing, however, it would have been viewed by Paul as an abandonment of their Christian commitment. Paul believed himself to be imprisoned for Christ's sake. To fail to stand with him would be tantamount to drawing back from Christ Himself.

Paul names two of the "all." Scripture nowhere else mentions Phygelus or Hermogenes. Why are they named? Perhaps they are specified because their defection was most grievous to Paul. Had he come to expect more from them?

---

[53] BAGD, 100.
[54] Fee, 236.

Or was it that they led the way in turning others from Paul? Obviously Timothy knew the answers to these questions, but our knowledge of them was deemed unnecessary. The simple fact of their defection tells us what is important for us to know.

> **Digging Deeper:**
> 1. What does this teach us about the power of personal rejection? Why do negative statements by one or two people seem to cancel out the positive feedback coming from many more people?
> 2. How are we to relate Paul's statement ("turned away from *me*") to Jesus' words: "The world cannot hate you, but it hates Me because I testify of it, that its deeds are evil" (John 7:7)? Why do we feel personal rejection when it is Christ and His cause that may bring the displeasure of others toward us? How does this help us learn to handle those feelings?
> 3. What are we to make of the fact that Paul personally named two individuals out of an apparently larger group of defectors? Were they ringleaders? Did those two level a particularly venomous attack on Paul? What does this tell us about forgiveness and the old adage "forgive and forget"?

1:16 The Lord grant mercy to the house of Onesiphorus, for he often refreshed me and was not ashamed of my chains;

Paul now sets forth a more positive example of the kind of faithfulness to which he has called Timothy. Paul's first verb ("grant"; δῴη) is in the optative mood, expressing a wishful desire on his part (Rom. 15:5; Eph. 1:17; 2 Thess. 3:16; 2 Tim. 1:18; 2:25). It is not addressed directly to "The Lord" and thus does not quite qualify as a prayer. Rather Paul addressed it to Timothy in an informational way. "The Lord" (ὁ κύριος) has been used in reference to Jesus (vv.2, 8). It is natural to understand it in the same way here.

Paul wanted the Lord to extend "mercy" (ἔλεος). Paul has already extended this to Timothy (v.2) and he will wish again for it to go out to Onesiphorus himself in the future (v.18). It is a term denoting compassion and pity toward others aroused by their suffering or hardship. Onesiphorus himself had demonstrated such "mercy" to the Apostle, now he wishes for this to rebound (Matt. 5:7) upon his family. The name "Onesiphorus" means *help-bringer*. He had indeed embodied such merciful care to Paul. He is not only the subject here in vv.16-18, but his household is mentioned again in 4:19. Beyond this we know nothing more of him in the NT.

The wish is directed not toward Onesiphorus himself, but toward his "house" (οἴκῳ). The word was used metaphorically to include one's family and also one's servants, if there were such. But why the well-wishing toward them, when apparently Onesiphorus had done the caring? Some suggest that this is an indicator that Onesiphorus had died by this time, perhaps while on the quest to care for Paul. They find support from the fact that Paul speaks of Onesiphorus' rewards on "that day" (v.18), rather than presently. Yet Paul uses that expression of himself as one who is still living (1:12; 4:8). Also, in supposed support, they indicate that at the close of the letter Paul again greets only "the household of Onesiphorus" (4:19), again suggesting this indicates his death. Others, however, suggest that it means nothing more than that he had not yet arrived back home from his mission of mercy to Paul.

The twofold reason (ὅτι) for Paul's desire is stated in the last half of the verse. First, "he often refreshed me" (πολλάκις με ἀνέψυξεν). The verb is picturesque, meaning to cool again or to revive by cool breezes. The cool wind of grace had blown into Paul's life when Onesiphorus arrived and ministered to him. The aorist tense looks at the visit and ministry of Onesiphorus as a singular event and sums up its character. The verb is found nowhere else in the NT (though see the noun in Acts 3:20). That such refreshing came "often" to Paul through this dear brother is emphasized by the emphatic position of the adverb (πολλάκις).[55] The second reason is that Onesiphorus "was not ashamed of my chains" (τὴν ἅλυσίν μου οὐκ ἐπαισχύνθη). The noun is singular ("chain") and is likely used literally of Paul's being tethered to a guard. To picture the Apostle of such far-flung mission now chained and confined must have been heart-wrenching to Timothy. It was a moment of utter degradation for Paul. Yet Onesiphorus had not been "ashamed" (ἐπαισχύνθη) of him, of his chain, or of the Christ he served. The verb is an aorist, again pointing to the time of Onesiphorus's ministry as a whole. It is in the passive voice indicating that he refused to allow Paul's imprisonment and defamation to move him into distancing himself from the Apostle. This verb provides a verbal link, tying the whole of this chapter together. Paul used it in v.8 to command Timothy, "do not be ashamed of the testimony of our Lord or of me his prisoner" and then used it to describe his own lack of shame over having trusted Christ (v.12). This confirms that Paul's purpose in mentioning Onesiphorus was to provide a positive illustration of the action to which he has called Timothy.

> **Ministry Maxim**
>
> It is impossible to shield my family completely from either the difficulties or rewards of my ministry.

---

[55] Mounce, 496.

1:17 but when he was in Rome, he eagerly searched for me and found me —

The actions of Onesiphorus stand in marked contrast (ἀλλὰ, strong adversative) to the thought of being ashamed of Paul's chain. The phrase "when he was in Rome" is literally "being in Rome" (γενόμενος ἐν ʽΡώμῃ). The participle is used with a temporal significance, yielding the translation "when he was".[56] The fact that this took place "in Rome" specifies at least where he believed the Apostle to be imprisoned, and no doubt his actual location (contrary to the hypothesis of a Caesarean imprisonment). This is the only specific mention of the location of Paul's imprisonment.

Onesiphorus had "eagerly searched" (σπουδαίως ἐζήτησέν) for Paul. The verb is vivid, picturing a search driven by a longing expectation and passion. The addition of the adverb "eagerly" (σπουδαίως) served to intensify the picture (the root elsewhere in Paul only in Phil. 2:28; Titus 3:13). It describes action undertaken earnestly, diligently, or urgently. The fact that Onesiphorus had to put such effort into locating Paul indicates that the conditions of this imprisonment were dramatically different from those mentioned in Acts 28, where friends and visitors were free to pass in and out of Paul's presence. Apparently the Apostle's location was not well known and his conditions, when he was finally located, were likely rather dire. Paul explained that in reward for such loving exploration Onesiphorus "found me." The object is not found in the Greek text and is simply,

> **Ministry Maxim**
>
> A person simply devoted to me as an individual is rare — I must appreciate him when I find him.

"and found" (καὶ εὗρεν). This may serve to heighten the sense of joy in Onesiphorus' discovery,[57] it could simply mean the object is understood from the preceding phrase ("me"; με),[58] or it could set up a wordplay in v.18.[59] Both "searched" and "found" are in the aorist tense and, though the search was surely a process, both the quest and discovery are pictured as singular events.

1:18 the Lord grant to him to find mercy from the Lord on that day — and you know very well what services he rendered at Ephesus.

As Paul moved toward completing the sentence and the description of Onesiphorus' positive example, he took up again the same optative verb form

---

[56] Riencecker, 639.
[57] Hiebert, *Second Timothy*, 48.
[58] Knight, 385.
[59] Mounce, 496.

of v.16. His wish this time is aimed at Onesiphorus himself, rather than his household. The double use of the verb forms an inclusion around this discussion of Onesiphorus. The verb is used in this letter to describe God giving us a spirit of power, love, and discipline (v.7), His purpose and grace (v.9), understanding (2:7), and repentance (2:25). Here the content of Paul's desire is for him "to find mercy," just as it had been for his family (v.16). Paul himself was giving away this "mercy" (ἔλεος) to Timothy as the letter opened (v.2; cf. 1 Tim. 1:2), but now he seems dependent upon God to extend it to Onesiphorus (vv.16, 18). The infinitive "to find" (εὑρεῖν) is a wordplay with the same word found in v.17. Onesiphorus had worked hard "to find" Paul (v.17) and now, because of his merciful ministry to him, the Apostle wished for him "to find" mercy himself from the Lord.

The double use of "Lord" has been the topic of much discussion. The first occurrence is accompanied by the definite article, the second is not. The word has been used three times already in this chapter, two of the three clearly referring to Jesus Christ (vv.2, 8). The other usage is in the parallel statement to this one in v.16. Some argue that the double usage here is because Paul used two expressions so common that they almost had become formulas ("the Lord grant" and "from the Lord"). The argument is that two familiar phrases rolled off the Apostle's tongue so easily that there was no thought of the grammatical awkwardness.[60] Others feel that the second usage of "Lord" was to avoid the confusion that a second use of the personal pronoun "him" (αὐτός) would have created.[61] Despite all the discussion, most conclude that the first usage is a reference to Jesus Christ and the second a reference to God the Father. God the Son in His redemptive ministry has given God the Father the legal means to extend His mercy to sinners. There is some evidence from the LXX that when referring to God the Father it is the custom to use the noun without the article as is the case with the second occurrence of the word here.[62]

> **Ministry Maxim**
>
> The sacrifices made in ministry can't buy me acceptance at God's judgment— only His mercy can provide me that.

Paul's wish for extended mercy upon Onesiphorus is focused upon "that day" (ἐκείνῃ τῇ ἡμέρᾳ). Paul has already shown his future orientation by using the phrase in v.12. He will become more specific in its usage in 4:8. Paul is picturing the day when Onesiphorus stands before Christ, as will all believers, for judgment and reward regarding his ministry (1 Cor. 3:12-15). Some have used this future wish for Onesiphorus, coupled with the present

---
[60] Kent, 257.
[61] Knight, 385.
[62] Mounce, 496.

wish for his household (v.16; 4:19), as a signal that he had died by the time of writing. This assumption is then extended by some to at least permit, if not call for, the practice of prayer for the dead. First, the focus upon Onesiphorus's household provides no definitive proof that he had died. It need only mean that he had not yet returned home from his journey and that the Apostle recognized that it had been some considerable sacrifice for his family to do without him while he traveled to minister to him. This also reads too much into the optative mood in vv.16 and 18. It does not read like a prayer, but more as a wish expressed toward a beloved brother. Careful exegetes will find here no justification for the practice of prayer for the dead.

Paul adds a personal note as he closes the sentence. He tells Timothy "you know very well" (βέλτιον σὺ γινώσκεις). The verb "know" (γινώσκεις) stresses the personal and experiential nature of the knowledge. It is the first time Paul has used this word, opting in vv.12 and 15 for οἶδα which stresses the informational nature of that knowledge. Paul used the present tense to stress that Timothy was in constant personal awareness of "what services he [Onesiphorus] rendered at Ephesus" (ὅσα ἐν Ἐφέσῳ διηκόνησεν). This may have been a ministry Timothy observed along with Paul when they ministered together there. It seems more likely, however, that it points to Timothy's possession of knowledge that even Paul himself did not have. This was a knowledge Timothy possessed "very well" (βέλτιον). The word functions adverbially here. It can be a comparative, indicating that Timothy knew better than Paul all that the ministry of Onesiphorus had entailed. Or it can serve in a superlative sense, meaning "very well."[63] In either case, Timothy was, for this reason, all the more compelled to imitate the example of service laid down by this humble brother. The vast variety of Onesiphorus's ministry is indicated by the neuter plural ὅσα ("in how many ways," NIV). It is thrust forward grammatically to give it an emphatic position. This was a brother who knew no limits to his service.

Digging Deeper:
1. What do I learn from Onesiphorus that helps me undertake a ministry of refreshment to someone else?
2. What do I learn about how one's ministry may bring both challenges and benefits to one's own family?
3. Why did Onesiphrous prove faithful (vv.16-18) in hard times when others did not (v.15)? What does this demand of me, if I am to be faithful to God and His people?

---

[63] BAGD, 139.

CHAPTER

2

2:1 You therefore, my son, be strong in the grace that is in Christ Jesus.

That this sentence flows directly out of what precedes is clear from the inferential conjunction "therefore" (οὖν). It looks back most directly upon the negative example of how not to stand fast in the truth (1:15) and the positive example of how to do so (1:16-18). However, it would seem that Paul's exhortation looks back even further to the whole of the first chapter, including the recounting of his godly heritage (v.5), the enduement of the Spirit (vv.6-7), and the charge to guard the Gospel (vv.8-14). In light of all these things Timothy was charged to be strong in the grace of God.

The personal pronoun "you" (Σὺ) is emphatic, being thrown to the head of the sentence for emphasis. Paul, as it were, looked Timothy directly in the eye when writing what follows. Paul designates Timothy "my son." This is streamlined from the more intimate "my beloved son" that opened the letter (1:2). Paul's heart is again showing.

The verb "be strong" (ἐνδυναμοῦ) is used six times by Paul, half of them in his correspondence to Timothy (cf. also 1 Tim. 1:12; 2 Tim. 4:17). It is a compound word, being composed of "in" (ἐν) and "power" (δυναμόω). In the NT it always points toward moral or spiritual strength.[1] The present imperative form demands that the action be undertaken repeatedly or continuously. The passive voice indicates that this strengthening can come only from outside of Timothy as he is acted upon by another. A meaning something like "take responsibility to allow yourself to be strengthened" may capture the intent. But how is one to take responsibility to make oneself strong in something that cannot be had by any amount of effort and must come from somewhere outside of oneself?

---

[1] BAGD, 263.

It is "in the grace that is in Christ Jesus" (ἐν τῇ χάριτι τῇ ἐν Χριστῷ Ἰησοῦ) that Timothy is to be strong. The preposition ἐν is used instrumentally designating the means by which God imparts this strength.[2] This grace has already been described at length (1:2, 3, 6, 9) and will return to close the letter (4:22). The source of such grace is "in Christ Jesus" (τῇ ἐν Χριστῷ Ἰησοῦ). The definite article is repeated twice to specify the specific grace intended, that which is only found "in Christ Jesus." Since all believers are "in Christ," then this grace and empowerment are available to all His people. It is in union with Christ ("in Christ Jesus") that such empowering grace flows into a believer's life. The believer is responsible to live in such dynamic union with Christ that the flow of this grace is unrestricted. As one obeys God's commands (1:6, 8, 13, 14) in dependence upon God's Spirit (1:7) God continually enables that one with the strength required to fulfill the will of God. The Jesus expressed it this way, "Abide in Me, and I in you. As the branch cannot bear fruit of itself unless it abides in the vine, so neither can you unless you abide in Me" (John 15:4). Being strengthened in grace is not a matter of trying harder, but of resting more intentionally.

> **Ministry Maxim**
>
> I am as strong in the grace of God as I want to be.

> **Digging Deeper:**
> 1. How can I be responsible to make sure God strengthens me in His grace?
> 2. How does the previous question potentially uncover a misunderstanding of grace and how God has determined to channel it into our lives?
> 3. Do you agree with this statement: we are each as satisfied in the grace of God as we want to be? Why or why not?

2:2 The things which you have heard from me in the presence of many witnesses, entrust these to faithful men who will be able to teach others also.

If chapter one was primarily about protecting the Gospel, then chapter two focuses on propagating the Gospel. The sentence begins with the conjunction (καὶ), which the translators of the NASU leave untranslated. It is a simple continuative and, while linking to what has been said in v.1, it serves to move Paul's thoughts along to what is next.

---
[2] Knight, 389; Marshall, 724; Mounce, 503-504.

Second Timothy 2

The focus here is upon "The things which you have heard from me" (ἃ ἤκουσας παρ' ἐμοῦ). The phrase is a near repeat from 1:13. The aorist tense verb gathers up as if it were one event the whole of what Timothy had heard from Paul's lips by way of instruction in the past. At this stage of the church's development the transmission of the Gospel was primarily oral. Paul began broadly by using the indefinite plural relative pronoun "things which" (ἃ) to arch across the whole spectrum of all he had said in Timothy's presence. The next phrase, however, narrows the field of all Paul said to those things which Timothy had heard "in the presence of many witnesses." The preposition (διὰ) with the genitive of persons normally denotes the personal agency through which something arrives. Its use here has given rise to much discussion. Over time it came to be used, at times, to refer not strictly to agency through a person, but to something done in the presence of another. This seems to be the intent here.[3] This surely was a simple way of referring to the Gospel Paul has already spoken of as "the standard of sound words" (1:13; cf. vv.8, 10).

But still we must ask what exactly this means. Does this limit the subject matter to those things publicly taught by Paul? Is this a way of telling Timothy to major on the main points, not necessarily the finer points, of debate they may have entered into in personal, private discussions? Or is this a way of protecting Timothy by having him teach only what others would have to stand up and confess had apostolic authority because they also had heard Paul teach these things? Perhaps something of all of these is in view. Whatever challenges Timothy faced in Ephesus, Paul wanted him aware of the fact that he did not stand alone. There were "many witnesses" (πολλῶν μαρτύρων) who would testify with him to the truth that Paul had handed down to them. Some take "many witnesses" as a reference to some formal occasion such as ordination when Paul handed the truth off to Timothy, but the text does not seem to require this. Nor is it necessary to press further for exact identification of who these "witnesses" may be. They no doubt came from a cross-section of society as Paul preached publicly to all who would hear. It may seem odd to the casual reader that Paul could swing from "all who are in Asia turned away from me" (1:15) to reassuring Timothy that there existed in Ephesus "many witnesses." Yet Paul was not attempting to speak in precise numbers, but in a very personal letter was expressing with accuracy the burden of his heart.

The truths thus taught, Timothy was to "entrust" strategically to others. This is the verbal form of the noun encountered already in 1:14. The verb was used earlier by Paul when he told Timothy "This command [regarding continuing in ministry in Ephesus] I entrust to you" (1 Tim. 1:18; and is used by Paul elsewhere only in 1 Cor. 10:27). Thus Paul's instructions here were nothing Timothy had not already experienced and observed in Paul's dealings with him. The aorist imperative form stresses the urgency of the matter, demanding that action be undertaken at once. The verb means simply "place beside" or "place before," but in the middle voice, as here, it carries the sense of entrusting or committing something to someone for safekeeping.[4] The expression "these things" (ταῦτα) is plural and points to the completeness of Paul's teaching. It refers back to "which you have heard from me" earlier in the sentence.

What Paul had entrusted to Timothy (1 Tim. 1:18; 2 Tim. 1:14) he is now charged with entrusting to others. In entrusting this to others, Timothy's primary concern is to be with the character of these individuals. They must be "faithful men" (πιστοῖς ἀνθρώποις). The adjective "faithful" is an important one in the PE. It can speak in an active sense of one who believes (1 Tim. 4:3, 10, 12; 5:16; 6:2) or in the passive sense of the quality of faithfulness. This can be said of statements of truth (1 Tim. 1:15; 3:1; 4:9; 2 Tim. 2:11; Titus 1:9). Faithfulness is measured fundamentally by its conformity to the character of God Himself, who is and must be faithful to His own character (2 Tim. 2:13).

Within the confines of this verse the faithfulness involves at least the ability to listen with faith to the things handed down as truth and then the ability to pass these on in a convincing way to another generation to the end that the truth finds similar root in those lives and they are equipped to continue the life-transference to yet another generation. This is captured in the closing words "who will be able to teach others also" (οἵτινες ἱκανοὶ ἔσονται καὶ ἑτέρους διδάξαι). The qualifications now include both character ("faithful") and skill ("able to teach others"). We would err, however, if we understood "able to teach" through eyes of the twenty-first century Western educational system. Formal classroom pedagogy is not implied. Rather Paul casts this is as broad a way as possible. He heads the phrase with the relative pronoun "who" (οἵτινες, whoever) in order to emphasize the inclusiveness of the potential group. The expression "will be able" translates two words (ἱκανοὶ ἔσονται). The first word literally describes that which is sufficient in filling up a specific measure—sufficient, enough, adequate. It emphasizes not excess, but sufficiency.[5] Some might shrink from such responsibility. Even Paul, using this word, at times seemed to have despaired regarding his sufficiency for the ministry God had given him (1 Cor. 15:9; 2 Cor. 2:16; 3:5a). Yet he found that Christ dwelling in him was his sufficiency (2 Cor. 3:5b). The second word is the simple verb "I am" in the future middle indicative form. The future points to a sufficiency yet

> **Ministry Maxim**
>
> I have precisely one lifetime to make certain the Gospel survives and thrives in another generation—I must labor faithfully and invest wisely.

---

[3] BAGD, 180.
[4] Friberg, 298.
[5] Ibid., 203.

to be proven (through a new enabling work of God's Spirit) and the middle voice emphasizes the inward nature of such a work of God. Paul leaves no room for opting out of this transmittal of truth for lack of qualifications. The skills necessary will be imparted by God Himself and a failure in character would be a failure in the most basic of all Christian graces. The word "also" (καὶ) points to the basic orientation of the Christian life—"others also." Being transformed by Christ changes our orientation from simply receiving to consistently looking beyond ourselves to others. Christ reorients every life He invades with a focus beyond itself. We become outwardly focused. The aorist infinitive "teach" (διδάξαι) points to the specific aim of that others-focused life.

McCalley well says, "This verse is describing true apostolic succession. Apostolic succession is not succession of office, but succession of message."[6] Success in ministry, according to this verse, is measured by two standards. First, the accuracy of the message conveyed to another generation. Second, the ability of the next generation to pass this message accurately to yet another generation. Paul envisioned this success spanning at least four generations: himself, Timothy, "faithful men," and "others also." This is the pattern of life-to-life transference that measures the success of the church in all ages.

> **Digging Deeper:**
> 1. What are some current measurements of success in ministry and how do Paul's words here help us understand how God might evaluate them?
> 2. Can you trace the transference over four generations of the Gospel and its ministry in your life? Who passed on to you the Gospel and its ministry? To whom are you similarly investing the Gospel and its ministry?
> 3. Who are some "faithful men" (or for you women, "faithful women") in your life to whom you can hand off the Gospel and its ministry? How are you going about this?

2:3 Suffer hardship with me, as a good soldier of Christ Jesus.

The entire phrase "Suffer hardship with" is required to render but one Greek word (συγκακοπάθησον). With this command Paul returns to the same verb he used in 1:8. Here too it is an aorist imperative demanding the action be undertaken at once. The word is a triple compound: suffer (πάσχειν), evil (κακὸς),

---
[6] McCalley, 44.

and with (σὺν). It means either "suffer together with" or "take your share in suffering."[7] The Greek text leaves unstated just who Timothy is to suffer along with, but, given his circumstances and history, it would clearly include Paul (*"me"* is supplied by the translators of the NASU). It would surely also include all those believers whose sufferings Paul and Timothy knew all too well. A kindred verb, simply removing the prefix "with" (σὺν) and leaving a double compound, is taken up by Paul in v.9 to describe his own sufferings and is reintroduced in 4:5 in the command for Timothy to "endure hardship." And the core verb by itself ("suffer," πάσχω) is used by Paul in 1:12 to describe himself.

To reinforce this imperative, Paul introduces the metaphor of military life. He will stretch this out into the next verse and then add two more metaphors—that of an athlete (v.5) and that of a farmer (v.6)—before exhorting Timothy toward reflective thinking on these word pictures (v.7). The word "soldier" (στρατιώτης) is used only here by Paul (though see it in compound in Phil. 2:25 and Philem. 2) and elsewhere is used literally rather than metaphorically. However, military imagery is found frequently in Paul (2 Cor. 6:7; 10:3-5; Eph. 6:10-18; 1 Thess. 5:8-9; 1 Tim. 1:18; 6:12; 2 Tim. 4:7). Here the soldier (Timothy) is exhorted to be "good" (καλὸς). This common adjective is used here in the sense of unobjectionable, blameless, and excellent.[8] The metaphorical nature of the allusion is signaled by the use of "as" (ὡς). This subordinating conjunction functions as a comparative highlighting those qualities of a literal soldier, which would be comparable to Timothy's fulfillment of God's call in Ephesus. Indeed, Timothy is a soldier "of Christ Jesus" (Χριστοῦ Ἰησοῦ). The genitive signals that Paul is qualifying the metaphor and designating Christ as the commanding officer. Not everything about a literal soldier is in view, only those qualities which illustrate the truth Paul intended. Spirit-guided reflection (v.7) will enable us to know what those points of legitimate comparison were intended to be.

> **Ministry Maxim**
>
> Suffering well is a ministry in itself.

2:4 No soldier in active service entangles himself in the affairs of everyday life, so that he may please the one who enlisted him as a soldier.

The military metaphor continues. The entire expression "soldier in active service" (στρατευόμενος) represents the verb form of the noun used in v.3. Here it is a present middle participle used to express the subject of the sentence. The

---
[7] Rienecker, 638.
[8] BAGD, 400.

verb is used in the NT only in the middle voice. The present tense stresses the ongoing nature of the service, a thought which "in active service" captures well. The pronoun οὐδείς is added to cast the statement in the negative ("No"). It both broadens the subject and makes it absolute.

Such a soldier never "entangles himself" (ἐμπλέκεται). The word is used to describe a sheep or rabbit being caught by the fur in thorns.[9] The only other NT use of the verb is in 2 Peter 2:20 where it describes becoming re-entangled in "the defilements of the world" after having put one's faith in Christ. The noun form, however, is used in 1 Peter 3:3 to describe the braiding of hair—an image that helps inform our metaphor here. The verb form here can be either middle or passive. The former is represented by the NASU translation ("entangles himself"), the latter would mean "become entangled." The good soldier of Christ is not to become entangled in or interwoven with "the affairs of everyday life" (ταῖς τοῦ βίου πραγματείαις). The noun "affairs" (πραγματείαις) is found only here in the NT and the plural form points to the multiplicity of issues and details that confront one in this world. The word βίος refers to life as it relates to this earthly world (cf. 1 Tim. 2:2) as opposed to ζωή which tends to be used in reference to spiritual life (cf. 2 Tim. 1:1, 10). Accordingly the former is used by Paul only twice, the latter thirty-seven times. The rendering "of everyday life" captures well the intent of the word.

Just what is intended by this illustration? Is this a call to a cloistered life? Is it a demand for celibacy? Does this forbid the minister's involvement in secular work? This passage has been used to teach all of these things. Such conclusions, however, probably press the metaphor beyond Paul's intent. In applying such metaphors, we are not permitted to push all possible comparisons between the two objects (i.e., a soldier and a Christian), but only those which were the intent of the original author. By using the word picture of a soldier to instruct Timothy about the Christian's life, he was not saying everything about being a soldier applies to the believer. The primary point of application is that of single-minded focus. A soldier exists to "please the one who enlisted him as a soldier." Nothing should distract him from that commission.

> **Ministry Maxim**
>
> God's pleasure is my first and highest calling.

The word βίος was used by Jesus in the parable of the sower and is helpful in understanding the warning Paul issues here. "The seed which fell among the thorns, these are the ones who have heard, and as they go on their way they are choked with worries and riches and pleasures of this life [βίος], and bring no fruit to maturity" (Luke 8:14). Timothy was to make certain that

---

[9] Ibid., 256.

the "worries and riches and pleasures of this life" were not permitted to thrive and grow and one day choke out the one supreme concern that was to be always upon his heart—the pleasure of his Lord.

The final clause employs a ἵνα with a subjunctive verb to show the purpose behind a soldier's denial of everyday pursuits. It is "so that he may please the one who enlisted him as a soldier." The entire phrase "the one who enlisted him as a soldier" translates but one word and its definite article (τῷ στρατολογήσαντι). It is used only here in the NT and refers to the enlisting of soldiers for an army. The participial form is used as a substantive ("the one who") and the aorist tense looks back to the moment of his enlistment. Timothy was being urged to look back upon that moment when he heard God's call and responded in faith and obedience to that call. He is urged to remember that his was not merely a personal choice to follow, but a commissioning for service by One in authority. From that moment his pleasure became secondary to the pleasure of Christ, for every soldier wants to "please" (ἀρέσῃ) the one he serves. Paul frequently uses the word to describe pleasing God (Rom. 8:8; 1 Cor. 7:32; 1 Thess. 2:4, 15; 4:1).[10] The Christian "is bound to his commander not only by duty and loyalty but by the stronger cord of love."[11]

> **Digging Deeper:**
> 1. What points of comparison between a literal Roman soldier and one who serves Christ Jesus is God intending to stress?
> 2. What "affairs of everyday life" threaten to distract you from a single-minded focus on the pleasure of your Commanding Officer?
> 3. How does/should it change your attitude toward Christ and obedience to Him to know that you are viewed not primarily as one who has chosen to be a soldier of Christ, but rather as one who was "enlisted" by Him?

2:5 Also if anyone competes as an athlete, he does not win the prize unless he competes according to the rules.

Paul introduces a second metaphor, this time that of an athlete. The connection is made with v.4 by the coordinating conjunction δέ (untranslated in NASU, but cf. "And" in NASB) and the adverbial use of καί ("also"), which clearly designates this as one in a series of metaphors.

The conditional clause is introduced by the conjunction ἐάν, which, with the subjunctive verb, forms a class three condition expressing the undetermined nature of the condition. That is to say, it is not at all clear that any particular individual will compete as an athlete, but, if they do, the things that follow will hold true for them. The illustration is general in nature and then is to be applied appropriately by Timothy and other believers as the case may apply. The general nature of the illustration is made the more obvious by the indefinite pronoun "anyone" (τις).

The entire phrase "competes as an athlete" translates but one word (ἀθλῇ). The present tense sets the picture as simply unfolding in the mind of the reader. The subjunctive mood used with the conjunction sets forth the action as a possibility, but not yet a reality. The same verb is used at the end of the sentence, but appears nowhere else in the NT.

The phrase "he does not win the prize" translates one word (στεφανοῦται) and its negation (οὐ). The verb pictures the practice of placing a laurel wreath upon the head of the champion of the Greek games. The noun form is used elsewhere to describe just such a wreath or crown. An athlete's crown wilts and the glory of victory passes with time, yet the believer's crown is imperishable (1 Cor. 9:25). Paul anxiously awaited his "crown of righteousness" (2 Tim. 4:8).

But there will be no such prize "unless he competes according to the rules." There is a condition to being crowned victorious ("unless," ἐὰν μὴ) . The reward hinges on whether or not he competes "according to the rules" (νομίμως). The word is rooted in the word for law (νόμος). Thus the competition must be undertaken "lawfully" (i.e., "according to the rules"). The word is used elsewhere only in 1 Timothy 1:8. Here it is thrust forward to emphasize the critical nature of conformity to the law of the competition.[12] There is debate as to just what is referred to by "rules." Some point to the strict ten-month period of training Greek athletes were required to abide by prior to the games; others point to the rules of the contest itself. Given the general nature of the illustration all of this is probably in view. In application, however, the point is that, according to the rules of our contest, the Christian "athlete" must take his share in suffering (v.3). "Indeed, all who desire to live godly in Christ Jesus will be persecuted" (3:12).

> **Ministry Maxim**
>
> How I do ministry is as important as the fact that I am doing ministry.

The final verb is repeated from the beginning of the sentence. There is a significant shift in verb tense from the head of the sentence to here at its close. The first use is present tense and pictures anyone in general participating in the games at any time. The latter usage is aorist and makes specific the particular

---

[10] Marshall, 729.
[11] Kent, 260.
[12] Knight, 394.

moment or event of competition and that it is there that the rules must be upheld.

For other uses of athletic imagery in Paul see 1 Corinthians 9:24-27, Galatians 5:7, Philippians 3:14, 1 Timothy 1:18, 6:12, and 2 Timothy 4:7.

2:6 The hard-working farmer ought to be the first to receive his share of the crops.

To the imagery of a soldier (vv.3-4) and an athlete (v.5), Paul now adds that of a farmer. The noun "farmer" (γεωργὸν) is not infrequent in the Gospels, and James uses it once (5:7), but it appears only here in Paul's writings. Yet Paul does allude to farming imagery elsewhere (1 Cor. 3:6-9; 9:7-11). To understand the metaphor we must not picture the twenty-first century farming industry, but the hands-on vine-dresser of the first century. He is designated "The hard-working" (τὸν κοπιῶντα) farmer. The present tense pictures the unending toil to which a farmer must give himself. The participial form is used as an adjective.[13] This verb stresses the wearisome nature of the toil. It might apply to the ministry of local church leadership generally (1 Thess. 5:12), to preaching specifically (1 Tim. 5:17), or to striving after godliness in one's personal life (4:10). Paul knew from experience what it meant to work to the point of weariness (1 Cor. 4:12; 15:10; Gal. 4:11; Phil. 2:16; Col. 1:29; 1 Tim. 4:10).

The verb "ought" (δεῖ) stresses "the compulsion of what is fitting."[14] The present tense pictures the ongoing, unending nature of this compulsive appropriateness. That which is rightly the farmer's is that he might "receive his share of the crops" (τῶν καρπῶν μεταλαμβάνειν). The verb is a compound meaning "to receive" (λαμβάνω) and "with" (μετά). Here it refers to receiving what is rightly his along with any others who may also have a claim upon his crop (i.e., land owner, family members, etc.). The moral obligation here, however, is not just that the farmer receive some of the crops, but that he might be "the first" (πρῶτον) to do so. Just what this means is a matter of some debate. Does it serve as an adjective modifying the noun (τῶν καρπῶν) or as an adverb modifying the infinitive (μεταλαμβάνειν)? Does it refer to the first of the fruits or to the order of his reception of those fruits? And what particular significance is this intended to convey regarding Timothy's situation? Or is this simply part of the fabric of the metaphor without designating a specific application to be drawn from it?

> **Ministry Maxim**
>
> My labor for Christ does not go unnoticed and will not go unrewarded.

If taken as an adjective it would mean that the first of the fruits goes to the

---

[13] Marshall, 730.
[14] BAGD, 172.

farmer. Presumably in the application this would mean that the Christian who labors for the Lord would enjoy here in this life at least some measure of reward for his labors. This could be taken as instruction for Timothy to receive pay for his ministry willingly. This, however, seems foreign to the context where a more eschatological reward seems to be in view.[15] It could, on the other hand, point to the spiritual fruits of his labors (e.g., seeing others come to faith in Christ). This too, however, seems beyond what the context calls for. If πρῶτον is taken as an adverb it refers to the order of reception. This could point to the Christian/pastor learning from the Scriptures before those he teaches as he prepares and seeks God for his teaching. Or it could point to the logical necessity to labor before enjoying the fruits of one's labor.[16] Others conclude that πρῶτον was simply part of the vivid color of the metaphor and not intended to be drawn out for significant, individual detail.[17] But this seems to dismiss the word too easily. Perhaps πρῶτον is used not in a linear sense of "first in line," but rather as first in priority. In this sense it could point more to the certainty of reward rather than the rank or order of that reward's reception.[18] This would encourage Timothy and other readers by gathering up the eschatological nature of the reward as well as the present joys of service to Christ and underscoring their certainty. No one who labors for the Lord will fail to be rewarded.

> **Digging Deeper:**
> 1. How does the training and competition of a world-class athlete illustrate what God desires from you in your daily walk with Him and ministry for Him?
> 2. How does the laborious, toilsome life of a farmer picture what God wants to motivate you?
> 3. When is it appropriate to be motivated to serve God in hopes of being rewarded and when may that be an inappropriate motivation?

2:7 Consider what I say, for the Lord will give you understanding in everything.

The present imperative "Consider" (νόει) demands that action be taken continuously and habitually. The word refers to comprehending something through contemplation and reflection. The import of the word has to do with

---

[15] Fee, 243.
[16] Knight, 395.
[17] Ibid.
[18] Kent, 262.

the ability to perceive, understand, and comprehend, particularly in the spiritual or religious realm.[19] The words "what I say" have specific application to the three metaphors Paul has just set forth (vv.3-6). The command, however, rests upon the broader principle that the Holy Spirit unfailingly gives spiritual insight to those who contemplatively meditate upon God's Word with a heart toward obedience (John 14:26; 16:13; 1 Cor. 2:12, 14-15). Within this specific context, the command to "Consider" is defined by the fact that the images of the soldier (vv.3b-4), athlete (v.5), and farmer (v.6) are all controlled by the previous imperative to "suffer hardship" (v.3a). Not any and every comparison between soldier, athlete and farmer is intended, but those which help us to flesh out the previous command to "suffer hardship." Likewise each seems to point to a future reward for such faithfulness in suffering, be it victory for the soldier, the "prize" for the athlete or the "crops" of the farmer.

By the use of the conjunction "for" (γάρ), Paul sets forth the reason why Timothy should take pains to obey his command. By "the Lord," Paul could mean either the Father or Son (cf. 1:18). What is certain is that Divine aid "will give" the necessary insight Timothy needs. The future tense verb points with confident certainty to God's willingness to grant insight to the hungry, seeking heart. And this hope Paul sets forth not simply as a general principle, but as a promise to Timothy personally ("you," σοι).

The anticipated gift is "understanding" (σύνεσιν) The word is a compound ("with, σύν; "bring," εἰμί) and is used to describe the coming or sending together of two things. It is used to describe the union of two rivers that flow together.[20] Here the two things coming into dynamic union are Timothy and God's Word spoken through Paul. These two converge with a divine spark to create an understanding that Timothy could not have previously enjoyed. This will be Timothy's experience "in everything" (ἐν πᾶσιν), says Paul. This points specifically to all the implications of the three metaphors Paul has been setting before Timothy (vv.3-6). It does not promise that God will give a complete working knowledge of every detail of creation or divine providence to every child of God. Yet it does broaden out into a general principle regarding illumination of the Scriptures by God to every sincere, seeking heart.

> **Ministry Maxim**
>
> Illumination generally follows cogitation.

Paul points to the dynamic at work between a believer's effort at reasoning and God's work within that believer to bring him to understanding. God will not "give . . . understanding" apart from the believer taking up the responsibility to

---

[19] DNTT, 3:128.
[20] Friberg, 366.

obey the imperative "Consider." Yet we will never reason ourselves into spiritual understanding. We must exercise ourselves in thinking over the Scriptures, yet we do so in dependence upon God the Spirit who we trust will guide our thoughts and add His insight to this thinking. The result will be an understanding of God's truth which lies beyond normal human rational processes. What an exciting interchange takes place over the written Word of God when we come with humble, teachable, hungry hearts, crying out for insight that we might obey and follow God! Let us, therefore, pray: "Open my eyes, that I may behold Wonderful things from Your law" (Psa. 119:18; cf. Eph. 1:17-19).

Digging Deeper:
1. How is this promise a great encouragement and incentive to the student of Scripture?
2. What should the recognition of this truth change, practically speaking, about how we spend our time with God each day in His Word?
3. Is spiritual understanding our responsibility or God's? Why?

2:8 Remember Jesus Christ, risen from the dead, descendant of David, according to my gospel,

Continuing on the theme of the mind ("Consider," v.7), Paul commands Timothy now to "Remember." The focal point is no longer metaphors (vv.3-6), but a Person—"Jesus Christ." "Remember" (Μνημόνευε) is a present imperative calling for continuous or habitual action. The verb means to call to mind, to recall, or to think about. The theme of memory is a rich one throughout this letter (cf. 1:3-6; 3:14-15).

The object of Timothy's purposeful recollections was to be "Jesus Christ." This is the only time the order "Jesus Christ" is found in 2 Timothy. Twelve times in the letter we find the order "Christ Jesus." This uniqueness may be in order to highlight a shift in emphasis. The order "Christ Jesus" may be understood as a stress of Christ's position as the Messiah ("Christ"), whereas the reversed order may emphasize the Personhood of Jesus Himself. What is abundantly clear is that Paul is concerned that Timothy keep Jesus at the forefront of all his thoughts. He was not worried that Timothy would entirely forget who Jesus was. Rather he was concerned that, under pressure, Timothy might not allow Christ the place of preeminence and supremacy in this thinking that He deserves. It is tantamount to saying, "Remember the Commanding Officer you seek to please (vv.3-4), the athletic Judge before whom you compete (v.5), and the Land Owner in whose fields you till your crops (v.6)."

There were two primary things about Jesus that Paul was concerned Timothy allow to fill the panorama of his vision. The first is that he is "risen from the dead" (ἐγηγερμένον ἐκ νεκρῶν). The verb's perfect tense sets forth Christ as having been raised from the dead at a point in the past and then emphasizes the fact that He continues to exist in this living state. The passive voice makes clear that it was another who raised Him out of ("from," ἐκ) the dead—God the Father (Gal. 1:1). The participial form serves either in an adverbial way, modifying the verb "Remember" ("Remember that Jesus Christ has been risen from the dead"),[21] or in an adjectival way, modifying the noun "Jesus"[22] (as per the NASU). The apparently parallel nature of the two phrases (lit., "risen out of the dead" and "out of David's seed) seems to point to the latter.[23] Mention of the resurrection implies the fact of crucifixion. Paul speaks specifically of the resurrection, however, because it is not simply the suffering of Christ he wants Timothy to dwell upon, but also His victorious triumph over death. The resurrection is the primary stamp of authenticity upon Jesus Christ's divinity (Rom. 1:4).

> **Ministry Maxim**
>
> Jesus is always the point — He must ever be at the center of all my thoughts and reasoning.

The second focal point of Timothy's recollections of Jesus was to be that He is a "descendant of David" or more literally "out of David's seed" (ἐκ σπέρματος Δαυίδ). This emphasizes both His humanity (cf. "born of a woman," Gal. 4:4) and His genealogical qualifications as Messiah (cf. Matt. 1:1; Acts 13:22-23). All the promises made to David have now found their fulfillment in Jesus. He is not only ever-living, but is currently enthroned and reigning over all things, including the suffering of His people. This dual emphasis is reflected in Romans where Paul referred to Jesus as He "who was born of a descendant of David according to the flesh, who was declared the Son of God with power by the resurrection from the dead" (Rom. 1:3b-4a).

Keeping the glorious Son of God before his mind would allow Timothy to remember Him who as a man had suffered far more than he could imagine and yet had triumphed over the ultimate foe of death through His resurrection and continuing life. Only this One can sustain His followers in their hour of trial and offer them life beyond it.

All of this Paul demands is "according to my gospel" (κατὰ τὸ εὐαγγέλιόν μου). The exact phrase is used elsewhere by Paul in Romans 2:16 and 16:25, but he

---

[21] Knight, 397.
[22] Mounce, 512.
[23] Ibid.

also speaks of "our gospel" in 2 Corinthians 4:3, 1 Thessalonians 1:5, and 2 Thessalonians 2:14. More often Paul refers to it as "the gospel of God" (Rom. 1:1; 15:16; 2 Cor. 11:7; 1 Thess. 2:2, 8, 9) or "the gospel of our Lord Jesus Christ" (2 Thess. 1:8) or "the gospel of Christ" (Rom. 15:19; 1 Cor. 9:12; 2 Cor. 2:12; 9:13; 10:14; Gal. 1:7; Phil. 1:27; 1 Thess. 3:2). This Gospel could only be designated "my gospel" in that Paul was "was appointed a preacher and an apostle and a teacher" of it (2 Tim. 1:11; cf. 1 Tim. 2:7). Christ is ever the substance of the Gospel, being sent by the Father to secure our salvation. The Gospel could only be spoken of as being Paul's, or anyone else's, in the sense that they had first been captured by it personally and then compelled by it through divine calling.

2:9 for which I suffer hardship even to imprisonment as a criminal; but the word of God is not imprisoned.

The sentence continues with "for which" (ἐν ᾧ) providing the link. The preposition ἐν can point to cause[24] and the relative pronoun ᾧ points back to "my gospel" (v.8).[25] So far every time Paul has mentioned the Gospel (1:8, 10; 2:8) he has linked it to suffering (1:8, 12). Once again Paul says that for this Gospel "I suffer hardship" (κακοπαθῶ). The word is a compound made up of "suffer" (πάσχειν) and "evil" (κακὸς). The main root was met in 1:10 and the same compound with a prefix added was used in 1:8. The present tense points simply to Paul's current ongoing circumstances. This, however, was no ordinary suffering, it was "even to imprisonment as a criminal" (μέχρι δεσμῶν ὡς κακοῦργος). The preposition μέχρι basically means "until," but when related to the degree or measure of something it can mean "to the point of."[26] The word "imprisonment" (δεσμῶν) refers literally to bonds, chains or fetters (e.g., Luke 8:29; Acts 16:26). By metonymy it can then be used to speak of imprisonment generally (e.g., Phil. 1:7; Col. 4:18).[27] The noun here (δεσμῶν) forms a wordplay with the verbal form at the end of the sentence (δέδεται, "is not imprisoned"). Modern translations generally opt for the literal sense of "chains" (ESV, NIV, NKJV, NLT, NRSV) rather than the metaphorical sense of "imprisonment" (NASU) in this passage. Paul's present conditions were not just suffering, nor were they simply "imprisonment," but they

> **Ministry Maxim**
>
> I may be silenced, but the Gospel I preach will never be silenced.

---

[24] BAGD, 261.
[25] Mounce, 513.
[26] BAGD, 515.
[27] Friberg, 106.

were also incarceration "as a criminal." In its only other NT usage the same word (κακοῦργος) describes the two criminals crucified on either side of Jesus (Luke 23:32, 33, 39). Paul, like his Lord, falsely bore the brand of evil-doer. The word speaks of "one who commits gross misdeeds and serious crimes."[28] It describes not a simple delinquent, but points toward a thieving insurrectionist; it points not toward a pick-pocket, but a thief who uses violence rather than stealth to achieve his goal.

Such a one could expect the harshest of sentences and the most cruel of punishments. Paul was clearly in serious trouble. Yet Paul chose to dwell not upon his imprisonment, but upon the unrestrainable nature of the Gospel. Paul used the strong adversative (ἀλλά) to contrast his chains with the free-ranging, unencumbered nature of "the word of God" (ὁ λόγος τοῦ θεοῦ). Paul uses this later phrase to describe the Gospel message and its truths (Rom. 9:6; 1 Cor. 14:36; Titus 2:5). Jesus could also use it to represent the Scriptures (John 10:35). The Gospel—its truths and the Scriptures which reveal them to us—"is not imprisoned" (οὐ δέδεται). The perfect tense of the verb points to the fact that "the word of God" has never at a point in the past been restrained and that right up to this day it continues to do its work freely and without encumbrance from human or demonic opposition. The passive voice pictures such futile attacks coming against the word from outside. The history of the church has repeatedly illustrated that you may bind or even kill the messenger, but the message of Jesus Christ can never be restrained (cf. Phil. 1:12-18). As the next verse will make clear, Paul is not merely inferring that while he is imprisoned the Gospel goes on (you can't imprison every Christian). Rather, Paul sees his imprisonment and impending death as a vital and active part of the Gospel reaching "those who are chosen, so that they also may obtain the salvation which is in Christ Jesus" (v.10).

Digging Deeper:

1. How do pressures sometimes displace Christ from being the preeminent focus of our thoughts? What problems does this invite?
2. Why is the resurrection of Christ a key point of meditation for those who suffer for Him?
3. How does the unstoppable power of the Word strengthen us when opposition arises?

---

[28] BAGD, 398.

2:10 For this reason I endure all things for the sake of those who are chosen, so that they also may obtain the salvation which is in Christ Jesus and with it eternal glory.

Paul now draws a logical conclusion from what he has just said about the unfetterable nature of the word of God (v.9) by employing the inferential expression διὰ τοῦτο ("For this reason"). What follows logically in a relationship to such an unstoppable force is that "I endure" (ὑπομένω). The word is a compound meaning to remain (μένω) under (ὑπό), but it came to refer to the patient steadfastness which does not flee from trouble. The present tense points to the unceasing nature of this endurance. Paul's example should become the pattern of every believer's life (v.12). That which Paul endures is referred to as "all things" (πάντα). The neuter plural form points to Paul's present imprisonment for the Gospel and all the hardships that it has brought. One could well list also the lifetime of sufferings that had come to Paul in his service to Christ (cf. 2 Cor. 6:4-10; 11:23-28). The weight of all of this is willingly borne "for the sake of [διὰ with the accusative] those who are chosen" (τοὺς ἐκλεκτούς). From Paul's earliest moments of faith in Christ he understood that being chosen by God and suffering for God are inseparable. God sent Ananias to him while he was still-blinded, saying, "Go, for he is a chosen instrument of Mine, to bear My name before the Gentiles and kings and the sons of Israel; for I will show him how much he must suffer for My name's sake" (Acts 9:15-16). God chose His own before the foundation of the world (Eph. 1:4). He set His love upon the lowliest of this earth so as to magnify the nature of His grace (1 Cor. 1:27ff). The one whom God chooses, no one can condemn (Rom. 8:33).

A common criticism of the doctrine of election is that it will weaken the evangelistic impulse of God's people. Note, however, that the fact of election did not undercut the Apostle's missionary zeal; rather it fed it. Paul endured all manner of suffering "so that they also may obtain the salvation which is in Christ Jesus." The purpose ("so that," ἵνα) for the grinding difficulty, depravation, disgrace and discomfort of Paul's life was so that the grace of God might reach those whom God had chosen to enjoy it. Far from sapping missionary fervor, the doctrine of election ought to heighten it. Paul knew that just as they had been chosen to enjoy the undeserved riches of God's grace in Christ, so too he was "a chosen instrument" (Acts 9:15) of Christ to take that message to them. There was no throwing up of the hands in the face of difficulty and saying, "If God has chosen them, He will find a way to get the gospel to them."

Paul had a clear sense that his obedience and endurance in spreading the Gospel was essential if these people "also may obtain the salvation which is in Christ Jesus" (καὶ αὐτοὶ σωτηρίας τύχωσιν τῆς ἐν Χριστῷ Ἰησου). What Paul and other believers enjoyed, he knew he must make certain every other person had the opportunity to enjoy ("also," καὶ). This salvation is "in Christ Jesus" (ἐν Χριστῷ Ἰησου). The exact phrase occurs forty-six times in Paul. Seven of the nine times it is used in the PE are here in 2 Timothy (1:1, 9, 13; 2:1, 10; 3:12, 13). As the end of what Paul possessed in this world drew near, he focused all the more on what he had "in Christ Jesus" by grace and what he knew others must also have the opportunity to embrace.

> **Ministry Maxim**
>
> The sovereign grace of God in election does not relieve me of my responsibility in evangelism.

Though they are elect they must "obtain" (τύχωσιν) this salvation. The word means to attain, gain, find or experience something, that particular thing being designated by the genitive (in this case "salvation").[29] Paul saw the *process* of reaching the elect as important as the *fact* of their having been chosen. There must be the sacrifice of reaching them with the Gospel. There must be the active reception of the Gospel. Yet the whole of the process is overseen by God's electing grace. The Apostle did the sacrificing and preaching. The people did the believing and receiving. Yet the whole was God's work of salvation in their hearts. The Apostle saw no contradiction in such a Divine arrangement. As Hiebert puts it, "election does not eliminate or put any restrictions on the exercise of human freedom in meeting the conditions for salvation."[30]

This "salvation" is something enjoyed in the present, for we "obtain" it here and now. Yet it is something enjoyed even more fully in eternity, for it comes "with . . . eternal glory" (μετὰ δόξης αἰωνίου). Paul has the entire panorama of salvation in view—from the first work of the Spirit in awakening the heart to the truth of the Gospel all the way to the final glorification in eternity. As Paul will soon show, the necessity of endurance stands between our initial profession of Christ and our final glorification with Christ (vv.11-13). Yet it is that very hope which enabled Paul (and all like him) to endure in the cause of the Gospel. Such endurance is produced by proclaiming an unstoppable message (v.9), by pondering an undeserved privilege (v.10a) and by pursuing an unsearchable prize (v.10b).

---

[29] BAGD, 829.
[30] Hiebert, *Second Timothy*, 61.

> **Digging Deeper:**
> 1. How does a correct understanding of the doctrine of election fuel, not defuse, the missionary impulse of God's people?
> 2. Look again at why Paul endured—what does this say about your endurance in the face of the things that confront you today? How does this help focus your life and purpose?
> 3. Why is it essential in endurance to keep the ultimate goal of the glory of God (and our sharing in it with Him) always before us?

2:11 It is a trustworthy statement: For if we died with Him, we will also live with Him;

Now Paul transitions from his example of endurance (vv.9-10) to an exhortation to endurance (vv.11-13). He sets forth this exhortation by means of what appears to be a familiar poem or hymn. It is introduced by the phrase, "It is a trustworthy statement" (πιστὸς ὁ λόγος). The verb is missing, but implied and thus supplied by the translators. Literally it reads, "faithful the word." Paul uses this same introductory formula elsewhere only in the PE (1 Tim. 1:15; 3:1; 4:9; Titus 3:8). In a time of transition, as the Apostles passed off the scene and as challenges from both within and without confronted the fledgling church, Paul used this expression with those responsible to carry the Gospel ministry to the next generation. It served as a familiar way of identifying truth they could count on and use as a fixed point of reference in confusing times.

While some dispute the poetic or hymnic nature of these lines, it appears self-evident that there has been some design in their composition. The four lines each begin with a first class conditional statement (indicative plus εἰ). The protasis in all four lines each employs first person plural ("we") verbs, dealing with actions of believers and setting the whole in the corporate context of the church. The protases of the first three lines progress through verb tenses from the past to the present to the future. In addition, the apodosis in the first three lines each employ an "also" statement. The apodosis in each case deals with the outcome in terms of Christ. The final line breaks ranks using two present tense verbs, containing no "also" statement, and surprising us with its conclusion.[31] There appears to be two couplets to the poem or hymn. In the first two, three out of the four verbs are prefixed with σύν, stressing the relationship Christians possess

---
[31] Fee, 249.

"with" Christ. These first two lines speak of the outcome of fulfilling the condition in positive terms. The two lines of the second couplet speak of the possible outcome either in negative terms ("will deny us") or of the inability of God to act contrary to His own nature in dealing with us ("cannot deny Himself").[32]

That Paul's "trustworthy statement" points forward seems self-evident, based on the personal nature of what has preceded in vv.8-10 and the ordered composition of what follows in vv.11-13. There are those, however, who insist that it must point backward to what has already been said. They normally base their arguments upon the presence of the conjunction "for" (γὰρ), insisting that this links what follows in vv.11-13 with what has come before. Some have countered that the "for" (γὰρ) was simply a part of the original hymn or poem and refers not to what precedes in this letter, but to what came before it in the original composition. Perhaps Paul's words in vv.8-10 were a personalized summation of what preceded in the original work or perhaps Paul simply began the quotation without stylizing it for the present context. Still others believe γὰρ means something like "namely" and is used to emphasize what follows in vv.11-13. This, however, stretches the normal meaning of the word beyond what seems reasonable.[33] Fee sees the γὰρ as explanatory, pointing back not to the expression "this is a trustworthy statement," but to the whole of all Paul has said in vv.1-10.[34] This poem or hymn then becomes the conclusion to a larger section of the letter. This seems to provide a most reasonable explanation for the presence of γὰρ and the purpose of the poem or hymn.

> **Ministry Maxim**
>
> The only assurance I have that I could die for Christ someday is that I have died to self today.

As for the saying itself, the first line sets before us the first of four first class conditional statements. These assume the condition to be true, in this case that the believers being referenced have already "died with" (συναπεθάνομεν) Christ. The compound verb means literally "to die" (ἀποθνῄσκω) "with" (σύν) another. It was used in its most literal sense in Mark 14:31 where Peter swore that he would not deny Christ even if he had to die with Him. Paul also used it more metaphorically in 2 Corinthians 7:3 of the intensity of his love both to live and to die together with the believers in Corinth. Here it could point either to one's willingness to be martyred for Christ or his union with Christ in the more mystical sense. Despite Paul's

---

[32] Knight, 402.
[33] Ibid., 401.
[34] Fee, 248.

impending death, the former possibility seems ruled out by the aorist tense which points to a past act. The latter seems the more likely (though surely the former is not lost entirely), given Paul's clear emphasis elsewhere on the believer's union with Christ in His death (cf. Rom. 6:3-5, 8, 11; 7:4-6; Gal. 2:20; Col. 2:20; 3:3). When Christ died for our sins upon the cross, God the Father counted this as our death. Each believer then must by faith reckon that death to be actual fact for himself (Rom. 6:11; Col. 3:5).

If we have counted ourselves dead with Christ—and note the assumption that believers do indeed so consider themselves—then "we will also live with Him" (καὶ συζήσομεν). It follows like the day follows the night ("also," καὶ) that identification with Christ in His death leads to an experience of His resurrection life. The verb ("live with," συζήσομεν) is found together with the previous verb in 2 Corinthians 7:3. It is also found in the same context of the believer's union with Christ in His death in Romans 6:8: "Now if we have died with Christ, we believe that we shall also live with (συζήσομεν) Him." Both there and here it is in the future active indicative form. Does this point only to what shall be experienced one day in heaven? Or does it promise an experience attainable in this life, but on the other side of identification with Christ in His death? Left to only this passage, the answer would be unclear. However, the context of Romans 6:8 points to the present experience of the believer: "Even so consider yourselves to be dead to sin, but alive to God in Christ Jesus" (6:11). The Christian life is simply the life of Christ Himself lived out in and through the believer. Christ is our life (Gal. 2:20; Col. 3:4). Indeed, the Apostle told the Corinthian believers that we are "always carrying about in the body the dying of Jesus, so that the life of Jesus also may be manifested in our body" (2 Cor. 4:10). This is at least part of what Paul meant when he began this letter: "according to the promise of life in Christ Jesus" (1:1). Christ has "brought life and immortality to light through the gospel" (1:10), and we see this hope as we see Him alive in and through other believers. This having been said, there are no doubt eschatological overtones to Paul's hope for life on the other side of his impending martyrdom.

In times of melancholy one may wonder if he would stand true and endure death for Christ if required. Such grace is only given when it is needed. The only assurance one has about his response in such a potential future moment is found in the present moment and whether he is living as one already dead and now alive again with Christ. Denying self now is not choosing a grim path of hard discipleship, but an opening of the soul to the inflow of Christ's own life!

The Pastoral Epistles for Pastors

> **Digging Deeper:**
> 1. How is life lived differently knowing we have not just one "trust worthy statement," but an entire Bible full of them? What becomes of us if we fail to see the "trustworthy" nature of the Scriptures?
> 2. In what sense can we as believers be said to have "died with" Christ? How do we experience union with Christ in His death? What does that change about your life each day?
> 3. Do you agree or disagree with this statement: "Too many Christians want the supernatural life of Christ without dying with Christ?" What becomes of those unwilling to experience union with Christ in His death?

2:12 If we endure, we will also reign with Him; If we deny Him, He also will deny us;

The second in the series of four conditions is also assumed true. Note the transition from the past tense ("we died with Him") to the present ("we endure"), from the assumed past fact to the assumed present responsibility. The verb ("we endure," ὑπομένομεν) is the same one Paul used in v.10 and likely points to his primary reason for citing this poem or hymn. The transition from the first person singular to the first person plural makes certain the indirect influence of Paul's testimony (v.10) is now underscored and made more direct. The broad, principled nature of the hymn assures that we understand that endurance of suffering is the lot of every believer, not simply a singular event for an Apostle, nor even a spasmodic event in the ongoing life of the church (cf. 3:12). The present tense of the verb presents endurance as an ongoing need in every believer's life. The verb ὑπομένω is used only four times by Paul (Rom. 12:12; 1 Cor. 13:7), two of them in this chapter (vv.10, 12), thus highlighting the emphatic nature of its use in the present context.[35]

The real emphasis ("also," καί), however, is upon the promised "reign with Him." The verb is in the future tense, standing in contrast to the present tense verb in the protasis. It points thus to the eschatological hope of the believer at Christ's return. The compound word (συμβασιλεύσομεν) means to reign with another. That the faithful believer is promised a share in Christ's throne in the next life is a promise that first arose from Christ's own lips during His earthly ministry (Matt. 19:28; Luke 22:29) and then during His subsequent resurrection ministry (Rev. 2:26; 3:21). His Apostles echoed this same hope (1 Cor. 6:2; Rev. 20:4, 6; 22:5).

---

[35] Mounce, 516.

The third line moves us from the past ("we died," v.11) and the present ("we endure," v.12a) and on to the future ("we deny Him," ἀρνησόμεθα). The condition is once again assumed to be true. However, the supposed denial is cast in the future tense, making it not a present reality for Paul or Timothy, but a future probability for some. The denial is only potential, though it is stated as an actuality. Yet the argument is made only if such a denial is possible. The persecution that Paul and other believers of his day faced made this more than theoretical philosophizing (1:15; 2:18; 4:10, 16). The middle voice pictures the inward nature of the denial. The verb is used by Paul only in the PE and he uses it twice in this verse and once in the next. Such a denial may not be audible and outward, but the inward attitude of the heart (3:5). Such a denial inevitably shows itself in one's actions (1 Tim. 5:8; Titus 1:16). The Gospel is to teach us "to deny [ἀρνησάμενοι] ungodliness and worldly desires" (Titus 2:12).

> **Ministry Maxim**
>
> The order of ministry is fixed: a cross then a crown.

The rejection of Christ brings a reciprocal denial of the individual by Christ. The demonstrative pronoun κἀκεῖνος ("He also") is thrust forward for emphasis—no one less than Christ Himself will deny the one who denies Him. The future tense points to the certainty of Christ's action and functions as a warning against defection. "But whoever denies Me before men, I will also deny him before My Father who is in heaven" (Matt. 10:33; cf. Mark 8:38; Luke 9:26; 12:9; Rev. 2:13; 3:8).

The denial in view is not a temporary denial in a moment of weakness, like Peter (Matt. 26:35-75), but a permanent denial like Judas Iscariot (Matt. 27:5; John 17:12).

2:13 If we are faithless, He remains faithful, for He cannot deny Himself.

Again the condition is assumed true. The present tense does not mean that Paul, Timothy or their fellow believers were "faithless," but that for the sake of argument he was assuming such a thought for the moment. The word "faithless" (ἀπιστοῦμεν) in most of its eight usages in the NT means to fail or refuse to believe something. Here, however, it clearly refers not to disbelief, but to unfaithfulness. That this is the case is clear in that "faithless" in the protasis is answered by "faithful" (πιστός) in the apodosis. It is Christ who is said to remain "faithful" and it would be wholly out of place to describe Him as "believing" in this case. On the other hand, to prove "faithless" may be a strong indicator of the absence of true faith in the first place. Paul uses the verbal form only twice (also in Rom. 3:3), but the noun form five times (Rom. 3:3; 4:20; 11:20, 23; 1 Tim. 1:13).

While v.12b pointed to permanent defection from the faith, this verse refers to the passing acts of unfaithfulness in every believer's life that are followed by conviction regarding the sin and repentance and restoration to Christ. Judas's sin was pictured in v.12b, while that of Peter is depicted here.

Following the first three lines we would expect a different echo here in the apodosis. What we find, however, is a strong statement of the opposite character of Christ. The demonstrative pronoun "He" (ἐκεῖνος) is set forward in an emphatic position and points to Christ. That He is "faithful" could be either a reassuring promise or a stern warning. But the word "faithful" (πιστὸς), when attributed to deity in the NT, is always a positive reassurance of His commitment to blessing by way of keeping His promises (1 Cor. 1:9; 10:13; 2 Cor. 1:18; 1 Thess. 5:24; 2 Thess. 3:3; Heb. 2:17; 3:2; 10:23; 11:11; 1 Peter 4:19; 1 John 1:9; Rev. 1:5; 3:14; 19:11), never a warning of His judgment. Despite the possible unfaithfulness of the believer, Christ "remains" (μένει) faithful. The present tense verb points to the ongoing and unceasing action. This is a powerful way of underscoring His covenant commitment to His people and the unilateral nature of His commitment to them. This "trustworthy [πιστὸς, v.11] statement" is ultimately grounded in the "faithful" (πιστὸς) nature of God (v.13).

> **Ministry Maxim**
>
> God requires my faithfulness, for He is Himself comfortingly, terrifyingly consistent.

The final line breaks off from the first three by adding an explanatory clause: "for [γὰρ] He cannot deny Himself." The explanation is necessary because the apodosis seems not to follow naturally the protasis. The reason God remains faithful to His covenant promises when His followers prove unfaithful is grounded in the very nature of His own character. It is fundamentally impossible for God to "deny Himself" and act contrary to His own nature. The verb ("deny," ἀρνήσασθαι) is the same one used twice in v.12, except that here it is in the aorist tense instead of the future, pointing to even one point in time where God might deny Himself. This utter impossibility is stated in the strongest of terms (οὐ δύναται). For God to act any other way than in accord with His own nature would require that He cease being God, which is impossible. The surety of God's covenant with and promises to the believer is grounded in the eternal constancy of God's nature, not in mere sentiment or sympathy. The future salvation of "those who are chosen" (v.10) rests in the character and nature of God. Hope lives because God is eternally faithful, not merely to us, but to Himself. The whole hymn (vv.11b-13) rightly leaves one either assured (vv.11b-12a, 13) or unsettled (v.12b) before the awful consistency of God.

> **Digging Deeper:**
> 1. What is at stake when we are called to endure for Christ?
> 2. Is there a difference between denying Christ and being unfaithful to Him? What is it? What is God's response to either or both?
> 3. How does the inner self-consistency of God's character both reassure and frighten us?

2:14 Remind them of these things, and solemnly charge them in the presence of God not to wrangle about words, which is useless and leads to the ruin of the hearers.

This verse functions as a janus—both pointing back and looking forward. The sentence opens with a present imperative ("Remind," ὑπομίμνῃσκε) calling for continuous action. The verb is used by Paul only here and Titus 3:1. He also uses the noun form only in 1:5. Paul has also used a related verb for memory (ἀναμιμνῄσκω, 1:6). The concentrated use in this context of such relatively rare words underscores Paul's interest in memory in the letter. The demonstrative plural pronoun opens the sentence in Greek ("these things," Ταῦτα) and may refer generally to the entire letter so far, but most specifically points to the truths summarized in the hymn just cited (vv.11-13). In view of the false teaching that is rife in the Ephesian congregation, Timothy must repeatedly underscore the serious nature of endurance and the potential of apostasy.

What follows serves to open up a new section that transitions from the basic theme of endurance in the face of suffering to the struggle against false teaching (2:14-4:5). Timothy is to move from persistent reminder to solemn warning ("solemnly charge," διαμαρτυρόμενος). Paul has leveled a solemn charge to Timothy previously (1 Tim. 5:21) and will do so again (2 Tim. 4:1). Now he calls upon Timothy to do the same toward the people under his charge. The verb describes an emphatic verbal admonition.[36] The participial form signals a dependence upon the previous imperative ("Remind," ὑπομίμνῃσκε), yet the fact that both are in the present tense signals that this is action to be taken concurrently with the reminder and that the participle has taken on some imperatival force.[37]

This serious admonition is to take place "in the presence of God" (ἐνώπιον τοῦ θεοῦ). Paul uses this exact phrase ten times (Rom. 14:22; 1 Cor. 1:29; 2 Cor. 4:2; 7:12; Gal. 1:20; 1 Tim. 5:4, 21; 6:13; 2 Tim. 2:14; 4:1).

---
[36] Kittel, abridged, 570.
[37] Knight, 410.

Paul's charges to Timothy were also made "in the presence of God" (1 Tim. 5:21; 6:13; 2 Tim. 4:1). This expression often served as an attestation of a statement made (Gal. 1:20), an attitude held (Rom. 14:22) or an action undertaken (1 Tim. 5:4). It served as a solemnifying part of matters most serious.

That which is so seriously warned of is "not to wrangle about words" (μὴ λογομαχεῖν). The infinitive is used to express what the content of Timothy's charge is to be.[38] The word (λογομαχεῖν) is found only here in the NT (though compare the related noun in 1 Tim. 6:4). Some believe Paul may have coined the word to describe the very problem besetting the Ephesian church.[39] It is a compound word made up of λόγος (word) and μάχεσθαι (to battle). It means to "dispute about words, split hairs."[40] The present tense with the negative can demand a cessation of action already in progress. It is clear from 1 Timothy that this was an ongoing problem for the church in Ephesus (1:4, 6; 4:7; 6:3-5, 20). It is equally clear that Paul's instructions there were not heeded and the war of words continued to the time of this, his final letter (2 Tim. 2:14, 16, 23).

> **Ministry Maxim**
>
> Never underestimate the ministry of reminder — familiar truth restated and reapplied by the Holy Spirit.

Paul concludes the sentence by adding "which is useless and leads to the ruin of the hearers" (ἐπ' οὐδὲν χρήσιμον, ἐπὶ καταστροφῇ τῶν ἀκουόντων). It is in reality two parallel phrases, both introduced by the preposition ἐπί. The prepositional phrases set forth the results of such word-wars.[41] Both results are negative. First is "which is useless" (ἐπ' οὐδὲν χρήσιμον). The adjective speaks of that which is profitable or beneficial. The negation is absolute ("useless," οὐδὲν)—such talk is utterly devoid of any profit at all (cf. Titus 3:8-9). Second is "*and leads* to the ruin of the hearers" (ἐπὶ καταστροφῇ τῶν ἀκουόντων). The NASU translators have added the conjunction and verb ("*and leads*") for stylistic purposes in English. The noun "ruin" (καταστροφῇ) has a range of meaning that includes turning against, overturning, subverting, and demoralizing.[42] We get our word *catastrophe* from it.[43] Such undermining and turning over is the opposite of the building up of edification.[44] This effect

---

[38] Rienecker, 641.
[39] Robertson, 4:219.
[40] BAGD, 477.
[41] Ibid., 287.
[42] Rienecker, 641.
[43] Hiebert, *Second Timothy*, 67.
[44] Guthrie, 147.

is found in "the hearers" (τῶν ἀκουόντων). The present tense participle points to their regular and ongoing exposure to such talk. Clearly one does not have to join in the talk, but only listen to it for its negative effects to accrue to one's account. Passive, but inquisitive, listening will yield the same result as active participation in this case. Little wonder Paul warns Timothy so emphatically about the danger of such talk. There are some arguments you lose just by entering them. Debate for the sake of debate is debunked.

> ### Digging Deeper:
> 1. Why does Paul speak so frequently of reminder and memory in this particular letter? What principles for ministry can we draw from this emphasis?
> 2. How did Paul intend for Timothy to defend the truth without succumbing to word-wars with the false teachers and others involved in the conflict?
> 3. What effects come from simply being exposed to such bickering? What should this call for from church leaders when complaining and bickering start to arise in the congregation?

2:15 Be diligent to present yourself approved to God as a workman who does not need to be ashamed, accurately handling the word of truth.

Having instructed Timothy in what to avoid (v.14), the Apostle now directs him in that to which he should give himself. Paul issues the command, "Be diligent" (σπούδασον), an aorist imperative that demands action be taken immediately. The word combines the notions of both urgency and effort. That which requires immediate action also calls for intense effort. Paul uses the same verb and form in 4:9, 21 to demand Timothy make haste to come to him in his Roman prison. Elsewhere Paul uses the word to describe an eagerness to minister to the poor (Gal. 2:10), to keep the unity of the Spirit (Eph. 4:3), and to describe the driving force behind wanting to see others (1 Thess. 2:17; Titus 3:12). To this imperative Paul adds the second person singular reflexive pronoun "yourself" (σεαυτὸν), placed emphatically before the infinitive, that he might show Timothy that this eager effort was not to be expended upon others, but exercised upon and within himself. This effort is applied that he might "present [himself] approved to God." The word "to present" (παραστῆσαι) can be used to describe the presentation of a sacrifice upon the altar (Rom. 12:1) or to picture a bride being presented to her husband (2 Cor. 11:2). The word, however, carries broad nuances of meaning and here becomes a near equivalent of "make" or "render."⁴⁵ The presentation is made "to God" (τῷ θεῷ), which calls to mind the solemn warning "in the presence of God" which Paul has just called for (v.14). The One in whose presence you must solemnly warn others is the One in whose presence you must also stand yourself. The goal is to be able to stand before this Judge "approved" (δόκιμον). The word means to be found authentic and approved after testing. The false teachers were looking for the approval of the audience (4:3), but Paul focused Timothy upon the pleasure of the audience of One. "For it is not he who commends himself that is approved, but he whom the Lord commends" (2 Cor. 10:18).

The imagery here is that of "a workman" (ἐργάτην). When used literally, the word can describe one skilled in a trade (Acts 19:25) or, more frequently, one who works in agriculture (e.g., Matt. 9:37-38; 20:1-2, 8; James 5:4). Metaphorically it is used to describe those who labor in spiritual matters, whether bad (2 Cor. 11:13; Phil. 3:2) or good, as here. The particular quality of the worker pictured here is that he is to be one "who does not need to be ashamed" (ἀνεπαίσχυντον). This adjective is used only here in the NT. However, the verbal root (minus the alpha privative) has been used three times by Paul in this letter, all speaking of shame before men (1:8, 12, 16). How much worse to stand ashamed before God!

> **Ministry Maxim**
>
> My success in ministry is in direct relationship to my commitment to gaining facility and skill in the use of the Scriptures.

That which has potential to produce such shame is the way one handles "the word of truth" (τὸν λόγον τῆς ἀληθείας). The exact phrase is used in Ephesians 1:13, where it is set in apposition to "the gospel of your salvation" (cf. Col. 1:5). It is this Gospel that has been in Paul's view from the beginning of the letter (1:8, 10; 2:8). That it is "the word *of truth*" (emphasis mine) stands in contrast to the empty chatter just warned of (2:14). Such folk either actively oppose the truth (3:8) or more passively turn their ears away from it (4:4). They give the impression of great learning (3:7), but refuse the repentance that would open the way to understanding the truth (2:25). Thus they wander from the truth themselves and take others with them (2:18).

That which will enable us to stand before God as workmen without shame involves "accurately handling" (ὀρθοτομοῦντα) the Gospel. The word occurs only here in the NT. The basic meaning of this compound word is "to cut straight." It has been linked to a farmer plowing a straight furrow, an engineer making a straight road, a stone mason cutting a square stone, and a priest cutting

---

⁴⁵ BAGD, 627-628.

an animal for sacrifice.[46] The word is used in the LXX translation of Proverbs 3:6 and 11:5, "where it . . . means 'cut a straight path in a straight direction' or 'cut a road across country (that is forested or otherwise difficult to pass through) in a straight direction', so that the traveler may go directly to his destination . . . Then ὀρθοτομοῦντα τὸν λόγον τῆς ἀληθείας would perh[aps] mean guide the word of truth along a straight path (like a road that goes straight to its goal), without being turned aside by wordy debates or impious talk."[47] The context here in 2 Timothy helps clarify the meaning. Paul has just called Timothy to warn people "not to wrangle about words, which is useless and leads to the ruin of the hearers" (v.14) and in v.16 he will charge Timothy himself to "avoid worldly and empty chatter." Paul is calling Timothy to be a man of the Word, to avoid being led off into pointless debate and controversy, to keep holding forth the Gospel in a clear and pointed manner. While others absorb themselves in pointless debate, the one whom God will approve keeps clear-headed and tenaciously faithful to the Gospel of Jesus Christ.

God will approve the workman who labors with the right effort ("Be diligent"), the right motive ("to present yourself approved to God"), the right ethic ("as a workman who does not need to be ashamed"), and the right skill ("accurately handling the word of truth").

> **Digging Deeper:**
> 1. Why is our addiction to approval so powerful? What does this verse tell us about how its power can be redirected?
> 2. Which has the greater power to effect behavioral change in you—the thought of being ashamed before others or of being ashamed before God?
> 3. How are we tempted (in relationships both inside and outside of the church) to be drawn away from the Word of God and the ministry of the Gospel by debate, argument and fruitless discussion? What can we do about that?

2:16 But avoid worldly and empty chatter, for it will lead to further ungodliness,

Paul's next instruction stands in contrast ("But," δέ) to the positive instruction of v.15, but returns to the denunciation of the verbal battles of the false teachers (v.14). In v.14 the instructions were given to Timothy to pass on to others, but here Timothy is directly charged himself, though surely with application for the

---
[46] Rienecker, 642.
[47] BAGD, 580.

people under his care. The imperative ("avoid," περιίστασο) is in the present tense demanding that action be undertaken continuously or habitually. The middle voice points to the inward nature of the decision to avoid such conversational combat. The verb is used only here and in Titus 3:9 where Paul used it in a similar vein. The compound word means literally to stand around (around, περί; stand, ἵστημι). It can describe literally gathering as a group around someone (John 11:42; Acts 25:7). But, with the accusative of the thing, it came also to describe, as it does here, going around something in the sense of avoiding it.[48]

That which Timothy is to avoid is "worldly and empty chatter." The "and" has been added by the translators to make good English sense of the noun and its adjective. The noun "empty chatter" (κενοφωνίας) is used elsewhere in the NT only in 1 Timothy 6:20, where it is again teamed with the same adjective. The compound word (empty, κενός; voice, φωνή) points simply to talk that carries no content. It is empty, vacuous babble. It is blah, blah, blah, blah; it is speech which makes plenty of sound, but never any point. The adjective (βεβήλους) is used three other times by Paul, all in 1 Timothy (1:9; 4:7; 6:20), and one time in Hebrews (12:16). It describes that which is ungodly, profane, irreligious, and vile. It can describe the character of people (1 Tim. 1:9; Heb. 12:16) as well as the words that proceed from their mouths (1 Tim. 4:7; 6:20; 2 Tim. 2:16). That there is one particular example of such talk in Paul's mind is clear from his use of the definite article (τὰς).[49]

> **Ministry Maxim**
>
> There are some arguments you lose simply by entering them.

The reason (causal use of γάρ) to avoid this kind of talk is now given in two parts, the first here and the second in v.17 ("and," καί). The first reason regards the direction such talk leads. The verb "will lead" (προκόψουσιν) describes progress or advance. Paul uses it five times, though all three of its usages in this letter describe progress in that which is negative (2:16; 3:9, 13). The area of advance is indicated by the genitive noun which follows the verb ("ungodliness," ἀσεβείας).[50] The word describes a contempt for God that is displayed in action.[51] It comes then to mean that which is ungodly, irreligious, impious, and irreligious. It is the opposite of what divine grace produces (Titus 2:11-12). It will characterize the last days (Jude 18) and is that which God does now (Rom. 1:18) and will in the end (Jude 15) pour out His wrath upon. It is that which Jesus came to remove from His people (Rom. 11:26). The subject of the verb is not stated, though the context and the pronoun "their" (v.17) make clear that it is the Ephesian opponents that are intended.[52]

---

[48] Thayer, 503.
[49] Mounce, 526.
[50] Knight, 413.
[51] Kittel, abridged, 1012-1013.
[52] Fee, 255; Lea and Griffin, 215.

To stress the issue even more, Paul asserts that this advance will be into "further" (ἐπὶ πλεῖον) ungodliness. Paul uses same expression again in 3:9 (cf. also Acts 4:17; 20:9; 24:4). Here the expression means "they will arrive at an ever greater measure of godlessness = become more and more deeply involved in godlessness."[53] The phrase is thrown to the head of the clause for emphasis.[54] The Ephesian opponents may well have viewed themselves as being progressive in matters religious. In such a case Paul may have been stealing their own favorite word and using it ironically in description of them. It is as though the Apostle declares, "They think themselves religiously 'progressive'? They're correct, they are ever making steady progress—into ungodliness!"

2:17 and their talk will spread like gangrene. Among them are Hymenaeus and Philetus,

The second reason to "avoid worldly and empty chatter" (v.16a) is now set forth. The word "and" (καὶ) is a coordinating conjunction holding the first half of this verse in parallel with "it will lead to further ungodliness" (v.16b), both clauses controlled by the "for" (γὰρ) of v.16.

The concern here is again "their talk" (ὁ λόγος αὐτῶν). It is a direct reference to the "worldly and empty chatter" (v.16a) of the errorists in Ephesus. The noun λόγος is in the singular, picturing all of their words as one collective whole. It is etymologically related to the verbal form in v.14 that is translated as "wrangle about words" (λογομαχεῖν) and it contrasts "the word of truth" (v.15). The definite article points to the particular words of particular people, as the naming of two individuals in the controversies at the end of the verse makes clear.

> **Ministry Maxim**
>
> Falsehood always faces less resistance to its advance than does the truth.

The concern is that this talk "will spread," or more literally "have pasture" (νομὴν ἕξει). The noun νομὴν literally means pasture or grazing (John 10:9), but can be used figuratively in medical contexts of the spreading of an ulcer.[55] The imagery is likely that of cattle spreading out to consume the fodder of a field as they graze. The future tense of the verb (ἕξει) points to what will happen if such talk remains unchecked. The spreading of such false teaching will be "like gangrene" (ὡς γάγγραινα). The noun is used nowhere else in the NT, but was common in other Greek writings as a medical term descriptive of gangrene or the "cancer of spreading ulcers."[56] The spreading cancer of false teaching will consume the flock

---
[53] BAGD, 689.
[54] Knight, 413.
[55] BAGD, 541.
[56] Ibid., 149.

of God if it remains unchallenged. If left unchecked, the deviants will not only progress in ungodliness personally (v.16), but their falsehood will progress throughout the church (v.17).

In 3:9 Paul assures Timothy regarding those opposed to the truth, saying "they will not make further progress." How are we to understand the relationship between the warning here and the reassurance there? Will their heresy make progress or not? The two passages are not contradictory. Paul, being a realist, can see the possibilities of unopposed falsehood (vv.16-17). Paul, being a man of faith, can also see God's sovereignty and find rest in His care (3:9). Ultimately God is in charge and will make sure the deceitful plots of the errorists fail (3:9), but He will use His vigilant people in the process (2:16-17). God's sovereignty does not deny the necessity of our obedience.

Paul goes on to name two individuals involved in the spread of the false teaching. The first is Hymenaeus. It seems likely that he is the same man referred to in 1 Timothy 1:20 as having been "handed over to Satan, so that [he] will be taught not to blaspheme." Interestingly, despite the fact that Paul had excommunicated the man from the church, he still wielded enough influence and had enough contact with the members that he was a danger. The conditions within the church at Ephesus must have made ministry most difficult for Timothy. The second individual, Philetus, is nowhere else mentioned in the NT and thus we know nothing more about him. In 1 Timothy 1:20 Hymenaeus was paired with a certain Alexander. In both places Hymenaeus is mentioned first and this may be a signal of his leadership in the false teaching. The fact that he is mentioned again in 2 Timothy, but with a different partner, points out the power, persuasion, and persistence of the man. These individuals and those who joined them stand as a testimony to the truth of Paul's previous prediction in Acts 20:29-30.

Digging Deeper:

1. What percentage of your words today were either empty of real value or more representative of the world's agenda than God's?
2. Why are verbal sins never an end in themselves, but an open door to ever increasing ungodliness?
3. Why do you think Paul chose to liken such talk to an ulcerous cancer?
4. How can you cut out the cancer of such verbal sins and close the door such sins of speech open?
5. How does the persistent problem of Hymenaeus' presence and influence in the Ephesian church underscore the need for church members to follow their leaders in practicing church discipline?

2:18 men who have gone astray from the truth saying that the resurrection has already taken place, and they upset the faith of some.

The opening plural relative pronoun ("who," οἵτινες) demonstrates that Paul is now enlarging upon the activities of the two false teachers just mentioned in v.17. Because two individuals have been named in the heresy (v.17), the plural relative pronoun is now used in place of the simple relative pronoun.[57] Their problem is that they have "gone astray" (ἠστόχησαν). The word means to miss the mark, to go astray or to deviate from.[58] It is used only three times in the NT, all by Paul and all in the PE to deal with the Ephesian heresy. In each case they are described as turning away from "a pure heart and a good conscience and a sincere faith" (1 Tim. 1:6), "the faith" (6:21), or, as here, "from [περὶ; "with regard or respect to"[59]] the truth" (τὴν ἀλήθειαν). Timothy has just been charged with "accurately handling the word of truth" (2:15) and thus must deal with such departures from it. The "truth" is a major theme throughout the PE (1 Tim. 2:4, 7; 3:15; 4:3; 6:5; Titus 1:1, 14) and becomes a rich vein in the remainder of this letter. Because the errorists "turn away their ears from the truth and . . . turn aside to myths" (4:4) and "oppose the truth" (3:8), they at some point become incapable of learning the truth (3:7). The only hope is that "God may grant them repentance leading to the knowledge of the truth" (2:25).

The major point of their departure from the truth was when they started "saying that the resurrection has already taken place." The participle ("saying," λέγοντες) is used to designate just how they have gone astray—again words are the problem. The present tense points to the continuous nature of their teaching. Their erroneous teaching centered on "the resurrection" ([τὴν] ἀνάστασιν). Though there is debate about the genuineness of the definite article, it seems likely that it should be accepted.[60] The dualism that was rife in the first century often brought confusion regarding the doctrine of the resurrection because of the dualism's emphasis upon the intrinsic evil of matter. A bodily resurrection had no place in such thinking. It led either to an inappropriately strict asceticism (1 Tim. 4:3) or to a disregard for sexual morality (2 Tim. 3:6). Paul, however, preached the bodily resurrection of Jesus Christ (1 Cor. 15:3-4) and the coming bodily

> **Ministry Maxim**
>
> Heresy usually results from an unbalanced view of some otherwise marvelous truth.

---

[57] Ibid., 587.
[58] Rienecker, 636, 642.
[59] BAGD, 645.
[60] Knight, 414.

resurrection of believers (15:44). The error in Corinth was the denial of any resurrection for the believer at all (15:12). In Thessalonica it may have been taught that the resurrection had already taken place (2 Thess. 2:1-2).

The particular problem in Ephesus was their assertion that the resurrection "has already taken place" (ἤδη γεγονέναι). The perfect tense of the verb points to that which has taken place in the past and the effects of which continue in the present. This time element is made the more definite by the use of the adverb (ἤδη, "already").[61] The problem in Ephesus was apparently closer to that in Thessalonica than in Corinth. It is likely that the opponents seized on Paul's teaching of a spiritual resurrection that is already the experience of the true believer (e.g., Rom. 6:5, 11; Col. 3:1-3) and taught that any further resurrection is unnecessary. The doctrine of the resurrection is the lynchpin of Christianity (1 Cor. 15:14-19) and thus a watershed for truth and error.

The predictable result is now added ("and," καὶ) to the description of the error: "they upset the faith of some." The verb "upset" (ἀνατρέπουσιν) is a compound word from "up" (ἀνὰ) and "to turn" (τρέπω). Its emphasis is on the upsetting, overthrowing and destroying of something. It is used literally in John 2:15 to describe Jesus upsetting the tables of the money changers in the temple. It is used in Titus 1:11 to describe the effect of false teachers in Crete who are "upsetting whole families."

That which was overturned and destroyed was "the faith of some" (τήν τινων πίστιν). The indefinite pronoun (τινων) makes clear, without designating numbers or names, that this destruction of faith took place in a portion of the congregation, though not universally.

> **Digging Deeper:**
> 1. How can a curiosity with falsehood lead to an inability to hear truth?
> 2. Why does the loss of the truth of the resurrection destroy one's faith?

2:19 Nevertheless, the firm foundation of God stands, having this seal, "The Lord knows those who are His," and, "Everyone who names the name of the Lord is to abstain from wickedness."

Despite the confusion created in the Ephesian church by the heretics, some things were still clear. "Nevertheless" (representing the particle μέντοι, which is

---
[61] Mounce, 528.

used as a strong adversative) introduces an affirmation that stands in contrast to the chaos that must have been rife in the church in Ephesus. There is certainty about "the firm foundation of God" (ὁ . . . στερεὸς θεμέλιος τοῦ θεοῦ). The word "foundation" (θεμέλιος) refers to the foundation under a building, upon which the superstructure rests. The use of the definite article makes clear reference to the unique and only foundation to which Paul refers. It is used metaphorically in the NT of the foundation of the church, which is Jesus Christ (Rom. 15:20; 1 Cor. 3:10-12). In another place Paul sees the apostles and prophets as being part of the foundation, but even then Christ is the cornerstone of that foundation (Eph. 2:20). While error and false teaching may dismay its members and worry its shepherds, ultimately the foundation of the church remains unmoved and unthreatened by what anyone may say or do, for that foundation is Christ Himself. Here the foundation is described as "firm" (στερεὸς), a word used by Paul only here (cf. other NT usages in Heb. 5:12, 14; 1 Peter 5:9). The word describes that which is solid, hard, firm, steadfast and strong.[62] The genitive "of God" (τοῦ θεου) describes the foundation as belonging to God, not that God Himself makes up the foundation (though Christ is indeed the foundation of the church). This foundation "stands" (ἕστηκεν). The verb is in the perfect tense pointing to the laying of this foundation at a point in the past and the continuing effects in the present of its having been laid. Jesus Christ was made the foundation of the church through His death and resurrection and He remains the unshakeable rock of His people.

Upon this foundation is a "seal" (τὴν σφραγῖδα). Paul uses the word three times. Once he describes Abraham's reception of circumcision as "a seal of the righteousness of the faith which he had while uncircumcised" (Rom. 4:11). He told the Corinthian believers that they were "the seal of [his] apostleship in the Lord" (1 Cor. 9:2). Paul also uses the verbal form (Rom. 15:28; 2 Cor. 1:22; Eph. 1:13; 4:30). The noun is used elsewhere thirteen times by the Apostle John in Revelation. It referred literally to the seal itself or to the mark left by it. When used of documents it referred to the hot wax or soft clay that would be affixed to official documents as a verification of the unspoiled nature of its contents. It could be used of buildings upon which was inscribed a message, often indicating the ownership or purpose of the building. Metaphorically it was used to describe that which authenticated something, such as the righteousness that came to Abraham by faith or the genuineness of Paul's apostleship.[63] Here, given the metaphor of a building (vv.20-21; cf. 1 Tim. 3:15), the seal seems to

---

[62] Rienecker, 642.
[63] DNTT, 3:497-501.

refer to an inscription upon the foundation that signifies the ownership of all who make up that building. Given the difficult situation in the Ephesian church, this was probably designed to reassure Timothy as the pastor that ultimately the church is God's and that His purposes will prevail in those who are truly His.

This seal upon the building that is the church is singular (feminine singular, σφραγῖδα), yet twofold. The two statements make up two sides of one truth.[64] First is the statement that, "The Lord knows those who are His." This statement is drawn from Numbers 16:5 in the LXX, where we read of the account of Korah and his rebellion. God was able then to differentiate those who were His from those who were not. He can do the same today. The rebellion of Korah was a grievous black-mark on the nation of Israel, but it did not destroy the nation. So, false teaching and defection from the church in the present is a terrible and confusing thing, but God assures the clarity of His knowledge and the enduring stability of His people. The verb "knows" (ἔγνω) is aorist in tense and points to the act of God knowing His own in the past. While we speak often of whether or not a person knows the Lord, ultimately it is far more important to ascertain whether the Lord "knows" him or her. This knowing is not merely the mental act of recognition, but the deeply personal and relational act of God's electing knowledge. Timothy may not know who stands where in the chaos of doctrinal dispute, but God does. Timothy may not know the final outcome of the controversy, but God does. Paul assures Timothy by reminding him that man cannot undo what God has done.

> **Ministry Maxim**
>
> In times of doctrinal disagreement, remember that only God infallibly knows those who are truly His.

The second part of the seal is "and 'Everyone who names the name of the Lord is to abstain from wickedness.'" The coordinating conjunction "and" (καί) holds the two statements in a parallel relationship. What is said applies to "Everyone who names the name of the Lord" (πᾶς ὁ ὀνομάζων τὸ ὄνομα κυρίου). The adjective "Everyone" (πᾶς) makes the reference a sweeping one, to cover all who so call upon the Lord. The participle "who names" (ὁ ὀνομάζων) is used substantivally and is in the present tense, indicating a continual calling upon the Lord. It is followed by its kindred noun, "the name" (τὸ ὄνομα). In the ancient mind a name could convey and carry the character and nature of the one it designated. Thus the double-emphasis upon "naming the name" signified that the one doing the calling was seeking for the one being named to live up to their promises and ascribed nature. Here the name is not just any name, as the

---

[64] Knight, 415.

definite article makes clear, but is the name "of the Lord" (κυρίου). Thus the calling upon the Lord is not simply a momentary plea for help, but a decisive cry for salvation. The angel instructed Joseph regarding the child to be born of Mary, "'you shall call His name Jesus, for He will save His people from their sins'" (Matt. 1:21). His very name designated His role and work—a Savior to His people. Thus to name His name is to seek His saving work in your own life.

Note how Paul holds in dynamic tension the twin truths of God's gracious electing knowledge and the necessity of man's cry to God for salvation. For Paul, God is always prior. Salvation begins and ends with God. It is all His work. There is nothing of man in it. Yet passivity and presumption find no place in his preaching. Man must call upon the name of the Lord in order to be saved (Rom. 10:9-10). God chooses us before we can choose Him. Yet our choosing is treated as a free act of our volition. How can it be both? Paul does not feel compelled to explain the mystery. Indeed, when, in another place, he presses forward in an attempt to delineate a more specific answer, he finds himself on his knees as a worshiper (Rom. 11:33-36). So should we.

There is a moral imperative laid upon all who would so call upon the Lord: "to abstain from wickedness." The verb (ἀποστήτω) is an aorist imperative, signaling urgent action that must be taken at once. Paul's only two other uses demonstrate that the word can be used to describe apostasy and falling away from God (1 Tim. 4:1) or, in a more general way, simply to "leave" (2 Cor. 12:8). Given that Paul in the context of 2 Timothy is discussing the defection from truth of some key individuals in the church in Ephesus (vv.17-18), it is possible that he uses the word here to say to Timothy, "any apostasy that takes place should be an apostasy from wickedness!" On the other hand this too like the first of the statements, may be an echo from the account of Korah's rebellion (cf. Num. 16:26-27). In such a case it may dredge up the imagery of that event and simply mean "let everyone stand off from."[65] Either way it is "from wickedness" (ἀπὸ ἀδικίας) that we are to distance ourselves. The noun designates the opposite of righteousness, being variously translated as "unrighteousness" (e.g., Rom. 1:18, 29; 2:8), "injustice" (Rom. 9:14), "wrong" (2 Cor. 12:13), or as here "wickedness" (2 Thess. 2:10, 12). Here it stands not so much as the opposite of righteousness *per se*, but as the opposite of the truth: contrast "handling accurately the word of truth" (v.15) and "have gone astray from the truth" (v.18).[66] Errors in doctrine open the door for errors in living.

Moral imperatives accompany the doctrine of free grace, without in any way diminishing the free nature of that grace. In context, for Timothy and his

---

[65] Rienecker, 642.
[66] Marshall, 758.

people, obedience to this moral imperative required distancing themselves from those who taught erroneous doctrine.

> **Digging Deeper:**
> 1. Summarize the comfort the Apostle gives to those who are distraught over division within the church.
> 2. While both are essential, which is more foundational: our knowing God or God knowing us? Why?
> 3. How can the Gospel of free grace (which saves us apart from our works) contain moral imperatives (which demand our good works)?
> 4. Why does wrong living ("wickedness") always find its root in wrong thinking ("doctrine")?

2:20 Now in a large house there are not only gold and silver vessels, but also vessels of wood and of earthenware, and some to honor and some to dishonor.

Building on the necessity for God's people "to abstain from wickedness" (v.19b), Paul now illustrates his command (v.20) and then applies the illustration (v.21). The coordinating conjunction ("Now," δέ) has no adversative force, but rather is transitional or continuative in nature. It introduces a new start, but one that builds on what has just been said. The illustration regards "a large house" and the various "vessels" that one would find in its kitchen. The "house" must be the visible church, made up of a mixed multitude, with "some to honor and some to dishonor." The "vessels" refer to the various individuals who make up the visible church.

That Paul is considering the church in its widest possible frame of reference is clear from the use of "large" (μεγάλῃ). He is not making final determinations about who is or isn't truly a child of God. He is looking at the church as Timothy surely had to view it in Ephesus—a place with people of varying strands of teaching, commitment, desire, and motive. This variety is seen in that, "there are not only gold and silver vessels, but also vessels of wood and of earthenware." The word "vessels" (σκεύη) refers to dishes, plates, pots and the like.[67] The verb "are" (ἔστιν) is in the singular, while its accompanying nouns ("vessels") are in the plural. Some of these dishes are "gold and silver" (χρυσᾶ καὶ ἀργυρᾶ) and some are "of wood and of earthenware" (ξύλινα καὶ ὀστράκινα). The differences between these two kind of "vessels" are marked by the strong adversative ("but,"

---
[67] BAGD, 754.

ἀλλά) along with the coordinating conjunction ("also," καί). This is the echo to the previous note of distinction, "not only" (οὐκ . . . μόνον). The former were presumably used during special occasions and in the presence of guests. The latter were common and ordinary and may refer to containers used for collecting and disposing of garbage or excrement. The first three words ("gold and silver . . . wood") are found together again in 1 Corinthians 3:12. The last word ("earthenware") describes that which is easily breakable and thus disposable.[68]

Paul further distinguishes between the two by saying that some were "to honor and some to dishonor." This is introduced by "and some" (καὶ ἅ). The conjunction is used explicatively, meaning something like "that is" or "namely."[69] The relative pronoun (ἅ) appears twice and in both cases it functions as a demonstrative pronoun, meaning "some . . . others."[70] The "honor" (τιμήν) or "dishonor" (ἀτιμίαν) of a vessel arises from its usage and purpose: that is to say, by what it contains and thus what becomes of it. By way of application it means that within the visible church the various individuals distinguish themselves by adherence to the truth (v.15) or attachment to error (vv.16-18). As Paul will make plain in the next verse, the vessels "to honor" distinguish themselves as such by distancing themselves from the vessels "to dishonor" (false teachers).

> **Ministry Maxim**
>
> The visible church will always be a messy place, filled with people of varied spiritual commitments.

2:21 Therefore, if anyone cleanses himself from these things, he will be a vessel for honor, sanctified, useful to the Master, prepared for every good work.

Paul now builds logically (οὖν, inference) upon the metaphor of the church as a building (v.20) and applies it. The condition is third class (ἐάν plus the aorist subjunctive) and is undetermined as to its fulfillment. It is not at all clear just whether a given individual will cleanse himself, but if he does (and it seems probable that he will, at least for the sake of argument) he will then be "a vessel for honor." The indefinite pronoun "anyone" (τις) makes the reference broad, covering anyone within the visible church. The requirement is that such an individual "cleanses himself" (ἐκκαθάρῃ ἑαυτόν). The verb is used elsewhere of the ritual cleansing of vessels (cf. the only other NT usage in 1 Cor. 5:7). The preposition (ἐκ) in compound intensifies the verb and conveys the notion of "cleanse thoroughly."[71] The

---

[68] Ibid., 587.
[69] Knight, 417.
[70] Ibid., 418.

aorist tense designates punctiliar action, indicating that such a step will require specific action at specific moments of time. These actions, we may surmise, will often be painful and difficult (note the excommunication of 1 Cor. 5:7-13).[72] Yet they will be necessary if the goal is to be achieved. The pronoun (ἑαυτὸν) is singular, indicating that each individual must make these decisions and take these steps. It is also reflexive, denoting the effect his actions have upon himself. No one can avoid the need for such discerning steps of action. That which he must cleanse himself from are "these *things*" (τούτων). The antecedent must be the vessels "to dishonor" of the previous verse. That it is the content of the teaching, rather than the teacher himself, that is in view is seen in that Paul sets forth steps to take to continue in relationship with the individual (vv.24-26), even while denouncing the false assertions they may set forth. Yet if in the end they do not respond to such efforts, this would include separating from even the teacher as well (3:5), which indeed had been the case with Hymenaeus (cf. v.17 and 1 Tim. 1:20).

The result of such painful and yet necessary steps is that "he will be a vessel for honor" (ἔσται σκεῦος εἰς τιμήν). It seems a bit odd that a vessel would cleanse itself, not by removing filth from within it, but by distancing itself from other vessels. Though the metaphor is perhaps a bit inconsistent, its point is clear. The future tense of the verb points out the discipline necessary to take painful steps in the present to achieve a future outcome that is more preferable than avoidance of pain in the present.

> **Ministry Maxim**
>
> Anything or anyone who diminishes my readiness to obey God is sin for me.

Paul then makes three statements as to what it means to be "a vessel for honor." Such a vessel is "sanctified" (ἡγιασμένον). The word is often translated "holy" and designates a thing separated from one purpose and set apart to another, special purpose. The perfect tense points to this action taking place in the past and continuing in the present. Hard decisions to stand with truth have enduring consequences. The passive voice could call for a translation of "having been sanctified" and highlights the present state of sanctification as arising from past choices.

Having come to such a position with regard to God and His truth, this one will be "useful to the Master" (εὔχρηστον τῷ δεσπότῃ). The adjective "useful" is used only two other times in the NT, both by Paul and both in reference to specific individuals (Mark, 2 Tim. 4:11; Onesimus, Philem. 11). It points to that which is serviceable.[73] Such a person has come to a position where he can be used to fulfill the purposes of God. Through such sanctification, they have designated Christ to be

---

[71] Robertson, 4:114.
[72] Guthrie, 152.
[73] BAGD, 329.
[74] Rienecker, 643.

Second Timothy 2

"the Master." "The term denotes absolute ownership and uncontrolled power."[74]

Only in such a position and through such a relationship can a person be "prepared for every good work" (εἰς πᾶν ἔργον ἀγαθὸν ἡτοιμασμένον). The participle is in the perfect tense, pointing to a point in the past when the preparation was accomplished and that such a one now stands in that state of preparedness. The passive voice, similar to the previous participle, might be translated "having been prepared" and shows that the present preparedness came about by past action. The same expression ("good work," ἔργον ἀγαθὸν) appears in Philippians 1:6 and there designates what God begins in each of us when He imparts to us new life. Paul uses it again in 2 Timothy 3:17 where it is the readiness to fulfill these deeds that is in view. There it is the Scriptures that prepare one for such acts (cf. also its use in 2 Cor. 9:8; Titus 1:16; 3:1).

> **Digging Deeper:**
> 1. How is our honor or dishonor determined by our response to truth?
> 2. Why does our response to truth and/or falsehood determine our usefulness to God?
> 3. What must we do, according to these verses, in order to be prepared to do anything God may call us to do?

2:22 Now flee from youthful lusts and pursue righteousness, faith, love and peace, with those who call on the Lord from a pure heart.

Enough of metaphor (vv.20-21); Paul now launches himself into direct commands. The conjunction "Now" (δέ) is left untranslated by many modern versions (e.g., NIV, NRSV). It is difficult to decide just what the function of the conjunction is intended to fulfill. It could carry some slight adversative force ("But," NET), but it also seems have to have some inferential qualities based on the context ("So," ESV).

There are two commands: one to "flee" (φεῦγε) and one to "pursue" (δίωκε). Both verbs are present tense imperatives, demanding action be taken repeatedly or habitually. The two are butted up against one another in the original text, highlighting the contrasting direction of each. Both were used previously in the very similar words of 1 Timothy 6:11.

The word "flee" (φεῦγε) can be used absolutely to describe literal flight from one place to another (cf. Matt. 2:13; 8:33; Mark 14:50; Acts 27:30). It also is used in a moral sense when accompanied with an accusative that designates the thing to be fled from.[75] Here it is "youthful lusts" (τὰς ... νεωτερικὰς ἐπιθυμίας)

---
[75] BAGD, 856.

that are to be shunned. The word "lusts" (ἐπιθυμίας) points to any strong and overwhelming desire. It can refer to everything from the desire to be told what one wants to hear (4:3) to illicit sexual desire (1 Thess. 4:5). False teachers thrive on those who never rise above their bondage to such impulses (2 Tim. 3:6). The adjective "youthful" (νεωτερικὰς) is used only here in the NT (though compare the noun form in 1 Tim. 4:12). While the emphasis could be on sensual desires, the context does not encourage such a view in this case. It is more likely that, without discounting the power of such sensual desires, the major emphasis here is upon relational tendencies that may accompany the inexperience of youth. This could be, as some see it, an impulsive and combative approach to conflict such as Timothy faced with the false teachers in Ephesus.[76] Yet everything we know of Timothy indicates that his natural tendency was in the other direction (i.e., passivity and avoidance; cf. 1:7-8). So, in this case, such "youthful lusts" might include the desire to back away from battles that ought to be fought. More broadly in application it would refer to any impulse or desire that has not been tempered by the wisdom of maturity and brought under the control of the Spirit.

> **Ministry Maxim**
>
> God never asks us to forsake one thing without asking us to embrace something much better.

The positive is now set off in distinction from the negative ("and," δὲ). That which Timothy is to "pursue" (δίωκε) is set forth in a list of four nouns. The first three also appear together in the list found in 1 Timothy 6:11. First is "righteousness" (δικαιοσύνην). The believer is declared righteous by God through justification (Rom. 3:21-26) and thus stands in the gracious gift of Christ's own righteousness (5:2). In what sense, then, does the believer need to pursue righteousness? This speaks of conformity to the character of Christ Himself. Paul's concern here is the imparted righteousness of sanctification, not the imputed righteousness of justification.

The second pursuit of the believer is to be "faith" (πίστιν). The word can describe the body of truth the church has embraced (1 Tim. 3:9; 4:1, 6; 6:10, 12). It also describes the personal trust of an individual in the God of that truth (2 Tim. 1:5; 3:15). It is the latter sense in which Paul uses it is here.

Also "love" (ἀγάπην) is to be pursued by the believer. Such love is the product of the Spirit's presence and power in a believer's life (1:7) and is to characterize a believer in all situations, especially contentious ones (1:13). Both love and faith had been modeled for Timothy by Paul (3:10).

Finally, the believer is to pursue "peace" (εἰρήνην). Often the word refers to objective peace *with* God (Rom. 5:1) or the subjective, inward peace *of* God

---

[76] Fee, 263.

experienced in the heart of the believer (2 Tim. 1:2). Given the context, the reference here probably points to the relational peace that both of these enable the believer to live in toward others. In the midst of the contentious debate with the false teachers in Ephesus, Timothy was to make it his pursuit to "be at peace with all men" (Rom. 12:18; cf. Eph. 4:3).

This quartet of virtues is not to be pursued simply as an individual, but "with those who call on the Lord" (μετὰ τῶν ἐπικαλουμένων τὸν κύριον). Paul uses this verb (ἐπικαλουμένων) five other times, in reference to an initial calling upon God for salvation (Rom. 10:12-14) and the continuing call of the believer to God (1 Cor. 1:2; 2 Cor. 1:23). The present tense here designates such people as those who are currently, continually calling upon the Lord. Mere profession in the past is not in view, but the continuing life of faith that keeps on calling out to God in faith. This may be used in a subtle way to distinguish those in Ephesus who would continue on with Timothy and Paul in the truth as opposed to those who side with the false teachers like and Hymenaeus and Philetus (v.17). That this is the case is seen in the qualifying phrase "from a pure heart" (ἐκ καθαρᾶς καρδίας). The same phrase is used in 1 Timothy 1:5 to describe the goal of all Paul's teaching. There it is also linked with "a good conscience and a sincere faith." The word "pure" comes from the same root as "cleanses" (v.21).[77]

2:23 But refuse foolish and ignorant speculations, knowing that they produce quarrels.

In contrast ("But," δὲ) to the "righteousness, faith, love and peace" that Timothy has been charged with pursuing (v.22), Paul now directly instructs him concerning dealing with the false teachers. He is to "refuse" (παραιτοῦ) their arguments. The present imperative demands that action be taken repeatedly and habitually. The word has a broad range of meaning, from request (Mark 15:6), to decline (1 Tim. 5:11), to a strong rejection, as here.[78] Paul uses the word four times, all in the PE, and always in the present middle imperative form (1 Tim. 4:7; 5:11; 2 Tim. 2:23; Titus 3:10). This says something profound about the demands of pastoral ministry. The use here is similar to its use in 1 Timothy 4:7 where Paul tells Timothy, "have nothing to do with worldly fables" (cf. also Titus 3:10).

That which is to be rejected is "speculations" (ζητήσεις). Again Paul's use of the word is limited to the PE (1 Tim. 6:4; Titus 3:9). Strictly speaking the word means "seek" and arose from the Greek philosophical quest for wisdom (cf. Acts 17:27 and 1 Cor. 1:22 for the concept). In the NT it can describe arguments, word battles and disputes.[79] These are further described as "foolish and ignorant"

---

[77] Ibid., 264.
[78] BAGD, 616.

(μωρὰς καὶ ἀπαιδεύτους). The first word basically describes mental dullness. Our English word "moron" is derived from it. As it is here, it is linked with speech in Ephesians 5:4 and Titus 3:9. Such words are not simply stupid, but dangerous, for they come from those espousing false teaching.[80] The second word is found only here in the NT. It describes that which is uninstructed and uneducated. What it thus designates is without the higher view that comes from thoughtful reflection and outside input. It is stupid talk. Such talk often gives the impression of great insight and learning, yet is devoid of any actual wisdom (cf. 1 Tim. 1:7).

This strong stand should be taken by Timothy because he understands ("knowing," εἰδὼς) something that these unenlightened opponents do not. The perfect tense is defective and has a present tense meaning. The participle sets forth the reason for the refusal to enter into such arguments. That which they miss, and Timothy understands, is that such debates only "produce quarrels" (ὅτι γεννῶσιν μάχας). The verb "produce" (γεννῶσιν) describes the fathering of or giving birth to a child (1 Cor. 4:15). The present tense points to that which always happens in such verbal wars. That which is given birth through such talk is "quarrels." The word originally described actual battles fought with weapons, but in the NT it describes fighting, quarrels, strife and disputes fought not with weapons, but with words. Three of its four NT usages are found in Paul (2 Cor. 7:5; 2 Tim. 2:23; Titus 3:9; James 4:1). It is always in the plural form in the NT.[81]

> **Ministry Maxim**
>
> Always be patient with people, but not necessarily with their ideas and opinions.

These apostolic commands, of course, do not mean that the truth should not be defended. It must, but in the process the Lord's servant must know what assertions to respond to and which ones to let wither from their own foolishness.

> **Digging Deeper:**
> 1. How can our obedience in contentious circumstances be at one and the same time both a fleeing and a pursuing?
> 2. Why is what "feels" right (whether "fight" or "flight") not always the way of wisdom when in contentious circumstances?
> 3. What does it imply about a pastor's responsibilities that Paul's only four uses of the verb "refuse" are found in the PE?

---

[79] DNTT, 3:532.
[80] Kittel, abridged, 620-621.
[81] BAGD, 496.

2:24 The Lord's bond-servant must not be quarrelsome, but be kind to all, able to teach, patient when wronged,

Rather than (δέ, untranslated in NASU) being drawn into senseless arguments (v.23), "The Lord's bond-servant must not be quarrelsome" (δοῦλον δὲ κυρίου οὐ δεῖ μάχεσθαι). The designation "The Lord's bond-servant" (δοῦλον . . . κυρίου) is used nowhere else in the NT, but the concepts are familiar. The word "bond-servant" is normally linked with "Christ" (Rom. 1:1; Gal. 1:10; Phil. 1:1; Col. 4:12; cf. Eph. 6:5) and thus "Lord" probably points to Jesus rather than the Father as it did in v.22.[82] The phrase may be a reflection on the Servant of the Lord found in the Servant Songs of Isaiah (Isa. 42:2; 50:6; 53:7).[83] The word "bond-servant" (δοῦλος) is often used to designate a literal slave (e.g., Col. 3:22). Metaphorically it describes the unredeemed person's bondage to sin (Rom. 6:17). Yet Paul often used the term to designate himself as a "bond-servant" of Christ (Rom. 1:1; Gal. 1:10; Titus 1:1), and in Philippians 1:1 he so designated both himself and Timothy (cf. also Epaphras, Col. 4:12). Christ Himself took "the form of a bond-servant" (Phil. 2:7) and thus it is the proper station of every follower of His (Rom. 6:16; 1 Cor. 7:22; Gal. 1:10; Eph. 6:6). At times it is even appropriate to call one's self a "bond-servant" of others to whom we are bound by Christ's call (2 Cor. 4:5). It originally designated the bottom rung of servitude, but then came to describe one who simply yields himself to another's will.[84] Thus Timothy as "The Lord's bond-servant" may not respond to the false teachers in Ephesus as he may please, but is obligated to the command of Christ. In this case Christ's command through his Apostle is that he "must not be quarrelsome" (οὐ δεῖ μάχεσθαι). The impersonal verb δεῖ ("must") describes the moral obligation of the believer to Christ. The negative particle οὐ negates the action ("must not"). The infinitive "be quarrelsome" (μάχεσθαι) is used by Paul only here (John 6:52; Acts 7:26; James 4:2), but is related to the noun just used in v.23 ("quarrels," μάχας). Used literally it describes armed combatants in a physical battle, but figuratively it pictures those who are armed with words and set on destroying their opponents.[85] Such a war of words is off limits to those owned by Christ.

Rather (note the strong adversative "but," ἀλλὰ), a servant of Christ must be able to do three things, all conveyed by adjectives. The first is "be kind to all." The adjective "kind" (ἤπιον) is used only here in the NT. The present

---

[82] Knight, 423.
[83] Marshall, 765.
[84] Vine, 141.
[85] Rienecker, 643.

infinitive "be" (εἶναι) governs all three adjectives ("kind . . . able to teach, patient when wronged") and requires that these be the continual practice of the believer. The prepositional phrase "to all" (πρὸς πάντας) describes the breadth of the obligation of kindness and includes not merely believers of like-mind, but the false teachers and their followers as well.

> **Ministry Maxim**
>
> Kindness is always in God's will.

The second adjective, "able to teach" (διδακτικόν), is found elsewhere only in the list of qualifications for overseers (1 Tim. 3:2). It describes one who is able to convey the truth of the Gospel accurately and powerfully (cf. v.15). The next two verses enlarge upon just what is meant—the manner and the goal of such teaching.

The third adjective is "patient when wronged" (ἀνεξίκακον). This word is used only here in the NT. It describes the ability to bear up under evil treatment without resentment or bitterness.[86]

2:25 with gentleness correcting those who are in opposition, if perhaps God may grant them repentance leading to the knowledge of the truth,

In an echo of the three positive actions set forth in v.24, Paul now parallels them with three matching statements here. The expression "with gentleness" is set alongside "be kind to all," "correcting" matches up with "able to teach," and "those who are in opposition" pairs up with "patient when wronged."[87]

The phrase "with gentleness" (ἐν πραΰτητι) is thrust forward to place it in an emphatic position.[88] Such "gentleness" is a fruit of the Spirit's work in an individual's life (Gal. 5:23). All of Paul's other uses of the noun regard confrontation or discipline (2 Cor. 4:21; 10:1; Gal. 6:1) or general instructions about avoiding difficulties in relationships (Eph. 4:2; Col. 3:12; Titus 3:2). It is usually set as the opposite of harsh, divisive, defiant, brusque attitudes and actions. It speaks of humility, courtesy, considerateness and meekness, in the sense not of weakness, but of power under control.[89]

Such is to be the controlling factor when "correcting" (παιδεύοντα) opponents. The present tense points to the ongoing and unending need for the ministry of correction. The word has a breadth of meaning from severe punishment to redemptive instruction. Paul uses it to describe the effects of church discipline (1 Tim. 1:20) and judgment by the Lord (1 Cor. 11:32) on the one hand and the gentle ways of grace on the other (Titus 2:12). The

---

[86] BAGD, 65.
[87] Knight, 424.
[88] Marshall, 766.
[89] BAGD, 699.

emphasis here seems to be upon the more gentle side of instruction, but never losing completely the strength inherent in the term. This is aimed at "those who are in opposition" (τοὺς ἀντιδιατιθεμένους). The word is found only here in the NT. It is either a present middle, referring to those who are continually setting themselves in opposition to the truth (i.e., the false teachers themselves) or a present passive, pointing to those who are repeatedly drawn into opposition by the false teachers (i.e., the deceived church members). The word "correcting" (παιδεύοντα) is used in the context of delivering two leaders in false doctrine over to Satan (1 Tim. 1:20) and here the goal is to rescue from his clutches (v.26). It would seem that the form is probably a middle voice and points primarily (though not exclusively) to those leading the way in falsehood. The participle is substantive in function.

Such corrective instruction is undertaken with an enduring hope: "if perhaps God may grant them repentance." The condition is set forward by means of an interrogative particle (μήποτε) that is used in an indirect question: "Will God perhaps grant them repentance?"[90] The word comes from μή (not) and ποτέ (at some time) and casts the question as being in some doubt.[91] The interrogative form is lost in most English translations, but the slim sense of hope is retained.

The goal is "repentance" (μετάνοιαν). The word points to a change of mind which issues in a change of behavior. Such radical change must come from outside an individual, so Paul wonders if "God may grant them" (δώῃ αὐτοῖς ὁ θεός) this repentance. The verb is aorist in tense, showing the pivotal nature of such a change, and subjunctive in mood, demonstrating that the reality of such change is possible, but not certain. Repentance is elsewhere depicted as a gift from God (Acts 5:31; 11:18), yet it is also held before us as our obligation (2:38; 3:19; 8:22; 17:30; 26:20).

> **Ministry Maxim**
>
> Some things can only be known by first passing through the door of repentance.

This divine gift of repentance is always "leading to the knowledge of the truth" (εἰς ἐπίγνωσιν ἀληθείας). The exact phrase "the knowledge of the truth" is found only in the PE and describes genuine saving faith (1 Tim. 2:4; Titus 1:1). Paul uses it a few verses later to describe those who by their own unrepentant efforts are "always learning and never able to come to the knowledge of truth" (2 Tim. 3:7). Ultimately the truth comes by way of illumination as a divine gift to the humble heart, not through self-reliant research. The word "knowledge" (ἐπίγνωσιν) is a compound pointing to full or complete knowledge. There are some things that can be known only after passing through the door of repentance.

---

[90] BAGD, 519.
[91] Friberg, 263.

2:26 and they may come to their senses and escape from the snare of the devil, having been held captive by him to do his will.

The coordinating conjunction "and" (καὶ) holds "they may come to their senses" in parallel with "God may grant" (v.25) and sets before us a second outcome of responding to conflict as God outlines. Thus the sense of contingency from the previous verse continues here. The verb "they may come to their senses" (ἀνανήψωσιν) is an aorist active subjunctive to match the parallel verb in v.25. The aorist again signals point action, a decisive turn which brings a person to a whole new understanding. The subjunctive mood again shows that the reality of the action is possible, but not yet certain. The word is a compound from ἀνὰ (again) and νήφω (sober). It appears only here in the NT, though the root word is found elsewhere in the NT (e.g., 2 Tim. 4:5). It literally describes becoming sober again or ceasing to be intoxicated.[92] It is used here figuratively to describe the effect of coming out of the deception of the devil. There is an intoxicating effect to deceit. Lies flatter and we easily imbibe too willingly and too deeply.

The NASU has added the words "and escape" to make good English out of a difficult expression. Literally it is that one "may become sober out of the snare of the devil" (ἐκ τῆς τοῦ διαβόλου παγίδος). Paul has mixed his metaphors, but the sense is clear. The word "snare" (παγίδος) was used in a literal sense of a trap or snare employed in catching birds.[93] It became a metaphorical way of describing the dangers of temptation in this life (Luke 21:35). Such traps may include the pursuit of wealth (1 Tim. 6:9) and, as here, false doctrine.

> **Ministry Maxim**
>
> Falsehood is ultimately illogical, and it takes more than logic to free someone from its grip.

Paul consistently sees the devil's hand in such traps (1 Tim. 3:7). Here he describes such folk as "having been held captive" (ἐζωγρημένοι). The perfect tense of the participle points to their having been taken captive at some point in the past and continuing in that captivity right up to the moment of their escape. The passive voice pictures them as having been acted upon by the evil one. It refers to taking a live captive. Interestingly the only other use of the verb is in Luke 5:10 where Jesus promises Peter that "from now on you will be catching men." We who have been taken captive by Christ must rescue those who are captive to the devil.

The closing phrase "by him to do his will" (ὑπ' αὐτοῦ εἰς τὸ ἐκείνου θέλημα) is difficult. At root is just who "him" (αὐτοῦ) and "his" (ἐκείνου) refer to. Both may refer to the devil. Or the first could refer to "The Lord's bond-servant"

---

[92] BAGD, 58.
[93] Ibid., 602.

(v.24) and the second to God (v.25; cf. NASU footnote on v.26). Or the first may refer to the devil and the second to God.[94] The latter two options both present difficulties, both of which are unnecessary and probably insurmountable enough to make them unrealistic possibilities. Both pronouns appear to point to the devil.[95] The change in pronouns is possibly for emphasis, the second (ἐκείνου) having the sense of "that notorious one."[96]

It should not pass us by that the devil has a will. It stands in opposition to God's will (2 Tim. 1:1; only other use of the word in the PE). He seeks to impose it upon us. We ought to be a captive of Christ (Luke 5:10) and not of the devil. But either one is possible. Christ holds us captive with cords of grace, while the devil enslaves with chains of deception. To fail to make oneself a captive of Christ (v.24, "bond-servant") is to live by default in bondage to the lies of the evil one (Rom. 6:16). Note the progressive pattern of the devil's schemes: *deception* (being kept from "the knowledge of the truth"), *intoxication* ("come to their senses"), *entrapment* ("the snare of the devil"), and *enslavement* ("having been held captive").

Digging Deeper:

1. Why is repentance a prerequisite to spiritual understanding? How does this trip up many "seekers"?
2. How should it change our approach to everyday life to know the devil has a will for our lives and that he is seeking to impose it upon us?
3. Can we be absolutely free, in the sense that we rule our own lives? What do these verses teach regarding this?
4. Ponder the pattern of the devil's schemes: *deception* (being kept from "the knowledge of the truth"), *intoxication* ("come to their senses"), *entrapment* ("the snare of the devil"), and *enslavement* ("having been held captive"). How can knowing his strategy help you stand firm in Christ?

---

[94] Robertson, 4:622.
[95] Fee, 267; Knight, 426-427; Marshall, 767-768; contra. Mounce, 537-538.
[96] Hiebert, *Second Timothy*, 80.

CHAPTER

3

3:1 But realize this, that in the last days difficult times will come.

Paul has just thoroughly counseled Timothy regarding the appropriate means of dealing with the Ephesian errorists (2:16-26), including holding out hope for their repentance and restoration (vv.25-26). In contrast ("But," δέ) to this hope, however, Paul now feeds Timothy a strong dose of reality (3:1-9). Paul opens with the command "realize this" (Τοῦτο ... γίνωσκε). The present imperative demands the action be taken repeatedly and habitually. Paul wants Timothy never to lose sight of the difficult reality of what awaits us in the future. The content of "this" (Τοῦτο) is expounded upon in the clause that begins with "that" (ὅτι).

A present look at what will take place "in the last days" (ἐν ἐσχάταις ἡμέραις) is healthy. The expression points not to some far distant period of time, but to the current age that was inaugurated with the coming of Jesus Christ (Heb. 1:2; James 5:3). The prophets predicted this age (Joel 2:28ff) and the Apostles acknowledged its arrival (Acts 2:16-17). It encompasses the entire period between the death, resurrection, and ascension of Christ and His second advent (1 John 2:18). That the intensity of evil would grow toward the close of this age was a given to the NT writers (2 Peter 3:3; Jude 18) as it had been for the OT prophets before them (Dan. 12:1). Paul has previously warned Timothy of the dark nature of these days (1 Tim. 4:1ff) and he does so now again.

These will be "difficult times" (καιροὶ χαλεποί). The noun "times" (καιροὶ) points to a period of time, not to the passing of time.[1] It appears here without the article, making it a reference to the character of the whole closing

---

[1] Mounce, 544.

age, rather than to a definite length of time.² That it is plural may point to periods of time occurring within the larger context of "the last days." The whole of the last days will be "difficult," but there will be seasons of pronounced difficulty.³ The adjective "difficult" (χαλεποί) refers to that which is hard, fierce, or troublesome. The only other use of the word in the NT is in Matthew 8:28 where it describes a demon-possessed man as "violent." Interestingly Paul has just spoken of the devil's work in these days and has done so previously (1 Tim. 4:1ff). These "times" will be marked by the savagery, brutality, and demonic darkness of Satan's work.

> **Ministry Maxim**
>
> Faithfulness may not yield easier times, but emergence into significantly more difficult ones.

These are days that "will come" (ἐνστήσονται). The word means to impend or to be imminent.⁴ The future tense seems to put the concern out into some yet-to-come time period. Yet the context required that Timothy understand these days as having already arrived. In v.5 Paul will demand a present-time wariness on Timothy's part in view of the days in which they lived.

Paul's warning debunks the notion that life will get better. We believe that hard work, faithfulness, and walking with God are components in an equation that must equal an easier life. We believe it is our right to arrive at a point of sufficiency and leisure in this life. Anything else would simply be unjust! God, however, reminds us to guard our expectations, for faithfulness may not yield easier times, but emergence into significantly more difficult ones.

> **Digging Deeper:**
> 1. How can we obey this command without becoming disheartened?
> 2. How does genuine faith include both a clear view of the difficulties of reality and optimistic hope?
> 3. How can we have such guarded expectations for the future and yet not lose hope?
> 4. What does this command do to "the American Dream" of hard work yielding a life of leisure and ease?

3:2 For men will be lovers of self, lovers of money, boastful, arrogant, revilers, disobedient to parents, ungrateful, unholy,

Paul now sets out to explain ("For," γὰρ) what he means by "difficult times"

---

² Hiebert, *Second Timothy*, 82.
³ Kent, 272.
⁴ BAGD, 266.

(v.1). The problem is that "men will be" (ἔσονται ... οἱ ἄνθρωποι) sinful. The future tense, as in v.1, should not lead us to relegate this to a far future age. These are current problems that Timothy is to avoid in the present (v.5). The middle voice confirms the inward nature of the problem. The problem is not just what men will *do*, but what men *are*. Doing flows from being.

Paul now proceeds with a list of vices which runs through v.4 and totals eighteen different qualities (if counting the final contrast as one). The list is not dissimilar to other such enumerations of sin (e.g., Rom. 1:29-31; Gal. 5:19-21).

The first vice listed is that men will be "lovers of self" (φίλαυτοι). This is the first of five compound words built from the root φίλος. The first two head the list and the last two are found near the end (v.4), serving as something of an inclusion. The first four terms are negative ("lovers of self, lovers of money," v.2; "haters of good" (lit., "not loving good"), v.3; "lovers of pleasure," v.4) while the last is the contrasting positive that these have replaced ("lovers of God," v.4). This seems to indicate that compounding sinfulness arises from misplaced affections.

Of these misplaced affections, being "lovers of self" (φίλαυτοι) seems to be the most foundational. Such people have chosen self-interest rather than the will of God as their basic operating procedure. They are thus destined to fail in the two greatest commandments from God (Matt. 22:37-39), for their affections have already been fixed upon themselves. "Christ did not please Himself" (Rom. 15:3) and thus "He died for all, so that they who live might no longer live for themselves" (2 Cor. 5:15). But these people are among those who "seek after their own interests, not those of Christ Jesus" (Phil. 2:21).

> **Ministry Maxim**
>
> The root of sin is not lack of love, but misplaced love.

The Apostle says people will also be "lovers of money" (φιλάργυροι). This is a compound word made up of "love" (φίλος) and "silver/money" (ἄργυρος). This was the problem with enough of the Pharisees that the label could be applied generally to them all (Luke 16:14). The noun form is also used in 1 Timothy 6:10 where it becomes "a root of all sorts of evil" and, Paul says, "some by longing for it have wandered away from the faith."

The term "boastful" (ἀλαζόνες) is found elsewhere only in the list of vices Paul enumerated in Romans 1:30. This seems to be the outworking of their love of self. Such a person "tries to impress others by making big claims. It was used of the braggart, the charlatan, the quack, the imposter. The word is probably used here with the graver end of its range of meaning in mind."[5]

Similarly they are "arrogant" (ὑπερήφανοι). This term is also found in

---

[5] DNTT, 3:32.

Romans 1:30. God opposes such people (James 4:6; 1 Peter 5:5) and works to scatter them (Luke 1:51). The word means to appear better than others or to be arrogant in thought and conduct.⁶ It points to one's attitude even as "boastful" points to one's speech.

Such people are "revilers" (βλάσφημοι). Paul used to count himself among these folk (1 Tim. 1:13). Peter uses it to describe false teachers (2 Peter 2:11). False witnesses were produced to bring this charge against Stephen (Acts 6:11). The word can point to either slanderous speech toward others or blasphemous speech concerning God. Either could be the emphasis here, but given the next word the former may be more likely.

Such people are "disobedient to parents" (γονεῦσιν ἀπειθεῖς). Romans 1:30 also uses the same phrase to describe those God has abandoned to their own ways. The breaking of the fifth commandment brings no twinge of guilt to those of such conscience (cf. use of the adjective in Luke 1:17). The same adjective ("disobedient," ἀπειθεῖς) is used by Paul to describe generally the pre-Christian condition of every human heart (Titus 3:3) as well as the particular problem of false teachers (1:16). This also begins a series of eight alpha privative words, obviously stating that such people lack some positive quality that can reasonably be expected from those created in God's image. The only break in that list is the word διάβολοι, placed between the fifth and sixth words (v.3).

If they are "disobedient to parents" it comes as no surprise that they are also "ungrateful" (ἀχάριστοι). The word is used elsewhere only in Luke 6:35 where it says God "Himself is kind to ungrateful and evil men." Such a mind sees graces received as rights deserved and thus is not provoked to gratitude.

Such folk are also "unholy" (ἀνόσιοι). The word is used elsewhere in the NT only in 1 Timothy 1:9 where it says the law of God was given for just such people, that it might expose their sinfulness. It refers generally to those "who impiously reject sacred obligations," and here points specifically to those who are "devoid of piety."⁷

3:3 unloving, irreconcilable, malicious gossips, without self-control, brutal, haters of good,

The adjective "unloving" (ἄστοργοι) appears elsewhere in the NT only in Romans 1:31. The verbal form without the prefix describes the appropriate and expected love that would exist between parents and children.⁸ Thus the translation "without natural affects" in the KJV. Note its close proximity to "disobedient to parents" (v.2). It then comes to describe in this form someone

---
⁶ Robertson, 4:332.
⁷ Kittel, abridged, 734-735.
⁸ Rienecker, 644.

who is heartless and inhuman. As an illustration of the word, Cranfield notes Seneca's justification of the drowning of infants who are sickly and deformed.[9]

In addition such people are "irreconcilable" (ἄσπονδοι). The root σπονδή refers to a drink offering or libation such as would normally be a part of a ratification ceremony for a treaty between two factions. The alpha privative here negates the word and means to be without a treaty. By extension it means unforgiving, implacable, and refusing peace.[10] Such a person is unable or unwilling to come to a resolution of his differences with others. He lives in constant friction with those around him.

Another description is "malicious gossips" (διάβολοι). The great majority of this word's usages occur in the singular form as a reference to the devil. Jesus did use the expression to refer to someone as "a devil" (John 6:70). He told a group of Jews they were of their father the devil (John 8:44; cf. Acts 13:10; 1 John 3:10). The devil is able to put ideas and thoughts into the hearts of individuals (John 13:2), to oppress (Acts 10:38) and ensnare them (2 Tim. 2:26), and he wishes to destroy them (1 Peter 5:8). He has organized schemes (Eph. 6:11) which he is actively working out. Yet Jesus Christ destroyed the works of the devil (1 John 3:8), and Christ's followers can successfully resist him (James 4:7). The word "devil" means slanderer. One of his tactics is not merely to slander others himself (Rev. 12:10), but to incite human agents to do the same. Little wonder then that in the plural form the word can refer, as it does here, to those who are slanderers themselves (1 Tim. 3:11; Titus 2:3).

> **Ministry Maxim**
>
> We never look more like the devil than when we gossip.

The words "without self-control" translate a single word in the Greek (ἀκρατεῖς). The adjective is found only here in the NT, but the root κράτος is found frequently and describes power or dominion. Here with the alpha privative added it speaks of those who lack power or the ability to rule themselves.

The word "brutal" (ἀνήμεροι) is also found only here in the NT. It means literally "untamed," and points to one who is savage and brutal.[11] Like wild animals, such people feast themselves upon whatever is at hand that might seem to quell their appetites. It is not difficult to see why it follows "without self-control."

Such people are "haters of good" (ἀφιλάγαθοι). The word is a compound made up of the alpha privative (ἀ), love (φιλ-), and good (ἀγαθός). There are no other NT usages of this word, but its opposite is found in Titus 1:8 where it

---

[9] DNTT, 2:542.
[10] Thayer, 81.
[11] BAGD, 66.

says that overseers must be "loving what is good" (φιλάγαθον). Similarly love "does not rejoice in unrighteousness, but rejoices with the truth" (1 Cor. 13:6).

> **Digging Deeper:**
> 1. Why do you think the Apostle describes people by what they "will be" rather than by what they "will do"?
> 2. What does it say about the nature of sin and the human heart that five of the key words in this list are built on the word "love"?
> 3. Take some moments to identify contemporary expressions of each of these qualities.
> 4. To which of these is your heart most vulnerable?

3:4 treacherous, reckless, conceited, lovers of pleasure rather than lovers of God,

By saying people in the last days will be "treacherous" (προδόται), Paul meant that betrayal would characterize their relationships. The word is used to describe Judas Iscariot (Luke 6:16) and the Jewish Sanhedrin which betrayed Christ (Acts 7:52). In the latter reference it is paired with "murdered." It is a derivative of the compound word προδίδωμι, which means "before" (πρό) and "give" (δίδωμι).

Such people are also "reckless" (προπετεῖς). The word means literally to fall before or fall ahead (i.e., fall headlong, and thus recklessly). In the NT it is used figuratively and describes hasty, impetuous or rash words and actions. It is used in Acts 19:36 where, during the riot in Ephesus, the city clerk urges the crowds to settle down and "do nothing rash" (i.e., something you'll regret later when you've had time to think).

In addition people will be "conceited" (τετυφωμένοι). Paul now switches from the list of adjectives to this perfect passive participle. It means literally to wrap or fill with smoke. In the NT it is used figuratively and always in the passive voice. By extension it comes, then, to describe one who is puffed up with pride or blinded by pride and conceit.[12] The perfect tense indicates that they became thus at some point in the past and still continue in that state. This was the trap the devil fell into, and he would love to drag others into it with him (1 Tim. 3:6). Thus the theme of the demonic continues (cf. 2:26; 3:3). Paul directly applies such conceit to the false teachers in Ephesus in 1 Timothy 6:4.

As the list draws to a close Paul returns to the theme of corrupted love by

---
[12] Thayer, 633.

making a comparison. Such folk are "lovers of pleasure" (φιλήδονοι). The word is used only here in the NT and is a compound made up of "love" (φίλος) and "pleasure" (ἡδονος). The latter is the word from which we get our word *hedonism*. It describes those who are addicted to pleasure (cf. Titus 3:3). They are driven not by good sense, but the sensate. They are ruled by their glands. They are unable to choose consistently the delayed gratification which leads to wisdom.

This they are "rather than lovers of God" (μᾶλλον ἢ φιλόθεοι). The combination of μᾶλλον ἢ is used in an absolute sense in order to remove "lovers of God" from any consideration in calculating what these people are.[13] The expression "lovers of God" translates but one word (φιλόθεοι). This compound ("love," φίλος; "God" θεὸς) is also found nowhere else in the NT. Knight says it "summarizes in one word what Jesus (citing the OT) said to be mankind's highest duty (Matt. 22:37-38 par. Mark 12:28-30/Luke 10:27-28) and is the concept Paul uses elsewhere to describe those who know God (Rom. 8:28; 1 Cor. 2:9; 8:3; Eph. 6:24)."[14]

By closing with two compound words using φίλος, Paul rounds off the list of vices that will characterize those in the last days. The inclusion created with the two opening φίλος–based words (v.2) is a powerful communication device. We should also note the use of "unloving" (v.3a) and "haters of good" (v.3b, lit. "not loving good") in the middle of the list. This brings the list to six out of eighteen vices being perversions of love. All of these, except "unloving" (v.3a), are φίλος–based words. This underscores that the basic problem of the last days will be perversions of love. It highlights the wisdom in Solomon's words: "Watch over your heart with all diligence, for from it flow the springs of life" (Prov. 4:23). Our root problem is misplaced affections.

> **Ministry Maxim**
>
> We are delivered from sin not by denial, but, as Thomas Chalmers said, by "the expulsive power of a new affection."

3:5 holding to a form of godliness, although they have denied its power; Avoid such men as these.

The list of vices (vv.2-4) paints a bleak picture of the fabric of humanity in the last days. Perhaps most frightening of all is that it describes not so much society at large, but those within the church, for they are "holding to a form of godliness" (ἔχοντες μόρφωσιν εὐσεβείας). The present participle points to the

---
[13] BAGD, 489.
[14] Knight, 430-431.

continuous habit of their lives. The noun "a form" (μόρφωσιν) describes an outward form or appearance.[15] The genitive noun "godliness" (εὐσεβείας) is used by Paul often in the PE, but never outside of them. It generally describes the genuine article of faith (1 Tim. 2:2; 3:16; 4:7, 8; 6:3, 6, 11; Titus 1:1). But it can be imitated for selfish ends (1 Tim. 6:5) as it surely is in this present context. Such "godliness" has become nothing but an outer shell, devoid of the true substance of genuine faith. It is outward and showy, not inward and authentic. It is codified and moralistic, not vital and living. This is the fact because the contrast ("although," δέ) speaks of inner substance. They "have denied" (ἠρνημένοι) the reality of true spiritual life. They were refusing or holding at a distance the very thing they strained through their empty religious forms to give the appearance of embracing. The perfect participle points to the fact that they had done this at a point in the past and continued into the present in such a stance toward the truth of the Gospel. The middle voice underscores that their stance toward the reality of the Gospel has arisen from deep within themselves. Titus faced similar such folks in Crete: "They profess to know God, but by their deeds they deny Him" (Titus 1:16a).

That which they have denied is "its power" (δύναμιν αὐτῆς). The antecedent of the pronoun (αὐτῆς) is "godliness" (εὐσεβείας) rightly considered. Paul does not elaborate on just what he means by the word "power" (δύναμιν), yet the word has been used twice already in this letter. It refers first to what the Holy Spirit produces in the one He indwells (1:6-7). In such a case they have embraced the things of God ("a form of godliness") while holding God Himself at a distance. The second use of the word follows on the heels of the first when Paul called on Timothy to join him in "suffering for the gospel according to the power of God" (1:8). The Gospel after all is "the power [δύναμις] of God for salvation to everyone who believes" (Rom. 1:16). Thus these people have rebuffed God and refused His salvation, yet want to be counted within the membership of the church.

> **Ministry Maxim**
>
> Spirit-less Christianity is just another powerless religion.

For this reason Paul commands Timothy, "Avoid such men as these." "Avoid" (ἀποτρέπου) is a compound word (ἀπό, "from"; τρέπω, "turn") found only here in the NT. The present imperative demands the action be taken continually and it again makes clear that "the last days" (v.1) and those who characterize them are upon us. The middle voice gives the sense of "turn yourself away from" these kind of people. The word is a strong one whose full sense is difficult to bring out in English. Some see an implication that

---
[15] BAGD, 528.

Timothy is to turn away from such people in horror.[16] This is a command to Timothy (second person singular); however, it applies not simply to him as a Christian, but to him as a pastor who tends a flock of believers. This must, then, demand of him not simply a personal response, but a pastoral response as well. Thus the word may have reference to some level of formal church discipline and instruction to the congregation in how to respond to such people who name themselves as one of them.

The NASU does not translate the conjunction καὶ (though cf. NASB) which heads this clause. Its function is to connect the present imperative with the previous imperative that leads this section (v.1, "realize this").[17] This section is thus wrapped in the bookends of responsibility, first to know the days in which we live and secondly to respond correctly to them.

The phrase "as these" translates one word (τούτους). It refers to those described in vv.2-5a. We are thus reminded that in the last days we must guard not only our expectations (v.1) and our affections (various φίλος–based words in vv.2-4), but also our associations (v.5). That concerns not so much those outside the church, but those who profess to be a part of it.

> **Digging Deeper:**
> 1. How does our culture (outside and inside the church) encourage people to be "lovers of pleasure" rather than "lovers of God"?
> 2. Why do such folk want to maintain "a form of godliness"? What advantage do they believe it affords them?
> 3. How can we reach the people described here if we "Avoid such men as these"? How does this command relate to the Apostle's counsel in 2:23-26?

3:6 For among them are those who enter into households and captivate weak women weighed down with sins, led on by various impulses,

If the description of such people (vv.1-5) has not been sufficient, Paul adds another reason ("For," γάρ) to avoid them (v.5b). Now he names the actions of some "among them" (ἐκ τούτων), or, perhaps more literally, of some who arise "out from" (ἐκ) them. Such men are the worst of the worst. They "are those who enter into households" (εἰσιν οἱ ἐνδύνοντες εἰς τὰς οἰκίας). The

---
[16] Rienecker, 645.
[17] Knight, 433.

action now is moved outside of the assembly of believers to the individual homes of the most vulnerable among the folk. They are "those who enter" (οἱ ἐνδύνοντες), a present participle with the definite article used in a substantive way to identify their character. The word is used only here in the NT and has the sense of worming their way into these homes.[18] There is something insidious in their methods.[19] Like wolves, they try to separate one sheep from the safety of the flock. The definite article with "households" (τὰς οἰκίας) may indicate the homes of well-known women. Just what makes these women identifiable is unclear; perhaps it is their wealth or social standing.[20]

Their target is "weak women" (γυναικάρια). This is also the only time this word is found in the NT. It is the diminutive form of γυνή, meaning literally "little women." It is used in a pejorative sense here, though not of all women generally, but of idle, frivolous, silly or morally weak women.[21] Such men scan the congregation trying to spot a woman who is vulnerable and unlikely to have either the discernment to see their subtle schemes or the strength to resist their advances.

Paul uses a series of four participles (vv.6b-7) to describe these vulnerable women.[22] First, what makes these women so susceptible is that they are "weighed down with sins" (σεσωρευμένα ἁμαρτίαις). The participle "weighed down" means to pile or heap something up, either in the sense of piling one thing upon another or in filling something up. It is found only twice in the NT. In Romans 12:20 it is used in a quotation of Proverbs 25:22 to describe heaping up hot coals upon the head of one's enemy (i.e., overwhelm evil with good). It is used differently here. It describes a woman who has never gotten out from under the burden of her sins; in fact, she is overwhelmed by them and is vulnerable to an approach on a number of fronts because of her preoccupation with them.[23] The passive voice of the participle shows that the sins and their guilt have overwhelmed such women. The perfect tense describes the abiding nature of their burden, one they have never found freedom from.

> **Ministry Maxim**
>
> Beware of those who prey upon other's vulnerabilities — they have hidden intentions.

The plan of such men is to "captivate" (αἰχμαλωτίζοντες) such women. The word describes capturing someone at spear point and making them a prisoner of war. In the NT it is used to describe the plight of the Jews during "the times of

---

[18] BAGD, 263.
[19] Guthrie, 158.
[20] Mounce, 548.
[21] Friberg, 102.
[22] Hiebert, *Second Timothy*, 88.
[23] Kittel, abridged, 1150.

the Gentiles" (Luke 21:24), of being a prisoner to the law of sin (Rom. 7:23) and positively of the believer "taking every thought captive to the obedience of Christ" (2 Cor. 10:5). Here it has the sense of gaining complete possession of such women.[24] These men gain a cultic grip upon the mind, emotions and wills of the most vulnerable.

Secondly, in addition to the downward weight of their sins, such potential victims are propelled forward by seemingly irresistible desires. They are "led on" (ἀγόμενα). The present tense of the participle points to the unceasing yearning that is never satisfied. The passive voice makes clear that they are not in control of themselves, but under the control of their lusts. That which tugs the halter into which they have placed themselves are "various impulses" (ἐπιθυμίαις ποικίλαις). By "impulses" is meant the strong desires or lusts that arise within from a person's unchecked sinful nature. We all once lived under their control (Titus 3:3), but the grace of God teaches us to deny them (2:12). Paul told Timothy to flee them (2 Tim. 2:22). The emphasis is often sexual, but goes far beyond just that to include covetousness (1 Tim. 6:9) and misguided religious impulses (2 Tim. 4:3). Indeed, here they are "various" (ποικίλαις), a word meaning many-colored and pointing to the variety and diversity of the urges and desires that can arise to control a person. The dative form, coupled with the passive voice of the verb, signals that these lusts are the instrument that drives such people.[25]

3:7 always learning and never able to come to the knowledge of the truth.

A third participle (see v.6) describes another characteristic of these weak women. They are "always learning" (πάντοτε μανθάνοντα). The participle refers to learning something through someone's instruction.[26] The present tense coupled with the adverb ("always," πάντοτε) underscores the constant and continual nature of their learning. Presumably it is the burden of their sins and their helplessness in the face of inner urges (v.6) that drive them to be ever seeking and always open to those with new information, ideas and possibilities of help.

> **Ministry Maxim**
>
> Curiosity that never matures into conviction is defective from the beginning.

Yet in their quest they are frustrated, for in addition to ("and," καὶ) their learning is their inability to arrive at the truth. Here the fourth participle describing these women marks

---
[24] Rienecker, 645.
[25] Ibid.
[26] BAGD, 490.

their inability to arrive at and settle in the truth ("never able," μηδέποτε ... δυνάμενα). The present tense of the participle again underscores the constant inability they experience. The middle voice points to the inwardness of their weakness and that no amount of resolve can deliver them into the knowledge of the truth. The adverb "never" (μηδέποτε) is an intensified compound form found only here in the NT.[27] It stands in direct contrast to "always" (πάντοτε). Their continual effort is matched by their continual inability.

The adverb and the participle stand on opposite ends of the clause. Between them is specified just what the continual inability consists of. They are unable "to come to the knowledge of the truth" (εἰς ἐπίγνωσιν ἀληθείας ἐλθεῖν). The aorist active infinitive "to come" (ἐλθεῖν) indicates action at a point in time. For all of their continual effort at learning, they never actually arrive at the point of knowing the truth. The goal is "the knowledge of the truth." The word for "knowledge" (ἐπίγνωσιν) is a compound word (ἐπὶ, "upon" and γνῶσις, "knowledge") which intensifies the root and points to fullness of knowledge. Such folk accumulate facts, theories, proposals, and philosophies, but are unable to arrive at the full embrace of the truth. The phrase "the knowledge of the truth" (ἐπίγνωσιν ἀληθείας) is used exclusively in the PE. It is nearly synonymous with salvation (2 Tim. 2:4), follows repentance (2 Tim. 2:25) and is tied directly to saving faith (Titus 1:1). "'To come into' that knowledge is to acknowledge and embrace the truth of the gospel and be converted by it so that the things associated with this phrase in the other PE occurrences (repentance, faith, being saved, living in godliness) become a reality in one's life."[28]

> **Digging Deeper:**
> 1. Why do those who feel most guilty often come under the power of domineering, opinionated leaders? Why are those at rest in God's grace less likely to do so?
> 2. What keeps these constant "seekers of truth" from ever really arriving at it?

3:8 Just as Jannes and Jambres opposed Moses, so these men also oppose the truth, men of depraved mind, rejected in regard to the faith.

Having just made mention of some women's inability to embrace the truth

---
[27] Knight, 434.
[28] Ibid.

(v.7), Paul now speaks of the stance of the false teachers toward the truth. He begins with a comparison. "Just as" (ὃν τρόπον) means "in the manner in which" and links with "so . . . also" (οὕτως καὶ) in the second clause.[29] The NASU does not translate the coordinating conjunction δέ, (but see NASB where it is translated "And"). It connects this sentence with vv.6-7 and provides another reason for withdrawing from such false teachers (v.5b).[30]

The comparison revolves around two Egyptian magicians who set themselves against Moses. "Jannes and Jambres" (Ἰάννης καὶ Ἰαμβρῆς) are the names tradition has assigned to Moses' two primary opponents in Pharaoh's court (Exod. 7:11ff).[31] These men "opposed" (ἀντέστησαν) him. The word always has the sense of the middle voice in the NT and means to set oneself against, to resist or withstand someone ("Moses") or something ("the truth").[32] Paul uses it again in 4:15 to describe the personal opposition of "Alexander the coppersmith." The opposition of Jannes and Jambres consisted of replicating the miracles of Moses, which were given him by God to authenticate his message as from God. Their false miracles instead reinforced the false thinking of Pharaoh and his "heart was hardened, and he did not listen to them, as the LORD had said" (Exod. 7:13). Those two, then, served to confirm and advance a lie, resisting the truth of God as announced by Moses.

In a similar fashion ("Just as . . . so . . . also") the false teachers in Ephesus had set themselves against "the truth" (τῇ ἀληθείᾳ). The verb is the same, but is in the present tense to contrast their continual stance toward the truth in the present with the historical reference to the passing encounter (aorist tense) of the magicians with Moses. The use of the definite article specifies the body of orthodox Christian doctrine against which these teachers have set themselves. The truth is that which every servant of God is to handle with accuracy (2:15), that from which false teachers have gone astray (2:18), and that into which repentance might deliver them (2:25). But people will increasingly have little taste for the truth (4:4). Given their opposition to the truth, it is little wonder their disciples are "never able to come to the knowledge of the truth" (v.7). Their opposition, like that of Jannes and Jambres, consists of an alternative presentation which then sets itself up as superior to the truth.

> **Ministry Maxim**
>
> Rejecting the truth renders the mind incapable of any longer seeing the truth.

They are "men of depraved mind" (ἄνθρωποι κατεφθαρμένοι τὸν νοῦν). The noun "men" (ἄνθρωποι) might apply equally to both genders, though here

---
[29] BAGD, 827.
[30] Knight, 435.
[31] BAGD, 368.

it is clearly males that are in view, considering they "captivate weak women" (v.6). The perfect participle means that at some point in the past they became depraved in their reasoning and they continue in that abiding state in the present. The passive voice indicates that their thinking was overtaken by the deception into which they placed themselves. The passive voice may be a hint regarding the devil's work as well (cf. 2:26).[33] It is a compound word (κατά, "against" and φθείρω, "destroy") meaning to corrupt or pervert utterly.[34] That which is ruined is the "mind" (τὸν νοῦν). It refers to the ability to reason and think. The definite article specifies that it includes the whole realm of their reasoning. For a similar phrase using only a slightly different compound of the root verb see 1 Timothy 6:5.

Such people are "rejected in regard to the faith" (ἀδόκιμοι περὶ τὴν πίστιν). Through their corrupted thinking and clinging to a false Gospel they have placed themselves outside "the faith" (τὴν πίστιν). The noun and the definite article ("the faith") refer to the body of truth which conveys the saving grace of God in Christ. They have failed to embrace it believingly. The definite article (as with "the truth" earlier in the sentence) serves to specify the one and only faith through which one might be rescued from sin and its judgment.

The adjective "rejected" (ἀδόκιμοι) describes that which is "worthless, rejected, not in the sense of that which is seen from the first to be unsuitable . . . but meaning that which has not stood the test, that which has been shown to be a sham, and has therefore been rejected (Rom. 1:28; 1 Cor. 9:27; 2 Cor. 13:5; 2 Tim. 3:8; Titus 1:16)."[35] The preposition περὶ with the accusative ("in regard to") specifies that which they are rejected from. The rejection of these teachers after testing stands as the opposite of the approval Paul calls God's servants to seek (2 Tim. 2:15).[36]

3:9 But they will not make further progress; for their folly will be obvious to all, just as Jannes's and Jambres's folly was also.

In what seems an abrupt reversal ("But," ἀλλ') Paul assures Timothy that these teachers "will not make further progress" (οὐ προκόψουσιν ἐπὶ πλεῖον). The verb "make . . . progress" (προκόψουσιν) is used by Paul five times, three of them in this letter (cf. also Rom. 13:12; Gal. 1:14). Elsewhere in 2 Timothy he uses it to say that ungodly talk "will lead to further ungodliness" (2:16) and that evil men "will proceed" from bad to worse (3:13). But here the verb is

---

[32] Ibid., 67.
[33] Mounce, 550.
[34] Rienecker, 645.
[35] DNTT, 3:808.
[36] Fee, 273.

negated ("not," οὐ) to indicate that the only advance they will make is in the degree of their sinfulness, not in real success. The only other use of the verb in the NT is by Luke. In stark contrast it describes the successful advance of the boy Jesus: "Jesus kept increasing in wisdom and stature, and in favor with God and men" (Luke 2:52). The future tense here gathers up the worries of Timothy and assures him of the ultimate failure of these opponents. It was hard to deny they had made an impact upon the Ephesian church, but it is "further" (ἐπὶ πλεῖον) progress that the Apostle denies. The combination of ἐπὶ πλεῖον ("further," lit., "to more") was used also in 2:16 (cf. also Acts 4:17; 20:9; 24:4) and has the sense of "to a greater degree."[37]

Paul now explains ("for," γάρ) the foundation for his optimism. The Apostle was convinced that "their folly will be obvious to all" (ἡ . . . ἄνοια αὐτῶν ἔκδηλος ἔσται πᾶσιν). The word "folly" (ἄνοια, used elsewhere only in Luke 6:11) describes ignorance or a want of understanding.[38] Paul is not calling the false teachers stupid, but it is within the realm of spiritual things that these false teachers are deficient. They do not know what they are talking about (1 Tim. 1:7) and this "will be obvious" (ἔκδηλος ἔσται). The future tense points to a more promising day down the road and the middle voice emphasizes the self-destructive nature of such foolishness. Their teachings are unconnected to reality and are self-contradicting. This will become self-evident and their façade of spirituality will cave in upon itself. The adjective "obvious" (ἔκδηλος) is used only here in the NT. It describes that which is clear or evident.[39] The prefixed preposition ἐκ intensifies the meaning and points to that which is abundantly clear.[40] The essential and ultimate folly of their teaching will eventually be unveiled to the world for what it really is. It is only a matter of time.

> **Ministry Maxim**
>
> Falsehood is ultimately self-defeating.

Who does Paul's "all" (πᾶσιν) encompass? Paul is speaking specifically to Timothy within the Ephesian context. Thus he would likely have had in mind those within the Ephesian church who had been hoodwinked into their deception. But is he really promising that no one will remain within the camp of the false teachers?

A more exact answer requires understanding the comparison Paul makes in his closing phrase ("just as Jannes's and Jambres's folly was also"). The NASU is an interpretive rendering, presumably for the purposes of clarity and easier reading. The NASB's original translation is more literal: "as also that of

---
[37] Marshall, 750.
[38] BAGD, 70.
[39] Rienecker, 645.
[40] Guthrie, 160.

those two came to be" (ὡς καὶ ἡ ἐκείνων ἐγένετο). The reference is to the folly of Jannes and Jambres (the definite article ἡ refers to the noun ἄνοια, "folly"),[41] so the NASU is accurate and helpful. Those two were able to duplicate the miracles that came from Moses's hand (Exod. 7:11) until it came to the plague of gnats. Then "The magicians tried with their secret arts to bring forth gnats, but they could not" (Exod. 8:18a). Indeed, by the time of the plague of boils their magic could not keep pace with the power of God and they were overtaken by the plague: "The magicians could not stand before Moses because of the boils, for the boils were on the magicians as well as on all the Egyptians" (Exod. 9:11).

The "all" here probably corresponds to "all the Egyptians" of Exodus 9:11. Ultimately in the end, the power of God's truth will outlast and overtake the inherent weakness of falsehood and all will observe the triumph of the truth. Yet in the short-term such false teachers will find some measure of success, as Paul seems to admit throughout the letter was the case in Ephesus.

Wise ministry in "the last days" requires guarding our expectations (v.1), our affections (vv.2-4) and our associations (vv.5-9).

> **Digging Deeper:**
> 1. Why is time always on the side of truth?
> 2. Why is it difficult, in the short term, to trust in the eventual vindication of the truth?
> 3. How do vv.8-9 help us in our offices, homes and schools when people oppose our testimony for Christ?

3:10 Now you followed my teaching, conduct, purpose, faith, patience, love, perseverance,

Having warned of the difficulties of ministry in the last days (vv.1-9), Paul now moves on to positive encouragements regarding Timothy's past faithfulness and exhortations to future faithfulness (vv.10-17). That Paul is contrasting Timothy with the false teachers is clear since the sentence begins with the second person singular personal pronoun Σὺ ("you") in an emphatic position. The contrast is made explicit by the use of the conjunction δέ ("Now") in an adversative sense (cf. "But," NASB, NKJV; "however," NIV, ESV). Paul will again use the formula of Σὺ δέ in 3:14 and 4:5 to place special emphasis upon Timothy's life and to contrast it with negative examples (cf. 1 Tim. 6:11).

---

[41] Mounce, 551.

Whereas the false teachers were constantly resisting the truth (v.8), Timothy "followed" (παρηκολούθησάς) what Paul taught. The aorist tense points to Timothy's past dealings with Paul. The word is used by Paul elsewhere only in 1 Timothy 4:6 where he speaks of "the sound doctrine which you have been following." It is used of the meticulous research Luke gave himself to before writing his Gospel (Luke 1:3). The preposition in compound gives the basic sense of "following beside" something. Then it comes to mean "follow closely." It describes following along with the mind, to understand and then to make that thing one's own.[42] It may also have become a technical term relating to the intimate relationship of a disciple to his master.[43] The word does not require that Timothy had been alongside Paul through all of his experiences (i.e., specifically the events and locations mentioned in v.11), but that at least he had knowledge of them and had thought deeply upon them, comparing and combining them with what he had observed first hand.

That to which Timothy paid such careful attention is specified by the use of nine nouns in the dative case and each accompanied by its definite article (running into v.11a). All nine are governed by the first person personal pronoun "my" (μου). Thus these were not abstract philosophical contemplations of Timothy, but the personal and relational observations of the life of God at work in Paul. This reminds us that a disciple of Jesus Christ is not primarily the product of a classroom, but of life invested and shared through personal relationship.

The first of these observed qualities was "my teaching" (μου τῇ διδασκαλίᾳ). This noun is used in the NT only two times outside of Paul's writings, but he uses it nineteen times—fifteen of them in the PE. It may refer to either the act of teaching or to that which is taught ("doctrine").[44] It is in this latter sense that it is used here. There may be the "doctrine of demons" (1 Tim. 4:1). But "the doctrine of God our Savior" (Titus 2:10) is "sound teaching/doctrine" (1 Tim. 1:10; 4:6; 2 Tim. 4:3; Titus 1:9; 2:1), "doctrine conforming to godliness" (1 Tim. 6:3) and "purity in doctrine" (Titus 2:7). It is this "teaching" that Paul has held forth and that is to be Timothy's preoccupation. This is the heart of Scripture's purpose (2 Tim. 3:16) and all our teaching is to arise from and be controlled by the Scriptures. Such a ministry requires careful attention (1 Tim. 4:13), perseverance, and meticulous study (4:16), if our "doctrine will not be

> **Ministry Maxim**
>
> Christian maturity involves more than the gathering of data, but is the transference of life through contemplative observation and study.

---

[42] BAGD, 619.
[43] Rienecker, 647.
[44] BAGD, 191.

spoken against" (6:1). Thus Timothy observed in Paul's teaching not merely orthodox content, but a commitment to the demanding disciplines of submission, preparation, thinking, delivery and personal obedience.

Naturally, then, "conduct" (τῇ ἀγωγῇ) comes after "teaching." The word is used only here in the NT. Its basic meaning is "a leading," but when used intransitively, as it is here, it comes to refer to the way one leads his life, the course or manner of one's life.[45] Paul is reminding Timothy that he had been given access to the most mundane and intimate of Paul's daily affairs and that Timothy had observed a manner of life that was governed by the Scriptures and what Paul taught from them. Can true disciples be made without such a relationship?

Timothy had also seen Paul's "purpose" (τῇ προθέσει). Paul uses this word five other times, all of them to speak of God's purpose (Rom. 8:28; 9:11; Eph. 1:11; 3:11; 2 Tim. 1:9). What Timothy had personally observed was that the purpose of God had become the guiding purpose of Paul's life. In the Gospels its three uses (Matt. 12:4; Mark 2:26; Luke 6:4; cf. also Heb. 9:2) describe David and his men eating the "consecrated" bread that had been set apart to God. Thus Timothy had observed that in life's details Paul's heart never failed to be sanctified to God.

Paul's "faith" (τῇ πίστει) was also observable by Timothy. Clearly the reference is not simply to "faith" as the body of truth embraced by the Apostle (cf. v.8), but also to the active trust Paul displayed in the God of truth. From his shared life with Paul, Timothy could easily recall many instances in which he had seen the Apostle exercise faith.

Timothy had also studied the "patience" (τῇ μακροθυμίᾳ) of Paul. The Apostle had used the word to describe God's great patience with him (1 Tim. 1:16) and other sinners (Rom. 2:4; 9:22). He in turn had extended this patience to all (2 Cor. 6:6); so should Timothy as well (2 Tim. 4:2). Only God can produce this within us (Gal. 5:22; Col. 1:11). The word has the sense of endlessly bearing up under ill-treatment at the hands of others.[46] This would also be a necessary virtue in Timothy's ministry to the troubled Ephesian church (2 Tim. 2:24-26).

In his careful observations of Paul, Timothy had also seen his "love" (τῇ ἀγάπῃ). For Paul this was the supreme virtue of Christianity (1 Cor. 13:13) and the goal of all his teaching (1 Tim. 1:5). It is found only in Christ (2 Tim. 1:13) and produced in the believer only by the indwelling Holy Spirit (1:6-7). It stands opposed to fleshly lusts and must be the constant pursuit of the child of God (2:22).

---

[45] Thayer, 10.
[46] Rienecker, 517.

The seventh quality which Timothy is said to have observed in Paul is his "perseverance" (τῇ ὑπομονῇ). This is a compound word which literally meant to "remain under." It pointed then to a patient endurance which held out long under difficulty with hope and courage.

3:11 persecutions, and sufferings, such as happened to me at Antioch, at Iconium and at Lystra; what persecutions I endured, and out of them all the Lord rescued me!

The string of descriptive nouns begun in v.10 continues here, but with a shift to the plural for the final two in the list. These final two are an outgrowth of the previous noun, "perseverance" (v.10), and make more concrete and specific the recollections to which Paul calls Timothy. Timothy knew all about Paul's "persecutions" (τοῖς διωγμοῖς) and "sufferings" (τοῖς παθήμασιν). The former word is used in the NT of religious persecution.[47] Paul used it twice in this verse, but only three times beyond this verse. He had learned to be content even in such conditions (2 Cor. 12:10), for he knew they could not separate him from God's love in Christ (Rom. 8:35). In 2 Thessalonians 1:4 he again linked it with "perseverance." The latter word, "sufferings," tells us the effect of these persecutions upon Paul.

The relative pronoun οἷα ("such as") helps makes specific which "persecutions and sufferings" Paul was referring to and focuses upon the qualitative nature of these events.[48] The aorist tense of the verb "happened" (ἐγένετο) points Timothy's mind to the past, and the dative first person pronoun "me" (μοι) fixed his attention upon the arena of the Apostle's life. Even more specifically Paul points to his past experiences "at Antioch, at Iconium and at Lystra."

The account of these specific sufferings is recorded for us in Acts 13-14 and took place during Paul's first missionary journey. In Antioch the Jews became jealous after observing the response to the preaching of Paul and Barnabas (Acts 13:45). Many among the Gentiles believed (v.48) and the word spread throughout the entire region (v.49). "But the Jews incited the devout women of prominence and the leading men of the city, and instigated a persecution against Paul and Barnabas, and drove them out of their district" (v.50). Having shaken the dust from their feet, Paul and Barnabas departed for Iconium (v.51). In that city they again preached in the synagogue and many Jews and Gentiles believed (14:1). "But the Jews who disbelieved stirred up the minds of the Gentiles and embittered them against the brethren" (v.2). Paul and Barnabas, however, did not flee, but stayed on for some time preaching

---

[47] BAGD, 201.
[48] Knight, 440.

boldly (v.3). The community was divided over their presence and preaching. Soon "an attempt was made by both the Gentiles and the Jews with their rulers, to mistreat and to stone them" (v.5). Paul and Barnabas fled the city, departing for Lystra (v.6). There Paul healed a lame man, which resulted in the residents identifying him and Barnabas as Zeus and Hermes (v.12). With great effort they stopped the crowds from sacrificing to them as gods, but then "Jews came from Antioch and Iconium, and having won over the crowds, they stoned Paul and dragged him out of the city, supposing him to be dead" (v.19). Yet Paul miraculously got up, returned to the city and stayed until the next day (v.20).

In the text of Acts there is no mention of Timothy until the second missionary journey, when Paul and Silas returned to Lystra (Acts 16:1). By that time he was well-spoken of and well-known to the church throughout the region, including not only his hometown of Lystra, but also Iconium (v.2). Thus, it is highly improbable that Timothy would have had first-hand knowledge of Paul's prior experiences in either Antioch or Iconium. He may well have been one in the crowd in Lystra who heard Paul preach, watched his stoning, and stood in amazement as he fearlessly walked back into town. Perhaps this was the turning point in Timothy's life when he put his faith in Christ, and during the intervening time between that first visit of the Apostle and his return in Acts 16:1 he grew and began preaching the Gospel himself. Since at that time he was well known even in Iconium (v.2), he would surely have heard the local believers' accounts of the Apostle's sufferings in their city. His dealings in each city probably became standard lore around fires at night, so all of these events were likely familiar to Timothy when he met Paul more personally (16:1). Then, during their travels together, the Apostle surely answered his many questions, correcting any misunderstandings and filling in details. But why would Paul make mention of these earlier persecutions in which Timothy was largely absent, rather than later persecutions which they went through together (Acts 16-17)? Fee may be very near the point when he insists that it was the Apostle's intention to underscore that Timothy had known from his earliest days that persecution was a part of faith in Christ and that he should therefore not lose heart in his current sufferings.[49]

> **Ministry Maxim**
>
> Sometimes God delivers "out of" and sometimes "through," but He always delivers His people.

The next clause is awkward to translate, as our various English versions demonstrate. It is probably best understood as an exclamation: "What

---
[49] Fee, 276-277.

persecutions I endured!" (NRSV). The relative pronoun "what" (οἵους) points to the quality of the thing and means something like "of what sort."[50] The word "persecutions" (διωγμοὺς) is the same word used earlier in this verse. The verb "I endured" (ὑπήνεγκα) is used by Paul elsewhere only in 1 Corinthians 10:13 where it is bearing up under temptation that is the concern (cf. also 1 Peter 2:19 for the only other NT usage). The compound word (ὑποφέρω) has the sense of bearing something by being under it. It describes bearing up under or carrying a heavy load.[51] The aorist tense points to a past fact already completed in the experience of Paul. It is a colorful compliment to "perseverance" (ὑπομονῇ), which appears in this same sentence (v.10b) with a somewhat similar meaning.

Paul then added a closing word of testimony which was to verbalize what Timothy had observed, "and out of them all the Lord rescued me!" (καὶ ἐκ πάντων με ἐρρύσατο ὁ κύριος). Paul may intentionally be echoing Psalm 34:19: "Many are the afflictions of the righteous, but the LORD delivers him out of them all." The conjunction "and" (καὶ) connects the grim fact of Paul's sufferings with the glorious testimony of God's deliverance. In the past God delivered Paul "out of" (ἐκ) all his persecutions. Paul's expectations regarding his current plight are somewhat different. He expected God not to deliver him "out of" this imprisonment, but to deliver him *through* death *into* his glorious presence (4:6-8; cf. Phil. 1:20). He may not be delivered "out of" his current plight as he had in the past, but he could still affirm, "The Lord will rescue me *from* [ἀπό] every evil deed" (4:18, emphasis added). The Apostle's exuberance is not dampened over God's past faithfulness. His experience has been complete ("them all," πάντων) and personal ("me," με). It has been none other than "the Lord" (ὁ κύριος) Himself who has accomplished this time and again. The verb "rescued" (ἐρρύσατο) is used twice as Paul closes this letter: "I *was rescued* out of the lion's mouth. The Lord *will rescue* me from [ἀπο] every evil deed, and will bring me safely to His heavenly kingdom" (4:17b-18a, emphasis added). Sometimes God delivers "out of" and sometimes "through," but He always delivers His people "from" persecution and suffering.

This sentence (vv.10-11) suggests a wise course of analysis when choosing spiritual leaders to follow: What do they believe ("teaching")? What do they do ("conduct")? What do they live for ("purpose")? What will they risk ("faith")? Who or what can rattle them ("patience")? What do they treasure ("love")? What will they endure ("perseverance")? What won't they negotiate ("persecutions and sufferings")?

---

[50] BAGD, 562.
[51] Rienecker, 646.

> **Digging Deeper:**
> 1. What do Paul's words tell us about how disciples are reproduced?
> 2. For each item in Paul's list think of someone you know who embodies that item. Who is an example of more of these than anyone else? What are you learning from that person?
> 3. Which of these nine items do you think people are most likely to see in you? Who are you inviting into your life that they might be close enough to observe these things about you? If the answer is "no one," how are you making disciples of Christ?
> 4. How would you explain this statement to a doubting person: "Sometimes God delivers 'out of' and sometimes 'through,' but He always delivers His people 'from' persecution and suffering."?

3:12 Indeed, all who desire to live godly in Christ Jesus will be persecuted.

The NASU has unfortunately dropped the "And" which heads the sentence in the NASB ("And indeed, all" καὶ πάντες δὲ). The combination of καὶ ... δὲ is both emphatic and connective, linking the general principle stated here with the specific "persecutions and sufferings" of Paul (v.11). The specifics of Paul's hardships for Christ (v.11) become here a general principle for "all" (πάντες).

The "all" is not universal, but encompasses the totality of those "who desire to live godly in Christ Jesus" (οἱ θέλοντες εὐσεβῶς ζῆν ἐν Χριστῷ Ἰησοῦ). The present participle "who desire" (οἱ θέλοντες) is used as a substantive to describe a class of people, highlighting their common and continuous quest. The verb describes the engaging of the will, either from a confirmed position of determination (to resolve, to purpose, to determine) or from a more wishful stance (to desire, to wish).[52] Paul has set the stage of this world as the battle between two wills: that of God (2 Tim. 1:1) and that of the devil (2:26). Here Paul speaks of those who continuously join their will to that of God and therefore draw the ire of the devil. The desire in view is "to live godly" (εὐσεβῶς ζῆν). Outside of the PE and 2 Peter, the adverb is never used of the Christian life or faith. But in the PE the word-group of this adverb describes a manner of life in relation to God, others, and self that brings honor to the Lord

> **Ministry Maxim**
>
> Suffering with Christ is inevitable for the one living in union with Him.

---

[52] Thayer, 285-286.

(1 Tim. 2:2; 3:16; 4:7, 8; 5:4; 6:3, 5, 6, 11; 2 Tim. 3:5, 12; Titus 1:1; 2:12).[53] In combination the two words describe not some super-class of Christians, but the normal life which results from true saving faith (cf. Titus 2:11-12).[54] This much-desired life is "in Christ Jesus" (ἐν Χριστῷ Ἰησοῦ). That is to say, it is experienced only in union with the living Lord of the church.

Those who pursue such a life "will be persecuted" (διωχθήσονται). This is the verbal form of the noun found twice in v.11. It was used in the LXX to describe the hunting down of humans by soldiers (Exod. 15:9) or other hostiles (Gen. 31:23).[55] In the NT it came primarily to describe the harassment, molestation or troubling of Christians. The future tense points to the certain outcome of such a life. The passive voice demonstrates that the persecution consists of external opposition that overtakes such believers.

As Christians we seek to live in union with Christ ("in Christ Jesus") and to increasingly bear a likeness to Christ ("desire to live godly"). We, therefore, share also in the sufferings of Christ ("will be persecuted"). Paul had announced this outcome for followers of Christ in the cities of his earliest persecution (v.11), including Timothy's home town of Lystra (Acts 14:21-22), and later in his letters (Rom. 8:17; Phil. 1:29; 1 Thess. 3:3-4). In doing so he was echoing his Master's prior warning (Matt. 10:22-25; Luke 21:12; John 15:20; 16:33).

Digging Deeper:
1. Explain how the desire to live in union with Christ and to be increasingly conformed to His likeness leads automatically to sharing also in His sufferings?
2. Is it appropriate to reverse the logic of v.12 to say also that if we are not being persecuted we are probably not seeking to live a truly godly life in Christ?

3:13 But evil men and impostors will proceed from bad to worse, deceiving and being deceived.

Paul has recounted his own sufferings and persecutions (v.11) and then broadened out to a general principle of persecution for all believers (v.12). This having been said, he now contrasts ("But," δέ) against these facts what will become of those who bring such persecution. He applies two labels to

---

[53] Kittel, abridged, 1012.
[54] Knight, 441.
[55] DNTT, 2:805.

these folk. First he calls them "evil men" (πονηροὶ ... ἄνθρωποι). The adjective can be used generally to refer to that which is bad, in poor condition, spoiled or worthless. Here, however, it probably carries the ethical sense of wicked, evil, bad, base, worthless, vicious and degenerate.[56] This characterizes them as "men" (ἄνθρωποι). The noun need not be a gender specific term, but, given that these were teachers, they were likely males (cf. vv.2-6). Secondly, he calls them "impostors" (γόητες). The word is found only here in the NT. It apparently comes from the word γοάω, meaning "to wail." It came then to refer to a wizard or magician who tried to exercise evil powers by verbally spoken incantations and spells. In later usage it could be used to refer to a charlatan or deceiver generally. Given the reference to the two Egyptian magicians in this context (v.9), it might be possible to translate here with the word "magician."[57] However, it seems more likely that the broadened sense of "impostors" is correct.

Having identified what they are, Paul now describes what will become of them. They "will proceed from bad to worse." The verb (προκόψουσιν) originally meant "to beat forward" and was used to describe the work of a metalsmith hammering out his product to lengthen it. Over time it began being used metaphorically, as it is here, to describe increase or the making of progress.[58] In the present case, however, the progress will be regress—"from bad to worse" (ἐπὶ τὸ χεῖρον). See 2 Timothy 2:16 and 3:9 for other uses of this verb. Note especially the latter for discussion of the seeming contradiction between "they will not make further progress" (3:9) and the statements here and in 2:16 regarding their apparent progress. Here the NASU is an idiomatic rendering to make sense of the Greek for the English reader. The preposition when used with indications of number or measurement has the sense of "to a greater extent" or "further."[59] The adjective is the comparative of κακός ("evil") and the presence of the definite article identifies this as "the" worst case scenario. The literal sense might be something like "unto the worse."

> **Ministry Maxim**
>
> Deception cannot remain static—the progression from deception to self-deception is inevitable.

Along this path these folk are "deceiving and being deceived" (πλανῶντες καὶ πλανώμενοι). The same verb is used both times and has the sense of being misled down a path that is not in reality what you thought it was. The first usage is a present active participle, describing their continuous influence upon those around them. The second is a present passive participle,

---

[56] BAGD, 690.
[57] DNTT, 2:558.
[58] Thayer, 540.
[59] BAGD, 289.

describing their own personal deception by another. There is some debate as to whether the second participle should be read as a middle or passive voice: the former indicating self-deception, the latter deception by an outside influence (i.e., the devil, cf. 2:25-26 and 1 Tim. 4:1-2). However, the subtleties of deceiving and being deceived are often difficult to trace out in fine detail. We may be assured that wherever deception takes place the deceiver and his minions are at work to compound and spread the lie. When we deceive others (1 John 1:6), we tend to believe our own lie (v.8) and may even come to call God's testimony a lie (v.10) in order to maintain the ruse.

> **Digging Deeper:**
> 1. Why does sin, once chosen, never remain static, but always seek deeper expressions of wickedness?
> 2. Which comes first, deceiving or being deceived? Does it matter? Why?
> 3. Is it more dangerous to be deceived by another or by ourselves? Why?

3:14 You, however, continue in the things you have learned and become convinced of, knowing from whom you have learned them,

As in v.10, Paul now makes a strong contrast between the false teachers (v.13) and Timothy (vv.14-15). He sets the second person personal pronoun ("You," σύ) in an emphatic position at the head of the sentence and adds to it the conjunction ("however," δέ) used in an adversative way (cf. v.10; 4:5).

The present imperative "continue" (μένε) demands that action be undertaken continually or habitually. The verb means to abide, remain, continue, stay put, live or dwell. It stands in direct contrast to the constant progress of the false teachers (v.13; cf. 2:16; 3:9). Whereas the errorists are driven by an appetite for deeper and deeper levels of sin, the child of God has already come to the source of unending truth and grace. We have now only to discover the fuller significance and meaning of the life of Christ into which we have already been placed by God. The verbal form may have the sense of "keep on continuing to continue."

That in which ("in," ἐν) Timothy was to remain are "the things you have learned and become convinced of." The relative pronoun (οἷς, "the things") is used as a demonstrative pronoun here and is explained by the two verbs that follow. The plural pronoun includes the Gospel (1:8, 10; 2:8), the Scriptures (vv.15-16), and the right doctrine and worldview which arise from them (vv.10-11). The first verb is "you have learned" (ἔμαθες). Paul used it in v.7 to describe those who are "always learning" yet never arriving at the knowledge of the truth. But that present tense has become an aorist tense here, which, when taken with the preceding imperative, points to the abiding nature of the things which Timothy has learned. Paul later closes this sentence with the same verb. It refers to learning something through the instruction of another.[60] Unlike the unsettled and ever-searching folk around us (vv.7, 13), we have come to the fountain and source of truth in Christ and His Scriptures (vv.15-17) and need only to learn more fully what has already been given to us. But Paul adds ("and," καὶ) a second verb, indicating that something in addition to knowledge is involved. He points also to those things Timothy had "become convinced of" (ἐπιστώθης). The word is used only here in the NT. It means to be firmly assured of or persuaded about something.[61] The aorist tense again points to a past action. The passive voice indicates that an outside force or power has done the convincing—perhaps pointing to the self-authenticating nature of the Scriptures (v.15), to the God who breathed them out (v.16), or to the family and friends who taught them (v.14b).

We do well to take note of the fact that we must not only learn, but also become convinced of—for they are not the same thing. They both have in view the same object, but relate to it from two different angles. The first ("have learned") points to mental recognition and assent; the second ("become convinced of") to personal conviction and commitment. We must not only believe the right things, but also believe them worthy of our trust to the very end.

> **Ministry Maxim**
>
> Knowledge and conviction are co-joined twins that should never be separated.

Paul then adds two motivating reasons for continuing in these things. The first is presented at the end of this verse and the second comprises the opening of the next. First is "knowing from whom you learned them" (εἰδὼς παρὰ τίνων ἔμαθες). The participle "knowing" is a defective perfect, with a present tense meaning. The verb (οἶδα, also used in 1:12, 15; 2:23; 3:14, 15) stresses the completeness of the knowledge, rather than the process of gaining that knowledge through experience or relationship (γινώσκω, used in 1:18; 2:19; 3:1).[62] The preposition ("from," παρὰ) with the genitive form of the interrogative pronoun ("whom," τίνων) prepare us to consider persons who have exerted tremendous influence

---

[60] BAGD, 490.
[61] Thayer, 514.
[62] Mounce, 32, 486.

over Timothy. The final verb "learned" (ἔμαθες) is precisely the same as earlier in the sentence. Who were these from "whom" (τίνων, plural) Timothy learned such things? They would have included Timothy's mother Eunice and grandmother Lois (1:5), since it was from childhood he knew the Scriptures (3:15). It most certainly included Paul himself (2:2; 3:10-11; cf. 1 Cor. 4:17; Phil. 2:22). The coupling of godly parents and godly mentors who focus their ministry upon the Scriptures provides a powerful influence upon young lives. A relationship with the teacher of the Scriptures compounds the effect upon the student's life, for he not only hears the truth taught, but sees it lived out. The church should complement the efforts of the home in bringing forth mature disciples of Christ.

3:15 and that from childhood you have known the sacred writings which are able to give you the wisdom that leads to salvation through faith which is in Christ Jesus.

Paul now adds a second reason to why Timothy should continue in what he had "learned and become convinced of" (v.14). The conjunction "and" (καὶ) coordinates this alongside the first reason. The conjunction "that" (ὅτι) introduces the second reason. That reason is "that from childhood you have known the sacred writings" (ὅτι ἀπὸ βρέφους [τὰ] ἱερὰ γράμματα οἶδας). The object of the sentence is "the sacred writings" (ἱερὰ γράμματα), an expression found only here in the NT. It was, however, a term used by Greek-speaking Jews to designate the Hebrew Scriptures of the OT.[63] The adjective "sacred" (ἱερὰ) points to the reverent view of the Scriptures held by the Jewish people. There is some debate about the genuineness of the definite article ("the," τὰ) found in some texts. It likely was a later addition, but even without it the expression was used to point to the Scriptures.[64] Paul told Timothy "you have known" (οἶδας) these Scriptures, using the same verb as in the first part of the sentence (v.14). The perfect tense has a present tense meaning—Timothy had continuously known these Scriptures "from childhood" (ἀπὸ βρέφους). The word can refer to a child still in the womb (Luke 1:41, 44) and to a newborn (Luke 2:12, 16). Here, however, it is likely that Paul is pointing to the requirement for Hebrew parents to begin teaching their children the Law in their fifth year.[65] From his earliest days Timothy's mother and grandmother (1:5) had been instructing him in what God says.

It is these Scriptures "which are able to give you the wisdom"

---

[63] BAGD, 165.
[64] Fee, 281.
[65] Rienecker, 646.

(τὰ δυνάμενά σε σοφίσαι). The present participle (τὰ δυνάμενά) points to the continuous, innate ability of the OT Scriptures to provide wisdom. This reminds us not to neglect the OT Scriptures, even though we now have the NT as well. That innate ability still resides in them.[66] That which they are able to do is made specific through the infinitive clause "to give you the wisdom" (σε σοφίσαι). The second person personal pronoun ("you," σε) makes clear the individual and personal nature of the Scripture's instruction—in this case to Timothy. The root of the infinitive is found only here and in 1 Peter 1:16. Here it is used in the active voice which gives it the meaning of to make wise, teach or instruct.[67] This wisdom is something the false teachers have missed (3:9, 13) because of their wrong approach to and misuse of the OT Scriptures (1 Tim. 1:4, 6-7, 14; 4:7; 6:20; 2 Tim. 2:16, 23; 4:4; cf. Titus 1:14).[68] They were "holding to a form of godliness, although they have denied its *power*" (2 Tim. 3:5, emphasis added; noun form of "are able" here). They are ever-searching, but "*never able* to come to the knowledge of the truth" (v.7, emphasis added; again the same root).

> **Ministry Maxim**
>
> God's Word unleashed early in a child's life will not fail to have a lasting influence.

The wisdom that the Scriptures impart is "that [which] leads to salvation" (εἰς σωτηρίαν). The Scriptures themselves, though living (Heb. 4:12), are not life—Jesus is, and it is to Him that they point. "You search the Scriptures because you think that in them you have eternal life; it is these that testify about Me" (John 5:39; cf. v.46). It is "the salvation *which is in Christ Jesus*" (2:10, emphasis added) which the Scriptures lead us to. Indeed, Paul insists that this salvation is "through faith which is in Christ Jesus." The preposition and noun ("through faith, διὰ πίστεως) are a favorite combination of Paul. He uses it to describe the righteousness of God that comes "through faith" (Rom. 3:22; Phil. 3:9), walking by faith (2 Cor. 5:7), justification by faith (Gal. 2:16), and being saved by faith (Eph. 2:8). The final clause, "which is in Christ Jesus" (τῆς ἐν Χριστῷ Ἰησοῦ), specifies the faith under discussion as that which has as its object the Person of the Lord Jesus Christ. The OT can be understood fully only through the revelation of Jesus Christ contained in the NT. Indeed, it is only through personal trust in the Lord Jesus Christ, held before us in shadowy form in the OT and in fuller brilliance in the NT, that we are able to know the salvation of God.

In the OT Scriptures we have *God's words* ("the sacred writings"), *wise words* ("which are able to give you the wisdom"), and *saving words* ("that leads to salvation"). These Hebrew Scriptures must be interpreted Christologically, for Christ is their main subject and only "through faith which is in Christ Jesus" may they be rightly understood and will their power be unleashed. Here too we have a powerful example concerning the wisdom of parents who begin early and continue faithfully in teaching their children the Scriptures.

> **Digging Deeper:**
> 1. When and how does it become clear whether a person not only has "learned," but also "become convinced of," the truth of the Scriptures?
> 2. What do these verses demand of parents? What do these verses tell us about how to fulfill these obligations?
> 3. What do these verses tell us about every child's most basic need?
> 4. How do these verses instruct us regarding how the church may complement the ministry of parents?

3:16 All Scripture is inspired by God and profitable for teaching, for reproof, for correction, for training in righteousness;

Having introduced the topic of the "sacred writings" (v.15), Paul now speaks more specifically about the origin and nature of these Scriptures. The opening three words comprise one of the most profound statements of the Bible regarding itself: "All Scripture is inspired by God" (πᾶσα γραφὴ θεόπνευστος). The profundity, as one might expect, has drawn some controversy. This leaves one with several key questions that must be answered. Is the noun "Scripture" (γραφὴ) used as a collective, referring to the whole of Scripture, or does it refer to the various passages of Scripture within the whole? If it is used as a collective, what makes up the collection to which it refers? Does "all" (πᾶσα) mean "all" or "every"? Does "inspired by God" (θεόπνευστος) function actively or passively? Does it relate to "All Scripture" as "all God-breathed Scripture" or as "All Scripture is God-breathed"? Where should we understand the verb "is" to belong, before or after "inspired by God" (θεόπνευστος)? Just how is the "and" (καὶ) to be understood?[69]

The noun "Scripture" (γραφὴ) is singular and anarthrous. Does this eliminate understanding it as a collective noun referring to the whole of the Scriptures? The noun can be used of writings in general, but the NT's fifty-one uses always refer to the Holy Scriptures. It is not of great import that it is not accompanied here by a definite article, for in view of its use as a technical term

---

[66] Kent, 280.
[67] BAGD, 760.
[68] Mounce, 565.
[69] Knight, 444.

for the Holy Scriptures it is understood as definite. The singular form can be used as either a collective noun referring to the whole of the Scriptures (e.g., John 20:9; Acts 8:32; 1 Peter 2:6) or as a reference to a particular writing within those Scriptures (e.g., Gal. 4:30; James 2:23). That the whole is in view here seems obvious from the context where "the sacred writings" (ἱερὰ γράμματα, v.15) has already pointed to the recognized body of the Hebrew Scriptures of the OT. The reference here clearly points to the same body of Scriptures, though Peter used the term (γραφὴ) to include Paul's own writings among those of the OT (albeit in the plural, 2 Peter 3:16). Thus we are justified in ultimately understanding Paul's words here to apply to both the OT and NT.

How does the coupling of this noun with the adjective "all" (πᾶσα) affect our understanding of it? Should this be read as "all Scripture" (ESV, JB, KJV, NASB, NASU, NIV, RSV, NRSV) or as "every Scripture" (ASV, NEB, NET)? That is to say, does Paul's statement view the Scriptures as a collective whole or in each constituent part? When πᾶς is used with an anarthrous noun it generally points to the individual members within the class indicated by the noun, thus yielding a meaning like "every."[70] However, when used with an anarthrous collective or proper noun, as here, it can have the sense of "the whole."[71] C.F.D. Moule wrote that the expression "is most unlikely to mean *every inspired Scripture*, and much more probably means *the whole of Scripture* [is] inspired."[72] Ultimately, the distinction may not be of great significance. E.J. Young well says, "If Paul means 'every scripture,' he is looking at the various parts of the Bible, that is, he is considering Scripture distributively. He is then saying that whatever Scripture we consider, it is inspired of God. On the other hand, if he means 'all scripture,' it is clear that his reference is to the Scripture in its entirety. In either case he is saying that whatever may be called 'scripture' is inspired of God."[73] Indeed, as Hendriksen, has pointed out, ". . . if 'every scripture' is inspired, 'all scripture' must be inspired also."[74] Yet it seems that the evidence may tip the scales in favor of the rendering "all Scripture."

The adjective θεόπνευστος, translated "inspired by God," is found only here in the NT. It is a compound word made up of the noun "God" (Θεός) and the aorist stem of the verb for "breath" (πνέω). To this is suffixed the ending -τος. The NIV's "God-breathed" is a literal translation. The more common rendering "inspired" is due to the influence of the Vulgate's Latin *inspirata*.[75]

---

[70] BAGD, 631.
[71] Thayer, 491.
[72] Moule, 95.
[73] Young, 19.
[74] Hendriksen, 301.
[75] Knight, 446.

The typical English translation of "inspired" is unfortunate, since that implies the action of breathing *in*, whereas the Greek word describes the act of breathing *out* (cf. "breathed out by God," ESV). "... man does not live by bread alone, but man lives by everything that *proceeds out of the mouth* of the LORD" (Deut. 8:3b, emphasis added; cf. Matt. 4:4; Luke 4:4). "The word *has gone forth from My mouth* in righteousness" (Isa. 45:23a, emphasis added). The Scriptures are not a preexisting body of human literature into which God breathed something divine, but rather they owe their very existence to the out-breathing of God's Spirit.[76] Apart from God's out-breathing in time and space through specific human authors under the power of His Holy Spirit, the Scripture would not exist. It is the Scriptures, not the writers of the Scriptures, which are inspired.

2 Timothy 3:16 states the fact of the divine origin and nature of the Scriptures, but does not define how that quality is passed on through the writers to the Scriptures they produced. That would be more fully answered by 2 Peter 1:20-21.

Is this adjective to be understood in a passive sense (the source of Scripture is the breath of God, i.e. "God-breathed") or in an active one (the Scripture is filled with God's breath and continues to "inspire")? When the ending –τος is compounded with the word Θεός, it is nearly always used in a passive sense.[77] 1 Timothy 4:4 is the only other NT passage with this same word order (if one allows for an additional word to intervene) that also has a following καὶ along with another adjective. In that case the adjective must be predicative. This seems to support a similar reading here of "inspired by God and useful."[78] Further argumentation can become complex,[79] but B.B. Warfield's evidence in favor of the passive sense has proven most difficult to refute.[80]

This opening clause is devoid of a verb, which must be understood as one reads the line. But should the verb "is" be read before or after "God-breathed" (θεόπνευστος)? Reading it before the adjective yields a translation of "All Scripture *is* God-breathed" (NIV, and most English translations). Reading it after yields something like "Every scripture inspired of God *is* . . ." (ASV, cf. NEB). The matter is important for the latter can be taken to mean that there may exist some portions of Scripture that are not inspired. Such a notion could not be further from the Apostle's mind. The former (placing the assumed verb between "All Scripture" and "God-breathed") seems logical given that the two adjectives separated by the conjunction ("God-breathed and . . . useful," NIV;

---

[76] Young, 22.
[77] Ibid., 20.
[78] Knight, 446.
[79] House, *Bibliotheca Sacra*, 55ff.
[80] Warfield, 245-296.

θεόπνευστος καὶ ὠφέλιμος) make the most sense when allowed to be read as parallel to one another, both serving in a predicative sense.[81] Understanding the verb between these two adjectives and before the conjunction (which would then have to be understood as "also") is not an impossible reading, but seems considerably less likely.

Having stated the divine origin and consequent authority of the Scriptures, Paul now speaks of their practical worth. They are "profitable" (ὠφέλιμος). The word is found only in the PE (1 Tim. 4:8 [twice]; Titus 3:8). It has the sense of helpful, beneficial, useful or advantageous.[82] The practical usefulness of Scripture in the daily affairs of this world is directly tied to its origins from outside of this world ("God-breathed"). The benefits of Scripture are spelled out by four nouns, all accompanied by the preposition πρὸς ("for"). Each noun is in the accusative, thus giving the preposition a sense of pointing toward the purpose or destiny of the Scriptures.[83] The very destiny for which the Scriptures were appointed by the God who breathed them out was that they might yield these four practical benefits in the daily lives of those who would embrace them with obedient faith.

> **Ministry Maxim**
>
> God's Word works in this world because it has its origins from outside this world.

The first benefit is "teaching" (διδασκαλίαν). The word is used in the NT only twice outside of Paul, and that in parallel passages (Matt. 15:9; Mark 7:7). Of the nineteen times Paul uses it, fifteen are in the PE. It may refer to either the act of teaching or to that which is taught ("doctrine").[84] It is in this former sense that it is used here, but with a view to producing the latter. Paul has just reminded Timothy of how he had followed "my teaching" (3:10). There may also be the "doctrine of demons" (1 Tim. 4:1), but that which the Scriptures hold forth is called "the doctrine of God our Savior" (Titus 2:10), "sound teaching/doctrine" (1 Tim. 1:10; 4:6; 2 Tim. 4:3; Titus 1:9; 2:1), "doctrine conforming to godliness" (1 Tim. 6:3), and "purity in doctrine" (Titus 2:7). The Scripture must be the source and controlling influence of all a minister's teaching. Paul elsewhere has said, "whatever was written in earlier times was written for our instruction [διδασκαλίαν]" (Rom. 15:4a). A Scriptural ministry requires careful attention (1 Tim. 4:13), perseverance, and meticulous study (4:16), so that our "doctrine will not be spoken against" (6:1).

The second benefit is "reproof" (ἐλεγμόν). The word is used only here in the NT. It describes correction or censure in the sense of refuting error or

---

[81] Blum, 46.
[82] BAGD, 900.
[83] Ibid., 710.
[84] Ibid., 191.

rebuking sin.[85] Scripture both exposes sin ("reproof") and illuminates truth ("teaching").

The third benefit is "correction" (ἐπανόρθωσιν). This word too is found only here in the NT. It describes restoring something to an upright state and in this sense means correction, improvement or restoration.[86] It is "reproof" that exposes and denounces. It is "teaching" which brings in the needed supplies (truth) and "correction" which restores and rebuilds.

The fourth benefit is "training" (παιδείαν). The noun is used elsewhere of a father's discipline (Eph. 6:4), whether of an earthly father (Heb. 12:5) or the heavenly Father (Heb. 12:7, 8, 11). Paul uses the verbal form to describe the discipline of God (1 Cor. 11:32) and of the church (1 Tim. 1:20). He has told Timothy to practice this toward the false teachers in Ephesus (2 Tim. 2:25). It is for this work in the believer's life that the grace of God appeared (Titus 2:12) and, though painful at times, it is always a signal of His love (Heb. 12:6; Rev. 3:19). Paul has personally experienced this work of God in his life (2 Cor. 6:9).

This instruction or training is "in righteousness" (τὴν ἐν δικαιοσύνῃ), or more particularly is "that training which leads us in righteousness."[87] The primary means by which God wishes to bring us to maturity and trains us to walk in His ways is through the Scriptures, though, if we consistently refuse its counsel, God will move to more direct means (cf. John 15:2-3).

It may well be, as several commentators have suggested, that these four words are to be read as two pairs: the first two dealing with doctrine/belief ("for teaching, for reproof") and the second two dealing with practice/behavior ("for correction, for training").[88] This would yield a chiastic arrangement in which the first and fourth elements are positive and the second and third negative. Marshall too sees a chiastic arrangement here; however, he reads it as a teaching/education emphasis set beside a conviction/correction emphasis.[89]

3:17 so that the man of God may be adequate, equipped for every good work.

The Scriptures were breathed out by God (v.16) for the express purpose ("so that," ἵνα plus the subjunctive) of enabling God's people to live differently. In the opening clause the verb ("may be," ᾖ) is in the present tense, emphasizing a continual adequacy and readiness. The desired outcome is that the individual

---

[85] Rienecker, 647.
[86] Thayer, 228.
[87] Alford, 3:398.
[88] e.g., Guthrie, 164; Knight, 449-450; Mounce, 570.
[89] Marshall, 795.

might be "adequate" (ἄρτιος). The word is used only here in the NT. It carries the sense of complete, capable, and proficient; that is to say, one who is able to meet all demands placed upon him.[90] The challenges of life and ministry are legion, as Paul has reminded Timothy throughout this letter. It is the word of God which fits us to face those multitudinous opportunities.

These Scriptures are aimed at "the man of God" (ὁ τοῦ θεοῦ ἄνθρωπος). Both nouns are accompanied by their definite articles, making specific the reference. That the genitive ("of God," τοῦ θεοῦ) is tucked between the nominative and its definite article (ὁ ... ἄνθρωπος) signals the uniqueness of the relationship which is in view. Perhaps this can be expressed by a translation such as "the-of God-man" (i.e., the man whose life is marked by its relation to God). The title "man of God" was used in the OT to designate a prophet (e.g., 1 Kings 13), and its use here may point to the pastor or the leaders of a local church (cf. 1 Tim. 6:11). But here it may be that it makes no such special designation. The word "man" (ἄνθρωπος) can have the broader connotation that encompasses both males and females, young and old, from every station of life. It is through the Scriptures that one becomes such a person and then continues in that course. Godliness comes to characterize a life that feasts on the Scriptures.

> **Ministry Maxim**
>
> God's Word is the primary means by which He fits us to carry out His will.

Paul then ends the sentence by adding an additional clause in apposition to the previous one. It serves to make more specific just what is meant by "may be adequate." The clause begins with a preposition (πρὸς, "for") which designates a purpose.[91] That purpose is pointed toward "every good work" (πᾶν ἔργον ἀγαθὸν). The same expression is used by Paul five times in the NT, four of those in the PE. He paralleled it with being "sanctified, useful to the Master" (2 Tim. 2:21). Some, Paul reminded Titus, are "worthless for any good deed" (Titus 1:16). Paul told him, therefore, to prepare everyone in the church ("older men ... older women ... young women ... young men ... bondslaves ... all men," Titus 2:2, 3, 4, 6, 9, 11) "to be ready for every good deed" (3:1). Indeed, "God is able to make all grace abound to you, so that always having all sufficiency in everything, you may have an abundance for every good deed" (2 Cor. 9:8). The singular noun and adjective ("good work," ἔργον ἀγαθὸν) point to each individual opportunity as unique among a vast variety of all the things that could rightly be called good works. This makes "each," rather than "all" (as in v.16), the correct translation for the adjective

---

[90] BAGD, 110.
[91] Ibid., 710.

(πᾶν). The goal is that we might be "equipped" (ἐξηρτισμένος) for these opportunities. The root of the verb is the same as the previous noun "adequate," only with ἐκ prefixed to it. The preposition in compound with the verb perfects its meaning. The result is a meaning of completely outfitted, fully furnished, fully equipped or fully supplied. It was used to describe a wagon or a rescue boat which was fully outfitted for its task.[92] It is used elsewhere in the NT only in Acts 21:5. The perfect tense points to an abiding state of readiness for God's will. The passive voice indicates the work of God through His out-breathed word in preparing us for all the "good works, which God prepared beforehand so that we would walk in them" (Eph. 2:10b).

Digging Deeper:
1. How does v.16 build your confidence in the Word of God?
2. Of the four benefits of Scripture listed in v.16, which do you most often experience? Least often? Why do you think this is so?
3. Assuming the truth of vv.16-17, what would be the result in a person's life if they neglect the Word of God?

---

[92] Rienecker, 647.

CHAPTER

4

4:1 I solemnly charge you in the presence of God and of Christ Jesus, who is to judge the living and the dead, and by His appearing and His kingdom:

The Apostle now gathers himself for one final, climactic and solemn charge to Timothy (vv.1-8), before giving final instructions (vv.9-18), sending various greetings (vv.19-21) and making his final farewell (v.22). Having set forth the source and sufficiency of the Scriptures (3:16-17), Paul now adjures Timothy to "preach the word" (v.2) faithfully.

The opening statement, "I solemnly charge" (Διαμαρτύρομαι), adds an air of solemnity and gravity to the following commands of the Apostle. The present tense verb emphasizes the ongoing nature of the charge. It is a deponent verb, thus the middle/passive form has an active meaning. "The first person singular form gives the charge a direct and forceful quality and conveys the fact that the charge is given by Paul in his apostolic authority (cf. 1:1)."[1] The word can speak of bearing a solemn witness or testimony to something (e.g., Acts 20:21, 23, 24; 23:11; 28:23); however, here it means to charge, warn, or adjure (cf. 1 Tim. 4:6; 5:21; 2 Tim. 2:14).[2]

Paul's charge is made all the more solemn by the building up of the atmosphere in which it is made, prior to actually leveling the charge in v.2. Paul exhorts Timothy "in the presence of God and of Christ Jesus" (ἐνώπιον τοῦ θεοῦ καὶ Χριστοῦ Ἰησοῦ). The expression "in the presence of" is the translation of but one Greek word (ἐνώπιον), which has the sense of "in the sight of" or "in the presence of" someone. It is a favorite expression in the making of assertions and oaths which call upon God (Gal. 1:20; 1 Tim.

---
[1] Knight, 452.
[2] BAGD, 186.

5:21; 6:13; 2 Tim. 2:14) as here.³ It is noteworthy that God and Jesus are mentioned together in such close connection. Some have suggested that τοῦ θεοῦ καὶ Χριστοῦ Ἰησοῦ might just as easily be translated "of God, even Christ Jesus,"⁴ though the NASU probably gives us the correct rendering. Nevertheless, it is not without significance that Paul so closely links Father and Son—they who are one in essence, yet distinct in Personhood.

Paul clearly believed that the presence of God is not simply something to be experienced in the far distant future, but a living reality in the present. As Paul told the Athenians, "in Him we live and move and exist" (Acts 17:28a). It is true that "now we see in a mirror dimly, but then face to face" (1 Cor. 13:12). And, yes, one day we will stand before His unveiled presence and be assayed by His searching eyes of omniscience. But it is equally true that He is all of that at the present moment as well, if we will have eyes to discern it. All that He will be then, He is now. This was not a psychological trick or a motivational technique. Remember, Paul had been "caught up to the third heaven" (2 Cor. 12:2) and had been in the very presence of God. He knew of what he spoke! The Apostle called Timothy to live and minister now in the awareness that he did so in the presence of the One who one day will be unveiled in all His magnificence and glory.

Paul goes on to a second assertion concerning the God before whom he and Timothy minister. Christ Jesus is the one "who is to judge the living and the dead" (τοῦ μέλλοντος κρίνειν ζῶντας καὶ νεκρούς). Having just mentioned both God and the Lord Jesus, Paul now uses a singular participle and its definite article ("who is," τοῦ μέλλοντος) to make reference to Jesus alone in the role of Judge. Jesus told the Jews that "not even the Father judges anyone, but He has given all judgment to the Son" (John 5:22). Paul told the people of Athens that God "has fixed a day in which He will judge the world in righteousness through a Man whom He has appointed, having furnished proof to all men by raising Him from the dead" (Acts 17:31). The articular participle is a present tense and is often followed, as here, by a present tense infinitive ("to judge," κρίνειν) as a periphrasis for the future.⁵ The Apostle saw a future day when "the living" (ζῶντας, plural present active participle) and "the dead" (νεκρούς, plural adjective used as a substantive⁶) would be judged. The exact expression is used again only in 1 Peter 4:5, but the concept is present also in Acts 10:42. Paul firmly believed that "we must all appear before the judgment seat of Christ, so that each one may be recompensed for his deeds in the body, according to what he has done, whether good or bad" (2 Cor. 5:10). Yet for him

---

³ Ibid., 270.
⁴ Wuest, 152.
⁵ BAGD, 501.
⁶ Ibid., 535.

this was a day of hope which held for him "the crown of righteousness," a reward also available to "all who have loved His appearing" (2 Tim. 4:8). Paul may not expect a just verdict from the Emperor, but it was the judgment of Christ to which ultimately he entrusted himself.

It is that very appearing to which Paul next points Timothy's attention: "and by His appearing" (καὶ τὴν ἐπιφάνειαν αὐτοῦ). With the final two modifiers ("His appearing" and "His kingdom") Paul uses a different grammatical approach (transitioning from the genitive participle to two articular accusative nouns), which makes translation difficult. The accusative can be used as a summoning of witnesses against a person.[7] Perhaps that is the sense here. Paul had previously charged Timothy to "keep the commandment without stain or reproach until the appearing of our Lord Jesus Christ" (1 Tim. 6:14). This "appearing" is something to be loved and longed for (2 Tim. 4:8). The word could also be used of Christ's first advent (1:10), but here refers to His second coming. The Apostle spoke to Titus of "looking for the blessed hope and the appearing of the glory of our great God and Savior, Christ Jesus" (Titus 2:13). This word "appearing" (τὴν ἐπιφάνειαν) was used by the Greeks of the appearance of a god to men. It was taken over by the Christians as a reference to the "shining forth" or "breaking forth" (English, *epiphany*) of Jesus Christ, whether in His first or second advent.[8] The use of the definite article makes obvious that the unique return of Jesus Christ is in view here. The third person singular pronoun "His" (αὐτοῦ) finds its antecedent in "Christ Jesus" (Χριστοῦ Ἰησοῦ). None other than the shining forth of the Anointed Savior in all of His glory and majesty is in Paul's view. In His light all will be seen for what it really is.

> **Ministry Maxim**
>
> I preach because God is watching and because Christ is judging, coming and ruling.

As the Apostle prepares Timothy to receive appropriately the imperatives of vv.2-5, he finally adds "and His kingdom" (καὶ τὴν βασιλείαν αὐτοῦ). Again the definite article and the third person singular pronoun make this a reference to the kingdom of Christ Jesus Himself. The exact phrase "His kingdom" (τὴν βασιλείαν αὐτοῦ) is found again in Paul only in v.18 where he is confident that "The Lord will rescue me from every evil deed, and will bring me safely to His heavenly kingdom." Paul preached (Acts 20:25; 28:31) and taught about (28:31) the kingdom. This kingdom is the present place of residence for believers, having been rescued from the domain of darkness (Col. 1:13). Servants of Christ are workers for that kingdom (4:11). Yet that kingdom is also something yet to be inherited (1 Cor. 6:9-10; 15:50;

---

[7] Marshall, 799.
[8] Thayer, 245-246.

Gal. 5:21; Eph. 5:5). In its present reality the kingdom is enjoyed through the ministry of the Holy Spirit in the believer's life (Rom. 14:17), but Paul also viewed the sufferings of this life as a part of preparation for that kingdom (Acts 14:22; 2 Thess. 1:5). Thus in light of his present imprisonment and impending martyrdom (vv.6-7), Paul's anticipation of entering the fullness of Christ's kingdom must surely have been brought to a climax (v.8). The use of the word "heavenly" to describe this kingdom in v.18 and Paul's use of the future tense verbs ("The Lord will rescue me . . . and will bring me safely into His heavenly kingdom") make clear that it is the future form of the kingdom that he has in mind here.[9]

The Apostle binds this opening verse of the section with its closing by picking up again themes he introduces here: "judge" (v.1) and "the righteous Judge" (v.8), "His appearing" (vv.1, 8), and "His kingdom" (v.1) and "crown" (v.8).

The nine imperatives that now follow in vv.2-5 find their climax and summary in the final command, "fulfill your ministry" (v.5b). This opening verse of the chapter reminds us that such faithfulness in ministry is laid upon us in seriousness and with solemnity—in the light of God's presence and the judgment, coming, and ruling of Christ Jesus.

> **Digging Deeper:**
>
> 1. How would you live differently today if you knew you did so "in the presence of God and of Christ Jesus"?
> 2. How should the knowledge of Christ's return affect our service to and for Him now?
> 3. What does it mean to be given a solemn charge to obedience "by … His kingdom"?

4:2 preach the word; be ready in season and out of season; reprove, rebuke, exhort, with great patience and instruction.

Paul has dramatically set the stage (v.1) to issue nine commands that will effectively pass the baton of ministry to Timothy. The first five of those imperatives are found in this verse and form the heart of the "charge" (v.1). The other four are found in v.5. All five imperatives in this verse are in the aorist tense, adding a sense of urgency to their thunder. They are unaccompanied by any connectives, the rapid-fire presentation contributing additional force to their urgency.

---

[9] Knight, 452.

The first imperative is "preach" (κήρυξον). It is the heart of the charge and flavors the understanding of the other four imperatives that follow on its heels. The verb κηρύσσω is used sixty-one times in the New Testament and is found throughout the Gospels, Acts and the epistles (e.g., Matt. 3:1; Mark 1:14; Acts 10:42; 1 Cor. 1:23; 2 Cor. 4:2). Friedrich tells us that it "does not mean the delivery of a learned and edifying or hortatory discourse in well-chosen words and a pleasant voice. It is the declaration of an event . . . Its true sense is 'to proclaim'."[10] The verb carried, in secular Greek usages, a distinct ring of authority.

While the New Testament authors were not shy about using the verb, the virtual lack of the kindred noun κῆρυξ indicates an aversion to its use. This noun is found only three times in the New Testament (1 Tim. 2:7; 2 Tim. 1:11; 2 Peter 2:5). The last of these refers to Noah, who obviously is a special case. The other two usages of the noun are references to the Apostle Paul and are mentioned in connection with his special calling as an apostle. Why this hesitancy to employ the noun form of such a dominant verb? The answer appears to lie in the secular Greek usage and the resultant meaning of the noun. In secular Greek a κῆρυξ (or herald) held a significant role in society. Every ruler had a herald to whom he entrusted messages and announcements. When speaking in official matters the herald had royal authority. Heralds were under obligation to deliver the message without alteration. A herald was accountable to his ruler for the exact representation and reproduction of the given message. The Greek herald was given no room for personal interpretation or negotiation in the proclamation process. This authority worked in their favor in that they were inviolable when under the sovereign direction of their prince. Religion and politics were inseparable in the ancient Greek mind, so heralds were considered to be under the protection of the gods. Thus those opposed to the message they bore were duly warned of the dangers of taking their displeasure out on the κῆρυξ.[11]

The question arises, Why do the New Testament writers show such an aversion to a noun which seems in many ways perfectly suited for use in describing the Christian preacher, while wholeheartedly employing the verb? Indeed, Marvin Vincent says, "The word herald is beautifully suggestive, at many points, of the office of a gospel minister."[12]

This hesitancy in the use of the noun may partially lie in the fact that not only were heralds of earthly rulers protected by the gods, but the very gods themselves had their heralds. The Stoic philosophers were often viewed as divine heralds.[13] Hermes was the special herald-god. Birds also were at times

---
[10] Kittel, 3:703.
[11] Ibid., 3:683-692.
[12] Vincent, 1:692.
[13] Kittel, 3:692.

seen to be messengers of the gods. This makes for a profound difference between the secular Greek usage of the noun and the New Testament view of the one who proclaims God's word.

The place of the verb in being retained and dominant over the noun makes a powerful point as to the nature of Biblical preaching:

> The Bible is not telling us about human preachers; it is telling us about preaching. Furthermore, the prior Greek history gives too specific meaning to κῆρυξ. The NT knows nothing of sacral personages who are inviolable in the world. . . . The messengers of Jesus are like sheep delivered to wolves (Mt. 10:10). As the Lord was persecuted, so His servants will be persecuted (Jn. 15:20). The servants of Christ are, as it were, dedicated to death (Rev. 12:11). But the message does not perish with the one who proclaims it. The message is irresistible (2 Tim. 2:9). It takes its victorious course through the world (2 Th. 3:1). Hence κηρύσσειν is more important than the κῆρυξ in the NT.[14]

The New Testament writers did not wish to draw attention to the one who does the proclaiming, but rather to the Savior being proclaimed. Indeed, it is specifically "the word" (τὸν λόγον) that Paul charges Timothy with preaching. Paul has already called it "the word of God" (2:9; cf. 1 Tim. 4:5; Titus 2:5) and "the word of truth" (2:15) so the simpler expression suffices here. In the PE the expression points to the Gospel message about Jesus Christ.[15] However, within this context, the phrase's meaning must be informed by the previous expressions "the sacred writings" (3:15) and "Scripture" (3:16). Additionally, its close proximity to warnings about those who will not endure "sound doctrine" and who will turn away from "the truth" (4:3, 4) enlarges the scope of its reference. The definite article sets this "word" off as distinct from the arguments (2:14), "worldly and empty chatter" (2:16), "foolish and ignorant speculations" (2:23), and "myths" (4:4) of the false teachers in Ephesus. Here "the word" (τὸν λόγον) refers to the saving message of God's redeeming work in Christ as announced, explained, and applied in its fullness through the written Scriptures.

The second imperative is "be ready" (ἐπίστηθι). Again the aorist tense makes obedient response an urgent matter. Paul uses the verb only three times, two of them in this chapter (v.6; cf. 1 Thess. 5:3). It is a compound word made up of the verb "to stand" (ἵστημι) and the prepositional prefix "upon" (ἐπί). It means to stand by or stand near, to approach or to appear and often with the added sense of suddenness about the action.[16] Grammatically this imperative may be understood to qualify the previous imperative or as standing on its

---

[14] Ibid., 3:696.
[15] Fee, 284; Marshall, 800.
[16] BAGD, 330.

own as a separate command. It is probably best understood in the former sense, as qualifying how the previous imperative is to be carried out.[17] It is accompanied by two adverbs which together make for a play on words: "in season" (εὐκαίρως) and "out of season" (ἀκαίρως). Both are built off of καιρός ("time" or "season") and form a word play. The former uses the prefix εὐ-, and refers to that which is well-timed, suitable or convenient. It is used elsewhere in the NT only in Mark 14:11 (though cf. the verbal form in Mark 6:31; Acts 17:21; 1 Cor. 16:12) where it describes Judas seeking to betray Jesus "at an opportune time." The latter uses the negative prefix ἀ-, and refers to that which is ill-timed or inconvenient.[18] It is not found elsewhere in the NT. But from whose perspective does Paul mean to measure the convenience or inconvenience of such opportunities? Should it begin with the preacher or with the hearers? Surely, given all that has been said to this point—the gravity of the circumstances and the solemnity of the situation—the Apostle is not telling Timothy to "preach the word" if it is convenient to him! Paul is laying upon Timothy the responsibility to proclaim the word whenever and wherever an opportunity opens itself or a way can be made. Paul uses the word καιρός three times in this letter. Once to describe the "difficult times" of the last days in which we live (3:1), once in the next sentence to describe the fickle-hearted nature of the listeners ("For the time will come," v.3), and finally to describe the impending nature of his own death ("the time of my departure has come," 4:6). Given the perilous nature of the times, the user-oriented nature of the culture, and the transitional nature of the immediate situation, Paul was charging Timothy—to use his own previous words to this church—with "making the most of your time, because the days are evil" (Eph. 5:16).

The third imperative is "reprove" (ἔλεγξον). It is the verbal cognate of the noun found in 3:16. It means to correct with the connotation of refuting.[19] It describes exposing another's position with overwhelming proof so that he is brought to the point of conviction of sin.[20] In the PE Paul uses it to describe publicly exposing an elder in sin (1 Tim. 5:20) and exposing the faulty thinking of opponents (Titus 1:9). Titus was to exercise it generally in his ministry because of the obstinate nature of the Cretans (1:13; 2:15). The aorist imperative once again adds punch to this already strong word.

The fourth imperative is "rebuke" (ἐπιτίμησον). The word is used twenty-seven times in the Synoptic Gospels, but only here by Paul. It is a compound word made up of the verb τιμάω (to honor) and the prepositional prefix ἐπὶ (upon). Strictly it meant to place honor upon, but then came to describe judging

---
[17] Knight, 453.
[18] Rienecker, 647.
[19] BAGD, 249.
[20] Rienecker, 647.

one worthy of receiving such honor and finally, as it does here, to a sharp censure of one's conduct. The cognate noun is found only in 2 Corinthians 2:6 and is translated "punishment." The verb was used of Jesus rebuking demonic spirits (e.g., Matt. 17:18; Mark 1:25; 9:25; Luke 4:35, 41), the wind and raging sea (Matt. 8:26; Mark 4:39; Luke 8:24), a fever (Luke 4:39), and even Peter (Mark 8:33). Jesus commanded, "If your brother sins, rebuke him" (Luke 17:3).

The fifth imperative is "exhort" (παρακάλεσον). It also is a compound word, coming from the verb καλέω (to call) and the prepositional prefix παρά (beside). Strictly speaking it means "to call alongside." It is a favorite verb of Paul used in every one of his letters (except Galatians). It is a word that has a range of meaning that can swing from the softer sense of "comfort" to the sharper edge of "exhort." It is translated variously according to context by words such as "appeal" (Philem. 9, 10), "comfort" (2 Cor. 1:4, 6), "encourage" (1 Cor. 16:12), "exhort" (1:10), "implore" (2 Cor. 12:8), and "urge" (Rom. 12:1). The masculine singular noun form became a title for the Holy Spirit (John 14:16, 26; 15:26; 16:7) and the Lord Jesus Christ (1 John 2:1).

Just as the first imperative "preach" was qualified by the second imperative ("be ready") and its two adverbs ("in season and out of season"), so the last three imperatives ("reprove, rebuke, exhort") are qualified by the prepositional phrase that follows them: "with great patience and instruction" (ἐν πάσῃ μακροθυμίᾳ καὶ διδαχῇ).[21] It is also possible this is meant to qualify all five imperatives. Timothy observed this "patience" (μακροθυμίᾳ) in Paul during their travels and ministry together (3:10). The word describes a long-suffering forbearance that is slow to avenge wrongs done.[22] The ability to maintain such an attitude in the face of opposition and the difficulties of ministry (2 Cor. 6:6) arises out of the awareness of God's own patience with you (Rom. 2:4; 1 Tim. 1:16). This "patience" is ours only as we allow the Holy Spirit to produce it within us (Gal. 5:22), but we must cooperate by making a conscious decision to put on this attitude (Col. 3:12). The word is often found in combination with other attitudinal and character qualities such as "kindness and tolerance" (Rom. 2:4; cf. 2 Cor. 6:6), "love, joy, peace . . . kindness, goodness, faithfulness" (Gal. 5:22), "humility and gentleness" (Eph. 4:2), "steadfastness" (Col. 1:11), "compassion, kindness, humility, gentleness" (3:12), and "love, perseverance" (2

> **Ministry Maxim**
>
> The purpose of preaching is to allow the Word of God to accomplish its divinely intended purpose.

---

[21] Knight, 454.
[22] Thayer, 386.

Tim. 3:10). Here, however, it is paired, via the coordinating conjunction "and" (καί), with the more unlikely "instruction" (διδαχῇ). The noun here can be used in a passive sense for what is taught or in an active sense to describe the act of teaching itself. It is in the latter sense that it is used here.[23] Paul did pair "patience" (μακροθυμίᾳ) with the related, but distinct and more frequent, noun "teaching" (διδασκαλίᾳ) in 3:10. Our noun here (διδαχῇ) is used but two times in the PE (4:2; Titus 1:9), whereas the noun διδασκαλία is used fifteen times in the PE (1 Tim. 1:10; 4:1, 6, 13, 16; 5:17; 6:1, 3; 2 Tim. 3:10, 16; 4:3; Titus 1:9; 2:1, 7, 10).

The combination of "patience and instruction" means more than "patience in teaching,"[24] but calls for both as the answer to the challenges that stand in the way of a biblical ministry (vv.3-4). As the faithful minister goes about preaching, reproving, rebuking, and exhorting, he does so with the "patience" that keeps him from attacking the people themselves, but rather with "instruction" that confronts false thinking with solid facts and not just emotional intensity. The foundation of truth conveyed through teaching is the bedrock upon which real life-change is built, long after the bluster of human personality has blown over. The addition of the adjective "great" (πάσῃ) is a reminder of just how challenging ministry will be. The use of the preposition ἐν ("with") reveals that such patience and instruction are "not the *accompaniment* of the actions, but the element, the temper in which they are to be performed."[25]

We do well to note that there is a continuity that transcends the chapter break here. Paul has said that Scripture has four primary purposes (3:16) and then has gone on to set forth four primary functions of a pastor's speaking ministry (4:2). There is a correspondence between these functions.

God-breathed Scripture	God-anointed preaching
Teaching	Preach
Reproof	Reprove
Correction	Rebuke
Training	Exhort

The words "teaching" (διδασκαλίαν) and "preach" (κήρυξον) pair up. The two are paired with one another not infrequently in the life and letters of Paul. The final verse of the Book of Acts has Paul "preaching [κηρύσσων] the kingdom of God and teaching [διδάσκων] concerning the Lord Jesus Christ" (Acts 28:31). Paul had earlier told Timothy, "I was appointed a

---
[23] BAGD, 192.
[24] Alford, 3:399.
[25] Ibid.

preacher [κῆρυξ] and an apostle . . . as a teacher [διδάσκαλος] of the Gentiles in faith and truth" (1 Tim. 2:7). He reminded him again in this letter that it was for the Gospel that he "was appointed a preacher [κῆρυξ] and an apostle and a teacher [διδάσκαλος]" (2 Tim. 1:11; cf. also Rom. 2:21). Both teaching and preaching were paired-up also in the ministry of Jesus (Matt. 4:23; cf. with parallels in Mark 1:39; Luke 4:15). Is there a difference between preaching and teaching? Many of our distinctions are matters merely of personal taste or cultural bias. All good preaching imparts and builds upon solid doctrinal content and all teaching of the Scripture is authoritative and persuasive in nature.

The words "reproof" (ἐλεγμόν) and "reprove" (ἔλεγξον) also match up. The noun and verb are cognates. Both point to the exposing of another's position with overwhelming proof so that he is brought to the point of conviction of sin.

The words "correction" (ἐπανόρθωσιν) and "rebuke" (ἐπιτίμησον) also line up. While they are not from the same root, the words are similar in meaning. The former refers to restoring something to an upright state and in this sense means correction, improvement or restoration. The latter points to censure in conduct so that it may be corrected.

Finally, the words "training" (παιδείαν) and "exhort" (παρακάλεσον) are paralleled. The former describes a fatherly discipline that lovingly trains a child in righteousness. The latter word means to come alongside another with the intent of lending aid, counsel and help. As can readily be seen, the two words describe very similar functions.

Why this parallel? It makes plain that God's purposes for the Scriptures (3:16-17) and for preaching (4:1-2) are one and the same. Preaching should allow the Word of God to dominate and arrive at its intended purpose. A sermon must be more than Scripture-based, it must be shaped and controlled by Scripture. We must allow our bibliology to inform our homiletics.

Digging Deeper:
1. Why does the NT give priority to the act of preaching (verb) over the one doing the preaching (noun)?
2. How does comparing the purpose of Scripture (3:16) with the practice of preaching (4:2) help us understand what God-pleasing preaching is like?

4:3 For the time will come when they will not endure sound doctrine; but wanting to have their ears tickled, they will accumulate for themselves teachers in accordance to their own desires,

Paul now states the reason ("For," γὰρ) for the urgent and solemn imperatives that precede (vv.1-2). That reason is not just because of present realities, but because "the time will come" (ἔσται . . . καιρὸς). Without denying the present troubles in Ephesus, the future tense verb points to a coming day, while the middle voice points to its coming on its own without outside influence. This will be the natural outcome of forces now at work. The passing of time will simply produce this. The noun "time" (καιρὸς) is related to the two adverbs of the previous verse ("in season and out of season," εὐκαίρως ἀκαίρως). It points to a season or period of time.[26] Paul has already called them "difficult times" (3:1). Now he characterizes it as a time "when they will not endure sound doctrine" (ὅτε τῆς ὑγιαινούσης διδασκαλίας οὐκ ἀνέξονται). All of Paul's uses of "sound" (ὑγιαίνω) are found in the PE. He connects it either with "words" (1 Tim. 6:3; 2 Tim. 1:13), "faith" (Titus 1:13; 2:2), or, as he does here, "doctrine" (1 Tim. 1:10; Titus 1:9; 2:1). Such words are "sound" in that they are healthy. The word was used literally of physical (e.g., Luke 5:31; 7:10) or mental health (e.g., 15:27). Here it speaks of that teaching which begets spiritual health as opposed to the false doctrine propagated by the errorists in Ephesus. Having just used the less frequent διδαχῇ ("instruction," v.2), Paul now returns to the word διδασκαλίας ("doctrine"). It is used twenty-one times in the NT, fifteen of those appearing in the PE (1 Tim. 1:10; 4:1, 6, 13, 16; 5:17; 6:1, 3; 2 Tim. 3:10, 16; 4:3; Titus 1:9; 2:1, 7, 10). Such teaching "they will not endure" (οὐκ ἀνέξονται). The future tense points to a coming attitude and stance toward the Gospel and the Scriptures which tell of its truth. This verb is always in the middle voice in the NT. It points to enduring something in the sense of listening to it willingly. It can have the connotation of putting up with something.[27] Here it is strongly negated (οὐκ, "not") so that it points to the opposite attitude.

In strong contrast ("but," ἀλλὰ) to the idea of enduring sound teaching, the people will act "in accordance to their own desires" (κατὰ τὰς ἰδίας ἐπιθυμίας). The preposition (κατὰ) with the accusative has a relational sense and means "according to." The problem is the "desires" or lusts (ἐπιθυμίας) of the listeners. The word can be used in a neutral (Rev. 18:14) or positive sense (1 Thess. 2:17), but the overwhelming number of uses in the NT point to the negative sense of desiring something forbidden.[28] Paul has already warned Timothy to

---

[26] Rienecker, 648.
[27] BAGD, 66.
[28] Ibid., 293.

flee his own "youthful lusts" (2 Tim. 2:22). Some women are "led on by various impulses" and it makes them vulnerable to the false teachers (3:6). The truth instructs us "to deny . . . worldly desires" (Titus 2:12), but these folk have already determined to listen only to those who are "in accordance to their own desires." Apart from the grace of God set forth in the Gospel, such desires would enslave us all (3:3). The adjective ἰδίας ("their own") points to what is one's own as opposed to what belongs to another.[29] They have closed their ears to all that contradicts their own inner emotions, feelings and urges. There is, for them, no fixed point of reference by which to judge truth or error. Their only standard of measure is their own subjective feelings at any given moment. The use of the article (τὰς) makes definite the reference to their own desires and no one else's.

> **Ministry Maxim**
>
> The measure of good preaching can never ultimately be people's response to it—a higher standard is needed.

The specific action that is "according to their own desires" is that "they will accumulate for themselves teachers" (ἑαυτοῖς ἐπισωρεύσουσιν διδασκάλους). The verb "they will accumulate" (ἐπισωρεύσουσιν) is found only here in the NT. Its future tense points to the end at which they will most certainly arrive, if they continue their current selfish course. It means to heap up or accumulate into piles.[30] They will stockpile a host of teachers who are filtered "in accordance to their own desires." The innate selfishness of their actions is emphasized by the use of the third person pronoun "themselves" (ἑαυτοῖς). They "themselves" have become their only standard of measure. The multiplicity of their collected preachers is seen in the plural form of the noun "teachers" (διδασκάλους).

The final participial phrase, "to have their ears tickled" (κνηθόμενοι τὴν ἀκοὴν), emphasizes the means by which these instructors made the cut. The present tense participle describes the continuous nature of their teaching and its content. The word can mean to tickle, to scratch, and to itch. In the passive voice, as here, it means "to feel an itching." It is used figuratively "of curiosity, that looks for interesting and spicy bits of information. This itching is relieved by the messages of the new teachers."[31] This is the only NT occurrence of the verb. Such teachers claimed expertise (1 Tim. 1:7), but peddled novelties and held their audience with sensationalized claims. That there is a constant turnover in this group of teachers is likely, for, as Paul has already stated, their clientele is "always learning and never able to come to the knowledge of the truth" (3:7). What tickles the ear today may not tomorrow when one's fickle moods have shifted.

---

[29] Thayer, 296.
[30] Ibid., 244.
[31] BAGD, 437.

4:4 and will turn away their ears from the truth and will turn aside to myths.

Paul now tacks on ("and," καὶ) a closing clause to underscore the outcome that their preacher-collecting, ear-tickling approach to truth produces. The effect is twofold. On the one hand (μὲν), they "will turn away their ears from the truth" (ἀπὸ μὲν τῆς ἀληθείας τὴν ἀκοὴν ἀποστρέψουσιν). The verb "will turn away" (ἀποστρέψουσιν) is in the future tense, pointing to what their present trend will most assuredly bring forth. It is a compound verb made up of "from" (ἀπὸ) and "to turn" (στρέφω). Paul has used it twice already in the PE. He used it in the aorist passive form to describe the rejection he felt from "all who are in Asia" (1:15). He also uses it in the present middle form in Titus: ". . . not paying attention to Jewish myths and commandments of men who turn away from the truth" (1:14). In both of these cases it has the sense of rejecting or repudiating someone. Here it is used transitively in the simple sense of "to turn away from."[32]

It is the "ears" (τὴν ἀκοὴν; cf. its use in v.3) which are turned away and it is "the truth" (τῆς ἀληθείας) which is left behind. Here "the truth" is the same as "the gospel" (1:8, 10; cf. 2:8), held forth in "the word" (4:2; cf. 2:9, 15). It is that saving message of Christ given us in the Scriptures (3:15-16).

When such a stance is taken an automatic second action is unavoidable. On the other hand ("and," δὲ), they "will turn aside to myths" (ἐπὶ δὲ τοὺς μύθους ἐκτραπήσονται). The verb "will turn aside" (ἐκτραπήσονται) is also a compound word from "out" (ἐκ) and "to turn" (τρέπω). It may have been a medical term used to describe the dislocation of a joint (cf. Heb. 12:13). It is used only three other times by Paul, all in the PE. Twice people are turning aside to either "fruitless discussion" (1 Tim. 1:6) or "Satan" (5:15). The other use is in a command to Timothy to turn away from "worldly and empty chatter and the opposing arguments of what is falsely called 'knowledge'" (1 Tim. 6:20). It describes a powerful transition from one thing to another.

> **Ministry Maxim**
>
> Listening only to teaching we "like" can be the first step toward embracing false-hood.

The first verb ("will turn away," ἀποστρέψουσιν) is in the active voice, meaning that the person chooses to reject the truth. The second verb ("will turn aside," ἐκτραπήσονται) is in the passive voice, probably used in a middle sense, and thus means that once the first choice is made, a person automatically moves himself into the second choice with unavoidable certainty. To turn

---
[32] Ibid. 100.

away from truth and reality is automatically to embrace "myths" (τοὺς μύθους). This has been a favorite way for Paul to describe the falsehood being taught in Ephesus (1 Tim. 1:4; 4:7) and Crete (Titus 1:14). Here he neither characterizes them as particularly "Jewish" (1:14) nor as related to "genealogies" (1 Tim. 1:4), thus allowing his words to reach across the ages and encompass all falsehood that asserts itself and is embraced rather than truth. Turn yourself away from God-defined truth and you unavoidably find yourself full-face before a fanciful, make-believe world constructed of your wishes and wants, but without the substance and support of reality.

> **Digging Deeper:**
> 1. How does modern mobility and technology enable these verses to become truer than ever?
> 2. Describe the danger in simply listening to teachers/preachers or reading authors we "like."
> 3. When we turn away from a truth we don't like, what is the inevitable result? Why is this so dangerous?

4:5 But you, be sober in all things, endure hardship, do the work of an evangelist, fulfill your ministry.

Having momentarily turned aside from his charge (vv.1-2) to focus upon the difficult days ahead for the Gospel and its messengers (vv.3-4), Paul now, in contrast ("But," δέ) to the fickle crowds, emphatically ("you," σύ) calls upon Timothy to live a life of disciplined ministry (cf. similar use of σὺ δέ in 1 Tim. 6:11; 2 Tim. 3:10, 14). In addition to the five commands that were at the heart of the Apostle's charge (vv.1-2), he now adds four more imperatives here, gathering up and summarizing much of what he has said to Timothy throughout the letter.

Paul first commands Timothy to "be sober" (νῆφε). It describes the opposite condition of drunkenness, though in the NT it is always used in a figurative sense. It means to be free from "every form of mental and spiritual 'drunkenness,' [from] excess, passion, rashness, confusion."[33] It means to be well-balanced and self-controlled. Paul used this verb only two other times. Both were made in the context of the eschatological hope of Christ's return (1 Thess. 5:6, 8). It was also a favorite word of Peter (1 Peter 1:13; 4:7; 5:8). The present tense verb demands action that is continuous and habitual. It is the

---
[33] Ibid., 538.

only one of the nine imperatives in this charge (vv.1-2, 5) which is in the present tense. This may be in order to match the requirements of the sweeping prepositional phrase "in all things" (ἐν πᾶσιν). His clear-headed vigilance must be all encompassing. Nothing must possess control of Timothy at any point, save the Spirit and purpose of God. Even small diversions may be dangerous, clouding the mind and impairing the judgment. The crowds will be possessed by their own desires (vv.3-4), so it will take constant attention and self-examination for the servant of God to maintain this vigilant watchfulness.

Next Paul calls Timothy to "endure hardship" (κακοπάθησον). The aorist imperative form calls for immediate action to be undertaken with a sense of urgency. The Apostle already used the verb when he earlier said, "I suffer hardship even to imprisonment as a criminal" (2:9). The word is a compound made up of "suffer" (πάσχειν) and "evil" (κακὸς). The same compound with an additional prefix (σύν) has been used twice already, both of which are also aorist imperatives: "join with me in suffering for the gospel" (1:8) and "Suffer hardship with me, as a good soldier of Christ Jesus" (2:3). Here also the military imagery will enter soon after this present command (v.7). Whereas the first command demanded sobriety in the face of intoxicating lusts, this imperative demands endurance in conflict. The first pictured an inward battle against one's own desires, the second an inward resolve in an outward battle against spiritual foes. Paul's own example throughout his ministry, and now especially at the close of that ministry as he faced an impending death (v.6), added a personal and powerful impact as Timothy felt the force of this command.

> **Ministry Maxim**
>
> Hardship may be the divine slap in the face that keeps me clear-headed in ministry.

Paul then charges Timothy, "do the work of an evangelist" (ἔργον ποίησον εὐαγγελιστοῦ). The aorist imperative form demands that this work be undertaken urgently and immediately. The noun "evangelist" (εὐαγγελιστοῦ) is used beyond this verse to describe only Philip the evangelist (Acts 21:8) and evangelists in Ephesians 4:11, alongside other gifted people given by God to the church, such as prophets, pastors and teachers. Here, however, the noun lacks the definite article, pointing to the quality of the work to be done, rather than a title or office. Timothy is not called "an evangelist," but told to "do the work of an evangelist" (cf. Phil. 2:22 and 1 Thess. 3:2 for reference to Timothy's work in the Gospel). Some, like Philip, may have their entire ministry identity wrapped up in their evangelistic fervor. The primary area of their gifting and role within the body of Christ may be related to evangelism. There will be, however, many others in ministry who prioritize the work of evangelism, despite their comparative lack of gifting. For them evangelism is "work" (ἔργον). It does not come naturally or easily, but is difficult and toilsome at times. Yet this is at the heart of the church's mandate, and the pastor must lead the way. Timothy had been trained in the work of evangelism through many long miles of travel with the Apostle Paul. It was from the base of the Ephesian church that "all who lived in Asia heard the word of the Lord, both Jews and Greeks" (Acts 19:10). One of their own paranoid pagans confessed, "You see and hear that not only in Ephesus, but in almost all of Asia, this Paul has persuaded and turned away a considerable number of people, saying that gods made with hands are no gods at all" (Acts 19:26). Paul did not want the strategic hold that had been gained in Asia Minor and its leading city to be lost in the scuffle of disunity that had broken out in the Ephesian church. One of Satan's craftiest ploys (2 Tim. 2:26) to keep the church from fulfilling it mission is to preoccupy her with inward matters of disunity. Throughout this letter Paul has vigorously guarded the Gospel from errorists and charged Timothy to do the same (1:13-14), but he knows that ultimately the greatest protection for the Gospel is found not in argument, definition, re-definition and debate, but through proclaiming the Gospel and releasing it to bring about in the lives of lost people that which it is designed to produce (1:10; cf. Rom. 1:16-17).

Finally, Paul commanded Timothy, "fulfill your ministry" (τὴν διακονίαν σου πληροφόρησον). The verb "fulfill" (πληροφόρησον) in the passive voice can describe being fully convinced of something (Rom. 4:21; 14:5; Col. 4:12). But here it is in the active voice with an object and means to add to something that which it lacks and thus to fill it completely or, as we might say it, to fulfill that thing.[34] In this case that which is fulfilled is "your ministry" (τὴν διακονίαν σου). The noun "ministry" (διακονίαν) is a broad word that gathers up all the diverse elements of what may be required by one who serves God. The definite article (τὴν), along with the second person singular pronoun (σου, "your"), makes clear that it is the particular ministry laid upon Timothy by God that is in view. There are specific good works "which God prepared beforehand so that we would walk in them" (Eph. 2:10). Note how Paul, with Timothy at his side (Col. 1:1), charged Archippus, "Take heed to the ministry which you have received in the Lord, that you may fulfill it'" (4:17). Ministry requires *this* of some and *that* of others, but we each must know what it is God has called us to do and must keep our hand to the plow until our fields of service have been plowed, planted, prayed over and readied for harvest.

It is possible, as some have suggested,[35] that the first of these four imperatives

---

[34] BAGD, 670.
[35] Hiebert, *Second Timothy*, 108; Lenski, 856

is primary and that the following three describe the arenas in which it is to be completed. Thus the primary call in this verse is for sobriety in ministry. The pastor maintains such clear-headed sobriety as he endures hardship within the church ("endure hardship"), holds forth the Gospel to those outside the church ("do the work of an evangelist"), and, with regard to himself, fulfills all that God requires of him in ministry ("fulfill your ministry").

> **Digging Deeper:**
> 1. What threatens to "intoxicate" you and keep you from being clear-headed spiritually?
> 2. How have you worked at evangelism this past week?
> 3. What remains to do if you are to fulfill the ministry God has ordained for you?

4:6 For I am already being poured out as a drink offering, and the time of my departure has come.

The charge having been delivered (vv.1-5), Paul now gives the powerful reason ("For," γὰρ) behind its serious and forceful delivery. The first person pronoun ("I," Ἐγώ) is set off in an emphatic fashion by thrusting it to the head of the sentence. Its emphatic nature matches the emphatic "you" (σὺ) of the previous verse. Timothy's actions (v.5) would be all the more important in light of what was about to befall the Apostle (v.6).

Paul says, "I am already being poured out as a drink offering" (ἤδη σπένδομαι). Drink offerings were common among the pagans (Deut. 32:38) and among the Hebrews before Sinai (Gen. 28:18; 35:14). But when the Law was given to Moses, God prescribed that drink offerings should accompany many of the sacrifices (Exod. 29:40, 41). Usually wine, it was poured out as the final act of the sacrifice (Num. 15:4, 5, 7, 10, 24) or continual burnt offering (28:7-8). It was a regular part of worship on all Sabbaths (28:9-10) and feasts (28:14-31; 29:6-39). The wine may have been used by the Israelites as a substitute for the blood of pagan libations (Psa. 16:4).[36] Hendriksen well says, "Since this wine *was gradually poured out*, was *an offering*, and was *the final act* of the entire sacrificial ceremony, it pictured most adequately *the gradual ebbing away* of Paul's life, the fact that he was presenting this life to God as *an offering*, and the idea that while he viewed his entire career of faith as 'a living sacrifice' (Rom. 12:1; cf. 15:16), he looked upon *the present* stage of

---

[36] Fee, 288-289.

this career as being *the final act of sacrifice*."³⁷

The drawn out or continual nature of this sacrifice is pictured in the present tense of the verb and its accompanying temporal adverb ("already," ἤδη). The passive voice shows that Paul is not pouring out his own life, but rather he is being acted upon by another. The most direct, active human agent might be the Roman Empire generally or Caesar more specifically. It seems, however, more likely that Paul is viewing God as the active agent. He thus pictures his impending martyrdom as his sovereign King pouring out His servant's lifeblood—which had long before been offered as a living sacrifice (Rom. 12:1)—in one final act of service and worship.

The verb is used elsewhere in the NT only in Philippians 2:17 when during an earlier imprisonment Paul said, "But even if I am being poured out as a drink offering upon the sacrifice and service of your faith, I rejoice and share my joy with you all." What Paul had contemplated as a possibility during an earlier imprisonment, he now sees as present reality in his current incarceration.³⁸

> **Ministry Maxim**
>
> Death is the believer's last act of faith and greatest act of worship.

How this must have moved Timothy! The great Apostle was no longer full of faith for deliverance (Phil. 1:9), but was now full of faith for death. It reminds us that unless one's life is lived as a sacrifice of worship to God (Rom. 12:1), one's death will not be an act of worship.

Paul adds ("and," καὶ) another metaphorical reference to his death, saying "the time of my departure has come" (ὁ καιρὸς τῆς ἀναλύσεώς μου ἐφέστηκεν). The word "time" (ὁ καιρὸς) has become an ominous one in this letter. Paul used it to describe "difficult times" coming in the last days (3:1) and a time when people "will not endure sound doctrine" (4:3). It points to a season or period of time.³⁹ Paul is not saying that his death will be immediate, but that he has entered the final season of his life. This is the final segment of time for Paul in this life. It is made the more definite by the presence of the article. This final season is marked by its primary event, "my departure" (τῆς ἀναλύσεώς μου). The noun is not used elsewhere in the NT (though see the cognate verb in Phil. 1:23). In its secular usage the word signified untying the ropes that hold a ship to its moorings, so that it could set sail on a new journey. It was also used to describe a party breaking camp in order to trudge on in the next stage of their march. It could describe an unloosing (as of things that had been woven) or a dissolving of something into different parts.⁴⁰

---

³⁷ Hendriksen, 313.
³⁸ Robertson, 4:630.
³⁹ Rienecker, 648.
⁴⁰ Thayer, 39.

All of this background richly flavors its imagery as a metaphor for death. The Book of Acts is rife with reference to Paul setting sail from one port to another (e.g., Acts 18:21; 21:1, 2; 27:21; 28:11). These scenes may have played in Timothy's mind and evoked great emotion as he read these words of the Apostle.

The verb "has come" (ἐφέστηκεν) is the same one found as an imperative in v.2 when Paul commanded Timothy to "be ready." Here it means something like "stand before" or "is imminent."[41] The perfect tense describes action that has already taken place at a point in time in the past and that continues to be true in the present. Paul's death is at hand, though perhaps not within the next few days or weeks or else his pleadings "Make every effort to come to me soon" (v.9) and "Make every effort to come before winter" (v.21) would be meaningless.

The brave faith of Paul in the face of death is not reserved for Apostles alone. For every believer in the risen Christ death is not the end, but the final act of faith-filled worship in this life and a departure on a new journey into the fullness of eternal life in God's presence.

> **Digging Deeper:**
> 1. Explain why the imagery of "a drink offering" pictures a Christian's stance toward death.
> 2. What needs to be true of you now if your death is to be an act of worship to God someday?
> 3. Why is the imagery of death as a "departure" so full of hope for a believer?

4:7 I have fought the good fight, I have finished the course, I have kept the faith;

Paul has succinctly described his present circumstances (v.6) and now he does the same with his personal past. He sums up in three tight lines the whole of his Christian life and ministry. His words of reflection have become words of direction for believers who want to finish this life well.

He says first, "I have fought the good fight" (τὸν καλὸν ἀγῶνα ἠγώνισμαι). The verb "I have fought" (ἠγώνισμαι), when used literally, can describe either competing for a prize in an athletic contest (1 Cor. 9:25) or engaging another in a battle with weapons (John 18:36). When it is used figuratively it often has the sense of contending or struggling with great effort against difficulties or

---
[41] BAGD, 331.

dangers generally (Col. 1:29; 1 Tim. 4:10) or of striving after something with strenuous zeal (Luke 13:24; Col. 4:12).[42] It is matched here by its cognate noun "fight" (ἀγῶνα), which can speak of an athletic contest such as a race (Heb. 12:1), but more often speaks of a conflict, struggle or fight for the Gospel (Phil. 1:30; Col. 2:1; 1 Thess. 2:2).[43] It seems, therefore, that if one must choose, the imagery of this first line is more likely that of an athletic event, rather than of a soldier in a pitched battle. Perhaps as in 1 Corinthians 9:26 Paul has in mind the boxer, which he, as here, sets next to the runner. Paul clearly is not afraid, however, to employ military imagery (2 Tim. 2:3). The words describe not just the outward engagement of such a fight, but also the inward turmoil inherent in such conflict. Our words "agonize" and "agony" are derived from this verb and noun. The enduring, drawn-out nature of the conflict is seen in the perfect tense of the verb which points to an action begun at a point in the past and continuing right up to the moment of writing. The voice is either middle or passive. If the former, it has the sense of Paul acting upon himself, forcing himself into faithful warfare for the Gospel. If the latter is correct then it has the sense of God really doing the battle through His servant. Though the latter is an attractive option theologically, it is more likely the former which we find here.

That which Paul has entered into and been faithful in is specifically "the good fight" (τὸν καλὸν ἀγῶνα). Just what this fight entails is not spelled out, but the imagery is clear. The article makes definite the solitary nature of the conflict he has entered into. Paul has previously commanded Timothy to "fight the good fight of faith" (1 Tim. 6:12), employing the same noun and verb. He employed a similar expression in 1 Timothy 1:18 ("fight the good fight"), but used a more specifically militaristic noun (στρατείαν). Paul demanded of himself what he commanded of others. We note that it is the fight itself that is "good," not the way Paul had engaged in it. At the end of his life and ministry he can rejoice in the fact that he has spent himself for that which matters.[44]

Secondly, Paul asserts, "I have finished the course" (τὸν δρόμον τετέλεκα). The noun "course" (τὸν δρόμον) was used in non-biblical writings to describe the path the stars or planets take in their movements. In the NT it figuratively describes a footrace. Its three usages all come from the mouth or pen of Paul. He used it when preaching to the people of Pisidian Antioch and summarized the whole of John the Baptist's life, saying, "And while John was completing his course, he kept saying . . ." (Acts 13:25). Later he used it again while speaking to the elders of Ephesus, "But I do not consider my life of any account as dear to myself, so that I may finish my course and the ministry which I

---
[42] Thayer, 10.
[43] BAGD, 15.
[44] Kent, 287.

received from the Lord Jesus, to testify solemnly of the gospel of the grace of God" (Acts 20:24). This latter reference is most telling in helping to determine just what Paul's words mean here in 2 Timothy. Not only was Paul speaking to the elders of the church Timothy was now pastor of, but Timothy apparently had been present for this earlier meeting and heard the Apostle's words spoken (Acts 20:4, 13-17). For Paul his "course" was the completion of "the ministry which [he had] received from the Lord Jesus" (20:24a). That, more specifically, was "to testify solemnly of the gospel of the grace of God" (20:24b). The presence of the article makes definite the reference to this course marked out for him by God. Note the parallels in the immediate context here in 2 Timothy. Paul commanded Timothy, "fulfill your ministry" (4:5) and said, "I solemnly charge you in the presence of God and of Christ Jesus . . . preach the word" (4:1a, 2a). Probably a decade or more spanned the time between when Timothy had heard Paul make this declaration to the elders from Ephesus and the writing of this letter to Timothy in Ephesus (*ca.*, A.D. 56 – A.D. 67). What Timothy had heard Paul so passionately describe as his life's purpose and goal those years before, he now hears him testify to as a completed assignment.

> **Ministry Maxim**
>
> Winning in the Christian life is often a matter of outlasting the opposition.

Paul says, "I have finished" (τετέλεκα) this race. The verb is the same one the Lord Jesus used when, with His final breaths, He said, "It is finished" (John 19:30). In both places the tense if perfect, pointing to a state of utter completion. Jesus spoke in reference to all the redemptive work He was sent by the Father to complete. Jesus had been on a very definable mission to procure the salvation of the lost. Paul too saw his life as the fulfillment of a mission: not the procuring of salvation, but the proclaiming of that salvation which Jesus provided completely. How fitting that the Apostle appointed by Christ Himself (Acts 9:15-16) could, as he faced death, look back over his own life and ministry and employ the same word his Master had used of His own life and ministry.

The third expression Paul makes in review of his life is, "I have kept the faith" (τὴν πίστιν τετήρηκα). The verb "I have kept" (τετήρηκα) can mean to guard or keep watch over something, to keep blameless or protect a thing. Here it seems to have the sense of to hold to something in the sense of following it.[45] Paul was saying he had remained faithful and true.[46] If the imagery of the first two clauses was athletic in nature, this may picture for us a sentry standing watch over something precious.

That which had been kept is "the faith" (τὴν πίστιν). Paul often used the

---
[45] DNTT, 2:133.
[46] Rienecker, 648.

same form with the definite article in the PE (1 Tim. 1:19; 5:8; 6:21; 2 Tim. 3:8). Does it designate Paul's own "believing" (subjectively) or that in which he believed (objectively)? Is Paul saying he has come to the martyr's block and refused to give up believing in Jesus? Or is he saying that as a faithful Apostle and preacher he has protected the content of the Gospel message under great pressure? The noun with the article often points to "the faith" as an objective body of essential doctrine. Yet how can one preserve such a body of truth without personally believing it? To force a distinction between the objective and subjective is to push beyond what Paul probably intended. He preserved the content of the Gospel precisely because he believed it to be true.

The thrust of these three images seems to be that of perseverance to the end. Some believe these expressions to be unworthy of a man like Paul, feeling they are self-exalting. But Paul spoke as a man possessed by a clarity of call (2 Tim. 1:1) and a singularity of purpose ("one thing I do," Phil. 3:13). To such a one these statements were not the boasting of an arrogant man, but the relieved presentation of a humble servant before his Master. Paul was abundantly aware of the grace of God that had enabled him to come to the end of his life and to have been found faithful. Such confessions were an exaltation of grace and the God who gives it, not of the servant through whom God had poured that grace.

Digging Deeper:
1. What "agony" in your life today may be a signal that you are in "the good fight"?
2. How does Jesus' statement "It is finished!" enable us to come to the end of our lives and say "I have finished"?
3. In what way have you had to guard "the faith" in your own life recently?
4. Do you see what God has called you to clearly enough to identify the arena of the fight you must fight today, the course you must run today, the threats from which you must keep "the faith" today?

4:8 in the future there is laid up for me the crown of righteousness, which the Lord, the righteous Judge, will award to me on that day; and not only to me, but also to all who have loved His appearing.

Paul now speaks to what awaits him "in the future" (λοιπὸν). Used here as an adverb related to time, λοιπὸν has the sense of "from now on" or "henceforth."[47]

---
[47] BAGD, 480.

Having reviewed his present circumstances (v.6) and his past ministry (v.7), all that remains is to consider what he confidently hopes for "in the future."

In that future "there is laid up" (ἀπόκειταί) something which Paul eagerly anticipates. The verb is used by Paul elsewhere only in Colossians 1:5 where he similarly speaks of "the hope laid up for you in heaven." It means to be laid away or reserved. With the dative of person, as it is here, it has the sense of "reserved for one" or "awaiting him."[48] The verb was used with reference to the rewards bestowed upon the champions of the Greek athletic games as well as metaphorically with reference to rewards for civic service.[49] Surely given the athletic imagery of v.7, the former sense is intended here. The present tense heightens the sense of the anticipation by revealing that no further action need be taken for it is already "laid up" for Paul. The passive voice signals that this is something that another, presumably God, has set aside for Paul's arrival.

That which is reserved for Paul is "the crown of righteousness" (ὁ τῆς δικαιοσύνης στέφανος). With the use of the noun "the crown" (ὁ στέφανος), Paul continues the athletic imagery of v.7 (cf. 1 Cor. 9:25). Of the twenty-five times the word is used in the NT, only four are found in Paul's writings (1 Cor. 9:24; Phil. 4:1; 1 Thess. 2:19), though see the related noun in 2 Timothy 2:5. It described the laurel wreath placed upon the head of the victor in the athletic games of Greece. Here it is specifically designated the crown "of righteousness" (τῆς δικαιοσύνης). Is this to be understood as a genitive of apposition, meaning that the crown consists of righteousness? Or is it to be understood as a possessive genitive, meaning that the righteousness describes the one receiving the crown (i.e., the crown is a reward for a righteous life)? Throughout the NT the noun is coupled with genitive nouns to describe the reward anticipated by faithful believers. We read of the "crown of exultation" (1 Thess. 2:19), the "crown of life" (James 1:12; Rev. 2:10), the "crown of glory" (1 Peter 5:4), and a "crown of twelve stars" (Rev. 12:1). These usages and the context here point toward understanding the crown as consisting of righteousness. But just what does that mean? Some suggest it hints at a finalization of the believer's justification in heaven, but this seems to fly in the face of Paul's theology (cf. Rom. 5:1, 9; 8:30; 1 Cor. 6:11; Titus 3:5). It is more likely to be descriptive of the state of perfect righteousness that will be enjoyed in the presence of God when Paul (and other faithful believers) are welcomed into His presence finally and forever.[50] The presence of the definite article would seem to point to just such a perfect and final righteousness. Paul has commanded Timothy to "pursue righteousness" (2:22) and exhorted him

---

[48] Thayer, 63.
[49] Marshall, 808.
[50] Knight, 461.

to cling to the Scriptures which are for "training in righteousness" (3:16). Yet that state of perfect righteousness is still before us. Thus, he says, "we through the Spirit, by faith, are waiting for the hope of righteousness" (Gal. 5:5). Or as Peter states it, "according to His promise we are looking for new heavens and a new earth, in which righteousness dwells" (2 Peter 3:13).

The Lord "will award" (ἀποδώσει) this crown to Paul. The verb is a compound from the words "from" (ἀπό) and "give" (δίδωμι), having the sense of paying something back. The word has a wide range of meaning, from paying back a debt owed (e.g., Matt. 5:26) to positively rewarding (1 Tim. 5:4) or negatively recompensing (2 Tim. 4:14) someone for something. Here it seems to have the simple meaning of give away, give up or give out.[51] The preposition in compound does not point here to that which is owed, but simply views the reward as having been stored away or laid up and then taken out of the treasury for presentation.[52] There is no sense of payment for services rendered; rather, the future tense is full of the anticipation of faith in the grace of God. The future tense looks forward to what will take place "on that day" (ἐν ἐκείνῃ τῇ ἡμέρᾳ). The same expression (minus the preposition) was used in 1:18 to describe Paul's prayer/wish for Onesiphorus's reward (cf. also 1:12). Paul is picturing the day when he and Onesiphorus and all other believers will stand before Christ for judgment and reward regarding their ministries (1 Cor. 3:12-15). Confronted as he is with his own impending death, Paul has had his eyes upon "that day" from the opening of the letter until its closing.

On that day we will all stand before "the Lord, the righteous Judge" (ὁ κύριος ... ὁ δίκαιος κριτής). The reference is surely to Jesus Christ, for as Paul told the Athenians, God "has fixed a day in which He will judge the world in righteousness through a Man whom He has appointed, having furnished proof to all men by raising Him from the dead" (Acts 17:31). Jesus Himself said, "For not even the Father judges anyone, but He has given all judgment to the Son" (John 5:22). The crown awarded will be one of righteousness so it must come from a Judge who is righteous. Frequently Paul links the judgment and righteousness of God together (Acts 24:25; Rom. 2:5; 2 Thess. 1:5). The Apostle had recently stood before a very different kind of judge (2 Tim. 4:16) and would soon enough be before him again, so the just verdict of Christ must have been an appealing hope.

> **Ministry Maxim**
>
> God never allows faithfulness to go unrewarded.

This crown, says Paul, will be presented "not only to me"

---

[51] BAGD, 90.
[52] Rienecker, 649.

(οὐ μόνον δὲ ἐμοί). This hope and reward is not reserved for Apostles only, "but also to all who have loved His appearing" (ἀλλὰ καὶ πᾶσι τοῖς ἠγαπηκόσι τὴν ἐπιφάνειαν αὐτοῦ). Paul uses the strong adversative (ἀλλά, "but") to demonstrate forcefully the availability of this hope to all who are in Christ. He specifically designates them as those "who have loved" (τοῖς ἠγαπηκόσι). The articular participle is used in a substantive way. The perfect tense points to a love that began in the past and now continues right up into the present as the abiding state of their hearts. What they love is "His appearing" (τὴν ἐπιφάνειαν αὐτοῦ). The third person singular pronoun (αὐτοῦ, "His") finds its antecedent in "the Lord" and "the righteous Judge." The noun "appearing" (τὴν ἐπιφάνειαν) is used only six times in the NT, all of them by Paul. Of his six uses, five of them are found in the PE. While it can refer to Christ's first advent (2 Tim. 1:10), it is used mostly for His second coming. It provides a motivating terminus point for this life and a believer's faithful service (1 Tim. 6:14). Every word Timothy preaches is to be done in light of this "appearing" of Christ (2 Tim. 4:1). The shining forth of the Lord Jesus Christ in all of His glory is the singular focus and hope of the believer's heart (Titus 2:13). Here it is accompanied by the article, as it usually is (except Titus 2:13), to make specific and definite the "appearing" that is in view.

Having looked back (v.6), having reviewed the present (v.7), and having anticipated the future (v.8), the Apostle brings the main body of the letter to a close. The words "Judge" and "appearing" intimately tie his personal testimony here to the charge he laid upon Timothy (v.1). And the verb "have loved" (τοῖς ἠγαπηκόσι) is used elsewhere in the PE only in v.10. There it describes Demas, who "having loved this present world, has deserted [Paul]." We are reminded that the primary battle in this world is a battle of loves—for Christ and His eternal purposes to be culminated at His return, or for this present, temporal world. Paul has warned us that as we face the future we must guard our affections (3:2, 4); now he demonstrates as much in his own life and that of a now-fallen co-laborer Demas (v.10).

Digging Deeper:

1. Is righteousness sufficiently attractive to capture your imagination, control your will and form your hope? What was it about righteousness that Paul understood that we might not?
2. Do you *love* (not know of, believe in, expect, anticipate, but *love*) Christ's appearing? How can you tell?

4:9 Make every effort to come to me soon;

The main body of the letter now behind him, Paul moves toward a conclusion (vv.9-22). What we encounter here, however, are not unimportant details. Indeed, it is in the mundane details of life that our hearts are often most readily seen, and it is so here with regard to the great Apostle. As Paul speaks of people and places and makes some parting exhortations, he shows us that he is still fully engaged in ministry, right up until the end.

The urgency of the command that we meet here has characterized the entire letter. Early on, Paul revealed that he was "longing to see" Timothy (1:4). That "longing" now becomes an imperative. With his final pen strokes Paul will repeat this command nearly verbatim (4:21a). The resolve of his faith in the face of death has not lessened his human desire for the comfort and fellowship of a beloved brother in Christ. What fuels this earnestness? Paul is in prison (1:8, 16), has gone through a first defense without any support and received an unfavorable ruling (4:16), knows he will soon die at the hands of Rome (4:6), has been deserted by key friends (4:10), has redeployed other faithful friends for ministry purposes (4:12), has been unable to help others still in need (4:20), feels as though he has lost the support of the church in major regions where he has ministered (1:15), and knows winter is coming on and he is unprepared to face its long cold nights (4:13, 21). In addition he recalls Timothy's loyal love and tears (1:4) and longs simply for the mutual comfort they may provide one another.

> **Ministry Maxim**
>
> A deepening faith does not deny the need for human relationship, but deepens it as well.

The imperative is thrust forward in the sentence to emphasize its critical importance: "Make every effort" (Σπούδασον). The aorist imperative demands that action be taken without delay. Paul uses the verb seven times (Gal. 2:10; Eph. 4:3; 1 Thess. 2:17), four of them in this same form, and three of those in this letter (2 Tim. 2:15; 4:9, 21; cf. Titus 3:12). The urgent nature of this letter becomes even more acutely obvious as Paul nears its end. The word can have the notion of being zealous or eager or exerting every effort toward something. Some of that may be present here where it seems to have the simple notion of hurrying or hastening to fulfill that which is expressed in the following infinitive.[53]

The demand is "to come" (ἐλθεῖν). The personal nature of the command is seen in the prepositional phrase "to me" (πρός με). Timothy is not simply summoned to a place (Rome), but to a person (the Apostle). The journey from Ephesus to Rome was no small trip and would have to be made at some

---
[53] BAGD, 763.

considerable expense, both financially and personally. Yet the bonds of brotherhood in Christ count such expenditures as tokens of love.

Some object that the time necessary for Tychicus (v.11) to have traveled from Rome to Ephesus with the letter and then for Timothy to ready himself, gather up Mark (v.11) and for them to make the return trip, stopping off in Carpus to collect some personal items of the Apostle (v.13), would have stretched out to months and thus been out of character with the rest of the letter. Yet Paul has revealed from the beginning that this has been his desire (1:4). Even here the sense of urgency makes it unclear whether Paul has full confidence that they will be able to arrive in time, though he is hopeful and urges him to make the attempt.

This action was to be taken "soon" (ταχέως). The adverb describes that which is quick, fleet or speedy.[54] Just what Paul means by "soon" is spelled out in the nearly parallel command of v.21: "before winter."

4:10 for Demas, having loved this present world, has deserted me and gone to Thessalonica; Crescens has gone to Galatia, Titus to Dalmatia.

Paul now provides several reasons ("for," γάρ) that stand behind his urgent request for Timothy's presence (v.9). These reasons all relate to the dispersion of several co-workers in the Gospel.

The first is Demas (Δημᾶς). Paul sent greetings to the Colossian believers from Demas and Luke (Col. 4:14). Paul mentioned Demas in Philemon 24 as one of "my fellow workers." This, then, was a man who had come to faith in Christ, advanced in the things of God to a level where he was recognized as having gifts for ministry, and then was chosen to travel and minister with Paul on his missionary journeys. It is possible that Demas was from Thessalonica since he is mentioned next to Aristarchus (Philem. 24) who was from that city (Acts 20:4; 27:2). This may explain why he had left Paul and "gone to Thessalonica" (ἐπορεύθη εἰς Θεσσαλονίκην); he was running for home. The church in Thessalonica was one of the most dear to Paul's heart (1 Thess. 2:7-8, 17-20; 3:9-10) and if Demas was an official representation of that congregation it would have meant that he was likely very close to the Apostle himself.

We thus rightly read Paul's words concerning Demas with a wince of pain: he "deserted me" (με ἐγκατέλιπεν). The verb is a triple compound composed of: "in" (ἐν), "down" (κατὰ), and "leave" (λείπω).[55] It means to abandon or desert someone. It can have the sense of forsaking or leaving one in the lurch.[56] The word is also used in 4:16 to say "all deserted" Paul at his first defense. Was

---

[54] Thayer, 616.
[55] Kent, 289.
[56] Rienecker, 649.

Demas deserting Christ as well as His Apostle? The personal pronoun (με) specifies only Paul, though abandoning the official bearer of the Gospel would call into question one's commitment to that Gospel (see the comments on 1:15). At Saul's conversion, Jesus had instructed Ananias to go to him because "I will show him how much he must suffer for My name's sake" (Acts 9:16). Paul now takes up the same word his Master used upon the cross to express His abandonment (Matt. 27:46; Mk. 15:34; cf. Psa. 22:1 in LXX). Yet, as he had earlier in his ministry described himself as "persecuted, but not forsaken" (2 Cor. 4:9), even now he knew he had been not forsaken by Christ (2 Tim. 4:17). Indeed, He is the One who said, "I WILL NEVER DESERT YOU, NOR WILL I EVER FORSAKE YOU" (Heb. 13:5). The faithfulness of God anchors our soul when forsaken by others, but it does not completely remove the pain.

The commentary Paul adds as to why Demas took such action is telling: "having loved this present world" (ἀγαπήσας τὸν νῦν αἰῶνα). The aorist tense has an ingressive sense, meaning something like "having fallen in love with" and giving the impression that the action still continues.[57] The only other place in the PE that Paul used the participle "having loved" is in 4:8 where he speaks of those "who have loved His appearing." There is an obvious contrast set up between true believers awaiting the coming age to be ushered in by Christ at His return and Demas who had abandoned such a hope for the seemingly sure comfort of "this present world" (τὸν νῦν αἰῶνα). In 4:8 the participle is in the perfect tense, pointing to a settled state; while here it is in the aorist tense, simply reporting the fact of Demas' love at the moment of his actions. Does this leave room for hope that he might yet abandon his love for "this present world" and return to Christ?

The expression "this present world" (ἀγαπήσας τὸν νῦν αἰῶνα) might be more literally rendered "this present age." Just what is meant by this? The exact phrase is found nowhere else in the NT, but the same elements are found in two other places in the PE. Earlier Paul had told Timothy, "Instruct those who are rich in this present world [τῷ νῦν αἰῶνι] not to be conceited or to fix their hope on the uncertainty of riches, but on God, who richly supplies us with all things to enjoy" (1 Tim. 6:17). He had also told Titus that the grace of God is "instructing us to deny ungodliness and worldly desires and to live sensibly, righteously and godly in the present age [τῷ νῦν αἰῶνι]" (Titus 2:12). The only other places in the PE where the noun "age" (αἰῶνα) is used provide a stark contrast. "Now to the King eternal [τῶν αἰώνων ; lit., "of the ages"], immortal, invisible, the only God, *be* honor and glory forever and ever [εἰς τοὺς αἰῶνας τῶν αἰώνων ; lit., "unto the ages of the ages"]. Amen" (1 Tim. 1:17). "The Lord will rescue me from every evil deed, and

---
[57] Marshall, 815.

will bring me safely to His heavenly kingdom; to Him *be* the glory forever and ever [εἰς τοὺς αἰῶνας τῶν αἰώνων ; lit., "unto the ages of the ages"]. Amen" (2 Tim. 4:18).

The expression "this present world" describes the tangible world of time and space. It is limited to the moment and the momentary, the immediate and the temporary. It has no anchor beyond time. It is consumable, but not constant. It is not worthy of our hope and trust, for it is passing away. Its tangible comforts are seductive for they can richly address our desires, but soon enough they disappoint and are no more.

> **Ministry Maxim**
>
> My feet follow my heart—thus I must guard my heart above all else.

In contrast to "this present age" is "the King eternal" (1 Tim. 1:17)! He resides outside of time and beyond this tangible world. Having created this present age, God sovereignly holds it in His hand and controls it in His providence. He owns this world and all it contains (Psa. 24:1) and can disperse its goods to His children for their legitimate pleasure (1 Tim. 6:17). But Demas had fallen in love with the gifts of God rather than with the God who gives them. This is ever the risk of those of us who, for the present, live in two worlds at the same time.

The second co-worker mentioned is "Crescens" (Κρήσκης). He is not mentioned elsewhere in the NT and thus we know nothing about this individual except what we find here. He apparently was a traveling companion of Paul and presumably had ministered alongside him. There is no verb in this clause or the next, making these clauses dependent upon the previous "has . . . gone" (ἐπορεύθη). They are not also dependent upon "has deserted" (ἐγκατέλιπεν), for that refers only to the actions of Demas. By "Galatia" Paul probably means the Roman province by that name (in modern Turkey) where he had spent time establishing churches (Acts 16:6; 18:23). Some later manuscripts change it to Gaul (*Gallia*, modern France), but this seems unlikely to be accurate, even though that region was at times referred to as "Galatia" in the ancient world.[58] Did he also defect from faith and run from the front lines of ministry, like Demas had? Or was he redeployed by the Apostle to a needed ministry in Galatia? The latter seems more likely, given that the words about Titus follow the same pattern.

Titus is the third person Paul makes mention of. Again the reading is literally, "Titus to Dalmatia" (Τίτος εἰς Δαλματίαν). "Dalmatia" was a Roman province situated along the eastern coast of the Adriadic Sea, directly across from Italy (modern Croatia, Bosnia, and Herzegovina).[59] Assuming that 2

---

[58] Knight, 465.
[59] Mounce, 590.

Timothy is Paul's last letter, and thus written after the letter to Titus, it means that Titus left his ministry in Crete (Titus 1:5) and moved on to Dalmatia for further ministry. Paul had asked him to join him in Nicopolis (3:12) from which Dalmatia might be reached. Apparently he had done so, then either stayed on or returned there at a later point.

It is highly unlikely that Titus was to be counted among those who fled the Apostle in his hour of need. Paul seems simply to be reporting the fact that he and Crescens have gone on to other fields of service, very likely at the bidding of Paul himself. The primary point is that, for a variety of reasons, Paul is alone (except for Luke, v.11) and this provides the incentive for his pleading request for Timothy's visit (v.9).

Digging Deeper:

1. Isn't Jesus enough? Why was Paul so desperate for Timothy to come to him in prison?
2. What does Paul's longing for Timothy's fellowship tell us about how God often ministers His grace to us in our most desperate circumstances?
3. How do you think the irony of the defection of Demas for "this present world" as the Apostle was about to leave "this world" through martyrdom affected Paul?

4:11 Only Luke is with me. Pick up Mark and bring him with you, for he is useful to me for service.

In contrast to those who have departed from Paul for one reason or another (v.10), Paul says, "Only Luke is with me" (Λουκᾶς ἐστιν μόνος μετ' ἐμοῦ). Luke was likely a Gentile who had come to faith in Christ through Paul's witness. He traveled extensively with the Apostle Paul in his missionary journeys (note the "we" sections of Acts; e.g., Acts 16:10ff) and had been with Paul in his first Roman imprisonment (Col. 4:14; Philem. 24). He was a physician (Col. 4:14) and likely was of great help to Paul in that regard. He was a learned man, capable of intricate research and writing (Luke 1:1-4; Acts 1:1). He was a trusted and loyal friend and co-laborer of the Apostle, thus "Only" (μόνος) should not be read with any sense of derision behind it. Luke never mentions himself in either his writing of the Gospel of Luke or in Acts. He seems to have been the epitome of a faithful, loyal friend and co-worker. It is a warm and reassuring word that Paul speaks of him here.

Paul's word here concerning Luke reveals that his "all" of v.16 (cf. the "all" of 1:15 and the immediate commendation of Onesiphorus in 1:16-18) will need at least some qualification. Some have seen an inconsistency with Paul's later greetings from several individuals and "all the brethren" (v.21). It is likely, however, that they represent believers from the church in Rome and that Paul is presently speaking about those who typically traveled and ministered alongside him in his missionary endeavors.

It has been suggested that perhaps Luke served as the amanuensis of this letter. This is a possibility, but only a conjecture.

It is a surprising command we meet next: "Pick up Mark and bring him with you" (Μᾶρκον ἀναλαβὼν ἄγε μετὰ σεαυτοῦ). The second person singular present tense imperative "bring" (ἄγε) commands Timothy personally to take up this action. The accompanying aorist participle "Pick up" (ἀναλαβὼν) may have some imperatival force or may describe antecedent action (i.e., "having picked up Mark, bring him with you").[60]

In contrast to Luke's loyal faithfulness, Mark had previously proven to be unreliable. He had been chosen to travel with Paul and Barnabas on their first missionary journey (Acts 13:5). Yet not long later he deserted Paul and Barnabas and returned to Jerusalem (13:13). At the beginning of the second missionary journey, Barnabas's insistence in bringing him along again led to a division between himself and Paul (15:37-39). Whether this was because of Barnabas's heart as an encourager (4:36) or because Mark was his cousin (Col. 4:10), we do not know. It is not until over a decade later that we hear again of Mark, at which time Paul's opinion of him has changed and he speaks of him positively

> **Ministry Maxim**
>
> A failure in faithfulness does not have to equal eternal uselessness.

(Col. 4:10; Philem. 24). Mark was with Paul in his first Roman imprisonment.

Now in his second imprisonment in Rome, the Apostle desires Mark to be with him once again. His stated reason ("for," γάρ) is that "he is useful to me for service" (ἔστιν γάρ μοι εὔχρηστος εἰς διακονίαν). The present tense of the verb speaks of the continual nature of Mark's value. The dative first person personal pronoun "to me" (μοι) speaks of the personal nature of such service. However, the use of the noun "service" (διακονίαν) has been used by Paul to describe both his ministry (1 Tim. 1:12) and Timothy's (2 Tim. 4:5) and may indicate that a more general usefulness in Gospel ministry is intended, instead of personal attendance to Paul in his need. The adjective "useful" (εὔχρηστος) is one used only by Paul in the NT and by him only three times. The word refers to the serviceable nature of someone.[61] He used it in 2:21 to speak of the one who has fully

---
[60] Mounce, 591.
[61] Rienecker, 649.

dedicated himself to God and has thus become "useful to the Master" (εὔχρηστον τῷ δεσπότῃ). He also uses it to commend Onesimus—a runaway slave who has now been converted—to his master, saying he "formerly was useless to you, but now is useful [εὔχρηστον] both to you and to me" (Philem. 11).

Paul clearly found room for grace after failure—both for Onesimus and Mark. Mark had overcome his failure and recaptured his position as a "helper" (Acts 13:5) to Paul in his ministry. In Mark's case he stands here as a hopeful contrast to the defector Demas (v.10). Perhaps there is yet room for repentance and restoration (2 Tim. 2:24-26)!

4:12 But Tychicus I have sent to Ephesus.

The first word we hear of Tychicus (Τύχικον), he is part of the party traveling with Paul back to Jerusalem with the famine relief collection (Acts 20:4). There we learn he was "of Asia," presumably referring to the Roman province of Asia Minor. At the close of Ephesians Paul makes mention of him again, calling him "the beloved brother and faithful minister in the Lord" (Eph. 6:21). He probably carried Paul's letter to the Ephesians and was to inform them about Paul's circumstances (vv.21-22). He had been with Paul when he met with the Ephesian elders along the journey to Rome (Acts 20:4). He was thus well-known to the Ephesian church by the time Paul wrote 2 Timothy and sent him to them again. Paul similarly referred to him as a "beloved brother and faithful servant and fellow bond-servant in the Lord" when he wrote to the Colossians (Col. 4:7). He was entrusted with the responsibility of returning the newly converted runaway slave Onesimus to his master and the church in Colosse (4:9). These latter two references would make Tychicus a veteran of Paul's first Roman imprisonment. He appears to have been in the running to fulfill a similar role of service in Titus's regard, for he similarly wrote to him saying, "When I send Artemas or Tychicus to you, make every effort to come to me at Nicopolis, for I have decided to spend the winter there" (Titus 3:12).

> **Ministry Maxim**
>
> There's always a place in God's service for those who do His will without recognition.

Clearly this was a man of outstanding character, loyalty and faithfulness. It is little wonder that Paul chose him to relieve Timothy so he could travel to Rome to be with the Apostle. In all likelihood, he was the courier of the letter of 2 Timothy on his way.

The verb "I have sent" (ἀπέστειλα) is in the aorist tense, pointing to past time not from the vantage point of the time of Paul's writing, but from the time of Timothy's reading the letter. The word is the verbal form of the noun "apostle." It has the sense of sending another on a mission and vesting them with authority.

Why would Paul use the conjunction "But" (δέ)? It normally functions as an adversative, but what is being contrasted here? It would seem that Tychicus's commission to Ephesus is contrasted with the command for Timothy to bring along Mark who would be useful to Paul in service (v.11). Given Tychicus's absence from Paul's presence to relieve Timothy in Ephesus, he would need someone (Mark) to take his place in serving the Apostle's commands in Rome. It is clear that individuals such as Mark and Tychicus were trusted and true servants who would carry out the bidding of the Apostle, but they did not hold the same place of personal intimacy with Paul that Timothy enjoyed.

As a long-time and faithful companion and fellow-minister of the Apostle Paul, Tychicus demonstrated humility in this assignment. When the Apostle longed for Timothy—a peer of Tychicus—and was willing to forfeit the presence of Tychicus to gain Timothy's fellowship, he appears not to have balked in fulfilling the wish of the Apostle. Would that all God's people could demonstrate such loyalty, love and humility in the cause of Christ!

We thus have exemplified in these men three portraits of godly servanthood: Luke, the faithful, enduring partner in ministry; Mark, the repentant, restored servant; Tychicus, the selfless, humble servant.

> **Digging Deeper:**
> 1. Who is a "Luke" to you—someone faithful, loyal and always at your side for service? What word of encouragement or thanks can you share with them today in view of their partnership in ministry?
> 2. Who is a "Mark" to you—someone who has failed, but has repented and now proves capable and valuable? How can you affirm them and their worth to Christ, to His mission and to you?
> 3. Who is a "Tychicus" to you—someone willing to serve, even if they are not recognized or honored as your "right hand man"? Is there a way you can lift them up and honor them?

4:13 When you come bring the cloak which I left at Troas with Carpus, and the books, especially the parchments.

The expression "When you come" (ἐρχόμενος) is the translation of but one word, a present tense participle used in a temporal way. The form could be either the middle or passive voice. The middle seems the more likely, giving a meaning of something like "as you are moving yourself along" on the way to Rome. The main verb is the imperative "bring" (φέρε). The present tense of the command means to undertake action continually, since once Timothy picked up the materials he would have to keep on bringing them until he reached Paul in Rome.

The Apostle names three items he wished for Timothy to bring to him. The first is "the cloak" (τὸν φαιλόνην). Rienecker says that this was "a large, sleeveless outer garment made of a single piece of heavy material w[ith] a hole in the middle through which the head was passed. It was used for protection against cold and rain, particularly in traveling."[62] This item of clothing had been "left at Troas with Carpus" (ὃν ἀπέλιπον ἐν Τρῳάδι παρὰ Κάρπῳ). Just when this took place is not certain, though perhaps the Apostle passed through Troas after his visit to Crete (Titus 1:5, note Paul "left" Titus on Crete) before being rearrested and placed in the prison in Rome. The verb "left" (ἀπέλιπον) is used by Paul only three times, all of them in the PE. It is used in v.20 to describe his leaving Trophimus sick in Miletus and in Titus 1:5 to describe his leaving Titus in Crete. Paul was apparently assuming the route of Timothy's journey from Ephesus to Rome. He would likely have traveled on foot from Ephesus northward to Troas, where he would have collected Paul's things. From there he would have crossed over to Greece, following the Egnatian Way to Dyrrachium, and then would have sailed to Brundisium. From there he would have completed the trip on foot to Rome.[63] We know nothing more of this Carpus than what we learn here, but he was obviously known well by both Timothy and Paul. Nor are we clear as to why these items would have been left in his possession. Perhaps Paul was rearrested while in Troas and was taken in such haste that personal items such as these were not able to be brought along.

> **Ministry Maxim**
>
> It's never too late for reading and learning.

Paul also ("and," καὶ) wanted Timothy to bring "the books" (τὰ βιβλία). Those "books" would have been in the form of scrolls, for it was not until later that written works began to be bound in the fashion we know them. Just what these volumes contained is a matter of speculation. There were among their number, however, some that were more valuable to Paul than others, thus he says "especially the parchments" (μάλιστα τὰς μεμβράνας). The "books" were probably made of papyrus, a cheaper method of manufacture made from the papyrus plant. The "parchments" would have been more expensive, having been made from the hides of animals. This material was more durable and was

---

[62] Rienecker, 649.
[63] Hiebert, *Second Timothy*, 118.

reserved for writings deemed to be of greater value. Paul marks these "parchments" off by the use of the adverb "especially" (μάλιστα). It is the superlative of the adverb μάλα and most commonly means something like chiefly, most of all, or above all.[64] It may be used, though less commonly, to narrow the description of what has already been mentioned. Here, then, the "parchments" would be a more particular description of "books" (i.e., "bring me the books, by that I mean the parchments"). Either could apply here, but the former sense seems the more likely.[65] In view of Paul's special interest in these "parchments," it seems likely—though it is still a matter of some conjecture—that these would have included personal copies of the OT Scriptures (cf. 3:15-16) and perhaps even some early copies of the accounts of Jesus' life and ministry.

This simple verse reminds us of two basic lessons. First, *physical comforts are not inherently unspiritual*. Paul had faced severe trials for Christ which included extreme physical suffering (e.g., 2 Cor. 11:23-28). He had counted the cost of physical hardship and even death (2 Tim. 4:6), but, with winter coming on (v.21), Paul was not afraid to ask for a coat to keep himself warm. Second, *intellectual stimulation is not inherently impractical*. Paul wanted to keep on learning right to the end. Even with his mobile, itinerate lifestyle, Paul was a reader. Paul was conversant with Greek poets and writers. When in Athens (Acts 17:28) he quoted Aratus of Soli in Cilicia (ab. B.C. 270) who has these exact words in his *Ta Phainomena*. Cleanthes, a Stoic philosopher (300-220 B.C.), had written similar words in his *Hymn to Zeus*. In 1 Corinthians 15:32 the Apostle quotes from Menander and in Titus 1:12 he quotes Epimenides. J. Rendel Harris claims he finds allusions in Paul's letters to Pindar, Aristophanes, and other Greek writers.[66] And, as has been advanced already, surely among these "books" and "parchments" were the beloved Scriptures, which Paul would pour over in search of strength from the Lord as his final day approached.

> **Digging Deeper:**
> 1. Why would Paul want reading material if he knows he is soon to die? What does this tell us about the place and value of ongoing learning?
> 2. What does Paul's facility in the Greek poets and philosophers tell us about the breadth of his personal reading? What might this suggest for our personal reading habits?

---

[64] Thayer, 387.
[65] BAGD, 489.
[66] Robertson, 3:289.

4:14 Alexander the coppersmith did me much harm; the Lord will repay him according to his deeds.

Just exactly who this "Alexander" (Ἀλέξανδρος) was is difficult to say. He is identified here simply as "the coppersmith" (ὁ χαλκεὺς). The word came also to describe workers in other metals as well. This does not aid us much in making an identification of the man. Others by the same name are mentioned in Acts 19:33 and 1 Timothy 1:20. It seems unlikely that this individual would have been the former, but there is some possibility that he could have been the latter. There he was paired with a Hymenaeus when they were "handed over to Satan, so that they will be taught not to blaspheme." This is likely the same Hymenaeus that is mentioned again in 2 Timothy 2:17, but is now paired with a Philetus. Perhaps, if we are to suppose him to be the same Alexander as in 1 Timothy 1:20 (which is by no means certain), following the excommunication of these two, Alexander left Ephesus—thus Hymenaeus is paired with someone else in 2 Timothy—and became an antagonist against Paul in another place. It is possible that he was in Troas (v.13) and brought charges against the Apostle Paul (a possible meaning of the verb "did") there which led to his arrest and current imprisonment. This could explain the mention of him here, since Paul had just spoken of Troas. This is speculative, of course, and in the end the designation of him as "the coppersmith" may just tell us that this is an entirely different Alexander, whose best identification is his occupation, not some past conflict with the Apostle.

Whoever Alexander was, Paul could say he "did me much harm" (πολλά μοι κακὰ ἐνεδείξατο). The attack had been personal ("me," μοι) and intense ("much," πολλά). The rendering "did" (ἐνεδείξατο) is a weak translation of the verb. It means "to show" or "to demonstrate," and is often used in legal contexts to mean "to inform against" another person.[67] If this latter sense is intended, it may mean that Alexander was responsible for Paul's most recent arrest or had presented evidence at his first defense (v.16) that swayed the decision against the Apostle. The aorist tense points to a definite episode in the past; it is found only in the middle voice in the NT.

> **Ministry Maxim**
>
> Vengeance belongs to the Lord; let Him handle evildoers.

That which Alexander did is called "harm" (κακά). The word means "evil," though its exact nuance often depends upon the context and it can have a broad range of meaning. No doubt "harm" is a good rendering here, if it is understood to have sinister overtones. The nature of this "harm" is made more specific in the next verse ("he vigorously opposed our teaching").

That this "harm" was indeed evil is evident in that Paul

---

[67] Fee, 296.

immediately adds, "the Lord will repay him according to his deeds" (ἀποδώσει αὐτῷ ὁ κύριος κατὰ τὰ ἔργα αὐτοῦ). This may well be an allusion to Psalm 62:12, though the thought is expressed elsewhere in the OT as well (e.g., Job 34:11; Psa. 28:4; Prov. 24:12; Jer. 17:10; 32:19; Ezek. 18:30). The notion of judgment based upon one's actions is thoroughly Pauline (cf. Rom. 2:6; 1 Cor. 3:8; 2 Cor. 5:10; and cf. Matt. 16:27; Rev. 2:23; 20:12; 22:12). The verb "will repay" (ἀποδώσει) is in the future tense, emphasizing the certainty of the event. Some manuscripts have the optative, which would make this an imprecation against Alexander. However, the manuscript support is not in favor of the optative.[68] This is the same verb Paul has just used in v.8 ("will award"), setting up a contrast between Paul's expected reward and this man's judgment. Paul leaves the judgment to God, but knows that, whatever this earthly court decides, his heavenly Judge will render a just verdict at the last. Indeed, here Paul calls Him simply "the Lord," but in v.8 He is "the Lord, the righteous Judge."

4:15 Be on guard against him yourself, for he vigorously opposed our teaching.

While in the future God will judge Alexander (and all like him), the Apostle commands Timothy in the present, "Be on guard against him yourself" (ὃν καὶ σὺ φυλάσσου). A more literal translation would be "whom also you be on guard [against]," with the relative pronoun "whom" (ὃν) connecting back to the previous clause. The imperative "Be on guard" is in the present tense, demanding continuous, vigilant action. The verb has been used in this letter to speak of God's ability to guard what has been entrusted to Him (1:12) and Timothy's responsibility to guard the treasure entrusted to him by God (1:14). Here the middle voice indicates that Timothy is to guard himself. That we may rest in God's ultimate judgment of Gospel opponents is true (v.14), but in addition ("also," καί) we must take steps to guard ourselves in the present time before that judgment is handed down. This is a personal (σύ) responsibility we each must exercise.

> **Ministry Maxim**
>
> Trust God to protect you, but keep your eyes open!

The reason ("for," γάρ) is stated at the end of the sentence, "he vigorously opposed our teaching" (λίαν γὰρ ἀντέστη τοῖς ἡμετέροις λόγοις). The verb "opposed" (ἀντέστη) was used in 3:8 to describe the resistance Jannes and Jambres brought against Moses. Here Alexander is placed in the same class. In the NT the word has the middle sense of "set oneself against, oppose, resist, withstand."[69] The aorist tense points to a definite encounter in the past. The action of the verb is

---
[68] Hiebert, *Second Timothy*, 120.
[69] BAGD, 67.

intensified by the adverb "vigorously" (λίαν), which is thrust forward for emphasis.[70] It has the general sense of "very (much), exceedingly" and here may have the meaning "vehemently."[71]

Specifically it was "our teaching" (τοῖς ἡμετέροις λόγοις) which was opposed. A more literal rendering would be "our words." This could be a reference to Paul's apostolic "teaching," as the NASU indicates. Or it could point to the words Paul offered in his defense at his first hearing (v.16). In the PE when the plural form λόγοις is used, it tends to be used more in the former sense (1 Tim. 4:6; 6:3). That these were "our" (ἡμετέροις) words, rather than simply Paul's, would add further support to this view. However, given the immediate context (vv.16-17), the latter is probably the intention here. In that case the "our" is a literary "we."[72] This, then, would mean that Alexander may have been the one who brought the charges against Paul which led to his arrest. He may, then, have appeared in court with a well-prepared and well-argued case which led to Paul's continued imprisonment and impending execution.

> ### Digging Deeper:
> 1. How are we to reconcile Paul's expectation of Alexander's judgment (v.14) with his instructions in 2:25-26?
> 2. How would you answer the objection, "Paul's stance toward Alexander is ungracious and unforgiving"?
> 3. In what sense must we trust the Lord to guard us from those who oppose the Gospel and in what sense must we protect ourselves (v.15)?

4:16 At my first defense no one supported me, but all deserted me; may it not be counted against them.

Paul reflects back now upon what happened "At my first defense" (Ἐν τῇ πρώτῃ μου ἀπολογίᾳ). The noun "defense" (ἀπολογίᾳ) was a legal, technical term for the case the defense presented in the face of charges brought in court. From this noun we derive our word *apologetics*. In Acts 22:1 the word is used to describe the speech Paul made in Jerusalem after his arrest (vv.1-21). The addition of the adjective and the definite article (lit., "the first," τῇ πρώτῃ) probably makes this a reference to a preliminary stage of the legal process through which Paul (μου, "me") would have had to pass.

---
[70] Knight, 468.
[71] BAGD, 473.
[72] Mounce, 594.

At this critical stage, when the tenor of the proceedings and the direction of their outcome would be set, Paul says, "no one supported me" (οὐδείς μοι παρεγένετο). This compound verb is made up of παρά ("by") and γίνομαι ("to stand"). It can mean simply "come," "arrive," or "be present." But here it has the sense of "stand by," or "come to the aid of."[73] The aorist tense points to a definite past action. The middle voice means something like "did not bring himself to my aid." The singular form means that Paul is looking at each possible supporter individually and laying the blame personally at each one's feet. The rejection was personal ("me," μοι) and total ("no one," οὐδείς).

Indeed, Paul added, "but all deserted me" (ἀλλὰ πάντες με ἐγκατέλιπον). The strong adversative ("but," ἀλλά) reveals the sense of utter abandonment Paul felt. Again the accusation is sweeping ("all," πάντες) and personal ("me," με). The verb "deserted" (ἐγκατέλιπον) is the same one used to describe Demas (v.10). It is now broadened out and made a universal statement. The plural forms signal that now his mind is sweeping the crowd of possible supporters. Of course, Paul's "all" is not universal, for Luke (v.11) and Tychicus (v.12) were still with him as he wrote, as well as at least some Christians from Rome (v.21). It is possible that Luke and Tychicus had not yet arrived when the preliminary hearing took place and that the Roman believers distanced themselves from Paul. But perhaps he thinks of others who might have rendered some weighty verbal testimony in his defense and those with him were not deemed sufficient as such witnesses in that cause.

Despite these disappointments and desertions, Paul is not bitter. In closing, he adds: "may it not be counted against them" (μὴ αὐτοῖς λογισθείη). The verb "counted against" (λογισθείη), a favorite of Paul, is an accounting term that means to reckon or to place to one's account.[74] The optative mood with the negative particle (μὴ) casts this as a

> **Ministry Maxim**
>
> Never excuse sin, but seek every way possible to extend mercy.

negative wish of the Apostle. The passive voice indicates that Paul is looking to God not to reckon the failures against these brothers. The aorist tense looks to that day in which the Lord will judge the hearts and actions of all (vv.1, 8).

Note the marked difference in Paul's attitude toward an obvious enemy ("the Lord will repay him according to his deeds," v.14) and his sentiments toward brothers who had failed him ("may it not be counted against them"). The former is not bitterness, but the intentional decision not to take their fate into his own hands, but to trust them to God. The latter is not excusing sin, but seeking divine mercy.

---

[73] BAGD, 613.
[74] Rienecker, 650.

Indeed, Paul echoes the words of the martyr Stephen, whose prayer he heard as he held the coats for his murderers (Acts 7:58), "Lord, do not hold this sin against them!" (v.60). And Stephen's words had been but an echo of His Lord's own prayer from the cross, "Father, forgive them; for they do not know what they are doing" (Luke 23:34).

4:17 But the Lord stood with me and strengthened me, so that through me the proclamation might be fully accomplished, and that all the Gentiles might hear; and I was rescued out of the lion's mouth.

In contrast ("But," δὲ) to the failures of earthly friends (v.16) is the utter faithfulness of "the Lord" (ὁ . . . κύριός). Five times in this chapter Paul makes reference to "the Lord" (vv.8, 14, 17, 18, 22). The context and combination of these makes clear it is Christ who is in view. He "stood with me" (μοι παρέστη), says Paul. The basic meaning of this compound verb is "to place beside" (παρὰ, "beside" and ἵστημι, "to place"), but here it is used intransitively and has the somewhat specialized meaning of "to come to the aid of, help, stand by . . . someone" (cf. Rom. 16:2).[75]

In addition (καὶ, "and"), Paul says, Christ "strengthened me" (ἐνεδυνάμωσέν με). The verb is a compound, made up of the preposition ἐν ("in") and the verb δυναμόω ("strengthen"). Paul used it earlier when he commanded Timothy, "be strong in the grace that is in Christ Jesus" (2:1; cf. imperatival form in Eph. 6:10). Paul earlier used the verb to tell Timothy he thanked the Lord "who has strengthened me, because He considered me faithful, putting me into service" (1 Tim. 1:12). And he used it in his first imprisonment to declare, "I can do all things through Him who strengthens me" (Phil. 4:13).

Here the aorist tenses of both verbs recall a definite event when the Lord appeared and strengthened the Apostle. How literally does the Apostle mean "the Lord stood with me"? Is this a figurative way of saying, "He drew near me spiritually"? Or did Jesus make a more tangible manifestation? On two other occasions, while he was in prison, Jesus appeared to Paul. The first was while still in Jerusalem, ". . . the Lord stood at his side and said, 'Take courage; for as you have solemnly witnessed to My cause at Jerusalem, so you must witness at Rome also'" (Acts 23:11). Later, while caught at sea in the deadly storm that overtook their ship, Paul told the crew, ". . . this very night an angel of the God to whom I belong and whom I serve stood before me, saying, 'Do not be afraid, Paul; you must stand before Caesar; and behold, God has granted you all those who are sailing with you'" (Acts 27:23-24). It is, therefore, not unreasonable to believe that Paul is referring here to a literal appearance of Jesus.

---
[75] BAGD, 628.

On the other hand, in view of Jesus' prediction of His disciples being dragged before Gentile kings as a witness (Matt. 10:17-18) and His promise that the Spirit would give them the words to say at such a time (vv.19-20), he may be referring to the inward work of His Spirit in his own life at that critical time.

> **Ministry Maxim**
>
> It is when others disappoint us that we come to know the faithful Christ most profoundly.

The next clause states the purpose ("so that," ἵνα plus the subjunctive verbs) for which the Lord stood with Paul, "through me the proclamation might be fully accomplished" (δι' ἐμοῦ τὸ κήρυγμα πληροφορηθῇ). When speaking of "the proclamation" (τὸ κήρυγμα), Paul used a word that refers to that which a herald is charged with proclaiming. The definite article designates this as the singularly important and authoritative message of the Gospel. The verb "might be fully accomplished" (πληροφορηθῇ) is used only five times by Paul (elsewhere only in Luke 1:1), two of those here in 2 Timothy. Paul has just used it to command Timothy to "fulfill your ministry" (4:5). Now the Apostle says that the Son of God Himself has been enabling him to do that very thing in his own ministry.

When Saul was first struck down by the Lord on the road to Damascus, Ananias was commanded by the Lord, "Go, for he is a chosen instrument of Mine, to bear My name before the Gentiles and kings and the sons of Israel; for I will show him how much he must suffer for My name's sake" (Acts 9:15-16). Now, standing in the heart and capital of the Gentile world, having had a preliminary trial before the Emperor or one of his designates, and awaiting the final stage of that trial, Paul saw that the last step of fulfilling that original commission was being fulfilled. Here the aorist tense of the verb signals Paul's arrival at the appointed end of that divine commission. The passive voice indicates that "the proclamation" has been acted upon by Paul in the power of God; it didn't fulfill itself.

Paul adds ("and," καὶ) a second prong to the purpose statement. This purpose is "that all the Gentiles might hear" (ἀκούσωσιν πάντα τα ἔθνη). The καὶ could be epexegetical (i.e., "namely"), indicating that the Gentiles' hearing is specifically what he was referring to by "the proclamation might be fully accomplished."[76] The exact phrase "all the Gentiles" (πάντα τα ἔθνη) is found in God's original promise to Abraham (Gal. 3:8; quoting Gen. 12:3, cf. 18:18; 22:18; 26:4). It is also found in the Great Commission passages of Matthew 28:19 and Luke 24:47 (cf. Mark 13:10). The phrase also came from Paul's pen when he wrote to the believers in the city of Rome (Rom. 15:11; 16:26). As the Apostle to the Gentiles (Rom. 11:13; 1 Tim. 2:7), the proclamation of the Gospel to all

---

[76] Mounce, 596.

nations was the benchmark of the completeness of his personal ministry as well as the redemptive purposes of God in Christ. The verb "might hear" (ἀκούσωσιν) is in the aorist tense, pointing to an eventually fulfilled task. The subjunctive mood matches that of the previous verb and holds these two clauses together as two expressions of the same purpose. Since Paul's original call was tied directly to preaching the Gospel to "the Gentiles and kings" (Acts 9:15), it is reasonable to believe that he stood before Nero himself, the king of the greatest Gentile power in the world, at his "first defense" (v.16) and thus is able to say that his commission has been completed. Oh that we could have record of Paul's words on this occasion!

One more clause adds ("and," καὶ) that on top of the fact that Paul not deserted, he was delivered: "I was rescued out of the lion's mouth" (ἐρρύσθην ἐκ στόματος λέοντος). The verb "rescued" (ἐρρύσθην) was used to describe the Lord's perfect record in past deliverances from danger (2 Tim. 3:11) and will be used to describe Paul's ultimate deliverance into God's presence (4:18). Here it refers to the fact that Paul's preliminary hearing (v.16) did not result in his immediate condemnation and death. The phrase "out of the lion's mouth" (ἐκ στόματος λέοντος) has been variously understood as a reference to the lions of the Coliseum, Nero, the Empire and its power, and Satan himself (1 Peter 5:8). Even though there is evidence of a Caesar being referred to as a lion and that Christians were thrown to the lions,[77] it seems doubtful these are the meaning here. The picture of Daniel being rescued from the lion's mouth because of the presence of God's angel (Dan. 6:20-22) and the use of such imagery in Psalm 22:21 lends support to the notion that Paul uses a familiar phrase for rescue from extreme danger. The aorist tense of the verb looks at the singular moment of rescue at the Apostle's first hearing. The passive voice surely makes "the Lord" the One exercising the rescue upon Paul.

Digging Deeper:

1. When and how have you felt abandoned by other Christians? From your experience, what does it take to maintain toward them the same attitude Paul displayed toward those who failed him (v.16b)?
2. Do you agree or disagree with this statement: it is only when others fail us that we truly come to know God's faithfulness? Why?
3. How does knowing one's specific mission in life help with facing the end of one's life?

---

[77] Mounce, 597.

4:18 The Lord will rescue me from every evil deed, and will bring me safely to His heavenly kingdom; to Him be the glory forever and ever. Amen.

"The Lord" (ὁ κύριος) is never far from the Apostle's mind in these closing words (vv.8, 14, 17, 22). What the Lord has done in the past ("I was rescued," v.17), Paul is confident He will finally and forever do in the future: "will rescue" (ῥύσεταί). The aorist passive form of the verb in v.17 has given way to the future middle form here. Jesus used the same verb to teach His disciples to pray (Matt. 6:13) and the lesson was not lost on Paul. He had supreme confidence that the Lord would answer the prayer He Himself had solicited from His people. This rescue would be personal ("me," με) and complete ("from every evil deed," ἀπὸ παντὸς ἔργου πονηροῦ).

The expression "every evil deed" stands in contrast to "every good work" (2:21; 3:17; cf. Titus 1:16; 3:1).[78] Paul's use of the adjective "every" (παντὸς) points to every single expression of evil. He was not expecting Christ to rescue him "out of" (ἐκ) death (cf. vv.6-8) as He had at his preliminary hearing (v.17), but through death to remove him "from" (ἀπὸ) the presence of such evil.[79] This ultimate spiritual deliverance is set alongside the physical deliverance he had just experienced (v.17) and is viewed with even more wonder and appreciation. Death is not defeat, but the doorway into Christ's ultimate deliverance (cf. Phil. 1:21, 23). Deliverance from a single evil act (even death itself) cannot compare with permanent separation from all evil!

Not only will Christ deliver the Apostle *from* evil, but He also ("and," καὶ) will deliver Him *into* heaven: "will bring me safely to His heavenly kingdom" (σώσει εἰς τὴν βασιλείαν αὐτοῦ τὴν ἐπουράνιον). The same verb (σώσει, "will bring me") Paul used earlier to speak of Christ's saving work at the beginning of a believer's experience (τοῦ σώσαντος, "who has saved us"; 2 Tim. 1:9) is used here to describe final salvation into His presence forever. Salvation is fully accomplished in this life, but is not fully experienced until the next. The kingdom Paul had in view at the beginning of the chapter as he made his final charge to Timothy (4:1) is now gloriously before his mind's eye with hopeful anticipation. These are the only two places in the PE where the kingdom is mentioned. Similarly the adjective "heavenly" (τὴν ἐπουράνιον) is used only here in the

> **Ministry Maxim**
>
> A day awaits you when God's greatest deliverance will not keep you *from* death, but will come *through* death.

---

[78] Fee, 298.
[79] Hiebert, *Second Timothy*, 123.

PE. This adjective marks off the nature of Paul's hope as distinct from the grim nature of his present realities.[80] As his final exit from this life draws near, Paul has his heart set upon a better life ahead.

The surpassing thrill of what is yet to come raised Paul's heart in a doxology of praise: "to Him be the glory forever and ever" (ᾧ ἡ δόξα εἰς τοὺς αἰῶνας τῶν αἰώνων). The verb ("be") is absent in the Greek text, but is rightly understood by the English translators. The pronoun "to Him" (ᾧ) ultimately finds its antecedent in "the Lord." The ascription of glory to Jesus reveals Paul's understanding of Christ's divinity. The expression "forever and ever" is more literally, "unto the ages of the ages" (cf. other Pauline usages in Gal. 1:5; Phil. 4:20; 1 Tim. 1:17). No greater expression of eternity could be found in the Greek language.

As he often did (cf. Rom. 1:25; 9:5; 11:36; 16:27; Gal. 1:5; Eph. 3:21; Phil. 4:20; 1 Tim. 1:17; 6:16), Paul caps this doxology with the solemn and emphatic affirmation "Amen" (ἀμήν). When so used it means something like "so it is," "so be it" or "may it be fulfilled."[81]

> **Digging Deeper:**
> 1. Sometimes God rescues us "out of" death and sometimes He rescues us "from" evil through death—how can we come to appreciate both acts as God's deliverance? What would have to take place in your life to come to that place?
> 2. In what sense is Christ's Kingdom both a present reality and a coming expectation? What does it mean to live in the kingdom *now*? What will it mean to live in the kingdom *then*? How does living in the kingdom now help us share Paul's anticipation of living in the kingdom more fully in the next life?

4:19 Greet Prisca and Aquila, and the household of Onesiphorus.

As he does here, Paul often closed his letters by commanding the recipients to "Greet" ("Ασπασαι) others in the Body of Christ (e.g. Rom. 16:3, 5-16; 1 Cor. 16:20; 2 Cor. 13:12; Phil. 4:21; Col. 4:15; 1 Thess. 5:26; Titus 3:15). He also often uses the indicative of this verb (cf. v.21) to convey personal greetings or those of others with him (e.g., Rom. 16:21-23; 1 Cor. 16:19-20; 2 Cor. 13:12; Phil. 4:21-22; Col. 4:10, 12, 14; Titus 3:15).

---

[80] Guthrie, 178.
[81] Thayer, 32.

On this final occasion the greetings are to go first to his old friends "Prisca and Aquila" (Πρίσκαν καὶ ᾽Ακύλαν). The Apostle first met these two when he came to Corinth. The couple had recently been expelled, along with all other Jews, from the city of Rome by Emperor Claudius (Acts 18:2). They, like Paul, were tentmakers. While in Corinth, Paul lived and worked with the couple (18:3). It seems unlikely that they were followers of Christ initially, for they are identified only as Jews. Paul would likely have used the hours of co-labor to share the Gospel, eventually seeing their hearts won to Christ. By the time Paul left Corinth, the couple had become sufficiently attached to him to depart with him for Syria (18:18). Along the route Paul left this couple in Ephesus (18:19). These two were in Ephesus when Apollos arrived and began his preaching in the city. They had become sufficiently versed in the truth that they were able to take Apollos into their home and instruct him more accurately (18:26). They were apparently still in Ephesus when Paul wrote 1 Corinthians (1 Cor. 16:19). Sometime later they were back in Rome (Rom. 16:3). Paul remarked that they had risked their lives for him and that all the churches of the Gentiles were grateful to them.

This husband and wife are always mentioned together. Luke used the diminutive form "Priscilla" (Πρίσκιλλαν), while Paul always used the more formal "Prisca" (Πρίσκαν). This may say something of the great respect of the Apostle for this woman. Their first mention places Aquila's name before that of his wife; however, in subsequent references her name is always mentioned first (except for 1 Cor. 16:19). This unusual fact has led to all manner of speculation (e.g., she had a stronger personality or she played a dominate role in their ministry), all of which is conjecture. What is clear is that their home was a vital part of their ministry (Acts 18:3, 26; 1 Cor. 16:19) and they had invested considerable time in the ministry in Ephesus. At some point they had made their way back to this capital city of Asia Minor where Timothy was shepherding the church. Paul could not send a letter without greetings to such dear friends.

> **Ministry Maxim**
>
> Develop deep friendships now, for at the close of life you'll understand their value.

Paul additionally ("and," καὶ) sends greetings to "the household of Onesiphorus" (τὸν ᾽Ονησιφόρου οἶκον). All we know about Onesiphorus is contained in 2 Timothy 1:16-18 (see the commentary there). The same question surrounds Paul's direction of greetings to this man's "household" as it did in the first chapter. It seems probable that he had died, in or had not yet returned from, his service to Paul in Rome.

4:20 Erastus remained at Corinth, but Trophimus I left sick at Miletus.

Paul, ever concerned for others, wants Timothy to have the facts about two important brothers in the Lord. He first speaks of "Erastus" ("Εραστος). This name appears three times in the NT. It is uncertain if they all refer to the same person. During Paul's ministry in Ephesus, we read, "having sent into Macedonia two of those who ministered to him, Timothy and Erastus, he himself stayed in Asia for a while" (Acts 19:22). It makes sense that the imprisoned Paul would want Timothy to know the whereabouts of one he had shared with in previous ministry. The next mention is at the close of Romans, where, writing from Corinth, Paul tells the Roman believers, "Erastus, the city treasurer greets you" (Rom. 16:23). An inscription has been found which bears the name of one Erastus who was "commissioner of public works."[82] Perhaps this was the same individual as our Erastus. Since Paul both here and there links Erastus with the city of Corinth, it seems likely—though not certain—that the name refers to the same person in both places. Some object, however, believing that a person who held the position of "city treasurer" would not be at liberty to travel in ministry with the Apostle. At first blush this seems an obstacle, but we know little about what such a position would have required or whether it refers to a post formerly held by Erastus. So, given the information we have, we might surmise that Erastus was a well-positioned person in Corinthian society (Rom. 16:23) who came to faith in Jesus Christ and showed evidence of ministry gifts. He was chosen to travel and minister both to and with the Apostle Paul and his band of missionaries (Acts 19:22). If Erastus had last been known to be with Paul, Timothy may rightly have wondered as to his whereabouts, particularly in view of Paul's present lack of support in Rome (2 Tim. 1:15; 4:10, 16).

Paul says simply that Erastus "remained at Corinth" (ἔμεινεν ἐν Κορίνθῳ). The aorist tense looks back to an action of Erastus at some indefinable time in the past. That he "remained" there seems to indicate that he (or they) had passed through Corinth, at which time Erastus chose to stay on in his hometown. We know nothing of Erastus's motives or thinking in this decision.

Next Paul makes mention of "Trophimus" (Τρόφιμον). This individual is also mentioned three times in the NT. The first is when he is listed with seven other traveling companions of Paul (including Timothy) as he left Greece and headed for Jerusalem (Acts 20:4; note the "us" in v.5 which adds Luke to the band of travelers). There he is mentioned in tandem with Tychicus (2 Tim. 4:12) and both are designated as "of Asia." He is mentioned next in Acts 21:29 and called "Trophimus the Ephesian." Thus is makes sense that Timothy, now living and ministering in the hometown of Trophimus, would appreciate news

---

[82] Knight, 476.

about this brother. In this latter context the Jews took Paul's association with this Gentile in the city of Jerusalem to imply that he had taken him unlawfully into the Temple. Trophimus thus unwittingly and unjustly became the cause of the Jews' riot and of Paul's arrest. That he apparently again became a ministry-partner and traveling companion of the Apostle after his first imprisonment speaks of both the Apostle's grace and Trophimus's value in ministry.

Regarding him, Paul tells Timothy simply, "I left [him] sick at Miletus" (ἀπέλιπον ἐν Μιλήτῳ ἀσθενοῦντα). The same verb and form was used in 4:13 to describe "the cloak which I left at Troas." Paul uses it again (the only three uses by Paul in the NT) when he tells Titus, "I left you in Crete" (Titus 1:5). The aorist, as in the first clause, looks back to an action at some indefinable point in the past. It is a compound verb made up of ἀπό ("behind") and λείπω ("to leave"). Paul left Trophimus behind because he was "sick" (ἀσθενοῦντα). The word means simply "weakness," here in the sense of bodily weakness due to sickness or disease.[83] The exact nature of the sickness will always be a matter of conjecture, but it was apparently sufficiently incapacitating to keep Trophimus from traveling the approximately 35 miles from "Miletus" (Μιλήτῳ) to his hometown of Ephesus (Acts 21:29), where Timothy was now ministering. This city had been the site of Paul's meeting with the elders of Ephesus during his journey back to Rome (Acts 20:15, 17). But now it was apparently the location of some sense of failure. Why did Paul, the great Apostle through whom the signs and wonders that marked an apostle (2 Cor. 12:12) were performed, not work healing upon this dear brother and fellow-servant of the Lord? The use of the adversative conjunction (δέ, "but") to separate the two clauses of this sentence seems to indicate that in the first case the decision to remain in Corinth was Erastus's alone, but in the second case it was Paul who decided to leave Trophimus behind in Miletus. Had Trophimus not been present up the coastline in Troas those years before when Paul raised Eutychus from the dead (Acts 20:7-12)? Did he wonder now, "Why not heal *me*?" What drama surrounded their parting and the difficult decision of the Apostle to continue on without his friend and brother? Answers will continue to elude us, but this does underscore the sovereign nature of God's decision to extend or withhold miraculous healing. Even apostles did not wield their gifts at their whim, but had to bow to the will of God and depend not only upon the power of the Holy Spirit, but upon His leading as well.

> **Ministry Maxim**
>
> Ministry gifts depend not only upon the power of the Holy Spirit, but also upon His will and leading.

---

[83] BAGD, 115.

4:21 Make every effort to come before winter. Eubulus greets you, also Pudens and Linus and Claudia and all the brethren.

The opening imperative ("Make every effort," Σπούδασον) and the infinitive ("to come," ἐλθεῖν) are identical to those in v.9. Both are in the aorist tense, calling for immediate action. That the command is repeated underscores the urgency with which Paul makes his plea. Here the two are separated by the clause "before winter" (πρὸ χειμῶνος), whereas in v.9 the clause "to me soon" (πρός με ταχέως) followed the infinitive. Just how far away the winter was is difficult to say. Travel being what it was, an arrival in Rome, even if Timothy moved in haste, could have taken up to several months. Travel on the Adriadic Sea was shut down during the winter months, and thus haste was needed. That winter was pressing in adds understanding to why Paul wanted Timothy to bring his cloak (v.13). The dungeon was no doubt cold and offered little in the way of comfort. Paul closes the letter with the same yearning he opened it with: "longing to see you, even as I recall your tears, so that I may be filled with joy" (1:4).

> **Ministry Maxim**
>
> Dependency upon Christ alone and desire for close friends are not mutually exclusive.

The four individuals Paul now enumerates are mentioned nowhere else in Scripture. Irenaeus in the second century speaks of a Linus as bishop of Rome. Whether that individual is identical with the one mentioned here is uncertain. The assumption is that they must be Christians from Rome (the last three names are Latin[84]). Apparently Timothy was familiar with them, else Paul would likely have simply wrapped these individuals with the others subsumed under the designation "all the brethren" (οἱ ἀδελφοὶ πάντες). The first three are men, the final one ("Claudia," Κλαυδία) is a female. This may indicate that the expression "all the brethren" was not intended to designate males only, but meant something more akin to "all the believers" or "all the brothers and sisters." It is unlikely that Claudia was the only woman in the Roman church or the only one who would have been likely to send greetings to Timothy.

Some feel that these names bring doubt upon Paul's earlier comments that he was alone (vv.11, 16). Yet in v.11 the Apostle is referring to trusted ministry associates and in v.16 he probably has in mind those whose testimony might have made a difference in the outcome of his preliminary hearing. Apparently the believers in Rome were not able to render such testimony, or, even if they had been able to do so and had failed, Paul had clearly extended grace to them by this time (cf. v.16b).

---
[84] Mounce, 601.

4:22 The Lord be with your spirit. Grace be with you.

Paul here pens his final recorded words. Not surprisingly, they are in the form of a benediction. What is unusual is that he issues a double benediction. The first benediction is directed to Timothy himself (σου "your," is singular) while the second is directed more broadly, presumably to the entire church in Ephesus (ὑμῶν "you," is plural).

To Timothy Paul says, "The Lord be with your spirit" (Ὁ κύριος μετὰ τοῦ πνεύματός σου). The absent verb must be supplied by the reader. Here once again, "The Lord" is a reference to Jesus Christ (cf. vv.8, 14, 17, 18), a fact that later scribes tried to make explicit by adding the words "Jesus Christ" to some manuscripts (cf. KJV). Paul often closed his letters by asking that the grace of the Lord be with the spirit of the recipients (e.g., 1 Cor. 16:23; Gal. 6:18; Phil. 4:23; Philem. 25). Only here, however, does he issue a benediction asking that the Lord *Himself* "be with your spirit." This serves to make the benediction more personal and intimate. By "with your spirit" Paul intends a spiritual presence of Christ with Timothy, rather than a physical manifestation of Christ to Timothy (cf. v.17-18).[85]

> **Ministry Maxim**
>
> Purpose to value in life that which will prove valuable at death: the presence and grace of Christ.

The second benediction is "Grace be with you" (ἡ χάρις μεθ᾽ ὑμῶν). Here too the verb must be supplied by the reader. Note the use of the definite article with "grace" (ἡ χάρις). It is no ordinary grace that Paul seeks for Timothy, but the unique and only grace—the grace of all grace—that comes exclusively from God the Father through Jesus Christ by the power of the Spirit. The letter has opened (1:2) and now closes on the blessing of extended grace. Does the use of the plural pronoun (ὑμῶν, "you") serve to remind Timothy and us that as difficult as it can be to live with and minister to other believers, we can only really know the fullness of God's grace in such a community?

This is a common blessing by Paul, issued in earlier letters (cf. the exact expression in Col. 4:18; 1 Tim. 6:21). Paul had valued in life what would be most important at death—the reality of God's grace. In fact, these closing verses (vv.19-22) remind us that when it's all been said and done, just three things really matter: the love of friends (vv.19-21), the presence of Christ (v.22a) and the reality of grace (v.22b).

---

[85] Knight, 478.

The Pastoral Epistles for Pastors

> **Digging Deeper:**
> 1. What does this teach us about how we view relationships the closer we draw to death?
> 2. Even in the face of an imminent death, Paul was focused on others. How can this instruct us about our relationships today?
> 3. Is the Lord with your spirit today, at this very moment? How do you know?

TITUS

CHAPTER

1

1:1 Paul, a bond-servant of God and an apostle of Jesus Christ, for the faith of those chosen of God and the knowledge of the truth which is according to godliness,

This letter characteristically begins with a salutation, in this case a lengthy one—a single sentence running through verse 4 (cf. Rom. 1:1ff, the only salutation longer in the Pauline letters). The name of the author of the letter heads the text: "Paul" (Παῦλος). This is his Roman name, as opposed to Saul, his Jewish name. He likely carried both names from birth, but he appears to have used his Roman name exclusively after accepting God's call as Apostle to the Gentiles (Acts 13:9).

Here he presents himself in a twofold self-identification. First, Paul saw himself as "a bond-servant of God" (δοῦλος θεοῦ). This is the only time Paul used this exact designation, usually preferring some form of "a bond-servant of Jesus Christ" (cf. Rom. 1:1; Gal. 1:10; Phil. 1:1). The term spoke of one who sold himself into utter servitude and submission to the will of another. Paul was not shy about using it to describe his relationship to Christ. He also used it to describe others like Epaphras (Col. 4:12), Timothy (Phil. 1:1), and all who serve Christ (2 Tim. 2:24). Paul even spoke of becoming a "bond-servant" to others "for Jesus' sake" (2 Cor. 4:5). Such a radical approach to life and ministry was only appropriate given that Christ "emptied Himself, taking the form of a bond-servant" (Phil. 2:7). The word, of course, was also used quite literally (cf. Titus 2:9).

Additionally ("and," δὲ), Paul saw himself as "an apostle of Jesus Christ" (ἀπόστολος δὲ Ἰησοῦ Χριστοῦ). The word "apostle" (ἀπόστολος) refers to one sent with a message and endowed with the full authority of the sender in delivering it. Paul routinely used some form of this designation as he opened his letters (Rom. 1:1; 1 Cor. 1:1; 2 Cor. 1:1; Gal. 1:1; Eph. 1:1; Col. 1:1; 1 Tim. 1:1; 2 Tim. 1:1). While Paul probably used the term humbly as an expression marking his submission to Christ, it also likely served the reader as a reminder of the authority of the words that followed. The order "Jesus Christ" is used by Paul here in Titus three times (1:1; 2:13; 3:6), while the reverse order "Christ Jesus" (as used almost universally throughout 2 Timothy, except for 2:8) is used only once (1:4).

Paul, as he opened this letter, simultaneously saw himself as one voluntarily bowed beneath the will of God and yet as someone raised up by God and sent on a mission of the highest priority. As such he tells Titus that he serves Christ "for the faith of those chosen of God" (κατὰ πίστιν ἐκλεκτῶν θεοῦ). The preposition κατὰ ("for") with the accusative points toward the end aimed at or the goal toward which a thing tends.[1] Thus the direction and goal of Paul's entire apostleship (and thus of this letter as an expression of that ministry) is the soundness of faith (1:13; 2:2, 10), not simply of Titus himself, but of the common faith (singular form of πίστιν, "faith"; cf. v.4) of all those who belong to Christ (plural form of the adjective ἐκλεκτῶν, "chosen"). By "faith," then, Paul refers on this occasion not to a definite body of truth, but the subjective response of trust that people give to that body of truth.[2] The identical form ἐκλεκτῶν θεοῦ ("those chosen of God") is found again only in Romans 8:33: "Who will bring a charge against God's elect?" (but cf. Col. 3:12). The adjective "chosen" (ἐκλεκτῶν) is used "of those whom God has chosen fr[om] the generality of mankind and drawn to himself."[3]

To this is affixed ("and," καὶ) another clause, also governed by the preposition (κατὰ, "according to"): "the knowledge of the truth" (ἐπίγνωσιν ἀληθείας τῆς). The "truth" (ἀληθείας τῆς), here with the definite article to establish it as the unique and only truth, is a major concern of the Apostle throughout the PE (1 Tim. 2:4, 7; 3:15; 4:3; 6:5; 2 Tim. 2:15, 18, 25; 3:7, 8; 4:4; Titus 1:14). The compound noun "knowledge" (ἐπίγνωσιν) is a favorite of the Apostle and rightly speaks of a full, precise and complete knowledge.[4] In the PE the verb is regularly linked with "truth" (ἀληθείας) in the genitive form as the thing which is known (1 Tim. 2:4; 2 Tim. 2:25; 3:7; Titus 1:1).[5] Clearly the truth has definite content and distinct parameters around it.

Such truth and knowledge, however, is not merely speculative and

---

[1] Thayer, 329.
[2] Mounce, 379.
[3] BAGD, 242.
[4] Thayer, 237.
[5] BAGD, 291.

philosophical in nature; it is "according to godliness" (κατ' εὐσέβειαν). Again the preposition κατά ("according to") with the accusative points toward the end aimed at or the goal toward which a thing tends.⁶ Knowledge can be misused ("Knowledge makes arrogant," 1 Cor. 8:1b), but the purpose of a full knowledge of the truth is so that our lives may bear the mark of "godliness." The position of the definite article following the noun and preceding this prepositional phrase (ἀληθείας τῆς κατ' εὐσέβειαν) highlights that the truth in view is that which pertains to such "godliness."⁷ The noun "godliness" (εὐσέβεια) is used by Paul often in the PE, but never outside of them. It generally describes the outward, visible witness of a genuine faith in and reverence for God (1 Tim. 2:2; 3:16; 4:7, 8; 6:3, 6, 11; Titus 1:1). False teachers could, with wrong motive, try to imitate it (1 Tim. 6:5; 2 Tim. 3:5). Here, however, Paul has the genuine article in view. Truth faith, while inward and spiritual, is never invisible. It is the manifestation in appropriate life action of this fuller knowledge of the truth that was the goal of Paul's apostolic ministry generally and of this letter specifically.

> **Ministry Maxim**
>
> Deeper knowledge of God and His will stands on the other side of my trusting obedience to what He has already shown me.

Two expressions in this opening verse carry strong OT overtones. The first is "a bond-servant of God" (δοῦλος θεοῦ). The LXX uses the expression of the nation of Israel as a whole (e.g., Isa. 42:1; 43:10), and also of key leaders throughout her history (e.g., Abraham, Psa. 105:42; Moses, Josh. 14:7; Psa. 105:26; Joshua, Josh. 24:29; Judg. 2:8; David, Psa. 89:3; 2 Sam. 7:5, 8; Elijah, 2 Kings 10:10). The second expression is "those chosen of God" (ἐκλεκτῶν θεοῦ). It, too, was used in the LXX to designate both the nation (1 Chron. 16:13) and individuals such as Abraham (Psa. 105:6) and David (89:3). As such, the Apostle Paul was not setting himself in the line of a new sect, but the fulfilled faith of his Jewish forefathers and in the train of Israel's most faith-filled leaders. Taking such designations for himself sent a strong signal as to the authority he wielded as an Apostle.

Note the course that true faith runs: there is the subjective response of trust in the God of the truth which was proclaimed ("for the faith of those chosen of God"), then a fuller intellectual grasp of the truth of the Gospel ("the knowledge of the truth"), and then the resulting quality-of-life action that results from true conversion ("which is according to godliness").⁸ Trust—knowledge—godliness: this is the order of God's dealings with us.

---

⁶ Thayer, 329.
⁷ Knight, 283.
⁸ Mounce, 379; Lea and Griffin, 267.

> **Digging Deeper:**
> 1. Why do you suppose the issue of trust precedes the gaining of fuller knowledge of God and His will and ways?
> 2. What does this tell us about why we may lack the specific knowledge of God's will which we desire?
> 3. What does this say about the way to increased godliness and victory over sin?

1:2 in the hope of eternal life, which God, who cannot lie, promised long ages ago,

Another prepositional phrase continues this lengthy opening sentence. Just how this phrase relates to what precedes is a matter of some uncertainty. It may qualify "the faith of those chosen and the knowledge of the truth" in v.1. Or, like the previous prepositional phrase ("for the faith of . . ."), it may relate to "an apostle of Jesus Christ" (ἀπόστολος δὲ Ἰησοῦ Χριστοῦ). The former would mean that all of the Christian life ("the faith . . . and the knowledge of the truth," v.1) is built on the firm base of "the hope of eternal life." The latter would mean that Paul's apostleship was founded on this hope and that he was sent to spread it abroad. Both are true. The latter would be more like the opening of 2 Timothy, where Paul is an apostle "according to the promise of life in Christ Jesus" (2 Tim. 1:1). In this case it would link Paul in common expectation with "those chosen of God" (ἐκλεκτῶν θεοῦ, Titus 1:1), for whose sake he was sent as an apostle.[9] This seems the more likely usage here. The preposition (ἐπ', "in") with the dative means "that upon which a state of being, an action, or a result is based."[10] In this case that base for ministry is "the hope of eternal life" (ἐλπίδι ζωῆς αἰωνίου). Paul uses the phrase again in 3:7 where he speaks of himself along with other believers as "heirs according to the hope of eternal life." The word "hope" (ἐλπίδι) is always used in the NT for a confident expectation of something good. Paul will use it again to speak of the common anticipation of all believers: "the blessed hope" (2:13). In 1 Timothy Christ Himself is our hope (1:1). Here it is the anticipation "of eternal life" (ζωῆς αἰωνίου). The phrase refers both to life in its duration (an unending continuation into the future) and to life in its essential quality (as it has appeared out of eternity in a totally different quality and kind of experience than life as we know it on this earthly plane). As such, "eternal life" is found in knowing

---
[9] Knight, 283-284.
[10] BAGD, 287.

God and His Son (John 17:3); indeed, Christ Himself is that life (Col. 3:4).

The relative pronoun "which" (ἣν), as a feminine singular, refers back to the words "eternal life" (ἐλπίδι ζωῆς αἰωνίου), which likewise are feminine singular in form. This "eternal life" is not some happenstance experience, but was "promised" (ἐπηγγείλατο). The aorist tense looks back to an event in the past counsels of God. The middle voice demonstrates that God was moved by no one and nothing other than His own gracious nature. Indeed, John can write, "This is the promise which He Himself made to us: eternal life" (1 John 2:25).

This promise was made by "God, who cannot lie" (ὁ ἀψευδὴς θεὸς). The adjective "cannot lie" (ἀψευδὴς) is found only here in the NT. It is made up of an adjective that means lying, false or deceitful (ψευδής, cf. Acts 6:13; Rev. 2:2; 21:8) and the alpha privative (ἀ) to negate it. By positioning the adjective between the definite article and noun, Paul stressed the qualitative nature of God as incapable of lying ("The non-lying God"[11]). That this is indeed the nature of God is set forth throughout Scripture (Num. 23:19; 1 Sam. 15:29; 2 Tim. 2:13; Heb. 6:18). Contrast this quality of God with the basic character of the Cretans ("Cretans are always liars," v.12). This is the God who "promised" this hope of eternal life. And He did so "long ages ago" (πρὸ χρόνων αἰωνίων) or, more literally, "before eternal times." Does this refer to God's eternal counsels (Eph. 1:4; 2 Tim. 1:9; Rev. 13:8) or to specific promises made in time and space (albeit long, long ago) to the Jewish forefathers (Acts 13:32; Eph. 2:12; Rom. 9:4)? The exact phrase is used elsewhere in the NT only in 2 Timothy 1:9 where it is an obvious reference to eternity past ("from all eternity"). Additionally, the adjective αἰωνίων ("long") was just used earlier in the verse to describe "eternal life" (ζωῆς αἰωνίου). But even if the phrase does refer to time in this created world, the fact that the promises were made "before" (πρὸ) would set it in previous times outside of human experience.[12]

> **Ministry Maxim**
>
> The promises of life in eternity future are anchored in eternity past so I may have firm hope in the present.

In eternity past God determined to provide eternal life for those He would create and in time and space. He committed Himself in specific promises to men whom He had created. The certainty of this purpose and these promises being fulfilled in us who believe rest upon the unchanging nature of God as One who is faithful and upon the eternal purpose that stands outside of the shifting sands of this world, which so often call us to doubt.

---

[11] Robertson, 4:597.
[12] Marshall, 126.

> **Digging Deeper:**
> 1. Why is our hope of eternal life in Christ a firm and certain hope?
> 2. How does a diminished view of God rob us of the hope of His promises?
> 3. What motivated God to make such amazing promises of eternal life to us?

1:3 but at the proper time manifested, even His word, in the proclamation with which I was entrusted according to the commandment of God our Savior,

In contrast ("but," δέ) to the promise of salvation made "long ages ago" in eternity past (v.2), Paul now speaks about what God did "at the proper time" (καιροῖς ἰδίοις). Paul uses this exact phrase two other times (1 Tim. 2:6; 6:15). The word for time used in v.2 (χρόνος) can refer to broad expanses of time or the succession of time—what we might call ages of time. The word used here (καιρός) views time as an occasion or event—a favorable moment. Its plural form may well be used as a singular, gathering up the whole of our Lord's life and viewing it as a whole.[13] The adjective "proper" (ἰδίοις) speaks of that which belongs to or is peculiar to an individual or thing.[14] Who or what determined when the "proper" time was? Does this mean that the time was peculiar to God's own will and determination or that the appropriateness of the time was related more to the nature of the message itself? Surely it is the former. It refers back to v.2 where a description of God's sovereign action has already begun ("now in his own time he has made his message evident," NET). God's sovereign initiative and timing in the outworking of redemption is a common emphasis in Paul's writings (Rom. 5:6; Gal. 4:4; Eph. 1:10; 1 Tim. 2:6; 2 Tim. 1:10).

The initiative of grace was made in the unfolding ages before time was (v.2), but at a specific moment in time (v.3) God "manifested, even His word" (ἐφανέρωσεν . . . τὸν λόγον αὐτοῦ). The verb "manifested" (ἐφανέρωσεν) is one which speaks of making something known, revealing it, and making it clear and plain. The aorist tense complements the word "time" (καιρός) by making the action happen at a point in time. Paul uses the word elsewhere in similar contrasts between what happened in eternity past with the saving events worked out in time and space through Christ (Rom. 16:25-26; Col. 1:26; 2 Tim. 1:9-10).

---

[13] Guthrie, 182.
[14] BAGD, 369.

That which was made known is "His word" (τὸν λόγον αὐτοῦ). The expression sounds more like John (John 4:41; 5:38; 8:55) than Paul (this is the only occurrence of the exact expression in his writings). Yet Paul does not use the expression as a direct designation of Christ, as John does. Paul often uses the word λόγος in the PE to designate the Gospel itself (e.g., 2 Tim. 2:9-10; Titus 2:5). It is probably in that sense he intends its use here. A word is a revelation of the mind of the speaker. God's intention in eternity past (v.2) was revealed at a point in time in history. This word, says Paul, was revealed "in the proclamation with which I was entrusted" (ἐν κηρύγματι, ὃ ἐπιστεύθην ἐγώ). The "proclamation" (κηρύγματι) refers not to the act of preaching, but to the thing that is proclaimed. It was used of the authoritative message a royal herald was commissioned with as he was sent out to make the king's will and mind known. It is God who sovereignly decreed salvation in the shrouded courts of eternity (v.2) then in time and space sent his Apostle forth with the news of His gracious and saving will. This revelation was "in" (ἐν, with the dative to express manner or means[15]) this proclamation—God has confined His mighty word to the speaking of men and His salvation to the faithfulness of human agents! This "proclamation," says Paul, was specifically the one "with which I was entrusted" (ὃ ἐπιστεύθην ἐγώ). The verb's aorist tense emphasizes the singularity of the event when Paul was confronted by God and entrusted with the Gospel. The passive voice makes clear that this life and mission was not Paul's decision, but was one put upon Him by God. The emphatic pronoun "I" (ἐγώ) underscores Paul's understanding of his unique role in salvation history and of his accountability before God for this message (1 Cor. 9:17; Gal. 2:7; 1 Thess. 2:4; 1 Tim. 1:11; 2 Tim. 1:11).

> **Ministry Maxim**
>
> Time and eternity meet in the speaking of the Gospel.

Indeed, the Apostle says this stewardship was "according to the commandment of God our Savior" (κατ' ἐπιταγὴν τοῦ σωτῆρος ἡμῶν θεοῦ). The phrase is nearly identical to that in 1 Timothy 1:1. The preposition "according to" (κατ') combines both the notion of a standard by which something is determined and the reason for which something is done.[16] That standard and reason are "the commandment" (ἐπιταγὴν). The word speaks of an injunction, mandate or command.[17] It drips with authority. It is used seven times by Paul and nowhere else in Scripture. Two of those seven appear here in Titus—God commanded Paul and thus he, and his associates, are able to command others (Titus 1:3; 2:15; cf. Rom. 16:25; 1 Cor. 7:6, 25; 2 Cor. 8:8; 1 Tim. 1:1).

---

[15] Knight, 285.
[16] BAGD, 407.
[17] Thayer, 244.

The expression "God our Savior" (τοῦ σωτῆρος ἡμῶν θεοῦ) is found only in the PE, most of those here in Titus (1 Tim. 2:3; Titus 1:3; 2:10; 3:4; cf. also 1 Tim. 1:1; 4:10). The Apostle is perfectly comfortable immediately transitioning into "Christ Jesus our Savior" (v.4; 3:6). Indeed, he understands Christ to be both God and Savior (2:13). The concentration of the expression "God our Savior" in Titus and its usage here gives an early hint as to the theological tone and purpose of this letter (cf. the later emphasis on salvation in 2:11-14; 3:3-8).[18]

The Apostle's sentiments here are similar to those expressed in Romans 16:25-26 where a number of the elements of this passage are duplicated: "Now to Him who is able to establish you according to my gospel and the preaching of Jesus Christ, according to the revelation of the mystery which has been kept secret for long ages past, but now is manifested, and by the Scriptures of the prophets, according to the commandment of the eternal God, has been made known to all the nations, leading to obedience of faith."

1:4 To Titus, my true child in a common faith: Grace and peace from God the Father and Christ Jesus our Savior.

Paul uses the dative case to designate the letter as addressed "To Titus" (Τίτῳ). A Gentile by birth, Titus was likely converted by the Apostle Paul himself. He traveled with Paul and Barnabas to Jerusalem where pressure began to mount upon Paul to have Titus circumcised. Paul, however, refused (Gal. 2:1-3, 6-10). Titus played a key role in Paul's ministry to the church in Corinth (2 Cor. 2:13; 7:6, 13, 14; 12:18), particularly relating to the collection for the poor (8:6, 16, 23). Titus later shared in evangelistic ministries with Paul on the island of Crete, where he has now been left to care for the believers (Titus 1:5). He would soon join Paul in Nicopolis, after either Artemas or Tychicus arrive in Crete to take responsibility for the pastoral work of the believers (3:12). At some later date he would go without Paul into the region of Dalmatia to do pioneer evangelism (2 Tim. 4:10). He may well have eventually returned to Crete, for tradition has it that he became the first bishop of the island and died an old man there.

Here Titus is designated as "my true child in a common faith" (γνησίῳ τέκνῳ κατὰ κοινὴν πίστιν). The word "true" (γνησίῳ) generally means something like genuine or sincere (2 Cor. 8:8; Phil. 4:3), but when used literally of children it means that they are legitimate, lawful or born in wedlock. The figurative extension, which applies here, is that Titus is spiritually a genuine child of the Apostle. Paul used nearly the same expression of Timothy (1 Tim. 1:2), only here he substitutes the preposition κατὰ for ἐν, (apparently

---
[18] Marshall, 131.

for stylistic reasons only[19]) and here adds the adjective "common" (κοινήν). That Titus is designated a "child" (τέκνῳ) means not that he was immature, but signals the kind and quality of relationship he enjoys with the Apostle. This relationship is "in a common faith" (κατὰ κοινὴν πίστιν). By the addition of the adjective "common" (κοινήν) Paul puts himself on level ground with Titus—as an encouragement to Titus and as a clear signal to those who would demand that Gentile believers must conform to the ceremonial law.[20] It is an interesting word choice, for it can simply describe that which is shared together in common (Acts 2:44; 4:32) or that which is unclean (Mark 7:2, 5; Acts 10:14, 28; 11:8; Heb. 10:29; Rev. 21:27). In Paul's only other use of the word, this is how he employed it (Rom. 14:14). During the controversy in Jerusalem over whether Titus must be circumcised (Acts 11:30; 12:25; Gal. 2:1-3, 6-10) it was surely a word often on the lips of Paul's opponents, being used in this latter sense. Yet here Paul took the word out of their mouths and turned it around to place Titus beside himself (and them!) as a brother standing on level ground before the cross of Christ (cf. Jude 3).

> **Ministry Maxim**
>
> Grace is both a joy and a judgment, for at once it both elevates the humble and denigrates the prideful.

The Apostle's next expression ("Grace and peace," χάρις καὶ εἰρήνη) is classic Paul, for this combination shows up in the salutation of every one of his thirteen NT letters. In all of his letters, except the PE, "grace" is followed by the second person plural pronoun in the dative case ("grace to you," χάρις ὑμῖν) which is then followed by "and peace" (καὶ εἰρήνη). For whatever reason, in the PE the formula changes ever so slightly. And in letters to Timothy Paul adds "mercy" (ἔλεος) to make a triad of blessing (1 Tim. 1:2; 2 Tim. 1:2). See on 2 Timothy 1:2 for the meanings of "grace" and "peace."

In every letter but one, Paul made these blessings extend "from God the Father" (ἀπὸ θεοῦ πατρὸς). Only in 1 Thessalonians is the expression slightly different (1:1). However, the expression "Christ Jesus our Savior" (Χριστοῦ Ἰησοῦ τοῦ σωτῆρος ἡμῶν) is found only here in Paul. Certainly the concept is present elsewhere in his writings (Eph. 5:23; Phil. 3:20; 2 Tim. 1:10), but here in Titus the Apostle develops the theme of Christ as our Savior as he does in no other letter (1:4; 2:13; 3:6). Paul's ease with calling "God our Savior" (v.3) and in the same breath calling "Christ Jesus our Savior" (v.4) is a testimony to the deity of Christ and the full involvement of the God-head in the work of salvation.

---

[19] Knight, 286.
[20] Ibid.

> **Digging Deeper:**
> 1. Would those who lived before the time of Christ and beyond the voice of the prophets have felt that God made His revelation of salvation in Christ "at the proper time"? How about those since Christ's earthly life and ministry, but before the ease of missionary travel or the technological dispersion of the Gospel message?
> 2. What made God's time "proper"?
> 3. What does Paul's ease in going back and forth between speaking of "God our Savior" (v.3) and "Christ Jesus our Savior" (v.4) tell us of his understanding of Christ's Person and work?
> 4. How does Paul's reference to "a common faith" both dignify Titus and silence his Jewish opponents?

1:5 For this reason I left you in Crete, that you would set in order what remains and appoint elders in every city as I directed you,

Paul now begins the body of the letter. He does so by making clear his purpose in leaving Titus in Crete. The purpose statement is introduced by "For this reason" (Τούτου χάριν). The accusative form of the substantive χάρις is used as a preposition with the genitive and indicates the goal of Paul's action.[21] As it almost always does in the NT, it stands behind the word it qualifies—"this" (Τούτου). This demonstrative pronoun will in turn be expanded and explained by the ἵνα clause. The action being explained is "I left you in Crete" (ἀπέλιπόν σε ἐν Κρήτῃ). The verb (ἀπέλιπόν) is a compound word, comprised of ἀπό ("behind") and λείπω ("to leave"). Paul only used the word two other times, both in 2 Timothy (4:13, 20). The aorist tense looks back to a specific action Paul took at a time in the past.

The island of Crete holds a dominating position in the Mediterranean Sea. It was no insignificant land mass—some 157 miles long and from 7 to 30 miles across. Crete "seems marked out by its position for an important role in the history of the eastern Mediterranean. But never since an age which was already legendary when Greek history began has Crete occupied a dominating position among the powers of the surrounding continents. Internal dissensions, due in ancient times to the diversity of races inhabiting its soil . . . have kept Crete in a position of political inferiority throughout the historical period."[22] Paul was correct; the Cretans, by the admission of one of their own, were a

---
[21] BAGD, 877.
[22] Orr, 2:744.

difficult people (v.12). There had long been a strong Jewish influence upon the island and some of their Jews had been present at Pentecost (Acts 2:11). This no doubt contributed to a Judaizing controversy among the believers (Titus 1:10). Paul's initial contact with the island came during the hazardous voyage to Rome for his first imprisonment (Acts 27:7-21). Paul may have gone ashore, but would have had no time for exploration of the interior of the island. Later, after having been released from his first Roman imprisonment, he returned to the island with Titus and apparently undertook evangelistic ministries.

The purpose for having then left Titus in Crete is explained through the next clause: "that you would set in order what remains" (ἵνα τὰ λείποντα ἐπιδιορθώσῃ). The main verb, "set in order" (ἐπιδιορθώσῃ), is a compound word comprised of ἐπί ("in addition"), διά ("thoroughly"), and ὀρθόω ("to set straight").[23] It is found only here in the NT. The aorist tense views this protracted work as a single event. The middle voice may emphasize that the responsibility for the order of the Cretan church falls upon Titus alone.[24] The subjunctive mood is coupled with the ἵνα ("that") to express purpose.

That which is to be so thoroughly "set in order" is "what remains" (τὰ λείποντα). The only other time Paul uses this word is in this letter when he commands Titus, "Diligently help Zenas the lawyer and Apollos on their way so that nothing is lacking [λείπῃ] for them" (3:13). It is used intransitively to mean "to be lacking or absent, to fail."[25] The participle with the definite article makes this a substantive use: "the things that are lacking." The present tense points to the continual absence of those things. The word may be a signal that Paul was not on the island long

> **Ministry Maxim**
>
> The church can never truly be "set in order" without godly leadership.

and that, when the people were found responsive to the Gospel, he left Titus to establish them in churches.

In addition ("and," καί) to setting in order what remains, Paul left Titus to "appoint elders in every city" (καταστήσῃς κατὰ πόλιν πρεσβυτέρους). The verb "appoint" (καταστήσῃς) means to appoint or put in charge. It was used in classical Greek to describe appointment to an office or position and that sense carries over here (cf. Acts 6:3).[26] The meaning of "ordain," though attested by some,[27] seems to go beyond its meaning in the NT.[28] The subjunctive mood

---

[23] Robertson, 4:598.
[24] Mounce, 387.
[25] Thayer, 375.
[26] DNTT, 1:471-472.
[27] BAGD, 390.
[28] Mounce, 387.

pairs it with the previous subjunctive ("set in order," ἐπιδιορθώσῃ) and the conjunction ἵνα to set this off as a second prong of Paul's purpose in leaving Titus in Crete. The conjunction ("and," καὶ) might be used epexegetically to mean, ". . . to set in order what remains, namely that you appoint elders in every city" or it could be a simple connective holding the two subjunctive clauses in parallel as two separate, but related, purposes. The aorist tense views the process of finding, selecting, training and setting apart such men as a single event. The word does not tell us just *how* elders were selected and appointed, but simply that they were (cf. Acts 14:23). This speaks of a flexibility in method, but a clarity of qualification. Elders would have had to meet certain qualifications (Titus 1:6-9). They were to be plural in number ("elders," πρεσβυτέρους). And the people of the church may well have had input into the selection from among their own (cf. the use of the verb in Acts 6:3).[29] Beyond this there would have been flexibility in the process of selection.

Elders were to be appointed "in every city" (κατὰ πόλιν). The preposition may be used distributively to mean "city by city."[30] This may indicate that the communities were so small as to have only one church, the churches were so young that they would not have had time to have multiplied into several house churches in the larger cities, or that Paul appointed elders over the whole of the church in a city rather than each individual house church. Given that it appears Paul had not spent a great deal of time in Crete before leaving Titus behind to establish the church, it seems more likely that the second option is the correct one here.[31]

The word "elders" (πρεσβυτέρους) originally spoke of men of advanced age, but is surely a carry over from the Jewish roots of the church. In the synagogue, elders were the leaders. It thus came to refer to the leaders of the church rather than simply the chronological age of an individual. The terms "overseer" (ἐπίσκοπος) and "elder" (πρεσβύτερος) are both used to describe one office and are used interchangeably (Acts 20:17, 28; Titus 1:5, 7). The distinction is often made by saying that "overseers" (ἐπίσκοπος) describes the duty of the office, while "elders" (πρεσβύτερος) depicts the honor and dignity of the office.

---

[29] Lea and Griffin, 276-277.
[30] Knight, 288.
[31] Mounce (386) lists the following indicators that the church in Crete was quite young: 1) Paul "left" Titus in Crete to appoint elders, which was normally an action taken early after initial evangelism; 2) There is no discussion of the removal of bad elders, only the appointment of initial leaders; 3) The elders are required to have "believing" children (v.6), but he argues that this means "faithful" children, not necessarily "believing," which would require the church to be older; 4) Unlike 1 Timothy 3:6, Titus is not warned against choosing a newly converted man to be an elder, for presumably all of them were new converts; 5) Titus was to appoint elders, but not deacons, perhaps a signal that the church had not developed sufficiently to need this additional leadership; 6) There are no other personal allusions in the letter other than to Titus himself; it seems unlikely that the church was solely the result of Paul's ministry.

All of this, says Paul, was to take place "as I directed you" (ὡς ἐγώ σοι διεταξάμην). The verb is a compound made up of διά ("through") and τάσσω ("appoint") and has the sense of "to arrange, appoint, ordain, prescribe, give order."[32] It is a word that bespeaks authority and not suggestion (cf. 1 Cor. 7:17; 9:14; 11:34; 16:1; Gal. 3:19). The aorist tense looks back to a specific instruction delivered by the Apostle to Titus, a time and a conversation Titus should well remember. Paul's reference to "I" (ἐγώ) is emphatic, adding to the authoritative nature of the directives.

> **Digging Deeper:**
> 1. Can the church ever truly be "set in order" without godly leadership ("elders") in place? Why or why not?
> 2. What particularly does the word "elders" contribute to the understanding of what spiritual leaders in the church are to be?
> 3. Why does Paul seem more concerned with the qualifications of elders than the method of their appointment? What does this teach us?

1:6 namely, if any man is above reproach, the husband of one wife, having children who believe, not accused of dissipation or rebellion.

The sentence continues in Greek with a first class condition (εἰ with the indicative verb ἐστιν), showing action that is determined as to its fulfillment. In this case it is assumed that some men will fit the qualifications listed and that they are the ones who are to be eligible as elders. The words "any man" represent the indefinite singular pronoun τίς, and broadens the sweeping options across any and all who as individuals might fit these qualifications. The singular stands in contrast to the plural ("elders" in v.5). Elders serve together in a plurality, but stand alone as individuals as to their qualifications.

First among these qualifications is the overarching term "above reproach" (ἀνέγκλητος). The word strictly means not having been called up or arraigned before a judge.[33] It then has the sense of being without charge or accusation, and thus irreproachable.[34] It is used to describe the state in which all believers will stand before God at Christ's return (1 Cor. 1:8; Col. 1:22) and of the present character and actions of those who may lead the church as deacons (1 Tim. 3:10) and elders (Titus 1:6-7; cf. the synonym in 1 Tim. 3:2). It is used here in a sweeping, unrestricted fashion, while in the next verse it will be tied directly

---
[32] Thayer, 142.
[33] Friberg, 54.
[34] Rienecker, 623.

to being above reproach "as God's steward." The term is generally understood to serve as a leading qualification that gathers up the intent of the others that follow. This will assist in resolving some sticky interpretational issues (e.g., "the husband of one wife").

The qualifications which follow serve to explain exactly the kind of things that go into making one "above reproach." Among these are being "the husband of one wife" (μιᾶς γυναικὸς ἀνήρ). More literally it might be rendered "a one woman man." This qualification stands not only for elders (1 Tim. 3:2), but also for deacons (3:12). But just what is meant by "a one woman man"? It is obvious that this refers to a male and establishes the office of elder as a position of male leadership. Beyond this it could mean: 1) that a man must be married to be considered for church leadership, 2) that, if he is married, he must only have one wife at a time (i.e., not be a polygamist), 3) that he is not divorced, 4) that he is not divorced and remarried, 5) that he is not widowed, or 6) that he is not widowed and remarried.

> **Ministry Maxim**
>
> All true spiritual leadership begins at home.

If #1 was the Apostle's intent, it seems an unnatural way to express it. As for #2, this surely is included, but is probably not the full extent of Paul's intention. Polygamy was a rare occurrence in the pagan culture of the day and would not likely have required space in such a list. And, as Fee shows, it would not fit the nearly identical expression when applied to widows (1 Tim. 5:9).[35] However, in this case Titus would be looking for someone who does not have the encumbrance of needing to work through applying the truths of Scripture to a twisted family relationship that could develop contention between multiple wives and their children. Paul surely did not intend these words to restrict a widower from serving as an elder (#5), nor would remarriage disqualify him (#6), since elsewhere he teaches that the death of a spouse frees a believer to remarry (Rom. 7:1-3; 1 Cor. 7:8-9; 1 Tim. 5:14). This leaves the matter of whether men who have been divorced or divorce and subsequently remarried are qualified to serve as elders in the local church. Given the apparently recent nature of the evangelistic work in Crete (see footnote #31 above), there may be some doubt as to whether the more modern arguments about when a divorce took place (i.e., before or after conversion) enter into the decisions here, for all would have been far too young in the Lord to have divorces and possible remarriages that took place subsequent to conversion. But must a man live under consequences flowing from decisions made while he was an unbeliever? Whether that is the Apostle's concern here, at least at times the answer is yes. While God forgives us, He does not always

---

[35] Fee, 80.

remove from us all the consequences of our sinful past. People who argue that acts committed while an unbeliever should have no bearing upon the current lives and circumstances of a believer discount the unique nature of marriage and its intention and design as God's first and primary institution of society. Remember also, the governing qualification is that a man be "above reproach." A broken marriage and/or illicit relationships of the past may threaten his current ministry with at least strife, if not scandal, even though they were committed while unredeemed. One can foresee at least some cases in which it would not be in the best interest of the church, the Gospel ministry, nor the man and his family to have him in the office of elder.

The next qualification is "having children who believe" (τέκνα ἔχων πιστά). The word for "children" (τέκνα) specifies no gender or age. The adjective πιστά ("who believe") is at the center of the decision about just what Paul intended by these words. It is unlikely that Paul intended this to restrict childless men from eldership. But does this require that the man be held responsible for his children's decisions? The answer is yes. But just what is demanded from his children? Does the adjective mean they are *"believing* children" or *"faithful* children"? The adjective could be rendered either way, though here it seems to point to the latter. In his instructions to Timothy regarding qualifications for an overseer, Paul said, "He must be one who manages his own household well, keeping his children under control with all dignity" (1 Tim. 3:4). This would seem to support the idea that the Apostle's intention here is that an elder have "faithful children," that is to say, children who are not wild and uncontrollable (thus the next explanatory clause).[36] What is clear is that the man's Christian faith has radically affected his marriage, parenting and home life.

By way of explanation Paul adds that such children be "not accused of dissipation or rebellion" (μὴ ἐν κατηγορίᾳ ἀσωτίας ἢ ἀνυπότακτα). The phrase "not accused of" (μὴ ἐν κατηγορίᾳ) more literally would be "not in an accusation." The noun was a legal technical term for a charge or accusation. It is used only three times in the NT. Pilate, concerning Jesus, asked the crowds, "What accusation do you bring against this Man?" (John 18:29). Paul used the word to instruct Timothy, "Do not receive an accusation against an elder except on the basis of two or three witnesses" (1 Tim. 5:19). It seems likely that the restriction here is not to gossip about one's parenting, but to a more formal charge against one's children. Whether it restricted the charge to the legal courts or was intended to encourage Titus to choose men whose parenting would not become the issue in their approval as elders before the congregation is not clear. But it would seem the latter is the more likely.

---

[36] Knight, 290.

The accusation Titus is to be concerned about is first that of "dissipation" (ἀσωτίας). Paul used the word in only one other place, where he set it alongside intoxication: "And do not get drunk with wine, for that is dissipation" (Eph. 5:18a). The only other NT use is by Peter where he speaks of avoiding "the same excesses of dissipation" as the unbelieving (1 Peter 4:4). The addition of "excesses" (ἀνάχυσιν) seem to speak of overindulgence. Peter's words are in the context of sins in the realms of sex and alcohol (1 Peter 4:3). The word itself refers to one who has abandoned himself to indulgence of his senses and appetites. As such, a person has placed himself beyond the safety of clear thinking and wise choices. He has utterly given himself over to reckless moral behavior. Such a life is often marked by wanton indulgence in alcohol, drugs and sexual misdeeds.

The second part of the possible accusation against the child is that of "rebellion" (ἀνυπότακτα). Paul elsewhere uses the word to describe those unwilling to live under God's law (1 Tim. 1:9) and of those in Crete who reject the truth (Titus 1:10). It is a compound word adjoining an alpha privative (ἀ) to negate the common verb ὑποτάσσω, which means "to arrange under" and commonly speaks of being in subjection to authority. An elder's children must not, through attitude ("rebellion") or action ("dissipation"), threaten to bring disrepute upon their father, his ministry and the church he serves.

> **Digging Deeper:**
> 1. Is anyone truly "above reproach"? How then can this be the leading qualification for church leadership?
> 2. Why do you suppose the Apostle Paul began the list of qualifications for church leadership with marriage and family issues?
> 3. How do the Apostle's instructions contrast the current cultural climate in which we live?

1:7 For the overseer must be above reproach as God's steward, not self-willed, not quick-tempered, not addicted to wine, not pugnacious, not fond of sordid gain,

The explanatory γὰρ ("For") opens this new sentence and expands upon the qualifications that have begun to be enumerated in v.6. The term "elder" (πρεσβυτέρους; v.5) now becomes "overseer" (ἐπίσκοπον). The two terms are used interchangeably of the same office (e.g., Acts 20:17, 28), though they each place a unique emphasis upon it. The term "elder" speaks to the dignity of the office, while "overseer" has its function more in view. The term used here is a compound word comprised of "over" (ἐπί) and "a watchman or observer" (σκοπός). The root noun is used in the NT only in Philippians 3:14 when he employs it to say, "I press on toward the *goal* [i.e., that which one set his eye upon] for the prize of the upward call of God in Christ Jesus" (emphasis added). Thus as an "overseer" the elder is charged with watching over the whole of the congregation not only to protect the congregation as a whole and its individual members, but also to guard the purpose and mission of the church. The singular form is not intended to designate a singular office in each church, but only carries on the shift to the singular made already in verse 6 ("if any man is").

See 1 Timothy 3:2 for a comparative listing of the qualifications for elders/overseers in 1 Timothy 3 and Titus 1. Of particular note, however, in comparing the two lists is the absence here of Paul's requirement in Ephesus that such a leader not be a new convert (1 Tim. 3:6). This may well speak to how recently the evangelistic work on Crete was begun and the youth of the church there in general. There simply may not have been any converts who were not young in the Lord.

To function effectively as an "overseer" Paul says again that the man "must be above reproach" (δεῖ . . . ἀνέγκλητον εἶναι). The verb δεῖ ("must") is thrust forward in the sentence to make emphatic the obligatory nature of the qualifications. The present tense underscores that these obligations for leadership never cease to apply. Paul then repeats the noun and verb from the previous verse (though here he uses the infinitive). The Apostle uses repetition as simply another means of stressing this as the overarching requirement under which all the other qualifications are subsumed. What is new here is that such irreproachableness is applied to the elder/overseer "as God's steward" (ὡς θεοῦ οἰκονόμον). The word "steward" (οἰκονόμον) originally referred to the manager of a household or estate. His responsibility was placed upon him by the owner of the house and the "steward" was held responsible for the welfare of that household and its goods. The entire expression reminds us that the church does not belong to the overseer, but that it is a precious possession of God Himself, who has placed it on deposit under his care. One day he will give an accounting for his care of this deposit. Indeed, more than that, the "steward" himself is called "God's." God owns the "steward" (elder/overseer). We are not our own. The church does not own the elder/overseer and the elder/overseer does not own the church. Both are God's own possession.[37] The word "steward" (οἰκονόμον) is a favorite of

---

[37] Fee, 174.

Luke (12:42; 16:1, 3, 8). Paul used it of himself (1 Cor. 4:1, 2) and Peter applied it to all believers (1 Peter 4:10). The emphasis of the word is upon the accountability and authority of the one serving in this role.

Paul continues to round out the portrait of a church leader: as an "elder" he is a man of dignity standing *among* the people, as an "overseer" he is a man of leadership standing *above* the people, and as a "steward" he is a man standing *before* the people on behalf of another.

Paul now begins a series of qualifications (running through v.9; the first five stated in the negative) which define something of what it means to be "above reproach." Such a man is to be "not self-willed" (μὴ αὐθάδη). The word describes one who is stubborn, self-willed and arrogant.[38] "It is the man who obstinately maintains his own opinion or asserts his own rights and is reckless of the rights, feelings and interests of others."[39] In its only other NT usage, Peter applies it to false teachers: "Daring, self-willed [αὐθάδεις], they do not tremble when they revile angelic majesties" (2 Peter 2:10b). Such a person cannot be trusted to have either the concerns of the Lord or the welfare of the people consistently in mind. The positive quality of gentleness (ἐπιεικῆ; 1 Tim. 3:3) may be the opposite Paul is looking for here.[40]

> **Ministry Maxim**
>
> The only one a self-willed man cannot conquer is himself.

Such leaders are to be "not quick-tempered" (μὴ ὀργίλον). The word is used only here in the NT and describes one who is prone toward anger. Anger is the natural and usual response of such an individual to stress, conflict and disagreement. Such a person will not be able to promote the harmony and peace that is to characterize the local assembly of God's people (Titus 3:2; cf. 1 Thess. 5:13). He will be unable to hear and listen, for he will jump to conclusions, become offended, and be defensive. Perhaps "peaceable" (ἄμαχον; 1 Tim. 3:3) is the corresponding positive trait called for.[41]

In addition such leaders are to be "not addicted to wine" (μὴ πάροινον). Paul had stressed this same qualification when writing to Timothy (1 Tim. 3:3). The concern here is not the advisability in a given culture of total abstinence from alcoholic beverages for church leaders, but with the more obvious problem of alcohol addiction. The word is a compound made up of "beside" (παρά) and "wine" (οἶνος).[42] It thus describes one who sits too long over his wine, thus drinking to excess and becoming drunk. Every usage of the word in Hellenistic Greek or Jewish literature describes one addicted to wine.[43]

---

[38] BAGD, 120.
[39] Rienecker, 652.
[40] Knight, 291.
[41] Ibid.
[42] Thayer, 490.

Titus 1

An overseer is to be "not pugnacious" (μὴ πλήκτην). Most literally the word describes "a striker." Thus our word "pugnacious" is related to the word "pugilist" (i.e., boxer). The word describes one who wants to settle disagreement by physical force. In application it need not be limited merely to hitting, but to any form of physical intimidation or violence employed to win an argument, make a point or manipulate others. Such tactics have no place in the church of God. This word is connected with the previous one in 1 Timothy 3:3 as a qualification for eldership. The connection in both contexts of physical violence with alcohol speaks to the nature of alcohol's effects upon the human mind and underscores why its use is discouraged.

An overseer must also be "not fond of sordid gain" (μὴ αἰσχροκερδῆ). The adjective is a compound made up of "shameful" (αἰσχρός) and "gain" (κέρδος). See v.11 for the two words separated, but used in union ("for the sake of sordid gain"). Since spiritual leaders are in view, it may refer to those who bend their teaching or use their pastoral care to manipulate people of means to give gifts to them. The same obligation is placed upon deacons in 1 Timothy 3:8. The synonym ἀφιλάργυρον ("free from the love of money") is found in the list of qualifications for elders in 1 Timothy 3:3. And the term αἰσχροκερδῶς ("sordid gain") is found in reference to elders in 1 Peter 5:2.[44] Obviously the position of spiritual leadership gives opportunity for and leaves a vulnerability to such sin.

Digging Deeper:
1. What does each of the following add to the fuller picture of what local church leaders are to be and do: elder, overseer, and steward?
2. How does a "self-willed" person become evident as such to those around him?
3. How might a person be "self-willed" and yet unable to control himself regarding his anger ("quick-tempered"), alcohol ("addicted to wine"), physical responses ("pugnacious") and covetousness ("fond of sordid gain")? What does this say about the basic nature of humanity?

1:8 but hospitable, loving what is good, sensible, just, devout, self-controlled,

Five times in v.7 Paul used the negative μὴ to define what an elder/overseer *is*

---

[43] DNTT, 1:514.
[44] Knight, 292.

not. Now he employs the strong adversative ἀλλά ("but") to list positively what he *is* to be. Heading the list is "hospitable" (φιλόξενον). The Apostle included it in the list of elder qualifications which he gave to Timothy (1 Tim. 3:2). The compound word strictly means "stranger-loving," being made up of φίλος ("love") and ξένος ("strange" or "foreign"). This is an interesting shift from the more common, and perhaps more expected, brotherly-love (φιλαδελφία) which is often called for. With "hospitable" there is no payback, no family obligation, no blood-lines to make one feel obligated. There is no earthly human reason to love the stranger. Yet just such a practical expression of love for strangers is made the obligation of all believers (Rom. 12:13; Heb. 13:2). While required of all, church leaders are to lead the way in showing the body of Christ how to do so. This was a vivid and regular part of Hebrew society. Community residents were almost under obligation to take in the traveling stranger who stopped in the city for a night of rest. But hospitality has fallen on hard times in a day when privacy and individuality are valued above community.

The expression "loving what is good" is the expression of but one Greek word (φιλάγαθον). It, like the previous word, is a compound built off of the root φίλος ("love"), but this time it is coupled with ἀγαθός ("good"). It is used only here in the NT. Such a man not only does good, but delights in good wherever and in whatever form he encounters it. He "does not rejoice in unrighteousness, but rejoices with the truth" (1 Cor. 13:6). There are those "Who delight in doing evil and rejoice in the perversity of evil" (Prov. 2:14). For them, "Doing wickedness is like sport to a fool" (10:23a). But the elder/overseer is not numbered among them.

He must be "sensible" (σώφρονα). This same quality is required of elders in 1 Timothy 3:2. It is also to be true of all older men (Titus 2:2) and the older women are to teach the younger to possess this quality as well (2:5). It means prudent, thoughtful, and self-controlled.[45] It describes a person "as having ability to curb desires and impulses so as to produce a measured and orderly life *self-controlled, sensible*."[46]

The elder/overseer must also be "just" (δίκαιον). The word has a wide range of meaning, depending upon its context. It is a quality possessed perfectly only by God (2 Tim. 4:8), but which He forges in His children who walk in faith and obedience after Him. Here it probably refers to the individual as law abiding, a man who is honest, fair and good in his dealings with others.[47] Such a man is easy to do business with, is trusted in delicate matters, and unswayed by personal interest or social pressure.

---

[45] BAGD, 802.
[46] Friberg, 373.
[47] BAGD, 195.

The man who would be an elder/overseer must be "devout" (ὅσιον). The word represented a life in conformity to what God says and does. "The word describes the pious, pure, and clean action which is in accordance w[ith] God's command."[48] Once again, only God (Acts 2:27; Rev. 15:4; 16:5) and Christ (Acts 2:27; 13:34-35; Heb. 7:26) perfectly fulfill the word. It can, however, also be used in a qualified way to describe that which is offered up to Him in worship (1 Tim. 2:8). The life of the elder/overseer is to be just such a life—fully dedicated to the glory of God and brought into conformity to the will and purpose of God.

Such a man must also be "self-controlled" (ἐγκρατῆ). The adjective occurs only here in the NT, but the noun is more common. It is a compound comprised of "in" (ἐν) and "power" (κράτος). It describes one who possesses power in or over something, in this case over one's self. The noun is used of an athlete's disciplined training regime (1 Cor. 9:25). It was one of the topics of discussion between Paul and Felix when he became frightened and sent the Apostle away (Acts 24:25). It can describe mastery of one's sexual desires (1 Cor. 7:9). It ultimately is a product of the Holy Spirit's presence in one's life (Gal. 5:23) and is not a static possession of the believer, but one that must be developed more and more over time (2 Peter 1:6, 8). Leaders within the church are to be men who have consecrated themselves and their desires to God and placed them under the control of the Holy Spirit. Both "sensible" (σώφρονα) and "self-controlled" (ἐγκρατῆ) describe a self-disciplined life. Any distinction is probably to be seen in that the former has its stress upon self-control in outward relations, while the latter has more to do with mastery of one's inner urges and desires.

> **Ministry Maxim**
>
> He who would rule over others must first rule himself.

1:9 holding fast the faithful word which is in accordance with the teaching, so that he will be able both to exhort in sound doctrine and to refute those who contradict.

One additional qualification for elders/overseers is set forth in v.9 and is more fully developed than any of the others. This may well be because it prepares the way for the instruction concerning false teachers that follow in vv.10-16.

They must be men "holding fast the faithful word which is in accordance with the teaching" (ἀντεχόμενον τοῦ κατὰ τὴν διδαχὴν πιστοῦ λόγου), or more literally, "holding fast the according-to-the-teaching faithful word." The present middle [it occurs only in the middle voice in the NT] participle "holding

---

[48] Rienecker, 620.

fast" (ἀντεχόμενον) describes clinging to something, holding it fast and thus being devoted to it.[49] It is the word both Matthew and Luke use when Jesus said that no one can serve two masters, for he will cling to one and despise the other (Matt. 6:24; Luke 16:13). So the elder/overseer must choose the Word of God over the other allurements that present themselves and devotedly cling to it at all costs. The present tense underscores that this should be the habit and pattern of his life. The only other NT usage is by Paul in a different sense (1 Thess. 5:14).

That which is to be thus held to is "the faithful word which is in accordance with the teaching" (τοῦ κατὰ τὴν διδαχὴν πιστοῦ λόγου). The definite article (τοῦ) leads the way and connects with the adjective/noun combination at the end of the phrase (πιστοῦ λόγου). Between them lies the prepositional phrase, "in accordance with the teaching" (κατὰ τὴν διδαχὴν). Thus enfolding the prepositional phrase between the definite article and the adjective/noun combination puts the phrase "in accordance with the teaching" in the attributive position—stressing what "word" we are talking about. The "word" under consideration is the one which jibes with what Paul and the other Apostles have taught. This differentiates it from the content of the false teachers (vv.10-16). This conformity to the apostolic teaching is also what makes this "the faithful word" (τοῦ . . . πιστοῦ λόγου). It is "faithful" in that it is in conformity to the apostolic teaching. Similarly the adjective "faithful" (πιστοῦ) is in the attributive position between the definite article (τοῦ) and the noun "word" (λόγου). Thus "the word" (τοῦ. . . λόγου) is qualified twice—it is not just any word, but the "faithful" (πιστοῦ) one and that which distinguishes it as "faithful" is that it is "in accordance with the teaching" (κατὰ τὴν διδαχὴν).

The purpose ("so that," ἵνα + subjunctive) for so clinging to the word is now stated. That purpose is twofold ("both . . . and," καὶ . . . καὶ). These two prongs of the purpose are set forth in two present infinitives. The first purpose is "he will be able both to exhort in sound doctrine" (δυνατὸς ᾖ καὶ παρακαλεῖν ἐν τῇ διδασκαλίᾳ τῇ ὑγιαινούσῃ). Clinging to the Word of God will enable a man continually to possess ("he will be," ᾖ, present subjunctive) power ("able," δυνατὸς) that he would not have had otherwise. This power will enable him to "exhort" (παρακαλεῖν). This present infinitive is a compound word meaning "to call" (καλέω) "beside" (παρά). It can range in meaning from encourage on the softer side, to exhort on the sterner side. It is one of the essential functions of Biblical preaching (1 Tim. 6:2; 2 Tim. 4:2). Paul uses it again when he tells Titus to "speak and exhort and reprove with all authority" (2:15; cf. also 2:6). The cognate noun is used as a title for both the Holy Spirit (John 14:16, 26; 15:26; 16:7) and Jesus Christ (1 John 2:1). When

---
[49] BAGD, 73.

a man clings to the Word of God he places himself in partnership with the Author and Subject of Scripture. They come alongside of him in his role of calling others to the walk of faith. Apart from so holding to the Word of God there will be no such ability.

The exhortation is to be "in sound doctrine" (τῇ διδασκαλίᾳ τῇ ὑγιαινούσῃ). The double use of the definite articles makes particular the teaching that is under consideration. The participle is in an attributive position, designating just what doctrine is in the Apostle's view. Such doctrine is "sound" in that it is healthy. The word was used literally of physical (e.g., Luke 7:10) or mental health (e.g., 15:27). In the PE it is always metaphorically attached either to "faith" (Titus 1:13; 2:2), "words" (1 Tim. 6:3; 2 Tim. 1:13) or "teaching/doctrine" (1 Tim. 1:10; 2 Tim. 4:3; Titus 1:9; 2:1). In this context, then, the word emphasizes the truthfulness, accuracy or correctness of the doctrine. It begets health by transmitting truth and a correct view of reality.

> **Ministry Maxim**
>
> A firm grip on the Word of God is required in order to get my arms around the work of God.

The second part of the purpose statement is "to refute those who contradict" (τοὺς ἀντιλέγοντας ἐλέγχειν). The participle and its definite article are used substantively. It is a compound word made up of "against" (ἀντὶ) and "to speak" (λέγω). It is used again in 2:9 where slaves are to be "not argumentative." Paul's only other use is in Romans 10:21 when he quotes from Isaiah 65:2 and describes God dealing with "OBSTINATE PEOPLE." Such people are always on the opposite side and always have something to say about it.

The elder/overseer must be able "to refute" (ἐλέγχειν) such folk. This infinitive word means "to prove w[ith] demonstrative evidence, to convict, reprove. It is so to rebuke another, w[ith] such effectual feeling of the victorious arms of the truth, as to bring one, if not always to a confession, yet at least to a conviction, of sin."[50] Out of his eight total uses of the word, Paul employs it three times here in Titus and five total in the PE. In view of the base nature of the Cretans (v.12), Titus is to "reprove [ἔλεγχε] them severely" (v.13). Later he instructs Titus to "reprove [ἔλεγχε] with all authority" (2:15). This is one of the basic functions of preaching (2 Tim. 4:2) and a duty the elders/overseers must exact upon one another, if need be (1 Tim. 5:20). Also, half of the uses were found in instructions to the Ephesian church or their pastor (Eph. 5:11, 13; 1 Tim. 5:20; 2 Tim. 4:2).

The two infinitives ("to exhort" and "to refute") are both in the present tense, emphasizing the ongoing and continual nature of the work of the elder/overseer in promoting the truth and contradicting error. The development

---

[50] Rienecker, 647.

of this final qualification is parallel to and elaborates upon the requirement that elders be "able to teach" in 1 Timothy 3:2. [51] In a similar way Paul required Timothy to be devoted to the Scriptures (2 Tim. 3:15-17) so that he would be able to "reprove" and "exhort" from it (4:2).[52]

> **Digging Deeper:**
> 1. What does it teach us that God included not only requirements about what an elder *is not* to be (v.7), but also what he *is* to be (v.8)?
> 2. How does "holding fast" the Word of God open the door for elders to receive what they need to fulfill their calling?
> 3. Why is an ability to handle the Word of God an indispensable matter for elders?

1:10 For there are many rebellious men, empty talkers and deceivers, especially those of the circumcision,

The immediate reason ("For," γὰρ) for establishing such qualified leadership (vv.5-9) in the church in Crete is now spelled out in some detail (vv.10-16). The situation in Crete was a difficult one, as the following verses make clear.

First, "there are many rebellious men" (Εἰσὶν ... πολλοὶ [καὶ] ἀνυπότακτοι). The adjective "rebellious" (ἀνυπότακτοι) has already been used in v.6 (which see) to describe what an elder/overseer's child(ren) must not be. It describes those who throw off authority and demand autonomy. God's purpose in giving the Law was to expose such rebellion (1 Tim. 1:9). These three uses in the PE represent Paul's total use of the word. The use of the word here is a signal that the problem was with professing believers, not unbelievers.

Such men tend to be "empty talkers" (ματαιολόγοι). This adjective is found only here in the NT, though the cognate noun is encountered in 1 Timothy 1:6. It is a compound word which describes those who idly talk about vain, senseless things.[53] Such folk sound impressive in their seemingly learned rhetoric, but the content of what they say is useless and of no value. This was the way of the pagans (Matt. 6:7).

They are, in the final analysis, "deceivers" (φρεναπάται). This noun is used only here in the NT, but the verbal form is encountered in Galatians 6:3. It describes one who deceives the mind or thinking of another.[54] They are dealers

---
[51] Knight, 294.
[52] Mounce, 391.
[53] Thayer, 392.
[54] Rienecker, 652.

in "myths" and season these with the "commandments of men" so that they may turn others "away from the truth" as well (v.14).

Such men come in many forms and can be found in many arenas, but Paul has "especially" (μάλιστα) in mind one group. The adverb is the superlative form of the adverb μάλα. It speaks of that which is the highest point in the extent of something.[55] In such a case it would mean that Paul was identifying just one part of a larger group of opponents. It may, however, also be used in the sense of "namely," in which case Paul would be identifying the whole of the group.[56] Here the height of all such talk and deception is found among "those of the circumcision" (οἱ ἐκ τῆς περιτομῆς). The definite article οἱ is used as a substantive ("those"). Paul refers to them as "of the circumcision," or more literally, "out of" (ἐκ) the circumcision. Paul may have been thus referring to Jewish Christians who arose out of the larger body of Jewish faith. It seems clear from Titus that the problem was one brewing within the church, so it seems likely this is his intention here.

> **Ministry Maxim**
>
> The current of rebellion runs along the conductor of deception.

That such folk were numerous ("many," πολλοί) made the situation all the more volatile and the need for thoroughly prepared elders/overseers (vv.5-9) all the more urgent.

1:11 who must be silenced because they are upsetting whole families, teaching things they should not teach for the sake of sordid gain.

Such false teachers (v.10) are people "who must be silenced" (οὓς δεῖ ἐπιστομίζειν). Just as the elder/overseer "must be" (δεῖ) a certain kind of man (v.5), so the false teachers "must be" (δεῖ) silenced. A moral obligation requires it. The infinitive "silenced" (ἐπιστομίζειν) is used only here in the NT. It is a compound word from ἐπί ("over") and στόμα ("mouth").[57] It strictly means to put a bridle, muzzle or gag in the mouth and thus by extension to bring to silence.[58] The present tense points to continuous action, so they are to be put to silence for good. It is not enough to ignore some words, expressions or teachings. They must be stopped. In this case such people are silenced by having their teachings refuted by godly leaders with sound answers to their foolishness (v.9). This should be done without quarreling and with great patience, holding out hope even for the false teachers themselves to be delivered from their

---

[55] Friberg, 252.
[56] Marshall, 195.
[57] Robertson, 4:600.
[58] Thayer, 248.

demonic deception (2 Tim. 2:24-26; cf. Titus 1:13). Yet Titus and the elder/overseers should not unendingly keep up the debate (Titus 3:9-11).

While hope may be held out for the false teachers themselves, ultimately the reason for silencing them is "because they are upsetting whole families" (οἵτινες ὅλους οἴκους ἀνατρέπουσιν). The relative pronoun (οἵτινες) is used "to emphasize a characteristic quality, by which a preceding statement is to be confirmed." It may mean something like "in so far as."[59] The verb "upsetting" (ἀνατρέπουσιν) is a compound word from "up" (ἀνὰ) and "to turn" (τρέπω). Its emphasis is on the upsetting, overthrowing and destroying of something. It is used literally in John 2:15 to describe Jesus upsetting the tables of the money changers in the temple. In its only other usage (2 Tim. 2:18) Paul employs it, as here, to describe the effect of false teachers upon the faith of others.

> **Ministry Maxim**
>
> There is a time to listen to those who disagree and there is a time to silence them.

In this case it is happening to "whole families" (ὅλους οἴκους). The word translated "families" is more literally "houses," but it can refer either to the structure in which a family dwells or the people who live in the dwelling. In this case the latter is in view. It is likely that the heads of the homes were being persuaded, and they thus took their entire household with them into the deception. It is also possible (though I think less likely) that, since churches probably met in homes, the congregations that gathered in those homes are in view.

This was happening because the false teachers were "teaching things they should not" (διδάσκοντες ἃ μὴ δεῖ). The present active participle "teaching" (διδάσκοντες) is used to express the manner or means of their deception.[60] It is the same word used by Paul when instructing Timothy to take the things he had taught him and "entrust these to faithful men who will be able to teach others also" (2 Tim. 2:2). The false teachers were employing the same strategy and raising up their own disciples to destruction. These were things which "should not" (ἃ μὴ δεῖ) be taught. The word "teach" at the end of the clause has been added by the translators of the NASU.

Their motives for such deception are laid bare, "for the sake of sordid gain" (αἰσχροῦ κέρδους χάριν). The preposition χάριν ("for the sake of") is used to indicate the goal of their activity.[61] The noun "gain" (κέρδους) describes whatever might be to one's profit, advantage, or gain. It is used only two other places in the NT, both by Paul (Phil. 1:21; 3:7). Both of those references are to

---
[59] BAGD, 587.
[60] Rienecker, 652.
[61] BAGD, 877.

non-monetary gain, thus Paul's intent here may not simply be financial, but could include social leverage, power and clout as well. Whatever form the "gain" may have taken, it was "sordid" (αἰσχροῦ). The word describes that which is shameful, ugly, or dishonest.[62] The word is used only by Paul in the NT and always of that which is either socially or spiritually shameful (1 Cor. 11:6; 14:35; Eph. 5:12). Paul has just used a compound word made up of "sordid" (αἰσχροῦ) and "gain" (κέρδους) to demand that this very impulse must be absent in potential elder/overseers (Titus 1:7). Paul asserted that Christian teachers could be paid (1 Tim. 5:17-18), but this was so that they could be more free to teach. These Cretan teachers were driven not to spread the truth, but to fill their pockets (cf. 1 Tim. 6:5).

> **Digging Deeper:**
> 1. What is the connection between rebellion and deception? Does one lead to the other?
> 2. When should wise church leadership patiently counsel those whose teaching is errant and when should they see that they are "silenced"?
> 3. How could Paul discern that the motives of these teachers were selfish ("for the sake of sordid gain")? Imputing motives to someone is dangerous business—how can church leaders today avoid error in this and discern accurately and wisely?

1:12 One of themselves, a prophet of their own, said, "Cretans are always liars, evil beasts, lazy gluttons."

To support his rather strong statements regarding the people among whom Titus is working (vv.10-11), Paul quotes one of their own. The introductory line prepares us to receive the quotation that will follow. The verb comes first in the sentence, rather than at the end, but this makes little sense in English (εἶπέν τις ἐξ αὐτῶν ἴδιος αὐτῶν προφήτης). The quotation appears to be from Epimenides a poet of Cretan birth in the 6th century B.C. Robertson says that Callimachus quoted the first part of it in a Hymn to Zeus.[63] That Paul calls him "a prophet" (προφήτης) means simply that he is projecting the current Cretan opinion of Epimenides, not that the Apostle was endorsing him as a prophet from God. It is also possible that Paul was using the term much like John did

---

[62] Ibid., 25.
[63] Robertson, 4:600.

in referring to Caiaphas (John 11:51) as one who unwittingly spoke the truth beforehand.[64]

What are we to make of Paul's familiarity with pagan poets and his liberty in quoting them in Scripture? Apparently Paul read widely. He was an expert student of Scripture, but he apparently was conversant with other material as well. When preaching in Athens, Paul said, "for in Him we live and move and exist, as even some of your own poets have said, 'For we also are His children'" (Acts 17:28). He appears to have been quoting the Cilician Aratus of Soli (ab. B.C. 270) in his *Ta Phainomena*. Cleanthes the Stoic philosopher (300-220 B.C.) has nearly the same expression in his *Hymn to Zeus*. And in 1 Corinthians 15:32 he may call upon the words of Menander.[65] The inclusion of these bits of foreign literature in Scripture does not mean that God inspired their original writers, only that the Holy Spirit moved Paul's heart to record these bits and, as he used them in their Scriptural context, they are what God would have had him say. It does not jeopardize the uniqueness of Scripture, but underscores that these were real letters, written under the inspiration of the Holy Spirit in real-life circumstances to people living in a certain place and in a certain time. They are at the same time the timeless, infallible, inerrant Scriptures.

Collectively the people of Crete had taken on certain consistencies of behavior. These characteristics are said to be "always" (ἀεί) true. The word refers to that which has been true from the beginning or "from time immemorial to the present."[66] It may appear that Paul is stereotyping or profiling in an inappropriate way, but he avoids such a charge by quoting from one of Crete's own favored sons. The Apostle's wise tact deflects the charge of inappropriateness. Three particular character traits of the Cretans are named here.

> **Ministry Maxim**
>
> Tactful honesty is more useful in ministry than servile political-correctness.

Cretans were known to be "liars" (ψεῦσται). The word is a favorite of the Apostle John. He uses it seven of the ten times it appears in the NT (John 8:44, 55; 1 John 1:10; 2:4, 22; 4:20; 5:10). The other three are by Paul (Rom. 3:4; 1 Tim. 1:10; Titus 1:12). The devil is the master-liar and all other lies are an imitation of him (John 8:44; 1 John 2:22). The Greek language had another word for lying which was cognate with the word for Crete (Κρής). The expression "to play the Cretan," then, was a way of designating a person a liar.

The people of Crete had also been branded as "evil beasts" (κακὰ θηρία). The word "beasts" (θηρία) describes simply a wild, untamed animal. It is,

---

[64] Marshall, 199.
[65] Ibid., 3:289.
[66] BAGD, 19.

however, used in significant contexts related to the devil. Mark said of Jesus during His temptation, "He was in the wilderness forty days being tempted by Satan; and He was with the wild beasts" (Mark 1:13). Thirty-one of the thirty-eight times the word is used in the NT are found in the Book of Revelation. There it often becomes a reference to the antichrist (e.g., Rev. 14:9, 11; 15:2). The word "evil" (κακὰ) can range in meaning from the harmful and calamitous to the morally wicked and evil. Here, however, it appears to tend toward the darker, more sinister, shades of meaning. The Cretans were unrestrained in their behavior and as such promoted the agenda of the evil one.

Finally, the Cretans were "lazy gluttons" (γαστέρες ἀργαί), or more literally, "idle bellies." In every other NT use of the word translated "gluttons" or "bellies" (γαστέρες) it refers to the womb or a woman who is with child. In seven of the other eight uses in the NT it refers in one way or to pregnancy (cf. the expression ἐν γαστρὶ ἔχουσα; "to be with child," Matt. 1:18).[67] Here, however, it refers more generally to the inward parts of a person, in this case the stomach, and then by extention to the appetites, thus the translation "gluttons." In Philippians 3:19 Paul speaks of those whose "god is their belly" (ESV). The word rendered "lazy" (ἀργαί) ranges in meaning from unemployed to lazy to useless and unproductive.[68] Here it points to the laziness that won't move to fulfill the appetites that the individual has allowed to rule his life. "The sluggard buries his hand in the dish; he is weary of bringing it to his mouth again" (Prov. 26:15).

> **Digging Deeper:**
> 1. For the careful student of Scripture, what positive impact can reading widely in even non-Christian literature have? What dangers might this hold?
> 2. How would you answer the charge that Paul was bigoted and racist in his characterizations of Cretans?

1:13 This testimony is true. For this reason reprove them severely so that they may be sound in the faith,

In characterizing the Cretans, the Apostle has quoted one of Crete's favored sons (v.12). This enables him to avoid the charge of bigotry or profiling. But now, having let the Cretan speak, he adds his opinion of what he has said: "This testimony is true" (ἡ μαρτυρία αὕτη ἐστὶν ἀληθής). Now the Cretans

---
[67] Thayer, 110.
[68] BAGD, 104.

would either have to disagree with one of their most famous citizens or stand in agreement with the Apostle Paul.[69]

Having established the basic character of the Cretans, Paul now uses it to make his point. "For this reason" (δι' ἣν αἰτίαν) is a strong causal statement (cf. Paul's only other uses of the phrase in 2 Tim. 1:6, 12) and it points back to the witness of Epimenides in v.12 and his confirmation of its truth (v.13a). Because that is true, Titus is to "reprove them severely" (ἔλεγχε αὐτοὺς ἀποτόμως). The verb "reprove" (ἔλεγχε) is one Paul used only in communication with the ministries in Ephesus (Eph. 5:11, 13; 1 Tim. 5:20; 2 Tim. 4:2) or Crete (Titus 1:9, 13; 2:15). The word is used in v.9 (which see) to outline the primary role of elders/overseers on Crete. Paul's use again here shows that what has come between the two references (vv.10-12) has served to underscore that last requirement of the elders/overseers and that, having underscored the need in Crete, he reaffirms his original point. This reproof is to be directed at the false teachers of Crete, not the ordinary people. Here he adds that this is to be done "severely" (ἀποτόμως; used elsewhere only in 2 Cor. 13:10). Robertson says it comes from an old verb meaning "to cut off." The adverb then comes to have the sense of "curtly" or "abruptly." He adds, "It is necessary to appear rude sometimes for safety, if the house is on fire and life is in danger."[70]

The goal in view is "so that they may be sound in the faith" (ἵνα ὑγιαίνωσιν ἐν τῇ πίστει). The conjunction ἵνα is used with the present subjunctive (ὑγιαίνωσιν) in a purpose clause. Such rebuke should be employed only with a redemptive purpose in mind. The false teachers have been in view (vv.10-11; cf. 2 Tim. 2:23-26), but the scope probably widens at this point to include the entire church body. The word "sound" (ὑγιαίνωσιν) is a word used only in the PE and he always uses it metaphorically, attaching it either to "faith" (Titus 1:13; 2:2), "words" (1 Tim. 6:3; 2 Tim. 1:13) or "teaching/doctrine" (1 Tim. 1:10; 2 Tim. 4:3; Titus 1:9; 2:1). Paul has just used it in v.9 (which see) and, connecting that key requirement for the elder/overseer with this purpose, reminds us that being "sound in the faith" (v.13) is directly connected to the church's teaching being "sound" in doctrine (v.9). The present tense points to a continuous, ongoing health that does not wane. The presence of the article with "faith" (τῇ πίστει) signals that a body of truth is in view more than is subjective trust, though the two are never entirely separated.

> **Ministry Maxim**
>
> The winds of reproof make the roots of my faith grow deep.

---

[69] Hiebert, "Titus," 11:433.
[70] Robertson, 4:601.

1:14 not paying attention to Jewish myths and commandments of men who turn away from the truth.

Paul continues the sentence and supplies for us something of the character of the opposition Titus faced on Crete. In opposition ("not," μὴ) to being "sound in the faith" (v.13) is "paying attention to Jewish myths" (προσέχοντες Ἰουδαϊκοῖς μύθοις). The verb "paying attention" (προσέχοντες) is used by Paul only in the PE (1 Tim. 1:4; 3:8; 4:1, 13). It is a compound word from "to" (πρὸς) and "bring" (ἔχω) and has the sense of "bring near" or "bring to." It is used in 1 Timothy 1:4 when Paul tells Timothy to teach men not "to pay attention to myths and endless genealogies." Such "myths" (μύθοις) were a problem in both Ephesus (1 Tim. 1:4; 4:7; 2 Tim. 4:4) and Crete. The word points to fanciful legends invented by man. It is always used in the NT in a negative sense. Here Paul calls these particular myths "Jewish" (Ἰουδαϊκοῖς; cf. v.10). We know that part of the problem in Ephesus was the morbid interest in "genealogies" and that these men wanted to be "teachers of the Law" (1 Tim. 1:4, 7). But they were speculative (1:4) rather than expository in their work, connecting dots that were not meant to be connected and thus creating meaningless—albeit high-sounding—gibberish for teaching (cf. Mark 7:2-8).

What they produced was ultimately nothing more than "commandments of men" (ἐντολαῖς ἀνθρώπων). Jesus told the Pharisees and teachers of the law that the traditions of the Jewish elders were "TEACHING AS DOCTRINES THE PRECEPTS OF MEN" (Matt. 15:9; Mark 7:7; quoting Isa. 29:13). The believers in Colossae were facing false teaching that was "in accordance with the commandments and teachings of men" (Col. 2:22). Whatever is not the true Gospel is a fabrication of mankind, or perhaps worse (1 Tim. 4:1; 2 Tim. 2:26). In 1 Timothy 4:3 Paul specified some of the "commandments of men" he was referring to there. The teachers would "forbid marriage and advocate abstaining from foods which God has created to be gratefully shared in by those who believe and know the truth."

Those who teach such things are they who "turn away from the truth" (ἀποστρεφομένων τὴν ἀλήθειαν). The verb is a compound word made up of "from" (ἀπὸ) and "to turn" (στρέφω). The present tense describes a continual turning away from the truth. The middle voice indicates that they are turning themselves away from the truth. Paul uses the verb two other times in the PE. He used it to describe the rejection he felt from "all who are in Asia" (2 Tim. 1:15). There and here he uses it in the sense of rejecting or repudiating someone or something. He also

> **Ministry Maxim**
>
> When you turn your ear to error, you turn your back to the truth.

used it in 2 Timothy 4:4. There it is employed transitively in the simple sense of "to turn away from."[71] It is "the truth" (τὴν ἀλήθειαν) that is repudiated. The definite article makes specific the subject—the truth of the Gospel of the Lord Jesus Christ as preached authoritatively by the Apostles. The definiteness of "the truth" stands in contrast to the anarthrous and general nature of "commandments of men." Also "the truth" is singular, whereas "commandments of men" is plural. If you choose not "the truth," any invention may grab your soul and carry you away. There are a million such varieties of falsehood being passed off as the truth. This was the problem in Galatia (Gal. 4:9) and Ephesus (2 Tim. 4:4) and was now true on Crete as well.

> **Digging Deeper:**
> 1. When confronting error how do you know when a severe reproof is in order (cf. 2 Tim. 2:23-26)? What danger and damage are found in the misuse of such a reproof? What danger and damage are to be found in failure to employ such a reproof when needed?
> 2. How does verse 14 illustrate the old adage that there are a million angles at which one can fall, but only one at which one can stand?

1:15 To the pure, all things are pure; but to those who are defiled and unbelieving, nothing is pure, but both their mind and their conscience are defiled.

The principle or proverb Paul sets forth now must be read in context as a development of what has been said regarding false teachers on Crete, and particularly what has just been said about the Jewish nature of their false teaching (vv.10, 14). The first assertion is that, "To the pure, all things are pure" (πάντα καθαρὰ τοῖς καθαροῖς). By "the pure" (τοῖς καθαροῖς) Paul means those who truly have believed in Christ and are free from the Law as a means of righteousness before God. They are pure before God in that their sins have been forgiven and they are pure in their conscience to eat what was previously forbidden by the Law. In Ephesus part of the problem was that the false teachers would "forbid marriage and advocate abstaining from foods which God has created to be gratefully shared in by those who believe and know the truth" (1 Tim. 4:3). But "the pure" knew "everything created by God is good, and nothing is to be rejected if it is received with gratitude; for it is sanctified by means of the word of God and prayer" (4:4-5). In Christ,

---
[71] BAGD, 100.

God had set aside the ceremonial law regarding clean and unclean foods (Mark 7:19; Acts 10:11-15). Thus Paul instructed the Colossians, "no one is to act as your judge in regard to food or drink or in respect to a festival or a new moon or a Sabbath day" (Col. 2:16).

To those who have obtained a righteousness that comes by faith, not the Law (Phil. 3:9), "all things are pure" (πάντα καθαρὰ). Such folk can eat what was once prohibited, but now declared "clean," without any spotting of their conscience before God. They have discovered that righteousness is not obtained before God on the basis of what they eat or don't eat, and they are thus free to eat or not eat without their sense of standing before God being affected. "All things indeed are clean, but they are evil for the man who eats and gives offense" (Rom. 14:20b).

In contrast ("but," δὲ) are "those who are defiled and unbelieving" (τοῖς δὲ μεμιαμμένοις καὶ ἀπίστοις). The participle with the definite article is used as a substantive ("those who are defiled"). The perfect tense points to the fact that at a point in the past they became defiled and they continue in that state at present. The passive voice shows that it was something outside themselves which defiled them. Paul uses the verb only here and at the end of the sentence. It can have a sense of ritual defilement to it (John 18:28; cf. Heb. 12:15; Jude 8). Given the context it seems to carry the sense of ritual uncleanness here. It refers, then, to people who have set up for themselves an external code of conduct by which they must gain God's favor and who have then failed to live up to it. In their own estimation they are defiled and unclean before God, because they have failed to live up to the code. By establishing such a codified basis for relationship with God they are automatically "unbelieving" (ἀπίστοις). The word simply takes the common word for faith (πιστὸς) and adds to it an alpha privative in order to negate it. Such a person, while highly religious and probably even using the title "Christian," is nevertheless "unbelieving" because he has not trusted in "the righteousness which is by faith" (Rom. 9:30b).

To such people "nothing is pure" (οὐδὲν καθαρόν). The verb is absent, but rightly supplied by translators. This is the third use of the word "pure" in this verse. The negation of "nothing" (οὐδὲν) is categorical, absolute, and without reservation. Such folk are forever drawing the circle of the acceptable smaller and smaller. Their consciences are always being offended by some new thing. Anticipating the next clause, Paul may have been hinting that their defiled inward nature defiles anything they put their hand to (Hag. 2:13-14).

In utter contrast (ἀλλὰ, "but") to the thought of finding anything pure is

> **Ministry Maxim**
>
> Legalistic righteousness sets in motion a journey that never arrives anywhere except despair.

the fact that "both their mind and their conscience are defiled" (μεμίανται αὐτῶν καὶ ὁ νοῦς καὶ ἡ συνείδησις). The verb is repeated from earlier in the sentence. It is again the perfect passive—pointing to an experience in the past where something from outside the person defiled them and has left them in a state of uncleanness. What is defiled is specifically designated. It is first their "mind" (ὁ νοῦς). Paul is pointing to the corruption of their reasoning. Having rejected the Gospel that promises righteousness through faith, they no longer think clearly or correctly about cleanness and uncleanness before God. Second, it is their "conscience" (ἡ συνείδησις) that is defiled. The word describes the moral awareness by which decisions are made. A person's conscience may be "good" (1 Tim. 1:5, 19) and "clear" (1 Tim. 3:9; 2 Tim. 1:3). Possessing such a conscience is always directly linked to living by faith (1 Tim. 1:5, 19; 3:9). Or a person's conscience can be "seared . . . as with a branding iron" (1 Tim. 4:2). Such injury comes when a person "fall[s] away from the faith" (1 Tim. 4:1). In other words, they abandon the righteousness that comes by faith and opt for a codified righteousness to be attained by works. In such an arrangement an infinitely holy God can never be pleased; every effort of righteousness falls short. Thus the code must constantly be refined and made more stringent. This only adds to the failure to keep the code, which produces guilt, which—according to their understanding—only distances them further from God. They stand defiled in thought and conscience and can find nothing in life that provides a "pure" experience.

Even though the pronoun is plural ("their," αὐτῶν), the "mind" (ὁ νοῦς) and "conscience" (ἡ συνείδησις) are singular. The group is characterized by a common way of thinking and of making moral evaluations.

> **Digging Deeper:**
> 1. Beyond "clean" and "unclean" foods, to what contemporary issues might these same principles apply?
> 2. In what way does legalism bind one to an ever increasing failure and hopelessness?
> 3. What does this verse teach us about the liberty of living by grace through faith?

1:16 They profess to know God, but by their deeds they deny Him, being detestable and disobedient and worthless for any good deed.

Such people are highly religious: "They profess to know God" (θεὸν ὁμολογοῦσιν εἰδέναι). The verb "profess" (ὁμολογοῦσιν) is a compound word, constructed from ὁμοῦ ("together") and λέγω ("to say"). Its basic root meaning is "to say the same thing." Here it has the sense of to declare something publicly.[72] The present tense tells us that such folk habitually claim "to know God." The infinitive (εἰδέναι, "to know") identifies that which is the substance of their profession. Paul does not use γινώσκω, which would have laid emphasis upon the personal, experiential and relational nature of their knowledge. Rather he uses οἶδα, stressing that the knowledge is that which is gained by information or intuition. It is a defective perfect which has a present tense meaning. The noun "God" (θεὸν) is thrown forward to emphasize it.

Their claim is not reality, however ("but," δὲ). In reality, "by their deeds they deny Him" (τοῖς δὲ ἔργοις ἀρνοῦνται). The pronouns "their" and "Him" do not exist in the Greek text, but it is obvious whose deeds are being spoken of and who is being denied, and thus they are supplied by the translators. More literally it reads simply, "by deeds they deny." This is the first usage of the word "deeds" (ἔργοις) in Titus. Here the dative case has an instrumental sense (i.e., their denial is made through the instrumentality of their actions). The word becomes a strong theme throughout the book, being used eight times. He calls upon the believers to prove their faith by their good deeds (2:7, 14; 3:1, 8, 14), while at the same time clearly declaring that none of us is saved "on the basis of deeds which we have done in righteousness" (3:5). Thus this statement and the usage of the word in the next clause are damning. It is proof positive, in the context of Titus, that such people are not followers of Christ and children of God at all. In fact they "deny" (ἀρνοῦνται) Him. Paul tells Titus, using the same verb, that the grace of God teaches us "to deny ungodliness and worldly desires" (Titus 2:12). But here the denial is of God Himself. As such they were very much like the false teachers in Ephesus, whom Paul told Timothy were "holding to a form of godliness, although they have denied its power" (2 Tim. 3:5; cf. 1 Tim. 5:8). Paul had warned Timothy, using the same verb, that "If we deny Him, He also will deny us" (2:12b; cf. Matt. 10:33; Luke 12:9). The present tense of the verb here reveals that their continual profession of faith in Christ is continually contradicted by their ongoing way of life. The middle voice is to be preferred over the passive—pointing out that their actions are taken upon themselves in the form of a denial of their words. These words of Paul make clear that he and James are not at odds about faith and works (James 2:14-16; cf. 1 John 1:6; 2:4; 3:6, 10; 4:7-8).

> **Ministry Maxim**
>
> Actions often tell a truer tale than words.

The basic nature ("being," ὄντες) of such folk makes them unacceptable to

---

[72] BAGD, 568.

God. The present participle points to the continuous nature of their character. Being "detestable" (βδελυκτοί) means they are abominable to God. The adjective is used only here in the NT, but the verbal form is used to describe the abomination of desolation (Matt. 24:15; Mark 13:14) and those whose portion will be the lake of fire (Rev. 21:8) and who are shut out from the new Jerusalem (v.27). It is a word-group used in the LXX in connection with the abomination of idolatry. "These persons who find 'abomination' everywhere are themselves 'abominable.'"[73]

Such folk are also ("and," καί) "disobedient" (ἀπειθεῖς). The adjective describes one who will not be brought under the authority of another; thus "impersuasible, uncompliant, contumacious."[74] Paul uses it to describe what became of those who originally rejected the light of God's revelation in creation (Rom. 1:30), what will characterize humanity in the last days (2 Tim. 3:2), and what was once true of those who now believe (Titus 3:3).

Finally ("and," καί), such folk are "worthless for any good deed" (πρὸς πᾶν ἔργον ἀγαθὸν ἀδόκιμοι). The phrase "for any good deed" is thrown to the front of the clause for emphasis. As mentioned above, the theme of good deeds is one that forms a central theme of this book (2:7, 14; 3:1, 5, 8, 14). The adjective "worthless" (ἀδόκιμοι) describes that which is "rejected, not in the sense of that which is seen from the first to be unsuitable . . . but meaning that which has not stood the test, that which has been shown to be a sham, and has therefore been rejected (Rom. 1:28; 1 Cor. 9:27; 2 Cor. 13:5; 2 Tim. 3:8; Tit. 1:16)."[75] Thus Paul is emphasizing that such a person is completely worthless for the purposes of God and does not bear the basic mark of being a child of God.

Digging Deeper:

1. In what way do your actions confirm or deny your profession of faith in Christ?
2. What does this verse tell us about the person who makes a "confession of faith," but never demonstrates any life change?
3. What do the final three adjectives tell us about God's opinion of those who profess faith without producing fruit?

---

[73] Dibelius and Conzelmann, quoted in Fee, 182.
[74] Thayer, 55.
[75] DNTT, 3:808.

CHAPTER

2

2:1 But as for you, speak the things which are fitting for sound doctrine.

Having thoroughly described the false teachers on Crete (1:10-16), Paul now contrasts ("But," δέ) what should be true of Timothy. The phrase "as for you" (Σὺ) renders the simple second person singular personal pronoun. The pronoun is emphatic and stresses the distinction between the false teachers (1:15-16) and Titus. Thus literally the sentence begins, "But you." Paul has used the same formula in his instructions to Timothy (1 Tim. 6:11; 2 Tim. 3:10, 14; 4:5). The command which Titus is to take up is "speak" (λάλει), used in the sense of teaching. The present tense imperative demands that action be taken repeatedly. In the face of falsehood and false teachers the pastor's primary strategy is to teach the truth. Such teaching may be preemptory or it may be corrective, but teach he must. The chapter opens and closes with this same imperative (vv.1, 15), forming an inclusion that shows the intent of what lies between the two commands.

> **Ministry Maxim**
>
> Teaching that claims orthodoxy (right + opinion) yet does not produce orthopraxy (right + practice) is erroneous from the start.

That which is to be spoken are "the things which are fitting for sound doctrine" (ἃ πρέπει τῇ ὑγιαινούσῃ διδασκαλίᾳ). The relative pronoun ἃ ("the things") broadens the scope out to include anything that would fit into the category. The teaching of the pastor is sweeping in its breadth. These teachings must be those which "are fitting" (πρέπει). The word describes that which is proper, suitable or fitting for a given context.[1] Here the teaching must thus conform to

---

[1] Rienecker, 653.

"sound doctrine" (τῇ ὑγιαινούσῃ διδασκαλίᾳ). The definite article reveals that there is a distinct and definite body of truth in Paul's mind. The word "doctrine" (διδασκαλίᾳ) harkens back to the primary duty of the elder/overseer—"holding fast the faithful word which is in accordance with the teaching, so that he will be able both to exhort in sound doctrine and to refute those who contradict" (1:9). And "doctrine" is the primary concern of this chapter (2:7, 10). Thus the first chapter revealed the kind of men necessary to teach sound doctrine and the second chapter the kinds of things that are to be taught in accord with sound doctrine. Yet the chapter addresses not so much the content of "sound doctrine" as it does the character and conduct which jibes with such truth. The doctrine is to be "sound" (ὑγιαινούσῃ). The word is a favorite in the PE and describes that which is healthy. The word was used literally of physical (e.g., Luke 7:10) or mental health (e.g., Luke 15:27). In the PE it is always metaphorically attached either to "faith" (Titus 1:13; 2:2), "words" (1 Tim. 6:3; 2 Tim. 1:13) or "teaching/doctrine" (1 Tim. 1:10; 2 Tim. 4:3; Titus 1:9; 2:1). Such doctrine begets health by transmitting truth. Here "sound doctrine" stands in direct contrast to the "Jewish myths and commandments of men" (1:14) which are espoused by the false teachers. They are defiling (1:15-16), while "sound doctrine" brings holiness and health.

Paul now outlines some of "the things which are fitting for sound doctrine" (vv.2-10). He proceeds according to groupings: "Older men" (v.2), "Older women" (v.3), "young women" (vv.4-5), "young men" (v.6), Titus himself (v.7-8), and "bondslaves" (vv.9-10).

> **Digging Deeper:**
> 1. Why do you think God demands not merely teaching right doctrine, but also "the things which are fitting for sound doctrine"?
> 2. Glancing ahead to what Paul demands be taught (Titus 2:2-10), what do you think is the distinction between "sound doctrine" and "the things which *are fitting for* sound doctrine"?
> 3. What are the implications of the fact that God requires one measure of a teaching's orthodoxy (right + opinion) to be whether it produces orthopraxy (right + practice)? Why is just "getting the truth right" not enough?

2:2 Older men are to be temperate, dignified, sensible, sound in faith, in love, in perseverance.

First are "older men" (πρεσβύτας). The word refers to men of some advanced age. It is cognate to the term for "elders" (1:5), but does not designate an ecclesiastical office. Paul, at the time of writing Philemon, considered himself an "old man" (Philem. 9), as did Zacharias when the angel appeared to him (Luke 1:18). The ancients divided life into various stages of age, and did not always agree with one another on those stages. Here Paul seems simply to divide human age into two stages—"older" (vv.2, 3) and "younger" (vv.4, 6). Just when one stage transitions into the next is somewhat subjective.

The Apostle designates four qualities that are to be true of such men. They "are to be temperate" (νηφαλίους εἶναι). The present tense infinitive proves that the first three qualities are to be continuously the habit of life of such men. The word "temperate" (νηφαλίους) literally means "holding no wine." Strictly speaking it referred originally to abstinence. However, the word then came to be used more broadly to describe self-control in the appetites and desires generally.[2] In view of 1:12 and 2:3 the word may retain some of its original, literal meaning.[3] Perhaps without entirely losing that sense, it probably tends here toward the broader, more general, meaning. Elsewhere Paul has said this should be true also of overseers (1 Tim. 3:2) and of deaconesses (3:11).

Such men must also be "dignified" (σεμνούς). The word describes that which is worthy of respect or honor, a person who is noble and dignified.[4] "The word denotes moral earnestness, affecting outward demeanor as well as interior intention."[5] This quality should be true of our thoughts (Phil. 4:8) and is the result of prayer (1 Tim. 2:2). Such should be true of overseers (3:4), deacons (3:8) and deaconesses (3:11). Shortly Paul will prescribe this as a goal for Titus himself (Titus 2:7).

A third quality is "sensible" (σώφρονας). Three of the word's four NT usages are here in Titus, describing overseers (Titus 1:8; cf. 1 Tim. 3:2), older men (2:2) and younger women (2:5). Add the cognates and this word-group is used six times in Titus, five times in this chapter alone (2:2, 4, 5, 6, 12). Another four are found in Paul's correspondence with Timothy (1 Tim. 2:9, 15; 3:2; 2 Tim. 1:7), making ten of Paul's twelve uses of the word-group show up in the PE (cf. also Rom. 12:3; 2 Cor. 5:13). The word-group generally describes a soundness of mind and thinking that shows up in a self-disciplined lifestyle. This is not the product of human

> **Ministry Maxim**
>
> We become sensible old men only by first striving to become sensible young men.

---

[2] Rienecker, 622.
[3] Marshall, 240.
[4] BAGD, 747.
[5] Rienecker, 619.

effort, but of the grace of God (Titus 2:12) by the Holy Spirit's ministry to the believer (2 Tim. 1:6-7) and through the sound teaching and good training of the church (Titus 1:8; 2:2, 4, 5, 6). If "older men" are to become "sensible," they must begin the pursuit as "young men" (v.6).

The fourth quality of older men is that they are to be "sound" (ὑγιαίνοντας). This word is the same one used in the previous verse. The present tense points to a continuous health and soundness. The word was used in v.1 to describe "sound" doctrine, and here it is used to describe the resulting "sound" character such doctrine produces.[6] The participle is modified by the three nouns which follow in the remainder of the sentence.

In the previous verse the soundness was to be in "doctrine;" here it is to be in three areas of character, each represented by a dative noun and its definite article. First is soundness "in faith" (τῇ πίστει). The noun and its definite article may better be translated "in *the* faith." It is possible this points to the objective body of Christian truth which comprises the Gospel of Jesus Christ; but, given its connection with the following two qualities, it more likely points to the subjective trust of the believer. The words "sound" and "faith" are used together also in Titus 1:13.

This soundness is also to be found "in love" (τῇ ἀγάπῃ) and "in perseverance" (τῇ ὑπομονῇ). The more normal trio is faith, hope and love (e.g., 1 Cor. 13:13). Here, however, "perseverance" (ὑπομονή) is substituted for "hope" (ἐλπίς). This particular trio of nouns, however, is not unfamiliar in Paul. He had seen these qualities evidenced in the young Thessalonican believers (1 Thess. 1:3). He told Timothy to make them the goal of his pursuit (1 Tim. 6:11) and reminded him that he had seen these modeled in the Apostle himself (2 Tim. 3:10). Jesus also said He had seen these in the church at Thyatira (Rev. 2:19).

Digging Deeper:
1. Why do you suppose Paul took so much space in this short letter to outline "the things which *are fitting for* sound doctrine" (the implications for living) rather than detailing the sound doctrine itself?
2. True or false: the implications of doctrine are as authoritative as the doctrine itself? Why?
3. What older man do you know who embodies these four qualities? What can you learn from him?

---

[6] Hiebert, "Titus," 11:436.

2:3 Older women likewise are to be reverent in their behavior, not malicious gossips nor enslaved to much wine, teaching what is good,

Paul transitions now to speak to "Older women" (πρεσβύτιδας). The word is used only here in the NT (but cf. use of πρεσβυτέρας in 1 Tim. 5:2) and describes women of advanced age. What the Apostle prescribes for such women in some way corresponds ("likewise," ὡσαύτως) to what he has just said to "Older men" (v.2). Six of Paul's usages of this adverb occur in the PE (Rom. 8:26; 1 Cor. 11:25; 1 Tim. 2:9; 3:8, 11; 5:25; Titus 2:3, 6). In nearly all of those usages it occurs, as here, in a listing of qualities for various groups. The correspondence between this verse and the one that precedes it is not to be found in the qualities prescribed, but in the fact that just as the Gospel has implications for "Older men," so too it similarly has implications for "Older women."

Such women "are to be reverent in their behavior" (ἐν καταστήματι ἱεροπρεπεῖς). The verb ("are to be") is absent in the Greek text and is rightly supplied by the translators. The adjective "reverent" (ἱεροπρεπεῖς) is used only here in the NT. It speaks of that which befits what is sacred to God. This attitude is to show up "in their behavior" (ἐν καταστήματι). This noun is also used only here in the NT. It describes the demeanor, deportment or behavior of a person. "They are to carry into daily life the demeanor of priestesses in a temple."[7] It describes outward presentation and action, but only as it arises out of a state of mind and a way of thinking.[8] Thus older women are to have come to a certain state of mind that is pervasive of all they are and do. Such women do not compartmentalize life, but see each and every part of their day as holy to the Lord.

> **Ministry Maxim**
>
> Life is lived rightly when it is lived from the inside out.

Older women are to be "not malicious gossips" (μὴ διαβόλους). The word translated "malicious gossips" is more literally "devils." The masculine singular form of the word is always used of the devil himself. Robertson suggests "she-devils" as a translation.[9] The word means "slanderer." And the feminine plural is used again as it is here in 1 Timothy 3:11 to require that wives of deacons be "not malicious gossips." The masculine plural is also used in 2 Timothy 3:3 to describe what will be

---

[7] Rienecker, 653.
[8] Guthrie, 192.
[9] Robertson, 4:575.

true of both males and females generally in the last days. Jesus told the unbelieving Jews "You are of your father the devil, and you want to do the desires of your father. . . . Whenever he speaks a lie, he speaks from his own nature, for he is a liar and the father of lies" (John 8:44). Similarly Satan is called "the accuser of our brethren . . . who accuses them before our God day and night" (Rev. 12:10). Those who in like fashion falsely accuse and slander others are operating in the devil's realm and advancing his cause. It is sad how often conversation in "Christian" circles can slip into such talk.

Similarly ("nor," μὴ) such women are not to be "enslaved to much wine" (οἴνῳ πολλῷ δεδουλωμένας). The word "enslaved" (δεδουλωμένας) is used of literal slavery (Acts 7:6), but is also used metaphorically. Such metaphorical usages can be negative in nature, such as enslavement to a bad marriage (1 Cor. 7:15) or to sin (Gal. 4:3; 2 Peter 2:19). Or they can be positive, describing enslavement to God (Rom. 6:22) or others (1 Cor. 9:19) for righteousness' sake (Rom. 6:18). Here it is a perfect tense, pointing to something that has taken place at a point in the past and continues to be true in the present. It is in the passive voice, showing that in this case the bondage is a negative one: "to much wine" (οἴνῳ πολλῷ). Paul has just quoted one of Crete's own citizens in saying that they are "always liars, evil beasts, lazy gluttons" (1:12). And he has instructed Titus to teach the older men to be "temperate" (2:2); and will lay the same obligation upon overseers (1 Tim. 3:2) and the wives of deacons (1 Tim. 3:11). There is no absolute prohibition in this verse against consuming some alcohol, though the wider context may make that the wiser course. Paul's personal course was, "All things are lawful for me, but not all things are profitable. All things are lawful for me, but I will not be mastered by anything" (1 Cor. 6:12). He called all believers to be under no other controlling influence than that of the Holy Spirit (Eph. 5:18). This seems to be the vein of counsel he urges here (cf. also 1 Tim. 3:8, 11).

After two negative instructions, Paul returns to a positive one: "teaching what is good" (καλοδιδασκάλους). This word is found only here in the NT. It is a compound word made up of "good" (καλός) and "teach" (διδάσκαλος). Thus older women are always to have others in mind, seeking to pass on what is virtuous, right and good to a younger generation of women. They live not for themselves, but for others and for the next generation. This refers not to an official teaching function within the church, but to the instruction passed on within the home through both life-example and intentional words.[10]

---

[10] Hiebert, "Titus," 11:436.

Titus 2

> **Digging Deeper:**
> 1. While the Gospel is for all regardless of generation or gender, what befalls us when we conclude that its *implications* are the same for all generations and genders?
> 2. Look up the word "deportment" in a dictionary. What have we surrendered as we have lost the use of this word in our functional vocabulary?
> 3. How does the work of the devil prosper in "Christian gossip"?

2:4 so that they may encourage the young women to love their husbands, to love their children,

This second chapter concerns what Titus should teach (v.1) the various groups of people within the church. This verse transitions to "young women" in mid-sentence by indicating that it is the "older women" (v.3) who are to teach them. The conjunction "so that" (ἵνα) with the subjunctive verb introduces the purpose of the "older women" living as they do (v.3). That purpose is that "they may encourage the young women" (σωφρονίζωσιν τὰς νέας). The verb "they may encourage" (σωφρονίζωσιν) is used only here in the NT, but is cognate to the adjective oft repeated in Titus and represented by the translation "sensible" (1:8; 2:1, 4, 5, 6, 12). It means simply to make someone be sensible and self-controlled, to restore someone to their senses. The person thus becomes moderate, controlled, disciplined, curbing appetites and actions that they might otherwise indulge.[11] It aims for a self-control that works from the thoughts outward into the words and actions. In that sense it can mean to encourage, to advise, or to urge.[12] Fee suggests the expression "wise them up" as representing the general idea.[13] As in v.3, this does not describe a formal teaching position within the church, but a consistent, steady (present tense verb) influence over and input into the lives of younger women in the course of daily life.

The ones receiving such a ministry are "the young women" (τὰς νέας). The adjective can mean simply new or fresh, but here is used substantivally and thus means those younger than the "older women" already mentioned (v.3).[14] The same word in the masculine form is used in v.6 to designate "the young men."

Part of such a call to sane living is "to love their husbands" (φιλάνδρους εἶναι) or, more literally, "to be husband lovers." The present tense infinitive speaks to a continuous, habitual love. The adjective

---
[11] Thayer, 613.
[12] BAGD, 802.
[13] Fee, 187.
[14] BAGD, 536.

(φιλάνδρους) is a compound from "love" (φίλος) and "man" (ἀνήρ) or, in this case, "husband." Similarly the older women are to teach young women "to love their children" (φιλοτέκνους). This is again a compound word, being comprised of "love" (φίλος) and "child" (τέκνον).

It is instructive that women must be taught "to love their husbands" and "to love their children." These apparently are not naturally obtained disciplines. And they are just that—discipline—for they are a part of what the Apostle intends by a self-disciplined life that grows out of a self-disciplined mind. In Titus's day, marriages were often arranged and love was an acquired thing. It is no less so in days when dating and romance are what lead up to marriage, for the settled discipline of marital love is a deeper and more advanced kind of love that does not arise naturally within us, but must be received from the Lord and taught by His church. There is such a thing as "natural affection" (2 Tim. 3:3, KJV) that should be expected from any human to his/her offspring, but the kind of Christian parenting Paul expects within the church must be inwardly produced by the Holy Spirit and encouraged by the fellowship of believers. In the last days the opportunities and pressures to be "lovers of self" (2 Tim. 3:2) only increase. Thus we must be diligent to live out the command of love the Lord Jesus laid upon us all, and to do so most obviously within our homes, for there is no greater proof of the reality of Christ's presence among us (John 13:34, 35; 15:12, 17; Rom. 12:10; 13:8). This instruction for wives to love their husbands balances the more dominant instruction to submit to them (v.5; cf. Eph. 5:22, 33; Col. 3:18; cf. 1 Peter 3:1).

> **Ministry Maxim**
>
> Mature love is not an emotion that wells up, but a discipline that is worked up.

2:5 to be sensible, pure, workers at home, kind, being subject to their own husbands, so that the word of God will not be dishonored.

Paul continues to list the qualities that "Older women" (v.3) are to teach "young women" (v.4) within the church. There is no verb, but the NASU translators have added "to be" for smoother English reading. The adjective "sensible" (σώφρονας) and its cognates are a staple in these lists of instructions (see on v.2). Younger women are also to be taught to be "pure" (ἁγνὰς). The word describes being chaste and modest. It originally referred to ritual cleanness, but over time its emphasis shifted to the moral realm. Here it likely has overtones of sexual purity.[15]

---
[15] Marshall, 248.

Such women are to be "workers at home" (οἰκουργοὺς). This is the more difficult and more likely reading, rather than οἰκουρός ("keepers at home," KJV). The word is a compound from "home" (οἶκος) and "work" (ἔργω). This does not strictly forbid women from working outside of the home, but it does say that there will be plenty of work awaiting her when she arrives home and that she must carefully balance any outside labor or activities to see that her home and family are prioritized appropriately (cf. 1 Tim. 5:14). Young women should also aim at being "kind" (ἀγαθάς). The word in general fashion describes that which is "good." Here the notion may be fit, capable, and useful[16] or kind, considerate, and benevolent.[17] It could qualify the preceding noun (i.e., "good workers at home"), but since the other qualities listed seem to stand alone, we should thus understand this one as well. It is a word used in Titus to qualify works (1:16; 3:1) or faith (2:10).

Also to be taught is "being subject to their own husbands" (ὑποτασσομένας τοῖς ἰδίοις ἀνδράσιν). The participle "being subject" (ὑποτασσομένας) is a compound verb from "under" (ὑπό) and "appoint" or "order" (τάσσω). It is a word that bespeaks authority and submission. It was a military word which described the ranks of soldiers arranging themselves under the leadership of their commander. Here the middle voice shows that it is a voluntary and personal choice and the present tense reveals that it is an abiding attitude, not a periodic whim. It is used again in this letter to describe the attitude of a servant (v.9) and of all believers to governing authorities (3:1). No one is exempt from submission to authority. In this case the submission is of the wives "to their own husbands" (τοῖς ἰδίοις ἀνδράσιν). It is true that ἀνήρ can refer simply to men in general, but here the addition of the adjective ἰδίοις ("their own") makes clear that the marital relationship is in view and not gender relations in general.

Authority and submission within the home was a hard sell then, and it continues to be today. Why should Christian wives take this seriously? It is "so that the word of God will not be dishonored" (ἵνα μὴ ὁ λόγος τοῦ θεοῦ βλασφημῆται). The conjunction (ἵνα) with the subjunctive verb and negation (μὴ) shows that this is a negative purpose statement. It is probably intended to modify the entire list of instructions toward younger women (vv.4-5), perhaps with special emphasis upon a wife's submission to her husband. When Paul speaks of "the word of God" (ὁ λόγος τοῦ θεοῦ), he probably means the Gospel and the Scriptures which convey it (see on 1:3). The passive voice of the verb shows that

> **Ministry Maxim**
>
> Obedience is only reasonable when the honor of God is my highest goal.

---
[16] BAGD, 2.
[17] Knight, 308; Marshall, 249; Mounce, 412.

"the word of God" is acted upon. The verb means to slander or to speak lightly or injuriously of sacred things.[18] This blasphemy could come from the unbelieving husband or from an unredeemed society that looks in upon the marriage. This is the first of three times in the letter when the motivating factor behind obedience is the response of unbelievers toward the Gospel message Christians are to convey (cf. vv.8, 10). This, combined with Paul's repeated exhortation to "good works" (1:16; 2:7, 14; 3:1, 8, 14), reveals that a major concern of the letter is to equip Titus so that he may equip the believers to become effective in living lives that propel the Gospel's advance to more and more lives.

> **Digging Deeper:**
> 1. What does it say about the nature of marital and parental love that it needs to be learned?
> 2. How do the requirements for a wife both to love and to be subject to her husband balance one another? Why are both required? What if she possesses one without the other? How would this distort God's intention?
> 3. True or false: one of our greatest evangelistic ministries as Christians is the quality of our home and family lives. Why?

2:6 Likewise urge the young men to be sensible;

Paul transitions to consider "the young men" by means of the adverb "Likewise" (ὡσαύτως). It has just been used in v.3 (which see). It signals not that the instructions for the young men are the same as for the young women (vv.4-5), but that for both groups alike true doctrine has implications for how life is to be lived. In designating "the young men" (τοὺς νεωτέρους) Paul used the same word employed in v.4 to speak of "the young women," only in the masculine form. The imperative "urge" (παρακάλει) is in the present tense, indicating that the action should be undertaken repeatedly or habitually. Training "young men" to be godly takes more than a one-time training seminar! The verb is the same one used earlier to urge Titus to train elders/overseers "to exhort" in sound doctrine (1:9) and is a stronger term than "speak" (λαλέω) in 2:1. Paul will use it again at the end of this chapter to wrap up how Titus should deliver all these instructions to various age groups within the church (2:15). The verb is a compound word meaning "to call" (καλέω) "beside" (παρά). It can range in meaning from encourage on the softer side, to exhort on the sterner side. It is one of the essential functions of

---
[18] Rienecker, 654.

Biblical preaching (1 Tim. 6:2; 2 Tim. 4:2). The cognate noun is used as a title for both the Holy Spirit (John 14:16, 26; 15:26; 16:7) and Jesus Christ (1 John 2:1). As Titus comes alongside the young men of the church in exhortations to godliness, he is making himself a channel through whom the Holy Spirit may work. It is not clear what, if any, significance is to be found in the difference in verb here from the one used in v.4 when older women are told to "encourage" the younger women.

> **Ministry Maxim**
>
> A self-controlled mind is the only path to a self-controlled life.

Everything in this verse has been met somewhere in the book already. What is unique is that the young men are given but one exhortation. The older men received four, the older women five, and the younger women seven. Why only one for the young men? It is not that as a general rule young men have less to be concerned about! It is probably closer to the truth that if they can be taught even just one thing, it should be this—"to be sensible" (σωφρονεῖν). The present tense underscores that this is to become a continuous habit of life. The verb is cognate to the word used throughout this second chapter for an obligation laid upon every age group (1:8; 2:2, 4, 5, 6, 12). See on v.2 above. True, the verb is used to describe one who is "in his right mind" (Mark 5:15; Luke 8:35) as opposed to the insanity of demon-possession. But in the bulk of its uses, it has the sense of having a self-controlled mind which enables a person to live a self-controlled life. If young men could be taught one thing, this would perhaps yield as great and far-reaching a benefit as any. If the goal is to become a "sensible" old man (v.2), then one must begin by becoming a "sensible" young man (v.6).

It is possible, though by no means required, that "in all things" (περὶ πάντα, v.7a) should be read with this verse instead of the next. The all-encompassing nature of σωφρονεῖν may make it a natural lead in to this phrase.[19]

Digging Deeper:
1. Why do you think the Apostle Paul gave but one exhortation to young men, after giving multiple exhortations to other age/gender groups?
2. Why do you think "to be sensible" won top billing as the most significant exhortation for young men?
3. Why must such instruction be not merely *spoken* to young men, but *urged* upon them? What significance is there in the fact that this is to be done *repeatedly*?

---

[19] Fee, 188; Mounce, 412.

2:7 in all things show yourself to be an example of good deeds, with purity in doctrine, dignified,

If "in all things" (περὶ πάντα) is meant to be read with the previous verse, that leaves "yourself" (σεαυτὸν) in an emphatic position, something that would seem likely given the instructions addressed now to Titus himself. Beyond just teaching sound doctrine (v.1), Titus is "to be an example" (παρεχόμενος τύπον). The present tense of the participle underscores the continual action required in setting forth an example. The middle voice affirms that this is action Titus must take upon himself and is reinforced by the use of the reflexive pronoun "yourself" (σεαυτὸν).[20] The participial form is used with the force of an imperative. Paul is not offering this as optional advice. It is a compound word made up of "beside" (παρά) and "to hold" (ἔχω). Here it has the sense of showing oneself to be something in particular.[21] The noun "example" (τύπον) originally referred to the mark left by a blow or an impression made under pressure. Then it described a copy or an image and came to refer to a type, pattern or model. Here the sense is that of being an example or pattern in the moral life.[22] The pastor's life must illustrate the truthfulness of his preaching. The same word was used similarly of Timothy (1 Tim. 4:12).

That which Titus is to present an example of is "good deeds" (καλῶν ἔργων). The Apostle's concern for the Cretan believers to perform good works is a major theme of this epistle (1:16; 2:14; 3:1, 8, 14); a concern echoed throughout the PE (1 Tim. 2:10; 3:1; 5:10, 25; 6:18; 2 Tim. 2:21; 3:17). Paul is careful to clarify that we are not saved "on the basis of deeds which we have done in righteousness" (3:5; cf. 2 Tim. 1:9), but that true salvation produces a life of grateful obedience that shows itself in "good deeds." Paul's instructions to Titus and through him to the Cretan believers are designed to produce the kind of life that "will adorn the doctrine of God our Savior in every respect" (2:10b). Paul is concerned for a church that will not hinder, but advance, the progress of the Gospel by their lives.

> **Ministry Maxim**
>
> When what we do matches what we say, we increase our effectiveness exponentially.

The arena (ἐν) of these "good deeds" should be "purity in doctrine" (τῇ διδασκαλίᾳ ἀφθορίαν). Note the presence of the definite article: "*the* doctrine." The word can refer either to the activity of teaching or what is taught.[23] Here it probably points to the former, since the words that follow seem more

---

[20] Mounce, 413.
[21] BAGD, 626.
[22] Ibid., 829-830.
[23] Knight, 311.

likely to apply to the action of teaching than to what is taught.²⁴ This "doctrine" concerns God (2:10). Paul's concern to this point has been that such doctrine be "sound" (1:9; 2:1). Here the concern is its "purity" (ἀφθορίαν). The adjective is used only here in the NT. The word describes that which is uncorrupted and unalloyed. "It is purity of motive, without desire of gain or respect of persons and purity of doctrine."²⁵ As such, Titus's teaching would stand in direct contrast to the self-motivated instruction of the false teachers active on Crete (cf. 1:10-16, esp. v.16).

Titus is also to be "dignified" (σεμνότητα). This noun, like the accusative singular nouns that proceed and follow ("purity," v.7; "speech," v.8) may describe what should be true of Titus's teaching or may stand independently to describe more general characteristics of his character and behavior. A definitive choice is difficult to make, and perhaps is ultimately unnecessary, for the point seems to be that the preacher's life must match his teaching. This noun is found only here and in 1 Timothy 2:2 (where it applies to all believers) and 3:4 (where it applies to overseers). The adjective is used to speak of what should characterize deacons (1 Tim. 3:8), their wives (3:11), and of older men (Titus 2:2). It describes the kind of dignity, gravity, majesty or sanctity which would mark a person as worthy of respect.²⁶

2:8 sound in speech which is beyond reproach, so that the opponent will be put to shame, having nothing bad to say about us.

Titus is also to be "sound in speech" (λόγον ὑγιῆ). The word "speech" is more simply "word" (cf. Titus 1:3, 9; 2:5; 3:8). Whereas "doctrine" (τῇ διδασκαλίᾳ, v.7) probably referred to the act of teaching, here "speech" (λόγον) probably points to the content of what is taught.²⁷ The adjective "sound" (ὑγιῆ) is used by Paul only here and elsewhere is used literally of being whole, sound and healthy. It is cognate to the verb met so often in Titus (1:9, 13; 2:1, 2) and elsewhere in the PE (1 Tim. 1:10; 6:3; 2 Tim. 1:13; 4:3). Titus's teaching is thus to be such as begets spiritual health and healing. Such speech is that "which is beyond reproach" (ἀκατάγνωστον). This word is found only here in the NT. It is a compound word made up of "against" (κατά), "know" (γινώσκω), and the alpha privative for negation. Thus the root idea is not knowing something against someone. It describes that which is unable to be accused and cannot be condemned.²⁸ The pastor must diligently labor to achieve and maintain such

---

²⁴ Mounce, 413.
²⁵ Rienecker, 654.
²⁶ Thayer, 573.
²⁷ Marshall, 255; Mounce, 413.
²⁸ Rienecker, 654.

a speaking ministry (1 Tim. 4:13-16).

Titus is to pursue all these qualities (vv.7-8) not simply because it is right, but because it is wise in the battle against false teachers. The ἵνα with the subjunctive is used in a purpose clause ("so that"). The designation "the opponent" translates ὁ ἐξ ἐναντίας. More literally it might be rendered, "the one out from opposite." It is a description of those on Crete who opposed the Gospel and Titus who represented it. It is in the singular here. Speculation as to the identity of some specific individual will remain just that, speculation. It is possible that the singular is employed because Paul views the opposition as a collective entity. There exist such opponents in every generation and location. The goal is that they "will be put to shame" (ἐντραπῇ). The word is a compound made up of "in" (ἐν) and "turn" (τρέπω). Strictly speaking it means to "turn back" or "turn about," but in the passive, as here, it means to be put to shame.[29] The aorist tense looks to a definite time when the opponents are put to shame. The subjunctive mood couples with the ἵνα to form the final clause. This is to take place both by superior teaching and by exemplary living (vv.7-8).

The shame should come because the opponent is "having nothing bad to say about us" (μηδὲν ἔχων λέγειν περὶ ἡμῶν φαῦλον). As in verse 5, Paul motivates Christian obedience by its effect upon the non-believing (cf. also v.10). The participle "having" (ἔχων) is in the present tense, underscoring that the opponent continually finds himself at a loss in trying to defame God's servant. The negation "nothing" (μηδέν) is absolute, having the sense of "not one single thing." No ground, even the tiniest toe hold or tidbit of truth, is given the enemy for his use against us. People can, of course, say whatever they wish, but there must be given them no just grounds for accusation. The infinitive "to say" (λέγειν) is also in the present tense, stressing the continual nature of the opposition's talk. If once they find any slanderous thing to say, we will never hear the end of it. The prepositional phrase "about us" (περὶ ἡμῶν) specifies the target they have made of us. And, of course, they are looking for something "bad" (φαῦλον) to say against us. It describes that which is worthless, of no account, base and wicked.[30] It is a word reserved almost exclusively for description of evil deeds, not words. Thus it is not simply the content of Titus's speech that is in view, but also his conduct and the manner in which that speech

> **Ministry Maxim**
>
> That which is right is also wise; that which is not right is never wise.

---

[29] Friberg, 152.
[30] Robertson, 4:229.

is presented. Titus's mastery of himself and success in these matters would reflect upon the whole Christian community, and perhaps especially upon its leadership (ἡμῶν, "us").

> **Digging Deeper:**
> 1. What would it look like if you lived a "dignified" life? What changes would be evident? What effect would it have?
> 2. Who do you know whose words beget spiritual health and healing to those who hear them? What from their example can you incorporate into your own speech?
> 3. As Christians should we be concerned with what others think of us? Or should we be concerned only to please the Lord?

2:9 Urge bondslaves to be subject to their own masters in everything, to be well-pleasing, not argumentative,

Paul, having directed Titus to instruct "Older men" (v.2), "Older women" (v.3), "young women" (v.4-5) and "young men" (v.6) in how to live and having directed Titus in how to conduct himself in the process (vv.7-8), Paul now comes to the last group whom Titus is to instruct (vv.9-10). There seems to be a finite verb missing. For smoother reading the NASU looks back to the command "urge" in v.6 and assumes it here, though it is not in the text of v.9. That probably captures the sense of Paul's intent, whether or not he was dependent consciously upon that imperative in his writing.

> **Ministry Maxim**
>
> Submission to our earthly authorities begins with our submission to our heavenly authority.

The sentence begins with "bondslaves" (δούλους). It is the title Paul metaphorically took for his self-identification: "a bond-servant of God" (δοῦλος θεοῦ, 1:1). Here, however, the word is used literally of those in servitude to another. How encouraging it must have been to folk in such a lot that the Apostle willingly adopted such a term for his self-designation. The term spoke of one who sold himself into utter servitude and submission to the will of another. What does the call of discipleship require of one in such a social station? They are "to be subject to their own masters" (ἰδίοις δεσπόταις ὑποτάσσεσθαι). The infinitive "to be subject" (ὑποτάσσεσθαι) describes that which wives are expected to render to their husbands (v.5) and all believers are to render to governing authorities (3:1). It is a compound word from "under" (ὑπό) and "appoint" or "order" (τάσσω). It is a word that bespeaks authority and submission. It was a military word which described the ranks of soldiers arranging themselves under the leadership of their commander. The present tense underscores that this is to be an abiding, constant attitude. The middle voice stresses that this is an attitude that each servant must adopt for himself. Outward discipline may bring the *actions* into submission, but the *heart* must be given in submission. This they are to give to "their own masters" (ἰδίοις δεσπόταις). The word "masters" (δεσπόταις) is used by Paul only in the PE, both of the literal master/slave relationship (1 Tim. 6:1-2) and metaphorically of the disciple/Christ relationship (2 Tim. 2:21). It is the word from which we derive our English word *despot*. The call here is not to slave owners in general, but to one's "own" (ἰδίοις) master. While such submission is restricted to one's own master, it is to him "in everything" (ἐν πᾶσιν). The phrase could be read with what follows, but it is rightly understood as being attached to what precedes it. The expression "in everything" would of course not include those matters a master might lay upon a slave which would require him to sin against the Lord. But all things short of this do appear to be included. The same expression is used to set the sweeping parameters of the instructions in v.10.

Another present infinitive adds a second responsibility for slaves: "to be well-pleasing" (εὐαρέστους εἶναι). The present tense stresses the continual nature of the action expected. The adjective "well-pleasing" (εὐαρέστους) is used by Paul eight of its nine times in the NT (Rom. 12:1, 2; 14:18; 2 Cor. 5:9; Eph. 5:10; Phil. 4:18; Col. 3:20; Titus 2:9; Heb. 13:21). The word describes that which is acceptable or pleasing and always in reference to God. It would be possible to understand the meaning here to be what is well-pleasing to a slave's master, but given its consistency of usage in the NT, it seems clear it is referring here not to a slave's earthly master, but to his heavenly Lord. Perhaps it should be said that the slave's new faith requires him to please his heavenly Master by seeking to please his earthly master. This would be a radical shift in thinking for a new believer who found himself in such a social station.

A slave is also to be "not argumentative" (μὴ ἀντιλέγοντας). Paul now begins a string of three participles (running into v.10). They describe more fully what it means for a slave to be "well-pleasing" unto God. He again stresses the continual nature of the action by use of the present tense in all three. The word here is a compound, made up of "against" (ἀντί) and "to speak" (λέγω). Two of Paul's three usages of the word are here in Titus (cf. Rom. 10:21). It is used also in 1:9 to speak of the false teachers as "those who contradict."

2:10 not pilfering, but showing all good faith so that they will adorn the doctrine of God our Savior in every respect.

The second of a string of three consecutive participles opens this tenth verse. A slave who is "well-pleasing" (v.9) is one who is "not pilfering" (μὴ νοσφιζομένους). The word is used again in the NT only in the description of what Ananias and Sapphira did in keeping back a portion of the proceeds after the sale of their land (Acts 5:2-3). Its root idea is that of setting apart, separating or dividing. Here it is in the middle voice and means to set apart to oneself.[31] The idea is that of misappropriation, embezzlement or stealing. A slave was in a unique position to be able to help himself to his master's property or wealth without detection. This was no doubt a widespread problem in the ancient world and the Apostle demands that believing slaves must behave differently.

In strong contrast ("but," ἀλλὰ) to arguing and stealing, more positively they should be "showing all good faith" (πᾶσαν πίστιν ἐνδεικνυμένους ἀγαθήν). The participle in the middle voice means to show or demonstrate oneself in something or show or demonstrate something in oneself.[32] Discerning just what is to be shown is a bit of a challenge. The participle separates "all faith" (πᾶσαν πίστιν) from "good" (ἀγαθήν). The key to understanding just what Paul meant appears to rest upon discerning how the adjective "good" (ἀγαθήν) is intended to function. Is it used attributively, as per the majority of English translations? Or is it used as a predicate, yielding a translation something like "showing that true faith is productive"? The separation of the adjective from the noun may point to the latter option.[33] Yet the likelihood, despite the unusual usage and position of "good" (ἀγαθήν), is that it is being used attributively. Here "faith" (πίστιν) has the sense of faithfulness, reliability or trustworthiness.[34] Perhaps, then, the notion is something like "showing yourself completely faithful in goodness." This would make this final quality for slaves a sweeping requirement that gathers up all unexpressed qualifications. This would allow Paul to complete his instructions to slaves on a broad basis just as he opened instructions to be subject to their masters "in everything" (v.9).

> **Ministry Maxim**
>
> A well-ordered life makes for a well-received witness.

---

[31] Thayer, 429.
[32] Ibid., 213.
[33] NET Bible.
[34] BAGD, 662.

Paul now adds a purpose clause ("so that," ἵνα + the subjunctive) to underscore why these instructions should be followed. The verb "will adorn" (κοσμῶσιν) is in the present tense and underscores the abiding, habitual nature of the action called for. It arose from the noun κόσμος ("world"), describing the ordered world. It has the root idea of placing things in order or arranging things and then to adorn or ornament something.[35] Our word *cosmetic* comes from this root. Paul used the word when he told Timothy that women should "adorn themselves with proper clothing, modestly and discreetly, not with braided hair and gold or pearls or costly garments" (1 Tim. 2:9; cf. 1 Peter 3:5). The word seems, then, to refer to drawing out the natural beauty of a thing by ordering and arranging it to look its best.

That which is to be thus adorned is "the doctrine of God our Savior" (τὴν διδασκαλίαν τὴν τοῦ σωτῆρος ἡμῶν θεοῦ). The noun "the doctrine" (τὴν διδασκαλίαν) is used passively, as so often in the PE (e.g., 1 Tim. 1:10; 4:6; 2 Tim. 3:10; Titus 1:9; 2:1, 7), to describe that which is taught. The specific teaching under consideration is made plain by a second use of the definite article (τὴν) after the noun and before the objective genitive phrase "of God our Savior" (τοῦ σωτῆρος ἡμῶν θεου).[36] The reference is probably to God the Father (1 Tim. 1:1; 2:3; Titus 1:3; 3:4), though similar phraseology will soon designate Jesus Christ (v.13).

This adornment is to be "in every respect" (ἐν πᾶσιν). This is the same phrase just employed in v.9 to mark out the sphere of a slave's submission. The form is probably to be understood as neuter ("in all things") rather than masculine ("among all men"). Paul is calling for the whole of life to be brought under the truth of the Gospel and made to serve its advance. No matter where someone may intersect our lives they should see the Gospel being set forth in its beauty. This is now the third time Paul has underscored his ethical instructions by noting the effect that a Christian's behavior will have upon the unbelieving (vv.5, 8, 10).

> ### Digging Deeper:
> 1. How does our commitment to pleasing our earthly authorities bring joy to our heavenly Master?
> 2. What do these two verses tell us about why Paul did not counsel slaves to overthrow the unjust system of slavery?

---

[35] Thayer, 356.
[36] Knight, 315.

2:11 For the grace of God has appeared, bringing salvation to all men,

We now come to the theological core of Titus (vv.11-14; these verses comprise one continuous sentence in the Greek text). Here Paul lays a foundation of truth upon which all the preceding instructions rest. The conjunction "For" (γὰρ) sets forth the reason that undergirds not simply the instructions to slaves (vv.9-10), but the whole of the chapter. The verb ("has appeared," Ἐπεφάνη) is thrust forward to the head of the sentence for emphasis. It emphasizes the revolutionary and transforming nature of the appearing. The aorist tense views it as an epical event in the past. The passive voice points to God's acting to reveal His grace to mankind. Paul uses the verb only twice, the second time being in 3:4. The two other NT usages speak either metaphorically (Luke 1:79) or literally (Acts 27:20) of the rising or appearing of the sun. It is a compound word made up of "upon" (ἐπί) and "to show" (φαίνω). The sense of the word, then, is to bring to light and then to appear or to show something. From this we derive our word *epiphany*.

That which has thus appeared is "the grace of God" (ἡ χάρις τοῦ θεοῦ). This exact expression is found again only in Romans 5:5 and 1 Corinthians 15:10. In using this expression Paul views the whole of Jesus' incarnation and redemptive work as one event. It is viewed from the vantage point of the benefit of man, thus the emphasis upon "the grace of God." Paul will similarly say, "But when the kindness of God our Savior and His love for mankind appeared, He saved us" (3:4-5a). Indeed, the same verb is used by Luke to speak of the incarnation: "Because of the tender mercy of our God, with which the Sunrise from on high will visit us, TO SHINE UPON [ἐπιφᾶναι] THOSE WHO SIT IN DARKNESS AND THE SHADOW OF DEATH . . ." (Luke 1:78-79a). The noun "the grace" (ἡ χάρις) serves as the subject of the entire sentence (vv.11-14).

This resulted in "bringing salvation to all men" (σωτήριος πᾶσιν ἀνθρώποις). There is no verb in the Greek text. It reads simply "salvation to all men." The predicate adjective "salvation" (σωτήριος) echoes the phrase "God our Savior" in v.10. The grace of God saves, instructs and empowers.[37] The phrase "to all men" properly attaches to the noun "grace" and not the verb "has appeared," as per the NASU translation (contra KJV, NKJV, NIV). Paul is not teaching universalism. Rather, he intends this statement in the spirit of what he said to Timothy about how God "desires all men to be saved and to come to the knowledge of the truth" (1 Tim.

> **Ministry Maxim**
>
> Light breaks through wherever the truth about Jesus is spoken.

---

[37] Knight, 318.

2:4). We "have fixed our hope on the living God, who is the Savior of all men, especially of believers" (4:10). Christ's atoning work is *sufficient* for all of humanity, though it is *efficient* only for those who actually repent and trust in Him. Thus Paul instructed Timothy to hold out hope even for the false teachers, "if perhaps God may grant them repentance leading to the knowledge of the truth" (2 Tim. 2:25). The universal scope of salvation is the justification for its ethical implications and instructions to all genders, ages and classes of people (vv.2-10).[38]

Digging Deeper:
1. Why is the expression "the grace of God" a fitting, concise way of describing the incarnation, life, death, resurrection and ascension of Jesus?
2. How did this appearing take place? How can it continue to take place for those still in darkness? What is our role in this?
3. In what sense is salvation "to all men"? Is there a sense in which it is not "to all men"? Explain.

2:12 instructing us to deny ungodliness and worldly desires and to live sensibly, righteously and godly in the present age,

The grace of God (v.11) has an educative purpose, for it is almost personified as a teacher who is "instructing us" (παιδεύουσα ἡμᾶς). The present tense points to continuous instruction. There is never a time in our Christian life and growth that we attain a plateau and cease to keep learning of grace. The participle qualifies the main clause of v.11: "the grace of God has appeared." The idea is the instruction of a child. It also often carries a sense of discipline or chastisement to the training it describes.[39] It is so used by Paul in the PE (1 Tim. 1:20; 2 Tim. 2:25) and elsewhere (1 Cor. 11:32; 2 Cor. 6:9). The purpose of the training is set forth by the conjunction ἵνα. That purpose is both negative ("to deny") and positive ("to live"). Paul begins with the negative. Grace teaches us "to deny" (ἀρνησάμενοι) certain things. All of Paul's usages of the word are in the PE. It is a strong word that normally points to a denial of the faith or of God (1 Tim. 5:8; 2 Tim. 2:12; 3:5; Titus 1:16). It can also describe God's denial of those who deny Him (2 Tim. 2:12). The aorist tense emphasizes the desired denial as action taken at a specific point in time. The middle

---

[38] Hiebert, "Titus," 11:440.
[39] Rienecker, 655.

voice emphasizes taking action upon oneself (cf. 2 Tim. 2:13 and God's inability to deny His own nature), thus denying oneself the opportunity to indulge in the vices that follow.

Those vices are described in two ways. First as "ungodliness" (τὴν ἀσέβειαν). The noun is used four times in Paul (Rom. 1:18; 11:26; 2 Tim. 2:16; Titus 2:12). God's wrath is currently being poured out against all such "ungodliness" (Rom. 1:18). It points to "the rejection of all that is reverent and of all that has to do with God."[40] It is the opposite of the "godly" life (εὐσεβῶς) that Paul will, later in this verse, say grace teaches us to live out. While God in His wrath is destroying such "ungodliness" in the world, He, by His grace, is actively teaching His own to distance themselves from it. The second vice to be avoided is "worldly desires" (τὰς κοσμικὰς ἐπιθυμίας). The noun "desires" (ἐπιθυμίας) can be a neutral term, but is used frequently by Paul and usually to describe strong impulses or lusts that arise within from a person's ungoverned sinful nature. We all once lived under their control (Titus 3:3). Paul told Timothy to flee them (2 Tim. 2:22). The emphasis is often sexual, but goes far beyond just that to include covetousness (1 Tim. 6:9) and misguided religious impulses (2 Tim. 4:3). Such lusts are described in the PE as "harmful" (1 Tim. 6:9), "youthful" (2 Tim. 2:22), "various" (2 Tim. 3:6; Titus 3:3), and one's "own" (2 Tim. 4:3). Here they are described as "worldly" (κοσμικὰς). That is to say they arise from and are fed by this fallen creation, rather than from and by God. They are what characterize "this present age" (see end of this verse). The definite article marks them as a distinct kind of impulse that stands opposed to God's will. They would include, in Titus's context, the kinds of things for which Cretans were so well known (1:12). The singular "ungodliness" coupled with the plural "worldly desires" shows that both the root problem ("ungodliness") and its multitudinous manifestations ("worldly desires") must be renounced.[41]

In addition to the negative orientation of grace's instruction ("to deny"), there is the positive function of showing us how "to live" (ζήσωμεν). The aorist tense corresponds to the aorist tense of the previous verb—showing that the living is to be done coterminous with the denying. The previous participle ("to deny") is dependent upon this main verb ("to live"). There is a substitution that is to go on. We cannot live the Christian life without saying "no" (cf. NIV) to certain things. However, we are not called simply to live a life of denial, but while denying certain desires we are to take up other pursuits as an active replacement for them. We don't just shun ungodliness, we also embrace godliness in its place. The Christian life is a positive life.

---

[40] Ibid.
[41] Knight, 320.

The verb "to live" (ζήσωμεν) is immediately qualified by three adverbs. The first is "sensibly" (σωφρόνως). It means with sound mind, soberly, temperately, discreetly.[42] It is cognate to the adjective and verb used so frequently by Paul in the instructions to various groupings in this chapter (1:8; 2:2, 4, 5, 6). The only way to live the life we ought to live is by the grace of God. A clear mind and accurate thinking do not arise simply from the absence of distraction, but from the presence of God's grace.

We should also ("and," καί) live "righteously" (δικαίως). This adverb is used by Paul only two other times, once to describe the uprightness of his own actions (1 Thess. 2:10) and again to describe what ought to be done (1 Cor. 15:34). It has a sense of moral obligation to it.

Then we should also ("and," καί) live "godly" (εὐσεβῶς). This adverb is used elsewhere only in 2 Timothy 3:12, but the word group is used extensively throughout the PE (1 Tim. 2:2; 3:16; 4:7, 8; 5:4; 6:3, 5, 6, 11; 2 Tim. 3:5, 12; Titus 1:1; 2:12). It describes a man's appropriate attitude and relationship toward God and the things of God.[43] It is the antithesis of the "ungodliness" (ἀσέβειαν) that Paul has just said grace teaches us to avoid. Thus the three adverbs point to a well-rounded life with oneself ("sensibly"), others ("righteously"), and God ("godly").

> **Ministry Maxim**
>
> Grace is both positive and negative—teaching me to embrace some things and to reject others.

The grace of God operates thus "in the present age" (ἐν τῷ νῦν αἰῶνι; lit., "the now age"). The exact phrase is found elsewhere only in 1 Timothy 6:17 where it used to discourage people from trusting in riches. It was "this present world" (τὸν νῦν αἰῶνα) which Demas loved so much that he deserted Paul (2 Tim. 4:10). The noun "age" (αἰῶνι) is frequently used in the expression "forever and ever" (εἰς τοὺς αἰῶνας τῶν αἰώνων; e.g., 2 Tim. 4:18) or "unto the ages of the ages." The emphasis seems to be, then, that the grace of God operates with such educative power right here, right now—in the midst of the very real world of spiritual struggle, temptation and opposition to God (cf. "worldly desires," just above in this verse). The hope of grace is found not merely in the eschatological triumph of Christ (though it is surely that as well, cf. v.13), but also in the present time and circumstances. Right here, right now, God's grace operates to make us the kind of people who live the kind of lives that honor God and benefit others and ourselves. The grace of God extends the power not just to rescue us from an evil world, but to transform us in the midst of it.

---

[42] Thayer, 613.
[43] BAGD, 326.

> **Digging Deeper:**
> 1. In what way does picturing God's grace as a teacher (as opposed to some other metaphor) give you hope in your growth in Christ?
> 2. How do the positive and negative aim of grace round out your understanding of what God's grace is and does?
> 3. In your own words explain how this verse reveals God's grace, positively impacting your relationships to self, others and God.

2:13 looking for the blessed hope and the appearing of the glory of our great God and Savior, Christ Jesus,

Grace not only saves us from the punishment of past wrongs (vv.11, 14a) and teaches us in the present (v.12); it also orients us rightly to the future. The participle "looking for" (προσδεχόμενοι) is a compound word made up of "to" (πρός) and "receive" (δέχομαι). The root idea is that of receiving to oneself. It came then to include the watchful, glad anticipation of some expected thing. It is used of Simeon (Luke 2:25), Anna (2:38), Joseph of Arimathea (Mark 15:43; Luke 23:51) and their watchful anticipation of the Messiah's first advent. It is used here and elsewhere (Luke 12:36) of anticipating Christ's second coming and His consummation of all things (Jude 21). The present tense stresses the continual nature of the anticipation and watchfulness, while the middle voice stresses the inward nature of the longing. The participial clause continues to clarify the verb "to live" (ζήσωμεν) of v.12 and thus describes the kind of life we live by God's grace—one full of hope and expectation.[44] All the previous moral instructions (vv.2-10) are undertaken with joy, in anticipation of the Lord's return (1 John 3:2-3).

The object of this anticipation is given a twofold description: "the blessed hope and the appearing of the glory" (τὴν μακαρίαν ἐλπίδα καὶ ἐπιφάνειαν τῆς δόξης). The word translated "blessed" (μακαρίαν) has a wide range of meaning—from "happy" to "blessed"—but in the PE it focuses more directly upon the Person of God Himself (1 Tim. 1:11; 6:15). Thus being combined here with the noun "hope" (ἐλπίδα) distinguishes this as a particularly divine event. The presence of the definite article marks this as a unique and singular "hope" characteristic of the Christian only. The position of the adjective ("blessed," μακαρίαν) between the definite article and the noun ("the . . . hope," τὴν . . . ἐλπίδα) emphasizes the qualitative nature of the "hope" that is anticipated. Another description of the same event is then given. The conjunction ("and," καὶ) is

---
[44] Knight, 321.

used epexegetically so that the former phrase ("the blessed hope") is given fuller definition and explanation by the second phrase ("the appearing of the glory")—the blessed hope of believers is the appearing of God's glory.[45] The one definite article ("the," τὴν) governs the two nouns, "hope" (ἐλπίδα) and "appearing" (ἐπιφάνειαν), showing this to be a singular event considered from two perspectives. The noun "appearing" (ἐπιφάνειαν) is used only by Paul in the NT. He uses it once of the first advent of Christ (2 Tim. 1:10), but otherwise it refers, as it does here, to His second advent (2 Thess. 2:8; 1 Tim. 6:14; 2 Tim. 4:1, 8). It was a word familiar to the Greeks who used it of the visible manifestation of one of the otherwise unseen gods. The manifestation might have been via a personal appearance or through some powerful deed done to show the presence of the god.[46] Paul took over the word, infusing it with Christian content and meaning, and used it of Christ. The cognate verb is used in v.11 (which see). It is a compound word stressing the brilliant shining forth of that which has previously been shrouded in darkness. We derive our word *epiphany* from it. It is not unusual, then, for Paul to speak of such a shining forth "of the glory" (τῆς δόξης). Note that the definite article is present to mark this as the distinctive and unique glory that belongs to God alone (Isa. 42:8; 43:7; 48:11; 49:3; 66:18, 19). Viewing the genitive as objective (i.e., "the appearing of the glory," NASB, ESV, RSV, NRSV) rather than descriptive (i.e., "glorious appearing," NIV, KJV, NKJV) is to be preferred.[47] Christ's first epiphany revealed God's grace (v.11); His second epiphany will unveil God's glory (v.13).

The anticipated appearance is "of our great God and Savior, Christ Jesus" (τοῦ μεγάλου θεοῦ καὶ σωτῆρος ἡμῶν Ἰησοῦ Χριστοῦ). A single definite article ("the," τοῦ) governs and holds together as one expression "great God" (μεγάλου θεοῦ) with "and Savior" (καὶ σωτῆρος).[48] This being affixed to "Christ Jesus" (Ἰησοῦ Χριστοῦ) makes for one of the strongest and clearest statements regarding the deity of Jesus Christ anywhere in the Scriptures. This understanding (as opposed to "the great God and our Saviour Jesus Christ," KJV) is further supported by the fact that the noun "appearing" (ἐπιφάνεια) is never used elsewhere to describe God the Father. Also the terminology "God and Savior" was in common usage in Hellenistic circles of the day. Such a

> **Ministry Maxim**
>
> Balanced faith looks back restfully upon the revelation of God's grace and looks forward hopefully to the revelation of God's glory.

---

[45] Marshall, 274; Mounce, 425.
[46] BAGD, 304.
[47] Fee, 195-196.
[48] Robertson, 4:604.

Christological reading of the text, Mounce says, is required because, "This the most natural reading of the text, is required by the grammar, concurs with Paul's use of ἐπιφάνεια, 'appearing,' accounts for the singular use of the phrase 'God and savior' in secular thought, and fits the context well."[49]

> **Digging Deeper:**
> 1. In what way should God's grace impact your past, your present, and your future?
> 2. Why is the revelation of God's "glory" a hopeful thing to the believer in Jesus Christ? Why might that sound to some as less than hopeful?
> 3. How can this verse be helpful in witnessing to cult members about the Person of Jesus Christ?

2:14 who gave Himself for us to redeem us from every lawless deed, and to purify for Himself a people for His own possession, zealous for good deeds.

The sentence begun in v.11 continues on, now expanding upon the reference to "Christ Jesus" made at the close of v.13. It is He "who gave Himself for us" (ὃς ἔδωκεν ἑαυτὸν ὑπὲρ ἡμῶν). The masculine singular relative pronoun "who" (ὅς) is the direct link back to "Christ Jesus" (Ἰησοῦ Χριστοῦ) in v.13. Indeed, here is a reverberation of our Lord's own words in Mark 10:45. The aorist tense of the verb "gave" (ἔδωκεν) may point to the whole of Jesus' redemptive mission considered as one event, but more specifically it points to the events of the cross when He bore our sins. The reflexive pronoun "Himself" (ἑαυτὸν) underscores the self-sacrificing and all-encompassing nature of Christ's sacrifice, stressing the high cost of our redemption. Such a gift is "for us" (ὑπὲρ ἡμῶν)! The combination of the preposition and pronoun is used often by Paul to describe Christ's sacrifice (Rom. 5:8; 8:32; 2 Cor. 5:21; Gal. 3:13; Eph. 5:2; 1 Thess. 5:10). The preposition "for" (ὑπέρ) means "in behalf of" or "for the sake of."[50]

Now a purpose clause spells out more specifically the aim of Jesus' sacrifice of Himself: "to redeem us" (ἵνα λυτρώσηται ἡμᾶς). The conjunction (ἵνα) plus the subjunctive mood of the two verbs mark this as a clause setting forth a double purpose. The first verb means "to obtain release by the payment of a

---
[49] Mounce, 431.
[50] BAGD, 838.

price."⁵¹ Surprisingly the verb is used only two other times in the NT (Luke 24:21; 1 Peter 1:18). Paul uses the verb only here and never uses the other cognates, though he does speak of Christ purchasing us (1 Cor. 6:20; 7:23; Gal. 3:13; 4:5).⁵² Jesus Himself used the cognate noun when He said, "the Son of Man did not come to be served, but to serve, and to give His life *a ransom for many*" (Matt. 20:28; Mark 10:45, emphasis added). The aorist tense again points to the events of Christ's suffering and death. The middle voice underscores Christ's acting upon Himself (i.e., sacrificing Himself) in order to redeem us.

With His own life Jesus redeemed us "from every lawless deed" (ἀπὸ πάσης ἀνομίας). The noun rendered "lawless deed" (ἀνομίας) refers to a contempt toward and violation of the law.⁵³ Such rebellion will find its fullest expression in the antichrist (2 Thess. 2:3, 7), but it is found active in the sin nature of every human (Rom. 6:19). It is the antithesis of what a believer is now to be (2 Cor. 6:14), but thankfully God through Christ provided forgiveness for such violations (Rom. 4:7). We were released from this bondage (6:19) when Christ purchased us at the cost of His own life. This phrase may be a reflection of Psalm 130:8 (129:8 in LXX).

The second ("and," καὶ) prong of this purpose clause is "to purify for Himself a people for His own possession (καθαρίσῃ ἑαυτῷ λαὸν περιούσιον). The verb (καθαρίσῃ, "to purify") is used thirty-one times in the NT, but only three of those are by Paul (cf. 2 Cor. 7:1; Eph. 5:26). It is the root from which we get our words *cathartic* and *cauterize*. It means simply to cleanse or to make clean. It can refer literally to cleansing from dirt (Luke 11:39) and also can be figuratively used of ritual cleanness (Acts 10:15), physical healing (Mark 1:40), and of religious and moral purity (1 John 1:7).⁵⁴ Knight says, "Whereas λυτρώσηται speaks of removing Christians from the control of sin, καθαρίσῃ speaks of removing the defilement of sin from Christians."⁵⁵ The aorist tense points to the singular act from which comes all cleansing from sin—the sacrificial death of Jesus Christ. Ezekiel 37:23 employs this verb in the LXX and must surely have been in Paul's mind as he penned this verse. This cleansed people are "for Himself" (ἑαυτῷ). The dative could be rendered "to Himself" and could be picking up on the previous idea of redemption. This is further expanded by

> **Ministry Maxim**
>
> Christ will not possess me fully until He has purified me thoroughly.

---

⁵¹ Rienecker, 655.
⁵² Vincent, 4:346.
⁵³ Thayer, 48.
⁵⁴ Friberg, 209.
⁵⁵ Knight, 328.

the expression "a people for His own possession" (λαὸν περιούσιον). It was not simply a single person whom Christ bought, but a whole "people." The collective singular form (λαὸν, "a people") pictures all the redeemed of all time as being the goal and desire of Christ's heart. And they are to Him "for His own possession," an expression that renders but one word in the Greek text (περιούσιον). The word is used only here in the NT. It refers to something that is a special and personal possession. It refers to that which is chosen and thus special. It is used in the LXX to speak of the Hebrews as God's special possession (e.g., Exod. 19:5). In secular Greek it could speak of a married man as "the chosen one."[56]

One last clause rounds out the sentence and further describes these people: "zealous for good deeds" (ζηλωτὴν καλῶν ἔργων). It might be rendered "a zealot for good works."[57] The singular form (ζηλωτὴν) is used to bring it into conformity to the singular "a people" (λαὸν). The term "zealous" (ζηλωτὴν) is used only two other times by Paul, once of his own zeal after his "ancestral traditions" (Gal. 1:14) and the other of the Corinthian's longing after spiritual gifts (1 Cor. 14:12). The theme of "good works" is a rich one in Titus (2:7, 14; 3:1, 8, 14). Paul acknowledges that though such deeds cannot save a person (3:5), they are the necessary evidence of one who is truly saved.

> **Digging Deeper:**
> 1. What does this tell us about the value Christ places upon His people: Christ died ("gave Himself") to buy us ("to redeem") for Himself ("for His own possession")?
> 2. How should it affect our choices to know that Christ has to purify us to possess us? Does He own you this thoroughly at this moment? If not, what does this tell you about why He does not thus own you?
> 3. Describe the difference between being *willing* to do good deeds and being *"zealous* for good deeds"? Which characterizes you?

2:15 These things speak and exhort and reprove with all authority. Let no one disregard you.

Using the demonstrative plural pronoun "These things" (Ταῦτα), the Apostle now gathers up the whole of what he has ordered in vv.1-14. He immediately charges Titus using three imperatives which speak to his responsibility with

---

[56] BAGD, 648.
[57] Robertson, 4:605.

"These things." All three are in the present tense, demanding that continual action be undertaken. The first two have been used already in this chapter, the third appeared in the previous chapter. The terms all become progressively more intense and strong—from "speak" to "exhort" to "reprove." First he must "speak" (λάλει). The same imperative opened this chapter (v.1) and now gathers up all that has been said since, forming an inclusion. By using the verb "speak," as in v.1, Paul points to the teaching ministry of Titus. Next ("and," καὶ) he orders Titus to "exhort" (παρακάλει). This command was used regarding Titus's instructions to the young men (v.6; cf. 1:9). It is a compound word meaning "to call" (καλέω) "beside" (παρά). It can range in meaning from the more gentle "encourage" to the stronger "exhort," depending upon the context. Paul also ("and," καὶ) ordered Titus to "reprove" (ἔλεγχε) the people. This third imperative harkens back to 1:13 where Paul charged Titus to "reprove them severely" (cf. also 1:9). It has the notion of proving something through demonstrable evidence and thus to reprove a person concerning their error and to produce conviction over his wrong.

> **Ministry Maxim**
>
> I must guard against my ministry being disregarded, but I must equally guard against my own selfish hunger to be respected by others.

Such teaching, exhortation, and reproof are to be "with all authority" (μετὰ πάσης ἐπιταγῆς). The three imperatives demand increasingly stronger forms of verbal instruction. Thus we may assume the appeal to authority would grow from an assumed authority ("speak") to a more overtly stated authority ("reprove"). The word translated "authority" (ἐπιταγῆς) is used only by Paul in the NT and speaks either of a command of God (Rom. 16:26; 1 Cor. 7:25; 1 Tim. 1:1; Titus 1:3) or the authoritative command of His Apostles (1 Cor. 7:6; 2 Cor. 8:8). Thayer suggests "with every possible form of authority" as a reasonable translation.[58] Or perhaps something along the lines of "with all impressiveness" gives the sense.[59] Titus may not have possessed the power to force obedience, but he did have the authority to demand it. Violations were then upon the conscience of the offender, not a reluctant shepherd. The pastor who holds forth and operates out of God's authoritative Word thereby ministers with divine authority.[60] With the reuse of these previous commands Paul gathers up all he has said to this point and underscores it with urgency and obligation. The Gospel truth (vv.11-14) and the practical instruction for various age groups (vv.2-10) are not simply good ideas or warm counsel, but God's divine will.

---

[58] Thayer, 244.
[59] BAGD, 302.
[60] Guthrie, 202.

Following on the three commands, Titus now issues a prohibition: "Let no one disregard you" (μηδείς σου περιφρονείτω). He similarly charged Timothy (1 Tim. 4:12). The verb is used only here in the NT. It is a compound word made up of "around" (περί) and "to think" (φρονέω). It thus means "to think around." It also came to mean to overlook someone and to disregard him.[61] The imperative is in the present tense and, with the negation, this demands that action now in progress be stopped. Titus was allowing others to, as it were, think circles around him. This must stop immediately. Robertson's counsel is sound, "The best way for the modern minister to command respect for his 'authority' is to do thinking that will deserve it."[62] The negative "no one" (μηδείς) is used as a substantive and makes the prohibition absolute and all-encompassing. The second person singular pronoun "you" (σου) lays the responsibility squarely upon Titus's own shoulders. This responsibility belongs to the pastor, and no one else can fulfill it for him.

> **Digging Deeper:**
> 1. Why does Paul use three commands ("speak," "exhort," and "reprove") when one might have sufficed?
> 2. How does a pastor exercise authority without becoming authoritarian?
> 3. What are appropriate steps a pastor—especially a younger one—can take to avoid being disregarded by people? How can he guard *his ministry* from being taken lightly without protecting *himself* from being taken lightly?

---

[61] Rienecker, 655.
[62] Robertson, 4:605.

CHAPTER

3

3:1 Remind them to be subject to rulers, to authorities, to be obedient, to be ready for every good deed,

Just as Paul had focused upon relationships among believers throughout the second chapter (vv.2-10) and then gave a theological undergirding for those instructions (vv.11-14), now the Apostle speaks of relationships to the non-believing (3:1-2) and gives a theological justification for these instructions (vv.3-7).

A fifth imperative follows quickly on the heels of the four in the previous verse and Paul continues on the theme of "authority" (2:15). The command "Remind them" ('Υπομίμνησκε αὐτοὺς) is in the present tense, demanding action be undertaken repeatedly. "Keep on reminding them" seems to capture the idea. Paul is calling for a new way of life and ministry—a lifestyle that apparently the Cretan believers have already been instructed in. A good deal of ministry, and thus also personal Christian growth, is taken up with reminder. Paul's only other use of the word was also in the form of a command to Timothy (2 Tim. 2:14). The theme of remembrance, however, is a rich one in the NT (Luke 22:61; John 14:26; 2 Peter 1:12; 3 John 10; Jude 5). Much of a pastor's energy will be spent on the ministry of reminder. The third person plural pronoun "them" (αὐτοὺς) points back specifically to the various age groups within the Cretan church (2:2-10) and generally to all the believers Titus has charge over. We never outgrow the ministry of reminder. The verb used here is a compound word, made up of "under" (ὑπό) and "remember" (μιμνήσκω). The preposition in compound may have the sense of "put them under remembrance" (i.e., under the weight of this reminder).

The command is here directed toward a sixfold responsibility, set forth by five infinitives (three here and two more in v.2) and a participle (v.2) that functions in much the same way. The grammar is compressed with the first two infinitives ("to be subject," ὑποτάσσεσθαι; "to be obedient," πειθαρχεῖν) and two nouns ("rulers," ἀρχαῖς; "authorities," ἐξουσίαις) compacted together without any connective words (such as "and," καὶ).

The first infinitive is "to be subject" (ὑποτάσσεσθαι). Here too is a compound word, made up of "under" (ὑπό) and "appoint" or "order" (τάσσω). It was a military word which described the ranks of soldiers arranging themselves under the leadership of their commander, and as such it addresses issues of authority and submission. Paul has already employed it in 2:5, 9 when speaking to wives in relation to their husbands and bondslaves in relation to their masters. Here he makes clear that submission is not the lot of a just a few, but that everyone lives under authority and must practice submission. The present tense demands continual action. The form could be either passive ("be subjected to") or middle voice ("subject yourselves"). The latter seems the more likely since Paul was probably calling for willing submission on the part of the believer. Such a stance is to be in direct contrast to "rebellion" (ἀνυπότακτα, 1:6) and the "rebellious" (ἀνυπότακτοι, 1:10) nature for which the unregenerate Cretans were infamous.[1] The subjection here pressed upon all believers is "to rulers, to authorities" (ἀρχαῖς ἐξουσίαις). As datives they serve as the object of the infinitive. The former word ("rulers," ἀρχαῖς) is used frequently by Paul (eight of his eleven usages) of unseen spiritual beings (angels or demons) at work in our world and the authority that has been delegated to them or usurped by them (Rom. 8:38; 1 Cor. 15:24; Eph. 1:21; 3:10; 6:12; Col. 1:16; 2:10, 15). The latter word, though used more broadly by Paul (e.g., Rom. 9:21; 1 Cor. 7:37; 2 Thess. 5:9), is also used to describe angels/demons. Virtually every time (except Col. 1:13, 16) that it is so used it appears in tandem with the former word (1 Cor. 15:24; Eph. 1:21; 2:2; 3:10; 6:12; Col. 2:10, 2:15). The latter word is used also in Romans 13:1-3, as it is here, to describe political rulers or their political entities. The two terms also appear together in that context in Romans 13:3. Paul develops this theme more fully there (Rom. 13:1-7), and that passage should be read as a fuller commentary of Paul's intent here.[2]

> **Ministry Maxim**
>
> Obedience may be compelled by eternal forces, but submission must arise from internal choices.

The second infinitive is "to be obedient" (πειθαρχεῖν). This too is in the present tense, demanding a continual lifestyle of obedience. The word is used only here by Paul and its other three NT usages are by Luke (Acts 5:29, 32;

---

[1] Marshall, 301.
[2] For more on this theme see the author's *Embracing Authority*, especially 61-76.

27:21). It is comprised of the roots of "to listen/obey" (πείθω) and "ruler" (ἀρχή, just used in this verse and translated "rulers"). It has specific emphasis upon obedience to authority. Set alongside the first infinitive, this describes the Apostle's intent when he demanded submission to earthly governing authorities. To live in submission to governing authorities is to live in obedience to them. The exception of being compelled to disobedience of a divine command is assumed (cf. Acts 5:29, where the same form of the word is found for the only other time in the NT). Those who dismiss Paul's words as antiquated and out of touch with reality need only remember that it was Nero who ruled even as Paul wrote.

The third infinitive is "to be ready" (ἑτοίμους εἶναι). Here too the present tense demands continual action, pointing to a lifestyle of readiness. The adjective "ready" (ἑτοίμους) is used by Paul only here and in 2 Corinthians (9:5; 10:6, 16). The believer is to be prepared "for every good deed" (πρὸς πᾶν ἔργον ἀγαθὸν). This phrase is thrown forward in the clause for emphasis, the infinitive being the last word. This exact expression was already used in 1:16 when Paul spoke of those who are "worthless for any good deed." In contrast, the believer's life is to stand at constant preparedness to undertake any and every good deed. In his typical way (2 Cor. 9:8; 2 Tim. 2:2; 3:17), the Apostle thus continues the theme of good deeds here in Titus (1:16; 2:7, 14; 3:1, 8, 14; cf. 3:5). By using the singular ("every," πᾶν) rather than the plural, Paul lays the stress upon each individual good work and thus demands readiness to perform whatever good deed might be called for in any given circumstance.[3]

> **Digging Deeper:**
> 1. Why does the NT so strongly emphasize the ministry of reminder? What does this tell us about ourselves?
> 2. What is the relationship between submission to authority and obedience to authority? How are they similar and dissimilar? Why might this be important?
> 3. Can either or both submission or obedience be compelled? Why or why not?

3:2 to malign no one, to be peaceable, gentle, showing every consideration for all men.

Paul continues on the theme of the believer's relationships to non-believers. Whereas Paul's initial concern was the believer's conduct toward the governing

---
[3] Knight, 333.

authorities (v.1), now he is concerned with those relations more broadly, to individual people in the unbelieving society (v.2). Just where that transition is made is sometimes in debate. Does "be ready for every good deed" (v.1) still refer specifically to the believer's response to the state? Or does it apply to his response to all peoples, and thus should be read with the instructions of v.2? What is clear is that God is concerned for the believer's attitude and conduct toward both the state, its officials, and the broader non-believing society. While he clearly has the former in view in v.1, and the latter in mind in v.2 ("all men"), the transition seems to take place in that final phrase in v.1. Thus "be ready for every good deed" likely includes both the state specifically and the broader society more generally.

> **Ministry Maxim**
>
> Slander not, lest God be slandered on account of you.

The infinitive "to malign no one" (μηδένα βλασφημεῖν) is subordinate to the imperative "Remind them" (v.1) and is the fourth such infinitive in this extended sentence. The infinitive is used of blasphemy of God (e.g., 1 Tim. 1:20) or disparagement of His Word (1 Tim. 6:1; Titus 2:5). It is also used more generally of slandering anyone (e.g., Rom. 3:8; 1 Cor. 10:30). It is in this latter sense that it is used here. The word was already used by Paul to give the reason for following the ethical instructions of chapter two: "so that the word of God will not be dishonored" (Titus 2:5). Now he uses it of the believer's actions toward unbelievers. Slander not, lest God be slandered on your account. The present tense extends this as a continuous prohibition.

A fifth infinitive ("to be," εἶναι) now follows and is accompanied by two accusative masculine plural adjectives: "peaceable" (ἀμάχους) and "gentle" (ἐπιεικεῖς). The infinitive actually stands between the two adjectives, governing both. The present tense calls for continuous action. The adjective "peaceable" is used elsewhere in the NT only in Paul's list of qualifications for overseers in 1 Timothy 3:3 (where the next adjective appears with it again). It comes from the root μάχη (rendered "disputes" in 3:9) and has the alpha privative affixed for negation. In extra-biblical Greek writings it meant "not to be withstood" or "invincible." In the NT it means not to fight, or, stated positively, as it is here, to be "peaceable."[4] The word "gentle" (ἐπιεικεῖς) is a compound made up of "over" (ἐπί) and "reasonable" (εἰκός). The preposition in compound intensifies the meaning. It "denotes a humble, patient steadfastness, which is able to submit to injustice, disgrace, and maltreatment without hatred and malice, trusting in God in spite of it all."[5] The adjective is found only five times in the NT, three of them in Paul's writings (Phil. 4:5; 1 Tim. 3:3; Titus 3:2; James 3:17; 1 Peter

---

[4] Thayer, 31.
[5] Rienecker, 485.

2:18). The noun form is found in Acts 24:4 and 2 Corinthians 10:1.

Paul moves to close this opening sentence by use of a participial phrase: "showing every consideration" (πᾶσαν ἐνδεικνυμένους πραΰτητα). The participle "showing" (ἐνδεικνυμένους) functions largely as the infinitives have, qualifying the imperative "Remind" in v.1.[6] It means to show, demonstrate or prove something, either by words or actions.[7] The middle voice could convey the notion of showing or demonstrating oneself in something or showing or demonstrating something in oneself (cf. 1 Tim. 1:16; 2 Tim. 4:14; Titus 2:10). The present tense demands that this be the case repeatedly and regularly. The specific thing to be shown is "consideration" (πραΰτητα). The noun points to a humble and gentle attitude which bears up under offense with patient submissiveness and without a move toward revenge.[8] It is found in combination with the noun form of the preceding adjective ("gentle") in 2 Corinthians 10:1 where together they describe "the meekness and gentleness of Christ." Such "consideration" must be thorough ("every," πᾶσαν) and unrestricted ("for all men," πρὸς πάντας ἀνθρώπους).

> **Digging Deeper:**
> 1. How would following these instructions toward unbelievers make the believers stand out in Cretan society (cf. 1:12)?
> 2. If 1:12 is an honest assessment of Cretan culture, how could people with the qualities in this verse avoid being used and abused by the unbelievers?

3:3 For we also once were foolish ourselves, disobedient, deceived, enslaved to various lusts and pleasures, spending our life in malice and envy, hateful, hating one another.

Paul now transitions to the doctrinal foundation (vv.3-7) for the exhortations he has just issued in vv.1-2. The conjunction "For" (γάρ) signals that what follows is an explanation of why the proceeding instruction should be embraced. The Apostle's point is that we believers once shared something in common with the unbelieving: "For we also once were foolish ourselves" (Ἦμεν γάρ ποτε καὶ ἡμεῖς ἀνόητοι). The verb "we were" (Ἦμεν) is thrust to the head of the sentence for emphasis. It is in the imperfect tense, pointing

---
[6] Mounce, 444.
[7] Thayer, 213.
[8] Rienecker, 485.

to the continuous habit of life in which we lived before we came to faith in Christ. The first person plural addresses this to all believers. We must remember who and what we were before the grace of God broke into our lives. We were once grouped among the lost and "also" (καὶ) operated from the same darkened mindset they do. The word "once" (ποτέ) is used here temporally and points to some time in the past and is thus translated "once" or "formerly."[9] Here it refers to the pre-Christian state of Paul's readers. The first person plural pronoun "ourselves" (ἡμεῖς) underscores again that before the grace of God came to us, we were no different from the unbelieving.

Paul now sets out in an extended series of statements just what we Christians "once were." First, we, like the unbelieving, were "foolish" (ἀνόητοι). The word means to be without understanding or thought. It is the opposite of "wise" (σοφός; cf. Rom. 1:14). In the only place the word is used in the NT outside of Paul's writings, it was used of the two disciples with whom the resurrected Jesus walked on the road to Emmaus and described their darkened, unenlightened view of the redemptive events and their correspondence to the prophetic Scriptures (Luke 24:25). Paul employed the word to describe the Galatians who were ready to depart from grace and return to works of the Law (Gal. 3:1, 3). It also described a money-hungry lust to become rich (1 Tim. 6:9). Thus we believers have had our hearts illumined by the Holy Spirit to see and understand the truth of Christ as it was prophesied in the Scriptures and have thus abandoned our own efforts at righteousness and the sinful urges that tug at our souls, and have received instead the free gift of life given to us in Christ (vv.4-7). But this was not always so, and we do well to remember this as we deal with the unbelieving around us.

We were also "disobedient" (ἀπειθεῖς). In Paul's other uses of the word it describes disobedience to God (Titus 1:16) and to parents (Rom. 1:30; 2 Tim. 3:2). Here it may be disobedience to the governing authorities (v.1), but, if so, it is only as an expression of disobedience to God. For "whoever resists authority has opposed the ordinance of God" (Rom. 13:2). The word describes one who will not be brought under the authority of another and is thus impersuasible, uncompliant and contumacious.[10] Paul uses it to describe what became of those who originally rejected the light of God's revelation in creation (Rom. 1:30) and of what will characterize humanity in the last days (2 Tim. 3:2). We too once were characterized by such an attitude.

We were once also "deceived" (πλανώμενοι). The word means to lead astray, but the passive form, as we have here, means to be led astray by another. The unbelieving are following a false guide to life and eternity. We

---
[9] BAGD, 695.
[10] Thayer, 55.

once followed in their train as well. The present tense describes this as a habitual course of life, ever stumbling down the path after false ideals. Paul used the word twice to describe the last days as full of people who are "deceiving and being deceived" (2 Tim. 3:13).

We also were "enslaved" (δουλεύοντες). The present tense of the participle "enslaved" (δουλεύοντες) points to the abiding and continuous nature of the unbeliever's bondage. Paul uses this word negatively to describe slavery to sin (Rom. 6:6), the Law (7:6), our appetites (16:18), idols (Gal. 4:8), and "weak and worthless elemental things" (4:9). He uses it positively in the sense of "service" to the Lord (Rom. 12:11; 14:18; Eph. 6:7; Col. 3:24; 1 Thess. 1:9), to one another (Gal. 5:13), to an earthly master (1 Tim. 6:2), and in the furtherance of the Gospel (Phil. 2:22). Here he uses it negatively to describe bondage to "various lusts and pleasures" (ἐπιθυμίαις καὶ ἡδοναῖς ποικίλαις). The noun "lusts" (ἐπιθυμίαις) can be a neutral term, but is used frequently by Paul and usually to describe strong impulses that arise within from a person's ungoverned sinful nature. They are tied to this fallen created order ("worldly desires," Titus 2:12). Paul told Timothy to flee them (2 Tim. 2:22). The emphasis is often sexual, but goes far beyond just that to include covetousness (1 Tim. 6:9) and misguided religious impulses (2 Tim. 4:3). Such lusts are described in the PE as "harmful" (1 Tim. 6:9), "youthful" (2 Tim. 2:22), "various" (3:6; Titus 3:3), and one's "own" (2 Tim. 4:3). The noun "pleasures" (ἡδοναῖς) is used only here by Paul. It is always elsewhere used negatively in the NT (Luke 8:14; James 4:1, 3; 2 Peter 2:13). We derive our word *hedonism* from it. Such desires may manifest themselves in many ways as the adjective "various" (ποικίλαις) indicates. Paul's only other use of this adjective is in 2 Timothy 3:6. It is a word meaning many-colored. It points to the multiplicity and diversity of the urges and desires that can arise to control a person.

> **Ministry Maxim**
>
> A poor memory makes for poor ministry.

Before meeting Christ we were "spending our life in malice and envy" (ἐν κακίᾳ καὶ φθόνῳ διάγοντες). A single participle stands behind the words "spending our life" (διάγοντες). It is a compound word meaning "through" (διά) and "to lead" (ἄγω). It is found elsewhere in the NT only in 1 Timothy 2:2 where Paul similarly commands that Timothy instruct the people to pray "for kings and all who are in authority" for the express purpose that "*we may lead* [διάγωμεν] *a tranquil and quiet life in all godliness and dignity*" (emphasis added). The present tense is descriptive of the ongoing unfolding of one's life. The preposition "in" (ἐν) indicates the sphere of life lived without Christ. Two nouns describe that life. The first is "malice" (κακίᾳ). Paul can use it more generally simply of "evil" (1 Cor. 14:20), but often also in the more specialized sense, as here, of "malice" (Rom. 1:29; 1 Cor. 5:8; Eph. 4:31; Col. 3:8). In this latter sense it describes "maliciousness or inward viciousness of disposition."[11] The second is "envy" (φθόνῳ). The two nouns appear together in Romans 1:29 where Paul also describes unregenerate humanity.

Being "hateful" (στυγητοί) also describes fallen humanity. The word is found only here in the NT. It may be understood in the passive sense ("hated," NIV, RSV, ESV) or in the active sense ("hateful," NASB, NET, KJV, NJB). Either way, being hated or being hateful makes for "hating one another" (μισοῦντες ἀλλήλους). Only four of the forty times the word is used in the NT are found in Paul's writings (Rom. 7:15; 9:13; Eph. 5:29; Titus 3:3). Again, the present tense points to a continuing and regular habit of relationships. Alford says, "It was our natural hatefulness which begot mutual hatred."[12]

We do well to recall that, in our non-believing state, when it came to our relationship to God we were deficient ("foolish," i.e., unenlightened), disobedient, and deceived. In regard to ourselves we were dominated ("enslaved") by our desires. And thus we destroyed our relationships through ill-will, envy and hatefulness.

> **Digging Deeper:**
> 1. Why does Paul urge remembrance of our non-Christian days? Aren't we supposed to be "forgetting what lies behind" (Phil. 3:13)?
> 2. What does remembering our former lives have to do with living in submission to God-ordained authorities (vv.1-2)?
> 3. How does this help us as Christian citizens heading into an election year?

3:4 But when the kindness of God our Savior and His love for mankind appeared,

Against the dark hues of our pre-Christian past (v.3), the bright light of God's grace shines brightly (vv.4-7). The conjunction "But" (δέ) is used as an adversative here, highlighting the stark contrast between what we were and what God, in Christ, has done for us. Verses 4-7 form one extended sentence in Greek. The conjunction "when" (ὅτε), used temporally, points to the pivotal moment when God's grace broke forth into this world in Christ (Rom. 5:8; Eph. 2:3-5).

---
[11] Robertson, 4:332.
[12] Alford, 3:423.

The NASB has rearranged the word order of this verse in an attempt for clarity. It more literally reads, "But when the kindness and love appeared of God our Savior" (cf. ESV, NIV).

God's saving activity in Christ is described by two nouns, both with their own definite article, thus marking them as distinct from one another. Yet they are obviously related because the verb governing both in is in the singular and demands they be viewed as two parts of one whole.[13] First is "the kindness" (ἡ χρηστότης). The word is used only by Paul in the NT. It refers to goodness, kindness and generosity, either of man (2 Cor. 6:6; Gal. 5:22; Col. 3:12) or, as here, of God (Rom. 2:4; 11:22; Eph. 2:7).[14] Naturally man has no such "kindness" in himself (Rom. 3:12). It can describe him only as God produces this "kindness" in him (Gal. 5:22).

The second noun is "love for mankind" (ἡ φιλανθρωπία). This noun is used elsewhere only in Acts 28:2. There it describes the extraordinary welcome extended to Paul and his shipwrecked traveling companions by the people of Malta. Here it is clearly a divine quality. It is a compound word made up of "friend" (φίλος) and "man" (ἄνθρωπος). We derive our word *philanthropy* from this word. While used sparingly in the NT, it was used liberally in the Hellenistic world and was considered the highest of their virtues.[15] The two nouns are often found in combination in the secular writings of the day to describe the qualities of gods and kings.[16] Paul, as he often did, took words common to the culture, infused them with new meaning and brought them into the service of Christ.

> **Ministry Maxim**
>
> The farther we are from acts of kindness the farther we are from acting like God.

Both of these "appeared" (ἐπεφάνη). Paul only uses the verb here and in 2:11 where he says, "the grace of God has appeared." The two other NT usages speak either metaphorically (Luke 1:79) or literally (Acts 27:20) of the rising or appearing of the sun. It is a compound word made up of "upon" (ἐπί) and "to show" (φαίνω). The sense of the word, then, is to bring to light and then to appear or to show something. From this we derive our word *epiphany*. The aorist tense looks back upon the epochal event of Christ's incarnation and encompasses the whole of His redemptive work as an accomplished fact. The passive voice describes God the Father as unveiling His "kindness" and "love for mankind" in the Person of Christ.

All of this is "of God our Savior" (τοῦ σωτῆρος ἡμῶν θεου). This points

---

[13] Knight, 338.
[14] BAGD, 886.
[15] Rienecker, 656.
[16] Mounce, 447.

to God the Father, as "through Jesus Christ" (v.6) makes clear. For the exact expression again see 1 Timothy 2:3 and Titus 1:3; 2:10. That we are no longer what we once were (v.3) is due completely to the merciful initiative and intervention of God. This extended sentence (vv.3-7) displays a Trinitarian understanding of salvation. God the Father initiated salvation (v.4), God the Son secured salvation (v.6), and God the Spirit produced salvation (v.5).[17]

3:5 He saved us, not on the basis of deeds which we have done in righteousness, but according to His mercy, by the washing of regeneration and renewing by the Holy Spirit,

The main verb of the first clause is pushed to the end so that the first words we meet are "not from works" (οὐκ ἐξ ἔργων). The negation is absolute, without exception. The negated preposition ἐκ points to that out of which the action of the main verb did not arise—"not *out of* our works." The theme of works is significant in this letter, but it is otherwise tied to the desirable good works that are produced in the life touched with salvation (2:7, 14; 3:1, 8, 14). Such works do not *effect* salvation, but *reflect* its presence through grace. The works in view here are those "which we have done in righteousness" (τῶν ἐν δικαιοσύνῃ ἃ ἐποιήσαμεν ἡμεῖς). The definite article (τῶν) is used without an accompanying noun and is employed as a relative pronoun, something akin to, "Not as a result of works, *those* in righteousness which we did."[18] These are not evil works, but acts done "in righteousness" (ἐν δικαιοσύνῃ). That is to say, they are done with the motive of attaining righteousness. But when works are done as a means to achieving righteousness before God, they become unworthy, for righteousness before God cannot be attained through human effort. Righteousness before God comes as a gift (v.7), not as the result of works. In the natural word order then comes the clause with the main verb: "which we have done" (ἃ ἐποιήσαμεν ἡμεῖς). The aorist tense looks at each work performed as an individual act.

In emphatic contrast ("but," ἀλλὰ) stands the true means of salvation. This means is "according to His mercy" (κατὰ τὸ αὐτοῦ ἔλεος). Half of Paul's usages of "mercy" (ἔλεος) are found in the PE (1 Tim. 1:2; 2 Tim. 1:2, 16, 18; Titus 3:5), reflecting perhaps something of his pastoral heart. It describes "the emotion roused by undeserved affliction in others."[19] It has the sense of compassion or pity. It was in accordance with this mercy that God "saved us" (ἔσωσεν ἡμᾶς). The aorist tense views the salvation as a decisive act performed

---

[17] Ibid.
[18] Rienecker, 656.
[19] Kittel, 222.

at a point in time. This is the main verb of the sentence stretching from vv.4-7. The preposition κατὰ ("according to") "points to his mercy as the yardstick for measuring the vastness of his saving grace."[20]

Salvation is described as taking place "by the washing of regeneration" (διὰ λουτροῦ παλιγγενεσίας). The preposition διὰ with the genitive, as here, means "by means of" or "through." The noun "washing" (here without a definite article) is used only twice in the NT (Eph. 5:26; Titus 3:5). In the larger culture it was used of a laver and the washing that took place there. In the NT it points to a spiritual cleaning and perhaps to baptism as a symbol of that cleansing. The only other use of the word in the NT (Eph. 5:26) points to the more general reference of "washing." Even if it does point to baptism, we must remember that the physical act of baptism is not the means of salvation. The reality of "regeneration" (παλιγγενεσίας) is effected by a direct act of the Holy Spirit in applying the saving work of Christ to the individual and is then pictured in the symbolic "washing" of baptism. The noun "regeneration" (παλιγγενεσίας) is found elsewhere in the NT only in Matthew 19:28. It is a compound word composed of "again/anew" (πάλιν) and "beginning" (γένεσις).[21] It was used in the broader culture to describe the restoration of a thing to its original, pristine state (e.g., life restored after death; the earth restored after the flood). The Jews expected such a restoration when Messiah came. And Christians await its fullest meaning when Christ returns (Matt. 19:28).[22] Here it points to what takes place when a person is brought to new life by the Holy Spirit (i.e., born again).

> **Ministry Maxim**
>
> Renewal without regeneration is cosmetic; regeneration without renewal is spiritual infanticide.

Thus salvation was also ("and," καὶ) accomplished through "renewing by the Holy Spirit" (ἀνακαινώσεως πνεύματος ἁγίου). The noun "renewing" (ἀνακαινώσεως) is used elsewhere in the NT only in Romans 12:2 where it speaks of being "transformed by the *renewing* of your mind" (emphasis mine). The kindred verb (ἀνακαινόω) is also found in 2 Corinthians 4:16 and Colossians 3:10 (and cf. ἀνακαινίζω in Heb. 6:6). The noun "regeneration" points to the act of entering new life, while "renewing" points to the qualitative nature of that new life.[23] This "renewing" takes place only by the power and personal ministry of "the Holy Spirit" (πνεύματος ἁγίου).

It is possible that "regeneration" and "renewing" are to be understood as

---

[20] Hiebert, "Titus," 11:445.
[21] Knight, 342.
[22] Thayer, 474-475.
[23] Guthrie, 205.

two descriptions of the same action, "renewing" thus being a further elaboration of what was meant by "regeneration." It is more likely, however, that the former describes the instantaneous entrance into a new existence at the moment a person trusts in Christ, while the second describes the ongoing ministry of the Holy Spirit within the believer to shape that new character after the nature of Christ.[24]

> **Digging Deeper:**
> 1. Honestly, at an emotional level, do you believe yourself to be the object of divine kindness and mercy? What becomes of us if we lose this sense?
> 2. Why is being clear regarding the basis of our acceptance before God so important?
> 3. Which one comes first, regeneration or renewing? Why? If we are truly regenerated, why is renewing necessary as well?

3:6 whom He poured out upon us richly through Jesus Christ our Savior,

The pronoun "whom" (οὗ) refers back to the Holy Spirit (v.5), the genitive case being due to that of the noun (πνεύματος ἁγίου) in v.5. The verb "He poured out" (ἐξέχεεν) points to the action of God the Father. Paul uses the verb only three of its twenty-seven appearances in the NT (Rom. 3:15; 5:5; Titus 3:6). He uses it twice in reference to the Holy Spirit (Rom. 5:5; Titus 3:6; cf. also Acts 2:17, 18, 33; 10:45). It is used literally of pouring out liquids such as wine (Matt. 9:17) and frequently describes the pouring out of blood in death (e.g., Matt. 23:35; Luke 11:50; 22:20) and metaphorically pictures the outpouring of other substances (e.g., John 2:15). The aorist tense may look back upon the outpouring of the Spirit at Pentecost (Acts 2:17, 18, 33; cf. Joel 2:28) and/or the coming of the Spirit to indwell each believer at the time of his salvation (as "upon us" [ἐφ' ἡμᾶς] indicates here; cf. Rom. 8:9; 1 Cor. 12:13). The latter is a perpetuation of the former, and Paul may have both in view.

This outpouring was "upon us" (ἐφ' ἡμᾶς), pointing to all who are in Christ through faith. The outpouring was done "richly" (πλουσίως). The adverb is used four times in the NT, three of those by Paul (Col. 3:16; 1 Tim. 6:17; Titus 3:6; 2 Peter 1:11). It is related to the more frequently used noun πλούσιος ("rich"). The adverb thus has the sense of richly, abundantly, and lavishly. "He gives the Spirit without measure" (John 3:34).

---

[24] Hiebert, "Titus," 11:445-446.

The Holy Spirit was sent by both the Father and the Son (John 15:26; Acts 2:33). He is pictured here as being given by the Father "through Jesus Christ" (διὰ Ἰησοῦ Χριστοῦ). Jesus said the Father would send the Spirit at His request (John 14:16) and in His name (v.26). Jesus is here designated as "our Savior" (τοῦ σωτῆρος ἡμῶν). Paul has already proven he can freely use "Savior" (σωτήρ) to designate the Father (1:3; 2:10) and immediately again use it in reference to the Son (1:4; 2:13). He does so again here (3:4, 6). Paul clearly believed in the deity of Jesus Christ. He here reveals the work of the Trinity in salvation: Father (vv.4-5a), Son (v.6), and Holy Spirit (v.5b).

> **Ministry Maxim**
>
> The only limits to God's self-giving exist within us.

3:7 so that being justified by His grace we would be made heirs according to the hope of eternal life.

Paul now completes the sentence begun in v.4 by speaking to the purpose ("so that," ἵνα) of God's saving work. The main verb here is "would be made" (γενηθῶμεν). The subjunctive mood combines with the conjunction ἵνα to designate the purpose of God's saving work. The aorist tense points out that this being "made heirs" happens at the moment of personal salvation and is not the result of the process of sanctification. The passive voice makes clear that our standing as heirs is divinely, not personally, produced.

The imagery of being "made heirs" is a favorite of Paul. We become such by believing God's promise (Gal. 3:29), not through observance of the Law (Rom. 4:13-14). Through faith we are moved from slavery to sin to the status of sonship and thus to the position of heirs (Gal. 4:1, 7). Indeed, we are "heirs of God and fellow heirs with Christ" (Rom. 8:17).

> **Ministry Maxim**
>
> In Christ we are legally righteous and rich.

The participial phrase "being justified by His grace" (δικαιωθέντες τῇ ἐκείνου χάριτι) proceeds the main verb. To be "justified" is to be declared legally righteous by God in heaven based on the atoning work of Christ on the cross. It takes place at a moment in time (aorist tense) rather than through an unfolding process. The passive voice underscores that no man justifies himself. Only God can declare one righteous in His sight. The participle is used either temporally ("after having been justified by His grace") or causally ("because we have been justified").[25]

Our having been appointed heirs is "according to the hope of eternal life"

---

[25] Rienecker, 656.

(κατ' ἐλπίδα ζωῆς αἰωνίου). Paul opened the letter saying he was writing "in the hope of eternal life" (1:2). The letter reaches something of a zenith when he speaks of "the blessed hope" of Christ's return (2:13).

Think of what this verse assures us! As believers in Christ our sin is atoned for, wrath no longer looms over us. Rather, we stand in the presence of God in the righteousness of Christ, declared righteous now and forevermore. Not only are we declared righteous, but we are made children of God and as children we are appointed as heirs of God and co-heirs with Christ. And we are present possessors of eternal life and wait with confidence for our entrance into the fullness of all that we have begun even now to experience!

> **Digging Deeper:**
> 1. What does the inclusion of the adverb "richly" add to our understanding of the role and ministry of the Holy Spirit in the believer's life?
> 2. What does it mean to be "heirs" of God?
> 3. In what sense is "eternal life" a present reality and in what sense is it a future hope?

3:8 This is a trustworthy statement; and concerning these things I want you to speak confidently, so that those who have believed God will be careful to engage in good deeds. These things are good and profitable for men.

"This is a trustworthy statement" (Πιστὸς ὁ λόγος) refers back to the sentence that comprises vv.4-7 and provides such a beautiful Gospel synopsis. It says more simply and literally, "faithful the word." This has by now become a familiar expression in the PE (1 Tim. 1:15; 3:1; 4:9; 2 Tim. 2:11). It normally is used before the statement (1 Tim. 1:15; 3:1; 2 Tim. 2:11), but can also be used after the statement (1 Tim. 4:9), as here. This expression was apparently becoming something of a stock statement and may point to words that similarly had become, among the early disciples, convenient ways of expressing basic theological or confessional truths. The two words also appear together in Titus 1:9 where Titus was charged with holding fast "the faithful word" (πιστοῦ λόγου; cf. also 1 Tim. 4:6, 12; 2 Tim. 1:13).

Following the previous theological statement (2:11-14), Paul gave Titus a strong exhortation regarding how he should speak those truths (2:15). So also here, Paul follows a theological statement (3:4-7) with an exhortation regarding how Titus was to handle these truths (3:8). This exhortation in turn leads on to a series of other exhortations regarding ministry more broadly, particularly how to handle the false teachers (vv.9-11).

Having affirmed the truthfulness of his previous words, Paul now adds ("and," καὶ) an exhortation "concerning these things" (περὶ τούτων). Specifically "these things" (τούτων) points to vv.1-7[26] (as "these things" [Ταῦτα] in 2:15 pointed to all of Paul's instructions in vv.1-14) or perhaps all that Paul has written thus far in this letter.[27] The Apostle says, "I want you to speak confidently" (βούλομαί σε διαβεβαιοῦσθαι). Paul was not afraid to express what he wanted ("I want," βούλομαι; cf. Phil. 1:12; 1 Tim. 2:8; 5:14), largely because he saw his desires as in harmony with God's will (the verb also used of the divine will in 1 Cor. 12:11). The present tense points to the ongoing nature of Paul's desire regarding these things. The form is that of the middle or passive voice, but, being a deponent verb, the meaning is active. The Apostle's desire is that Titus ("you," σε) "speak confidently" (διαβεβαιοῦσθαι). The only other NT use of this verb is from Paul's pen as he describes false teachers who "do not understand either what they are saying or the matters about which *they make confident assertions* [διαβεβαιοῦνται]" (1 Tim. 1:7, emphasis added). Titus, with words of truth, should match and exceed the confidence of those who boldly spew forth falsehoods. The present tense demands ongoing or habitual action. This too is a deponent—middle/passive in form, but with an active meaning. The infinitive is used with the force of an imperative. It is a compound word made up of "through" (διά) and "to make firm/establish" (βεβαιόω). The preposition (διά) in compound implies persistence and thoroughness in the affirmation.[28] The verb, then, comes to mean speaking confidently or strongly about something, to insist upon it.[29]

Such dogmatism has a definite purpose ("so that," ἵνα plus the subjunctive). The object of this purpose is "those who have believed God" (οἱ πεπιστευκότες θεῷ). The perfect tense points to a definite point in the past at which they believed and that they are viewed as continuing in that belief up to the present moment. The abiding state of their faith remains since that day. The participle is use substantively and the definite article marks them out as a specific people—"those who have believed." Their faith rests upon God—specifically "God our Savior" (3:4) who works His salvation as defined in vv.4-7. The goal of Titus' preaching (v.8a) is that these believers "will be careful to engage in good deeds" (φροντίζωσιν καλῶν ἔργων προΐστασθαι). The verb "will be careful" (φροντίζωσιν) is used only here in the NT. It has the sense

---

[26] Fee, 207; Knight, 350; Mounce, 452.
[27] Guthrie, 207.
[28] Alford, 3:426.
[29] BAGD, 181.

of "think of," "be intent upon," or "be careful or concerned about."[30] The subjunctive mood couples with the ἵνα to make this a purpose clause. The present tense points to this as an abiding way of life—believers should be continually thinking of how to do "good deeds" (καλῶν ἔργων). As we have seen, this is one of the main themes of Paul's letter to Titus. Though such deeds do not produce salvation (3:5), true salvation will produce such good deeds (2:7; 14; 3:1, 8, 14). As believers, we are "to engage" (προΐστασθαι) in such works. This word is used only by Paul in the NT and six of its eight occurrences are in the PE (1 Tim. 3:4, 5, 12; 5:17; Titus 3:8, 14). It is used of overseers (1 Tim. 3:4, 5) and deacons (3:12) leading their own families and of overseers leading the church (5:17). In Titus it is used more generally with all believers in view. It is a compound word meaning "before" (πρό) and "to put/place" (ἵστημι). The middle voice which we meet here means to "put one's self forward." It thus can mean to take the lead or to busy one's self with something.[31] It is the believer's calling to busy himself in performing good deeds (2:14). The exact phrase "to engage in good works" (καλῶν ἔργων προΐστασθαι) will be met again in v.14.

Indeed, Paul can say, "These things are good and profitable for men" (ταῦτά ἐστιν καλὰ καὶ ὠφέλιμα τοῖς ἀνθρώποις). The identification of "these things" (ταῦτά) is the "good deeds," both being neuter plural forms. Fee points out that since "these things" are called "profitable" (ὠφέλιμα) and the corresponding word "unprofitable" (ἀνωφελεῖς) is used in the next verse for the bad deeds of the false teachers, it seems likely "these things" refers to the "good works" of the believers.[32] It may seem redundant to call "good" (καλῶν) deeds "good" (καλὰ), but the first refers to the inherent nature of the deeds themselves, while the second refers to the benefit that comes to those for whom they are done. Not only are they "good," but in addition ("and," καὶ) they are "profitable" (ὠφέλιμα). The word is used only in the PE, speaking of the comparatively little profit from physical exercise when compared to godliness (1 Tim. 4:8 [used twice]) and the inherent profit found in the Scriptures (2 Tim. 3:16). It has the sense of helpful, beneficial, useful or advantageous.[33] This is true "for men" (τοῖς ἀνθρώποις). This designates the good of both those who perform them and those who receive them. Or it may be that a reference to the unbelieving (cf. v.2 where ἄνθρωπος is used of the unbelieving)

> **Ministry Maxim**
>
> A lack of conviction in the pulpit breeds a lack of consecration in the pews.

---

[30] Ibid., 866-867.
[31] Rienecker, 656.
[32] Fee, 208.
[33] BAGD, 900.
[34] Knight, 352.

is primarily in view.[34]

Clearly there is a connection between the conviction of the preacher ("This is a trustworthy statement") and his confidence in the pulpit ("concerning these things I want you to speak confidently"). But there is also a connection with both the conviction of the preacher and his confidence in the pulpit and the desired change in the people ("so that those who have believed God will be careful to engage in good deeds").

> **Digging Deeper:**
> 1. What are the connections between *conviction* in the preacher ("This is a trustworthy statement"), *confidence* in the pulpit ("speak confidently") and *consecration* in the parishioners ("so that those who believe God will be careful to engage in good deeds")?
> 2. In what way are "good deeds" good both for those who perform them and those who receive them?

3:9 But avoid foolish controversies and genealogies and strife and disputes about the Law, for they are unprofitable and worthless.

Paul now changes directions ("but," δέ) and addresses how Titus and the believers are to deal with the false teachers (vv.9-11). There are certain things they are to "avoid" (περιΐστασο). It is a compound word meaning "around" (περί) and "to place" (ἵστημι). John (John 11:42) and Luke (Acts 25:7) use it to describe standing around. But in the middle voice, as here, it means "*to turn oneself about* namely, *for the purpose of avoiding something, hence, to avoid, shun.*"[35] The present tense imperative demands that action be undertaken continually. Paul uses it in the same form to command Timothy to "avoid worldly *and* empty chatter" (2 Tim. 2:16).

Here there are four things that Titus is instructed to have nothing to do with. These four give us some idea of the nature of the opposition faced by Titus and the Cretan believers. We should read this in connection with 1:10-16 and Paul's earlier treatment of the false teachers and their teaching that faced Titus and the believers on Crete. The first is "foolish controversies" (μωρὰς ... ζητήσεις). The same combination is found in 2 Timothy 2:23, with the addition of "and ignorant" (καὶ ἀπαιδεύτους) between the two words. The

---

[35] Thayer, 506.

noun "controversies" (ζητήσεις) refers to an investigation. Paul uses it only in the PE and it may describe the investigation of religious and theological problems that arise in the struggle against false teachers (1 Tim. 6:4; 2 Tim. 2:23; Titus 3:9).[36] While theological clarification and investigation are necessary both for growth in and defense of the Gospel, they can, at some point, become profitless and counterproductive for all involved. Indeed, they may become "foolish" (μωράς). Paul used the adjective elsewhere in 1 Corinthians in an ironic way to speak of the "foolishness" of God (1 Cor. 1:25) and the believers (1:27; 3:18; 4:10) in comparison to the "wisdom" of the world and the unbelieving. But here the word has its more typical meaning of dull, stupid or foolish.[37] We derive our word *moronic* from this word. No doubt Paul's evaluation of the heretics in Ephesus would fit those of Crete as well, "they do not understand either what they are saying or the matters about which they make confident assertions" (1 Tim. 1:7).

> **Ministry Maxim**
>
> Doing something constructive is always more important than saying something controversial.

The second ("and," καὶ) is "genealogies" (γενεαλογίας). The word is used elsewhere only in 1 Timothy 1:4 where Timothy is warned to avoid "endless genealogies." This probably points to the Jewish nature of the opposition both in Ephesus (1 Tim. 1:4) and here in Crete. The Jewish people meticulously investigated and documented their family lines since their inheritances and holdings of land were thus determined. It, rather than the Gospel, became the defining element of whether a person was "in" or "out."

The third ("and," καὶ) thing to be avoided is "strife" (ἔρεις). The noun describes contention and wrangling between people.[38] Such "strife" arises, as Paul told Timothy, out of the "controversial questions" (ζητήσεις; 1 Tim. 6:4). It is characteristic of the sinful nature, not the Spirit-filled life (1 Cor. 3:3; Gal. 5:20).

The fourth ("and," καὶ) is "disputes about the Law" (μάχας νομικὰς). The adjective "Law" (note the noun is anarthrous) is used by Paul elsewhere only in v.13 when he speaks of "Zenas the lawyer" (Ζηνᾶν τὸν νομικὸν). Obviously, then, the word can be used to speak of legal matters generally. Here, however, it refers to the Mosaic Law. Robertson says the prohibition is against "Wordy fights about Mosaic and Pharisaic and Gnostic regulations."[39] The noun "disputes" (μάχας) should be compared to the requirement that all believers be "peaceable" (ἀμάχους, 3:2), which comes from the root μάχη (here

---

[36] BAGD, 339.
[37] Rienecker, 656.
[38] Thayer, 249.
[39] Robertson, 4:608.

rendered "disputes") and has the alpha privative affixed for negation.

These things are to be avoided because ("for," causal use of γὰρ) "they are unprofitable and worthless" (εἰσὶν γὰρ ἀνωφελεῖς καὶ μάταιοι). The present tense of the verb points to the ongoing, constant nature of such things. The adjective "unprofitable" (ἀνωφελεῖς) is a negated cognate of the noun "profitable" (ἀνθρώποις) in the previous verse. Whereas good works are profitable (v.8), these arguments and controversies are not. This particular adjective is used elsewhere in the NT only in Hebrews 7:18 where it speaks of the "uselessness" of the old priesthood now that Christ, our High Priest, has come. This usage is notable in our regard for it is argued that Christ became our High Priest "not on the basis of a law of physical requirement" according to the Law, "but according to the power of an indestructible life" (v.16). Here too such OT legalities are now found to be "unprofitable."

Such arguments are also ("and," καὶ) "worthless" (μάταιοι). It refers to that which is idle, empty, fruitless, useless, powerless, and lacking truth.[40] It can describe idols (Acts 14:15), man's wisdom (1 Cor. 3:20), faith in a non-resurrected Christ (1 Cor. 15:17), religion that doesn't change a person's behavior (James 1:26), and life without Christ (1 Peter 1:18). We are well reminded that there are some arguments which cannot be won no matter how adroit one's debating skills and well-reasoned one's logic, for they in and of themselves are "unprofitable and worthless."

> **Digging Deeper:**
> 1. How can we discern when a debate has moved beyond the good goal of clarifying and defending the truth and become a foolish waste of time?
> 2. What does the word "strife" tell us about the nature of unprofitable debate and dispute?
> 3. If such debates are present within a congregation, how does it help for the leadership to "avoid" them?

3:10 Reject a factious man after a first and second warning,

The problem is "a factious man" (αἱρετικὸν ἄνθρωπον). The adjective "factious" (αἱρετικὸν) is found only here in the NT, though Paul uses the cognate noun (αἵρεσις) to describe "factions" (1 Cor. 11:19; Gal. 5:20). The root of the word describes one who possesses the power of choice. The noun thus may

---
[40] BAGD, 495.

speak of "a self-chosen party or sect or it could mean 'a self-chosen teaching,'" and from this the concept of heresy may be implied[41] (we derive our English word *heresy* from this Greek noun; cf. the noun translated as "heresies" in 2 Peter 2:1). Alford calls them "divisions gathering round forms of individual self-will."[42] Thus "a factious man" is "one who founds or belongs to . . . a self-chosen and divergent form of religious belief or practice."[43] The case in view here may not yet have graduated into heretical teaching, but was on its way because of the self-will and independent spirit of the one involved. The essence of self-will is underscored when the noun is listed as one of the works of the flesh (Gal. 5:20), which stand in contrast to the fruit produced when living under the control of the Spirit (5:22-23). Paul's counsel to the Roman's is apt here as well, "Now I urge you, brethren, keep your eye on those who cause dissensions and hindrances contrary to the teaching which you learned, and turn away from them" (Rom. 16:17).

> **Ministry Maxim**
>
> Self-will always self-destructs.

The answer for the church in dealing with such folk is to issue "a first and second warning" (μίαν καὶ δευτέραν νουθεσίαν). The noun "warning" (νουθεσίαν) is a compound word composed of "mind" (νοῦς) and "to put" (τίθημι). Thus the root idea is that of putting something into someone's mind. It has the sense of instruction, warning, admonition, and exhortation. The noun is used only here and 1 Corinthians 10:11 and Ephesians 6:4 in the NT, though the cognate verb is employed by Paul in Romans 15:14, 1 Thessalonians 5:14, and 2 Thessalonians 3:15. Significantly, both of the last two references find the verb used in instructions on how to deal with the unruly within the church. In what may be a deliberate echo of Jesus' teaching (Matt. 18:15-17), Paul calls for "a first and second" occurrence of such an admonition. Such exhortations should be *direct* (so that the person knows exactly what he is being confronted about), *didactic* (instructing him in the truth in addition to pointing out his error) and *redemptive* (seeking to restore him to the fellowship of God and His church). While this verse demands strong action, we should not miss the spirit of hope with which these warnings are to be undertaken (cf. the many parallels to Titus 3:9-11 in 2 Tim. 2:23-26).

If such overtures are rejected ("after," μετὰ with the accusative) and the individual continues in his divisive error, the church's next step is to "reject" (παραιτοῦ) him. What began as the shunning of the man's arguments (v.9) must now become the rejection of the man himself because of his impertinent persistence in the error (v.10). Paul's usages of this verb are confined to the

---

[41] Rienecker, 657.
[42] Alford, 3:427.
[43] Ibid.

PE and are always used, as here, in the present middle imperative form (1 Tim. 4:7; 5:11; 2 Tim. 2:23). When used, as here, with the accusative of person, it means to reject or refuse a person or to refuse to do something to them.[44] It might go further in this instance and mean to dismiss or drive someone out.[45] The present imperative demands that action be taken continually. This is not a one-time act, but an ongoing stance toward the rebel (Matt. 18:17). The middle voice points to the inward nature of the rejection—there is no fellowship possible with such a person, for he has chosen his own path, not the one God's people seek to walk with him. The second person singular form lays this responsibility upon the leader, but it may be assumed that the non-divisive congregants will follow his lead in similarly refusing fellowship to the anarchist.

3:11 knowing that such a man is perverted and is sinning, being self-condemned.

The reason for the strong action of v.10 is now detailed. It is to take place because certain facts have come to light ("knowing," εἰδὼς). The participle is a defective perfect, having a present tense meaning—Titus (or, by way of application, other spiritual leaders in the local church) should have continually become aware of these facts. The participle is used in a casual sense. The same verb was used in 1:16 to indicate that some people "profess to know God" when in fact they do not. Here it is used to point out what others do know about them. This knowledge presumably becomes obvious during the various confrontations described in v.10. The conjunction ὅτι ("that") is used to point out the content of what is known. The adjective with a definite article is used as a substantive ("such a man," ὁ τοιοῦτος).

The qualitative nature of "such a man" is described with a series of terms. First, he "is perverted" (ἐξέστραπται). This verb is used only here in the NT. It is a compound word composed of "out" (ἐκ) and "to turn" (στρέφω). It thus means to turn inside out or to turn from. It came over time to signify twisting or perverting something.[46] The perfect tense describes one who at some point in the past turned away from the truth and has now come to remain in such a condition. The passive voice pictures some

> **Ministry Maxim**
>
> Church discipline is the collective affirmation of the sentence already handed down by the culprit himself.

other person turning the individual away from the truth—it could have in mind a false teacher, the false teaching itself or, more likely, the evil one who

---

[44] BAGD, 616.
[45] Marshall, 338.
[46] Rienecker, 657.

is behind all such falsehood (1 Tim. 4:1-2; 2 Tim. 2:26).

In addition ("and," καί) this person "is sinning" (ἁμαρτάνει). This verb is used frequently by Paul and the other writers of the NT. Its basic meaning is "to miss the mark." The present tense points to the ongoing nature of this person's sin as he remains in his deception and continues in his divisive ways.

Finally, this perversion and sinning takes place with the person "being self-condemned" (ὢν αὐτοκατάκριτος). The present active participle "being" (ὢν) describes the ongoing state of such a person. Paul says they are "self-condemned" (αὐτοκατάκριτος), employing a rare compound word used only here in the NT. It is made up of "self" (αὐτός), "against" (κατά), and "judge" (κρίνω). Any verdict Titus (or the local church leader) makes of such a person is only secondary to the one he has already pronounced over himself by his actions (cf. Gal. 2:11). They have professed to know God, but by their deeds they have denied Him (1:16; cf. Luke 19:22).[47] Proverbs warns, "Do not answer a fool according to his folly, or you will also be like him" and exhorts "Answer a fool as his folly deserves, that he not be wise in his own eyes" (Prov. 26:4-5). Paul's counsel in these verses may help the local church leader know when the time is right for either option.

An interesting parallel to vv.9-11 is found at the end of Romans (16:17-20) where the Apostle similarly warns the Romans to be alert to divisive people and counsels them on how to deal with them.[48]

Digging Deeper:
1. How can one discern the difference between "a factious man" and simple spiritual immaturity?
2. What is learned in the process of the "first and second warning" that helps answer the first question?
3. What dynamics in many contemporary churches make application of these verses unlikely?

3:12 When I send Artemas or Tychicus to you, make every effort to come to me at Nicopolis, for I have decided to spend the winter there.

Paul now begins to move toward closing the letter. He does so by giving directions to Titus regarding his assignment (v.12) and other believers (v.13), a closing exhortation (v.14), and a farewell and benediction (v.15).

---

[47] Mounce, 455.
[48] Fee, 212.

We learn now that the Apostle's intent was to relieve Titus of his duties so that he might link up with him again. "When I send" ("Οταν πέμψω) indicates that Paul is making plans for Titus's replacement on Crete. "When" ("Οταν) is a temporal conjunction used with the aorist subjunctive verb ("I send," πέμψω) to indicate action that should take place before the main verb (in this case "make every effort," σπούδασον).[49] Paul's intent was to send "Artemas" ('Αρτεμᾶν). We know nothing more of this individual from the NT. His name may be a masculine form of Artemis the goddess of Ephesus. Tradition tells us that he was one of the seventy disciples and became bishop of Timothy's hometown of Lystra. Paul's plan, he tells Titus, is to send him "to you" (πρὸς σε). Interesting that Paul pictures sending a replacement to Titus and not to Crete or to the church. This may simply be because he was primarily being sent as Titus's replacement and so he can join Paul, or it may be because he intended Titus to brief Artemas on the situation in Crete before being presented before the church.

The fact that "or Tychicus" (ἢ Τύχικον) appears at the end of the clause in the Greek text may be an indication that Artemas had been Paul's first thought for a replacement, but this is conjecture. Tychicus was a well-known disciple from Asia Minor, who had been one of Paul's traveling companions as he journeyed toward Jerusalem with the Gentile offering (Acts 20:4) and must have been present for Paul's emotional farewell to the elders from Ephesus (vv.17-38). There Luke identifies him as "of Asia" (v.4). He was apparently with Paul in his first Roman imprisonment and was expected to brief the people in Ephesus and Colossae regarding the Apostle's condition there (Eph. 6:21; Col. 4:7). He was likely the carrier of those letters from Rome. His mention here in Titus indicates that Tychicus apparently rejoined the Apostle after his release from his first Roman imprisonment. The last reference to him reveals that he had been with Paul in his final imprisonment shortly before his death and that the Apostle has dispatched him on that occasion to travel to Ephesus (2 Tim. 4:12) with the letter of 2 Timothy and then to replace Timothy so he could journey to join Paul in Rome (vv.9, 21). All we find of Tychicus is that he must have indeed been a "beloved brother and faithful servant and fellow bond-servant in the Lord" (Col. 4:7). He was a "faithful minister in the Lord" (Eph. 6:21) who was willing to carry out faithfully any assignment given him by the Apostle.

Paul's command to Titus was to "make every effort to come to me" (σπούδασον ἐλθεῖν πρός με) once his replacement arrived. This is the precise phrase Paul would later use to urge Timothy to come to him in his last Roman imprisonment shortly before his martyrdom at the command of Caesar (2 Tim.

---
[49] BAGD, 588.

4:9). The aorist imperative demands that action be taken without delay. Paul uses the verb seven times (Gal. 2:10; Eph. 4:3; 1 Thess. 2:17), four of them in this same form, and three of those in his last letter (2 Tim. 2:15; 4:9, 21; Titus 3:12). The word can have the notion of being zealous or eager or exerting every effort toward something. Some of that may be present here where it seems to have the simple notion of hurrying or hastening to fulfill that which is expressed in the following infinitive.[50] The demand is "to come" (ἐλθεῖν). The personal nature of the command is seen in the prepositional phrase "to me" (πρός με). Paul was "at Nicopolis" (εἰς Νικόπολιν), so Titus's obedience would require some significant travel. The precise identification of Nicapolis is disputed by some. The name means "city of victory," being made up of "victory" (νῖκος) and "city" (πόλις). It was, however, most likely a major city situated near the eastern shores of the Adriatic Sea in Greece. It was a main route for travel both by land and sea. The fact that Paul was planning on wintering in a site west of most of his previous labors may indicate that his sights were set on further travel to the west come springtime, perhaps to fulfill his longing to reach Spain with the Gospel (Rom. 15:24, 28).

> **Ministry Maxim**
>
> The strategic advance of the Gospel requires many people and much change.

Paul explained his reason for being in Nicopolis: "for I have decided to spend the winter there" (ἐκεῖ γὰρ κέκρικα παραχειμάσαι). The conjunction "for" (γάρ) is explanatory. "I have decided" (κέκρικα) translates a word that usually means "to judge." Paul had made a judgment call that it was best to spend the winter in that locale, probably for strategic ministry reasons. The perfect tense means that the evidence had been weighed and a decision reached at a point in the past and that the Apostle was now settled in that conviction. The words "to spend the winter there" are the translation of but one word (παραχειμάσαι). The word appears also in Acts (27:12; 28:11) and 1 Corinthians 16:6. The frequency of usage speaks of the dangers of travel in the ancient world during the winter (of which Paul was acutely aware, cf. Acts 20:13-44; 2 Cor. 11:25) and the wisdom needed in selecting the place to hunker down for those months of restricted travel. It is possible that from Nicopolis Titus then later launched a mission into Dalmatia which lay to the north, where, by the time of Paul's last letter, he is said to have gone (2 Tim. 4:10).[51] Whether a strategic advance of the Gospel into that region was in the Apostle's mind at this time is unknowable, but is not unlikely, for he was always looking for new territory in which to spread the Gospel. The word

---

[50] BAGD, 763.
[51] Robertson, 4:608.

"there" (ἐκεῖ) indicates that Paul has not yet reached Nicopolis himself, but is likely soon to depart so as to meet up with Titus upon his arrival.[52]

We may assume since Titus is later mentioned as being in Dalmatia (2 Tim. 4:10), and Tychicus was later sent to Ephesus to allow Timothy to come to Paul in Rome (4:12), that it was indeed Artemas who was finally sent to Crete to free Titus to join Paul in Nicopolis.

> **Digging Deeper:**
> 1. Why do you think the Holy Spirit included seemingly mundane instructions like these in Scripture?
> 2. How do you think the Apostle's shuffling of servants among different ministry assignments and locations affected them and their families?
> 3. What made these men so willing to live mobile, transient lives of ministry? What might make us less likely to live such lives today?

3:13 Diligently help Zenas the lawyer and Apollos on their way so that nothing is lacking for them.

This is the only mention of "Zenas" (Ζηνᾶν) in the NT. We know nothing about him beyond what we learn here. He and Apollos may have been the couriers of this letter to Titus. He is designated as "the lawyer" (τὸν νομικὸν). The word is used in the Gospels to describe an expert in the Mosaic Law (Matt. 22:35; Luke 7:30; 10:25; 11:45, 46, 52; 14:3). The only NT usages of the word outside the Gospels are here in Titus. We met it in 3:9 where Titus was instructed to "avoid foolish controversies and genealogies and strife and disputes about *the Law*" (emphasis added). Zenas is a Greek name and thus he may have been an expert in Roman law. But the other NT usages, his association with Apollos (see below), and the circumstances in Crete suggest he may well have been a Jewish lawyer who had come to faith in Christ. Perhaps he was sent to Titus along with Apollos, who was early on known to be "mighty in the Scriptures" (Acts 18:24), because they would have been adept at dealing with some of the detailed arguments the false teachers were setting forth about the Law.

"Apollos" (Ἀπολλῶν) was an individual well-known to many of the early churches. He is first mentioned for showing up in Ephesus (Acts 18:24). He was a Jew of Alexandrian birth, having apparently imbibed of all the educational opportunities that great city afforded, for he is noted as "an eloquent

---
[52] Fee, 214.

man" ("a learned man," NIV). He was, as already mentioned, "mighty in the Scriptures" as well. He was "fervent in spirit" and "was speaking and teaching accurately the things concerning Jesus," but he was "acquainted only with the baptism of John" (v.25). When Priscilla and Aquila heard him speaking out boldly for Christ in the synagogue, "they took him aside and explained to him the way of God more accurately" (v.26). Apollos displayed the humility of true faith and learned from this godly couple and was then gladly sent on his way as a select servant of the Lord (v.27). He had become a great help to the believers in Corinth (Acts 19:1) and some felt especially drawn to his ministry (1 Cor. 1:12; 3:4-6, 22; 4:6). Despite what could have become a rivalry, Paul was glad to commend Apollos and his ministry to the Corinthians (1:12; 16:12). Here again, in the case of the church in Crete, Paul gladly is calling upon this godly and gifted man to help advance the purposes of God's kingdom.

Titus is to "Diligently help . . . on their way" (σπουδαίως πρόπεμψον) these two servants of God. The verb "help . . . on their way" (πρόπεμψον) is a compound word made up of "before" (πρό) and "send" (πέμπω; this latter part of the compound was just used in v.12, "send," πέμψω).[53] Its root meaning is that of "send on forth" or to "send on." It frequently also implied providing money or supplies for the needs of the journey ahead.[54] Paul's normal use of the word is at the end of letters to describe the assistance the recipients are to provide him or someone he is sending to them as they pass through their region (Rom. 15:24; 1 Cor. 16:6, 11). He uses it in a similar way at the beginning of 2 Corinthians (1:16) where, because of circumstances, he felt compelled to explain his travel plans upfront. It is the word of a man constantly on the move and who is seeking to enlist others in that mission. The aorist imperative form demands that the action be undertaken at once, as soon as they arrive and are ready to depart. The addition of the adverb "Diligently" (σπουδαίως) serves to intensify the picture (the root elsewhere in Paul only in Phil. 2:28; Titus 3:13; cf. also Luke 7:4). It can describe action undertaken either earnestly or urgently. It is the former sense that is intended here. The cognate verb was just used in the previous verse, "make every effort" (σπούδασον).[55]

> **Ministry Maxim**
>
> Our most fruitful service may be found in helping others bear fruit.

The purpose (ἵνα plus subjunctive) in this assistance is "so that nothing is lacking for them" (ἵνα μηδὲν αὐτοῖς λείπῃ). Paul's only two usages of the verb "is lacking" (λείπῃ) are found here in Titus. Titus had been left in Crete

---

[53] Mounce, 458.
[54] Rienecker, 657.
[55] Mounce, 458.

to set in order what "remains" (1:5). It is used intransitively to mean to be wanting or absent or to fail.[56] Its use at the opening and closing of the letter forms an inclusion and underscores the kind of ministry Titus was to have not only to the Cretan church, but to his fellow-ministers as well.

> **Digging Deeper:**
> 1. Why do you think Paul marks Zenas as "the lawyer"? How might his training as a lawyer have helped him serve the Lord?
> 2. Why might Paul have wanted Zenas and Apollos to travel and minister together?
> 3. Do you think Paul was urging Titus and the church primarily to support these two financially, materially or spiritually?

3:14 Our people must also learn to engage in good deeds to meet pressing needs, so that they will not be unfruitful.

As he moves to close, the Apostle sets forth one more time the primary exhortation of this epistle. The sentence begins with an imperative, thrust to the front of the sentence for emphasis: "must . . . learn" (μανθανέτωσαν). It refers to learning something through the instruction of another.[57] This means that there must be an instructor, and that ultimately must point to Titus. A pastor's instruction includes more than standing in the pulpit, but must also include acting out the implications of what he preaches. It also assumes the humility and readiness of the people to learn. The fact that such behavior must be learned reminds us that it is not the normal course of the human heart and will, but that we must be reprogrammed to be concerned for other's needs and to do something to help them. The present tense imperative demands that action be undertaken repeatedly or habitually. That which is to be learned is in addition to ("also," καὶ) the other assistance given to Zenas and Apollos (v.13). Note that the NASU has left untranslated the conjunction δὲ ("*And* let our people also learn . . ." NASB).

Those who are to be taught are designated as "Our people" (οἱ ἡμέτεροι). The first person plural pronoun "Our" (ἡμέτεροι) is coupled with the definite article (οἱ) and used substantively. Paul has had little good to say about the people of Crete (1:12-13) or the false teachers pressing upon the church (1:10-11, 14-16; 3:9-11). Even when the believers have been in view, it has frequently

---
[56] Thayer, 375.
[57] BAGD, 490.

been from a negative slant (1:5; 2:1-10; 3:1-2). But the Apostle closes with this expression of identity, affinity and unity with those who profess Christ.

That which they are to learn is most basically "to engage in good deeds" (καλῶν ἔργων προΐστασθαι). The precise expression has just been used in v.8 (which see). The theme of "good deeds" (καλῶν ἔργων) has dominated the letter (1:16; 2:7, 14; 3:1, 5, 8, 14). The present tense of the infinitive demands action that is habitual and continual. The finer focus of their perpetual "good deeds" are those which are aimed "to meet pressing needs" (εἰς τὰς ἀναγκαίας χρείας). The preposition εἰς with the accusative normally means something like "into," "unto," "to" or "for." Here it is used in the sense of "for the supply of"[58] or "because of."[59] The plural noun "needs" (χρείας) is used only here in the PE, but is frequent throughout the NT and is used by Paul a total of fourteen times (e.g., Rom. 12:13; 1 Cor. 12:21, 24; Eph. 4:28-29). It describes a need, lack, want or difficulty.[60]

> **Ministry Maxim**
>
> Do not expect people to do good deeds; train them to do them.

The adjective "pressing" (ἀναγκαίας) is a less frequent word, used by Paul five of its eight times (Acts 10:24; 13:46; 1 Cor. 12:22; 2 Cor. 9:5; Phil. 1:24; 2:25; Titus 3:14; Heb. 8:3). It describes those things which are necessary and indispensable.[61] With it in the attributive position (tucked between the definite article and its noun) it emphasizes the quality of those needs that are in view. Followers of Christ are, like their Master, to be ever devoted to others and are to show that concern in tangible expressions of grace (cf. JB which wrongly makes this about meeting one's personal needs: "doing good works for their practical needs as well"; cf. also NEB, NIV).

The purpose ("so that," ἵνα plus the subjunctive) of this lifestyle is "so that they will not be unfruitful" (ἵνα μὴ ὦσιν ἄκαρποι). The adjective "unfruitful" (ἄκαρποι) is a compound made up of the noun "fruit" (καρπός) and the alpha privative for negation. It literally means "without fruit." Outside of Paul it is used in the parable of the soils for what happens to the seed when thorns grow up around it and choke it out (Matt. 13:22; Mark 4:19). False teachers are described as "autumn trees *without fruit*" (Jude 12, emphasis added). Peter speaks of laboring to lead a life that is neither "useless nor *unfruitful* in the true knowledge of our Lord Jesus Christ" (2 Peter 1:8, emphasis added). Elsewhere in the NT it is used only by Paul. He speaks of the "*unfruitful* deeds of darkness" (Eph. 5:11, emphasis added) and the state of the mind when a person prays in a tongue (1 Cor. 14:14).

---

[58] Alford, 3:428.
[59] Dana and Mantey, 104.
[60] BAGD, 885.
[61] Thayer, 36.

Paul approaches the subject from a negative slant, the concern of being "unfruitful." Jesus stated the same concern positively, "My Father is glorified by this, that you bear much fruit, and so prove to be My disciples" (John 15:8). Indeed Christ said, "Truly, truly, I say to you, unless a grain of wheat falls into the earth and dies, it remains alone; but if it dies, it bears much fruit" (12:24).

Jesus and Paul agree that the person who lives his life focused on meeting other's needs will find he is more fruitful. We gain by giving. We grow by cultivating the benefit of others.

Digging Deeper:
1. Why does Paul place the emphasis on "good deeds" as a *learned* behavior? What does this say about our basic nature as humans?
2. How would your experience change if you did not *expect* the people around you to do "good deeds," but took seriously the command to *train* them to do them? How would they respond to your lessons in "good deeds"?
3. How would moving from expectation to training in shepherding our own children change the environment of our families?

3:15 All who are with me greet you. Greet those who love us in the faith. Grace be with you all.

The Apostle now closes the epistle with greetings, as is typical in his letters. He begins with greetings from his side: "All who are with me greet you" (Ἀσπάζονταί σε οἱ μετ' ἐμοῦ πάντες). The verb "greet" (Ἀσπάζονταί) is used by Paul forty times, always in the final chapter of one of his letters. He always uses it in the middle/passive form, but the meaning is that of the active voice. The present tense simply reports the present reality of the greetings at the time of Paul's writing. The third person plural form along with the adjective "all" (πάντες) indicate that there are multiple people with the Apostle who probably know and care for Titus. The greeting is to Titus himself, not the church as a whole since "you" (σε) is the second person singular. Just who all these people might be is unclear. They are designated only by their connection at the moment to Paul ("who are with me," οἱ μετ' ἐμοῦ). Paul regularly had a cluster of believers around him, and Titus likely was well-known throughout the churches. It must have heartened Titus to know, while he labored alone on the island of Crete among its often difficult populace and confronted difficulties inside and outside the church, that he was much loved and many people were in prayer for him.

Next Paul demands that Titus "Greet" ("Ἀσπασαι) others on their behalf. The verb is the same as in the previous sentence, but the form is that of an aorist imperative. Paul is demanding that action be taken at once. Titus's reading of the letter to the church would have fulfilled the command. Those for whom the greeting was intended were designated as "those who love us in the faith" (τοὺς φιλοῦντας ἡμᾶς ἐν πίστει). Just who the "us" (ἡμᾶς) includes is not clear. It could mean simply Paul and Titus, or it could have in view all who are with Paul and send the greeting (v.15a). Or it could be a way of indicating all true believers. Those to be greeted are specifically designated as "those who love" (τοὺς φιλοῦντας), using a participle and its definite article as a substantive. The present tense points to an ongoing love. The word describes love that is brotherly and filial in nature. Elsewhere Paul uses this verb only in 1 Corinthians 16:22. There too it is used in a restrictive sense: "If anyone does not love the Lord, he is to be accursed." This may signal that here too Paul was indicating that the greetings were to go out only to those who stood in the truth and loved those who stood with them (i.e., excluding the false teachers and their followers). Indeed, the nature of this love is made more specific by the addition of the phrase "in the faith" (ἐν πίστει). The original does not have the definite article (lit., "in faith"), but the major English translations read the definite article into the expression (e.g., ESV, NASU, NIV, NLT, NRSV). This little phrase is used by Paul nine times (elsewhere in NT only in James 1:6 and 2:5). Eight of those nine times are in the PE (1 Tim. 1:2, 4; 2:7, 15; 3:13; 4:12; 2 Tim. 1:13; Titus 3:15). Without the article the phrase could mean "faithfully" or "loyally," but it seems likely that on this occasion it is correct to understand the definite article and view the love as that which exists among those who have embraced in personal faith the body of truth known as "the faith."

> **Ministry Maxim**
>
> Genuine greetings can be sinews that hold the scattered body of Christ together.

As is often Paul's manner, the letter closes with the bestowal of a blessing: "Grace be with you all" (ἡ χάρις μετὰ πάντων ὑμῶν). As Paul has done in the other two PE (1 Tim. 1:2; 6:21; 2 Tim. 1:2; 4:22), he opens and closes this letter on the theme of "grace" (χάρις; 1:4; 3:15). Indeed the noun is found in the first and last chapters of every one of Paul's letters.[62] Note the use of the definite article with "grace" (ἡ χάρις). This is no boilerplate blessing. Paul extends to Titus the unique and only grace, that grace which stands out as distinct from all others. He extends the grace that comes only from God the Father through Jesus Christ by the power of the Spirit.

This grace is to be (the verb is absent, but is to be understood) "with you

---
[62] Knight, 360.

all" (μετὰ πάντων ὑμῶν). The plural form makes clear that the blessing goes out not merely to Titus, but to the whole of the church in Crete. Obviously, though the letter is addressed to Titus, it was intended to be read to the believers and was for their edification as well. The first greeting went to Titus alone, but the final grace is extended to all. There are dimensions of God's grace that can be enjoyed only in the context of Christian community, even with all of the inevitable challenges such fellowship brings. This provides a good reminder to the pastor and people at the close of the PE.

The final "Amen" (ἀμήν) of the KJV, though present in the majority of Greek manuscripts, is missing in key early ones. It was likely an addition made by later scribes.

Digging Deeper:

1. How can genuine greetings serve as the connective tissues that hold the scattered body of Christ together? How might this sense of connectivity have aided Titus in his mission?
2. Why do you suppose Paul greeted only Titus, but spoke grace to the entire church on Crete?
3. From what you have learned from the Book of Titus as a whole, how does it demonstrate that there are dimensions of God's grace that can be enjoyed only in the context of Christian community?

APPENDICES

APPENDIX A

A PASTOR'S SELF-GUIDED STUDY OF THE PASTORAL EPISTLES

he Pastoral Epistles for Pastors can assist you in growing as a man of God and as a shepherd of His people. You might approach this in one of three ways. First, you might systematically study through the PE using the pattern listed below under Consecutive Training Schedule. Second, you might want to peruse the topical listing of Ministry Maxims (see Appendix C) and set out to meet a felt need in your life and personal ministry. Third, the Qualifications Training Schedule will allow you to systematically pursue the qualifications for leaders listed in 1 Timothy 3 and Titus 1.

Consecutive Training Schedule

By establishing and using a Consecutive Training Schedule you may walk systematically through the PE. This can be done by selecting any one of the three PE and beginning there. Set for yourself a Consecutive Training Schedule by predetermining how long you will take to study through any one of the books or all three of the PE. Then determine how much you will read and study each day, week, or whatever interval you choose.

In whatever way your plan shapes up, make certain to allow plenty of time for reflection on the Ministry Maxim for each verse. Don't let the Digging Deeper questions slip by without answering them.

Topical Training Schedule

Employing the Topical Training Schedule allows you to focus upon specific needs that are currently facing you and your church. In Appendix C you will discover that all the Ministry Maxims found throughout the text of the commentary have been listed according to topics. By using one or more of these texts at a time you will be able to pursue the Scripture's teaching in regard to any of these key leadership issues. The benefit of using the Topical Training Schedule is that it allows you to deal in real time with the issues facing you and your church, but to do so directly from the Scriptures.

Qualifications Training Schedule

Using the Qualifications Training Schedule enables you to focus your study upon the qualities of life that are imperative for the faithful completion of your God-given ministry assignment.

The following list of qualifications is comprised of the terms from 1 Timothy 3:2-7 and Titus 1:6-9. The order begins with those qualifications listed in 1 Timothy 3:2-7. Where identical/similar terms or parallel concepts are found again in Titus 1:6-9 the reference (for identical expressions) or wording and reference (for similar terms or parallel expressions) are listed with the first entry. The terms used only in Titus 1:6-9 follow at the end of the list.

> above reproach (ἀνεπίλημπτον; 1 Tim. 3:2; cf. ἀνέγκλητος; Titus 1:6)
> the husband of one wife (μιᾶς γυναικὸς ἀνήρ; 1 Tim. 3:2; Titus 1:6)
> temperate (νηφάλιον; 1 Tim. 3:2)
> prudent (σώφρονα; 1 Tim. 3:2; "sensible," Titus 1:8)
> respectable (κόσμιον; 1 Tim. 3:2)
> loving what is good (φιλάγαθον; Titus 1:8)
> hospitable (φιλόξενον; 1 Tim. 3:2; Titus 1:8)
> able to teach (διδακτικόν; 1 Tim. 3:2)
>> "holding fast the faithful word which is in accordance with the teaching, so that he will be able both to exhort in sound doctrine and to refute those who contradict." (ἀντεχόμενον τοῦ κατὰ τὴν διδαχὴν πιστοῦ λόγου, ἵνα δυνατὸς ᾖ καὶ παρακαλεῖν ἐν τῇ διδασκαλίᾳ τῇ ὑγιαινούσῃ καὶ τοὺς ἀντιλέγοντας ἐλέγχειν; Titus 1:9)
> not addicted to wine (μὴ πάροινον; 1 Tim. 3:3; Titus 1:7)
> not pugnacious (μὴ πλήκτην; 1 Tim. 3:3; Titus 1:7)
> gentle (ἐπιεικῆ; 1 Tim. 3:3)
>> not self-willed (μὴ αὐθάδη; Titus 1:7)
> uncontentious (ἄμαχον; 1 Tim. 3:3)
>> not quick-tempered (μὴ ὀργίλον; Titus 1:7)
> free from the love of money (ἀφιλάργυρον; 1 Tim. 3:3)
>> not fond of sordid gain (μὴ αἰσχροκερδῆ; Titus 1:7)
> manages his own household well (τοῦ ἰδίου οἴκου καλῶς προϊστάμενον; 1 Tim. 3:4)
>> having children who believe (τέκνα ἔχων πιστά; Titus 1:6)
> keeping his children under control with all dignity (τέκνα ἔχοντα ἐν ὑποταγῇ,

Appendix A

μετὰ πάσης σεμνότητος; 1 Tim. 3:4)
not accused of dissipation or rebellion (μὴ ἐν κατηγορίᾳ ἀσωτίας ἢ ἀνυπότακτα; Titus 1:6)
not a new convert (μὴ νεόφυτον; 1 Tim. 3:6)
a good reputation with those outside (μαρτυρίαν καλὴν ἔχειν ἀπὸ τῶν ἔξωθεν; 1 Tim. 3:7)
just (δίκαιον; Titus 1:8)
devout (ὅσιον; Titus 1:8)
self-controlled (ἐγκρατῆ; Titus 1:8)

You also may contemplate a study which considers these qualifications thematically under the following four headings.[1]

Relationship to God

above reproach (ἀνεπίλημπτον; 1 Tim. 3:2; cf. ἀνέγκλητος; Titus 1:6)
not a new convert (μὴ νεόφυτον; 1 Tim. 3:6)
"holding fast the faithful word which is in accordance with the teaching, so that he will be able both to exhort in sound doctrine and to refute those who contradict." (ἀντεχόμενον τοῦ κατὰ τὴν διδαχὴν πιστοῦ λόγου, ἵνα δυνατὸς ᾖ καὶ παρακαλεῖν ἐν τῇ διδασκαλίᾳ τῇ ὑγιαινούσῃ καὶ τοὺς ἀντιλέγοντας ἐλέγχειν; Titus 1:9)
able to teach (διδακτικόν; 1 Tim. 3:2)
just (δίκαιον; Titus 1:8)
devout (ὅσιον; Titus 1:8)
loving what is good (φιλάγαθον; Titus 1:8)

Relationship to Self

self-controlled (ἐγκρατῆ; Titus 1:8)
temperate (νηφάλιον; 1 Tim. 3:2)
free from the love of money (ἀφιλάργυρον; 1 Tim. 3:3)
not fond of sordid gain (μὴ αἰσχροκερδῆ; Titus 1:7)
prudent (σώφρονα; 1 Tim. 3:2; "sensible," Titus 1:8)
not pugnacious (μὴ πλήκτην; 1 Tim. 3:3; Titus 1:7)
not addicted to wine (μὴ πάροινον; 1 Tim. 3:3; Titus 1:7)
not quick-tempered (μὴ ὀργίλον; Titus 1:7)

---

[1] These headings are suggested by H. Wayne House, *Charts of Christian Theology and Doctrine*, 119.

Relationship to Others

respectable (κόσμιον; 1 Tim. 3:2)
hospitable (φιλόξενον; 1 Tim. 3:2; Titus 1:8)
uncontentious (ἄμαχον; 1 Tim. 3:3)
gentle (ἐπιεικῆ; 1 Tim. 3:3)
a good reputation with those outside (μαρτυρίαν καλὴν ἔχειν ἀπὸ τῶν ἔξωθεν; 1 Tim. 3:7)
not self-willed (μὴ αὐθάδη; Titus 1:7)

Relationship to Family

the husband of one wife (μιᾶς γυναικὸς ἀνήρ; 1 Tim. 3:2; Titus 1:6)
manages his own household well (τοῦ ἰδίου οἴκου καλῶς προϊστάμενον; 1 Tim. 3:4)
having children who believe (τέκνα ἔχων πιστά; Titus 1:6)
keeping his children under control with all dignity (τέκνα ἔχοντα ἐν ὑποταγῇ, μετὰ πάσης σεμνότητος; 1 Tim. 3:4)
not accused of dissipation or rebellion (μὴ ἐν κατηγορίᾳ ἀσωτίας ἢ ἀνυπότακτα; Titus 1:6)

APPENDIX B

TRAINING LOCAL CHURCH LEADERS FROM THE PASTORAL EPISTLES

The *Pastoral Epistles for Pastors* can assist you in training the leaders or prospective leaders of your church. This can be accomplished in one of three ways. First, you might systematically walk them through the PE using the pattern listed below under Consecutive Training Schedule. Second, you can train them thematically by using the Topical Training Schedule you will find below. Third, you can use the Qualifications Training Schedule to train your leaders in the various qualifications listed for their offices in 1 Timothy and Titus. Whichever schedule you employ, if you feel the information in the commentary is too technical for your people, you can simplify and select those parts that will enable you to communicate to your people the God-breathed intent of each passage.

Consecutive Training Schedule

Using the Consecutive Training Schedule you may walk your leaders systematically through the PE. This can be done by selecting any one of the PE and beginning there. Additionally, each of these books may be progressed through at different rates. I will give two examples for each book. Using the Consecutive Training Schedule enables you to train your leaders using the content of these epistles, but also enables you to train them in good Bible study methods and hermeneutics.

If you are able to meet face-to-face with your leaders, spend a few minutes teaching the text before you in each unit. Then engage your leaders in discussion using the Digging Deeper questions and others you contribute on your own. You can finish by sharing the Ministry Maxim and launch into a season of prayer with your leaders. If you are not able to gather your leaders frequently, consider using these studies as the basis for a weekly e-mail to your leaders. This is how I have used these materials in our church.

1 Timothy

A six-month daily study – By studying one verse a day for five days a week, you will complete a study of 1 Timothy in just under six months.

A two-year weekly study – By using the Digging Deeper questions as dividing points, you will find that 1 Timothy offers ninety-six units of text. This will afford you the material for a once-a-week study which will span approximately two years.

2 Timothy

A one-year weekly study – By using the Digging Deeper questions as dividing points, you will find that 2 Timothy is divided into fifty-two units of text.

A one-year monthly study – By dividing these fifty-two sections by twelve, you can easily develop a once-a-month training regime that will cover one year.

Titus

A one-year weekly study – By using one verse per week, you'll find that Titus will provide you one year's worth of study material (with six weeks free for holidays and vacation).

A month of daily studies – Using the Digging Deeper questions as dividing points, you'll find that Titus breaks nicely into thirty-six units for study. This provides a full month (with a few additional days) of daily nourishment and training for your leaders.

Topical Training Schedule

Employing the Topical Training Schedule allows you to train your leaders based upon specific needs facing them and your church. In Appendix C you will discover all the Ministry Maxims found throughout the commentary have been assigned according to topics. By using one or more of these texts at a time you will be able to train your people directly from the Scriptures in regard to any of these key leadership principles. The benefit of using the Topical Training Schedule is that it allows you to deal in real time with the issues facing your leaders and your church, but to do so directly from the Scriptures. You might, for example, use the three passages and Ministry Maxims listed under "Vigilance" and develop a three-part training experience (taught face-to-face or via e-mail) or as one lesson with three points. By reducing and expanding the information provided in the text of *The Pastoral Epistles for Pastors,* you will be able to make these lessons expand or contract to the time frame and circumstances that best serve God's purposes for you and your people.

Qualifications Training Schedule

Using the Qualifications Training Schedule enables you to train your leaders in the qualifications that are imperative for the faithful completion of their God-given ministry assignments.

Overseers/Elders – The following list of qualifications is comprised of the terms from 1 Timothy 3:2-7 and Titus 1:6-9. The order begins with those qualifications listed in 1 Timothy 3:2-7. Where identical/similar terms or parallel concepts are found again in Titus 1:6-9 the reference (for identical expressions) or wording and reference (for similar terms or parallel concepts) are listed with the first entry. The terms used only in Titus 1:6-9 follow at the end of the list.

above reproach (ἀνεπίλημπτον; 1 Tim. 3:2; cf. ἀνέγκλητος; Titus 1:6)
the husband of one wife (μιᾶς γυναικὸς ἀνήρ; 1 Tim. 3:2; Titus 1:6)
temperate (νηφάλιον; 1 Tim. 3:2)
prudent (σώφρονα; 1 Tim. 3:2; "sensible," Titus 1:8)
respectable (κόσμιον; 1 Tim. 3:2)
loving what is good (φιλάγαθον; Titus 1:8)
hospitable (φιλόξενον; 1 Tim. 3:2; Titus 1:8)
able to teach (διδακτικόν; 1 Tim. 3:2)
  "holding fast the faithful word which is in accordance with the teaching, so that he will be able both to exhort in sound doctrine and to refute those who contradict." (ἀντεχόμενον τοῦ κατὰ τὴν διδαχὴν πιστοῦ λόγου, ἵνα δυνατὸς ᾖ καὶ παρακαλεῖν ἐν τῇ διδασκαλίᾳ τῇ ὑγιαινούσῃ καὶ τοὺς ἀντιλέγοντας ἐλέγχειν; Titus 1:9)
not addicted to wine (μὴ πάροινον; 1 Tim. 3:3; Titus 1:7)
not pugnacious (μὴ πλήκτην; 1 Tim. 3:3; Titus 1:7)
gentle (ἐπιεικῆ; 1 Tim. 3:3)
  not self-willed (μὴ αὐθάδη; Titus 1:7)
uncontentious (ἄμαχον; 1 Tim. 3:3)
  not quick-tempered (μὴ ὀργίλον; Titus 1:7)
free from the love of money (ἀφιλάργυρον; 1 Tim. 3:3)
  not fond of sordid gain (μὴ αἰσχροκερδῆ; Titus 1:7)
manages his own household well (τοῦ ἰδίου οἴκου καλῶς προϊστάμενον; 1 Tim. 3:4)
  having children who believe (τέκνα ἔχων πιστά; Titus 1:6)

keeping his children under control with all dignity (τέκνα ἔχοντα ἐν ὑποταγῇ, μετὰ πάσης σεμνότητος; 1 Tim. 3:4)
not accused of dissipation or rebellion (μὴ ἐν κατηγορίᾳ ἀσωτίας ἢ ἀνυπότακτα; Titus 1:6)
not a new convert (μὴ νεόφυτον; 1 Tim. 3:6)
a good reputation with those outside (μαρτυρίαν καλὴν ἔχειν ἀπὸ τῶν ἔξωθεν; 1 Tim. 3:7)
just (δίκαιον; Titus 1:8)
devout (ὅσιον; Titus 1:8)
self-controlled (ἐγκρατῆ; Titus 1:8)

You also may contemplate a study which considers these qualifications thematically under the following four headings.[1]

Relationship to God

above reproach (ἀνεπίλημπτον; 1 Tim. 3:2; cf. ἀνέγκλητος; Titus 1:6)
not a new convert (μὴ νεόφυτον; 1 Tim. 3:6)
"holding fast the faithful word which is in accordance with the teaching, so that he will be able both to exhort in sound doctrine and to refute those who contradict." (ἀντεχόμενον τοῦ κατὰ τὴν διδαχὴν πιστοῦ λόγου, ἵνα δυνατὸς ᾖ καὶ παρακαλεῖν ἐν τῇ διδασκαλίᾳ τῇ ὑγιαινούσῃ καὶ τοὺς ἀντιλέγοντας ἐλέγχειν; Titus 1:9)
able to teach (διδακτικόν; 1 Tim. 3:2)
just (δίκαιον; Titus 1:8)
devout (ὅσιον; Titus 1:8)
loving what is good (φιλάγαθον; Titus 1:8)

Relationship to Self

self-controlled (ἐγκρατῆ; Titus 1:8)
temperate (νηφάλιον; 1 Tim. 3:2)
free from the love of money (ἀφιλάργυρον; 1 Tim. 3:3)
not fond of sordid gain (μὴ αἰσχροκερδῆ; Titus 1:7)
prudent (σώφρονα; 1 Tim. 3:2; "sensible," Titus 1:8)
not pugnacious (μὴ πλήκτην; 1 Tim. 3:3; Titus 1:7)
not addicted to wine (μὴ πάροινον; 1 Tim. 3:3; Titus 1:7)
not quick-tempered (μὴ ὀργίλον; Titus 1:7)

---

[1] These headings are suggested by H. Wayne House, *Charts of Christian Theology and Doctrine*, 119.

Appendix B

Relationship to Others

respectable (κόσμιον; 1 Tim. 3:2)
hospitable (φιλόξενον; 1 Tim. 3:2; Titus 1:8)
uncontentious (ἄμαχον; 1 Tim. 3:3)
gentle (ἐπιεικῆ; 1 Tim. 3:3)
a good reputation with those outside (μαρτυρίαν καλὴν ἔχειν ἀπὸ τῶν ἔξωθεν; 1 Tim. 3:7)
not self-willed (μὴ αὐθάδη; Titus 1:7)

Relationship to Family

the husband of one wife (μιᾶς γυναικὸς ἀνήρ; 1 Tim. 3:2; Titus 1:6)
manages his own household well (τοῦ ἰδίου οἴκου καλῶς προϊστάμενον; 1 Tim. 3:4)
having children who believe (τέκνα ἔχων πιστά; Titus 1:6)
keeping his children under control with all dignity (τέκνα ἔχοντα ἐν ὑποταγῇ, μετὰ πάσης σεμνότητος; 1 Tim. 3:4)
not accused of dissipation or rebellion (μὴ ἐν κατηγορίᾳ ἀσωτίας ἢ ἀνυπότακτα; Titus 1:6)

Deacons – The following list of qualifications is comprised of the terms from 1 Timothy 3:8-10, 12. These will be useful in training the deacons within your fellowship.

Dignity (σεμνούς; v.8)
Not double-tongued (μὴ διλόγους; v.8)
No addicted too much wine (μὴ οἴνῳ πολλῷ προσέχοντας; v.8)
Not fond of sordid gain (μὴ αἰσχροκερδεῖς; v.8)
Holding to the mystery of the faith with a clear conscience (ἔχοντας τὸ μυστήριον τῆς πίστεως ἐν καθαρᾷ συνειδήσει; v.9)
Tested (δοκιμαζέσθωσαν; v.10)
Beyond reproach (ἀνέγκλητοι; v.10)
Husbands of only one wife (μιᾶς γυναικὸς ἄνδρες; v.12)
Good managers of their children and their own households (τέκνων καλῶς προϊστάμενοι καὶ τῶν ἰδίων οἴκων; v.12)

APPENDIX C

A TOPICAL INDEX TO THE MINISTRY MAXIMS

What follows is a topical index of the Ministry Maxims found in each verse of the commentary. In many cases each verse could have multiple Ministry Maxims formulated for it, so this does not serve as a comprehensive index of all that the PE teach. Rather this index serves as a quick guide to locating some of the PE's teaching on various subjects, as capsulated in the Ministry Maxims. These topics may provide a starting point in dealing with particular issues in your personal study (see Appendix A) or in training church leaders (see Appendix B).

Abandonment	2 Tim. 1:15
Accountability	1 Tim. 3:10; 5:25; 2 Tim. 4:1
Actions	Titus 1:16; 2:1, 3, 6, 7; 3:4, 9
Aging	2 Tim. 4:13, 19; Titus 2:2
Apostasy	1 Tim. 1:19; 3:9; 5:12; 6:21; 2 Tim. 2:12, 13
Appreciation	2 Tim. 1:17
Arguments/debate	1 Tim. 1:4, 6; 4:7; 6:5; 2 Tim. 2:16, 17, 19, 23, 24, 26
Authenticity	2 Tim. 1:5
Authority	1 Tim. 1:1; 2:11, 12; 4:11; Titus 2:9, 15; 3:1, 10
Balance	2 Tim. 2:18
Boldness	2 Tim. 1:8
Call/calling	1 Tim. 2:7; 3:1, 10; 2 Tim. 1:9, 11; 4:1
Change	Titus 3:12
Character	1 Tim. 2:9, 10; 3:2, 5, 6; 4:12; 5:7; 2 Tim. 2:5
Children	1 Tim. 5:4, 16; 2 Tim. 3:15; Titus 1:6
Church	1 Tim. 2:8; 3:11, 15; 6:1; 2 Tim. 2:20; Titus 1:5
Church discipline	1 Tim. 5:20; Titus 3:11

Circumstances	2 Tim. 1:1, 2
Commitment	2 Tim. 2:20
Compensation (financial)	1 Tim. 5:17, 18; 6:6, 7, 8, 10
Conscience	1 Tim. 1:19; 3:9; 4:2; 2 Tim. 1:3
Contentment	1 Tim. 6:6, 7, 8, 10, 17
Conviction (of belief)	1 Tim. 1:10, 18; 2 Tim. 3:7, 14; Titus 3:8
Conviction (of sin)	1 Tim. 1:8
Correct	Titus 2:8
Covetousness	1 Tim. 6:10
Deaconesses	1 Tim. 3:11
Deacons	1 Tim. 3:8, 9, 10, 12, 13
Death	1 Tim. 6:7; 2 Tim. 4:6, 18, 19, 22
Desire	2 Tim. 2:1
Devil/Satan	1 Tim. 3:7; 4:1; 5:14, 15; 2 Tim. 2:26; 3:3
Deception	1 Tim. 2:14; 2 Tim. 3:13; Titus 1:10
Deliverance	2 Tim. 4:18
Deportment	1 Tim. 2:9, 10
Despair	Titus 1:15
Devotion	2 Tim. 1:17
Diet	1 Tim. 4:4, 5
Disappointment	2 Tim. 4:17
Discernment	2 Tim. 2:19, 23
Discipleship	2 Tim. 1:8
Disrespect	1 Tim. 4:12
Effectiveness	Titus 3:3
Elders/overseers	1 Tim. 3:1, 2, 3, 4, 5, 6, 7; Titus 1:5, 6, 7, 8, 9
Election	2 Tim. 2:10
Emotions	2 Tim. 1:4, 15; Titus 2:4
Endurance	1 Tim. 5:5, 12; 6:13, 14; 2 Tim. 1:8; 2:12; 3:11; 4:7
Escape	2 Tim. 3:11
Eternal life/heaven	2 Tim. 2:11; Titus 1:2
Eternity	Titus 1:3
Example	2 Tim. 2:2; 3:10
Exclusivity (of Christ)	1 Tim. 2:5, 6
Failure	1 Tim. 5:4; 2 Tim. 1:13; 3:9, 13; Titus 3:10, 11
Faith	1 Tim. 1:14, 20; 5:8, 23; 2 Tim. 1:12
Faithfulness	1 Tim. 3:9, 13; 5:5; 6:13, 14, 15, 16, 21; 2 Tim. 1:11, 12, 14, 17; 2:2, 3, 12, 13; 3:1; 4:7, 8, 10, 11, 12
False teachers	2 Tim. 3:6, 13

Appendix C

Family	2 Tim. 1:16
Fatherhood	1 Tim. 3:4, 12
Fear	2 Tim. 1:7
Focus	2 Tim. 2:8
Forgiveness	2 Tim. 4:11, 16
Forsake	2 Tim. 2:22
Freedom	2 Tim. 1:8; 3:4
Friendship	2 Tim. 1:17
Fruitfulness	1 Tim. 2:2; 4:10
Gender	1 Tim. 2:14
Generations	2 Tim. 2:2
Giving	1 Tim. 5:9, 10; 2 Tim. 1:2
God's	
Character	1 Tim. 6:14, 16
Faithfulness	2 Tim. 1:14; 2:13
Giving	Titus 3:6
Glory	1 Tim. 1:11; Titus 2:5
Kingdom	2 Tim. 4:1
Knowledge	2 Tim. 2:19
Law	1 Tim. 1:8, 9
Love	1 Tim. 2:5, 6
Patience	1 Tim. 1:16
Pleasure	1 Tim. 2:3; 2 Tim. 2:4
Presence	1 Tim. 5:21; 2 Tim. 4:22
Promises	Titus 1:2
Reproof	2 Tim. 4:5
Will	2 Tim. 3:17; 4:20; Titus 1:1
Godliness	1 Tim. 3:16; 5:4, 7, 14; 6:6, 11, 13; 2 Tim. 2:21, 22; Titus 2:14; 3:4
Gospel	1 Tim. 1:11; 2 Tim. 1:10, 12; 2:9; Titus 1:3; 2:13
Gossip	2 Tim. 3:3
Grace	1 Tim. 1:2, 12, 13, 14; 4:3; 5:9; 2 Tim. 2:1; 4:16, 22; Titus 1:4; 2:12, 13
Gratitude	1 Tim. 1:12, 15
Greed	1 Tim. 5:18
Guard (the truth)	1 Tim. 1:20
Gullible	2 Tim. 3:6
Hardship	1 Tim. 1:18; 5:7; 6:1, 10, 12; 2 Tim. 1:2, 16; 2:3, 9; 3:1, 11, 12; 4:5
Heart	2 Tim. 4:10
Heirs/inheritance	Titus 3:7

Heresy/falsehood	1 Tim. 6:20; 2 Tim. 2:17, 18, 23, 24, 26; 3:8, 9; 4:4, 14; Titus 1:10, 11, 14, 16; 2:1
Holy/holiness	1 Tim. 3:16; 4:5; 5:6; 6:3, 11, 13; 2 Tim. 2:21, 22; 3:4; Titus 2:14; 3:4, 8
Holy Spirit	1 Tim. 4:14; 2 Tim. 1:6, 7, 8, 14; 3:5; 4:20; Titus 3:6
Honest/honesty	1 Tim. 1:15; Titus 1:12
Honor	1 Tim. 5:3
Hope	1 Tim. 4:10; 5:5; 2 Tim. 1:1; Titus 1:2; 2:13
Humility	1 Tim. 1:15, 16; 2 Tim. 4:12; Titus 1:4; 3:3
Hypocrisy	2 Tim. 3:5, 13
Ignorance	1 Tim. 1:7
Illumination	2 Tim. 2:7, 25; Titus 2:11
Influence	1 Tim. 2:15
Jesus	2 Tim. 2:8
Judgment	2 Tim. 4:1
Kindness	2 Tim. 2:24; Titus 3:4
Knowledge	1 Tim. 1:7, 10; 4:3; 6:4; 2 Tim. 3:7, 10, 14, 17; 4:13, 17; Titus 1:1, 9
Labor/hardwork	2 Tim. 2:6, 15
Last days	2 Tim. 3:1
Leaders/leadership	1 Tim. 1:3; 2:1, 15; 3:1, 2, 3, 4, 5, 6, 7, 8, 9, 10, 12, 13, 15; 4:16; 5:1, 9, 18, 19, 20, 21, 22, 24, 25; 6:21; 2 Tim. 2:2; Titus 1:5, 6, 7, 8, 9, 11, 16; 3:10, 14
Learning	1 Tim. 1:7, 10; 4:3; 5:20; 6:4; 2 Tim. 3:7, 10, 14, 17; 4:13, 17; Titus 1:1, 9
Legalism	Titus 1:15
Listening	Titus 1:11, 14, 16
Loneliness	2 Tim. 1:15
Loss	2 Tim. 1:4
Love	1 Tim. 1:5; 3:15; 5:8; 2 Tim. 3:2, 4
Lying	2 Tim. 3:13
Manhood	1 Tim. 2:13; 3:12; 5:2
Marriage	Titus 1:6
Martyrdom	2 Tim. 4:6
Maturity	1 Tim. 3:6; 4:15; 2 Tim. 3:7, 10, 17; Titus 1:13; 2:4, 13; 3:5
Medicine	1 Tim. 5:23
Meditation	2 Tim. 2:7, 8; 3:10
Membership	2 Tim. 2:20

Appendix C

Mentoring	2 Tim. 2:2; 3:10; Titus 3:14
Mercy	1 Tim. 1:2; 2 Tim. 1:18
Ministry	1 Tim. 1:13, 18; 2 Tim. 1:2; Titus 3:3
Money	1 Tim. 6:8, 9, 17, 18, 19
Motherhood	1 Tim. 2:15
Motivation	1 Tim. 4:16; Titus 2:3
Obedience	1 Tim. 1:10; 5:14; 6:14, 16; 2 Tim. 1:14; 2:21; 3:17; 4:3,10, 12; Titus 1:1, 16; 2:5, 8, 10, 12; 3:1
Obscurity	2 Tim. 4:12
Others	2 Tim. 1:2
Parenting	1 Tim. 2:15; 3:4, 12; 5:16; 2 Tim. 3:15; Titus 1:6
Partiality	1 Tim. 5:21
Pastor's faith	2 Tim. 1:5
Patience	2 Tim. 2:23
Peace	1 Tim. 1:2; 2:2
Persecution	2 Tim. 2:9; 3:11, 12; 4:6, 14
Perseverance	1 Tim. 5:5, 12; 6:13, 14; 2 Tim. 1:8; 2:12; 3:11; 4:7
Perspective	1 Tim. 1:17; 6:7
Pleasure	1 Tim. 5:6; 6:9
Power	1 Tim. 1:12
Prayer	1 Tim. 2:1, 2, 4, 8; 4:5; 5:5
Preaching	1 Tim. 1:5, 9; 4:1, 6, 11, 13; 5:17, 18; 6:3; 2 Tim. 4:1, 2, 3, 4; Titus 1:9; 2:1; 3:8
Pride	1 Tim. 6:4; Titus 1:4
Promises	2 Tim. 2:13
Protection	2 Tim. 4:15, 18
Purity	2 Tim. 2:21
Purpose	1 Tim. 2:8; 6:1, 21
Quitting	2 Tim. 1:7
Reading	1 Tim. 4:13; 2 Tim. 4:13
Reality	1 Tim. 1:17
Rebellion	Titus 1:10; 3:10, 11
Rebuke/reproof	1 Tim. 5:20; Titus 1:11, 12, 13
Regeneration	Titus 3:5
Relationships	1 Tim. 2:11, 13, 14; 3:14; 5:1, 2; 2 Tim. 4:9, 17, 19, 21; Titus 3:13, 15
Religion	2 Tim. 3:5, 6
Reminder	Titus 3:3
Repentance	1 Tim. 5:22; 2 Tim. 2:25
Respect	1 Tim. 3:3; 4:12; 5:1, 3, 11, 17; Titus 2:15

Responsibility	1 Tim. 6:2; 2 Tim. 2:10
Revenge	2 Tim. 4:14
Revival/renewal	Titus 3:5
Reward	1 Tim. 5:10; 6:12, 14, 15, 18, 19; 2 Tim. 2:5, 6, 12; 4:8
Righteousness	Titus 3:7
Sacrifice	2 Tim. 1:18
Salvation	Titus 3:5
Scripture/Word of God	1 Tim. 1:4; 4:4, 13; 2 Tim. 2:9, 15; 3:15, 16, 17; 4:2
Second Coming	1 Tim. 6:14; Titus 2:13
Self (death to)	2 Tim. 2:11
Self-control/discipline	1 Tim. 3:3, 4; 4:6, 8, 14, 15; 5:6; 6:11, 12; 2 Tim. 1:6; Titus 1:8; 2:4, 6, 12
Selfish	1 Tim. 5:15
Self-will	Titus 3:10
Servant/servanthood	1 Tim. 1:3; 3:8, 11, 13; 2 Tim. 1:8; Titus 3:13
Shame	2 Tim. 1:10
Sickness	1 Tim. 5:23
Sin	1 Tim. 1:9; 2 Tim. 2:21; 3:2, 4; 4:16; Titus 1:7
Single-minded	2 Tim. 2:4, 8
Speaking/speech	1 Tim. 1:4, 6, 7; 4:7, 9; Titus 1:12; 2:1, 7; 3:2, 9
Spiritual gifts	1 Tim. 3:2; 2 Tim. 4:20
Strength	2 Tim. 2:1
Study	1 Tim. 4:6, 13; 2 Tim. 2:15
Submission	1 Tim. 1:1; 2:11; 6:14, 15; Titus 2:9; 3:1
Success	1 Tim. 2:2; 4:10, 14; 2 Tim. 1:9, 12, 13, 18; 2:5, 15, 17; 3:9, 17; Titus 2:7; 3:12, 13
Suffering	1 Tim. 1:18; 5:7; 6:1, 10, 12; 2 Tim. 1:8; 2:3, 9, 10, 12; 4:5
Teaching	1 Tim. 1:5, 9; 4:1, 6, 11, 13; 5:17, 18; 6:3; 2 Tim. 2:2; 4:1, 2, 3, 4; Titus 1:9; 2:1, 12
Temptation	1 Tim. 3:7; 5:13, 14, 15, 19
Thanks	1 Tim. 1:12, 15
Thinking	1 Tim. 4:11; 2 Tim. 2:7, 8; 3:8; Titus 2:6
Time	Titus 1:3
Tongue	2 Tim. 3:3
Training	2 Tim. 2:2
Trust	2 Tim. 4:15, 21
Truth	1 Tim. 1:20; 2:5; 3:15; 4:1, 2, 5; 6:3; 6:5; 2 Tim. 1:13; 2:18; 3:8; 4:4; Titus 1:14

Appendix C

Unbelievers	2 Tim. 2:20
Usefulness	2 Tim. 4:11
Values	1 Tim. 4:8, 9; 2 Tim. 4:22
Victory	2 Tim. 3:11; 4:7
Vigilance	1 Tim. 1:19, 20; 2 Tim. 4:15
Wise/wisdom	1 Tim. 1:7; 4:7; 5:1, 2, 19, 22; 6:9; Titus 2:8
Will	2 Tim. 2:1
Witness/evangelism	1 Tim. 1:11; 2:4; 2 Tim. 1:10; 2:10; Titus 1:3; 2:10, 11; 3:2, 12
Womanhood	1 Tim. 2:9, 10, 13, 15; 3:11
Work	1 Tim. 5:13
Worship	1 Tim. 2:3; 2 Tim. 4:6
Writing	1 Tim. 3:14; 4:9
Youth	Titus 2:2

APPENDIX D

PREACHING/TEACHING THE PASTORAL EPISTLES

Preaching is one of the great privileges of a pastor. The PE have much to say about faithfully preaching God's Word (see especially the commentary on 2 Timothy 4:1-4). It is my conviction that expository preaching should be the regular practice of every local church pastor.[1] Of course, even among those of similar conviction, there is not always consensus on just what constitutes expository preaching. Similarly, each pastor is comfortable preaching passages of different lengths and series of varying duration. Local circumstances also permit (or require) sermon series of differing lengths. What follows are suggestive attempts at projecting both preaching series and their individual sermons. First, I offer exegetical outlines of each of the PE. Then I offer three possibilities for preaching each one of the PE—a single message covering the entire book, a shorter series of messages, and a more extended series of messages. These may, of course, be expanded even further. In some cases you may divide the books differently than I have suggested here. My hope is that these suggestions will provide fodder for your preaching of these portions of sacred Scripture.

"I solemnly charge you in the presence of God and of Christ Jesus, who is to judge the living and the dead, and by His appearing and His kingdom: preach the word; be ready in season and out of season; reprove, rebuke, exhort, with great patience and instruction" (2 Tim. 4:1-2).

---

[1] See the author's *Revival in the Rubble* (chapter 9) for more on the primacy and practice of expository preaching.

1 Timothy

EXEGETICAL OUTLINE

I. **The Salutation. (1:1-2)**
   A. The author. (1)
   B. The recipient. (2a)
   C. The greeting. (2b)

II. **The Church's Proclamation. (1:3-20)**
   A. **God's Law confronts false teaching. (3-11)**
      1. The proper use of God's message. (3-5)
         a. Timothy's goal in Ephesus. (3-4)
         b. Paul's goal in teaching. (5)
      2. The proper use of God's Law. (6-11)
         a. The false use of God's Law. (6-7)
         b. The correct use of God's Law. (8-11)
            i. God's Law is good when used properly. (8)
            ii. God's Law is glaring when used properly. (9-10)
            iii. God's Law is in harmony with God's grace. (11)
   B. **God's grace overcomes our sin. (12-17)**
      1. Paul's gratitude for God's call. (12)
      2. Paul's guilt before God's call. (13a)
      3. God's grace was given with a purpose. (13b-16)
         a. Paul was called by virtue of grace. (13b-14)
         b. Paul was called as an example of grace. (15-16)
      4. God's glory is seen through His grace. (17)
   C. **God's call compels our faithfulness. (18-20)**
      1. The faithfulness of Timothy is required. (18-19a)
      2. The faithlessness of others is recounted. (19b-20)

III. **The Church's People. (2:1-3:16)**
   A. **God's people worshiping in the truth. (2:1-15)**
      1. The role of prayer in worship. (1-7)
         a. The various kinds of prayer. (1a)
         b. The various objects of prayer. (1b-2a)
         c. The various reasons for prayer. (2b-4)
            i. Reasons for prayer with respect to the church. (2b)
            ii. Reasons for prayer with respect to God. (3-4)
         d. The vicarious foundation for prayer. (5-7)
            i. God's mediator. (5-6)
            ii. God's messenger. (7)
      2. The role of people in worship. (8-15)
         a. The role of men in worship. (8)
         b. The role of women in worship. (9-15)
            i. The proper adornment of women in worship. (9-10)
            ii. The proper activity of women in worship. (11-15)
               aa. A command for women in worship. (11)
               bb. A prohibition for women in worship. (12)
               cc. An explanation for women in worship. (13-15)
                  (i.) An explanation regarding the order of creation. (13)
                  (ii.) An explanation regarding the lesson from the Fall. (14-15)
   B. **God's leaders walking in the truth. (3:1-13)**
      1. The required qualities for overseers. (1-7)
         a. The passionate desire to serve as an overseer. (1)
         b. The personal qualities of an overseer. (2-7)
            i. The overseer's relationship to his family.

Appendix D

    ii. The overseer's relationship to God.
    iii. The overseer's relationship to himself.
    iv. The overseer's relationship to others.
  2. The required qualities for deacons and deaconesses. (8-13)
    a. The personal qualities for deacons. (8-9)
    b. The congregational testing for deacons. (10)
    c. The personal qualities for deaconesses. (11)
    d. The familial qualities for deacons. (12)
    e. The hopeful prize for deacons. (13)
 C. God's servants working together in the truth. (3:14-16)
  1. The cause of this letter to Timothy. (14-15b)
  2. The calling of the church. (15c)
  3. The confession of the church. (16)

IV. The Church's Pastor. (4:1-16)
 A. Confronting the false teachers. (1-5)
  1. The prediction of apostasy. (1a)
  2. The profile of apostasy. (1b-3a)
    a. Deceived in their thinking. (1b)
    b. Seared in their conscience. (2)
    c. Ascetic in their practice. (3a)
  3. The practice of apostasy. (3b-5)
    a. What God created they reject. (3b)
    b. What God created should be received. (4-5)
 B. Continuing as a faithful minister. (6-12)
  1. A faithful minister teaches the people truthfully. (6)
  2. A faithful minister disciplines himself spiritually. (7-9)
  3. A faithful minister fixes his hope firmly. (10-11)
  4. A faithful minister sets an example consistently. (12)
 C. Growing as a faithful minister. (13-16)
  1. A faithful minister reads Scripture publicly. (13)
  2. A faithful minister develops his spiritual gift. (14)
  3. A faithful minister works hard. (15)
  4. A faithful minister guards himself and his teaching. (16)

V. The Church's Practice. (5:1-6:2)
 A. The pastor's practice with his people. (5:1-2)
  1. The pastor's relationship to older men. (1a)
  2. The pastor's relationship to younger men. (1b)
  3. The pastor's relationship to older women. (2a)
  4. The pastor's relationship to younger women. (2b)
 B. The church's practice toward its widows. (5:3-16)
  1. The church is commanded to honor widows. (3)
  2. The church is commanded to classify widows. (4-7)
    a. Identify widows who have children to care for them. (4)
    b. Identify widows who have qualified for church support. (5)
    c. Identify widows who have disqualified themselves for church support. (6)
    d. Impartiality in applying these instructions. (7)
  3. The church is commanded to insist on familial support of widows. (8)
  4. The church is commanded to support widows. (9-16)
    a. The widows qualified for the church's support. (9-10)
    b. The widows disqualified for the church's support. (11-13)
    c. The widows directed during their younger years. (14-16)
 C. The church's practice with its leaders. (5:17-25)
  1. Remunerating elders. (17-18)
    a. The standard for remuneration is stated. (17)
    b. The standard for remuneration is supported. (18)

The Pastoral Epistles for Pastors

      2. Reprimanding elders. (19-21)
          a. The required basis for considering an accusation is outlined. (19)
          b. The required rebuke of sinning elders is commanded. (20)
          c. The required impartiality in applying these principles is demanded. (21)
      3. Recognizing elders. (22, 24-25)
          a. The church needs discernment regarding a candidate's standing. (22)
          b. The church needs discernment regarding a candidate's sin. (24)
          c. The church needs discernment regarding a candidate's service. (25)
      4. Remedying Timothy's sick stomach. (23)
   D. The slave's practice toward his master. (6:1-2)
      1. Christian slaves must honor their unbelieving masters. (1)
      2. Christian slaves must honor their Christian masters. (2)

VI. The Church's Problem. (6:3-21)
   A. The Apostle gives final instructions regarding false teachers. (3-10)
      1. The identity of the false teachers is outlined. (3-5)
          a. Spotting the false teachers is described. (3)
          b. Sentencing the false teachers is described. (4-5)
      2. The instruction against the false teachers is enjoined. (6-10)
          a. The delight of contentment is outlined. (6-8)
             i. Contentment comes through piety. (6)
             ii. Contentment comes through perspective. (7-8)
          b. The danger of discontentment is outlined. (9-10)
             i. The trap of discontentment is described. (9)
             ii. The trigger of discontentment is described. (10)
   B. The Apostle gives final instructions regarding Timothy's ministry. (11-16)
      1. Flee sin and pursue sanctification. (11)
      2. Fight for faith and take hold of eternal life. (12)
      3. Keep the commandment and praise the Lord. (13-16)
   C. The Apostle gives final instructions regarding the rich. (17-19)
      1. The pastor must identify the rich. (17a)
      2. The pastor must instruct the rich. (17b-19)
          a. The wrong object of hope is set forth. (17b)
          b. The correct object of hope is set forth. (17c)
          c. The correct outworking of hope is set forth. (18-19)
   D. The Apostle gives a final charge to Timothy. (20-21)
      1. The Apostle's final charge is delivered. (20-21a)
      2. The Apostle's final benediction is delivered. (21b)

EXPOSITIONAL OUTLINES

A Single Message: Called to Greatness

I. We are called to proclaim a great message. (1:3-20)
   A. We must proclaim God's Law rightly. (3-11)
   B. We must proclaim God's grace rightly. (12-17)
   C. We must fulfill God's call rightly. (18-20)
II. We are called to prepare a great people. (2:1-3:16)
   A. We must prepare believers for worship. (2:1-15)
   B. We must prepare leaders for leadership. (3:1-13)
   C. We must prepare servants for service. (3:14-16)
III. We are called to prepare great leaders. (4:1-16)
   A. We must prepare leaders who confront falsehood. (1-5)
   B. We must prepare leaders who continue in faithfulness. (6-12)

C. We must prepare leaders who are committed to growth. (13-16)
IV. We are called to establish great churches. (5:1-6:2)
   A. We must prepare a church for godly relationships. (5:1-2)
   B. We must prepare a church for needy widows. (5:3-16)
   C. We must prepare a church for following leaders. (5:17-25)
   D. We must prepare a church for the workplace. (6:1-2)
V. We are called to overcome great challenges. (6:3-21)
   A. We must prepare a church to overcome errant teaching. (3-10)
   B. We must prepare a church to endure to the end. (11-16)
   C. We must prepare a church to overcome materialism. (17-19)

A Shorter Series: Five Messages

Series Title: Becoming the Church God Desires.

Message #1: The Church's Message Must Be Articulated (1:3-20)
I. **The church must correct what is in error. (3-11)**
   A. **Truth flourishes under a godly preacher. (3-5)**
   B. **Truth flourishes under an illuminating Law. (6-11)**
II. **The church must teach what is true. (12-20)**
   A. **Truth is preached when we proclaim God's Gospel. (12-17)**
   B. **True is preached when we fulfill God's call. (18-20)**

Message #2: The Church's People Must Be Unified (2:1-3:16)
I. **God's people worship together. (2:1-15)**
   A. **God's people worshiping in prayer. (1-7)**
   B. **God's people worshiping in propriety. (8-15)**
II. **God's people work together. (3:1-16)**
   A. **God's leaders lead well. (1-13)**
   B. **God's servants serve well. (14-16)**

Message #3: The Church's Pastor Must Be Clear (4:1-16)
I. **The pastor is a defender of the truth. (1-5)**
II. **The pastor is a disseminator of the truth. (6-16)**

Message #4: The Church's Practice Must Be Holy (5:1-6:2)
I. **The church's practice with its people. (5:1-2)**
II. **The church's practice with its widows. (5:3-16)**
III. **The church's practice with its leaders. (5:17-25)**
IV. **The church's practice within its marketplace. (6:1-2)**

Message #5: The Church's Problems Must be Confronted (6:3-21)
I. **The church will always face false teachers. (3-10)**
II. **The church will always face temptation. (11-16)**
III. **The church will always face materialism. (17-19)**
IV. **The church will always face threats. (20-21)**

A Longer Series: Twenty Messages

Series Title: God's Household Living in Harmony.

Message #1 The Preacher of God's Word (1 Timothy 1:1-5)
I. A master preacher. (1-2)
    A. Masterful preaching speaks with authority. (1a)
    B. Masterful preaching speaks with hope. (1b)
    C. Masterful preaching speaks with grace. (2)
II. A misguided preacher. (3-4)
    A. Misguided preaching promotes strange doctrines. (3)
    B. Misguided preaching promotes speculation. (4)
III. A mature preacher. (5)
    A. Mature preaching produces love which looks at others with good motives. (5a)
    B. Mature preaching produces love which looks at self in self-judgment. (5b)
    C. Mature preaching produces love which looks at God without ulterior motives. (5c)

Message #2 The Place of God's Law (1 Timothy 1:6-11)
I. When God's Law is used wrongly it is disastrous. (6-7)
II. When God's Law is used rightly it is demanding. (8-11)
    A. God's Law exposes our sin. (8-11)
    B. God's Law prepares us for grace. (11)

Message #3 The Products of God's Gospel (1 Timothy 1:12-17)
I. The Gospel creates gratitude. (12-14)
    A. I am grateful for Christ's strength in me. (12a)
    B. I am grateful for Christ's confidence in me. (12b)
    C. I am grateful for Christ's appointment of me. (12c)
    D. I am grateful for Christ's mercy toward me. (13)
    E. I am grateful for Christ's grace to me. (14)
II. The Gospel creates assurance. (15)
III. The Gospel creates mission. (16)
IV. The Gospel creates praise. (17)

Message #4 The Power of God's Call (1 Timothy 1:18-20)
I. We are called to a fight which we must win. (18)
    A. We must fight to keep God's charge.
    B. We must fight to keep our destiny.
II. We are called to a journey which we must finish. (19-20)
    A. Keeping the faith is a journey. (19a)
    B. Keeping a good conscience is a journey. (19b-20)

Message #5 The Role of Prayer in Public Worship (1 Timothy 2:1-8)
I. We must pray for our rulers. (1-2)
II. We must pray for our witness. (3-8)
    A. This is in line with God's thinking. (3)
    B. This is in line with God's heart. (4)
    C. This is in line with God's sacrifice. (5-6)

D. This is in line with God's commission. (7-8)

Message #6 The Role of Women in Public Worship (1 Timothy 2:9-15)
I. A woman must guard her public adornment. (9-10)
   A. A woman must guard her adornment personally. (9)
   B. A woman must guard her adornment interpersonally. (10)
II. A woman must guard her outward behavior. (11-15)
   A. A woman is to learn submissively. (11)
   B. A woman is to follow quietly. (12)
   C. A woman is to think biblically. (13-14)
   D. A woman is to parent hopefully. (15)

Message #7 The Ministry of Elders (1 Timothy 3:1-7)
I. The church must be confident their elders are called. (1)
II. The church must be confident their elders are qualified. (2-7)
   A. Observe a man's relationship to God.
   B. Observe a man's relationship to family.
   C. Observe a man's relationship to himself.
   D. Observe a man's relationship to others.

Message #8 The Ministry of Deacons and Deaconesses (1 Timothy 3:8-13)
I. A church is blessed by the ministry of godly deacons. (8-10, 12-13)
   A. Deacons must control themselves. (8)
   B. Deacons must keep their faith. (9)
   C. Deacons must maintain their testimony. (10)
   D. Deacons must lead their families. (12)
   E. Deacons must deserve their rewards. (13)
II. A church is blessed by the ministry of godly deaconesses. (11)
   A. In their hearts, deaconesses must be dignified. (11a)
   B. In their conversations, deaconesses must be discreet. (11b)
   C. In their appetites, deaconesses must be temperate. (11c)
   D. In their responsibilities, deaconesses must be faithful. (11d)

Message #9 The Ministry of Waiting (1 Timothy 3:14-16)
I. We wait well when we remember the primacy of our responsibilities. (14-15)
II. We wait well when we remember the power of our message. (16)

Message #10 Life in the Last Days (1 Timothy 4:1-5)
I. The last days will be marked by apostasy. (1a)
II. The last days will be marked by deception. (1b-2)
III. The last days will be marked by legalism. (3-5)

Message #11 The Pastor as a Faithful Minister (1 Timothy 4:6-12)
I. The faithful pastor teaches his people truthfully. (6)
II. The faithful pastor disciplines himself spiritually. (7-9)
III. The faithful pastor fixes his hope firmly. (10-11)
IV. The faithful pastor sets his example consistently. (12)

The Pastoral Epistles for Pastors

Message #12 The Pastor as a Preacher of God's Word (1 Timothy 4:13-16)
I. **Preaching God's Word must be our practice. (13)**
II. **Preaching God's Word must be our passion. (14)**
III. **Preaching God's Word must be our priority. (15)**
IV. **Preaching God's Word must be our perseverance. (16)**

Message #13 The Pastor and His People (1 Timothy 5:1-2)
I. **Respect must mark the pastor's relationship to older men. (1a)**
II. **Collegiality must mark the pastor's relationship to younger men. (1b)**
III. **Affection must mark the pastor's relationship to older women. (2a)**
IV. **Purity must mark the pastor's relationship to younger women. (2b)**

Message #14 The Church and Its Widows (1 Timothy 5:3-16)
I. **The church must honor its widows. (3)**
II. **The church must help families honor their widows. (4-8)**
III. **The church must honor its widows wisely. (9-16)**

Message #15 The Church and Its Leaders (1 Timothy 5:17-25)
I. **The church should remunerate its leaders appropriately. (17-18)**
    A. Such remuneration is appropriate. (17)
    B. Such remuneration is commanded. (18)
II. **The church should reprimand its leaders appropriately. (19-21)**
    A. Discipline of leaders must be insightful. (19)
    B. Discipline of leaders must be instituted. (20)
    C. Discipline of leaders must be impartial. (21)
III. **The church should recognize its leaders appropriately. (22-25)**
    A. Discernment is needed regarding a potential leader's standing. (22)
    B. Discernment is needed regarding a potential leader's sin. (24)
    C. Discernment is needed regarding a potential leader's steps. (25)

Message #16 The Godly Employee (1 Timothy 6:1-2)
I. **There is a right way to work for a non-Christian employer. (1)**
    A. Work with a commitment to honor your employer.
    B. Work with a commitment to witness to your employer.
II. **There is a right way to work for a Christian employer. (2)**
    A. Your shared faith should not lead to lessened honor.
    B. Your shared faith should lead to increased honor.

Message #17 The Church's Response to False Teaching (1 Timothy 6:3-5)
I. **The church must be trained to spot false teachers. (3)**
    A. Their teaching does not agree with God's Word. (3a)
    B. Their living does not agree with God's character. (3b)
II. **The church must be trained to see through false teachers. (4-5)**

Message #18 The Perils of Possessions (1 Timothy 6:6-19)
I. **We will possess more through godly contentment. (6-10)**
II. **We will possess more through godly character. (11-16)**
III. **We will possess more through godly hope. (17-19)**

Appendix D

Message #19 The Dangers and Delights of Material Things (1 Timothy 6:17-19)
I. **Material things carry possible dangers. (17)**
   A. Material things bring the danger of pride. (17a)
   B. Material things bring the danger of presumption. (17b)
II. **Material things carry potential delights. (18-19)**
   A. Material things are a delight when shared. (18)
   B. Material things are a delight when invested. (19)

Message #20 Faithfulness to the End (1 Timothy 6:20-21)
I. **Faithfulness requires retaining the truth. (20a)**
II. **Faithfulness requires running from falsehood. (20b-21a)**
III. **Faithfulness requires relying upon grace. (21b)**

2 Timothy

EXEGETICAL OUTLINE

I. **The Salutation and Thanksgiving. (1:1-5)**
   A. **The Apostle's salutation. (1-2)**
      1. The author. (1)
      2. The recipient. (2a)
      3. The greeting. (2b)
   B. **The Apostle's thanksgiving. (3-5)**
      1. The Apostle gives thanks with a clear conscience. (3a)
      2. The Apostle gives thanks with a longing memory. (3b-4)
      3. The Apostle gives thanks with a grateful recognition. (5)

II. **The Necessary Qualities for Ministry. (1:6-18)**
   A. **Ministry necessitates faith-filled courage through the Sprit. (6-7)**
      1. The cultivation of God's Spirit. (6)
      2. The character of God's Spirit. (7)
   B. **Ministry necessitates faithful suffering for the Gospel. (8-12)**
      1. Suffering without shame. (8a)
      2. Suffering by God's power. (8b)
      3. Suffering by God's grace. (9-10)
      4. Suffering by God's appointment. (11)
      5. Suffering with God-confidence. (12)
   C. **Ministry necessitates faithful stewardship of the Gospel. (13-14)**
      1. The pattern of stewardship of the Gospel. (13)
      2. The power of stewardship of the Gospel. (14)
   D. **Ministry necessitates faithful friendships. (15-18)**
      1. A sample of failed friendships. (15)
      2. A snapshot of a faithful friendship. (16-18)
         a. A blessing to the family of Onesiphorus. (16)
         b. A blessing for the search of Onesiphorus. (17)
         c. A blessing for the service of Onesiphorus. (18)

III. **The Necessary Direction for Ministry. (2:1-26)**
   A. **Ministry requires the power of God's grace. (1-6)**
      1. Ministry requires us to be strong sons. (1)
      2. Ministry requires us to be discerning mentors. (2)

The Pastoral Epistles for Pastors

      3. Ministry requires us to be focused soldiers. (3-4)
      4. Ministry requires us to be scrupulous athletes. (5)
      5. Ministry requires hardworking farmers. (6)
  B. Ministry requires pondering Paul's pattern. (7-13)
      1. The call to ponder Paul's words. (7)
      2. The call to ponder Paul's Gospel. (8-10)
         a. Paul defined the Gospel. (8)
         b. Paul suffered for the Gospel. (9)
         c. Paul endured for the Gospel. (10)
      3. The call to ponder Paul's poem. (11-13)
         a. Death with Christ brings life with Christ. (11)
         b. Endurance for Christ brings reigning with Christ. (12a)
         c. Denying Christ brings denial by Christ. (12b)
         d. Faithlessness to Christ brings faithfulness from Christ. (13)
  C. Ministry requires the poise of God's minister. (14-26)
      1. God's minister is a shameless workman. (14-19)
         a. A shameless workman rejects worthless words. (14)
         b. A shameless workman handles God's Word. (15)
         c. A shameless workman avoids poisonous words. (16-18)
            i. Bad words lead to a bad walk. (16-17a)
            ii. Bad men lead to an abandoned faith. (17b-18)
         d. A shameless workman rests in God's words. (19)
      2. God's minister is a holy vessel. (20-21)
         a. There are different sorts of vessels. (20)
         b. There is different serviceability of vessels. (21)
      3. God's minister is a patient servant. (22-26)
         a. A patient servant in relationship to allurements. (22)
         b. A patient servant in relationship to arguments. (23)
         c. A patient servant in relationship to antagonists. (24-26)
            i. The guidelines for dealing patiently with antagonists. (24-25a)
            ii. The goal in dealing patiently with antagonists. (25b-26)

IV. The Necessary Contexts of Ministry. (3:1-17)
  A. Ministry in the world: Guard your affections! (1-9)
      1. A prediction of apostasy. (1)
      2. A portrayal of apostates. (2-5)
         a. The description of apostates. (2-4)
         b. The deception of apostates. (5a)
         c. The danger of apostates. (5b)
      3. The path of apostates. (6-9)
         a. The pattern of apostates is stated. (6a)
         b. The prey of apostates is stated. (6b-7)
         c. The principle of apostates is stated. (8)
         d. The progress of apostates will be stopped. (9)
  B. Ministry in the church: Follow godly examples! (10-13)
      1. Timothy had Paul's profile. (10-11)
      2. Timothy heard Paul's promise. (12-13)
  C. Ministry in the Word: Cling to the Scriptures! (14-17)
      1. The pattern of early instruction must be remembered. (14-15)
         a. Timothy received instruction from his mentors. (14)
         b. Timothy received instruction from his mother. (15)
      2. The power of Scripture must be relied upon. (16-17)
         a. The source of Scripture is set forth. (16a)
         b. The serviceability of Scripture is set forth. (16b-17)

V. The Necessary Faithfulness for Ministry. (4:1-22)
  A. Faithfulness means preaching God's Word faithfully. (1-4)
      1. The motive of faithful preaching. (1)

Appendix D

      2. The method of faithful preaching. (2)
      3. The milieu of faithful preaching. (3-4)
  B. Faithfulness means finishing God's work faithfully. (5-8)
      1. Paul's charge to Timothy. (5)
      2. Paul's example to Timothy. (6-8)
          a. Paul's example of present endurance. (6)
          b. Paul's example of past faithfulness. (7)
          c. Paul's example of future hopefulness. (8)
  C. Faithfulness means following Paul's directions faithfully. (9-22)
      1. One final direction to be obeyed. (9-15)
          a. Paul directed Timothy to come personally. (9-12)
              i. Paul asked Timothy to come to him. (9-11a)
              ii. Paul asked Timothy to bring Mark to him. (11b)
              iii. Paul asked Timothy to receive Tychicus from him. (12)
          b. Paul directed Timothy to bring his possessions. (13)
          c. Paul directed Timothy to avoid his persecutor. (14-15)
      2. One final testimony to be heard. (16-18)
          a. Paul was abandoned by all at his first trial. (16)
          b. Paul was attended to by the Lord at his first trial. (17)
          c. Paul was assured by the Lord of deliverance from every trial. (18)
      3. One final explanation to be received. (19-21)
          a. Paul sent greetings to special friends. (19)
          b. Paul sent explanations to Timothy. (20)
          c. Paul solicited Timothy's presence. (21a)
          d. Paul sent greetings to Timothy. (21b)
      4. One final blessing to be received. (22)

EXPOSITIONAL OUTLINES

A Single Message: Faithful to the Finish Line

I. Perseverance requires being faithful in ministry. (1:1-18)
    A. We must minister with gratitude. (1-5)
    B. We must minister with courage. (6-7)
    C. We must minister through suffering. (8-12)
    D. We must minister with stewardship. (13-18)

II. Perseverance requires being faithful as a minister. (2:1-26)
    A. We must be faithful as a purposeful mentor. (1-2)
    B. We must be faithful as a loyal soldier. (3-4)
    C. We must be faithful as a scrupulous athlete. (5, 8-13)
    D. We must be faithful as a hardworking farmer. (6-7)
    E. We must be faithful as a shameless workman. (14-18)
    F. We must be faithful as a holy vessel. (19-22)
    G. We must be faithful as a patient servant. (23-26)

III. Perseverance requires being faithful in relationships. (3:1-17)
    A. We must be faithful in relationship to the world. (1-9)
    B. We must be faithful in relationship to the church. (10-12)
    C. We must be faithful in relationship to the Scriptures. (13-17)

IV. Perseverance requires being faithful to the end. (4:1-22)
    A. We must be faithful in our preaching. (1-4)
    B. We must be faithful in our assignments. (5-8)
    C. We must be faithful in our relationships. (9-22)

The Pastoral Epistles for Pastors

A Shorter Series: Four Messages

Series Title: The Faithful Ministry of a Faithful Minister

Message #1 Qualities of a Faithful Ministry (1:3-18)
I. **We must minister with fond gratitude. (3-5)**
II. **We must minister with faith-filled courage. (6-7)**
III. **We must minister with faithful suffering. (8-12)**
IV. **We must minister with faithful stewardship. (13-18)**

Message #2 Images of a Faithful Minister (2:1-26)
I. **The minister must be an intentional mentor. (1-2)**
II. **The minister must be a faithful soldier. (3-4)**
III. **The minister must be a scrupulous athlete. (5, 8-13)**
IV. **The minister must be a hardworking farmer. (6-7)**
V. **The minister must be a shameless workman. (14-18)**
VI. **The minister must be a holy vessel. (19-22)**
VII. **The minister must be a patient servant. (23-26)**

Message #3 Contexts of Faithful Ministry (3:1-17)
I. **We live faithfully in the world by cultivating godly affections. (1-9)**
II. **We live faithfully in the church by following godly examples. (10-12)**
III. **We live faithfully in the Word by clinging to God's Word. (13-17)**

Message #4 Measure of Faithful Ministry (4:1-22)
I. **We finish well by preaching God's Word faithfully. (1-4)**
   A. We must preach with the right motive. (1)
   B. We must preach with the right method. (2)
   C. We must preach in the face of the right challenge. (3-4)
II. **We finish well by completing God's work faithfully. (5-8)**
   A. We have a charge to keep. (5)
   B. We have an example to follow. (6-8)
III. **We finish well by following godly directions faithfully. (9-22)**
   A. We must relate rightly to those over us. (9-18)
   B. We must relate rightly to those next to us. (19-22)

A Longer Series: Seventeen Messages

Series Title: The Things That Last

Message #1 The Measure of My Circumstances (2 Timothy 1:1-2)
I. **My circumstances are not inconsistent. (1a)**
II. **My circumstances are not incidental. (1b)**
III. **My circumstances are not irredeemable. (1c)**
IV. **My circumstances are not incapacitating. (2)**

Message #2 Gratitude that Lasts (2 Timothy 1:3-5)
I. **Enduring gratitude depends upon a commitment to serve. (3)**

II. Enduring gratitude depends upon an informed memory. (4a)
III. Enduring gratitude is informed by an intense desire. (4b)
IV. Enduring gratitude is motivated by a living example. (5)

Message #2 A Ministry that Lasts (2 Timothy 1:6-12)
I. A ministry that lasts is a courageous ministry. (6-7)
   A. Courage comes by reliance upon the Spirit gifted to us. (6)
   B. Courage comes by remembering the Spirit given to us. (7)
II. A ministry that lasts is a contented ministry. (8-12)
   A. I suffer contentedly because God has given me a calling. (9a)
   B. I suffer contentedly because God has given me a purpose. (9b-10)
   C. I suffer contentedly because God has given me an appointment. (11)
   D. I suffer contentedly because God has given me a confidence. (12)

Message #3 A Gospel that Lasts (2 Timothy 1:13-14)
I. We must battle for the truth of the Gospel. (13)
   A. Orthodoxy must define itself. (13a)
   B. Orthodoxy must reproduce itself. (13b)
   C. Orthodoxy must examine itself. (13c)
II. We must guard the truth of the Gospel. (14)
   A. Guarding the Gospel is a humanly impossible work. (14a)
   B. Guarding the Gospel is a humanly internal work. (14b)
   C. Guarding the Gospel is a heavenly invested work. (14c)

Message #4 Relationships that Last (2 Timothy 1:15-2:1)
I. The pain of relationships. (1:15)
II. The possibility of relationships. (1:16-18)
III. The power of relationships. (2:1)

Message #5 A Legacy that Lasts (2 Timothy 2:2)
I. A legacy that lasts has a treasure to pass on. (2a)
II. A legacy that lasts has a person to invest in. (2b)
III. A legacy that lasts has a goal to strive toward. (2c)

Message #6 A Minister that Lasts (2 Timothy 2:3-7)
I. A minister that lasts possesses the focus of a soldier. (3-4)
II. A minister that lasts possesses the discipline of an athlete. (5)
III. A minister that lasts possesses the patience of a farmer. (6-7)

Message #7 A Mission that Lasts (2 Timothy 2:8-13)
I. Remember to guard your thinking. (8)
   A. Keep Jesus central in your mind. (8a)
   B. Keep Jesus clearly in your mind. (8b)
II. Remember to guard your endurance. (9-10)
   A. Proclaim an unstoppable message. (9)
   B. Ponder an undeserved privilege. (10a)
   C. Pursue an unsearchable prize. (10b)
III. Remember to guard your faithfulness. (11-13)

A. God rewards faithfulness. (11-12a)
B. God repays unfaithfulness. (12b-13)

Message #8 Words that Last (2 Timothy 2:14-18)
I. **Articulate worthy words. (14)**
   A. We need to be reminded of what does matter. (14a)
   B. We need to be reminded of what does not matter. (14b)
II. **Aim for welcome words. (15)**
   A. We need to work with the right effort. (15a)
   B. We need to work with the right motive. (15b)
   C. We need to work with the right ethic. (15c)
   D. We need to work with the right skill. (15d)
III. **Avoid worthless words. (16-18)**
   A. The character of a worthless conversation. (16a)
   B. The consequences of a worthless conversation. (16b-17a)
   C. The characters of a worthless conversation. (17b-18)

Message #9 Service that Lasts (2 Timothy 2:19-22)
I. **Service that lasts is built on God's foundation. (19)**
   A. The church's foundation is solid. (19a)
   B. The church's fate is sealed. (19b)
   C. The church's foundation is simple. (19c)
II. **Service that lasts is a part of God's house. (20-21)**
   A. Guarding my life assures I will be sanctified to God's work. (20-21a)
   B. Guarding my life assures I will be serviceable in God's work. (21b)
   C. Guarding my life assures I will be supplied for God's work. (21c)
III. **Service that lasts is a picture of God's character. (22)**
   A. Where you end up depends upon what you run from. (22a)
   B. Where you end up depends upon what you run to. (22b)
   C. Where you end up depends upon whom you run with. (22c)

Message #10 A Conversation that Lasts (2 Timothy 2:23-26)
I. **Know when to shut your mouth. (23-24a)**
II. **Know when to open your mouth. (24b-25a)**
III. **Know when to open your arms. (25b-26)**

Message #11 A Battle that Lasts (2 Timothy 3:1-9)
I. **Perseverance requires guarding my expectations. (1)**
II. **Perseverance requires guarding my affections. (2-4)**
III. **Perseverance requires guarding my associations. (5-9)**

Message #12 A Path that Lasts (2 Timothy 3:10-13)
I. **Following Christ-like leaders. (10-11)**
II. **Following a Christ-like legacy. (12)**
III. **Forsaking Christ-less leaders. (13)**

Message #13 A Guide that Lasts (2 Timothy 3:14-17)
I. **Cling to the Word of God. (14-15)**

Appendix D

    A. Cling to Gods' Word because of who taught us. (14)
    B. Cling to God's Word because of what was taught us. (15)
II. Follow the Word of God. (16-17)
    A. Follow God's Word because of its divine origin. (16a)
    B. Follow God's Word because of its practical usefulness. (16b)
    C. Follow God's Word because of its complete sufficiency. (17)

Message #14 Preaching that Lasts (2 Timothy 4:1-4)
I. The provocation to preaching. (1)
    A. We must preach because Christ is listening. (1a)
    B. We must preach because Christ is judging. (1b)
    C. We must preach because Christ is coming. (1c)
    D. We must preach because Christ is ruling. (1d)
II. The preparation for preaching. (2b)
III. The purpose in preaching. (2, 3-4)
    A. We must preach. (2a)
    B. We must reprove. (2c)
    C. We must rebuke. (2d)
    D. We must exhort. (2e)
IV. The pattern for preaching. (2f)
    A. We must preach with great patience.
    B. We must preach with great instruction.

Message #15 Work that Lasts (2 Timothy 4:5-8)
I. Finish your work well. (5)
    A. With regard to the church: Stand firm! (5a)
    B. With regard to the world: Win others! (5b)
    C. With regard to God: Be faithful! (5c)
II. Finish your life well. (6)
    A. For the believer death is an act of worship. (6a)
    B. For the believer death is a departure for home. (6b)
III. Finish your journey well. (7-8)
    A. Running well is costly. (7)
    B. Finishing well is worth it. (8)

Message #16 The Stamina to Last (2 Timothy 4:9-18)
I. **If you are going to last you will have to deal with being lonely.** (9-12)
    A. Loneliness is lifted when people embrace us. (9)
    B. Loneliness is intensified when people betray us. (10a)
    C. Loneliness is confirmed when people replace us. (10b)
    D. Loneliness is bearable when people support us. (11a)
    E. Loneliness is lightened when people encourage us. (11b)
    F. Loneliness is dissipated when people obey us. (12)
II. **If you are going to last you will have to deal with being uncomfortable.** (13)
    A. Physical comforts are not inherently unspiritual. (13a)
    B. Intellectual stimulation is not inherently impractical. (13b)
III. **If you are going to last you will have to deal with being wronged.** (14-15)
    A. True forgiveness does not demand forgetfulness. (14a)
    B. True forgiveness does not demand frivolity. (14b)

The Pastoral Epistles for Pastors

    C. True forgiveness does not demand foolishness. (15)
IV. If you are going to last you will have to deal with being let down. (16-18)
    A. The failure of people is inevitable. (16)
    B. The faithfulness of Christ is indisputable. (17-18)
        1. Count on Christ's faithfulness in the present. (17)
        2. Count on Christ's faithfulness in the future. (18)

Message #17 The End at Last (2 Timothy 4:19-22)
I. When it's all been said and done, the love of friends matters ultimately. (19-21)
II. When it's all been said and done, the presence of Christ matters ultimately. (22a)
III. When it's all been said and done, the reality of grace matters ultimately. (22b)

Titus

EXEGETICAL OUTLINE

I. **The Salutation. (1:1-4)**
    A. **The author. (1-3)**
        1. Paul described his profile. (1a)
        2. Paul described his purpose. (1b)
        3. Paul described his passion. (2-3a)
        4. Paul described his proclamation. (3b)
    B. **The recipient. (4a)**
    C. **The greeting. (4b)**

II. **The Instructions for Titus. (1:5-16)**
    A. **The appointment of elders. (5-9)**
        1. Appointing godly elders. (5)
        2. Identifying godly elders. (6-9)
            a. Look for men who are above reproach. (6a)
            b. Look for men who have sound families. (6b)
            c. Look for men who have sound character. (7-8)
            d. Look for men who have skill with Scripture. (9)
    B. **The silencing of false teachers. (10-16)**
        1. The false teachers on Crete. (10-11)
            a. The spirit of the false teachers. (10)
            b. The silencing of the false teachers. (11)
        2. The ungodly populace of Crete. (12-16)
            a. The testimony of their own poet. (12)
            b. The testimony of their own words. (13-14)
            c. The testimony of their own behavior. (15-16)

III. **The Instructions for all believers. (2:1-3:11)**
    A. **Instructions regarding the pattern for living properly. (2:1-10)**
        1. How older men ought to live. (1-2)
        2. How older women ought to live. (3)
        3. How younger women ought to live. (4-5)
        4. How younger men ought to live. (6-8)
        5. How slaves ought to live. (9-10)
    B. **Instructions regarding the power for living properly. (2:11-15)**
        1. The resource of God's grace. (11-14)
            a. The appearance of God's grace provides salvation. (11)

Appendix D

        b. The instruction of God's grace provides direction. (12)
        c. The hope of God's grace provides motivation. (13-14)
    2. The responsibility of God's servant. (15)
- **C. Instructions regarding the problem of living presently. (3:1-11)**
    1. The problem of living with ungodly people is stated. (1-7)
        a. The right conduct and attitude. (1-2)
            i. The right conduct and attitude toward ungodly rulers. (1)
            ii. The right conduct and attitude toward all people. (2)
        b. The reason for such conduct and attitude. (3-7)
            i. The fact of our sinful past. (3)
            ii. The fact of God's saving grace. (4-7)
                aa. The motive of God's saving grace. (4)
                bb. The basis of God's saving grace. (5a)
                cc. The means of God's saving grace. (5b-6)
                dd. The hope of God's saving grace. (7)
    2. The problem of living with false teachers is stated. (8-11)
        a. Instruct the targets of the falsehood. (8)
        b. Refuse the arguments of the falsehood. (9)
        c. Discipline the leaders of the falsehood. (10-11)

IV. The Final Instructions. (3:12-15)
    A. Titus is to join Paul in Nicopolis. (12)
    B. Titus is to help Zenas and Apollos on their way. (13)
    C. Titus is to instruct God's people to do good works. (14)
    D. Titus is to receive greetings and a blessing. (15)

EXPOSITIONAL OUTLINES

A Single Message: Living as God's People in God's World

I. God's people need leadership to live for God's purpose. (1:1-16)
II. God's people need order to live as God's people. (2:1-15)
III. God's people need counsel to live in God's world. (3:1-15)

A Shorter Series: Four Messages

Series Title: A Godly People in an Ungodly World

Message #1 The Leadership of God's People (Titus 1:5-16)
I. The appointment of godly leaders over God's house. (5-9)
    A. God's people must appoint godly leaders. (5)
    B. God's people must identify godly leaders. (6-9)
II. The silencing of false teachers in God's house. (10-16)
    A. Leaders are called to silence false teachers. (10-11)
    B. Leaders are called to serve an ungodly populace. (12-16)

Message #2 The Order of God's People (Titus 2:1-10)
I. Older men are to live well-ordered lives. (1-2)
II. Older women are to live well-ordered lives. (3)
III. Younger women are to live well-ordered lives. (4-5)
IV. Younger men are to live well-ordered lives. (6-8)
V. Employees are to live well-ordered lives. (9-10)

The Pastoral Epistles for Pastors

Message #3 The Power of God's Grace (Titus 2:11-15)
I. **God's grace provides salvation. (11)**
II. **God's grace provides instruction. (12)**
III. **God's grace provides hope. (13)**
IV. **God's grace produces holiness. (14)**
V. **God's grace provides authority. (15)**

Message #4 The Wisdom of God's People (Titus 3:1-15)
I. **Wisdom is seen in a correct response to ungodly rulers. (1-8)**
   A. The right conduct and attitude to ungodly rulers. (1-2)
   B. The reason for such conduct and attitude to ungodly rulers. (3-8)
II. **Wisdom is seen in a correct response to ungodly teachers. (9-11)**
   A. We must shun wrong teaching. (9)
   B. We must discipline wrong teachers. (10-11)
III. **Wisdom is seen in a correct response to godly leaders. (12-15)**

A Longer Series: Ten Messages

Series Title: Being God's People in Painful Places

Message #1 Being God's Servant (Titus 1:1-4)
I. **Being God's servant requires knowing your calling. (1)**
   A. I am sent for service. (1a)
   B. I am sent for Christ. (1b)
   C. I am sent for others. (1c)
II. **Being God's servant requires knowing your message. (1-3)**
   A. We call out for faith. (1c)
   B. We call out to the chosen. (1d)
   C. We call out the truth. (1e)
   D. We call out with hope. (2)
   E. We call out God's word. (3)
III. **Being God's servant requires knowing your audience. (4)**

Message #2 Being Christ's Church (Titus 1:5-9)
I. **If the church is to be the church, leaders must be established. (5)**
II. **If the church is to be the church, leaders must be identified. (6-9)**
   A. Observe a man's relationship to his family. (6)
   B. Observe a man and his relationship to himself. (7)
   C. Observe a man and his relationship to others. (8)
   D. Observe a man and his relationship to God's Word. (9)

Message #3 Being Faithful With Difficult People (Titus 1:10-16)
I. **We are called to deal with false teachers. (10-11)**
   A. We must know the profile of false teachers. (10)
   B. We must know the fruit of false teachers. (11)
II. **We are called to deal with unruly people. (12-16)**
   A. Know what to confront with unruly people. (12-13)
   B. Know what to ignore with unruly people. (14)

Appendix D

    C. Know what to think with unruly people. (15)
    D. Know what to believe about unruly people. (16)

Message #4 Being God's People – Part I (Titus 2:1-4a)
I. The profile of a godly pastor. (1)
II. The profile of a godly older man. (2)
III. The profile of a godly older woman. (3-4a)

Message #5 Being God's People – Part II (Titus 2:4b-8)
I. The profile of a godly younger woman. (4b-5)
II. The profile of a godly younger man. (6)
III. The profile of a godly pastor. (7-8)

Message #6 Being God's Employee (Titus 2:9-10)
I. The attitude of a godly employee. (9)
II. The actions of a godly employee. (10a)
III. The aim of a godly employee. (10b)

Message #7 Being a People of Grace (Titus 2:11-15)
I. God's grace moves us to salvation. (11)
II. God's grace moves us to sanctification. (12)
III. God's grace moves us to suspense. (13)
IV. God's grace moves us to service. (14-15)

Message #8 Being a Godly Citizen (Titus 3:1-8)
I. The profile of a godly citizen. (1-2)
II. The power of a godly citizen. (3-8)
    A. Remember the truth of our sin. (3)
    B. Remember the fount of our salvation. (4)
    C. Remember the basis of our salvation. (5a)
    D. Remember the Spirit of our salvation. (5b-6)
    E. Remember the hope of our salvation. (7)
    F. Remember the fruit of our salvation. (8)

Message #9 Being a People of Discipline (Titus 3:9-11)
I. We must practice careful discernment. (9)
    A. Discern the nature of a divisive person's folly. (9a)
    B. Discern the nature of a divisive person's fruit. (9b)
II. We must practice church discipline. (10-11)
    A. The actions of church discipline. (10)
    B. The reasons for church discipline. (11)

Message #10 Being a People of Holy Appetites (Titus 3:12-15)
I. God's people long for fellowship. (12, 15)
II. God's people long for faithfulness. (13)
III. God's people long for fruitfulness. (14)

APPENDIX E

ANNOTATED BIBLIOGRAPHY

This annotated bibliography is provided to help pastors determine how to invest their money in commentaries before preaching the PE. I believe a pastor should interact with the Greek text at the greatest depth his training and available tools afford him. My comments will come from this perspective.

As I prepare to preach a book of the NT, I seek several commentaries that work closely and carefully with the Greek text, engage in technical discussions and provide exegetical insights. I then look for two or three commentaries that are either exegetical or theological in nature. Finally, I want one or two that are more expositional or homiletical in nature. After my own exegetical work, I work through the commentaries in that order. Those in the first category help me with analysis (taking the pieces apart). Those in the second category assist in the transition from analysis to synthesis (putting the pieces back together). Those in the last category help me move from text to message. To that end, then, I would want to have (in addition to this current volume!):

Group #1: Knight, Marshall, Mounce, and Towner (NICNT).
Group #2: Fee, Guthrie, and Hiebert.
Group #3: Stott and Wiersbe.

In the annotations that follow, I have generally attempted to identify the author's view of authorship, given the foundational nature of that question in approaching the PE. My observations are personal reflections and each reader may come to different conclusions about a given commentary.

Alford, Henry. *Alford's Greek Testament: An Exegetical and Critical Commentary*. 5 vols. Grand Rapids, Michigan: Baker Book House. Reprint 1980, from the 1871 version.
> Based on the Greek text. Its age limits its usefulness, but there are occasional gems to be found here.

Arichea, Daniel C. and Howard A. Hatton. *A Handbook on Paul's Letters to Timothy and to Titus*. UBS Handbook Series. New York: United Bible Societies, 1995.
> Not touted as a commentary *per se*, but as a handbook for those seeking to translate these letters. Virtually no interaction with introductory matters. Leans toward Pauline authorship. One may find some helpful material here, though you'll want more than just this in your stack of commentaries.

Barclay, William. *The Letters to Timothy, Titus, and Philemon*. Revised edition. Daily Study Bible. Philadelphia: Westminster, 1975.
> Believes a disciple of Paul pieced together fragments of genuinely Pauline letters and amplified them for a later purpose. Barclay is not always where we would like him to be on some matters, but he sometimes provides great background material.

Barrett, C.K. *The Pastoral Epistles*. Oxford: Clarendon, 1963.
> Brief work. Late dating of the PE (A.D. 90-125). Of limited helpfulness.

Bassler, Jouette M. *Abingdon New Testament Commentaries: 1 Timothy 2 Timothy Titus*. Nashville: Abingdon Press, 1996.
> Supports pseudepigraphic authorship. Dismisses some instructions as merely culturally based and of limited applicability for today's church.

Bernard, J.H. *The Pastoral Epistles*. Thornapple Commentaries. Cambridge: Cambridge University Press, 1899. Reprint. Grand Rapids: Baker, 1980.
> Affirms Pauline authorship. Strong on the Greek text. Dated, but still of some help.

Blaiklock, E.M. *The Pastoral Epistles: A Study Guide Commentary to the Epistles of I and II Timothy and Titus*. Grand Rapids, Michigan: Zondervan Publishing House, 1972.
> Affirms Pauline authorship. A light overview of the contents of the PE.

Briscoe, Stuart. *Purifying the Church – What God Expects of You and Your Church. A Topical Commentary on Titus*. A Regal Bible Commentary for Laymen. Ventura, California: Regal Books, 1987.
> Affirms Pauline authorship. An eight-part exposition of Titus. The outlines may be suggestive as you develop your own homiletical work.

Collins, Raymond F. *I & II Timothy and Titus: A Commentary*. Louisville: Westminster John Knox Press, 2002.
> Conjectures pseudepigraphic authorship by one he dubs "the Pastor." He comments from the perspective that "the Pastor" wants the readers not to wrestle with his authority, but to respond to the appeal he makes in Paul's name. Limited usefulness for the pastor serious about the text of the PE.

Appendix E

Demarest, Gary W. *1, 2 Thessalonians, 1, 2 Timothy, Titus*. The Communicator's Commentary Series, vol. 9. Waco, Texas: Word Books, 1984.
<blockquote>Tentatively affirms Pauline authorship. His comments are intended to help preachers in their preparation. I have found little help in this series.</blockquote>

Dibelius, Martin and Hans Conzelmann. *A Commentary on the Pastoral Epistles*. Hermeneia—A Critical and Historical Commentary on the Bible. Translated by Philip Buttolph and Adela Yarbro. Philadelphia: Fortress Press, 1972.
<blockquote>Rejects Pauline authorship. A fair representative of the critical view of the PE. I don't find much help here for the pastor.</blockquote>

Earle, Ralph. "1, 2 Timothy," in *The Expositor's Bible Commentary*, vol. 11. Grand Rapids, Michigan: Zondervan Publishing House, 1978.
<blockquote>Affirms Pauline authorship. A good commentary that provides some discussion of the Greek text. One wishes it could have been longer.</blockquote>

Erdman, Charles R. *The Pastoral Epistles*. Philadelphia: Westminster, 1923.
<blockquote>Affirms Pauline authorship. An older work of some brevity which contains some helpful applicational comments.</blockquote>

Fairbairn, P. *Commentary on the Pastoral Epistles*. Grand Rapids, Michigan: Zondervan Publishing House, 1874 T&T Clark. Reprint 1957.
<blockquote>Affirms Pauline authorship. Some help on the Greek text. Dated by its age, but still has some valuable comments.</blockquote>

Fee, Gordon D. *1 and 2 Timothy, Titus*. New International Biblical Commentary. Peabody, Massachusetts: Hendrickson Publishers, Inc., 1984, 1988.
<blockquote>Affirms Pauline authorship. Conservative, insightful, consistently helpful. Buy this one and refer to it often.</blockquote>

Gromacki, R.G. *Stand True to the Charge: An Exposition of I Timothy*. The Woodlands, Texas: Kress Christian Publications, 2002.
<blockquote>A brief, but insightful set of thirteen expositions. A good outline frames the comments. Best suited for adult Sunday School teachers and lay readers.</blockquote>

Guthrie, Donald. *The Pastoral Epistles: An Introduction and Commentary*. Tyndale New Testament Commentaries. Grand Rapids, Michigan: William B. Eerdmans Publishing Company, 1957.
<blockquote>Affirms Pauline authorship. A quality commentary that is of significant usefulness. Purchase the revised edition (1990), published by InterVarsity Press.</blockquote>

Hanson, A.T. *The Pastoral Epistles*. The New Century Bible Commentary. Grand Rapids, Michigan: William B. Eerdmans Publishing Company, 1982.
<blockquote>Rejects Pauline authorship and does so with flair. Comments are scanty and generally of little help to the preacher.</blockquote>

Hendriksen, William. *Exposition of The Pastoral Epistles*. New Testament Commentary. Grand Rapids, Michigan: Baker Book House, 1957.

Affirms Pauline authorship. A fine commentary filled with rich insights. Well worth the investment.

Henry, Matthew. *Matthew Henry's Commentary on the Whole Bible: Complete and Unabridged.* Peabody, Massachusetts: Hendrickson Publishers, Inc., 1991.
Dated, but devotionally warm and thus sometimes helpful in homiletical development.

Hiebert, D. Edmond. *First Timothy.* Everyman's Bible Commentary. Chicago: Moody Press, 1957.
Affirms Pauline authorship. Great exegetical outline. I am consistently amazed at what Hiebert packs into a small package. It is worth your time to hunt down a copy of all Hiebert's works on the PE.

_____*Second Timothy.* Everyman's Bible Commentary. Chicago: Moody Press, 1958.
See entry just above.

_____"Titus," *The Expositor's Bible Commentary*, vol. 11. Grand Rapids, Michigan: Zondervan Publishing House, 1978.
Affirms Pauline authorship. As always, a great exegetical outline. Hiebert always makes the most of his words.

_____*Titus and Philemon.* Everyman's Bible Commentary. Chicago: Moody Press, 1957.
See entry just above on other contributions by Hiebert in this series. You will want to own one, but won't need both Hiebert's volumes on Titus. If given a choice I would opt for his newer commentary in *The Expositor's Bible Commentary.*

Hughes, R. Kent and Bryan Chappel. *Guard the Deposit: 1 & 2 Timothy and Titus.* Preaching the Word. Wheaton, Illinois: Crossway, 2000.
Affirms Pauline authorship. Fine contemporary expositions by Hughes (1 & 2 Timothy) and Chappel (Titus). Can be helpful when it comes time for homiletical work.

Ironside, H.A. *Timothy, Titus and Philemon.* New York: Loizeaux Brothers, 1948.
Affirms Pauline authorship. Classic, but dated expositions.

Johnson, Luke Timothy. *The First and Second Letters to Timothy: A New Translation with Introduction and Commentary.* The Anchor Bible. New York: Doubleday, 2001.
Affirms Pauline authorship. Interacts with much of the scholarly material on the PE. A wealth of information which may prove helpful to the exegete.

Kelly, J.N.D. *A Commentary on the Pastoral Epistles.* Black's New Testament Commentaries. Henry Chadwick, ed. London: Adam & Charles Black, 1963. Reprint 1972.
Supports Pauline authorship. A work highly regarded by many scholars. Can be of help in wrestling with the text.

Appendix E

Kent, Homer A., Jr. *The Pastoral Epistles: Studies in 1 and 2 Timothy and Titus*. Winona Lake, Indiana: Brethren Missionary Herald Books. Reprint 1995.
> Affirms Pauline authorship. Helpful introduction on 1 Timothy. Helpful exegetical outlines embedded in the text of the commentary. I consistently found valuable insights here.

Knight, George W., III. *The Pastoral Epistles*. The New International Greek Testament Commentary. Grand Rapids, Michigan: William B. Eerdmans Publishing Company, 1992.
> Affirms Pauline authorship. Based on the Greek text. Conservative, thorough, insightful. A must-have before you preach the PE.

Kostenberger, Andreas, J. T. Schreiner, H.S. Baldwin, eds. *Women in the Church: A Fresh Analysis of 1 Timothy 2:9-15*. Grand Rapids, Michigan: Baker Books, 1995.
> Not a commentary on the whole of the PE. Conservative, level-headed and helpful in understanding this controversial text. Get this and read it carefully before preaching on this passage.

Larson, Knute. *1 & 2 Thessalonians, 1 & 2 Timothy, Titus, Philemon*. The Holman New Testament Commentary, vol. 9. Nashville: Broadman & Holman Publishers, 2000.
> Affirms Pauline authorship. Little to no interaction with the Greek text. An interesting mix of commentary, outlines, principles, and applications. The preaching pastor may find some suggestive help here when it is time for the transition from exegesis to exposition.

Lea, Thomas D. and Hayne P. Griffin, Jr. *1, 2 Timothy, Titus*. The New American Commentary. Nashville: Broadman Press, 1992.
> Affirms Pauline authorship. Good exegetical outlines of the books. A helpful commentary.

Lenski, R.C.H. *The Interpretation of St. Paul's Epistles to the Colossians, to the Thessalonians, to Timothy, to Titus and to Philemon*. Minneapolis: Augsburg Publishing House. Copyright 1937; Lutheran Book Concern, 1946; The Wartburg Press. Copyright assigned to Augsburg Publishing House, 1961.
> Affirms Pauline authorship. The classic Lutheran commentator. Because of its age, some newer developments are not touched upon; yet often helpful and intriguing on the Greek text. For a Lutheran perspective, get this one rather than Moellering.

Liefeld, Walter L. *The NIV Application Commentary: 1 & 2 Timothy, Titus*. Grand Rapids, Michigan: Zondervan Publishing House, 1999.
> Affirms Pauline authorship. Some help in bridging from exegesis to application.

Litfin, A. Duane. "1 Timothy." *The Bible Knowledge Commentary*, vol. 2. Wheaton, Illinois: Victor Books, 1983.
> Affirms Pauline authorship. Good as far as it goes, but too brief to be of great help to the serious expositor.

Lock, Walter. *A Critical and Exegetical Commentary on The Pastoral Epistles*. The International Critical Commentary. Edinburgh: T&T Clark, 1924.
>Leans toward Pauline authorship, but hesitant to take a strong stand. Good on the Greek text, but a surprisingly brief work. An older work which may therefore prove to be somewhat dated.

MacArthur, John. *1 Timothy*. The MacArthur New Testament Commentary. Chicago: Moody Press, 1995.
>Affirms Pauline authorship. One could wish for a fuller introduction, but provides strong work in the text. Conservative and consistent. A valuable resource for the preaching pastor.

_____ *2 Timothy*. The MacArthur New Testament Commentary. Chicago: Moody Press, 1995.
>See entry just above.

_____ *Titus*. The MacArthur New Testament Commentary. Chicago: Moody Press, 1996.
>See entry just above.

Marshall, I. Howard and Philip H. Towner. *A Critical and Exegetical Commentary on The Pastoral Epistles*. International Critical Commentary. London: T&T Clark International, 1999, 2004.
>Believes the PE are "based on authentic Pauline materials" and "produced by a group which included Timothy and Titus themselves" (92). Thorough work in the Greek text. Helpful and insightful discussion of the issues. A must-have for the serious expositor.

Martin, Harold S. *1 & 2 Timothy and Titus*. Brethren New Testament Commentary. Ephrata, Pennsylvania: Brethren Revival Fellowship, 2004.
>Affirms Pauline authorship. Perhaps helpful for lay teachers in the Brethren renewal movement, but it lacks the depth serious expositors seek.

Martin, Sydney. *Beacon Bible Expositions: Thessalonians, Timothy, Titus*. vol. 10. Kansas City: Beacon Hill Press, 1977.
>Affirms Pauline authorship. Brief expositions from a Nazarene perspective.

McCalley, Chester A. *Commentary and Outline of I and II Timothy*. Kansas City: Word of Truth Cassettes and Literature, n.d.
>Affirms Pauline authorship. Self-published expository notes. Too brief to be of great benefit to one looking for more than a concise survey.

Moellering, H. Armin. *1 Timothy, 2 Timothy, Titus*. Concordia Commentary. St. Louis: Concordia Publishing House, 1970.
>Affirms Pauline authorship. A Lutheran commentary. No interaction with the Greek text. For a Lutheran perspective use Lenski instead, even though it is an older work.

Moo, Douglas. "What Does It Mean Not to Teach or Have Authority over Men?," in *Recovering Biblical Manhood and Womanhood*, John Piper and Wayne Grudem, eds. Wheaton, Illinois: Crossway Books, 1991.
> Not a commentary on the whole of the PE, but very helpful in working through the issues in 1 Timothy 2:11ff.

Moss, C. Michael. *1, 2 Timothy & Titus*. The College Press NIV Commentary. Joplin, Missouri: College Press Publishing Company, 1994.
> Affirms Pauline authorship. An exposition from an Arminian perspective. The comments are not as thorough as one would wish for. Sometimes asserts what the text means without showing from the text why he deems this to be so.

Moule, H.C.G. *Studies in II Timothy*. Kregel Popular Commentary Series. Grand Rapids, Michigan: Kregel Publications, 1977.
> Affirms Pauline authorship. Dated, overly brief, scanty help to be found here.

Mounce, William D. *Pastoral Epistles*. The Word Biblical Commentary, vol. 46. Nashville: Thomas Nelson Publishers, 2000.
> Affirms Pauline authorship. A massive work. One appreciates the thorough nature of the work, but perhaps it can seem a bit much to wade through at times. It is a must-have for anyone preaching the PE.

Oden, Thomas C. *First and Second Timothy and Titus*. Interpretation. Louisville: Westminster John Knox Press, 1989.
> Argues for Pauline authorship. Oden's wish to return to a classical Christianity as represented by the early church can be seen in his comments here.

Plummer, Alfred. *The Pastoral Epistles*. The Expositor's Bible. New York: Funk & Wagnalls Company, 1888.
> Affirms Pauline authorship. Because of its age it is a dated work, but provides some fine expositions of these books. There is little here you cannot find in a newer commentary.

Quinn, Jerome D. *The Letter to Titus*. The Anchor Bible, number 35. New York: Doubleday, 1990.
> A thorough work contributed by a Catholic scholar.

_____ and William C. Wacker. *The First and Second Letters to Timothy: A New Translation with Notes and Commentary*. Grand Rapids, Michigan: William B. Eerdmans Publishing Company, 2000.
> A massive work by a Catholic scholar. Published posthumously by one of Quinn's students following Quinn's death.

Rowland, Alfred. *Studies in First Timothy*. London: James Nisbet & Co., 1887. Minneapolis: Klock & Klock Christian Publishers. Reprint 1985.
> Affirms Pauline authorship. Very brief introduction. Evidences a warm heart and a sharp mind, but its age diminishes it usefulness today.

Scott, E.F. *The Pastoral Epistles*. The Moffat New Testament Commentary. London: Hodder & Stoughton, 1936.
Rejects Pauline authorship. I found little help here.

Simpson, E.K. *The Pastoral Epistles: The Greek Text with Introduction and Commentary*. London: The Tyndale Press, 1954.
Affirms Pauline authorship. Brief work on the Greek text. Contains some useful material.

Sparks, Irving Alan. *The Pastoral Epistles*. San Diego: Institute of Biblical Studies, 1985.
Rejects Pauline authorship. A brief work written for laymen. Not much help here for the expositor.

Stanton, Knofel. *Timothy-Philemon*. Standard Bible Studies. Cincinnati: Standard Publishing, 1988.
Affirms Pauline authorship. Expositions of these epistles. Some may find some spark for their own homiletical development of the passages, but not of much help with the text of Scripture itself.

Stibbs, A.M. "1 Timothy," "2 Timothy," and "Titus." *The New Bible Commentary: Revised*. D. Guthrie and J.A. Motyer, eds. Grand Rapids, Michigan: William B. Eerdmans Publishing Company, 1970.
Affirms Pauline authorship. As part of a one-volume commentary his comments are helpful, but are generally too brief to be of significant help to the serious expositor.

Stott, John R.W. *Guard the Gospel: The Message of 2 Timothy*. The Bible Speaks Today. Downers Grove, Illinois: InterVarsity, 1973.
Affirms Pauline authorship through an amanuensis. Helpful for thinking through the flow of thought in the PE and with some interpretational issues. Great resource as you do preliminary study and plan your preaching series.

_____ *Guard the Truth: The Message of 1 Timothy and Titus*. The Bible Speaks Today. Downers Grove, Illinois: InterVarsity Press, 1996.
See entry just above.

Towner, Philip H. *1-2 Timothy and Titus*. The IVP New Testament Commentary Series. Downers Grove, Illinois: InterVarsity Press, 1994.
Affirms Pauline authorship. Helpful, but purchase Towner's NICNT volume instead.

_____ *The Letters to Timothy and Titus*. New International Commentary on the New Testament. Ned B. Stonehouse, F.F. Bruce, Gordon D. Fee, gen. eds. Grand Rapids, Michigan: William B. Eerdmans Publishing Company, 2006.
Affirms Pauline authorship. A massive work that the preaching pastor will want to own and interact with regularly. Suggests the title PE is unhelpful and has shackled the letters, keeping us from their intended message. Urges us to read each of the PE on their own merits rather than as a package of three.

Appendix E

Wallis, Wilbur B. "The First Epistles to Timothy," "The Second Epistle to Timothy," "The Epistle to Titus." *The Wycliffe Bible Commentary*, ed. Charles F. Pfeiffer and Everett F. Harrison. Chicago: Moody Press, 1962.
> Affirms Pauline authorship. Brief works for a one-volume commentary. The comments are typically too brief to provide much depth on the text.

Ward, Ronald A. *Commentary on 1 & 2 Timothy & Titus*. Waco, Texas: Word Books, 1974.
> Regards Paul as the author. The outlines can be suggestive for one's own sermon development. Does not deal deeply with the text of Scripture itself, but may be helpful as you transition from exegesis to homiletical development and application. Use only after completing solid exegetical work of your own.

Wiersbe, Warren W. *The Bible Exposition Commentary*. New Testament, vol. 2. Colorado Springs: Victor, 2001.
> Affirms Pauline authorship. A much-loved Bible teacher who has faithfully opened the Scriptures for countless hungry hearts. Because of the size and nature of the volume, much technical material is untouched, yet Wiersbe seldom fails to provide some useable homiletical tidbit.

Woychuk, N.A. *An Exposition of Second Timothy: Inspirational and Practical*. Old Tappan, New Jersey: Fleming H. Revell Company, 1973.
> Affirms Pauline authorship. No technical work in the text. Warm devotional comments and applications.

Wright, Tom. *Paul for Everyone: The Pastoral Letters*. Louisville: Westminster John Knox Press, 2003, 2004.
> Little interaction with the text. Broad applicational comments. Limited in usefulness to the serious expositor.

www.ingramcontent.com/pod-product-compliance
Lightning Source LLC
Chambersburg PA
CBHW050417240426
43661CB00055B/2180